Learning and Memory

Learning and Memory

CHARLES F. FLAHERTY

LEONARD W. HAMILTON

RONALD J. GANDELMAN
Rutgers University

NORMAN E. SPEAR
*State University of New York
at Binghamton*

Rand McNally College Publishing Company / Chicago

COMPLETE CITATIONS FOR ALL WORKS CITED IN THIS
VOLUME ARE TO BE FOUND IN THE REFERENCE LIST.

Copyright © 1977 by Rand McNally College Publishing Company
All Rights Reserved
Printed in U.S.A.
Library of Congress Catalog Card Number: 75-20650

78 79 80   5 4 3

Preface

Our intent in this text is to acquaint undergraduates with the experimental analysis of learning and memory. We have attempted to treat both data and theory and to place current research in both a historical and biological perspective. In order to accomplish the latter we have included sections on possible genetic and developmental influences on learning and memory and by integrating behavioral and physiological data where this seemed feasible and appropriate. The great majority of the data we have included was derived from research on lower animals. However, data from experiments using humans has been included where it seemed appropriate and relevant. We have, for the most part, excluded coverage of learning and memory that seems to depend on linguistic capabilities. This has been done not from a lack of interest, but because there is more than enough material available for a separate course on verbal learning and memory.

In writing this text an attempt was made to overcome problems inherent in multi-authored texts by repeatedly editing and contributing to each other's chapters. In the initial writing C.F. was primarily responsible for Chapters 2, 3, 4, 5, 6, 8, 10, and 11; L.H. for Chapters 1, 7, and 15; N.S. for Chapters 12, 13, and 14; and R.G. for Chapter 9. We would like to acknowledge our intellectual debt to our students and colleagues, particularly George Collier and Michael D'Amato, in the Rutgers College Psychology Department, and we would like to thank the following people for their specific comments on sections of the text: Robert Erhart and Elizabeth Webber of Rand McNally, Dalbar Bindra, William Safarjan, and Milton Schwartz. For their assistance in typing, proofreading, and general preparation of the manuscript we would like to thank Joanne Bellezza, Regina M. Hill, Gail Petroski, Peggy Reich, and Olga Dubas.

And finally, for their patience while we worked on the manuscript, we would like to thank our wives.

C.F.
L.H.
R.G.
N.S.

ACKNOWLEDGMENTS FOR FIGURES AND TABLES

We would like to thank the following for permission to reproduce the indicated tables and figures:

Academic Press, 4-7; 6-7; 10-9; 13-5; 13-8. *American Association for the Advancement of Science,* 2-3; 7-4; 7-10; 9-1; 9-2; 9-3; 10-3; 10-6; T7-1. *American Psychological Association,* 2-4; 2-5; 3-2; 3-6; 3-7; 4-1; 4-2; 4-4; 4-5; 4-6; 4-8; 4-9; 4-10; 5-1; 5-2; 5-4; 5-5; 6-1; 6-2; 6-3; 6-4; 6-6; 8-1; 9-4; 9-6; 10-1; 10-2; 10-4; 10-7; 11-1; 11-2; 13-2; 13-6; 13-7; T4-1; T5-1; T8-1; T9-2. *Brain Research Publications,* 5-7; 9-2; 14-5. *Butterworth Publishing Company,* quote on p. 429-30. *Cambridge University Press,* 15-4. *Elsevier Publishing Company,* 14-1. *Hemisphere Publications,* 3-3. *Irvington Publishers,* 3-4. *Kimble, Gregory,* 3-1; T2-2. *Macmillan Publishing Company (Nature),* 14-2; 14-3; 14-4. *McGraw-Hill Book Company,* 11-3. *New York Acadamy of Sciences,* 4-3. *Prentice Hall,* 2-1; 2-6; 5-8; 5-9; 5-10; 7-3; 10-5; 11-5; 11-6; T2-1; T11-1; T11-2. *Plenum Press,* 7-2; 13-1. *Psychological Record,* 5-11. *Psychonomic Society,* 6-2; 7-1; 13-1. *San Francisco Book Company,* 7-8. *Scott, Foresman & Company,* 5-11. *Society for the Experimental Analysis of Behavior,* 5-12; 6-5; 10-10; 11-4; 13-4. *Van Nostrand Reinhold Company,* 15-5. *W. H. Freeman & Company,* 7-5; 7-6; 7-7; 15-6; 15-7. *Yale University Press,* 3-5. ·

Contents

Abbreviations Used in This Text

CER	Conditioned Emotional Response
CR	Conditioned Response
CS	Conditioned Stimulus
DRH	Differential Reinforcement for High Rates of Responding
DRL	Differential Reinforcement for Low Rates of Responding
DRO	Differential Reinforcement for Other Behavior
ECS	Electroconvulsive Shock
FE	Frustration Effect
FI	Fixed Interval Schedule of Reinforcement
FR	Fixed Ratio Schedule of Reinforcement
GSR	Galvanic Skin Response
IRT	Interresponse Time
ISI	Interstimulus Interval
ITI	Intertrial Interval
N	Nonreward
NCE	Negative Contrast Effect
NR	Nonreward-Reward Transition
OR	Orienting Response
ORE	Overlearning Reversal Effect
PCE	Positive Contrast Effect
PREE	Partial Reinforcement Extinction Effect
R	Reward
R to E	Resistance to Extinction
$r_f\text{-}s_f$	anticipatory frustration response

R_G Goal Response

r_g fractional anticipatory goal response

R_I Instrumental Response

S_A Apparatus Stimulus

s_g stimulus component of fractional anticipatory
           goal response

S^N Stimulus Aftereffects (Memory) of Nonreward

S^R Stimulus Aftereffects (Memory) of Reward

S–R   Stimulus—Response Association

S–R–O   Stimulus—Response—Outcome

SSDR   Species Specific Defense Response

UCR   Unconditioned Response

UCS   Unconditioned Stimulus

VI   Variable Interval Schedule of Reinforcement

VR   Variable Ratio Schedule of Reinforcement

Learning and Memory

CHAPTER *1*

An Introduction to the Study of Learning

*When we no longer look at an organic being as a savage looks
at a ship, as something wholly beyond his comprehension;
when we regard every production of nature as one which
has had a long history; when we contemplate every complex
structure and instinct as the summing up of many con-
trivances, each useful to the possessor, in the same way
as any great mechanical invention is the summing up of the
labour, the experience, the reason, and even the blunders
of numerous workmen; when we thus view each organic
being, how far more interesting . . . does the study of
(that organic being) become!*

Charles Darwin, *On the Origin of Species*

I. THE ADAPTIVE NATURE OF BEHAVIOR

More than a billion years ago, when warm tropical waters were opulent with complex organic molecules, there occurred the first self-contained and self-sustaining set of biochemical reactions which we call life. This unit of life was probably not unlike the simple single-celled organisms which exist today, and in all likelihood this ancestral protoplasm shared the same characteristics that can now be observed in all protoplasm.

Perhaps the most fundamental characteristic of protoplasm is *reactivity*, or the ability to change the nature of its complex chemical reactions as a result of changes in the environment, e.g., changes in temperature, illumination, pH, etc. A second characteristic of protoplasm is *conductivity* or the ability to carry information about environmental changes throughout the entire protoplasmic mass. Thus, changes that are produced by a localized alteration in an environmental condition will be conducted or transmitted to the remainder of the organism. A third characteristic of protoplasm is *motility* or the ability to move away from adverse environmental conditions and toward favorable environmental conditions.

As multicellular organisms developed through the process of evolution, the cells of the various subdivisions of the organisms have specialized according to these three characteristics: cells which specialize in reactivity are called *receptors* or sense organs; those which specialize in conductivity are known as *nerve tissue;* and those which specialize in motility are called *effectors* or the muscle and gland systems.

It is, of course, impossible to consider any of these three systems in a vacuum because each complements the other two in the functional organism. But as psychologists, we are primarily interested in the function of those cells which have specialized in conductivity, that is, those cells which carry information about environmental changes. With respect to more advanced organisms, this population of cells comprises the nervous system and is responsible for conducting information obtained from the environment (via the receptors) to higher centers where it is translated into signals which result in action upon the environment (via the effectors).

The nervous system of the organisms that most psychologists use for experimentation are, of course, much more sophisticated in function than the protoplasm of a single undifferentiated cell. Investigation of both the developing and the mature nervous system has revealed that much of its circuitry has been preprogrammed according to the diagram provided by the genetic code. At birth or hatching, then, a large number of cells are restricted either to carrying environmental information into the central nervous system or carrying processed information out of the central nervous system. Interposed between these two populations of cells is a third population of cells that connects the input and output systems.

In simple cases the sequence of neural impulses generated by these cells constitute what is known as a *reflex arc*. An example of such a reflex is the withdrawal of the hand from a hot plate. This particular reflex is the flexor reflex and involves only relatively few cells in the spinal cord.

At a more complex level of organization these prewired or preprogrammed pathways mediate more sophisticated forms of behaviors known collectively as *innate behaviors*. Much of what is known about this type of behavior has been obtained by investigators in the field of ethology—the study of the behavior of animals in their natural environment. One of the most widely cited examples of a prewired behavioral pattern is the response of the male stickleback to a female that is laying eggs (Tinbergen, 1951). While the female fish is laying her eggs, the male engages in a stereotyped sequence of behaviors in the process of fertilizing the eggs. The analysis of the stimuli which elicit this sequence of responses provides a good example of the general organization of innate behaviors. The presentation of models of a female stickleback, even though highly accurate in color and other detail, will not evoke the sequence of responses in the male unless the model includes a red bulge in the abdominal region similar to that of the egg-filled abdomen of the female. The presentation of very crude models will readily elicit fertilization behavior provided that the bulge is present. The bulge has been referred to as a *releasing stimulus* and the neural mechanism underlying the response to the releasing stimulus as an *innate releasing mechanism*.

It must be emphasized that the response sequences that are preprogrammed are not necessarily simple, nor is the apparent degree of complexity necessarily correlated with the complexity of the organism. It seems the only general characteristics of these behaviors is that they occur in all members of the species and contribute, directly or indirectly, to their survival. By way of example, we shall describe a very complicated sequence of responses which occurs during the life cycle of the liver fluke (*Dicrocoelium dendriticum*) that infests sheep (Olsen, 1962).

The eggs of the parasite are deposited in the intestine of sheep and, subsequently, excreted in the feces. Should another sheep accidentally ingest some of this fecal material, the eggs will *not* hatch; therefore some alternate route is essential to the completion of the life cycle. This alternate route is via the snail and the ant. First, the eggs are ingested by the snail where they develop into an aggregation in the body cavity. This aggregate is then ejected in the form of a slime ball. The eggs in the slime ball are eaten by the ant and subsequently hatch (usually in large numbers) inside the gut cavity of the ant. Once hatched, the resulting army of tiny creatures bore through the walls of the ant's gut cavity and into the space between the gut and the outer shell of the ant's body. The resulting damage would almost certainly result in the death of the ant (and its contents), were it not for the fact that the tiny creatures *repair* the holes which they bored through the ant's gut.

After the parasites are secure in their new quarters, one of their members (and apparently only one) engages in a journey through the cavities of the ant's body up into the head region where a specific area of the brain is located and destroyed. As a result of this brain damage, the ant engages in a bizarre pattern of behavior: When the environmental temperature is relatively low (e.g., early in the morning), the ant climbs to the top of the nearest blade of grass and hangs from the tip of it. This unconventional bit of behavior sets the stage for the completion of the life cycle—the sheep, which prefers to graze during the cool hours of the early morning, consumes the ant and becomes the host for a new generation of parasites.

The examples outlined above are illustrative of the manner in which the nervous system has evolved to ensure that certain behaviors are displayed, thereby contributing to the survival of the species. Despite the efficiency of these preprogrammed patterns of behavior, it is not difficult to imagine situations for which prewired or preprogrammed behaviors would not be suitable. Indeed, one could argue that as organisms became more complex and developed the capacity to be exposed to a broader range of environments, the probability of encountering situations for which preprogrammed behavioral sequences were unavailable increased dramatically.

In order to appreciate both the importance and the range of behaviors that can change to fit a changing environment, we will consider first some behavioral patterns that are not directly genetically determined, but rather are "stamped in" at some stage of development. It seems likely that this intermediate form of flexibility developed at an earlier stage of evolutionary history than did the much more malleable changes that we call learning.

As an example of a rather primitive form of change, we will consider the alteration of a behavioral pattern which was once thought to be genetically determined and not subject to change. It had been observed that certain moths always laid their eggs on the leaf of the same species of plant (e.g., hackberry leaves), even though these leaves did not serve as a source of food for the adult form (the female dies shortly after laying the eggs). However, once the larvae hatched, these leaves served as a source of food for the developing larvae. The question was: How does the adult form know where to lay the eggs? Although this would appear to be a clear case of genetic control an ingenious experiment showed that it was not that simple. If the eggs were transferred to a new species of plant (e.g., to apple leaves), the emerging larvae ate these leaves and developed into the adult forms many of which laid their eggs on *apple* leaves. Thus, it is clear that the egg-laying site is not entirely genetically determined, but based in part on prior experience. The chemical nature of the food that is consumed during the larval stage somehow permanently influences this very primitive nervous system in such a way that the adult form can detect the "appropriate" location to deposit the eggs (cf., Beach, 1955).

This type of a permanent stamping in of a behavioral pattern that is retained into adulthood is not restricted to simple organisms such as insects. Similar, though somewhat more complex examples of such changes are fairly widespread, especially among birds. It has been shown, for example, that baby ducklings will follow the first moving object that is seen during a particular period of time following hatching (Hess, 1959). Although this tendency, called *imprinting*, is subject to some modification, there is a strong likelihood that this particular object will continue to attract the organism into adulthood. In most cases, this change in the nervous system is quite appropriate—the moving object most likely to be seen is the mother. But mistakes can and do occur, leading to inappropriate and usually maladaptive consequences.

To reiterate, the examples above indicate three relatively simple methods by which the nervous system can provide the organism with an appropriate repertoire of behavior: (1) The behavior can be preprogrammed genetically, with virtually no flexibility, as in the case of the life cycle of the sheep larva, or the mating behavior of the stickleback; (2) the behavior can be established on the basis of some chemical input into the organism, as in the case of the egg-laying site of moths; or (3) the behavior can be established by the performance of other behaviors (which may be largely under genetic control) as in the case of ducklings being imprinted to follow a moving object. Regardless of the mechanism by which the behavioral pattern is established, it tends to be very resistant to change once it has been established.

But what about more complicated interactions with the environment? Clearly, a complex organism in a changing environment requires the ability to adapt its behavior to the day-to-day and even minute-to-minute changes in the environment. In order to engage in these more flexible patterns of behavior, some of the connections of that population of cells that are interposed between the input and output systems must remain uncommitted and ready to guide the organism through a constantly changing environment.

It is probably safe to say that one of the most important of all evolutionary developments was the development of the ability to alter the population of these uncommitted cells so that the behavior of the organism is appropriate to a particular set of environmental circumstances for as long as that set of circumstances exists.

It is this ability, this plasticity or malleability of the central nervous system, that we call *"learning."*

II. THE DEFINITION OF LEARNING

A prerequisite for the study of any phenomenon is that it be clearly defined. Accordingly, in a book which revolves around the process of learning, we are obliged to provide a rather precise definition of the phenomenon of learning. Toward this end, we see little need to alter the definition provided by Kimble (1961, p. 2) in his revision of Hilgard and Marquis' *Conditioning and Learning.* He defined learning as a " . . . more or less permanent change in behavior potentiality which occurs as a result of repeated practice." We will now dissect this definition in order to make its salient features more explicit.

The phrase "more or less permanent change" is important to distinguish the process of learning from changes which are either very transient or very permanent, and which are apparently not subserved by the population of cells that mediate the flexible types of behaviors that we are discussing. Transient changes in behavior result from processes such as receptor *adaptation* or muscle *fatigue;* e.g., the maximal running speed of the average individual is greatly reduced within a few hundred yards. This is clearly a change in behavior, but not of the type which we classify as learning because the effect is only temporary and primarily involves the inability of the muscles to maintain a sustained level of forceful contraction.

At the opposite end of the spectrum are the permanent changes in behavior that are primarily associated with such processes as *maturation*, e.g., the physical ability to lift a 20-pound weight does not develop for a number of months following birth, but once developed, the ability remains throughout the lifespan of the individual. Also included in this category of permanent changes in behavior are the innate behaviors elicited by certain environmental situations as a result of preprogrammed behaviors (as outlined above). It should be noted that many of these behaviors also have a maturational component, in that the pattern of behaviors may not appear for some time after birth.

The behavioral changes that reflect the process of learning are *relatively* permanent in that they fall between the two categories outlined above, i.e., these changes in behavior typically remain in effect as long as they are appropriate to the environment, but can change relatively quickly as the environmental requirements change.

The phrase "behavior potentiality" refers to the fact that the behavioral changes that result from learning need not necessarily be manifested by an immediate and overt response. For example, it is possible to learn a sequence of numbers without any overt response. The fact that learning has occurred can easily be demonstrated at a later time by dialing the sequence of numbers on the telephone.

The phrase "repeated practice" refers to the observation that under most conditions repeated experience with the appropriate stimuli is necessary before learning can be demonstrated. We will give examples in later chapters of both extremes; in some cases learning occurs very gradually over many trials, in other cases learning appears to take place in a single trial.

Simply stated, learning is a *process* which permits the organism to adapt to the changing conditions of the environment. This process determines, to a large extent, much of the observable behavior of mammals and other complex vertebrates. The goal of psychologists interested in learning has been to provide a set of *general principles* to account for the resulting change in behavior.

But one might ask: *How can a set of general principles be developed to describe a process which has been selected for its ability to change?*

The ability to change need not imply the lack of a set of rules. There are an infinite number of ways to complete a chess match following a simple set of rules that govern the movement of 32 pieces. It has been the hope of students of behavior that the central nervous system may also follow a rather simple set of rules—relying on the ten billion or so cells (in humans) for the observed complexity of behavior.

We now know that the nervous system does not follow a simple set of rules. The precise influence of a particular environmental event upon an organism's central nervous system depends upon that organism's past history, present state, genetic background, and the presence or absence of certain other environmental events. No two members of the same species will show exactly the same response to the same environmental event. But neither will they show completely unpredictable behaviors. We know from our everyday experience that most dogs will respond to a friendly voice and outstretched hand by approaching and wagging the tail; some will not. Most people will respond to a smile and a greeting by returning a smile and a greeting; some will not. It is the belief of those who study behavior that within these similarities of behavior lie the general principles that can increase our understanding and appreciation of the process of learning. The search for these principles is obviously beset with many difficulties. In the final section of this chapter, we will outline some of the approaches to this problem along with an introduction to some of the terminology which will be used throughout the remainder of the book.

III. EXPERIMENTAL PROCEDURES FOR THE STUDY OF LEARNING

Some Basic Principles

One of the major difficulties in the study of learning arises from the fact that learning is a process and not (at this stage of our technology) a discrete physical entity. Although there is almost universal acceptance of the notion that learning involves some relatively permanent biochemical (e.g., changes in protein) or anatomical (e.g., growth of new connections) changes in the brain, we do not yet have the technology required to assess these changes in appropriate detail. Accordingly, we must *infer* that the process of learning has occurred on the basis of the resulting changes in behavior. Thus, the study of learning is by necessity the study of behavior, and the process of learning per se is a *hypothetical construct*.[1]

The major goal of experimentation in any field of science is to

---

1. The term "hypothetical construct" refers to a process or structure that cannot be directly observed, but the existence of which is implied by the observable data.

determine the effects of one type of event upon another type of event. It has been determined, for example, that the amount of force exerted upon a piece of iron varies as the distance of the iron from a magnet is varied. Similarly, the amount of water that can flow through a hose per unit of time varies as the pressure of the water varies. Events which influence other events in varying degrees are called *variables*. The goal of the scientist is, therefore, to determine the influence of different variables upon a particular event.

In order to determine the relationship between one particular variable and a particular event, the scientist attempts to *control* or maintain constant all other variables. In the example given above, the relationship of distance to the force exerted could not be accurately determined if magnets of differing strength were used for each differing distance. Similarly, the relationship between rate of flow and water pressure could not be determined accurately if the cross-sectional diameter of the hose were not held constant. The use of these *control procedures* is really the essence of experimentation. If more than one variable is introduced concurrently (e.g., distance *and* strength of the magnet, or pressure *and* cross-sectional diameter), the variables are said to be *confounded,* i.e., it is impossible to determine which variable produced the observed change. These fundamental principles of experimentation have allowed very precise relationships to be determined in the physical sciences.

The problems of control are somewhat more difficult for the biological scientists in general and for the behavioral scientists in particular. A biological system, by definition, is not a stable system but one which is undergoing constant change. The central nervous system, which controls the behavior of biological organisms, *specializes* in change and is quite likely the least stable of all biological systems. The question arises: How can the behavioral scientist exercise control over such a system to allow him to define the relationship between certain behaviors and certain environmental events?

The control procedures used by the behavioral scientist investigating learning are logically the same as those used by the physical scientist studying magnetism, though perhaps more difficult to perfect. The typical procedure is to divide the organisms being tested into two groups, a *control group* and an *experimental group*. Attempts are made to match these groups in terms of past experience, genetic background, the present state of the organism, etc. Then the investigator introduces a *single* change into the environment of the experimental group to determine, for example, if this change will influence the learning rate of the experimental group relative to the control group. The change that is introduced by the experimenter is termed the *independent variable*. The term "independent" is used because the experimenter decides whether or not to administer the variable—the decision is made independently of the subject.

(It should be noted that it is sometimes desirable to design an experiment so that each subject serves as its own control, i.e., the control and experimental *procedures* are administered successively to the same subject. This can be a powerful procedure, used in some cases to control such variables as age, past experience, genetic background, etc.).

We must recall, however, that the investigator of learning cannot measure his phenomenon directly. He must measure yet another variable, the behavior of the organism. This variable is termed the *dependent variable*. The term "dependent" is used because the variable is dependent upon the organism and (hopefully) dependent upon the organism's reaction to the independent variable.

The imprinting phenomenon described earlier can be used as a simple example of this type of an experimental design. For example, Hess (1959) devised a standardized procedure for testing imprinting that involved the exposure of the newly hatched duckling to a moving decoy. One of the hypotheses derived from some early experiments was that the amount of effort expended in following the decoy was related to the strength of the imprinting. To test this hypothesis, one group of ducklings (the control group) was exposed to the standard testing procedure, while the other group (the experimental group) was forced to climb over several four-inch hurdles to follow the decoy. As expected, the results showed that the group that expended the greater effort showed significantly higher scores of imprinting on a later test. In this example, the independent variable was the presence or absence of the hurdles, and the dependent variable was the time spent following the decoy during the testing session.

IV. RESEARCH STRATEGIES

Although all scientists follow similar sets of principles in the design and analysis of their experiments, there are probably as many different strategies of experimentation as there are scientists. We are using the term strategy to refer to the following types of questions: What type of behaviors should be measured? What type of subjects should be used? What type of independent variables should be used? The answers to these questions probably reflect, more than anything else, the biases of a particular scientist. This being the case, it is appropriate that we should indicate some of our biases. It is, after all, these strategies and biases that have determined our selection of a relatively small amount of material from a massive literature to help the reader gain an appreciation for what we consider to be one of the most challenging and exciting areas of research: the study of learning and memory.

Throughout this volume, there will be a recurrence of two major themes, both of which are extensions of the evolutionary principles that were outlined by Darwin over a century ago. These principles are: (a) *the continuity of behavior across species* and (b) *the specialization of behavior within a species*. The remainder of this first chapter will further develop these notions to alert the reader to viewpoints that will not always be explicitly stated in the chapters to follow.

The Continuity of Behavior

During the past 400 years, man has gone through some stormy periods in terms of trying to maintain his place in the sun. In the middle of the sixteenth century, Copernicus revealed that the earth was not the center of the universe. In the middle of the nineteenth century, Darwin revealed that birds were related to reptiles, and dogs to horses, and apes to men. In short, man learned that he was just one of many creatures sharing an infinitesimal speck of the universe. For those who would not see the beauty of this, these ideas were bitter pills to swallow. There is still a reluctance on the part of many to accept the notion that the similarity between man and other animals goes beyond the liver and the kidneys to include the brain, i.e., that the brain is another organ of the body—no more and no less—and that the functions of this organ are modifiable and heritable as are the functions of other organs.

In addition to the philosophical importance of the notion of the continuity of behavior across species, there is a great practical significance in terms of increasing our potential to understand behavior. Once this principle is accepted, the door is opened for the analysis of simpler and more easily controlled systems of less complicated organisms. These simpler systems may reveal the general principles that apply to all systems, but which are masked by the complexities of the brain of man.

An analogy from the physical sciences may be useful. It is highly unlikely that any amount of looking to the heavens would have led to a simple explanation of the orbital pathways of the planets about the sun; the information is simply too complicated. But once the principles of gravitation on earth were determined by studying falling objects, the broader application of these principles simplified what appeared to be an unanalyzable body of information. The simplification of behavior through the choice of the subject, the control of the environment, and in some cases the reduction of the capacities of the central nervous system, may be equally useful in providing us with the principles for understanding otherwise hopelessly complicated behavior.

One of the essential requirements for the continuity of behavior is, of course, the heritability of behavior. This is very easily demonstrated in the case of such innate behaviors as the mating of sticklebacks (i.e., specific responses performed by all members of a species). In some instances closely related strains show slight differences in the nature of genetically programmed behaviors, and crossbreeding leads to predictable intermediate forms of behavior.

The issue of heritability becomes somewhat more clouded in the case of the more flexible, learned behaviors. We must avoid the point of view that acquired skills are passed on to the next generation just as we avoid the notion that giraffes have long necks because of generations of stretching to reach leaves. The heritable factor is the *potential* for acquisition. As an example of this, it is relatively easy to develop strains of rats that can acquire maze tasks either very easily or with great difficulty by selectively breeding animals on the basis of their performance of this task (Tryon, 1940). The heritability of behavioral potentials provides the basis for the natural selection of those characteristics that enhance the probability for the survival of the species in the same manner that the heritability of morphological and physiological characteristics are selected.

In the chapters that follow we will be discussing particular areas of research in some detail. In each case, we will be using experimental data to support the general conclusions that are reached. In most cases the experimental subject will be the rat, because of the widespread use of this animal as a subject. But is it reasonable to base general conclusions on the behavior of a specific organism? Would these same generalities apply to a sea slug, an insect, a chimpanzee, a fish, or a college sophomore? In many cases, the differences in behavior that would be observed by using another subject would be trivial; the purpose of this text is to develop an understanding of the basic principles of learning, and it is the contention of the authors that these principles are applicable across species. We shall see, for example, in the chapters on classical conditioning that the important temporal relationships between the conditioned stimulus and the unconditioned stimulus are remarkably constant across species, as are temporal and quantitative parameters of the unconditioned stimulus. In the chapters on instrumental conditioning, we shall see that the characteristic patterns of responding in the presence of various schedules of reinforcement are likewise similar across species. The characteristics of memory storage and retrieval will also prove to be widely applicable.

The Specialization of Behavior

A second theme will appear, at first glance, to be directly opposed to the first. The basic tenet of this theme is that the behavior of a particular species is, in part, characteristic of that species and none other. How, then, can we maintain that continuity exists?

The specialization of behavior is related, to a large extent, to the response repertoire of the particular organism. The most obvious case involves the morphological characteristics of the organism. Anyone who has been to a circus knows that lions jump through hoops and elephants pick up logs; it would be difficult or impossible to teach either animal the other trick. Does this mean that their central nervous systems do not share certain principles of learning? This is possible, but it would seem more reasonable to attribute the differences to structure—lions don't have trunks and elephants are too big to leap through hoops. Each could learn its respective task via the same principles of reinforcement that will be explicated in a later chapter.

We must point out, however, that the response repertoire of the organism depends upon more than external structures and physical abilities; the central nervous system of each species has evolved along with the structure of the species, and there is almost certainly a powerful mutual interaction between the two. To put it bluntly, the lion and the ferret are predisposed to attack, whereas the deer and the rabbit are predisposed to flee. Both the structure of the organism and the brain of the organism are specialized for the ecological niche that is occupied. When the organism is taken out of its niche and brought to the laboratory, one must be very careful not to overemphasize or underemphasize these characteristics. If we overemphasize specialization, we will falsely conclude that all organisms are different, and that different sets of rules will have to be discovered for each species before the behavior can be understood. If we underemphasize specialization, we will falsely conclude, for example, that the rabbit is more intelligent than the cat because only the former will learn to run through a maze for the opportunity to eat a lettuce leaf.

Although our major purpose is to develop the general conclusions that apply to virtually all organisms, we will also examine a variety of situations in which the nature of the organism clearly interacts with the nature of the task. For example, some organisms easily acquire an active, running response but have difficulty learning to be passive and sit still; other organisms show the opposite pattern. Similarly, it will be seen that birds tend to respond to the color of the food, whereas rats respond more to the taste. Even within an organism it will be seen that the precise way in which a pigeon pecks a key differs, depending upon whether the reward is water or grain. In summary, we shall see that different organisms may be biologically prepared to learn different types of behaviors even though the principles of learning may be the same.

CHAPTER 2

Pavlovian Conditioning: History and Basic Phenomena

*It seems evident that animals as well as men
learn many things from experience, and infer,
that the same events will always follow from
the same causes. By this principle they become
acquainted with the more obvious properties
of external objects. . . .*

David Hume,
An Enquiry Concerning Human Understanding

What is the principle by which animals and men note and remember the properties of external objects, learn from experience, and infer causal relationships? Philosophers who have speculated on these topics have recognized that there are probably several principles or conditions that must be met in order for memory or learning to occur.

I. HISTORICAL BACKGROUND

Aristotle, for example, recognized six conditions important for the formation of a memory. The first of these conditions was *contiguity*. If two events occur close together in space or time, then the reoccurrence or recollection of one of the events is likely to lead to the recall or expectation of the other event. The odor of smoke leads to the thought or expectation of fire, because the two nearly always occur contiguously. Other principles or conditions that Aristotle thought important for memory were *similarity* between events, *contrast* or differences between events, the *repetition* of the event, the presence of a strong *emotion*, and the *organization* of the material or events to be remembered.

Although Aristotle was able to list the conditions that seem important for memory, he was not able to explicate or clarify the operation of them. For example, one might wonder about contiguity: How close in time or space did two events have to be in order for contiguity to be important in the recall of the events? Or about similarity: What determines similarity? When are similarities and when are differences important for memory? Or about repetition: Does the amount of repetition required depend on how contiguous the events are? One can think of many interesting questions bearing on the elaboration and specification of the principles developed by Aristotle. Aristotle himself probably wondered about the answers to these or similar questions, but he was unable to obtain answers because the appropriate methods had not yet been developed in the fourth century B.C.

Little additional progress was made concerning the nature of learning and memory until the seventeenth through the nineteenth centuries, when there developed in England a group of philosophers who were concerned with the general problem of where knowledge comes from. These philosophers are usually grouped together as *empiricists* because they held that all knowledge comes from experience. As did Aristotle, they believed that the mind at birth is a blank, a *tabula rasa*. They assumed a network of ideas was fixed upon this blank tablet by information coming in through the senses. For example, one of these philosophers, John Locke, wrote that ideas are the elements of the mind, and these ideas derive from sensation, i.e., from experience. Simple ideas are combined into more complex ideas by *association*. By simple ideas Locke meant such things as hardness, redness, roundness, etc.; and these ideas, together with such others as a particular taste might be compounded into a more complex idea as an "apple." That is, ideas (or sensations) that frequently occur together become *associated*.

The principles by which these associations are constructed were generally thought to be the same as those elaborated earlier by Aristotle as principles of memory. For example, Bishop Berkeley, another British empiricist, wrote that contiguity leads to the use of a single term (e.g., apple) for a group of sensations that always occur together. David Hume was another of these empiricists. He believed that there were two fundamental principles of association, resemblance (similarity) and contiguity. Other writers (including James Mill and John Stuart Mill) emphasized one or another or several of Aristotle's principles as conditions important for the formation of associations and as the means by which knowledge of the external world is acquired.

However, the elaboration of these principles had still not left the realm of philosophical speculation. There was an abundance of systematic thought about the principles of association or learning but little in the way of systematic study or data. Then there came a radical change in the late nineteenth and early twentieth centuries, a change that was to lead, some would say, to a current imbalance in the other direction—an abundance of data and not enough systematic thought.

Ivan Pavlov, a Russian physiologist who had already made Nobel prizewinning contributions to the study of the digestive processes, turned to the study of learning and became the original investigator of the type of learning now known as classical or Pavlovian conditioning. (The main concern of the present chapter is Pavlovian conditioning and we will see below that many of the principles enunciated by Aristotle and the British empiricists have experimental counterparts in the work of Pavlov.)

It was observations that Pavlov had made while studying digestion that directly led to his investigation of the learning process. Pavlov noted that saliva and gastric secretions, which were initially elicited by the placement of food in a dog's mouth, eventually came to be elicited by a number of other stimuli that antedated the actual receipt of food by the dog. For example, salivation would eventually be elicited by the sight or smell of food, by the bowl that usually contained the food, or even by the sight of the person who usually brought in the food bowl.

The important observation here was that stimuli initially ineffective in eliciting a biologically important *reflex* (secretion of digestive juices) began to elicit this **reflex** after the animal had some experience with the stimuli regularly preceding the food. If Pavlov had had different training, or lived at a different time, he might have been content merely to note these interesting observations and perhaps relate them to a principle of contiguity or repetition; or maybe mention them as an example of Hume's statement that animals and men learn from experience and infer that the same events will always follow from the same causes. But, for Pavlov, these observations were not the end but the beginning of the systematic study of the conditions that influence learning.

The concept of a reflex was important in Pavlov's analysis of learning. The origin of this concept may be traced back at least to René Descartes, the French philosopher and mathematician of the seventeenth century. Descartes was a mechanist. He believed that the body was a machine and that all of the behavior of animals and most of the behavior of man could be explained in strictly physical terms without the need of concepts such as mind or soul. According to Descartes, involuntary behavior (all animal behavior was thought to be "involuntary") resulted from the passage of sensory information through the nerves to the brain where it was *reflected* out (in the form of "animal spirits") through the "hollow tubes" that were the nerves to the appropriate muscles causing the organism to behave. This behavior was viewed as a "necessary reaction to some external stimulus," and the characteristics of the behavior were entirely determined by the nature of the stimulus and the internal "construction" of the organism.

This trend in thought was continued by Sechenov, a Russian physiologist whose writings appear to have influenced Pavlov and anticipated in several details Pavlov's interpretations of conditioning phenomena. Sechenov was even more of a mechanist than Descartes. He believed that the higher mental functions (as well as simple responses) were amenable to an explanation in terms of reflexes. According to Sechenov, all forms of human behavior, including thought, were involuntary and reflexive in nature. This interpretation implied that higher mental functions could be subject to scientific investigation and analysis, and further, that the study of simple reflexes might have something to tell us about more complex forms of behavior. Pavlov undertook the scientific investigation of a form of learning apparently based on reflexes at the turn of the century.

II. EXAMPLES OF PAVLOVIAN CONDITIONING

Before continuing with a detailed analysis of Pavlovian conditioning, we will present several examples of Pavlovian conditioned responses, some of which you may be familiar with, some not. Perhaps the example of Pavlovian conditioning familiar to most people comes from Pavlov's own research and concerns the conditioning of salivary secretions. If a hungry dog is presented with food, it will salivate. Salivation is a natural part of the digestive process. The salivary fluid, in addition to containing water that helps put the food substance into solution, also contains enzymes that begin the digestive process. Pavlov's initial observations indicated that environmental objects not biologically related to food (objects such as the room or bowl used to present the food) would also elicit salivation after the animal had some experience with the objects that immediately preceded the presentation of food.

In order to investigate this apparent learning, Pavlov selected a stimulus which did *not* normally elicit salivation, for example, the sound of a bell or the beating of a metronome. By presenting these stimuli at the same time that food was presented, Pavlov could determine how long it would take these stimuli to acquire the property of producing salivation and determine the variables that influenced this putative learning process. Of course, it was found that this procedure of pairing a bell with the presentation of food did indeed eventually lead to the bell alone producing salivation. In some ways the learning to salivate at the presentation of a stimulus regularly paired with the occurrence of food is an extrapolation of a normal biological process. The presence of food in the mouth normally initiates the secretion of digestive juices in the stomach sometime before the food actually arrives there to be digested. As a result of the Pavlovian conditioning process, salivation occurs in the mouth before food arrives there to be ingested and digested.

For another example of Pavlovian conditioning let us again turn to a process related to digestion. Insulin is a hormone secreted by the pancreas in response to high levels of sugar (glucose) in the blood. Insulin causes the removal of sugar from the blood and the storing of sugar in the liver. If a dose of insulin is injected into an animal, it also removes sugar from blood, thereby producing a temporary state of lowered blood sugar or *hypoglycemia*. The question of interest here is whether or not learning can take place within this system. Can environmental events regularly correlated with the injection of insulin produce an effect on blood sugar even if, on some occasion, no insulin is actually injected? The answer is apparently yes.

In one experiment (Siegel, 1972) rats were given an injection of insulin on each of four different days. On the fifth day, the animals were again injected but this time with a saline solution rather than with insulin. On each of the first four injections the insulin produced a regular drop in blood sugar level. Following the fifth injection, when the insulin was omitted, there was also a reliable change in blood sugar, but this time the level of blood sugar was *increased*. In other words, injection of insulin itself always led to a drop in blood sugar, but the stimuli usually associated with this injection, when presented alone on the fifth day, led to a rise in blood sugar (*also see* Siegel, 1975).

Was this change a reflection of learning based on the insulin injections? Apparently it was because a second group of rats which was given an injection of physiological saline on each of the five test days (they were never injected with insulin) did not show any rise in blood sugar in response to the injection procedure or the physiological saline. The hyperglycemic response found in the first group must therefore have depended on the prior association of the injection procedure with the physiological effects of insulin.

An interesting aspect of this experiment is that the learned response to the stimuli correlated with the insulin injection is in the opposite direction (hyperglycemia) to the natural response produced by insulin itself (hypoglycemia).[1] It is as if the physiological system controlling the level of blood sugar learns to "anticipate" the artificially lowered level of blood sugar produced by the external injection of insulin and "prepares" for this effect by raising the level of blood sugar when the stimuli associated with the insulin injection

---

1. This response might not be expected in human diabetics receiving insulin injections because, in their case, the blood sugar level is high and needs to be reduced by the insulin. This contrasts to the experimental situation where the blood sugar level is normal and is artificially reduced by the insulin injection. It should also be noted that some investigators (e.g., Woods et al., 1969) find conditioned hypoglycemia rather than hyperglycemia. The reason for this discrepancy has not yet been determined.

are presented. We will have more to say about this interpretation of Pavlovian conditioning as we proceed through the text.

For a third example of Pavlovian conditioning we shall go to another species and quite different response. The male Siamese fighting fish *(Betta splendins)* engages in a ritualistic pattern of behavior associated with fighting when it encounters another male of the same species. The behavior displayed includes frontal approach, fin erection, gill-cover erection, and undulating movements. In an interesting experiment, Thompson and Stürm (1965) constructed an apparatus in which one side of the fish tank became a mirror when a light placed behind it was extinguished. Thompson first determined that when the fish encountered its own reflection in the mirror it would go through its regular aggressive display pattern. Thompson then arranged for the illumination of a red light at one end of the fish tank that preceded the availability of the mirror by five seconds. After just a few pairings of the red light with the mirror image, the fish began its aggressive display when the red light alone was activated.

These three examples of Pavlovian conditioning involved different species and quite different responses: salivation, change in blood glucose, and a complex aggressive display, and yet they share a similarity. The similarity is that stimuli which were originally neutral in regard to these responses came eventually to lose their neutrality as a result of having been presented contiguously with other stimuli that themselves reliably elicited these responses. Sometimes, as in the case of salivation and the aggressive display, the response elicited by the originally neutral stimuli was quite similar to the responses reflexively elicited by the food and fish image; at other times, as in the case of blood sugar, the learned response was in the opposite direction to the innate response. And yet, the similarity remains; neutral stimuli acquiring new properties as a result of contiguous pairing with nonneutral stimuli. We proceed now to some terminology and a more detailed analysis of Pavlovian conditioning.

III. ELEMENTS OF CONDITIONING

There are four basic elements in the conditioning paradigm: (1) the *Unconditioned Stimulus* (UCS); (2) the response that it reflexively elicits, the *Unconditioned Response* (UCR); (3) an originally neutral stimulus, the *Conditioned Stimulus* (CS); and (4) the response that it eventually comes to elicit, the *Conditioned Response* (CR).

The UCS and UCR

We have already mentioned several UCSs and UCRs; the placement of food in the mouth (a UCS) reflexively elicits salivation (a UCR), insulin (a UCS) elicits a decrease in blood sugar (a UCR), etc. Many other UCSs have been used in the study of conditioning. For example, electric shock has been used as a UCS for such UCRs as heart-rate changes, vasomotor reactions, leg-flexion reflexes, eyelid-closure reflexes, and others. Morphine or such poisons as lithium chloride have been used to produce UCRs of nausea, vomiting, or general malaise. A number of UCSs and the UCRs they elicit are presented in Table 2–1.

Table 2–1.   Unconditioned Responses and the Stimuli Used to Elicit Them*

RESPONSES	STIMULI
Salivation	Dry food, acid
Clocking of EEG Alpha Rhythm	Light
Change in skin resistance (GSR)	Electric shock
Pupillary reflex	Change in illumination, shock
Gastrointestinal secretions	Food
Vasomotor reactions	Shock, thermal stimuli
Nausea, vomiting, etc.	Morphine
Immunity reactions	Injection of toxin and antigen
Diuresis	Increased water intake
Flexion reflex	Electric shock
Knee jerk	Patellar blow
Eyelid reflex	Shock, sound, air-puff
Eye movements	Rotation
Change in respiration	Electric shock
Change in pitch of voice	Electric shock
Withdrawal movements	Electric shock
Mouth opening, swallowing	Food
Locomotion	Shock
Instructed responses	Various
Previously conditioned (higher order) responses	Various
Novel food aversion	X-irradiation, lithium chloride ingestion, apomorphine injection, others
Change in blood sugar	Insulin injection

*Modified from Kimble, 1961, by permission of Prentice-Hall.

The CS

Almost any stimulus can be utilized as a CS. The two principal requirements for the selection of a stimulus as a CS are (1) that it can be perceived or attended to by the subject, and (2) that it does not itself elicit the UCR, that is, it should be initially neutral. The first requirement is often indexed by the behavior of the subject. For example, Pavlov noted that when a *novel* stimulus, such as the beat of a metronome, was first presented, the dog would turn in the direction of the sound. This response, called the investigatory reflex by Pavlov but now more frequently termed the *Orienting Response* (OR), provides behavioral evidence that the subject is attending to the stimulus.

The requirement that the CS be originally neutral with regard to the elicitation of the UCR is related to the definition and measurement of learning. If we want to measure the course of learning (the effects of experience), then it is reasonable to start with a stimulus that does not initially elicit the response that will be used as the dependent variable to measure learning. For example, if the sound of a metronome always elicited salivation in dogs, then it would be a relatively poor choice for a CS if food was to be the UCS, because it would be difficult to measure any changes in behavior, any learning, that occurred as a result of placing this sound in close contiguity with the food.

In practice, the selection of a neutral stimulus is sometimes a problem. Consider what happens when electric shock is used as a UCS. The application of the shock elicits a general activation of the sympathetic division of the autonomic nervous system. This general activation has many specific effects, the nature of which depends upon the organ system that the sympathetic branch innervates. For example, electric shock leads to an increase in heart rate, an increase in blood pressure, a constriction of peripheral blood vessels, and a decrease in skin resistance. This last measure, a change in skin resistance, is termed a *galvanic skin response* (GSR) and is a frequently used measure in classical conditioning. The popularity of this measure probably relates to its relative ease of measurement and its covariation with the experience of emotion in humans. That is, events that produce emotions in humans also tend to produce GSR changes.

However, the use of the GSR for conditioning presents difficulties for the selection of a neutral stimulus. This is so because GSR changes are also part of the orienting response and, therefore, the presentation of any novel stimulus produces a decrease in skin resistance, which is the same response that the shock UCS produces. How then is one to study the acquisition of a conditioned GSR with, say, light onset as the CS and shock as the UCS when both produce a GSR change from the beginning, without any training?

There are several ways around this problem; we shall mention two. First of all, as you may have guessed, the GSR to shock is usually considerably larger than the GSR to something such as a light onset. Size of the skin resistance change, then, could be used to discriminate between the two responses. The second solution to this problem deals with the fact that the organism eventually habituates to the novel stimulus. Thus, the OR is no longer exhibited. Therefore, if the light is presented by itself for a few times before the start of conditioning it will eventually cease to elicit a GSR change. At this point, the conditioning trials can be initiated.

The basic facts to remember about the selection of a CS, then, are (a) the stimulus should be within the sensory capacities of the subject; (b) the stimulus should not initially elicit the same response as the UCS; and (c) if the CS does elicit a component of the UCR, certain procedures must be used to circumvent this problem.

The CR

The last of the four basic elements of conditioning we have to mention is the CR. It is the occurrence of the CR, upon the presentation of the CS, that tells us that learning has taken place. The CR is often quite similar in form to the UCR, as we have seen already in the case of salivation and the aggressive display of Siamese fighting fish. However, although grossly similar, the CR often differs in detail from the UCR. For example, the CR occurs before the UCR and it may be of smaller magnitude than the UCR. An example of some of these relationships between a CR and a UCR is presented in Figure 2–1.

The figure illustrates the development of a CR at several different stages of conditioning. In this experiment the UCS was a puff of air directed at the eyelid of human subjects. The onset of the UCS is indicated by the bottom line in each panel of the figure. The UCR elicited by the UCS is a reflex closure of the eyelid. This response is indicated on the line labeled "eyelid" and marked UCR. The CS was the onset of a light and this is indicated by the downswing in the line marked "light." After the light and air puff have been presented together a number of times the light begins to elicit an eyelid closure (CR) just before the air puff (UCS) is presented. This initial CR, shown in the second and third panels of Figure 2–1, is a smaller and less smooth closure of the eyelid than the response elicited by the UCS. Eventually, as in the fourth panel of the figure, after a number of pairings of the CS and UCS the CR

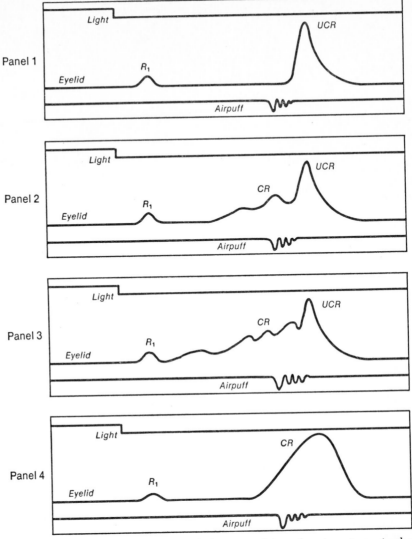

Figure 2–1. Records from a single human subject showing stages in the development of a conditioned eyelid response. Notice that at no point is the CR simply substituted for the UCR, nor is it completely identical to the UCR. The point labeled R_1 is a reflex response to the light that does not change during the course of conditioning. (From Hilgard & Marquis, 1940, by permission of Prentice-Hall.)

merges with the UCR resulting in a smooth and more gradual closure of the eyelid that *precedes* or anticipates the presentation of the UCS (*see also* Levey & Martin, 1968).

Sometimes the CR is quite different from the UCR. We have seen one example of this in the case of the conditioned response to insulin. Another example occurs in heart-rate conditioning when the UCS is electric shock. The UCR to shock is an *increase* in heart rate. However, the response that occurs to a CS after a number of conditioning trials is a *decrease* in heart rate (Fitzgerald, Martin, & O'Brien, 1973).

There is one final comment to make concerning the conditioned eyelid response. The eyelid closure response is under voluntary control. How is an experimenter to tell if a particular eyelid closure is a conditioned reflex that resulted from Pavlovian training procedures or simply a voluntary closure on the part of the subject? It has been found that the voluntary eyelid closure tends to have a different form than the conditioned eyelid response. In particular, the voluntary closure tends to have a steeper slope (faster rate of closure), shorter latency (starts sooner after CS presentation), and a longer duration of closure than conditioned responses (Spence & Ross, 1959). So we see that experienced workers in the field are able to distinguish among reflex eyelid responses to a CS, voluntary eyelid closures, and unconditioned eyelid closures to a UCS. (There is more to a blink than meets the eye.) We will have more to say about each of these basic elements of conditioning as we proceed into a more detailed analysis of Pavlovian conditioning experiments and the principles (laws) that can be derived from these experiments.

Now, however, let us stop a minute and consider what the term "conditioned reflex" meant to Pavlov. Pavlov entertained a number of other terms that could possibly be used instead of conditioned and unconditioned reflex. For example, Pavlov thought that the term unconditioned reflex might be replaced with "inborn reflex" and that conditioned reflex might then be replaced with "acquired reflex"; or perhaps "species reflex" could be substituted for UCR since all members of the species would possess that particular reflex, and then CR could be replaced with "individual reflex" since these reflexes vary depending on the differential experience of each individual organism. In the end Pavlov chose the terms unconditioned and conditioned reflexes because "these new reflexes actually do depend on very many conditions, both in the formation and in the maintenance of their physiological activity (Pavlov, 1927, p. 25)."

In a sense then, the study of classical conditioning is the study of the conditions that are necessary for the formation of new associations in the way the British empiricists used the term. A stimulus will acquire properties it did not formerly possess if certain conditions are met. One of these conditions, as we have already implied several times, is that the stimulus to be conditioned (invested with new properties) must be presented contiguously with a stimulus that already elicits a response (i.e., a UCS). We will go on now to a more detailed study of classical conditioning.

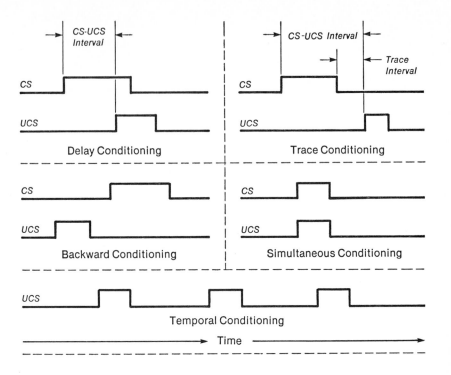

Figure 2–2. Temporal Relationships in Basic Conditioning Paradigms. A number of different conditioning paradigms are labeled in accordance with the temporal relationships between CS onset and UCS onset.

In *Delay Conditioning*, CS onset precedes UCS onset, and the offset of the CS either overlaps the UCS or coincides with UCS onset.

In *Trace Conditioning*, the CS terminates before UCS onset, thus there is a gap between CS termination on UCS onset. The length of this gap is referred to as the *trace interval*.

In both delay and trace conditioning, the time between CS onset and UCS onset is termed the *CS–UCS interval*.

In *Simultaneous Conditioning*, there is no *CS–UCS interval*, the CS and UCS coincide.

In *Backward Conditioning*, the UCS precedes the CS and may or may not overlap with it.

In *Temporal Conditioning*, the UCS is presented at regular temporal intervals; there is no explicit CS. Conditioning may be demonstrated in this paradigm by omitting the UCS occasionally and determining whether or not a response occurs.

IV. BASIC CONDITIONING PHENOMENA

A diagrammatic representation of the conditioning paradigm is presented below. The schematic illustrates several aspects of conditioning:

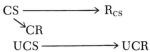

A response (the CR) will eventually be elicited by an originally neutral stimulus (the CS) if it has been presented contiguously with the UCS. The schematic also indicates that the CS itself often elicits a response (R_{CS}) that usually habituates and/or is not recorded by the experimenter because it is not of central interest to the conditioning experiment. The schematic illustrates one other aspect of conditioning. From Aristotle down through the British empiricists contiguity was emphasized as important for the formations of associations. Pavlov, however, added another dimension to contiguity. He found that the CS and UCS should be presented not only contiguously, but that the CS should precede the UCS and overlap with it (termed *delayed conditioning*) if conditioning was to be efficient and effective. In other words, conditioning proceeded very poorly or not at all if the CS followed the UCS (*backward conditioning*), or if the CS preceded the UCS but did not overlap with it (*trace conditioning*). Some of the temporal relationships between the CS and UCS are illustrated in Figure 2–2.

Acquisition

The progress of conditioning is measured by recording the presence or absence of the CR on a trial by trial basis, a trial being defined by the presentation of the CS and UCS. An example of an acquisition function is presented in Figure 2–3. The response conditioned in this experiment was the rabbit's eye blink. The UCS was a puff of air directed at the eye, the CS was a tone, and the time between CS onset and UCS onset (the *CS–UCS interval*) was 0.5 seconds. Notice that learning under the conditions of this experiment was very gradual, requiring some 500 trials for the subjects to reach an apparent asymptotic level of responding. But, in the end, the tone had acquired a property it did not originally possess, the property of causing the rabbit to close its eyelid. In some ways this may seem like a simple and even unimportant response to be concerned with. However, it is interesting in that (a) the response is of possible biological (adaptive) importance to the animal, and (b) the response is quantifiable and may be able to tell us something about general principles of learning.

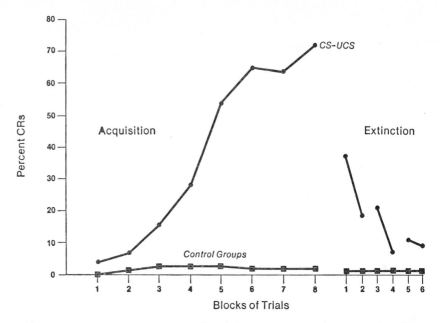

Figure 2–3. Mean percentage of eyelid responses as a function of trials in acquisition and extinction. The curve labeled CS–UCS represents the conditioning group, the other curve represents four control groups. One group received the CS alone on each trial, another received the UCS alone on each trial. A third received random presentations of the CS, and a fourth received random presentations of the UCS. Only the group in which the CS and UCS were paired showed conditioning. The data are plotted in terms of 82-trial blocks in acquisition and 41-trial blocks for the 82 trials per day of extinction. (From Schneiderman, Fuentes, & Gormezano, 1962, © Am. Assoc. Adv. Science.)

A second example of an acquisition function is presented in Figure 2–4. In this experiment the subjects were humans (male college students) and the response conditioned was the GSR. The parameters of the experiment included a red light as the CS, electric shock applied to the fingertips as the UCS, and a 5-second CS-UCS interval in a delay conditioning paradigm (*see* Figure 2–2). The group labeled "unpaired" was a control group that experienced all the same parameters as the experimental group except that the CS and UCS were not paired. That is, whether the CS or UCS came first on any given trial was randomly determined. Note that acquisition was very rapid in the experimental group (labeled "paired"), asymptote being reached in essentially four conditioning trials. Very rapid acquisition is fairly typical in Pavlovian conditioning experiments conducted with humans as subjects.

Also note that the control group in this experiment (and all four control groups in the eyelid experiment) showed no signs of conditioning. In both experiments only the groups in which the CS was paired with the UCS showed an acquisition function. It was this

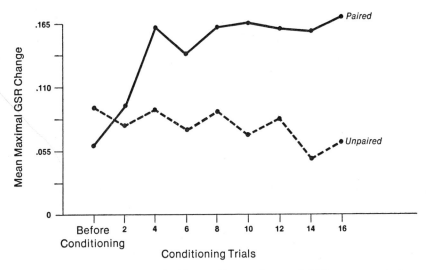

Figure 2–4. Acquisition of a classically conditioned GSR response in humans. The CS and UCS were presented equally often but not paired in the group labeled "unpaired." See text for further explanation. (Modified from Kimmel, 1967.)

type of effect that led Pavlov to use the term *reinforcement* to describe the function of the UCS. The term was used in an essentially descriptive way by Pavlov to describe the effect of a UCS following a CS on the acquisition of a CR. With the UCS applied in this way the CR grew in magnitude or probability (was reinforced); without it the CR did not occur. When we use the term reinforcement, we shall be using it in this descriptive sense.

Recording the CR

The actual measurement of the CR is often obtained on a special type of trial termed a test trial. On test trials the UCS is *not* presented. If a response occurs following the CS on these trials, it clearly must be a CR since the UCS was not presented. Test trials are generally presented infrequently, perhaps one of every ten trials may be used as a test trial. A *frequency* or *percentage* score is then obtained by recording the number or percentage of CRs that occur over a block of trials, and this score is used to represent the progress of conditioning.

The test trial procedure is one of the two basic methods of recording the progress of conditioning. The second method, the recording of *anticipatory* CRs, can be used whenever there is a relatively long CS–UCS interval as in the GSR experiment mentioned above. Anticipatory CRs are those responses to the CS that can be clearly seen to occur before the onset of the UCS (*see* Figure 2–1). When the anticipatory response method of scoring is used, it is possible to keep a continuous record of the increase in the frequency or magnitude of the CR across training trials, and there is no need to include special test trials where the UCS is omitted.

Nonassociative Behavioral Changes

Referring again to Figure 2–3 and 2–4 note that both experiments included control groups. Note also that there was no sign of conditioning in any of these control groups, indicating that the pairing of the CS and UCS was critical for conditioning. If the simple repeated presentation of either the CS or UCS was important for conditioning, then one of the control groups should have shown an increase in the frequency of CRs across acquisition trials; none occurred.

Control groups are often used in classical conditioning studies to obviate the possibility that the behavioral changes observed are due to something other than the formation of an association between the CS and UCS. We shall briefly mention two behavioral changes that occur often enough to warrant special names to distinguish them from associative learning. The first of these is termed *pseudoconditioning*. It sometimes happens that if a UCS is presented by itself for a few trials and then the CS is presented, a response much like that elicited by the UCS will occur in response to the first presentation of the stimulus designated as the CS. This would not be termed a CR because it is not based on CS–UCS pairings; it is not due to an association between the CS and UCS. Pseudoconditioned responses are probably based on a general startle reaction rather than on associative learning. The inclusion of control groups where the CS and UCS are not paired will allow one to distinguish pseudoconditioning from associative conditioning.

The second type of behavioral change not due to CS–UCS pairings per se is *sensitization*. Sensitization refers to an increase in the response originally elicited by the CS as a result of presentations of the UCS. Sensitization is more difficult than pseudoconditioning to

pseudoconditioning

sensitization

control and interpret, and it is particularly a problem when responses under the control of the sympathetic nervous system are used in conditioning studies. This is so because these responses are generally elicited by any neutral stimulus (as we have previously discussed) and because these responses are particularly sensitive to any general arousal effects that might result from the presentation of an aversive UCS. However, sensitization effects can usually be monitored and distinguished from associative learning if the proper controls are used.

To summarize, sensitization and pseudoconditioning are phenomena that may occur as a result of CS and UCS presentation, but they are not the result of the *pairing* of the CS and UCS. Both phenomena are probably motivational in nature and related to the arousal-producing effects of the UCS. The two phenomena differ primarily in terms of whether the response that occurs is similar to the one initially elicited by the CS or by the UCS. If the response is similar to one initially elicited by the CS (e.g., heart-rate deceleration), it is termed sensitization; if it is similar to the response initially elicited by the UCS (e.g., heart-rate acceleration to a shock UCS), it is termed pseudoconditioning.

Sensitization and pseudoconditioning are interesting phenomena in their own right, but should be distinguished from associative learning which is based on the contiguous pairing of the CS and UCS.

Alternative Response Measures

Percent of test trials on which a CR occurred was the dependent variable used to measure the course of conditioning in the data presented in Figure 2–3. Percent (or frequency) of CR occurrence is often used as a measure of conditioning. Both percent and frequency measures may be assumed to reflect the probability of CR occurrence.

Two other response measures of conditioning, somewhat less frequently used than frequency or percent, are the *magnitude*[2] of the CR and the *latency* of the CR. Pavlov, working with a small number of dogs, typically used a magnitude measure, recording the total number of drops of saliva secreted after the presentation of the CS. In an eyelid conditioning experiment the magnitude of eyelid closure usually increases during conditioning (this is somewhat evident in a comparison of panels 2 and 3 of Figure 2–1), and the magnitude of GSR response usually changes across trials in GSR conditioning.

---

2. It is possible to make a distinction between magnitude and amplitude (*see* Pennypacker, 1967). For our purposes we will simply refer to magnitude as an index of *amount* of CR change.

Latency refers to the lag between the presentation of the CS and the occurrence of the CR. For most conditioning paradigms (but not all) it is reasonable to assume that as conditioning becomes stronger, the latency of the CR should decrease. Of course, it is possible to take more than one of these measures in any given experiment; and when this is done, it is usually found that the measures vary together, giving the same general impression of the degree of conditioning. However, as the data in Table 2–2 indicate, these measures are not perfectly correlated, and therefore are not measuring exactly the same thing. Perhaps these various measures should be interpreted as related, but different, peripheral manifestations of the "true" conditioning which is occurring in the central nervous system.

Table 2–2. *Intercorrelations Among Measures of Conditioned Response Strength*

	Frequency & Amplitude	Latency & Amplitude	Latency & Frequency	Magnitude & Frequency	Magnitude & Amplitude	Magnitude & Latency
Leg Flexion (Dog)	.94	−.22	−.18			
Knee Jerk (Man)	.63	−.27	−.27			
Eyelid (Man)	.63	−.15	−.54			
Eyelid (Man)*	.68	−.65	−.79	.59	.86	−.71

*Data obtained from Pennypacker, 1967. Other data obtained from Hilgard and Marquis, 1940, by permission of Prentice-Hall.

There is one other general point about acquisition measures that we should mention. The data in Figures 2–3 and 2–4 represent averages obtained across a number of subjects. Average curves such as these may mask wide differences among individual subjects in both rate and final level of conditioning and, therefore, it is not feasible to rely on averaged data to infer fundamental processes of conditioning. For example, it would not be wise to infer from Figure 2–3 that learning was very gradual in *all* the subjects, some few subjects may well have acquired the response quite rapidly, but their rapid learning would not be visible in the group average. Averaged learning curves are much like average income figures for a community, they do not say that every individual is learning at the same rate or making the same amount of money. Average curves are useful for a summary statement, but more detailed information can be derived from an inspection of the data from each individual subject.

Extinction and Related Phenomena

If, after acquisition training, the CS is presented over a number of trials without the UCS, the CR becomes weaker and less likely to occur. The term extinction is applied to both the procedure of presenting the CS without the UCS and to the resultant phenomenon, the decrease in the probability of a CR occurring. An example from Pavlov of a response that extinguished rapidly is presented in Table 2–3. Another example of extinction, somewhat more gradual, was presented previously in Figure 2–3. Note that in the experiment presented in Figure 2–3 there is both within-session and between-session extinction apparent in the way the data are plotted. Note also that there tends to be a slight recovery of the CR between days (compare extinction Block 2 with 3 and 4 with 5). Pavlov also noted this phenomena (*see* Table 2–3) and termed it *spontaneous recovery;* spontaneous because no experimental procedures were performed during the interval between tests that would tend to produce relearning. The spontaneous recovery of an extinguished CR tends to be small in magnitude but, nevertheless, the phenomenon is important because it indicates that the association that had been acquired during the acquisition phase is not completely eliminated by the extinction procedure, even when, at the end of extinction, the subject is no longer responding to the CS (*see* Table 2–3).

Pavlov's interpretation of extinction was that the CR was being inhibited. According to Pavlov, the extinction procedure led to the development of *internal inhibition,* a hypothetical process that occurs within the organism and is responsible for the reduction in CR strength. Additional support for Pavlov's hypothesis that the CR

*Table 2–3. Demonstration of Extinction and Spontaneous Recovery**

Presentation of CS alone	CR, Secretion of Saliva
Time	*c.cs.*
11:33 a.m. _ _ _ _ _ _ _ _ _	1.0
11:36 a.m. _ _ _ _ _ _ _ _ _	0.6
11:39 a.m. _ _ _ _ _ _ _ _ _	0.3
11:42 a.m. _ _ _ _ _ _ _ _ _	0.1
11:45 a.m. _ _ _ _ _ _ _ _ _	0.0
11:48 a.m. _ _ _ _ _ _ _ _ _	0.0
Interval of 2 hours	
1:50 p.m. _ _ _ _ _ _ _ _ _	0.15

*The data were obtained in Pavlov's lab by Babkin.
(From Pavlov, 1927.)

was being inhibited, not eliminated, by the extinction procedure was obtained from the observation that a novel stimulus presented during the course of extinction served to increase the probability or magnitude of an otherwise diminishing CR. This re-emergence of the CR, under what might be termed distracting conditions, Pavlov referred to as *disinhibition*. The inhibitory process itself was somehow blocked.

An analogous effect of a novel stimulus sometimes occurs during acquisition. Here, the presentation of a novel stimulus serves to *decrease* the probability of a CR, particularly if the organism has not had extensive acquisition training. Pavlov referred to this effect as *external inhibition* (cf., extinction, which is *internal inhibition*). Although the effects produced by a novel stimulus on the CR are opposite in direction in acquisition and extinction, these effects can probably be related to the same underlying mechanism, inhibition. What is inhibited is simply the dominant, on-going process. In acquisition this is an increase in the strength of a CR (or "excitation"), but in extinction it is a decrease in the strength of a CR, or inhibition itself, that is inhibited. Thus, disinhibition is another way of saying inhibition of inhibition. As the reader may have guessed, both of these effects (external inhibition and disinhibition) are probably related to the occurrence of the OR to novel stimuli.

A third line of evidence (in addition to spontaneous recovery and external disinhibition) that extinction does not completely eliminate the effects of acquisition training comes from experiments where the animal was retrained on the original response after extinction. These studies usually find that reacquisition is faster than original acquisition, indicating that some aspect of the original learning has been maintained through extinction.

We have now covered a number of the basic phenomena related to extinction, and it is interesting to briefly consider what a biologically adaptive advantage a process such as extinction (especially an extinction process that does not completely reverse the effects of prior learning) must give to an organism. The extinction process permits the organism to modify its behavior when the environment changes, it permits a "tracking," as it were, of fluctuations in biologically important environmental events. It is also interesting to note that, given the apparent importance and complexity of extinction related phenomena, a comparable process for eliminating unnecessary or no longer accurate associations was hardly considered by those philosophers who speculated about learning without the availability of experimental data. This is perhaps just one of many examples from the history of science where the availability of systematic objective data has revealed interesting subtleties and interpretations that were not reached by methods of pure speculation.

Generalization and Discrimination

When an animal learns an association by classical conditioning procedures, how narrowly defined is that association? For example, when Pavlov's dog began salivating at the sight of the vessel that usually contained its food, did it salivate only to that particular vessel or to any container that faintly resembled it? What does "faintly resemble" mean? What are the principles by which an organism learns to associate the occurrence of an event (the presentation of food) with one stimulus but not with a closely related stimulus? These are all questions that relate to the phenomena of generalization and discrimination. We will have a great deal to say about this topic in Chapter 10, but now, however, we shall briefly describe some of the procedures used to investigate these phenomena within the context of the classical conditioning paradigm.

Pavlov noted that when conditioned responses were in the initial stages of acquisition virtually any stimulus in the testing environment would acquire some propensity for eliciting the CR. For example, if the beat of a metronome was the specific CS paired with a food UCS, the dogs would not only salivate and show other CR behaviors when the metronome was sounded, but also when they were first brought into the testing room itself, or perhaps even when presented with any of several other stimuli from the area. However, as training proceeded those ancillary stimuli would gradually lose some, but not all, of their ability to elicit the CR.

The tendency for stimuli other than the specific CS to elicit the CR Pavlov referred to as *generalization*. As was usually the case, Pavlov's incidental observations were followed by systematic experimentation in order to further explore and understand the phenomena. Research from Pavlov's laboratory indicated, for example, that if the CS was tactile stimulation of a restricted area on a dog's back, then stimulation of other areas of the dog's body would also tend to elicit the CR; but the further away these areas were from the location of the original CS, the less likely they were to elicit the CR. Similarly, if the CS was a 1000 Hz tone, then tones of other frequencies, higher or lower, also tended to elicit the CR, but again, the further away in frequency they were from the original CS the less the probability (with some exceptions) that they elicited the CR. An example of generalization obtained in a Pavlovian conditioning experiment with rabbits is presented in Figure 2–5. In this experiment the rabbits were first conditioned with a 1200 Hz tone as the CS, and then presented tones of other frequencies. It is apparent that the greatest proportion of responses were made to the original CS, but also other stimuli elicited the CR, even though they were never paired with a UCS.

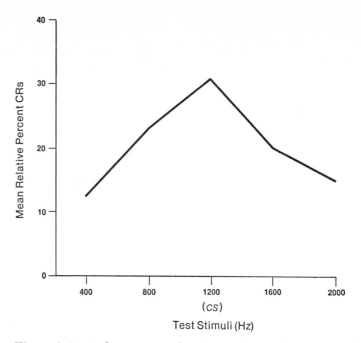

Figure 2–5. Relative generalization gradient: Percentage of responses elicited by the stimulus used in conditioning (CS) and by stimuli never paired with the UCS. (Redrawn from Liu, 1971.)

The generalization process is quite possibly related to the development and treatment of some forms of abnormal behavior such as phobias. Phobias are not only characterized by an extreme and unrealistic fear of some object or circumstance (e.g., snake or confinement in a "small" space) but also by the spread of this fear to anything vaguely resembling the object or circumstance. For example, individuals who are abnormally afraid of snakes will fear not only snakes but will refuse to go near any object that resembles a snake or near any area such as a zoo, woods, or fields that may contain a snake, and they may even find the word "snake" itself repulsive.

It is known that phobiclike behavior can be induced by Pavlovian conditioning procedures. For example, in the famous (or infamous) Watson and Raynor experiment (1920) a rat, which initially elicited no fear responses in an eleven-month-old child, was paired with a loud noise, an event which produced obvious startle and fear responses. It will be recognized that the rat was the CS and loud noise the UCS in this experiment. After a few pairings the presentation of the rat alone began to elicit conditioned fear responses. As described in the protocol of Watson and Raynor, "Rat suddenly presented alone, [Albert] puckered [his] face, whimpered and withdrew body sharply to the left." And, on a later trial, "The instant the rat was shown the baby began to cry. Almost instantly he turned sharply to the left, fell over on left side, raised himself on all fours and began to crawl away so rapidly that he was caught with difficulty before reaching the edge of the table." These conditioned responses were not only elicited by the original CS, the rat, but also generalized to other stimuli such as a rabbit, a dog, a fur coat, a package of cotton, and a Santa Claus mask. These stimuli had been presented to Albert prior to conditioning and none had elicited fear responses at that time. The fear response did not generalize to wooden blocks.

The preceding discussion gives some indication of the importance of generalization as a basic phenomena of conditioning. Pavlov himself gave an ethological interpretation to generalization, indicating, perhaps, why generalization should have evolved as an adaptive corollary of conditioning. In Pavlov's words:

> . . . natural stimuli are in most cases not rigidly constant but range around a particular strength and quality of stimulus in a common group. For example, the hostile sound of a beast of prey serves as a conditioned stimulus to a defense reflex in the animals which it hunts. The defense reflex is brought about independently of variations in pitch, strength and timber of the sound produced by the animal according to its distance, the tension of its vocal cords and similar factors (Pavlov, 1927, p. 113).

It is important that an organism generalize a conditioned response, but it is also sometimes important that an organism differentiate among stimuli that are followed by biologically important events and those that are not. Pavlov initially believed that if one stimulus was followed often enough by a UCS, then the organism would eventually respond to only that stimulus and no other. However, research in Pavlov's lab indicated otherwise. Complete differentiation between a stimulus consistently followed by a UCS and other stimuli was never obtained by this method, despite, in some instances, of over a thousand presentations of the CS–UCS pair. If, however, two stimuli are presented, one termed the CS+, always followed by a UCS and another, termed the CS−, never followed by a UCS, the subject quickly came to respond to the CS+ only. This procedure of presenting one stimulus that is consistently reinforced and another that is consistently nonreinforced is termed a _discrimination learning_ paradigm. It is through such research paradigms that we can investigate how environmental stimuli come to acquire differential control over an organism's behavior.

For example, in Pavlov's laboratory it was found that dogs could be conditioned to salivate only when a circle (the CS+) was presented and not when a square (the CS⁻) was presented. Pavlov and his colleagues investigated discrimination learning with many other stimuli including tones of different frequencies, several different geometric shapes, tactile stimuli, and even the sounds of metronomes and bubbling water.

An example of a discrimination formation is presented in Figure

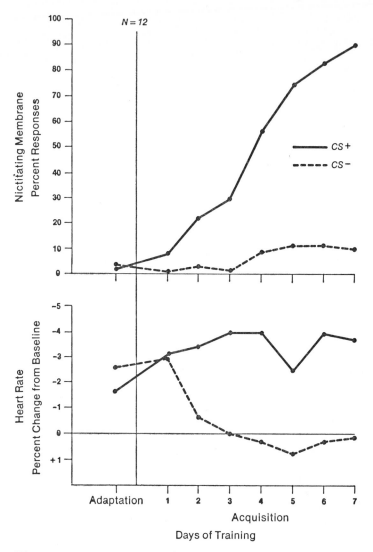

Figure 2–6. Discrimination learning. Acquisition of nictitating membrane and heart rate discriminative responses to an electric shock UCS applied near the rabbit's eyelid. See text for further explanation. (From Schneiderman, 1972, by permission of Prentice-Hall.)

2–6. This experiment by Swadlow, Schneiderman, and Schneiderman (1968) is interesting for several reasons. The differential stimuli (CS⁺ and CS⁻) were internal to the animal. Specifically, the CS⁺ was electrical stimulation (through implanted electrodes) of a visual relay nucleus (lateral geniculate body of the thalamus) on one side of a rabbit's brain, and the CS⁻ was stimulation of the contralateral visual relay nucleus. The UCS was a brief electric shock applied near the rabbit's eyelid. Note that two responses were measured, the nictitating membrane closure (one of the rabbit's three "eyelids") and heart rate, and that both showed differential conditioning to the same UCS and CS. Also note that during an adaptation phase both stimuli that were to serve as CSs elicited a decelerative heart-rate response, but as conditioning was initiated and developed, only the CS⁺ came to elicit the heart-rate deceleration.

This experiment, then, illustrates several general points. First is the phenomenon of discrimination learning itself; the CR comes to be elicited only by the reinforced stimulus (CS⁺). Second, it is possible for the differentially reinforced stimuli to be internal to the organism as well as external. Third, a number of responses may be conditioned simultaneously. In this particular experiment two response measures were taken and both demonstrated differential conditioning. Although only a single response is measured in the majority of experiments, we should remember that the actual learning that is occurring may be quite complex, involving several responses and probably occurring in a number of different brain areas simultaneously.

V. SUMMARY

Philosophical speculation through two millenia focused attention on just a few principles that seemed critical for the formation of associations between stimuli or events. Most important among these principles were *contiguity, frequency,* and *similarity.*

The experimental investigation of associative learning was begun by the Russian physiologist Ivan Pavlov just at the turn of the century. Pavlov found that if a stimulus (the UCS) which naturally elicited a reflex response (UCR) was presented in close temporal contiguity with an originally neutral stimulus (the CS), then that originally neutral stimulus would eventually come to elicit a response (the CR) which had many of the characteristics of the original reflex response. Conditioning was found to proceed most efficiently if the CS preceded the UCS.

The presentation of the UCS was said to *reinforce* conditioning in the sense that as long as the UCS was presented the probability of a CR increased or remained high *(acquisition)*, but when the UCS was not presented the probability of a CR decreased (extinction). Both an acquired and an extinguished conditioned response tend to *generalize* to similar stimuli.

However, if one stimulus is specifically reinforced (CS$^+$) and another stimulus not reinforced (CS$^-$), then an organism will eventually develop a discrimination between the stimuli so that the CR is more likely to be elicited by CS$^+$ than by CS$^-$.

The experimental investigation of the associative processes has revealed a number of complexities that had not been considered in the earlier philosophical speculations on the subject. Some of these complexities are the number and importance of various temporal relationships between the CS and UCS, alternative ways to measure the behavioral consequences of the new association (the CR), and the likelihood that a number of different responses are learned at the same time, perhaps in different levels of the nervous system.

Pavlov believed that the phenomenon of classical conditioning had important adaptive consequences for the organism because the acquisition of an association between a CS and a UCS provided the organism with a signal (the CS) indicating the impending occurrence of a biologically important event (the UCS). The study of classical conditioning is a study of how these signaling functions are acquired.

CHAPTER 3

Pavlovian Conditioning: Parameters and Theories

> *At present, after having acquired some knowledge of its (conditioning's) general principles, we feel surrounded, nay crushed, by the mass of details, all calling for elucidation.*
>
> Ivan Pavlov, 1927

Any phenomenon or process is understood only to the extent that we have knowledge of the variables that influence the phenomenon or process, knowledge of the manner in which these variables exert their influence, and knowledge of the extent of the influence. In this chapter, we shall examine how some of the most frequently investigated variables influence classical (Pavlovian) conditioning, and then we will turn to a consideration of several theoretical interpretations of the conditioning process.

I. VARIABLES THAT INFLUENCE CONDITIONING

Temporal Relationships Between the CS and UCS

The CS–UCS Interval

The CS–UCS interval refers to the time between CS onset and UCS onset in either a delayed or trace conditioning paradigm. In a sense, then, investigation of CS–UCS interval functions represents a direct investigation of the importance of contiguity in classical conditioning. In at least one area, eyelid conditioning, this investigation has yielded some remarkably consistent results. Figure 3–1 summarizes the results of eyelid conditioning studies conducted with humans. Note that a CS–UCS interval of approximately 450 milliseconds appears to produce maximal conditioning and that the degree of conditioning falls off rather sharply on either side of this optimal interval. Functions quite similar to this have been found in a number of other investigations with humans and lower animals. For example, in an investigation of eyelid conditioning in the rabbit Frey and Ross (1968) found that a 400-millisecond interval produced the most rapid conditioning in the range investigated (250, 400, 600, 1000 and 2000 milliseconds).

A more detailed examination of the lower end of the CS–UCS interval function is presented in Figure 3–2. The data presented in this figure were obtained from a study of the conditioned nictitating membrane response in rabbits (Smith, Coleman, & Gormezano, 1969). It is evident from the figure that (a) no conditioning occurs with CS–UCS intervals of 50 milliseconds or less (the –50 millisecond point represents a backward conditioning paradigm); (b) there is apparently a sharp break in the conditionability of this system between CS–UCS intervals of 50 and 100 milliseconds; and (c) there is an optimal CS–UCS interval in the 200 to 400 millisecond range with rate of conditioning and final level of performance falling off on either side of that range.

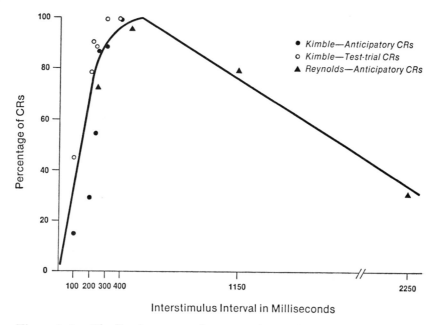

Figure 3–1. Idealized interstimulus interval (ISI) function, obtained from eyelid conditioning in humans. (From Kimble & Reynolds, 1967.)

Although there is rather impressive species generality in the CS–UCS interval functions obtained in eyelid (and related) conditioned responses, the generality does not extend to all forms of classically conditioned responses. For example, Noble and Harding (1963) conditioned the gross bodily movements elicited in Rhesus monkeys by an electric shock. The CS in this experiment was a change in illumination. The range of CS–UCS intervals investigated was 0.5, 1.0, 2.0 and 4.0 seconds, and optimal conditioning was found with the 2.0-second interval. In a study using an appetitive UCS (a

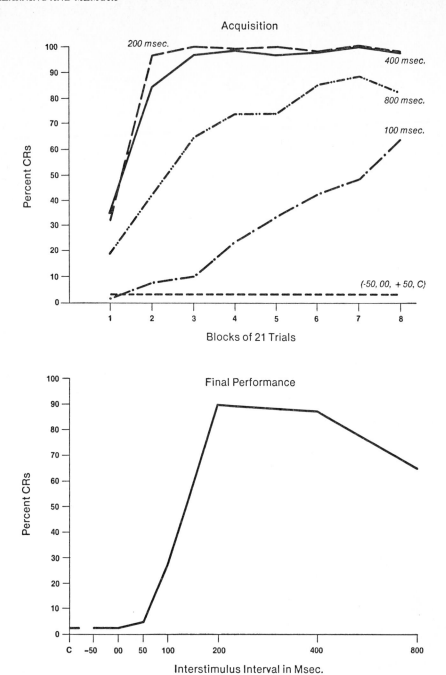

Figure 3–2. CS–UCS interval function in rabbit nictitating membrane conditioning. The top panel presents the acquisition functions obtained with the various ISI conditions and the right panel summarizes terminal performance level as a function of ISI. (Data from Smith, Coleman, & Gormezano, 1969.)

small amount of a saccharin solution squirted directly into a rabbit's mouth which produced a jaw movement UCR), Gormezano (1972) found that a 4.0-second CS–UCS interval produced the best conditioning in the range employed (0.25, 0.5, 1.0, 2.0 and 4.0 seconds).

In summary, then, the CS–UCS interval is a variable which clearly influences the effectiveness of conditioning. Forward conditioning, in which CS onset precedes UCS onset, is generally much more effective than either simultaneous conditioning or backward conditioning and, within at least some forward conditioning paradigms, there exists an optimal CS–UCS interval for conditioning. The exact value of the optimal CS–UCS interval itself appears to depend on the nature of the UCS and UCR involved in the experiment.

Why should there be an optimal CS–UCS interval for conditioning? Speculation concerning the mechanism behind these interstimulus interval (ISI) functions has taken two general directions. One explanation offered by Hull (1943, 1951) was based on events that were assumed to occur in the central nervous system as a result of the presentation of an external stimulus such as a CS. On the basis of a small amount of available data, Hull (1943) hypothesized that neural activity following the presentation of a CS reached a maximum in about 450 milliseconds after the presentation of the external stimulus. Hull further assumed that the resultant conditioning would be strongest if the UCS was presented at a time when the neural aftereffects of the CS were maximal.

These assumptions are clearly consistent with much of the eyelid conditioning data. However, Hull's theory of ISI effects is no longer considered to be generally applicable for at least two reasons. One reason is that the data from a number of studies clearly show that the optimal ISI is not always 450 milliseconds, and a second difficulty is that Hull's assumptions concerning the presumed neural aftereffects of CS presentation were probably much too simple, given our current knowledge of brain functioning.

A second approach to explaining the ISI data has been concerned with the latency of the response system involved in the conditioning task. It has been suggested by several investigators (e.g., Hilgard & Marquis, 1940) that the effects of the CR on the UCS are important for conditioning and that the opportunity for the CR to modify the UCS would depend on the ISI used in the experiment *and* on the latency of the response system. For example, the eyelid closure reflex has a short latency, and therefore short ISIs should be effective in the conditioning of this system since the UCS would then be presented at a time when its effects could be ameliorated by the CR of eyelid closure. However, with slower acting response systems, such as those mediated by the autonomic nervous system, conditioning might be effective with much longer ISIs, and, indeed, heart-rate conditioning has been reported with an ISI of 20 seconds (Church & Black, 1958), an interval much longer than those usually effective in eyelid conditioning. However, at the present time there are no clear data on exactly what the *optimal* ISI is for a variety of responses mediated by the autonomic nervous system (heart rate, GSR, salivation, etc.).

A further dimension is added to this interpretation of ISI effects by a fact noted in a large number of conditioning studies. That is, the latency of the CR often changes during the course of conditioning. Sometimes the change is an increase in latency (e.g., Kimmel, 1965) and sometimes a decrease (e.g., Suboski, 1967). In addition to a change in latency, there may also be a change in the form of the CR with different CS–UCS intervals. An example of this change is presented in Figure 3–3. These changes in CR latency and in form, in themselves, may be related to the effectiveness of the CR in modifying the effects of the UCS, but this is not entirely clear at the present time.

Although the details of ISI functions with different response systems are quite complex and by no means completely worked out, it is clear that the potential effectiveness of the CR on the impact of the UCS will have to be taken into account in any explanation of the

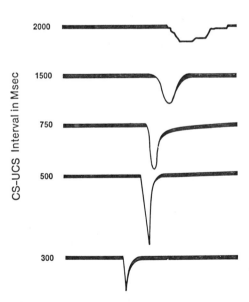

Figure 3–3. Typical forms of the conditioned paw-movement response in cats at different interstimulus intervals. (From Wickens, 1973.)

CS–UCS interval function. In general, though, it may be useful to remember now that the CS probably prepares the organism for the presentation of the UCS and that the measured CR may be just one aspect of the preparation. Sometimes the CR may be directly adaptive (such as salivation when the UCS is food in the mouth or eyelid closure when the UCS is a puff of air to the eye), and sometimes it may just reflect some general preparatory function (such as gross bodily movement when the UCS is electric shock). But in any case, the idea that Pavlovian conditioning involves a preparatory response has occurred to a large number of investigators and we shall return to this point later in this chapter (*see* pp. 69-72).

Trace Conditioning

Conditioning was found in Pavlov's laboratory with trace intervals (time between CS *termination* and UCS onset) as long as several minutes. However, in these experiments, the dogs were first trained with contiguous presentation of the CS and UCS and only gradually introduced to the long trace intervals. In most cases, trace intervals longer than a few seconds greatly reduce the degree of conditioning. For example, in a discriminative salivary conditioning experiment, Ellison (1964) found that conditioning was about equally effective with an 8-second trace interval and an 8-second ISI in a delay paradigm, but a 16-second trace interval led to poorer conditioning than a 16-second ISI in a delay paradigm. In a heart-rate discriminative conditioning study it has been found (Manning, Schneiderman, & Lordahl, 1969) that delay conditioning was superior to trace conditioning at all intervals investigated (7, 14 and 21 seconds) and that a 21-second trace interval led to very little discriminative conditioning at all.

It is a general finding that trace conditioning is possible, but that it tends to be inferior to delay conditioning. Furthermore, the longer the trace interval the greater the difference is likely to be. As was the case in CS–UCS interval functions, the nature of the response being conditioned is likely to have a great effect on the boundaries of the effective trace interval. For example, it has been found that a 1-second trace interval seriously disrupts nictitating membrane conditioning but not heart-rate conditioning in the rabbit (Meredith & Schneiderman, 1967).

Long-Delay Conditioning

The final type of temporal relationship between the CS and UCS that we shall consider here is the long-delay conditioning paradigm. Pavlov found that when there was a relatively long CS–UCS interval such as two or three minutes (the CS remaining on during the entire interval), a very interesting phenomenon occurred. Early in training the CR tended to be elicited by CS onset, but as conditioning proceeded, the latency of the CR became longer and longer, so that eventually it did not occur until just before the UCS was scheduled to be delivered. Pavlov labeled this phenomenon *inhibition of delay* and interpreted it to mean that the dog was forming a temporal discrimination and actively inhibiting the occurrence of the CR until the UCS was imminent, perhaps because this was the point at which the CR had its maximal adaptive influence on the UCS.

Pavlov found that inhibition of delay, like internal inhibition or extinction, could be disinhibited by the application of a novel external stimulus. An example of inhibition of delay and of its disinhibition is presented in Table 3–1. The development of inhibition of delay as a function of training trials is presented in Figure 3–4.

Characteristics of the UCS

UCS Intensity

In general the more intense the UCS (up to some limit), the greater the final level of conditioning. When an appetitive response is being conditioned, there are two ways to manipulate UCS intensity: One is to vary it indirectly by varying the deprivation state of the subject, and the second is to vary the levels of the UCS itself. Considering first variations in deprivation state, Pavlov himself reported that little or no conditioning could be obtained in his dogs unless they were deprived of food for some time before the experiment began.

Surprisingly little has been done in the way of systematic investigation to follow up Pavlov's observation. However, it has been found that the classical conditioning of licking in rats with water squirted into the mouth as the UCS varies directly as a function of the degree of water deprivation, with no conditioning occurring when the subjects were completely satiated (DeBold, Miller, & Jensen, 1965). When the amount of food used as the UCS is varied, it has been found that dogs given greater amounts of food show greater anticipatory salivation (Gantt, 1938: Wagner, Siegel, Thomas, & Ellison, 1964).

Results similar to these have been found in aversive conditioning situations. For example, the degree of eyelid conditioning varies directly with the intensity of the air puff used as a UCS (Spence, 1956). An example of the effects of UCS intensity on eyelid conditioning may be seen in Figure 3–5.

Table 3-1. Inhibition of Delay*

Time	Stimulus (Experiment of 15th September, 1907)	Drops of Saliva
2:28 p.m.	Tactile	0, 0, 0, 0, 2, 8
2:40 p.m.	Tactile	0, 0, 0, 5, 20, 17
2:55 p.m.	Tactile + thermal stimulus at 0.5°C	2, 2, 3, 4, 20, 24
3:10 p.m.	Tactile	1, 0, 0, 0, 10, 17

*The table presents salivary secretion for each 30-second period during a 3-minute CS–UCS interval. The application of a novel stimulus on Trial 3 produced "external disinhibition." (Data from Pavlov, 1927.)

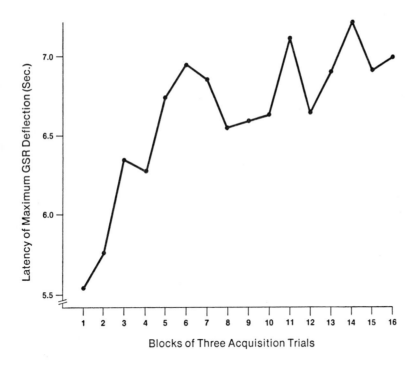

Figure 3-4. Average time from CS onset to peak GSR deflection. Nonresponse trials were omitted. (From Kimmel, 1964, © Irvington Publishers, New York.)

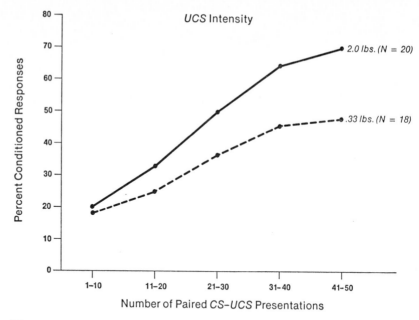

Figure 3–5. Frequency curves of eyelid conditioning as a function of the intensity of air puff used as the unconditioned stimulus, with average puff strength held constant. Both groups received 50 presentations of the air puff alone interspersed between 50 conditioning trials. The upper curve presents the data of a group given 2.0-lb. puffs on the conditioning trials and .33-lb. puffs alone; the lower curve shows the data of a group given .33-lb. puffs on the conditioning trials and 2.0-lb. puffs alone. (From Spence, 1956.)

UCS Duration

Variations in UCS duration have very small or no effects at all on conditioning. These results have been found in a number of studies including GSR conditioning with shock UCS durations of 0.5, 3.0 and 15.0 seconds (Coppock & Chambers, 1959), heart-rate conditioning with shock UCS durations of 0.1, 2.0, 6.0 and 15.0 seconds (Zeaman & Wegner, 1958) and with eyelid conditioning with air puff UCS durations of 0.05 and 1.0 seconds (Runquist & Spence, 1959).

However, a more thorough exploration of brief UCS durations has indicated that this variable may have an effect (Frey & Butler, 1973). In this study it was found that a UCS duration of 100 milliseconds produced better conditioning than UCS durations of either 50 milliseconds or 200 milliseconds. Frey and Butler speculate that the relationship of UCS offset to the point of the maximal UCR may be an important variable in determining the differential effectiveness of UCS durations. In their study the 100-millisecond duration led to UCS offset just as the UCR reached its maximum.

All in all, though, the effects of UCS duration appear to be small, and it would seem that the time of UCS *onset* is a far more critical variable than the time of UCS *offset* (as manipulated by UCS duration).

Characteristics of the CS

CS Intensity

Several studies have indicated that CS intensity has virtually no effect on acquisition of a CR with humans (e.g., Grant & Schneider, 1949; Walker, 1960). The Walker study was particularly interesting in that she varied UCS intensity (0.5 psi or 5.0 psi air puffs) as well as CS intensity (1000-Hz tones at 30 db or 80 db). This manipulation is interesting because it is possible that CS intensity would be effective at only a high or only a low UCS intensity; in other words, there may have been an interaction between CS intensity and UCS intensity. However, Walker did not find an effect of CS intensity at either level of the UCS.

There does appear to be at least two conditions under which substantial CS intensity effects are obtained. One of these conditions simply involves the use of lower animals as subjects. Kamin (1965) and Gormezano (1972) both reported considerably better conditioning with more intense CSs in experiments using rats and rabbits, respectively, as subjects. A second procedure that leads to large CS intensity effects involves the within-subjects manipulation of the intensity variable. That is, if the same subjects experience both high and low intensity CSs, then CS intensity does have a fairly large effect on conditioning in humans and lower animals (Grice & Hunter, 1964; Gormezano, 1972). The results of the Grice and Hunter study are presented in Figure 3–6. Since these results are quite interesting in their own right and also illustrate several general principles, specific instances of which will occur at other places in this text, we shall go into the study in some detail.

The experiment was a study of eyelid conditioning in humans with a 1.0-psi air puff as the UCS, and a 0.5-second CS–UCS interval. There were three groups in the experiment; for one group the CS was a 100-db tone, for a second group the CS was a 50-db tone, and the third group (two-stimuli group) received half of its trials with the 50-db tone as a CS and half with the 100-db tone as the CS. It is quite clear from Figure 3–6 that the CS intensity effect was much greater in the group that experienced both stimuli than it was when the CS

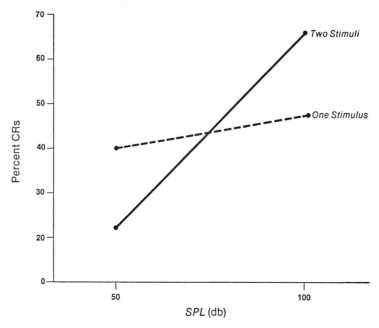

Figure 3–6.   Percent CRs during last 60 trials to loud and soft tones under one- and two-stimulus conditions. (From Grice & Hunter, 1964.)

intensity variable was manipulated between groups. We shall see several examples throughout this text where the effects of a variable are quite different when the same subjects experience different levels of the variable than when the variable is manipulated between subjects. In fact, many of the effects we will be referring to as within-subject effects are, in common usage, referred to as "psychological" effects. That is, effects of a variable that would not be large in any absolute sense but are apparently magnified when a subject compares different levels of the variable.

Before leaving the topic of CS intensity, we should mention that intensity effects, when they are obtained, are probably not entirely due to some enhanced "energizing" effect of the more intense stimuli. Instead, the CS intensity effects are probably related to the degree of difference between the CS and the average level of background stimulation. We can say this because the offset of a stimulus has been shown to be effective as a CS, and the offset of a more intense CS is more effective than the offset of a less intense CS (Champion, 1962). In general the greater the change or difference between the stimulus functioning as a CS and the background stimuli, the more effective the CS will be, and it does not make too much difference whether the change is in the direction of increasing or decreasing intensity in the CS (Kamin, 1965).

Other Characteristics of the CS

COMPOUND STIMULI

The use of multiple or compound stimuli as CSs represents a very interesting variation of CS parameters. A compound stimulus is a stimulus that is composed of two or more elements such as a tone and a light. These elements can be presented simultaneously (simultaneous compounding) or successively (successive compounding). Apparently the first compound conditioning experiment was conducted by Palladin in Pavlov's laboratory in 1906 (Pavlov, 1927; Razran, 1965). Palladin paired a thermal stimulus of 0°C. with a tactile stimulus that had already been used as a CS. He found that the tactile stimulus and the compound of tactile plus thermal stimuli would both elicit the CR; but the second stimulus added to the compound, the thermal stimulus, never did come to elicit a CR if presented by itself, despite repeated pairings with the UCS as part of the compound.

Results of this type in which one stimulus in the element does not acquire conditioned properties were found a number of times in Pavlov's laboratory and by later investigators (e.g., Kamin, 1969). These effects, referred to as "overshadowing" or "blocking," are likely to occur when the two stimuli are from different modalities and particularly likely to occur when one of the stimuli is more intense than the other and/or has been previously presented singly as a CS. These results seem to be explicable, at least on a superficial level, by assuming that if one element of the compound sufficiently predicts the impending occurrence of the UCS, then the subject will not attend to, and will learn nothing about, the second element of the compound (cf., Kamin, 1969; Rescorla & Wagner, 1972). We will have more to say about this interesting line of research in Chapter 11.

A second result that sometimes occurs with compound conditioning is that *neither* of the elements will elicit a CR when presented singly; only the joint presentation of both elements in the compound is sufficient to elicit the CR. Table 3–2 presents the results of one of the subjects in an experiment by Platanov (in Razran, 1965). In this experiment, the elements of the compound eventually became ineffective in eliciting the CR after extensive overtraining. This type of compound conditioning, in which only the compound elicits the CR, has been termed *configural conditioning* by Razran (1965) and is clearly a situation in which the whole means something different than its elements in isolation (*see also* Booth & Hammond, 1971).

Table 3–2.   Configural Conditioning

Session	Percent CRs elicited by each CS*		
	Compound	Bell	Light
1	77	66	35
2	67	50	32
3	89	80	25
4	90	21	13
5	95	20	13
6	95	15	10
7	100	0	0

*Percent of occurrence of compound and component plantar conditioning in an adult human subject with a simultaneous compound of an electric bell and a light as the CS, shock as the UCS, and approximately 40 trials per session. (After Platanov, from Razran, 1965, © Irvington Publishers, New York.)

Table 3–3.   Successive Compound Conditioning *

Time	Conditioned stimulus	Secretion of saliva in drops during 30 seconds	
3:10 p.m.	H-T_1-T_2-B	4	Reinforced
3:17 p.m.	H-T_2-T_1-B	0	Not reinforced
3:27 p.m.	H-T_1-T_2-B	3	Reinforced
3:32 p.m.	H-T_1-T_2-B	4	Reinforced
3:38 p.m.	H-T_2-T_1-B	0	Not reinforced
3:46 p.m.	H-T_1-T_2-B	2	Reinforced

*Different sequences of stimuli used as CS+ and CS− in a successive compound conditioning experiment by Ivanov-Smolensky. (From Pavlov, 1927.)

More recently, Rescorla (1973b) has reported evidence that a compound stimulus, AB, can be considered as three stimuli, each element separately and a unique stimulus associated with the combination of the two.

An example of the compounding of successively presented stimuli is provided by an experiment by Ivanov-Smolensky working in Pavlov's laboratory (Pavlov, 1927). The experiment was a study of discrimination learning with the CS+ and CS−, each composed of a four-stimulus sequence. The CS+ was made up of a hissing sound (H), a high frequency tone (T_1), a low frequency tone (T_2) and the sound of a buzzer (B). The stimuli were presented in the order stated with the last stimulus followed by the UCS. The CS− in the experiment differed from the CS+ only in that the order of the two middle components was reversed. The results presented in Table 3–3 show that very good differential conditioning was established despite the complex nature of the stimuli and the subtle differences between the stimuli. Further information on compound conditioning may be found in Razran, 1965; Baker, 1968; and Weiss, 1972.

INFORMATION STIMULI

Another interesting use of stimuli as CSs in conditioning experiments has been pursued in a number of human eyelid conditioning studies by David Grant and his students (e.g., Fleming, Grant, & North, 1968; Fleming, Grant, North, & Levy, 1968; Grant 1972). In these experiments the stimuli used as CSs have ranged from words flashed on a screen to the truth or falsity of brief statements (e.g., "bees make honey," "horses can fly") and to solutions of simple arithmetic problems also flashed on a screen. These studies have indicated that true statements and correct solutions to arithmetic problems tend to elicit more eyelid CRs than false statements and incorrect solutions to arithmetic problems, even when both types of CS are equally reinforced. Furthermore, differential conditioning tends to be better when incorrect solutions or false statements are used as CS$^+$ and true statements or correct solutions are used as CS$^-$, than when the reverse pairings are used.

If these findings seem somewhat paradoxical, remember that the reinforcement in eyelid conditioning is an aversive event (air puff in these studies), and apparently an aversive event as reinforcement following an incorrect statement produces better conditioning than an aversive event following a correct statement. It is clear that the use of stimuli that convey information adds yet another dimension to Pavlovian conditioning research, a dimension that some day may have something to tell us about the interaction between processes that we could call cognitive and conscious, and processes that are normally noncognitive and nonconscious.

Percentage of Reinforced Trials

Acquisition Effects

One of the methods of measuring the course of conditioning is the test trials procedure. Occasionally, a UCS is omitted and the data are examined to determine whether a CR occurred. But how often can the test trials be presented before the progress of conditioning itself is affected? The few studies that were conducted in Pavlov's laboratory indicated that conditioning was virtually impossible if only one of every four trials was reinforced. Research since Pavlov has indicated quite strongly that the final level of conditioning is considerably reduced if fewer than 100 percent of the acquisition trials are reinforced. This result has been obtained from humans and infrahuman organisms in situations using salivary conditioning with a food UCS (Wagner, Siegel, Thomas, & Ellison, 1964) and with a dilute acid UCS (Fitzgerald, 1963); it has been found in heart-rate conditioning (Fitzgerald, Vardaris, & Teyler, 1966), activity conditioning (Longo, Milstein, & Bitterman, 1962), and eyelid conditioning (Humphreys, 1939; Grant & Schipper, 1952). The results of the Grant and Schipper study are presented in Figure 3–7. The data are quite orderly, with 100 percent and 75 percent reinforcement producing approximately equal performance, both greater than 50 percent reinforcement which was greater than 25 percent reinforcement which was greater than no reinforcement.

These decremental effects of partial reinforcement occur over a wide range of UCS intensities, at least in eyelid conditioning (Ross & Spence, 1960), and they seem to be asymptotic; i.e., there is no indication that a partially reinforced group will ever "catch up" with a continuously reinforced group even after many trials; (for somewhat different results obtained with conditioning of the rabbit's nictitating membrane response *see* Gormezano & Coleman, 1975). This asymptotic effect is apparent in the 50 percent and 25 percent groups in the previously mentioned Grant and Schipper (1952) study (*see* Figure 3–7) and also in a study by Ross (1959).

The Ross study is somewhat complicated but interesting and instructive, and so we shall spend a little time describing it. There were five groups of subjects (college students) used in an eyelid conditioning study: One group (Group C) received continuous reinforcement throughout the 220 acquisition trials; a second group (Group P) received 50 percent reinforcement throughout acquisition; a third group (Group C20–P) received continuous reinforcement for the first 20 trials and was then shifted to partial reinforcement; a fourth group (Group C100–P) received continuous reinforcement for the first 100 trials and then was shifted to partial reinforcement; and a final group (Group P40–C) received 40 partially reinforced trials and was then shifted to continuous reinforcement.

The results of this experiment indicate the following: (a) the decrement associated with partial reinforcement persists even after extensive training (Groups P versus C); (b) subjects shifted from continuous to partial reinforcement drop abruptly to the level of the partially reinforced group indicating that, whatever the process is that is producing the decrement associated with partial reinforcement, it does not develop gradually; (c) on the other hand, subjects shifted from partial to continuous reinforcement show a slow rise to the level of the continuous group, indicating that the process involved in this change is one that is gradually acquired. Ross's interpretation of his data was that partially reinforced subjects develop a set not to respond (an "inhibitory set"), and, thus, the decrement

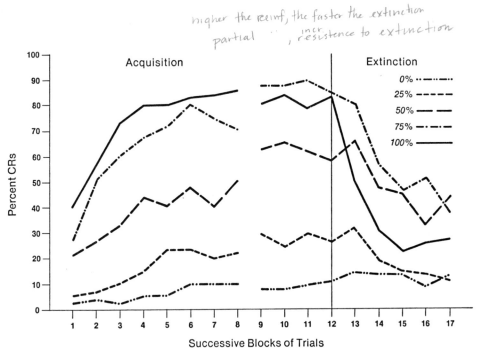

higher the reinf, the faster the extinction
partial ", incr resistence to extinction

Figure 3–7. The course of acquisition and extinction of the eyelid CR with varying percentages of reinforced trials during training. Percent frequency of CRs is plotted against successive blocks of trials. The size of the block during training (1–12) is eight trials except for Block 8 which is four trials. The size of the block during extinction (13–17) is five trials. (From Grant & Schipper, 1952.)

associated with partial reinforcement is a motivational or performance effect not a learning effect. This interpretation is certainly consistent with Ross's results and with other experiments using human subjects (*see* Spence, 1966, for a review of these experiments), but it does not seem applicable to studies on infrahuman organisms in which a partial reinforcement acquisition decrement is also found. A complete explanation of these data will have to await further research.

Extinction Effects

Partial reinforcement in acquisition also produces some very interesting effects in extinction. Note in the Grant and Schipper study previously presented (Figure 3–7) that the group given 100 percent reinforcement in acquisition extinguished faster than the groups given 75 percent and 50 percent reinforcement in acquisition. This greater resistance to extinction following partial reinforcement is a frequent finding in Pavlovian conditioning, having been found in human eyelid conditioning (Humphreys, 1939; Grant & Schipper, 1952); salivary conditioning with an acid UCS (Fitzgerald, 1963); salivary conditioning with a food UCS (Wagner, Siegel, Thomas, & Ellison, 1964) and in heart-rate conditioning (Fitzgerald, Vardaris, & Teyler, 1966). However, see Gormezano and Coleman (1975) for a recent study conducted with rabbits in which there was no effect of partial reinforcement on resistance to extinction.

This partial reinforcement extinction effect (PREE) is in some ways paradoxical, particularly if one thinks that each reinforcement adds in some way to the "strength" of an association and that resistance to extinction reflects this strength. If this were true, the subjects that receive 100 percent reinforcement ought to be more resistant to extinction. This is clearly not the case. There is no completely adequate account of the PREE in classical conditioning, and we will defer any theoretical discussion of partial reinforcement until later in the text (*see* pp. 120-38) after we have discussed instrumental learning in which a good deal more systematic research has been done on partial reinforcement (*see* Chapter 5).

Distribution of Trials

The last variable we will consider in detail is the intertrial interval (ITI), the time between successive trials. If you look back at any of the several tables that we have reproduced from Pavlov's book (e.g., Table 2–3, p. 35 and Table 3–1, p. 51), you will note that several minutes were typically allowed to elapse between successive trials. There was a good practical reason for this, perhaps discovered informally in Pavlov's laboratory, but since demonstrated quite clearly in systematic studies. That is, both the rate and final level of conditioning tend to be retarded when conditioning trials occur close together in time. For example, a human eyelid conditioning study by Prokasy, Grant, and Meyers (1958) found that final level of conditioning was better in a group given a 135-second ITI than in a group given a 45-second ITI, and both of these showed better conditioning

Table 3–4.   Summary of Parametric Effects

CS–UCS Interval	Optimal interval in eyelid conditioning and nictitating membrane in range 250–450 milliseconds.
	Good conditioning obtained with longer intervals with other responses (e.g., heart rate), optimum not clearly specified.
Trace Interval	Trace conditioning possible, but performance usually inferior to delay conditioning.
Long-delay Conditioning	With a long CS–UCS interval in delay conditioning the CR latency usually increases during training; this is termed inhibition of delay.
CS Characteristics	Asymptotic performance greater with more intense CS. CS intensity more effective if varied within subjects.
	CS duration has little effect on conditioning.
	Compound stimuli and informational stimuli can serve as CSs.
UCS Characteristics	Conditioning tends to vary directly with UCS intensity.
	UCS duration has apparently minor effects on conditioning.
Partial Reinforcement	Decrement in acquisition performance, but usually greater resistance to extinction.
Intertrial Interval	Acquisition hampered by very short ITIs.
	Resistance to extinction enhanced by long ITIs in extinction.

than a group given a 15-second ITI. Most of the detrimental effects of short ITIs appear to come with ITIs shorter than a minute or two. Very long ITIs would probably also have a detrimental effect, but there has been almost no systematic research conducted in standard classical conditioning paradigms with ITIs beyond a few minutes.

The various parametric relationships discussed in this section are summarized in Table 3–4.

II. VARIATIONS ON
THE BASIC CONDITIONING PARADIGM

Interoceptive Conditioning

When either the CS or UCS, or both, is delivered directly to the internal organs of the subject (human or lower animal), the conditioning paradigm is often referred to as *interoceptive conditioning.* Most of the research utilizing this technique has been conducted in Russia, perhaps because Russian investigators of conditioning are trained as physiologists. Some of this work has been summarized in English by Razran (1961). In this section we shall briefly describe a few of the experiments presented by Razran and indicate the presumed importance of this paradigm.

In one experiment the CS was the inflation of the duodenum of a dog (Laska) with 30–40 cc of air over a 5-second period. The UCS was a shock applied to the dog's left hind paw during the fifth second of the CS. The UCR was paw withdrawal. The first CR (withdrawal of the paw to the CS of duodenum inflation) occurred after only five trials and remained stable over an extended conditioning period.

In another experiment the CS was a rhythmic distension (90–100 per minute) of surgically formed intestinal loops in dogs. The UCS was a change in the gaseous composition of air to a 10 percent carbon dioxide mixture. This UCS was reported to produce severe hypercapnic (overbreathing) and defensive reactions (including contraction of the spleen). When the intestinal CS was paired with the respiratory UCS, the first hypercapnic CRs occurred within 3–6 trials and were stable within 16 trials. Futhermore, when a discrimination paradigm was introduced with the original CS as the CS^+ and with a rhythmic distension of the same intestinal loop at a rate of 15 per minute (and a lower pressure) as the CS^-, the dogs quickly developed differential responding, the hypercapnic reactions occurring only to the CS^+. These same dogs were used in another experiment in which the hypercapnic reactions were shown to be conditionable to auditory stimuli.

In another study the intestinal fistula of a human subject was irrigated with cold water at 6–8°C. When this UCS had been preceded only eight times by the flash of a red lamp as a CS, the subject began to report that he felt cold (the CR) whenever the red light was flashed.

Razran (1961) has referred to the interoceptive conditioning paradigm as a method of making the unconscious observable. This is so because activity of the visceral organs is not usually consciously experienced, but this activity can readily serve as either a CS or UCS for the conditioning of measurable response. Interoceptive conditioning research is also important because, in Razran's terms ". . . interoceptive conditioning (is) an almost built-in function that is constantly generated and regenerated in the very process of living and acting (Razran, 1961, p. 97)." The potential relevance of interoceptive conditioning research for psychosomatic medicine should also be obvious (*see also* Chapter 9).

Higher-Order Conditioning

When a CS is paired with a UCS, it eventually acquires the property of eliciting a CR, a response that is usually much like the original response elicited by the UCS. Does this mean that the CS also acquires reinforcing properties much like the original UCS had? Can the CS itself support conditioning to a new stimulus? The answer is yes. This higher-order conditioning paradigm is illustrated diagrammatically below.

$$\text{I. } CS_1$$
$$\searrow$$
$$CR$$

$$UCS \rightarrow UCR$$

$$\text{II. } CS_2$$
$$\searrow$$
$$CR$$

$$CS_1 \rightarrow CR$$

The first phase of the paradigm is a standard conditioning sequence, and in the second phase the original CS (CS_1) was used like a UCS and paired with a new stimulus (CS_2). As an example of this procedure, we can refer to a continuation of one of the interoceptive conditioning studies cited above. Recall the experiment on the dog Laska in which the CS was an inflation of the duodenum with air and the UCS was shock to the left hind paw. After 129 trials of this original conditioning, the shock was no longer presented and a new stimulus, the sound of a buzzer, was paired with the duodenal inflation. The buzzer (CS_2) lasted for 15 seconds and preceded duodenal inflation (CS_1) by 10 seconds. After 18 trials, the buzzer came to elicit left-paw withdrawals as well as respiratory changes. Note that the buzzer was never itself paired with shock to the paw.

Relatively few studies have been conducted with the higher-order conditioning paradigm, and those that have been done have indicated that higher-order conditioning is often difficult to establish and is not a particularly robust phenomenon once established. One of the reasons for difficulties encountered in this line of research is that the higher-order conditioning procedure (Phase II in the above diagram) is also an extinction procedure for the original CS. See studies by Kamin (1969) and Rizley & Rescorla (1972) for recent examples of higher-order conditioning and a discussion of the methodological issues involved.

Sensory Preconditioning

The third paradigm we will mention here, sensory preconditioning, is similar to higher-order conditioning, but the experimental manipulation of particular interest comes *prior* to the basic conditioning procedure. This paradigm is illustrated in a study by Brogden (1939). Brogden first paired a bell and a light for some 200 trials. Then, in the second phase of the experiment, Brogden paired one of these stimuli with a leg shock UCS in dogs. In the third phase of the experiment, the stimulus from Phase I that had not been paired with shock was presented to the dogs, and it was found to elicit the leg withdrawal CR. Dogs that were treated identically, except that Phase I was omitted, did not show the transfer of the CR to another stimulus. A diagrammatic outline of the sensory preconditioning paradigm is presented below.

$$\text{I. } CS_1 \qquad\qquad \text{II. } CS_2 \qquad\qquad\qquad \text{III. } CS_1$$
$$CS_2 \qquad\qquad\qquad\qquad \searrow CR \qquad\qquad\qquad\qquad \searrow CR$$
$$UCS \rightarrow UCR$$

For a second example of the operation of this paradigm, we can return to another one of the studies presented as an example of interoceptive conditioning; the second example given, in which the CS was a distension of the small intestine and the UCS was an electric shock to the dog's paw. Prior to the conditioning phase, the intestinal distension stimulus had been paired with other stimuli (e.g., smell of ammonia, sound of a whistle). After conditioning to the intestinal CS had been established, the other stimuli were presented and it was found that they now elicited the paw withdrawal CR.

Sensory preconditioning is particularly important for theories of learning because it demonstrates that associations can be formed between two stimuli, neither of which is a particularly potent elicitor of a response other than, perhaps, an orienting response. The actual performance of a sensory preconditioning experiment is somewhat more complicated than indicated here because a number of control conditions are needed to equate for familiarity with the two stimuli used as CSs and to insure that the results are not simply due to generalization. The interested reader may consult Seidel (1959) for a consideration of the appropriate experimental designs and Rizley and Rescorla (1972) for an interesting theoretical interpretation of sensory preconditioning.

Semantic Conditioning

The final variation on the basic Pavlovian theme that we shall discuss here, semantic conditioning, grew out of some research in Pavlov's laboratory that indicated that a CR could be transferred from an object used as a CS to the word for that object when humans were used as subjects. For example, if a light was used as a CS, it was found that the CR would occur if the word "light" was presented to the subjects. This paradigm was extended to the situation in which words themselves are used as CSs, and then transfer was tested to words that did not look alike but had similar meaning. For example, Razran (1939) found that college students transferred a conditioned salivary response from the CS word "style" more to the word "fashion" than to the word "stile"; and, similarly, the salivary CR transferred from "surf" to "wave" more readily than from "surf" to "serf."

A somewhat incredible experiment performed in Russia was briefly described by Razran. The UCS in this experiment was an electric shock and the UCR was the reduction in blood coagulation time. The initial CS in a study with human subjects was the flash of a lamp. It was not only found that the coagulation response was conditioned, but it generalized from the lamp to the word "lamp" and to the related words "lantern" and "light," but not to the word "whistle" (Markosyan, 1958, reported by Razran, 1961, p. 104). For a more extensive review of semantic conditioning *see* Feather (1965) and Hartman (1965).

III. THEORETICAL INTERPRETATIONS OF CLASSICAL CONDITIONING

We have now covered some of the procedures used and some of the data obtained in classical conditioning research. We have seen that the various "principles" of association elaborated by earlier writers (e.g., Aristotle and the British empiricists) have counterparts in the experimental investigation of conditioning, and that these principles are indeed important in conditioning. For example, contiguity becomes translated into temporal relationships between the CS and

UCS, and these relationships, while quite complex, are undoubtedly very important in determining the degree, course, and manner of conditioning. The principle of resemblance or similarity finds expression as the process of generalization. Forming an association by pairing one CS with a UCS tends also to form associations of lesser strength between stimuli similar to the original CS and that UCS. In fact, generalization tests provide a method of quantifying similarity and of determining just what it is that subjects, even nonverbal subjects, do find similar. The semantic conditioning procedure is a particularly interesting type of generalization procedure for use with human subjects. The principle of repetition or frequency finds expression as the number of acquisition trials. We can determine with some degree of accuracy the average number of repetitions or trials necessary to produce a given level of conditioning.

Beyond finding an empirical basis for these principles, the laboratory investigation of association revealed a number of other variables, and interactions between variables, that influence the effectiveness of conditioning. For example, we have seen that the level of conditioning varies as a function of the CS–UCS interval, but the CS–UCS function itself depends on what response is being conditioned. Similarly, the effect of CS intensity on conditioning depends to a large extent on whether a between-subject or within-subject testing procedure is used.

Given these basic empirical relationships, we will now turn to attempts to explain classical conditioning in theoretical terms. Why does classical conditioning occur? Is there a basic process or processes common to all classical conditioning? There have been numerous theoretical accounts of classical conditioning. We shall sample but a few starting, naturally, with Pavlov.

Pavlov's Theory of Conditioning

Pavlov's interest in conditioning arose primarily from his interest in physiology, not from his interest in behavior. Pavlov believed that the conditioning paradigm provided a means of studying the functioning of the cerebral cortex, the most "advanced" part of the brain. Accordingly, Pavlov's theory of conditioning was a theory of the cortical and subcortical events that underlie the observed behavior.

There are three important concepts in Pavlov's theory, *excitation, inhibition,* and *irradiation.* When a stimulus impinges upon the receptor organs it initiates neural activity or excitation in an area of the cerebral cortex which receives input from that sensory modality. Pavlov assumed that this excitation spreads out or irradiates to other areas of the brain much as the disturbance created by tossing a rock into a pond spreads out away from the initial point of contact. When two stimuli, such as a CS and UCS, are presented, the irradiation of excitation from both focal points meets at some intermediate locus in the cortex, forming a *temporary connection* between the two centers of excitation. This connection does not persist unless it is reinforced by the repeated presentation of the CS and UCS. It is this connection between the CS and UCS areas that is the physical basis of the association that, in some sense, allows the CS to substitute for the UCS.

One can see how these few concepts mentioned thus far might be used to account for some of the conditioning phenomena. For example, one could say that it is the irradiation of excitation that is the basis of the generalization gradient. Or, consider the demonstrated importance of temporal contiguity in conditioning. The explanation for this phenomenon in Pavlovian terms can be easily imagined by considering again the analogy of ripples produced by a rock thrown in water. This time, imagine two rocks thrown in close but spatially separated locations. If the irradiating waves from the two disturbance centers are to meet, then the two rocks must be thrown within a reasonably close time span. If not, the irradiation from the first thrown rock will have dissipated by the time the second rock is thrown. Similarly, if the UCS follows too long after the CS, there will be no opportunity for a temporary connection to be formed because the irradiation of excitation from the CS will have diminished.

Pavlov also hypothesized that a CS not followed by a UCS-generated inhibition in the CS receiving area, and this inhibition irradiated across the cortex, actively blocking the expression of a CR. This is essentially Pavlov's theoretical account of *internal inhibition*, the phenomenon that accounted for behavioral extinction. This irradiation of inhibition would also account for the generalization of extinction.

There were a number of other interesting aspects to Pavlov's theory that we will not be able to cover here. The interested reader is referred to Pavlov himself (1927) or to Kimble (1967) for a more detailed account. We can say that Pavlov's theory of conditioning has relatively little contemporary impact on other investigators of conditioning, particularly those outside of Russia. This stands in stark contrast to the methodology and data elaborated by Pavlov, both of which have had a great influence on behavioral research. There are probably several reasons why Pavlov's theory is not now influential. One reason is the continuing lack of any experimental data supporting Pavlov's hypothesis concerning cortical neurophysiology. Physiological research has yet to reveal any phenomena isomorphic with Pavlov's concepts of the irradiation of excitation and inhibition, nor of the formation of a connection between CS and UCS areas in the manner specified by Pavlov. In fact, very little is yet known about the neurophysiology of conditioning. The experimental data that are available clearly indicate that subcortical areas may be more important than cortical areas for conditioning (e.g., Doty & Rutledge, 1959). Another reason for the lack of influence of Pavlov's theory is that his theoretical terms provide little in the way of deductive information that was not already available in the data.

Stimulus-Response Theory

When Pavlov's work became known in the United States, it was quickly welcomed into the growing behaviorist approach to psychological issues. The receptive atmosphere had already been set by John Watson with the publication of an article entitled "Psychology as the Behaviorist Views It" in 1913. In the behaviorist treatment, the emphasis was placed on the association between the CS and the CR, not between the CS and the UCS. There were probably at least two reasons for this emphasis. One was that the CR was the objective measure taken during conditioning, and there was no way of measuring directly the strength of an association between a CS and UCS. The second probable reason was that the emphasis on the response was consistent with the major form of learning research in America—instrumental learning, the study of response learning itself (*see* Chapter 4).

We shall briefly mention two theoretical issues that occupied the attention of stimulus-response psychologists in the early behaviorist tradition. The first of these was whether the occurrence of the behavioral response itself was necessary for conditioning to occur. Those who believed that the association learned in classical conditioning was between the CS and the CR would have to predict that no learning could occur if the CR did not occur. However, extensive research has now shown quite convincingly that classical conditioning does occur in organisms that are completely paralyzed by curare or related drugs. These experiments (e.g., Solomon & Turner, 1962; Leaf, 1964) show that performance of an overt behavioral response is not necessary for Pavlovian conditioning to occur. However, there may well be changes that occur during conditioning in the area of the cerebral cortex controlling responding (cf., Wagner, Thomas, & Norton, 1967), but this is a different question than the original behaviorist position of the necessity of overt responses (*see* Chapters 8 and 15 for a further discussion of the S–R view of learning).

The second theoretical issue was whether contiguity was necessary and sufficient for conditioning, or whether contiguity was necessary but not sufficient. Those who felt that contiguity alone was insufficient postulated the importance of a second factor, motivation. This issue has never been satisfactorily resolved, perhaps because motivation is itself such a nebulous concept. However, there have been a number of interesting experiments conducted in pursuit of an answer and the reader is referred to Beecroft (1966), Grossman (1967), and Seward (1970) for further discussion of this issue.

Conditioning as Preparatory Response Learning

A number of investigators have noted that much of the behavior that occurs after a CS is presented seems to function as preparation for the impending UCS. For example, in a salivary conditioning experiment, Zener observed the dog's behavior when the CS was presented as

> ... anthropomorphically describable as looking for, expecting, the fall of food with a readiness to perform the eating behavior which will occur when the food falls. Furthermore ... movements occur which do not appear as parts of the unconditioned response to food: all the restless behavior of stamping, yawning, panting (Zener, 1937, p. 393).

A similar interpretation has been given to behavior occurring when the UCS is an aversive shock to a dog's paw;

> ... suppose a bell be rung before the shock. After a few times we witness a display of behavior (as soon as the sound begins) which seems to duplicate the actual [UCR]; indeed, so realistic is the animal's performance that I have sometimes been misled into thinking that shock was being inadvertently applied along with the bell. ... Thereafter [the UCR and CR] diverge, each in accord with its own function. ... After a dog is often shocked, the same charge applied in the same place no longer yields this loose and widespread activity. It yields a quick effective removal of foot, which is then slowly replaced. ... The CR is changing, but its function is not to *react* to [UCS] itself, but to *get ready* for [UCS], to make preparatory adjustments for an oncoming stimulus (Culler, 1938, as quoted in Osgood, 1953).

Similarly, it has been noted that rats hop around and breathe rapidly when shocked to the foot, but when the shock is preceded by a CS, they "hold their breath and wait tensely (Warner, 1932, as cited in Osgood, 1953)."

There are other data, not of an observational nature, that indicate that the subject's behavior consequent to CS administration is in the nature of preparation for the UCS. For example, in a study on human eyelid conditioning (Kimble & Ost, 1961) it was found that the amplitude of the UCR gradually diminished during the course of conditioning, but when the CS was omitted, the UCR showed an abrupt increase in amplitude. A possible interpretation of these data is that some aspects of the subject's behavior produced by the CS have an ameliorative effect on the UCS and thereby reduce the amplitude of the UCR. When the UCS is presented "unannounced" by the CS there is no opportunity for the subject to prepare for the UCS and, therefore, a large amplitude UCR occurs.

In a subsequent study, it was found that the increase in UCR amplitude following omission of the CS is greatest in subjects conditioned with a 0.5-second ISI, the value that generally leads to the best eyelid conditioning (Kimble & Ost, 1961). These UCR dimunition effects have also been found in GSR conditioning and, in general, the greater the prior number of acquisition trials, the greater the increase in UCR amplitude subsequent to a CS omission (Kimmel & Pennypacker, 1963). It has also been found (Kimmel, 1964) that the latency of the initial GSR deflection to the CS and the latency of the maximal GSR deflection to the CS both increase during the course of conditioning (*see* Figure 3–3). These effects are examples of the inhibition of delay phenomenon, the CR moving closer in point of time to UCS onset, possibly because it is at this point that the CR may have its greatest ameliorative effect on the UCS.

Two experiments that are particularly enlightening in regard to the matter of preparatory responses were conducted in the Yale laboratories by Wagner, Thomas, and Norton (1967) and by Thomas (1971). The first of these experiments was an attempt to condition a leg-flexion response in dogs when the UCS was direct electrical stimulation of the motor area of the brain controlling the leg-lifting response. The rationale for conducting this type of experiment was that, if conditioning occurred, then it presumably would be an example of conditioning by simple CS–UCR contiguity since a UCS applied directly to the motor cortex was assumed to have no motivational properties. The outcome of the experiment, however, served a somewhat different purpose.

In this first experiment a conditioned leg-flexion response was obtained in two of three dogs in which an auditory stimulus was paired with the brain stimulation UCS. However, the most interesting aspects of the results came on certain trials when the UCS was presented without the CS. On these trials the leg-lifting responses tended to be more abrupt and vigorous than usual, so much so in one dog that it often fell over against its restraints when the UCS was presented without being "announced" by the CS. These data are clearly consistent with the eyelid and GSR data cited above and indicate that CS onset allowed the dogs to make some postural adjustment to prepare for and perhaps minimize the effect of the UCS–UCR combination. Supporting evidence for this contention was derived by Wagner et al. (1967) from the fact that the two dogs that did condition were required to stand up during the conditioning trials, whereas the one dog that did not condition was allowed to sit, perhaps minimizing the need for postural adjustments.

To further investigate this preparatory response hypothesis, Wagner and his colleagues set up a situation in which their dogs could obtain food by pressing on either of two panels. Both delivered the same amount of food and both were also programmed to deliver the brain stimulation UCS aperiodically. The two panels differed, however, in that the UCSs delivered by one panel were always preceded by the CS, whereas the UCSs delivered by the other panel were not preceded by a CS. If the dogs were indifferent to whether or not the UCS was preceded by a CS, then one would expect no difference in the frequency of presses on the two panels. However, this was not the case. The dogs preferred the panel where the UCS was preceded by a CS. This experiment indicated that the dogs preferred to make a UCR that is modified by a CR rather than one that is unmodified. The CR, some sort of postural adjustment or set, apparently reduces the abruptness or other aversive consequences of the UCS–UCR combination. In this sense, the preparatory response provides a motive for the development of the CR.

Further support for the role of postural adjustments in conditioning where the UCS was direct stimulation of the motor cortex was found in a later experiment by Thomas (1971). Thomas varied the amount of postural adjustment the dogs were required to make, and his results indicate that the greater the adjustment necessary, the more effective conditioning was.

Earlier, in Chapter 2, we presented some evidence that is consistent with the possibility of preparatory response learning on a physiological level. Recall that Siegel (1972) demonstrated that the UCR to insulin injection was hypoglycemia, but the CR was hyperglycemia. The hyperglycemic response to the CS could be thought of as preparing, in a homeostatic sense, for the effects of the UCS. Data supporting this result, but with a response in the opposite direction, has been obtained by Deutsch (1974). Deutsch found that stomach-loading rats with a glucose solution led, naturally enough, to blood hyperglycemia. But if the stomach-loading was preceded by a CS (the taste of Sanka), then the CR is hypoglycemia, a response in the opposite direction from the UCR. Both of these studies indicate that conditioning leads to the development of a CR, the effects of which are to oppose the action of a UCS.

Recently, Siegel (1976) has investigated the possibility that this type of Pavlovian conditioning may be at the basis of tolerance developed to the analgesic effects of morphine. Siegel found that rats injected repeatedly with morphine showed less and less of an analgesic response. The conditioning interpretation of these data offered by Siegel was that a compensatory CR developed to the stimuli associated with drug injection and that this compensatory CR, which opposes the action of the UCS, was at the basis of the tolerance. In support of this interpretation, Siegel found that there was a loss of tolerance when rats were injected with morphine but tested in an environment different from the one in which they had received all their previous injections. That is, the morphine tolerance appeared to be specific to stimulus environment in which the injections were administered. Further, and extensive, support for the role of preparatory responses in the classical conditioning of human subjects (in this case preparatory responses are often called cognitive factors) may be found in the writings of Kimble (1971), Spence (1966), and Grings (1973).

Perhaps a summary of what we have said thus far would be in order. When a CS and UCS are presented in a Pavlovian conditioning paradigm, the subject learns an association between the two stimuli. There is currently no definitive knowledge concerning the neurophysiological nature of the association. As the subject learns the association between the CS and the UCS, a conditioned response begins to develop. The CR often, but not always, resembles the UCR in topological characteristics. A major effect of this CR seems to be the alteration of the impact of the UCS or the UCS–UCR combination. That is, the CS, once the association between the CS and UCS has been learned, induces a response that anticipates, and partly compensates for, the effects of the UCS (cf., Jones, 1962; Liu, 1964). The preparatory response may be rather simple, such as salivation, or it may be more a complex homeostatic mechanism involving insulin secretion, or it may involve general postural adjustments. It is also quite likely that not a single response is being learned, but rather a number of responses being acquired more or less simultaneously. The complexity of the response that is acquired probably depends on the nature of the UCS and the nature of the organism.

Contingency and Predictability

We shall now examine our last theoretical account of Pavlovian conditioning, an account that is compatible with the preparatory response notion presented above.

We shall approach this account through a discussion of the control groups appropriate for Pavlovian conditioning, a discussion closely following an article written on the topic by Rescorla (1967). The acquisition of a classically conditioned association has traditionally been viewed as depending upon the *pairing* of the CS and UCS. In order to insure that the behavior changes which occur in a conditioning experiment result from this pairing and not from other factors, most studies have included one or more control groups (*see* Figures 2–3 and 2–4 on pp. 30 and 31).

The essence of a control group is that it should include all the factors that may influence the outcome of an experiment *except* for the one factor being investigated; i.e., the control group and the experimental group should differ in this one factor only. This would mean that, in the simplest conditioning study, the experimental group should have the CS and UCS paired and the control group should have the CS and UCS unpaired. If both the CS and UCS are to be presented to the control group and they are to be unpaired, the logical procedure would be to randomize the occurrence of the CS and UCS in relation to each other. In this way the control group and the experimental group could each experience the CS and UCS an equal number of times but differ only in whether the CS and UCS were paired or unpaired.

In actual practice, many investigators that have presented both the CS and UCS to a control group have not randomized the occurrence of the two. Instead, two alternative procedures have frequently been used. One procedure involves the use of a semirandom sequence in which the CS and UCS are randomly presented *except* that no CS is allowed to immediately precede the UCS (that is, during an effective CS–UCS interval). The second procedure involves the use of a backward conditioning paradigm in which the CS immediately *follows* the UCS, again a procedure that is usually ineffective in promoting conditioning. The use of the semirandom and the backward conditioning paradigms as control procedures is based on empirical data showing that little or no conditioning occurs with these paradigms. Both of these control groups include the basic elements of conditioning, the CS and UCS, but both differ from the experimental group in that the CS never immediately precedes the UCS.

The reason for including control groups such as these in a conditioning situation is as follows. If the presentation of the CS and UCS produce changes in the behavior of the control groups that are similar to the changes occurring in an experimental group, then it would be clear that these changes are not due to the pairing of the CS and UCS, and hence do not represent associative learning. The function of these control groups, then, is to provide a means of detecting behavioral changes due to phenomena such as *sensitization* and *pseudoconditioning* rather than to associative learning.

Rescorla has argued that to specify the pairing of the CS and UCS in a forward conditioning paradigm as the essential element in conditioning represents a misinterpretation of the conditioning process. It is not the pairing per se that is important, but rather it is the *contingency* between the CS and UCS that is the effective element in conditioning. That is, the occurrence of the UCS is dependent on the prior occurrence of the CS in the standard forward conditioning paradigms. It is this contingency that the organism learns in the usual classical conditioning situation.

A contingency is like a conditional probability; if the CS occurs, then the UCS is likely to follow. If the organism can learn this kind of contingency or probability, it is likely that it can learn another kind of contingency, e.g., if the CS occurs, then there will be no UCS for some time period. Rescorla has argued that this kind of learning is likely.

Specifically, organisms presented with either a backward conditioning paradigm or the semirandom control paradigm might well be learning a contingency between the occurrence of the CS and the *nonoccurrence* of a UCS for some time period. This type of learning would not be detected in the typical conditioning experiment because these experiments are set up to measure unidirectional changes in behavior, i.e., an increase in the probability of a CR. In order to test whether an organism learns negative as well as positive contingencies, one needs a conditioning situation in which deviations both above and below a baseline can be measured. The baseline itself would be represented by the case of zero contingency —no relationship or correlation between the CS and UCS. Such a situation has been devised, and we shall describe, in general terms, the outcome of one experiment conducted to test the contingency learning idea.

This experiment (Rescorla, 1966) involved three stages. First dogs were taught to jump over a low hurdle in order to avoid receiving an electric shock. Shocks were programmed to occur at regular time intervals (e.g., every 20 seconds) *unless* the dog jumped from one side of the apparatus to the other. Every time the dog jumped from one side to the other the clock timing the interval between shocks would reset back to zero and start running again. There was no signal indicating when shock would occur other than the animals' own internal representation of the passage of time. When dogs are exposed to this type of situation, they learn to jump frequently enough to avoid most shocks. It is this jump *rate* that can be used as a baseline on which to measure the effects of positive and negative contingency learning.

After the dogs were performing this hurdle-jumping response well, they were removed from the apparatus and subjected to a Pavlovian conditioning procedure. For the Pavlovian conditioning treatment the dogs were divided into three groups. One group received a standard forward conditioning procedure in which the CS (an auditory stimulus) preceded the UCS (an electric shock). A second group was exposed to a backward conditioning procedure in which the shock UCS preceded the CS. Note that this procedure should lead to the learning of a negative contingency if Rescorla's speculations were correct. A third group was exposed to both the CS and UCS, but the occurrence of either one of these events was not correlated at all with the occurrence of the other event. That is, the occurrence of the CS was randomized with respect to the occurrence of the UCS. This procedure should lead to the learning of a zero contingency or no relationship between the CS and UCS.

The critical test of these predictions came in the third stage of the experiment when the dogs were placed back in the hurdle-jumping apparatus and the CS from the classical conditioning phase was presented. When the CS was presented to the forward conditioning group, they *increased* their rate of jumping, as if they had learned that the CS predicted the impending occurrence of shock. The group that was exposed to the backward classical conditioning paradigm *decreased* its rate of jumping when the CS from the conditioning stage was presented. This decrease in jump rate could be interpreted as indicating that the backward conditioning group had learned that the CS indicated a period free from the occurrence of shock, or, in other words, that they had learned a negative contingency between the CS and shock. When the CS was presented to the third group, the group that had been given a random sequence of CS and UCS presentations in the classical conditioning stage, they showed *no change* in their rate of jumping, indicating, perhaps, that they had learned that the CS could not be used to predict the occurrence of shock.

These results support Rescorla's original hypothesis about the importance of the CS–UCS contingency in classical conditioning. There are many other terms that we think of as nearly synonymous with contingency as used by Rescorla; terms such a correlation, conditional probability, and prediction. Which of these is the best way of conceptualizing the Rescorla view of conditioning we cannot say at the present time. It is clear, though, that this interpretation of conditioning represents a more dynamic view of the conditioning process than alternative views which stress simply the importance of CS–UCS pairings.[1] We will return to Rescorla's ideas on contingency and prediction in Chapter 11 when we discuss discrimination learning. For now, it should be obvious to the reader that Rescorla's contingency learning theory is consistent with the data and theories emphasizing the role of preparatory responses in conditioning.

IV. SUMMARY

The acquisition of a classically conditioned response is strongly influenced by the temporal relationships between the CS and UCS. For some responses, such as the eyelid or nictitating membrane, there is a clearly specified optimum in the CS–UCS interval function in the vicinity of 0.25–0.50 seconds. However, other responses (e.g., GSR, heart rate) can be conditioned with longer CS–UCS intervals and, as yet, there is no clear optimal interval indicated for these responses. Responses can be conditioned if there is a break between CS offset and UCS onset, however, this trace conditioning tends to be inferior to delay conditioning (where the CS remains on until UCS onset). With long CS–UCS intervals the CR latency tends to increase over training so that the CR tends to occur just prior to UCS administration.

Final level of conditioning tends to vary directly with the intensity of the UCS and CS. The CS intensity effects are usually greater if the different levels of the CS are experienced by the same subjects.

If fewer than 100 percent of the trials contain a UCS or if the intertrial intervals are very short, then acquisition tends to be hampered. However, less than 100 percent reinforcement in acquisition tends to prolong the course of extinction. Similarly, resistance to extinction is increased by relatively long intertrial intervals in extinction.

A review of some theories of conditioning indicated that Pavlov's cortical theory has little empirical support. The performance of the

---

1. Use of Rescorla's random control group has sometimes led to evidence of conditioning (Benedict & Ayres, 1972; Kremer & Kamin, 1971). One of the factors that seems to influence whether or not a chance pairing in a random group will lead to an increment in conditioning is when the chance pairing occurs. If the pairing occurs early in training, then some evidence of conditioning is likely to develop. Recently Ayres, Benedict, and Witcher (1975) have provided evidence indicating that chance pairings do not lead to conditioning if they have been preceded by some number of trials in which the subject has experienced the UCS alone. Apparently, initial experiences with the UCS alone "block" conditioning that might have otherwise occurred on chance pairing trials (*see also* Rescorla, 1972).

behavioral response is probably not necessary for conditioning to occur; however, when the CR does occur there is evidence that it serves the function of preparing the subject for the effects of the impending UCS. The neural basis for this preparatory response may still occur when the subject is prevented from responding by paralytic agents. There is some evidence that changes occur during conditioning in the area of the cortex controlling motor responses.

The final theory we reviewed hypothesizes that organisms learn a contingency or correlation between the CS and UCS in the classical conditioning paradigm. This theory further hypothesizes that organisms learn not only a positive contingency when the CS precedes the UCS, but also a negative contingency when the UCS precedes the CS, and they learn that there is no correlation when the CS and UCS occur randomly with respect to each other. There is some indirect support indicating that organisms may learn all three of these relationships in appropriate conditioning paradigms.

4

Instrumental Learning: History and Reinforcement Variables

> *. . . animals (may), by the proper application of rewards and punishments, . . . be taught any course of action, and most contrary to their natural instincts and propensities.*
>
> David Hume, *An Enquiry Concerning Human Understanding*

I. HISTORICAL BACKGROUND

In 1896, a Harvard graduate student named Edward Thorndike was attempting to conduct experiments in "mindreading" by young children for his master's degree in psychology. Thorndike was discouraged from pursuing these experiments, and as a result he turned to another line of research, the study of the intelligent and instinctive behavior of chickens. Within a few short years of research at Harvard and Columbia, Thorndike developed research techniques, discovered empirical relationships, and stated theoretical principles that have endured and generated additional research up to the present day.

Some feeling for Thorndike's research may be obtained by considering a typical experiment. Thorndike would place a hungry cat inside of a "puzzle box" like the one illustrated in Figure 4–1. Outside of the puzzle box there would be a small amount of food visible to the animal. If the cat made a "correct" response, the door to the puzzle box would fall open and the cat could obtain the food. The correct response designated by Thorndike could have been any of a number of responses. Notice that the door could be held closed by one or two sliding bolts or by one or two wooden bars or by any combination of these restraints, all of which could be manipulated by the cat from inside of the box. For example, one of the bolts would be retracted if the cat stepped on a pedal connected to the bolt through a series of pulleys, the other bolt could be retracted, perhaps by having the cat pull at a loop in a string connected to the bolt, the wooden bars could be manipulated directly if the cat stuck its paws through the slats in the box, and so on.

Whatever the response selected as being correct in a particular experiment, Thorndike would place the cat inside the box and then measure how long it took the cat to get out and obtain the food. With

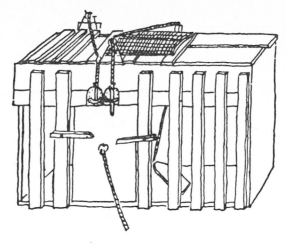

Figure 4–1.   A Thorndikian puzzle box for cats. (From Bitterman, 1969.)

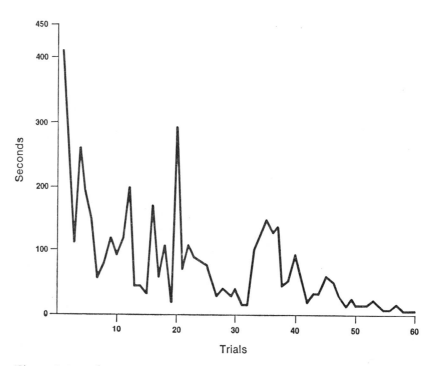

Figure 4–2.   A learning curve showing a decline in the time, as a function of trials, required for a cat to make the response releasing the exit door in one of Thorndike's puzzle boxes. (From Bitterman, 1969.)

repeated experiences or trials in a particular puzzle box, the cat would escape and obtain the food in shorter and shorter times. From these data Thorndike constructed learning curves, one of which is shown in Figure 4–2.

Now all this may seem quite simple. These experiments are something that could be done at home with the family pet and very little equipment. But Thorndike was the first to systematically investigate this type of learning in animals. Before Thorndike, there was only anecdotal evidence concerning the learning abilities of animals. As Thorndike wrote:

> Dogs get lost hundreds of times and no one ever notices it or sends a scientific account of it to a magazine. But let one find his way from Brooklyn to Yonkers and the fact immediately becomes a circulating anecdote. Thousands of cats on thousands of occasions sit helplessly yowling, and no one takes thought of it or writes to his friend, the professor; but let one cat claw at the knob of a door supposedly as a signal to be let out, and straightway this cat becomes the representative of the cat-mind in all the books (Thorndike, 1898; cited by Bitterman, 1969, p. 444).

Many individuals before Thorndike had undoubtedly known that animals could be brought to behave in specified ways by the proper application of rewards and punishments. But it was Thorndike's research procedures that provided a means of obtaining *quantitative* data on the course of learning, data and conditions that were relatively free of influence from the experimenter, and that *could be reproduced* by other investigators in other laboratories. As with many other concepts and inventions, once the basic idea was developed hundreds of variations became quickly evident, such variations as: Would the animals learn faster if given a large amount of food as compared to a small amount? Do they have to be hungry and, if so, how hungry? Do they remember what they have learned? And for how long? What if they are given food on only some of the trials, will they still learn? Once they learn their way out of one box, will they find it easier to get out of other boxes? We will be looking at data relevant to these and other questions in the following chapters. But first, let us speculate on the characteristics of the learning that takes place in the puzzle box.

Stimulus-Response Theory

Thorndike described the behavior of his animals as "learning by trial and error with accidental success." This phrase emphasized that there was apparently no contemplative analysis of the surroundings; the cat did not sit calmly in the puzzle box until it had "figured" a way out. Instead, the cats were quite active, engaging in a variety of species typical behaviors such as scratching and poking. Eventually, one of these responses moved the correct manipulandum (floor pedal, wooden bar, etc.), the door opened and the cat escaped and consumed the food. As a function of repeated trials in the puzzle box, the time taken to make the correct response decreased (Figure 4–2).

But what is the nature of this "trial and error learning with accidental success"? A common sense view might be that the animals eventually learn a relationship between the stimulus environment defined by the puzzle box, the response requirements, and the availability of food. That is, the animal might learn that, in the stimulus context provided by the puzzle box (S), if it makes a particular response (R) such as stepping on a footswitch, then a given outcome (O) such as the availability of food occurs. This type of relational learning we shall call S–R–O learning. The symbols S–R–O meaning that the animals learn a relationship between the *stimulus* context, the *response* requirement, and the *outcome* produced by that response.

However, this was not Thorndike's interpretation of what occurred in the puzzle box. Thorndike proposed that an association is learned between the stimulus provided by the manipulandum and the appropriate response to the manipulandum (e.g., if the stimulus is the presence of the foot pedal, the correct response is pressing the foot pedal). But this learning of an association between the stimulus and the response (S–R learning) does *not* also involve the expectation of the outcome produced by the response. That is, the cat does not anticipate food if it steps on the pedal; it learns simply to step on the pedal. What then is the role of the food?

Thorndike reasoned that the food served to strengthen the connection (association) between the stimulus and the response. The food "stamps-in" or *reinforces* the tendency to step on the foot pedal; but the animal does not learn to anticipate the receipt of the food; it does not operate the foot pedal *in order* to obtain the food. Thorndike's interpretation of learning was stated as the *law of effect.* This law or principle can be summarized by saying that the association between a stimulus and a response is either strengthened or weakened by the *effect* produced by the response.

If the effect of the response is to produce a "satisfying state of affairs" (e.g., food for a hungry animal), then the association is strengthened (reinforced), but if the effect of the response is to produce an aversive event (e.g., electric shock), then any association between that stimulus and response is weakened. The important thing to remember is that the response outcome reinforces the association between a movement pattern (response) and a stimulus context, but that response outcome is not anticipated the next time the stimulus situation is repeated.

Why would this nonintuitive S–R explanation for the behavior of cats in the puzzle box be accepted? The reasons were several, but perhaps the most important was that the S–R–O interpretation assumes that the animals develop an expectancy of reward (or of the response outcome). And while the idea of an expectancy seems perfectly appropriate when applied to humans who can and do verbalize their expectancies, an expectancy is a good deal more difficult to characterize in an animal that does not share these verbal capacities. The S–R interpretation seems to be more parsimonious and scientifically sound in that it is more closely tied to a measurable and observable stimulus and response. An expectancy is not measured per se but only inferred.

The difference between the S–R and S–R–O interpretations of simple learning go beyond the experimental investigations that were conducted at the turn of the century. These differences in interpretation are related to centuries-old philosophical speculations concerning the behavior of animals and men. For example, in Chapter 2, we mentioned that the French philosopher René Descartes believed that the behavior of animals and much of the physiological functioning of man was machine-like. In fact, Descartes wrote that animals were "flesh and blood machines." The S–R view of learning is more consonant with this mechanistic interpretation than is the S–R–O view. We can imagine an automatic response to a stimulus being "stamped-in" to a machine, but it is a little more difficult to imagine a machine that anticipates the outcome of its own behavior (S–R–O). In fact, it was just this issue, a complex machine (computer) that could anticipate and plan, that was one of the more interesting aspects of the film, "2001: A Space Odyssey."

Cognitive Theory

The S–R view dominated early research and theorizing concerning simple learning. The notion of S–R associationism was championed by John Watson, the founder and advocate of behaviorism, which is the philosophy that psychology was the study of measurable responses. Later influential researchers (B. F. Skinner, for example) have held quite closely to this behavioristic, S–R tradition.

Despite this strict behavioristic influence, there were those who thought that other interpretations of simple learning might be fruitful. Edward Tolman published a text in 1932 titled *Purposive Behavior in Animals and Men.* This title indicated Tolman's belief that the anticipation of the goal or reward (the purpose) was an important factor in the behavior of even lower organisms such as the rat. Tolman felt that a food reward for a hungry animal does not simply strengthen an association between a stimulus and a response, but rather the food itself comes to be expected. In other words, Tolman's interpretation of the learning that occurs in a puzzle box was quite similar to the "common-sense" S–R–O view outlined above. Tolman's theory is often classified as a cognitive theory in the sense that cognition means knowledge and Tolman believed that animals acquire knowledge of their environment, knowledge of where the rewards are, and how to get to them when there is a need. In this regard, it is perhaps significant that Tolman did most of his research with mazes.

The maze apparatus is particularly well suited to an interpretation of an animal learning the structure of its environment, or forming "cognitive maps" as Tolman put it. Also the use of the maze (apparently first introduced by Small in 1899 [Boring, 1957]) provides an additional dependent variable, errors (entry into blind alleys) which may be used along with time scores to index the course of learning.

If time and errors are measured as responses, how are the cognitions and expectancies to be measured? Tolman, although not an S–R theorist, was a behaviorist, and he recognized the importance of measurable behaviors for science. He saw his problem as one of getting these "central processes" (expectancies, etc.) out onto "objective pointer readings," something which could be measured (Tolman, 1959). He never quite solved the problem. Expectancies and cognitions could only be inferred from behavior as something that intervened between the stimulus situation and the animals' response to it. However, there were some interesting early experimental observations that strongly supported Tolman's contention that animals developed expectancies concerning the rewards they received.

For example, Tolman (1932) described an experiment by Tinklepaugh (1928) in which a monkey was trained on a delayed-response problem. This problem involved placing food under one of two containers with the monkey watching, and then a screen was placed between the containers and the monkey for a certain amount of time (the delay interval). The object of the experiment was to determine how well the monkey could choose the container with food after different delay intervals. But the manipulation of particular interest here is what happened when the experimenter changed the food during the delay interval.

As described by Tinklepaugh:

> With the same setting as before, the experimenter displays a piece of banana, lowers the board and places the banana under one of the cups. The board is then raised, and working behind it, with his hands hidden from the view of the monkey, *the experimenter takes the banana out and deposits a piece of lettuce in its place.* After the delay, the monkey is told to "come and get the food." She jumps down from the chair, rushes to the proper container and picks it up. She extends her hand to seize the food. But her hand drops to the floor without touching it. She looks at the lettuce but (unless very hungry) does not touch it. She looks under and around her. She picks the cup up and examines it thoroughly inside and out. She has on occasion turned toward observers present in the room and shrieked at them in apparent anger. After several seconds spent searching, she gives a glance toward the other cup, which she has been taught not to look into, and then walks off to a nearby window. The lettuce is left untouched on the floor (Tinklepaugh, 1928, p. 224).

The apparent searching behavior of the monkey conforms to Tolman's view that animals acquire an expectancy of the response outcome in simple learning situations.

Anticipatory Response Theory

A third general theoretical position, one intermediate between the nonexpectancy S–R view of Thorndike and the cognitive theory of Tolman, can be classified as anticipatory response theory. This approach is intermediate because it specifies that animals can behave as if they expect a particular outcome, but the theory specifies that the mechanism of this apparent anticipation is a measurable response. This viewpoint, most closely associated with the names Clark Hull and Kenneth Spence, relies heavily on principles and data derived from Pavlovian conditioning experiments.

We have seen in Chapters 2 and 3 that Pavlovian CRs become anticipatory, that is, come to precede UCS onset, and that they may generalize to stimulus situations similar to the original CS. Hull believed that, in addition to any overt responses that may be learned in an apparatus such as a puzzle box or a maze, Pavlovian CRs are also acquired and may become anticipatory. For example, if a rat is given food for running in a maze, then eventually the rat may begin to salivate (as a CR) to the stimulus complex early in the maze because it is similar to the stimulus complex in the goal area where the food is presented. The point here is that the specification of a particular response, salivation, provides for the possibility of objective measurement to determine whether anticipatory responding does indeed occur.

As a second example of an anticipatory response, we can cite an early study by Neal Miller (1935). Miller trained one group of rats to run down a simple maze to obtain water and a second group to run down to obtain food. The food receptacle in the goal region was constructed so that the rats would have to twist their heads around to the right and, similarly, the water receptacle was constructed so that the rats in this group would have to twist their heads around to the left to get at the water. The interesting aspect of this study was that the rats in each group began to twist their heads in the appropriate direction *as they ran down the maze,* and the closer they were to the goal box, the more pronounced the twisting became. In other words, a part of the goal response had become anticipatory and was directly observable.

Now, the question is whether these anticipatory responses indicate that the animal is expecting the reward at the end of the maze in the way that Tolman meant, or are these responses simply stamped in or reinforced by the food in the way Thorndike meant? This is a most difficult question to resolve and further detailed consideration of it will be postponed until Chapter 8 after we have reviewed some data. We should point out, however, that when the anticipatory response theory was first formulated by Hull in the early 1930s, it was closer to Thorndike's S–R view than to Tolman's cognitive view, but over the years and through extensive research and writing (Hull, 1932, 1943, 1951; Spence, 1956; Logan & Wagner, 1965), anticipatory response theory has now become similar to Tolman's original cognitive theory.

Instrumental Learning and Pavlovian Conditioning

It is time now to compare the learning that occurs in mazes and puzzle boxes with Pavlovian conditioning. In the process of making this comparison, we shall introduce some terms that will be needed in the next few chapters.

The receipt of food by the cat in the puzzle box is dependent upon the cat's first making a response that has been designated as correct by the experimenter. For example, the cat cannot get out of the box and obtain food until it has stepped on the foot pedal and released the door. This type of learning is often described as *instrumental learning*[1] in the sense that the animal's response is

---

1. There is an asymmetry in the standard terminology in the sense that *Pavlovian conditioning* has become more popular than the synonymous *classical conditioning,* perhaps because the latter term, like the term "classical music," is potentially ambiguous. However, *instrumental learning* seems to be preferred over the designation "*Thorndikian learning*" (suggested by Bitterman, 1966).

instrumental in making the reward available. Compare this with Pavlovian conditioning in which the delivery of the UCS is directly under the control of the experimenter and is *not* dependent upon any response made by the animal. Accordingly, one difference between Pavlovian and instrumental conditioning is procedural: In Pavlovian conditioning, the presentation of the reinforcer (UCS) is completely controlled by the experimenter; in instrumental learning, the delivery of the reward is more under the control of the subject in the sense that the presentation of the reward must await the correct response on the part of the subject.

This distinction sometimes becomes blurred. For example, during the course of Pavlovian conditioning, the CR becomes anticipatory and thus may *modify* the effectiveness of the UCS. When this happens the CR is somewhat like an instrumental response in that it gives the animal some degree of control over the UCS. However, it does not, by our definition, constitute an instrumental response because the delivery of the UCS is still not dependent on whether or not the CR occurs. Thus, in Pavlovian conditioning paradigms, the UCS is presented independently of the animals' behavior; in instrumental learning paradigms, the presentation of the reward depends upon the animals' behavior.

A second difference between Pavlovian and instrumental learning concerns the nature of the responses that are measured to index learning. As we mentioned in Chapter 2, the UCR of Pavlovian conditioning is a reflex response that is *elicited* by the UCS. The term *elicited* is also used to characterize the CR. The connotation is that the CR is forced or pulled from the animal by the CS, much as the UCR is forced reflexively from the animal by the UCS. In instrumental learning, however, the response that changes during the course of learning (e.g., stepping on the foot pedal) is not forced from the subject by the availability of food but, rather, the response is *emitted* by the subject. This "elicit/emit" distinction roughly parallels the distinction between reflexive movement and voluntary movement as applied to humans.

Research Methods

We have seen that, in addition to Thorndike's puzzle box, the maze was introduced quite early into the investigation of animal learning. In addition to seeming more appropriate for the study of rat behavior, the maze was also thought to have several other advantages. For example, entries into *culs-de-sac*, as well as time to traverse the maze, could be readily scored. The two dependent variables provided the opportunity of determining whether these measures were differentially affected by experimental treatments. Such studies, in turn, provided further insight into the nature of animal learning. The maze possessed other advantages in that its pattern and complexity could be varied readily, and it was suitable for use with a wide variety of animals from mouse to man.

Some investigators were interested in a more detailed analysis of behavior at choice points and began using elements of complex mazes containing only a single choice point (the T-maze). The trend towards simplification of the complex maze reached its culmination in the straight runway, an apparatus with no choice point at all. Much of our information of how reinforcement affects simple behavior has been derived from the straight runway.

Variations of the maze are typically used in *discrete-trial* investigations of learning. That is, the subject is placed in the start region of the maze or runway, allowed to traverse the apparatus to the goal area where a reward is located, and then is removed from the apparatus after the reward has been consumed. The number of errors made and/or the time to traverse the apparatus are recorded as the dependent variables. After some time (the intertrial interval), the subject is returned to the start region for the next trial.

A somewhat different research strategy is associated with the use of the operant chamber or the Skinner box, another apparatus frequently used in the study of animal behavior. An animal is placed in the chamber and left for a relatively long period of time (e.g., an hour or longer) and its *rate of responding* is measured. The response selected for reinforcement depends upon the animal being tested. This decision is based upon the animal's physical capacities. For example, rats are usually required to press a lever, whereas birds are required to peck a disc.

The Skinner box is reminiscent of the original Thorndikian puzzle box, except that in the Skinner box the food is automatically delivered into the chamber and the subject only needs to pause for a short time to consume the reward before returning to responding. In the puzzle box, the animal must leave the apparatus to obtain the food. One advantage of the Skinner box, then, is its suitability for automation. The recording of the response and the delivery of the reward at the appropriate time can be accomplished through the use of electronic equipment without constant monitoring by the experimenter. Besides the obvious advantages in efficiency, the operant chamber also provides for better experimental control than the maze or runway in that the subject's behavior is less susceptible to influence by the experimenter. In the maze or runway, where the experimenter must be present to initiate the trials and monitor the animal's behavior, it is all too easy to alter the animal's speed of running or perhaps even its entry into incorrect arms by the slightest noises or movements.

However, the advantage gained by automation in the Skinner box may be offset if the experimenter does not occasionally watch the animal's behavior. Such monitoring often provides the experimenter with fruitful insights and hypotheses concerning the behavioral mechanism under investigation. We have already seen one example of this in Neal Miller's study of anticipatory head-turning. Similarly, we speak of lever-presses by a rat, but observations inform us that many rats do not press the lever with their paws, as the word "press" might lead us to imagine, but instead they bite the lever, or grasp it between their teeth and shake their head, or push the lever down with the side of their face, etc. Such observations give us a different picture of what it means when we say a rat "presses" a lever.

When we introduced the topic of the Skinner box, we also called the apparatus an "operant chamber." Operant, a term introduced by Skinner, is derived from the word *operate*. The animal's response operates on or changes the environment, and it is the effect of this response-produced change in the environment that determines whether the response will increase or decrease in frequency. As stated in Thorndike's law of effect, some response outcomes (e.g., food for a hungry animal) increase the probability that the response will be made again; other outcomes (e.g., an aversive event) decrease the probability that the response will be made again. Although the term "operant" generally refers to the same class of behaviors as the term "instrumental," operant has also acquired a connotative meaning relating it to certain research strategies, particularly to situations where *rate of responding* is the dependent variable (cf., Skinner, 1969). This distinction is also sometimes made in terms of free-operant versus discrete-trials procedures. We shall use instrumental as the more general term.

The maze and its derivatives *and* the puzzle box and its derivatives represent the equipment most widely used in the laboratory study of animal learning. However, many experiments directed toward a specific hypothesis about learning require variations in equipment and research strategies that will be mentioned at the appropriate time in later chapters.

Learning and Performance

When defining learning, it is customary to specify a number of factors that can influence behavior but are not thought of as learning. For example, in Chapter 1 we mentioned that the behavior changes attributed to learning were the result of practice, were relatively permanent, and were not due to factors such as fatigue and disease. The distinction between learning and performance is necessary because learning is not measured directly but only inferred from changes in performance. Performance is an imperfect measure of learning, and it can change independently of learning.

The idea that there are conditions other than learning that can affect behavior is a common sense notion, and, in fact, it is an idea that is invoked quite often by students to explain their performance on an examination. In distinguishing between learning and other influences on behavior, the terms "relatively permanent" and "result of practice" are critical. Variables which have a temporary effect on behavior are said to be performance variables. Fatigue is one example of a performance variable. Rare is the teacher who has not heard the lament, "I studied all night and was so tired during the exam that I didn't do well, but I really knew the material"— the implication being that the student would have done much better if the exam had been taken after a good night's rest. That is, the effects of learning were relatively permanent but the effects of the sleepless night were only temporary. Of course, not everything that has a relatively permanent effect on behavior is classified as a learning variable. Physical injury may have a permanent effect on behavior but this effect is not usually the result of practice!

The performance variable that will be of particular concern to us in this text is the deprivation state of the subject. Recall that when we first introduced the topic of Pavlovian conditioning in Chapter 2 and when we were describing Thorndike's experiments earlier in this chapter, we specified that the animals used as subjects in these experiments were hungry. If the animal were not hungry, food would not function as a particularly effective reward in instrumental learning. Food deprivation is, then, one of the conditions that influences behavior in a learning experiment in which food is the reward. Yet, the deprivation state is usually considered to have its effect on performance, not learning per se, and this is so because the effects are temporary and relatively easily reversed.

For example, it has been shown that a rat's behavior in a complex maze varies with its deprivation state (Tolman, 1932). Rats deprived of food run faster in the maze than rats deprived of water when food was the reward; but the relative speeds of these two groups were reversed when the reward was changed to water. It is not reasonable to assume that the switch in reward had erased the previous learning on the part of the hungry group of rats. Therefore, the change in behavior is attributed to a performance effect, not a learning effect. The previous learning of the maze is still there, some place, but it is no longer being measured because the animals' deprivation state is not appropriate to the reward.

Deprivation state is one of a number of conditions that are sometimes grouped together as motivational variables; that is, variables that affect performance. In the experiment just described, it could be said that the deterioration in the performance of the food-deprived group occurred because the rats in that group were no longer motivated. This is simply a shorthand way of saying that the deprivation state was not appropriate for the reward.

The distinction between variables that influence performance and those that influence learning is quite complicated and one that we cannot go into in any great detail in this text (*see* Kimble, 1961, Chapter 5; Bolles, 1967). For now it is sufficient to remember that the distinction between learning and performance has served as a useful distinction, and it is a distinction based primarily on "relative permanence."

Before leaving this topic we should mention that not all researchers make a distinction between learning and performance. Many investigators in the operant tradition refer simply to what is measured (e.g., response rate). As we said above, those who make a distinction between learning and performance contend that learning is estimated indirectly from performance, learning itself is not directly measured. Many prefer to confine their speculations to what is measured directly, and avoid speculation on what cannot be directly measured.

For those who prefer to speak about learning and performance separately, learning has the logical status of a *hypothetical construct*. A hypothetical construct is something that is assumed to exist and influence events—behavior, in the case of learning—but which cannot be measured directly. Hypothetical constructs have had a long history of successful usage in other areas such as physics. For example, atoms were postulated to exist and to be responsible for the physical properties of matter for over two millenia before the first "atom" was ever directly visualized. Similarly, the concept of gravity was something that was postulated to influence events before the recent first attempts to measure "gravity waves." A more recent concept in physics that seems to have the status of a hypothetical construct is the "black hole" or collapsed star, something whose effects can be measured only indirectly at the present time.

Of course, the careless postulation of hypothetical entities to explain behavior can itself be dangerous. Sometimes a postulated entity or process can serve to provide a false sense of understanding and to misdirect research. The concept of phlogiston, a substance postulated to explain combustion, is perhaps an example of a hypothetical construct that did not advance the science of chemistry. The history of psychology is replete with examples of postulated events or processes which intervene in behavior and which were used to explain behavior. Examples such as the way the term "instinct" was used at the turn of the century, and the way some concepts such as id and ego have been misused since, serve to deter psychologists from being too loose in their postulation of hypothetical constructs. It is this danger of misleading ourselves into thinking we understand behavior because we have postulated the existence of a process or entity to explain behavior that cautions against the abuse of hypothetical constructs.

However, the use of a hypothetical construct such as learning—something that results from practice, is relatively permanent, influences behavior but can only be imperfectly estimated from performance—seems to be a useful concept. There is little danger of being greatly misled if this concept is kept closely tied to observable data.

We turn now to an analysis of some of the variables that have been found to influence instrumental behavior. In the remainder of this chapter and in the next chapter we will present data concerned with appetitive reinforcers, and in Chapter 6 we will concentrate on aversive reinforcers.

An appetitive reinforcer is a stimulus that an organism will approach and the presentation of which will support the learning of approach responses. In Thorndike's terms, an appetitive stimulus would be something that constituted a "satisfying state of affairs." Other terms that are often used to designate an appetitive reinforcer are "positive reinforcer" or a reward. Some obvious examples of appetitive reinforcers are food for a hungry animal, sugar solutions or other sweet-tasting substances (e.g., saccharin, cyclamates), some salt solutions, a warm temperature for a cold animal, etc.

The effectiveness of many, but not all, positive reinforcers is dependent upon the subject being deprived of the specific substance for some time before it is to be used as a reinforcing stimulus. Deprivation itself has systematic effects on behavior, and it is these effects that we shall now examine.

II. DEPRIVATION STATE
Acquisition Effects

When an animal is deprived of food, many aspects of its behavior appear to become more energetic. For example, the data in Figure 4–3 show a very large increase in the amount of activity by rats in a running wheel as a function of food and water depriva-

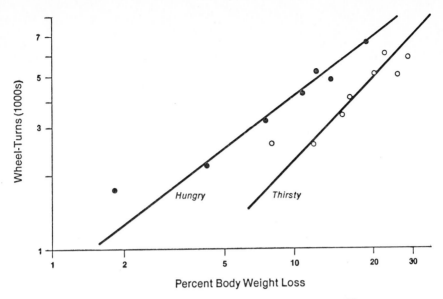

Figure 4–3. Log number of wheel-turns as a function of log percentage body weight loss in hungry and in thirsty rats. (From Collier, 1969.)

tion. The independent variable in this study was the amount of weight (in percentages) the rats had lost as a function of being deprived of food or water. It is important to note that wheel-running in this experiment was not an instrumental response. That is, running in the wheel did not obtain a reward for the rats, yet their wheel-running behavior was increased by deprivation. This study is one of many showing that activity levels are increased by deprivation, sometimes even by deprivation of specific nutritional substances such as proteins (Collier & Squibb, 1967).

This increase in activity may have adaptive functions if, in the natural environment, such increases in activity are likely to carry the animal to a different location, perhaps one where it is more likely to encounter the substance needed to satisfy the deprivation condition (cf., Craig, 1918; Eibl-Eibesfeldt, 1970). However, under laboratory conditions, deprivation does not always increase activity; it seems most likely to do so when there is opportunity for extensive physical movement and/or where there are changing environmental stimuli (Campbell & Sheffield, 1953; Bolles, 1967; Collier, 1969).

Instrumental behavior also increases in vigor as a function of deprivation. The data presented in Figure 4–4 illustrate the effects of food deprivation on running speed for a food reward (Weiss, 1960). The experiment was conducted in a straight runway, and the data are presented in terms of running speed in the various segments of the runway. It can be seen that running speed increased as food deprivation was increased from 2 through 48 hours and that the greatest speeds occurred in the middle section of the runway. The latter result is interesting in regard to a theoretical concept called the *goal gradient*. According to the goal gradient hypothesis, a positive reinforcer exerts an increasingly greater effect on behavior the closer an organism is in its approach to the reinforcer (Hull,

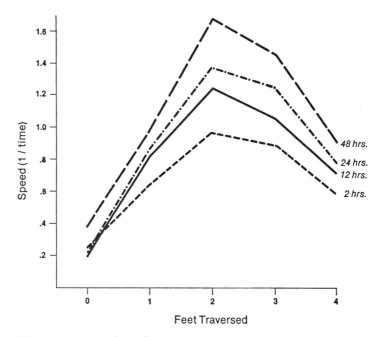

Figure 4–4.   Goal gradient at four levels of deprivation. (From Weiss, 1960.)

1934). This might lead to the prediction that a rat in a straight runway should run faster and faster the closer it gets to the goal box. However, there are obvious physical limitations on the applicability of the goal gradient hypothesis to an apparatus like the straight runway; the rat must slow down and stop at some point and, therefore, the ordering of the speeds in the runway is responsible (*also see* Knarr & Collier, 1962).

One interpretation of the effects of deprivation on runway behavior is that the rats do not really run *faster* as deprivation increases; they take less time to get from the start box to the goal box because such responses as sniffing and grooming that would normally compete with running forward become eliminated to an increasing degree as deprivation increases (cf., Estes, 1958). This interpretation implies that behavior does not become more vigorous or energetic as a function of deprivation, it simply becomes more direct.

However, the latter interpretation has not received complete support from the data. For example, Porter, Madison, and Senkowski (1968) carefully observed rats' behavior in the runway and recorded

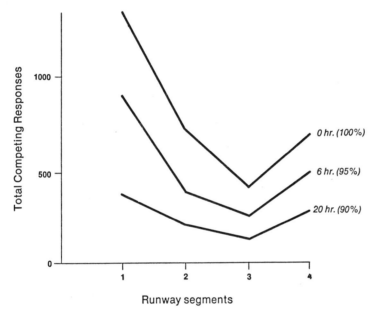

Figure 4–5. Competing responses in different runway segments (from start to goal) as a function of deprivation. Each curve is labeled by the hours of food deprivation (0, 6, and 20) and the correlated percentage of free-feeding weight (100, 95, and 90). (From Porter, Madison, & Senkowski, 1968.)

the trials and runway sections in which competing responses occurred. As can be seen from Figure 4–5, there was a decrease in competing responses as deprivation increased and, furthermore, competing responses were at a minimum in the middle sections of the runway, data which nicely parallel the speed data presented in Figure 4–4. However, these investigators went one step further and examined their data with the effects due to competing responses removed. They did this by examining the effects of deprivation on trials where no detectable competing responses at all occurred and/or by subtracting the time consumed by the competing responses themselves. When this was done, a relationship between deprivation and running speed was still found. The greater the deprivation the faster the rats ran.

So it appears that competing responses are eliminated as deprivation increases but, in addition, it also appears that rats run faster as deprivation increases. In other words, it is meaningful to think of an organism's behavior as becoming more energetic or vigorous as deprivation increases, as well as more direct (fewer competing responses). These energizing effects of deprivation have been found in a variety of other situations such as operant bar-pressing tasks (e.g., Carlton, 1961), with other rewards such as sucrose solutions (e.g., Collier, 1962) and saccharin, a nonnutritive sweet-tasting substance (e.g., Snyder, 1962).

Extinction Effects

When an animal is no longer rewarded for performing an instrumental task, its performance deteriorates. These effects of the removal of a reward appear to be directly analogous to the extinction effects that occur in Pavlovian conditioning when the CS is no longer followed by the UCS. The deprivation state of the animal has an effect on the rapidity with which this extinction occurs: Animals under more extreme conditions of deprivation during extinction take longer to extinguish (e.g., Barry, 1958; Pavlik & Reynolds, 1963; E. D. Capaldi, 1972).

It is also possible to shift the deprivation state between acquisition and extinction. The question of interest in such shifts is whether or not there is a carry-over effect from acquisition to extinction. In other words, does the rate of extinction depend only on the level of deprivation in extinction, or is it also influenced by the deprivation levels that prevailed in acquisition but are no longer in effect? The answer to this question has not been easy to come by, and it appears that the degree of carry-over between acquisition and extinction may depend on the apparatus used (cf., Bolles, 1967) and the deprivation parameters. But, to the extent that generalizations can be made, it appears that high deprivation during either the acquisition or extinction phase retards extinction; but this effect is more pronounced when deprivation is manipulated during the extinction phase (E. D. Capaldi, 1972; Barry, 1958, 1967).

III. AMOUNT OF REWARD
Acquisition Effects

It seems reasonable that amount of reward ought to have an effect on instrumental behavior, and the effect should be such that the larger the reward the better the performance. By and large, this is what the data indicate. For example, in one of the earliest studies in the area, Grindley (1929) rewarded different groups of chickens with either 0, 1, 2, 4 or 6 pieces of rice and found that the larger the reward the faster the chickens ran. Similarly, Crespi (1942) rewarded different groups of rats with either 1, 4, 16, 64 or 256 units of laboratory rat food (each unit weighed .02 gm) and found that the final level of running speed (after approximately 20 trials) was directly related to the amount of reward. These basic results have been found in a large number of studies (*see* Pubols, 1960), and we can say quite confidently that in simple instrumental tasks performance bears a direct relationship to the amount of reward proffered.

As straightforward as these studies seem to be, the design of the reward magnitude experiment becomes complicated by the subtleties inherent in the definition of amount of reward. For example, a number of investigators (*see* Pubols, 1960) have noted that the phrase "amount or quantity of reinforcer" may actually refer to several possible dimensions of the reward substance. That is, amount may refer to quantity of reward in terms of weight or volume; or it may refer to the duration or rate of consummatory activity involved in ingesting the reward; or it may refer (in part) to the perceptual stimuli received from the reward prior to ingestion. There are a number of studies that demonstrate the effectiveness of the consummatory and/or perceptual dimensions independent of the physical amount of the reward. For example, Wolfe and Kaplon (1941) found that chickens rewarded with a piece of popcorn cut into four sections ran faster in a runway than chickens rewarded with a single whole piece of popcorn! Similar effects have been found in studies with rats (e.g., Campbell, Batsche, & Batsche, 1972).

The quality of reward has also been shown to influence instrumental behavior. This can be seen in a study by Guttman (1954) which examined the effects of different concentrations of two sugar solutions, sucrose and glucose, on rate of bar-pressing. Guttman found that, in general, the higher the concentration of the two sugars, the higher the rate of bar-pressing, and that sucrose produced a higher rate of bar-pressing than did glucose. These results are consistent with human judgments of sweetness; the higher the concentration of sucrose and glucose the sweeter they taste, and at equivalent concentrations sucrose tastes sweeter than glucose (cf., Pfaffman, 1960).

Reward Contrast Effects

The effects of reward quantity or quality are usually greater when the levels of the reward are varied within-subjects rather than between-subjects. For example, the data in Figure 4–6 show the lick rates of rats drinking either 32 percent or 4 percent sucrose solutions. There are three groups in this experiment: Group 1 receives only the 32 percent solution, Group 2 receives only the 4 percent solution, and Group 3 sometimes receives the 32 percent and sometimes the 4 percent solution. It can be seen that the difference in the rate of licking the two solutions is greater in Group 3 (the

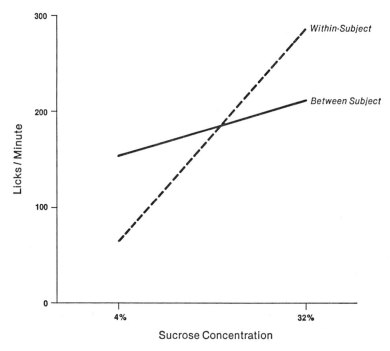

Figure 4–6. Lick-rates for 4 percent and 32 percent sucrose under two test conditions. The curve labeled "within-subjects" represents data obtained from rats that had concurrent experience with both solutions. The curve labeled "between-subjects" represents data obtained from two separate groups of rats: One responding for 4 percent only and the other for 32 percent only. (Redrawn from Flaherty & Largen, 1975.)

within-subjects comparison) than it is between Groups 1 and 2 (the *between-subjects* comparison). You may have noticed that these data are quite similar to the CS intensity effects obtained by Grice & Hunter (cf., Figure 3–6 on p. 54). In both cases the within-subjects manipulation of the variable (sucrose solutions or CS intensity) led to greater effects than between-subjects manipulations.

This difference must be related to the opportunity for comparison that exists in the within-subjects design but does not exist in the between-subjects design. These within-subjects effects could be termed "psychological" since the response to the stimuli (CS intensity or sucrose) seems to be exaggerated beyond any differences attributable to the physical dissimilarity of the stimuli (as measured by the between-groups comparison). In the research literature, the difference in results obtained under comparison (or within-subject) and noncomparison (or between-subject) conditions are termed *contrast effects.*

Perhaps the earliest study of contrast was conducted by Elliott in 1928. Elliott trained two groups of rats to run through a complex maze. One of these groups was rewarded with bran mash and the other group was rewarded with sunflower seeds. This difference in the quality of reward led to a difference in performance; the rats receiving the bran mash ran faster and made fewer errors. On the tenth trial Elliott changed the reward of one group; the rats that had previously received bran mash were shifted to sunflower seeds, the group originally receiving sunflower seeds were maintained on that reward. The performance of the animals whose reward had been shifted deteriorated quickly, and they were soon making more errors and running more slowly than the animals whose reward was not changed.

Note that in the postshift phase of this experiment both groups were receiving the same reward, sunflower seeds, but their performance was quite different. The group with the prior history of receiving the bran mash, apparently the more preferred reward, performed more poorly than the group that had always received the sunflower seeds. This difference in performance must, in some way, be related to the comparison of the sunflower seeds with the bran mash in the shifted group, the only group that had the opportunity to make this comparison. (Note the similarity of this study to the Tinklepaugh experiment described earlier on pp. 84–85).

In a later study Crespi (1942) found that shifting rats in amount (rather than quality) of reward also produced contrast effects. Specifically, Crespi found that shifting rats from a small to a large reward led to faster running in these rats than in rats that had experienced only the larger reward. Conversely, shifting rats from a large to a smaller reward led to slower running in the downshifted rats than in rats that had experienced only the smaller value of reward. Crespi termed the enhanced running obtained with the upshift in reward an *elation* effect and the reduced running obtained with the downshift in reward a *depression* effect. These labels clearly reflected Crespi's interpretation of contrast as being emotionally based. In support of his interpretation, Crespi (1942, 1944) described some of the behaviors of the rats downshifted in reward. These behaviors included failures to eat the smaller reward when first encountered, attempts at retracing or running back away from the goal box in the runway, peering into the foodbox, attempts to jump out of the goal box, and hesitant running. Other than the fact that the animals ran faster, Crespi was unable to observe any differential behavior in the upshifted rats.

In the years since Crespi's experiment, many investigators have been reluctant to use the terms elation and depression to describe the Crespi phenomena. This reluctance stems, in part, from the dangers of anthropormorphizing or describing the phenomena in terms appropriate to man. We have no way of knowing (and most likely never will) whether the phenomenon associated with a change in the reward conditions of nonverbal organisms is, in any way, similar to emotional states of elation and depression that we may use to describe our own experiences.

Zeaman (1949) replicated the Crespi phenomena but used the more neutral term, *contrast effects*, to describe them. The "elation" effect is now frequently termed a *positive contrast effect* (PCE) and the "depression" effect is termed a *negative contrast effect* (NCE). The term "contrast" was carried over from research in perception where contrast effects have been known and investigated for some time. In perception, the term "contrast" was applied to situations where the effects of a given stimulus were exaggerated or altered by the context in which that stimulus was presented.

Most of the research with reward contrast has been concerned with negative contrast effects. The reason for this is that, despite the clear evidence from Crespi and Zeaman, other investigators were not able to reproduce the positive contrast phenomenon. Negative contrast, on the other hand, was readily obtained by a large number of investigators. In fact, evidence was so one-sided that by 1968 many investigators assumed that positive contrast was not a real phenomenon and that theories need account for only negative contrast (*see* Black, 1968; Dunham, 1968).

However, a number of investigators had made note of a possible artifact that would prevent the measurement of positive contrast effects when the underlying phenomenon might indeed be present. You will recall that positive contrast is generally defined by *faster* running in a runway by a group of animals shifted up in reward than by a group of animals receiving the same current reward but without the prior experience of a smaller reward. But what if the unshifted animals are already running as fast as is possible in the given situation? If this were the case, then the shifted animals could not possibly run faster and, therefore, no positive contrast could be measured. This possible artifact is known as a "ceiling effect." But how to get around (or below) it?

One answer has apparently come from the combination of reward shifts with another variable that is known to influence instrumental behavior, *delay of reward.* It has been known for some time that instrumental behavior suffers if the delivery of reward is delayed until some time after the completion of the response. In fact, in the runway apparatus there seems to be a direct relationship between the delay of reward and the speed of running; the longer the delay the slower the running (cf., Logan, 1960).

The use of delayed reward to alleviate the ceiling effects problem was demonstrated by Shanab, Sanders, and Premack (1969) and by Mellgren (1972). Mellgren's experiment was similar in basic

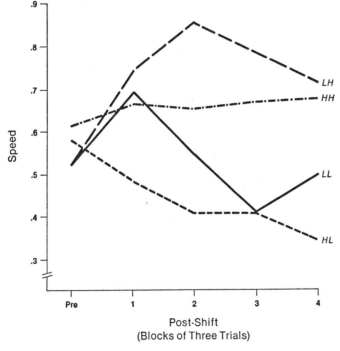

Figure 4–7. Mean speed of running as a function of reward conditions. Curves labeled LL and HH refer to animals maintained on the Low and High reward conditions; curves labeled LH and HL refer to animals shifted from low to high reward and to animals shifted from high to low reward. (From Mellgren, 1972.)

design to the Crespi study but the various groups were run with a constant 20-second delay of reward. There were four groups of rats in this experiment: Group HH received eight pellets reward throughout the experiment; Group LH received one pellet in the first phase of the experiment and then was shifted to eight pellets; Group HL received 8 pellets in the first phase of the experiment and then was shifted to one pellet and, finally, Group LL received one pellet throughout the experiment. From the results presented in Figure 4–7, it can be seen that both positive and negative contrast effects were obtained. Similar bidirectional contrast effects have been obtained in other test situations (e.g., Trowill, Panksepp, & Gandelman, 1969; Flaherty & Largen, 1975), and there now seems little doubt that the positive contrast effect is a real phenomenon.

In what terms are contrast effects to be explained? Crespi's original interpretation of contrast as being a reflection of an emotional response produced by the comparison of the new with the old reward receives some support from more recent experiments. For example, Goldman, Coover, and Levine (1973) varied the *frequency* of reward and measured plasma levels of adrenal corticosterone (one of several hormones secreted by the adrenal cortex under conditions of stress). They found that the adrenal response was *elevated* when the conditions involved a negative contrast paradigm. When reinforcement frequency was shifted in the other direction, so that rats were receiving more reinforcement than they had previously (a positive contrast paradigm), there was a *reduction* in the adrenal response.

Thus, there was a bidirectional shift in the levels of circulating corticosterone that corresponded to the bidirectional shift in reward. The elevated adrenal response following a decrease in the frequency of reward is certainly consistent with the hypothesis that reduction in reward produces an aversive emotional state: The adrenal response in this situation is similar to that produced by physical stressors such as electric shock or physical injury. The change in the adrenal response produced by an increased frequency of reward is a little more difficult to interpret because there are little other data concerned with the adrenal response in such situations.

There is another line of research relating negative contrast to an emotional state termed "frustration." According to this interpretation, frustration occurs whenever an obtained reward is less than an expected reward. An expectancy, for our present purposes, can simply be defined as prior experience with reward of a particular quality or quantity. Thus, in the Elliott experiment mentioned earlier, the rats in the shifted group could be described as having developed an expectancy for bran mash. When the reward was shifted to the sunflower seeds, the discrepancy between the new reward and the expected reward resulted in an emotional response of frustration. This emotional response includes behaviors which interfere with the response of approaching the goal area, behaviors such as those described by Crespi and mentioned above.

This interpretation of negative contrast contains two theoretical terms, expectancy and frustration, that some would refrain from applying to animal data. However, both terms occur frequently in the literature, can be closely tied to the procedures and results of experiments, and have served to focus research and thinking in several topic areas of research; they provide good examples of how the careful use of hypothetical constructs can be useful in research.

Let us look briefly now at some of the negative contrast data that can be interpreted around the concept of frustration. A number of studies have shown that the greater the difference between the large and small rewards, the greater the negative contrast effect (DiLollo & Beez, 1966; Ludvigson & Gay, 1966). If frustration is elicited following a shift from large to small reward, then it is reasonable to assume that the greater the difference between the two rewards, the greater the frustration should be; and if degree of frustration is related to size of the negative contrast effect, then the greater the negative contrast effect should be. Thus, these reward-disparity studies are consistent with a frustration interpretation. Also consistent are studies in which the deprivation state of the subject has been varied. These studies (e.g., Ehrenfreund, 1971; Flaherty & Kelley, 1973) indicate a direct relationship between degree of deprivation and negative contrast; the greater the deprivation, the more likely it is that a sizable negative contrast will occur when the amount of reward is shifted downward. Again, in frustration terms, it seems reasonable that the hungrier the rats are the more "frustrating" it would be to have the magnitude of a food reward reduced. There also seems to be a relationship between deprivation state and reward disparity such that relatively large differences between the two amounts of reward may offset less than optimal deprivation conditions in leading to a negative contrast effect (Capaldi, 1974).

These effects of deprivation and degree of reward disparity, while consistent with a frustration interpretation, provide no independent evidence that there is an emotional response involved in negative contrast effects. Somewhat more convincing evidence comes from pharmacological studies. It has been shown that negative contrast effects are reduced or eliminated by appropriate doses of the tranquilizer chlordiazepoxide (Librium) and by appropriate doses of the central nervous system depressant, sodium amytal, which may lower arousal level (Rosen & Tessel, 1970; Rosen, Glass, & Ison, 1967). Perhaps related to this latter effect, destruction of certain regions of the brain (e.g., the hippocampus) that have been implicated in modulating arousal level also eliminated negative contrast effects in some situations (Franchina & Brown, 1971).

Thus, while there is no definite evidence that an emotional response is at the base of contrast effects, there is certainly enough evidence to support continued thinking and research along these lines. However, an emotional reaction to changed conditions of reward is only one of several possible explanations of the occurrence of contrast effects. We have space to mention but briefly three others.

The first of these relates to sensory-perceptual processes. Judgments of physical stimuli can be made to vary without changing the judged stimulus itself, but by changing the context in which that stimulus is experienced (cf., Helson, 1964). For example, the apparent brightness of an object can be altered by varying the illumination of the surrounding field. Similarly, judgments of hue, temperature, size, etc., can be altered by changes in the environment in which the stimulus is perceived. It may be that reward contrast effects are, at least in part, a manifestation of a similar sensory process. For example, it may be that the contrast effects that result from a shift in sucrose solutions (as shown in Figure 4–6) result from the fact that the 4 percent solution simply tastes less sweet after experience with the 32 percent solution and, conversely, the 32 percent solution tastes sweeter after experience with the 4 percent solution. When solid food is used and shifts are made in amount of reward it may be that the animals, subsequent to the shift, "misjudge" the amount of food they are receiving as a function of their previous experience with greater or lesser amounts.

Some evidence supporting this view is provided by experiments showing that a rat's and a person's response to changing conditions of reinforcement can be interpreted in terms of changing internal frames of reference against which environmental stimuli are compared (e.g., Bevan, 1966; 1968) and by experiments showing that a rat's intake of sucrose solutions under conditions of repeatedly changing concentrations seems to follow the same psychophysical laws as a human's judgment of the sweetness of sucrose solutions (Flaherty & Sepanak, 1974). The question is whether all of contrast effects are due *only* to altered sensory responses or whether some of the behavioral changes that occur when rewards are shifted are perhaps due to both sensory and emotional responses. At the present time there is no definite evidence on this point.

A third view of contrast seems to apply principally to negative contrast. Capaldi (1972) has suggested that depressed performance subsequent to a downshift in reward may simply be the result of generalization decrement; the greater the difference between the stimulus originally conditioned and the test stimuli, the less the generalization. This *decrease* in responding that occurs when a new stimulus is substituted for the conditioned stimulus was termed a generalization decrement. A similar phenomenon occurs in instrumental behavior and has been used as an explanation for negative contrast effects.

The basic idea is that the substitution of a new reward for an old reward produces a change in stimulus conditions, and, thus, there should be a decrement in behavior. The difference between shifted and unshifted animals in the negative contrast paradigm is assumed to be due to the generalization decrement experienced by the shifted animals but not by the unshifted controls. This explanation certainly has face validity and is difficult to rule out experimentally. In fact, there is some experimental evidence (Huang, 1969) that generalization decrement does occur when rewards have equal reinforcing values when tested independently. What seems to matter is that the new rewards are different and this difference leads to a temporary decrement in behavior.

Although generalization decrement may well be a part of all contrast experiments, it is unlikely that it can serve as a sole explanation for contrast. For example, generalization decrement cannot explain positive contrast at all. Generalization decrement can only detract from positive contrast and, therefore, it cannot explain the occurrence of positive contrast. Generalization decrement also has problems as the sole explanation of negative contrast.

There are numerous experiments in the literature in which negative contrast occurs over a long period of time with repeated shifts between the large and small rewards (e.g., Bower, 1961; Flaherty & Largen, 1975). According to generalization decrement interpretations of contrast, the disruptive effects of the reward shift should become minimal with repeated experience with the different stimuli (Capaldi & Lynch, 1967) and, therefore, negative contrast should disappear. This is not always the case. So we are left with generalization decrement as a phenomenon which is likely to be consequent to all reward shifts but which cannot fully explain contrast effects. Even in the negative contrast paradigm in which the subjects experience a single shift from large to small reward, it seems quite likely that emotional factors play a major role.

The last factor that we shall mention as a possible contributor to contrast effects, particularly negative contrast effects, is concerned with exploratory behavior. In the Elliott (1928) experiment mentioned above (*see* p. 99) recall that there was both an increase in time to traverse the maze and an increase in *cul-de-sac* entries subsequent to the shift to a less preferred reward. Elliott did not interpret the increase in blind alley entrances as necessarily representing an increase in mistakes on the part of the rat. He believed that they might represent the rat "looking for" the missing preferred reward. Since Elliott's study there has been little in the way of systematic study of the possibility that the failure to obtain an accustomed reward will lead to the initiation of exploratory behaviors and that these behaviors may contribute to instrumental negative contrast effects by competing with the measured instrumental response.

It is clear that contrast effects are pervasive and complex phenomena that involve a comparison of two or more stimulus events. However, whether the comparison leads to an emotional response, a perceptual change, a generalization decrement, the initiation of exploratory behaviors, or perhaps all four, is not yet clear.

Extinction Effects

The extinction procedure is formally similar to a negative contrast experiment in that the subjects are downshifted in amount of reward. The difference, of course, is that in extinction the new reward is always zero. The question we are asking here is whether or not there is any relationship between amount of reward received in acquisition and resistance to extinction (R to E).

A number of studies have indicated that there is an inverse relationship between amount of reward in acquisition and resistance to extinction. That is, large rewards in acquisition apparently lead to faster extinction than do small rewards in acquisition (e.g., Hulse, 1958; Armus, 1959; Wagner, 1961; Ison & Cook 1964). If one assumes that R to E reflects the strength of a learned S–R association and that rewards strengthen this association between a stimulus and a response (as Thorndike did) and that larger rewards lead to stronger associations (as Hull, 1943, did), then these results are somewhat puzzling. It would seem that larger rewards should lead to greater resistance to extinction.

There are a number of plausible explanations for these results. One is that the larger the reward in acquisition, the greater the frustration in extinction. Frustration may, in turn, lead to behaviors which interfere with the performance of the instrumental response. You will recognize this explanation as quite similar to the frustration explanation of negative contrast effects. Thus, we might expect that the behaviors associated with extinction would be similar to those described by Crespi in relation to the negative contrast effect. Similarly, we might expect that the variables which influence contrast effects would also influence the effects of amount of reward on resistance to extinction. There is some evidence that this is the case. For example, both negative contrast and extinction shifts lead to behaviors that could be classified as irritable; both types of shift also lead to increases in plasma corticosteroid levels (Goldman et al.,

1973); both negative contrast and resistance to extinction are influenced in a similar fashion by pharmacological agents; and both negative contrast and the effects of magnitude of reward on resistance to extinction are influenced in a similar fashion by comparable retention intervals (Gonzalez, Fernhoff, & David, 1973). However, there is not enough evidence yet to justify the conclusion that frustration is a complete account of the effects of acquisition reward on R to E. At the present time, the frustration account can be regarded as an interesting hypothesis deserving of further research.

There are two complicating factors to this relationship between acquisition reward magnitude and resistance to extinction. One problem is that some studies have not shown the inverse relationship, finding instead a direct relationship—the greater the reward, the greater the R to E (e.g., Hill & Spear, 1962). Faced with this confusing state of affairs, D'Amato (1970) suggested that the effects of amount of reward on R to E may, in turn, be related to the number of acquisition trials. Specifically, D'Amato speculated that the inverse relationship might be found only after extended acquisition training, whereas after minimal training there may be direct effects, or possibly no effects of amount of reward during acquisition. There is some evidence in the literature that supports this line of reasoning (e.g., Ison & Cook, 1964; Wilton & Strongman, 1967).

Thus, we can see that even the investigation of a seemingly simple relationship can lead to some complicated results and interpretations. One lesson that these data should teach us is that the effects of any given variable on behavior depend on what other variables may be operating at the same time. Thus, the effects of amount of reward on R to E apparently interact with the amount of acquisition training. Interactions such as these prevent us from making any blanket statements concerning the effects of a variable without the addition of some qualifier such as "other things being equal." In the case of R to E we now know that amount of training and magnitude of reward must be jointly taken into account. There are probably other factors also that will be discovered in the future. Interactions such as these make the analysis of behavior difficult and slow work. But they also make it challenging, and they are what we can expect as we pursue the investigation of such a complex topic as behavior, human or infrahuman.

IV. DELAY OF REWARD

It is well established that delaying the presentation of a reward until some time after completion of the instrumental response results in a decrement in behavior (*see* Renner, 1964, for a review). Much of the research in this area has been conducted in attempts to: (a) determine the relationship between length of delay and behavior in a given task, (b) determine or infer what the mechanisms are that an animal uses to "bridge the gap" between the performance of a response and the presentation of a delayed reward, (c) determine whether the effects of delay of reward are due to influences on acquisition of the response or due to influences on the performance of the response (i.e., motivational variables), (d) determine how delay interacts with other reward variables, and (e) determine the effects of delay of reward in acquisition on later resistance to extinction.

The Delay Gradient

Perhaps the earliest research concerned with points (a) and (b) was conducted by John Watson (1917). Watson had two groups of rats dig through sawdust in order to obtain a food reward. The reward was presented immediately to one of the groups and delayed by 30 seconds for the other group. Watson found no difference between the groups. However, later studies have consistently found a regular delay gradient such that the longer the time between completion of the response and the receipt of the reward, the poorer the performance. The exact parameters of the gradient may depend on the learning task used and, perhaps more importantly, on the presence, during the delay interval, of stimuli correlated with the presence of food and/or the performance of the response. For example, in the Watson experiment, the rats waited out the 30-second delay interval in the presence of the cup in which food was presented. When Perkins (1947) had rats wait in special delay chambers (where reward was never received), he found that delays of 15 seconds substantially interfered with the learning of a simple T-maze position habit (e.g., turning consistently to the left at the choice point).

An even steeper delay gradient was found by Grice (1948). Grice trained rats on brightness discrimination in a two-choice apparatus (*see* Figure 4–8). In this task one brightness (e.g., black) is consistently rewarded and the rats must learn to approach this stimulus. To insure that the rats are learning to approach a brightness cue and not learning to respond to a position (e.g., right side), it is usual to change the position of the brightness stimuli from side to side repeatedly throughout the course of acquisition. When this was done, Grice found that delays in reward of only a second or two substantially interfered with the rats' performance (*see* Figure 4–9).

The apparent reasons for the differences in temporal gradients found in these studies are the following: (a) introducing a delay chamber in which there are no stimuli correlated with the delivery of food appears to steepen the delay gradient (comparison of Watson-type experiment with Perkins experiment), and (b) having a delay chamber plus removing stimuli correlated with the performance of a particular response steepens the delay gradient even further (comparison of the Perkins experiment with the Grice experiment). Thus, it appears that rats can use stimuli correlated with the presence of food and/or stimuli correlated with the performance of a particular

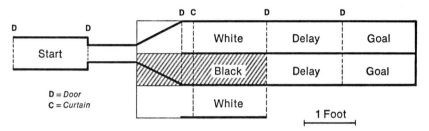

Figure 4–8. Apparatus used by Grice to investigate influence of delay of reward on discrimination learning. The delay compartment was devoid of secondary reinforcing stimuli. (From Grice, 1948.)

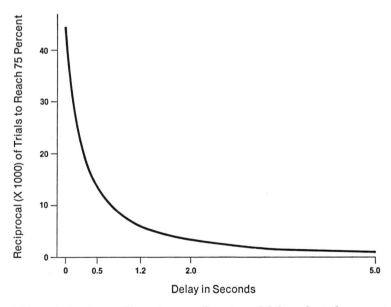

Figure 4–9. Rate of learning as a function of delay of reinforcement. The reciprocal x 1000 of the number of trials to reach the level of 75 percent correct choices is plotted against the time delay. Experimental values are represented by black dots and the smooth curve is fitted to these data. (After Grice, 1948.)

response to help "bridge the gap" between the performance of a response and the presentation of a delayed reward. When these stimuli are taken away from the rat, its performance is seriously disrupted by even very short delays (*see also* Keesey, 1964).

Performance Effects

The great majority of reward-delay studies have been conducted to determine the acquisition effects of delay. That is, an experimental group has been trained on a task with a given delay of reward, and the behavior of this group has been compared with a control group in which reward was not delayed. The interpretation of any differences existing between the groups generally has been that the delay of reward interferes with learning. This may well be true. However, other studies have shown that delay of reward has deleterious effects on the performance of responses that were well learned before the delay was introduced. As an example of these performance effects, we will mention an experiment by Shanab and Biller (1972). In this experiment, it was found that when rats were shifted from a 0-second to a 15-second delay of reward in a runway task, there was a decrease in running speeds to a level approximately one-quarter of what prevailed before the shift. Interestingly, it was also found that if the reward was shifted up from 1 pellet to 12 pellets at the same time that the delay of reward was added, there was considerably less of a decrement in performance. We will return to this point below when we discuss interactions between delay of reward and other variables (*see* pp. 111–13).

Similar decremental effects of delay of reward on well learned behavior have been found in other rat experiments (e.g., Shanab, Sanders, & Premack, 1969; Mackintosh & Lord, 1973) and in some recent experiments conducted with monkeys. In these latter studies D'Amato and Cox (1976) have found that the introduction of a delay of reward as short as only 8 seconds can lead to the decline from virtual 100 percent correct responding to change responding (50 percent correct) in a simple two-stimulus discrimination problem. The point here is that the monkeys apparently "knew" what the correct stimulus was—they had been performing at a very high level for hundreds of trials—and yet they began selecting the incorrect stimulus as often as the correct stimulus when the 8-second delay was introduced.

A motivational rather than a learning interpretation would seem to be appropriate for these effects of delayed reward on well learned tasks. Such an interpretation has been advocated in the past (e.g., Tolman, 1932; Spence, 1956), and the general idea is that delays reduce the reward value of the goal event. Tolman, consistent with his cognitive orientation to animal behavior, wrote that reward delays would serve to reduce that animal's "demand" for the goal object, demand having more or less equivalent meaning to incentive. We shall now review some studies that are consistent with this motivational interpretation of reward delay.

Interaction of Delay with Other Variables

In a series of experiments, Davenport (1962) and Logan (1965) have studied the behavior of rats given a choice between responding for a small reward presented after a short delay or a larger reward that was available only after a longer delay. For example (in Davenport's experiment), rats were given a choice of going to one side of a Y-shaped chamber for a 2-pellet reward delivered after a 1-second delay, or going to the other side for an 8-pellet reward delivered after a 10-second delay. There were actually many such combinations (*see* Table 4–1); Davenport found that the rats would eventually develop consistent choices for one side or the other and that, in general, larger rewards could offset longer delays, at least to some degree. The percentage choice of the various alternatives after 72

Table 4–1. Relationship Between Delay and Magnitude of Reward*

Delay of Reward (seconds)

		1 vs. 1	4 vs. 1	7 vs. 1	10 vs. 1	15 vs. 1	30 vs. 1
Amount of Reward (number of pellets)	16 vs. 2	100%	100%	100%	100%	60%	50%
	8 vs. 2	100%	100%	100%	60%	85%	25%
	4 vs. 2	100%	100%	50%	25%	0%	0%

*Percent choice of large reward as a function of reward and delay differences. The row labels indicate the reward differences associated with the two-choice alternatives. The column labels indicate the delays associated with each choice. The longer delays were always associated with the larger rewards. The percentages listed in the cells represent final level of choice of the large reward side. Separate groups of rats were tested under each condition. (After Davenport, 1962.)

training trials are presented in Table 4–1. It should be noted that preferences in some cases changed quite a bit over the course of acquisition and that the final level of preferences shown in Table 4–1 represent the result of an as yet little understood dynamic process. For example, the data in Table 4–1 show that the rats ended up never choosing 4 pellets at a 30-second delay when this alternative was pitted against 2 pellets at a 1-second delay. And yet, early in training under these conditions the rats tended to go to the larger reward side of 75 percent of the choice opportunities. Thus, during training preference—the choice of the larger reward in this case—dropped from 75 percent to 0 percent. There were other, but less striking, changes in preference in some of the other conditions of the experiment.

From these data Davenport was able to construct equal-reinforcement contours showing that, for example, an 8-pellet reward delivered after an approximate 20-second delay would be about equal to a 2-pellet reward delivered after a 1-second delay. This equal reinforcement contour (presented in Figure 4–10) shows conditions under which choice would be about equal for the two alternatives.

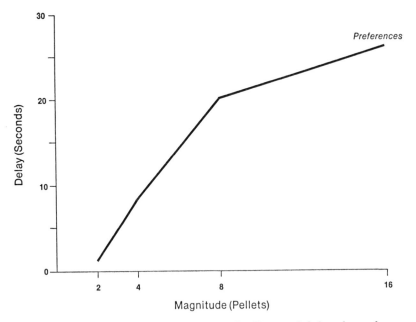

Figure 4–10. Different combinations of pellets and delays have the same reinforcement value. The figure shows that a 2-pellet reward presented after a 1-second delay was approximately equal in reinforcing properties to a 4-pellet reward presented after an approximate 8-second delay, etc. (After Davenport, 1962.)

A more extensive investigation (as well as a mathematical treatment) of this "decision making" by rats was undertaken by Logan (1965). Logan's data were remarkably consistent with Davenport's in those cases where similar delay and reward values were employed. Taken together, these experiments as well as those mentioned above in which delay was introduced late in training, indicate quite strongly that the effects of delay may be interpreted in motivational terms; i.e., delay of reward detracts from the reward value of the goal event but this detraction may be offset somewhat by increasing the amount of reward. The finding of Shanab and Biller (1972), also mentioned above, that the detrimental effects of the introduction of a 15-second delay may be offset by a simultaneous increase in reward from 1 pellet to 12 pellets is also clearly consistent with this interpretation. Other studies (e.g., Renner, 1963) have shown that the detrimental effects of delay of reward are also offset by higher levels of deprivation. That is, the more food deprived an animal is, the less effect a reward delay has on the performance of the instrumental response. Clearly, all of these variables (delay, reward magnitude, deprivation) may be interpreted as influencing the same thing, the reward or incentive value of the goal event (or, in Tolman's terms, the demand for the goal event).

An interesting variation on these studies was recently published by Ainslie (1974). Ainslie set up a situation with pigeons in which they had a choice of pecking at one key that would deliver a small reward after a short delay, or pecking at another disc that would deliver a larger reward after a longer delay. Ainslie found that, under these conditions, the pigeons virtually always chose the small reward and short delay. However, if the pigeons were given the opportunity to shut off the stimulus indicating that the small-immediate reward was available, they would do so, and then respond on the key giving them the larger reward after the longer delay. In other words, the pigeons could choose the longer delay and larger reward, but only if they could first get rid of the stimulus indicating the availability of the short-delay reward. Ainslie termed his findings a demonstration of impulse control in the pigeon.

Extinction Effects

The effects of delayed reward in acquisition on resistance to extinction are not entirely clear at the present time. Some studies (e.g., Fehrer, 1956) have found that experience with delays in acquisition leads to an increased resistance to extinction. However, other studies (e.g., Culbertson, 1970) have found no effect.

If the temporal value of the reward delay is varied, then it has sometimes been found that resistance to extinction is increased. For example, Logan, Beier, and Kincaid (1956) varied the reward delay between 1 and 30 seconds and found that this procedure led to an increased resistance to extinction in comparison to no delay. However, other investigators (e.g., Wike & Kintsch, 1959) have found no effects of varying delay over a less wide range.

Perhaps related to these effects of varied delay is the finding that presentation of delayed reward on only *some* of the trials does enhance resistance to extinction. These effects of partial delay are found in situations where delaying reward on every trial (constant delay) does not seem to enhance resistance to extinction (Shanab & Birnbaum, 1974).

Thus, it seems likely that delay of reward in acquisition will, under some conditions, lead to an increased resistance to extinction. The amount of research conducted up to the present time does not allow any definitive statement as to what these conditions might be. However, it does seem that varying the delay or presenting the delay on just some of the acquisition trials maximizes the likelihood that an extinction effect will be obtained.

V. SUMMARY

Instrumental behavior differs from Pavlovian conditioning operationally in terms of the degree of control the subject's response has over the reinforcing event. In Pavlovian conditioning the CR may or may not modify the UCS, but in instrumental learning the subject's response is *necessary* for the presentation of the reinforcer. The effect that the subject's emitted response has on the environment determines whether the probability of that response occurring again will increase or decrease.

Degree of deprivation increases general activity, in most situations, and both the vigor and directedness of instrumental behavior.

The vigor of instrumental behavior also tends to vary directly with both amount and quality of the reinforcement. Reinforcements have relative as well as absolute value. That is, shifting from a more preferred to a less preferred reinforcement will have deleterious effects on performance and shifting from a less preferred to a more preferred reinforcement will tend to enhance performance. There are several possible, and not mutually exclusive, theoretical explanations for these contrast effects.

The relationship between amount of reward in acquisition and resistance to extinction is a complex one, but it seems that, at least in some situations, a larger reward in acquisition leads to faster extinction.

Delay of reward impedes instrumental behavior. Many of the deleterious effects of delay can be attributed to motivational factors in that they may be offset, to some extent, by increasing the amount of reward. Also consistent with a motivational interpretation is that the effects of delay become manifest even when delay is introduced in a highly trained task. It is likely that delay of reward in acquisition also interferes with the formation of associations between the performance of the instrumental response and the availability of reinforcement.

CHAPTER 5

Instrumental Learning: Schedules of Reinforcement

---

*We need to go beyond mere observation to a study
of functional relationships. We need to establish laws by
virtue of which we may predict behavior, and we may
do this only by finding variables of which behavior is
a function.*

B.F. Skinner, *Behavior of Organisms*, 1938

In life rewards often come intermittently, and behavior is often quite different when only some responses are rewarded than when all responses are rewarded. We saw in Chapter 3 that the presentation of a UCS on less than 100 percent of the trials leads to a decrement in the acquisition of a CR but an enhanced resistance to extinction. The effect of partial reward in instrumental behavior shares a *similarity* and a *difference* with these effects of partial UCS presentation in Pavlovian conditioning.

The similarity is in resistance to extinction: *Subjects rewarded on a partial schedule for instrumental responses are more resistant to extinction than subjects rewarded on every trial.*

The difference is in acquisition: *There is usually no decrement in the acquisition of an instrumental response when subjects are partially rewarded unless the actual percentage of rewarded trials is very low; and, in some cases, there is an actual enhancement of the acquisition behavior of partially rewarded subjects as compared to subjects rewarded on 100 percent of their trials.*

In order to discuss these effects of partial reward on instrumental behavior we shall have to make a distinction between experiments concerned with an analysis of events that take place during the early stages of acquisition and those experiments concerned with the behavior generated after extensive experience with a particular schedule of reward. These latter effects may be termed the "steady-state" effects of reward schedules.

In practice, two different sets of experimental procedures have been used to investigate these two problems. The steady-state experiments have, for the most part, been free-operant experiments conducted in a Skinner box with rate of responding as the major dependent variable. The subjects in these experiments are given extensive experience, often hundreds of hours, on a particular schedule of reinforcement. On the other hand, the experiments concerned with the early acquisition effects of partial reward are generally conducted in runways, use a discrete trial procedure, and provide relatively little acquisition experience, sometimes as few as two to four trials. We shall start our discussion of partial reinforcement with these latter experiments.

I. DISCRETE-TRIAL EXPERIMENTS

We have already stated the basic result of the partial reward experiment; viz., generally equal or better performance in acquisition and greater resistance to extinction following partial than following continuous reward. An example of the extinction effects may be found in an experiment by Weinstock (1954). Weinstock found that there was an orderly inverse relationship between percentage of reinforcement in acquisition and resistance to extinction. That is, a group reinforced on only 30 percent of its acquisition trials was more resistant to extinction than a group reinforced on 50 percent of its trials; and this latter group was more resistant than a group reinforced on 80 percent of its trials; and least resistant of all, was a group given 100 percent reinforcement in acquisition.

Weinstock found little difference among these groups in acquisition; i.e., there was no decrement in performance associated with the lower reward percentages. In a further study of the acquisition effects of partial reward, Goodrich (1959) found that the relationship between a 50 percent group and a 100 percent group depended on where in a straight runway performance measures were obtained. That is, Goodrich found that the partially rewarded group ran faster than the 100 percent group in the start region of the runway, but slower in the goal region. These data are presented in Figure 5–1. It can be seen in this figure that the performance of the rats in the middle section of the runway was similar to their performance in the start region, but it took longer (more acquisition trials) to develop.

There have been many experiments demonstrating these basic relationships, and there have been almost as many theoretical accounts trying to explain the results (*see* Robbins, 1971, for a recent review). As we mentioned in Chapter 3, partial reinforcement effects are interesting because the greater persistence of partially rewarded animals in extinction is not consistent with two seemingly reasonable assumptions of simple S–R associationism; namely, that resistance to extinction should be directly related to the strength of an association, and the strength of an association, in turn, should vary directly with the number of reinforced trials. But in Weinstock's study the 50 percent group had only half as many reinforced trials as

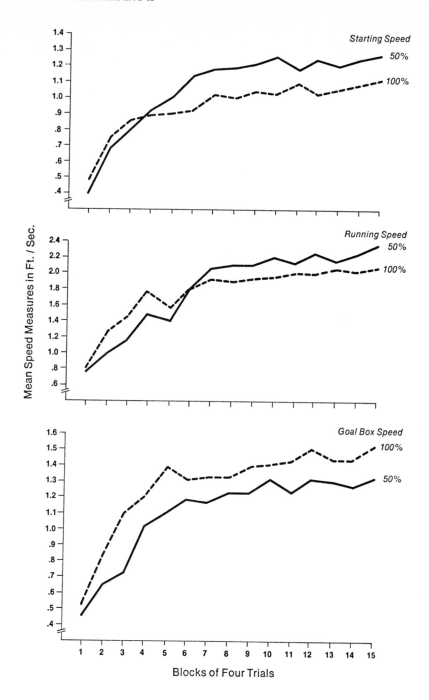

Figure 5–1. Mean starting, running, and goal-box speeds for groups given either 50 or 100 percent reinforcement. (From Goodrich, 1959.)

the 100 percent group, and yet it showed much greater resistance to extinction. How are these results to be explained? We will examine several attempts at explaining these data on a theoretical level, and we shall start with the frustration theory of Abram Amsel.

Frustration Theory

To understand the development of frustration theory we have to consider again the anticipatory response theory discussed in Chapter 4. Recall that in the previous discussion we developed the following ideas: The reward in an instrumental learning task is delivered in some stimulus context (e.g., the goal area of a runway or complex maze, the stimuli provided by a Skinner box, etc.), and the subject consumes the reward. This sequence of events is essentially the same as that which occurs in an appetitive Pavlovian conditioning experiment; food is presented in the presence of an originally neutral stimulus and the subject consumes the food. In the Pavlovian conditioning paradigm the neutral stimulus eventually comes to elicit a CR, a response that in some ways is a fractional component of the UCR and in some ways preparation for the UCS (salivation can be considered both). Clark Hull (e.g., 1943) used this similarity between the goal events that occur in instrumental learning and the procedures of Pavlovian conditioning to explain some of the events that occur in instrumental behavior.

Specifically, Hull termed the consumption of the food reward that occurs in instrumental learning situations a goal response and symbolized it as R_G. Hull assumed that this response was elicited by the food reward, much as a UCR is elicited by the UCS of food. Hull further assumed that fractional components of the goal response would be conditioned to the environmental stimuli (e.g., those stimuli in the goal region of a runway) that were highly correlated with the presence of the food. Again we can see the analogy to Pavlovian conditioning where components of the UCR (such as salivation) come to be elicited by originally neutral stimuli present in the environment where the UCS is delivered. These fractional components of R_G were termed r_g.

The situation we have described thus far could be summarized as follows: After a number of instrumental training trials, the apparatus stimuli, S_A, present in the area where food is regularly presented elicit a fractional component of the consummatory response, or in symbols $S_A \searrow r_g$. In other words, there is a "built-in" Pavlovian conditioning paradigm in every instrumental learning experiment.

Hull then made use of the principle of generalization (*see* Chapter 2) and assumed that stimuli similar to those present in the goal region would also acquire some tendency to elicit r_g. Important examples of these other stimuli might be those stimuli present in earlier portions of the maze or runway. These other stimuli (designated S_A') would thus tend to elicit r_g before the goal region was reached.

To what end was this theoretical mechanism elaborated? Assuming that these or similar processes occur, do they have any value in explaining instrumental behavior? The r_g mechanism has been used in several different ways since its development in the 1930s (*see* Bolles, 1967; Seward, 1970) but most recent applications have been in terms of a motivational mechanism. The Pavlovian conditioning of the fractional anticipatory goal response provides a mechanism for explaining how an animal *anticipates* the presence of motivationally relevant events.

Some theorists have assumed that this anticipation has both a response component (r_g) and a stimulus component (s_g). For example, one aspect of anticipation might be salivation; the salivation itself can be considered a response (r_g) and, as a result of this response, certain stimuli (s_g) are produced, e.g., the detection of saliva in the mouth. This r_g–s_g mechanism has become virtually synonymous with the development of an expectancy, an expectancy that a reward will be received in a given stimulus context. It should be emphasized that peripheral responses such as salivation are assumed to represent only a part of the total r_g–s_g mechanism; the goal box of a runway does not act directly on the salivary glands but produces its effect indirectly via the central nervous system. These central responses are at present difficult to measure but are likely to be the basis of the anticipatory reactions.

Thus, when r_g–s_g is elicited by environmental stimuli (S_A') it provides a source of motivation for the performance of the instrumental response. When used in this way, the symbol r_g–s_g represents a centrally occurring response, emotional or otherwise, that is correlated with the anticipation of reward (Miller, 1959; Logan & Wagner, 1965).

Now we will consider how Amsel (1958, 1962) made use of this construct in the development of frustration theory. He assumed that once an expectancy for reward had been acquired, then the occurrence of nonreward was frustrating. In other words, a nonreward becomes important only after a reward is expected. Frustration is viewed as an emotional response which can become anticipatory through the same conditioning and generalization mechanisms by which r_g–s_g becomes anticipatory to the goal area. The anticipatory frustration response, termed r_f–s_f, is assumed by Amsel to mediate tendencies to avoid the goal area.

Now, let us go back to the partial reinforcement experiment and see how these mechanisms can be used. During the early stages of acquisition the subject develops an expectancy of reward in the goal region. Once this expectancy (r_g–s_g) develops, then the nonreward that occurs on some percentage of the trials becomes frustrating. This frustration then becomes anticipatory (r_f–s_f), that is, it comes to be expected. Now, according to Amsel, r_g–s_g should mediate approach tendencies, and, since frustration is presumably aversive to the organism, r_f–s_f should mediate avoidance tendencies. The subject should thus be in a state of conflict—to approach where reward is sometimes received, or to avoid where frustration is sometimes experienced. (Remember, in a partial reinforcement experiment there are no cues to tell an animal on which trial it will receive reward.) The data tell us that subjects continue to respond in a partial reinforcement situation, thus the conflict assumed by Amsel must be resolved in favor of approaching the goal region. Subjects trained on a schedule of partial reward learn to approach a goal in the presence of stimuli signaling both reward and frustration.

Compare this with what happens to subjects trained on a 100 percent reward schedule. These subjects learn to approach a goal with the expectancy of reward only. They never experience frustration during acquisition.

In extinction all rewards are stopped for both groups and this should lead to frustration in both groups. Subjects trained under partial reinforcement have learned to approach the goal in the presence of anticipatory frustration (r_f–s_f), whereas the subjects trained under conditions of continuous reward have not had the opportunity for this kind of learning. Thus, for the 100 percent group, the avoidance tendencies elicited by r_f–s_f during extinction should predominate, and this group should stop performing before a partially rewarded group, which, of course, is what the data indicate. Thus, Amsel's explanation of the partial reinforcement extinction effect is essentially an explanation in terms of differential learned tendencies to persevere in the presence of stimuli indicating possible frustration.

Amsel's theory is potentially integrative because the concept of frustration occurs in the context of a number of different experimental paradigms (we have already used it as a potential explanation for negative contrast) and in several different areas of psychology (e.g., social, clinical).

Within the context of partial reinforcement itself, frustration has been used to explain some interesting findings. For example, consider an experiment by Hulse (1958) in which amount of reward as well as schedule of reward was varied. Hulse found that rats

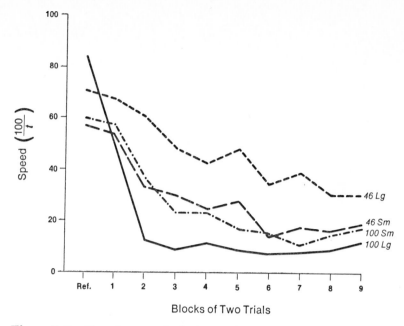

Figure 5–2. Running speeds during extinction as a joint function of percentage of reinforcement and amount of reinforcement. The rats had been reinforced 100 or 46 percent of the time with either a 1.0-gram (Lg) or an 0.08-gram (Sm) food reward. The reference point includes data from the last training trial and the first extinction trial. (From Hulse, 1958.)

rewarded on 100 percent of the trials extinguished faster following a large reward than following a small reward. But, in groups receiving partial reward the relationship was reversed; the small reward group extinguished faster than the large reward group (*see* Figure 5–2). How is this interaction between amount of reward and percentage reward to be interpreted?

In frustration terms, these data can be explained in the following way. Extinction following large reward elicits a greater frustration response than extinction following small reward (because of a greater reward expectancy in the former group), and this greater frustration response leads to greater avoidance tendencies and thus faster extinction in the 100 percent large reward group than in the 100 percent small reward group. In the case of partial reward, the frustration is experienced in acquisition, and thus, the large reward partial group should learn to approach under greater levels of frustration than the small reward partial group. This differential tendency to approach carries over into extinction (which is presumably maximally frustrating) leading to more persistent behavior in the large reward partial group than in the small reward partial group.

It can be seen that these joint effects of amount of reward and percentage reward can be explained by principles developed to account for the effects of each variable separately. Explanations such as this represent a large plus for frustration theory. We shall now briefly review several other experimental results which support the hypothesis that there is a frustration response, that it is aversive, and that it is related to extinction.

The Frustration Effect

Evidence that it is reasonable to think of a primary frustration response that occurs with nonreinforcement was obtained in an experiment by Amsel and Roussel (1952). This experiment made use of a double runway apparatus like the one diagrammed in Figure 5–3. Notice that this apparatus has two runway sections (A_1 and A_2) and two goal boxes, a middle goal box (GB_1) and an end goal box (GB_2). In the first stage of the Amsel and Roussel experiment the rats were rewarded in both goal boxes. After a number of trials (and presumably the acquisition of an expectancy of reward) the rats were shifted to a 50 percent reward schedule in GB_1. They were still rewarded on every trial in the second goal box. The data of interest were the running speeds in A_2, which showed that the rats ran faster following a nonreward trial than they did following a rewarded trial. Amsel interpreted this difference in

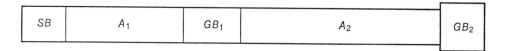

Figure 5–3. Diagram of a double runway similar to the one used by Amsel and Roussel (1952). The apparatus had a start box (SB), two alleyways (A_1 and A_2), and two goal boxes (GB_1 and GB_2). Rats were rewarded on 50 percent of the trials in GB_1 and 100 percent of the trials in GB_2. The data of interest were the running speeds in A_2 after rewarded and nonrewarded trials in GB_1.

running speed as representing an energizing effect of frustration, termed the *Frustration Effect* or *FE*. In order to understand these data, remember that the rats are running away from a place (GB_1) where they just experienced frustration and toward a place (GB_2) where they receive 100 percent reward. Thus, the FE, which by

Amsel's interpretation represents an enhancement of behavior, is to be distinguished from anticipatory frustration (r_f–s_f) which usually leads to avoidance tendencies and thus a decrement in behavior.

The FE experiment is more complicated than first appearances might indicate, and not all investigators agree with Amsel's interpretation. Some feel that the difference in A_2 running speeds after rewarded and nonrewarded trials in GB_1 may represent a *slowing down* after rewarded trials and not a speeding up after nonrewarded trials, and thus the data should not be interpreted as supporting an energizing effect of frustrative nonreward. And, indeed, there are some experiments that have demonstrated a slowing down after a rewarded trial (e.g., McHose & Ludvigson, 1965). However, other research has indicated that slowing down does not always occur (e.g., Patten, 1971, 1973), particularly if some time period such as 10 seconds is allowed for the rats to consume the food in GB_1 before access to A_2 is allowed.

Support for the frustration interpretation of the FE comes from experiments in which a control group devised by Wagner (1959) is employed. In Wagner's experiment there were two groups of rats; one group, as in the Amsel and Roussel study, received 50 percent reward in GB_1 and 100 percent reward in GB_2, the second group was never rewarded in GB_1 but received the regular 100 percent reward in GB_2. If frustration is responsible for the faster running after nonrewarded trials in the partially rewarded group, then the running speeds of this group after nonrewarded trials should also be faster than the running speeds in Group 2, which never receives reward in GB_1. This is so because nonreward in GB_1 should not be frustrating for Group 2 since it would have had no occasion to develop an expectancy for reward in GB_1. The results of the Wagner experiment supported the frustration theory in that the post nonreward speeds in A_2 of the partially rewarded group were faster than the postrewarded speeds of the same group, and faster than all trials of Group 2. These results have been replicated often enough (e.g., Hughes & Dachowski, 1973; *also see* Scull, 1973 for a review) to provide some measure of confidence in the assertion that nonreward when reward is expected may energize behavior, at least temporarily.

Also in agreement with this interpretation are other studies that show: (a) that when the reward on R trials is greater, the FE is greater, (Daly, 1968; Krippner, Endsley, & Tacker, 1967), (b) that the FE is more likely to occur under states of more severe deprivation (Dunlap & Frates, 1970), and (c) an increase in activity occurs under conditions correlated with the demonstration of an FE (Patten, 1973).

Frustration Is Aversive

A second line of evidence supporting the Amsel frustration account of partial reward comes from studies indicating that frustration is an aversive event. These studies have demonstrated that rats will learn to escape from the presence of a stimulus that had previously been associated with nonreward.

For example, Daly (1969A, 1969B) first gave rats a series of rewarded trials and then shifted the rats to extinction. Concurrent with the introduction of nonreward was the presentation of a new stimulus (e.g., a light onset) in the goal region. In the final phase of this experiment, the rats were placed in the start box of a hurdle-jumping apparatus and the stimulus that had previously been paired with nonreward was introduced. The rats could terminate this stimulus by jumping over a hurdle into a neutral goal box. The rats that had the stimulus paired with nonreward rapidly learned to jump over the hurdle to escape the stimulus. In comparison, rats that also had the same stimulus paired with nonreward, but that had never been rewarded in the apparatus (and therefore the nonreward should not have been frustrating), showed little tendency to jump the hurdle. Again, these results support the hypothesis that the occurrence of nonreward after a history of reward is frustrating and this frustration is an aversive state.

Thus, there is a fair degree of support for several aspects of Amsel's frustration account of the PREE (for some possible neurophysiological correlates of frustration and the PREE *see also* Gray, 1970; Glazer, 1974; and Henke, 1974). However, as attractive as frustration theory is, it cannot be a complete explanation for the effects of partial reward. The incompleteness of frustration theory has been highlighted in particular by the research and theorizing of Capaldi to which we now turn.

Sequential Theory

E. J. Capaldi (1966) has noted that most theories of partial reward characterize a schedule of reward in terms of the percentage of trials on which a reward is delivered, e.g., 100 percent, 50 percent, etc. In order to obtain a schedule of reward which is less than 100 percent, some intermixture of rewarded and nonrewarded trials must be arranged. For example, consider an experiment in which four trials a day will be given and only two of these trials will be rewarded (i.e., a 50 percent schedule). It is obvious that several sequences of reward (R) and nonreward (N) are possible (i.e.,

RNNR, RRNN, RNRN, NRRN, NRNR, NNRR). All of these are 50 percent schedules of reward, but they differ in the actual sequence of rewarded and nonrewarded trials. In the usual partial reinforcement experiment the sequence is determined randomly.

However, Capaldi has found that the sequences themselves may have differential effects on behavior and that characterizing a schedule of reward only in terms of percentage of rewarded trials and not in terms of the actual sequence of rewarded and non-rewarded trials may be imprecise. For example, note that the sequence NRNR contains two transitions between nonrewarded and rewarded trials (NR transitions); the sequence RNRN contains only one NR transition, and the sequence RRNN contains no NR transitions. Thus, the number of NR transitions is a sequential variable that can be manipulated independently of percentage of reinforcement (all three sequences just mentioned are 50 percent reward sequences).

It has been shown that NR transitions are very important in determining many of the effects associated with partial reward schedules. For example, Spivey (1967) found that after only ten acquisition trials a group that had experienced three NR transitions in acquisition was more resistant to extinction than a group that had received one NR transition, and this latter group was in turn more resistant to extinction than a 100 percent reward group. These effects of NR transitions were found independent of differences in resistance to extinction produced by differing percentages of rewarded trials.

As a second example of the operation of sequential variables, let us consider an experiment by Seybert, Mellgren, and Jobe (1973, Exp. I). In this experiment two groups were given a total of 16 acquisition trials (one trial per day). Ten of the 16 trials were rewarded (a 62 percent schedule) in both groups, but the groups differed in the sequences of rewarded and nonrewarded trials. The actual sequences each group experienced are presented in Table 5–1. We can see that the groups differed in number of NR transitions; one group experienced six NR transitions whereas the second group experienced only two NR transitions. The results of this experiment (shown in Figure 5–4) again illustrate that sequential variables can produce differences in R to E with percentage of reward held constant.

What accounts for the apparent effects of trial sequence, and why, in particular, do NR transitions seem to be so important in determining resistance to extinction? Capaldi's explanation of the effectiveness of sequential variables involves two assumptions. The first assumption is that subjects remember whether the outcome of

Table 5–1. Rewarded (R) and Nonrewarded (N) Trial Sequences Received by the Three Groups in Experiment 1 by Seybert, Mellgren, and Jobe (1973)*

Group	Trial Sequence
1N	R R N R R N R N R R N R N R N R
3N	R R R N N N R R R N N N R R R R
CRF	All Rewarded

*There was a total of 16 acquisition trials.

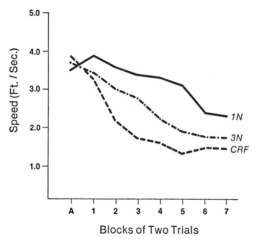

Figure 5–4. Mean running speeds for the last day of acquistion (A) and 14 days of extinction. (1N refers to group receiving a reinforced trial after each nonreward trial; 3N refers to group receiving a reinforced trial after 3 consecutive nonreward trials; CRF refers to continuously reinforced control group. (From Seybert, Mellgren, & Jobe, 1973.)

a just completed trial was a rewarded or a nonrewarded event. These memories can be symbolized as S^R and S^N respectively and can be considered to function as stimuli (stimuli internal to the subject). The second assumption that Capaldi makes, one common in the S–R interpretation of learning, is that the stimuli present when the performance of an instrumental response is reinforced become *associated* with that response so that when these stimuli occur again the instrumental response is likely to be made.

Given these basic assumptions, let us now consider what events might transpire on the second trial of four different two-trial sequences; NR, RR, RN, and NN. First, in the NR sequence, the animal performs the instrumental response on the second trial presumably remembering that it was nonrewarded on the previous trial. Another way to say this is that S^N is part of the stimulus complex present (along with external stimuli such as those arising from the apparatus, etc.) when the subject makes the instrumental response (R_I). This second trial is reinforced, so that S^N, along with other stimuli present, acquires a degree of association with R_I; when S^N occurs again, the subject is now more likely to perform the instrumental response. Thus, we can say that the following association is reinforced on a NR transition trial; $S^N \searrow R_I$.

Now consider the two-trial sequence RR. During the performance of the instrumental response on the second trial, the subject presumably remembers that the first trial was rewarded. In other words, S^R is part of the stimulus complex present during trial 2. Since this trial is rewarded in the RR sequence, S^R acquires some degree of association with R_I, so that when S^R occurs again, R_I is likely to be performed. Thus, the association that exists at the end of the RR sequence is $S^R \searrow R_I$.

Now in the two remaining sequences, RN, and NN, the second trial is not rewarded and therefore, in accordance with the assumption that we are working with in this discussion, no association is reinforced in these sequences. Thus, no associations should be formed between the memories S^N or S^R and the instrumental response on these two types of trial sequence.

In order to see how these differential associations might influence R to E, let us now consider the memory events that occur on extinction trials. Since all trials in extinction are nonrewarded, S^N must be the memory stimulus present on all trials after the first extinction trial. Therefore, subjects that have learned to make the instrumental response in the presence of S^N should persist longer in extinction than subjects that have not had the opportunity for this type of learning. These relationships are summarized in Table 5–2. Note that a group that received a 100 percent reward schedule would experience all RR transitions in acquisition, and thus, there would be no opportunity for S^N to be associated with the performance of R_I. Therefore, the memories of nonreward produced by consecutive extinction trials would not provide stimulus support for the performance of the instrumental response in a 100 percent reward group. Note also that in any partially rewarded group, the greater the number of NR transitions, the stronger the

Table 5-2. Assumed Memory Stimuli and Associations Operating in Acquisition and Extinction for Different Possible Two-Trial Acquisition Sequences

	ACQUISITION		EXTINCTION	
Two-Trial Sequence	Memory Stimulus Present on 2nd Trial	Reinforced Association	Memory Stimulus Present After 1st Extinction Trial	Association Functional
NR	S^N	$S^N \searrow R_I$	S^N	$S^N \searrow R_I$
RR	S^R	$S^R \searrow R_I$	S^N	None
RN	S^R	None	S^N	None
NN	S^N	None	S^N	None

association between S^N and R_I might be, and, therefore, the more stimulus support the nonrewarded extinction trials should provide for the performance of the instrumental response. These deductions, of course, conform to the experiments we have so far reviewed.

This analysis has been concerned with only a small part of the events that may actually take place. We have focused on the formation of associations between the stimulus aspects of memory and an instrumental response, and we have ignored other associations that may also form. For example, as we mentioned in the consideration of Amsel's theory, associations may form between apparatus stimuli and the instrumental response, and these associations should be present in all groups that are reinforced and thus be available to support performance in extinction in all groups. The associations formed between memories and the R_I would be something in addition to these associations between apparatus stimuli and the response.

Thus far, we have considered only two-trial sequences. The typical experiment is much more complicated in that a long series of trials is experienced and thus, three, four, or more trial sequences may become important. Before going on to a consideration of other possible sequential variables, however, let us remain a little longer with the two-trial sequence. Now that we have a theoretical mechanism to explain why the NR transition trial should be so effective in promoting increased resistance to extinction, let us go back again to the data and examine some additional results that demonstrate this experimentally.

Memory Interpretations of NR Transitions

INTERTRIAL REINFORCEMENTS

We have just seen that the presumed mechanism by which the NR transition trial exerts its influence in enhancing resistance to extinction is through the formation of an association between memories of nonreward and the response performed on rewarded trials. If this is true, then any treatment that interferes with the memory of nonreward prior to performance on the rewarded trial should diminish resistance to extinction.

One such treatment that has been attempted in a number of studies is the presentation of a reward to the subjects between N and R trials. In the usual procedure subjects are given instrumental training in a runway apparatus on a partial reward schedule. One group of these subjects is then given a reward in a situation different from the runway (usually just a plain box) between each NR transition. A control group is given an equal number of extra rewards but between other types of transition trials and never between NR trials. It is usually found that the group receiving the extra rewards between NR transitions shows less resistance to extinction than the control group (e.g., Capaldi, Hart, & Stanley, 1963; Capaldi & Spivey, 1964). The explanation for these effects is that the extra rewards between N and R trials have the effect of interfering with S^N or replacing S^N with S^R so that on the next trial S^N is not available to form an association with R_I, and thus the conditioning mechanism based on the memory of nonreward is not available to promote resistance to extinction. The results of the intertrial reinforcement experiments, then, support Capaldi's interpretation of the PREE.

INTERTRIAL INTERVAL

Another type of experiment relevant to the memory interpretation of NR transition effects is one involving the manipulation of the intertrial interval. Mackintosh (1970) has found that a partial reward schedule with long intertrial intervals (40–50 min.) produces *less* resistance to extinction than a partial reward schedule with short intertrial intervals (30 seconds). Mackintosh then went on to show that this effect of relatively long intertrial intervals is still obtained if the long intertrial interval is placed just between N and R trials, all other transitions having a short intertrial interval. This result implies that the effect of long intertrial intervals on reducing resistance to extinction is due just to the influence it is having on NR transition trials. What is this influence? One reasonable interpretation is that the long intertrial interval is interfering with the memory of nonreward that occurred on the N trial, and thus the association formed between S^N and R_1 is not as strong after a long intertrial interval as after a short intertrial interval. Again, the results of this experiment support a memory interpretation of the effects of NR transition trials. It should be noted here that the 40–50 minute intertrial interval used in the Mackintosh experiment, although reducing the PREE, does not eliminate it. In fact, effects of partial reward can be found quite readily with a 24-hour intertrial interval (Weinstock, 1954; Capaldi & Spivey, 1964).

SMALL TRIALS PREE

Another experimental situation that indicates the importance of the NR transition and supports Capaldi's interpretation of the PREE is the so-called "small-trials PREE." This research, pioneered by Garvin McCain, has demonstrated that a PREE may be obtained after a few acquisition trials, as few as four and perhaps just two acquisition trials, only one of which is rewarded (McCain, 1965, 1966, 1969). In the most extreme case, one group of rats is given the acquisition sequence NR (50 percent reward!) and a control group is given two rewarded trials. It has been found that the NR group is more resistant to extinction. These results are interesting in several ways. First of all they are interesting because one of the assumptions of frustration theory has been that some number of trials is necessary for an expectation of reward (r_g–s_g) to develop before nonreward can be frustrating. But with the small trials PREE there would seem to be little time for such an expectancy to be learned. Secondly, nonrewarded trials are assumed to be frustrating only when a reward is expected. But if the subjects never receive a reward before the nonreward (as in the extreme two-trial NR studies), then there can be no expectancy of a reward. Yet, the single nonreward has an effect of enhancing R to E. These effects of initial nonrewards (nonrewards preceding any rewarded trials) have also been demonstrated in experiments other than small-trial PREE studies (e.g., Spear, Hill, & O'Sullivan, 1965; Spear & Spitzner, 1967). Thus, there must be some explanation other than frustration for the results of these experiments, and Capaldi's sequential hypothesis clearly fits the data (Capaldi, 1971).

PATTERNING

One final example supporting Capaldi's thinking concerning the importance of the NR transition will be presented. In the standard partial reward study, where R and N trials are irregularly presented across a number of acquisition trials, there is no cue that the subject can use to predict the occurrence of reward and nonreward. Even if the trials are presented in some regular sequence such as RNRNRN etc., there is still no cue in the environment that the subject can use to predict reward. However, if the subjects can remember the reward outcome on a previous trial, then this outcome could perhaps be used as a discriminative stimulus for predicting when reward would occur. In other words, if the subject can remember outcomes of previous trials, then it might be able to discriminate the regular sequence of R and N trials. Such discrimination does indeed occur, and it is evidenced in behavior by faster running on R trials than on N trials (*see* Figure 5–5).

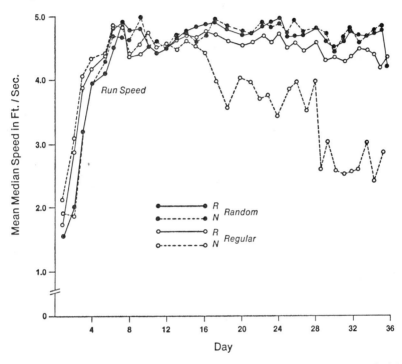

Figure 5–5. Mean median speeds on rewarded (R) and nonrewarded (N) trials. In the regular group the six trials per day were in the regular sequence RNRNRN. In the random group the sequence was randomized from day to day. (From Flaherty & Davenport, 1972.)

An explanation of patterning in terms of Capaldi's theoretical constructs takes the following form: Consider the sequence RNRNRN. As can be seen in Table 5–3, the memory stimulus operating on any given trial lags behind the actual reward contingencies by one trial. Thus, on trial 2, a nonrewarded trial, the memory stimulus in effect is S^R, and on trial 3, a rewarded trial, the memory operating is S^N, etc. In accordance with our previous assumptions, associations are reinforced on rewarded trials, and therefore, an association between S^N and R_I is acquired on trials 3 and 5. Now, note that this association means that whenever an animal remembers nonreward, it should run fast (because of the association between the memory and the instrumental response). On the other hand, there is no association formed between the memory of reward and R_I and, therefore, running should not be as fast whenever reward is remembered. This is, of course, the state of affairs on nonreward trials. Thus, making no assumptions beyond

Table 5–3. *Explanation of Patterning Behavior by Conditioning of the Memory of Nonreward (S^N)* *

Trial	1	2	3	4	5	6
Reward Event	R	N	R	N	R	N
Memory Stimulus in Effect	= =	S^R	S^N	S^R	S^N	S^R
Association Reinforced	= =	= =	$S^N \searrow R_I$	= =	$S^N \searrow R_I$	= =

*S^N is assumed to become associated with the instrumental response (R_I) when a trial terminates in reward.

what we made in the earlier treatment of NR transitions, we can see that Capaldi's interpretation of partial reward effects can explain patterning, including the seemingly paradoxical condition that the memory of reward should lead to slow running and the memory of nonreward should lead to fast running.

The reader may ask at this point why the rats run at all on N trials if they can discriminate the sequence. There are several possible answers to this question. First of all, we again must bear in mind that in our discussion of Capaldi's theory we are narrowing our focus and considering the role played by memory stimuli. At the same time that a subject is learning about the relationship between memory stimuli and rewards, other kinds of learning may be taking place. For example, in the runway apparatus it is reasonable to conceive of apparatus cues as acquiring some associative relationship with the instrumental response or with the expectation of food (as Amsel does assume). Thus, any learning of this type that does take place will support running on all trials because it is nondiscriminatory, the subject cannot use associations with apparatus stimuli to predict on which trials a reward will occur. In addition to the apparatus stimuli obvious to an experimenter there may be other cues such as odors in the environment that also acquire some degree of associative relations to the instrumental response or with the anticipation of reward.

Another possibility is simply that the discrimination formed between memories of reward and nonreward is imperfect, and thus, a complete separation of running speeds is not obtained. Given the number of trials it takes for patterning to develop in the rat (*see* Figure 5–5), it is reasonable to assume that it involves a difficult discrimination. There are still other possibilities that are not feasible to discuss in this text.

In sum, we can see that the consideration of what may happen on an apparently simple two-trial NR sequence leads to the potential integration of data from a number of different experimental paradigms. As complicated as it seems to get, the NR sequence is only one of several sequential variables that Capaldi has identified as being related to the PREE. We do not have space to consider these other sequential variables in any detail, but interested readers might want to consult Capaldi (1966), Campbell, Knouse, and Wroten (1970), and Seybert et al., (1973).

Summary of Frustration and Sequential Theory

Subjects given partial reward in acquisition are more persistent in extinction than subjects rewarded on every trial. We have so far considered just two of many explanations for this basic fact and have found that these explanations can become quite complicated and that both the frustration and the sequential interpretations of these data have some support. The sequential interpretation has emphasized the importance of the actual sequence of R and N trials that subjects receive and related experiments have demonstrated quite convincingly that trial sequence is a very potent variable in determining resistance to extinction. The aspect of Capaldi's explanation for these effects that we have considered revolves around the concept of memory; memory serving as an internal stimulus that may be associated with an instrumental response. The association of the memory of nonreward with the particular instrumental response serves to enhance R to E because all trials in extinction are N trials and, therefore, S^N should be the only memory stimulus operating in extinction.

Amsel's frustration theory has also emphasized stimuli generated by processes internal to the organism becoming associated with the performance of a particular instrumental response, and this association is then the basis of the prolonged R to E that occurs following partial reward. However, for Amsel the stimulus is not simply a memory of the rewarding event on the previous trial (although this memory may be present); instead, the stimulus is part of a frustration response generated when reward is expected but not received. Evidence in support of this theory has been mainly of the type demonstrating that frustration is a viable theoretical construct that can serve to organize a substantial amount of data.

These two currently prominent theories of the PREE are certainly not mutually exclusive. It is quite possible that both the conditioning of memories based on trial sequence and the conditioning of an emotional response based on unfulfilled expectations are somehow involved in the PREE. As yet there is little in the way of experimental evidence indicating the potential fruitfulness of combining these two approaches, although Capaldi has indicated that he recognizes that emotion-related stimuli may be involved in some types of persistent behavior (Capaldi, 1972).

Other Theories of Partial Reward

We have spent a great deal of time on the theories of Amsel and Capaldi because they seem to be generating the most research at the present time. However, there are many other theoretical accounts of the PREE, and we cannot leave the discrete-trial literature without some mention of a few of these. Two theories that have historical precedence in the area are the *Discrimination Theory* and the *Generalization Decrement Theory*. These two theories are quite similar, as we shall see, differing primarily in the degree of active role they attribute to the subject demonstrating the PREE.

The discrimination theory was offered by Humphreys (1939) to explain the PREE obtained following the extinction of a partially reinforced eyelid response (*see* Chapter 3). Humphreys reasoned that subjects who have had a history of 100 percent reinforcement will find it easier to discriminate the onset of extinction than subjects who have had a history of partial reinforcement. That is, the subjects in a 100 percent group detect sooner that they are no longer receiving reward and, therefore, the learned response ceases to be performed. The discrimination theory was put forth initially by Humphreys after research with human subjects, and the theory often seems to imply an active and perhaps conscious role of the subject in discriminating the extinction contingency.

However, the discrimination theory has been applied to animal data also (e.g., Tyler et al., 1953), and therefore an interpretation of the theory in terms of conscious processes need not be assumed. Briefly, the main bit of evidence against this theory is that subjects that are trained initially on a 50 percent reward schedule, then shifted to a 100 percent reward schedule for some number of trials, and then extinguished, still show a PREE (Theios, 1962; Shanab, Melrose, & Young, 1975). It is true that the extent of the PREE is often reduced in these groups, but the fact that a PREE is obtained, is usually taken as evidence that the discrimination theory cannot be the entire story of why a PREE occurs.

The generalization decrement theory is essentially a more passive version of the discrimination theory. As we saw when we discussed generalization in Chapter 2, there is a decrement in performance whenever the stimulus conditions are changed from those prevailing when the response was acquired. This decrement in performance is termed a generalization decrement. The generalization decrement interpretation of the PREE simply assumes that the prolonged resistance to extinction that occurs in partially rewarded groups is due to the fact that the shift from acquisition to extinction represents less of a change in the reward stimulus conditions for these rats than for rats that have been reinforced on every trial in acquisition. In other words, there is less generalization decrement following a shift from partial reinforcement to extinction than there is following a shift from continuous reinforcement to extinction.

The generalization decrement theory is difficult to test experimentally and seems to be partly true by definition (the definition of generalization decrement). However, we will describe the results of one experiment conducted to test the basic idea of generalization decrement. In this experiment (Hulicka, Capehart, & Viney, 1960) rats were trained in an apparatus with a compound stimulus composed of five separate elements correlated with the presence of reinforcement. In extinction it was found that the fewer the number of the separate elements present, the faster extinction was. Thus, this experiment provides evidence that extinction proceeds faster the greater the change in stimulus conditions from acquisition to extinction.

In summary, generalization decrement and/or discrimination may play some role in the occurrence of a PREE, but it is unlikely that they can account completely for the increased persistence in extinction. We can say this because neither version of the theory has much to say about many of the variables that we discussed in connection with frustration and sequential theory. For example, would the generalization decrement interpretation predict that a group given the repeated sequence NNRR would be more resistant to extinction than the group given the repeated sequence RRNN? Seemingly not, since there is equal stimulus change for both groups. The discrimination theory might even predict the opposite of sequential theory since there is a more abrupt transition from acquisition to extinction for the NNRR group. However, we have already seen that the sequential theory can make some fairly precise predictions such as the one just mentioned.

On the other hand, the basic idea of generalization decrement can easily be incorporated into both frustration and sequential theory. In frustration terms, a group that experienced partial reward in acquisition experiences less change than a 100 percent reward group when shifted to extinction because frustration is assumed to be elicited by nonrewards in both acquisition and extinction. In sequential terms, a group that experienced partial reinforcement in acquisition experiences less change than a 100 percent reinforcement group when shifted to extinction because the memory of nonreward (S^N) is common to both acquisition and extinction for partially reinforced groups.

This concludes our discussion of the discrete-trials literature on partial reinforcement. It is obvious that the basic phenomenon of increased resistance to extinction following partial reinforcement has produced a very large amount of research and theoretical activity in an attempt to arrive at an adequate explanation for this effect. It is equally obvious that there are many variables that influence the conditions under which a PREE will occur and/or which influence the extent of the PREE. As yet, no theoretical account of the PREE has been able to comprehensively handle all of the variables and results obtained in experimentation. The area remains a particularly interesting one for research and theoretical speculation. This is particularly so because intermittent reward is so characteristic of real life situations for both humans and other animals.

II. FREE-OPERANT EXPERIMENTS

The effect of intermittent reinforcement on well practiced behavior has been investigated almost exclusively with the free-operant research paradigm. As you will recall from Chapter 4, in free-operant research, subjects (usually rats or pigeons) are placed in an operant chamber for long time periods (an hour is typical), and during this time the response-object (a lever for rats or a lighted disc for pigeons) is continually available. Thus, the subject is free to make the instrumental response at any time (hence the term *free-operant*), a characteristic of many real life situations.

Free-operant experiments typically examine the effects of reinforcement schedules over numerous test sessions and many hours of experience (in contrast to the discrete-trials experiments in which even a relatively long experiment involving 60 or so acquisition

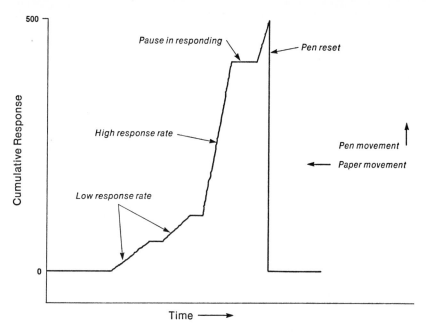

Figure 5–6.   Operant behavior is often studied with the help of cumulative response records. Above is an illustration of how differences in rate of responding appear on a cumulative record. This illustration was obtained with paper moving from right to left and each response served to deflect a pen slightly from the bottom towards the top of the page. The faster the rate of responding the steeper the slope of the cumulative record. Pauses in responding produce horizontal lines due to continued paper movement. At the top of the recording paper the pen resets to the bottom, ready to continue recording. Later in this chapter we shall see how different schedules of reinforcement produce characteristic response topographies, as measured by a cumulative record.

trials may take only a half-hour of actual subject time). Such long testing sessions measure steady-state behavior rather than acquisition and are made possible through the use of automated equipment that minimizes the time demand on the experimenter and tends to maximize control over variables in the environment that are extraneous to the experiment. Another difference between the discrete-trial studies and the free-operant paradigm is in the dependent variables typically employed. Whereas such time measures as latency or speed are typically used to measure runway performance, rate of responding is the dependent variable of choice in free-operant experiments. Response rate illustrated in Figure 5–6 is recorded on a cumulative recorder and provides a continuous record of behavior over long test sessions.

Simple Reinforcement Schedules

Fixed Ratio

The first of four simple schedules of intermittent reinforcement that we shall describe is the fixed ratio schedule (FR). On this schedule the ratio of responses to reinforcements is fixed and regular so that, for example, every fifth response that the subject makes produces reinforcement. This schedule is analogous to piecework pay rates in industry where, for example, an employee may be paid a certain amount or given a certain bonus for every fifth electronic device assembled. Fixed-ratio schedules of reinforcement produce a high rate of responding with, if the ratio is long enough, a pause in the rate after the delivery of the reinforcement.

The development of characteristic fixed-ratio behavior in a rat across successively more stringent ratios is shown in Figure 5–7. In this experiment by Collier, Hirsch, and Hamlin (1972) all of the rat's food was obtained in the experimental apparatus. By using this technique of making all food contingent upon the completion of a ratio response, Collier and his students have found that rats and guinea pigs will reduce their food intake to one meal per day and

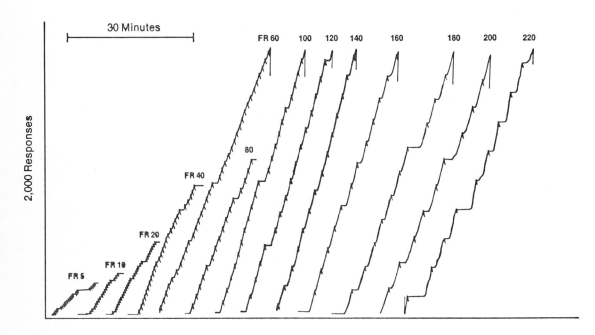

Figure 5–7. Samples of cumulative FR records taken at each ratio for a single rat. (From Collier, Hirsch, & Hamlin, 1972.)

respond on a fixed-ratio up to 5,120 in order to obtain that meal (Hirsch & Collier, 1974). Cats (Kanarek, 1974) respond on an FR schedule as high as 10,240 for one meal per day. Even at these extreme ratios the characteristics of fixed-ratio behavior are maintained: There is a post-reinforcement pause that lasts many hours followed by sustained responding at a high rate until reinforcement is obtained.[1] The high rate of responding obtained in fixed-ratio schedules seems reasonable since there is a direct contingency between the subjects' rate of responding and the delivery of reinforcement; the faster the subject responds, the sooner reinforcement is obtained.

Variable Ratio

In a variable-ratio (VR) schedule there is also a relationship between the number of responses the subject makes and the delivery of reinforcement, but the relationship is varied rather than fixed. For example, the first reinforcement may be delivered after 10 responses, the next after 20 responses, the third after 15 responses, etc. The VR schedule is characterized by the average number of responses it takes to produce a reinforcement. For example, if the three ratio values given just above were the only ones used, and they were presented in an irregular order, then the schedule could be characterized as a VR–15 since, on the average, it would take 15 responses to produce a reinforcement. A more complete description of a VR schedule would include a specification of the actual ratios reinforced and their sequence of presentation.

The behavior associated with VR schedules is similar to the behavior produced by FR schedules in that there is generally a high rate of sustained responding interrupted by occasional pauses. However, on VR schedules these pauses are less frequent and are not correlated with the delivery of a reinforcement. An example of performance on a VR schedule is presented in Figure 5–8.

Fixed Interval

In a fixed-interval (FI) schedule the delivery of a reinforcement depends upon both the passage of a time interval and the occurrence of a response. For example, in a fixed-interval one-minute schedule (FI–1′) the first response after the passage of one minute produces a reinforcement. Note that in FI schedules the subject may ideally

---

1. It should be noted that in Collier's experiments the reinforcement involves free access to a food supply (i.e., a meal) rather than a single pellet. These high ratios cannot be obtained with small rewards.

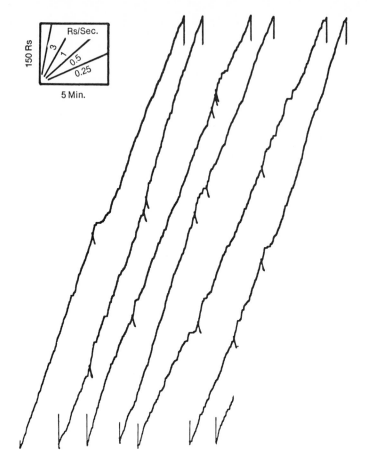

Figure 5–8. Performance of a pigeon on a VR-360 schedule. (From Ferster & Skinner, 1957, by permission of Prentice-Hall.)

obtain reinforcement by making only one response each interval; responses that occur before the interval has passed have no bearing on the availability of reinforcement. Although the behavior produced by FI schedules does not match this theoretical ideal, it is influenced in a systematic fashion by the passage of the time period. Generally, there is a pause after the delivery of the reinforcement and then a gradual increase in the rate of responding as the availability of a reinforcement draws near. This behavior produces a pattern termed a *scallop* on a cumulative record (*see* Figure 5–9). In comparison with FR schedules, FI schedules produce lower overall rates of responding and the transition from the pause after reinforcement to responding tends to be less abrupt on FI than on FR schedules.

The rate of responding on FI schedules is related to the length of the interval—the longer the interval the lower the overall rate of responding. This lower overall rate of responding is, in turn, quite likely related to the length of the pause after reinforcement which appears to increase directly with the length of the fixed interval (Wilson, 1954; Sherman, 1959).

In speculating about the processes controlling the typical FI

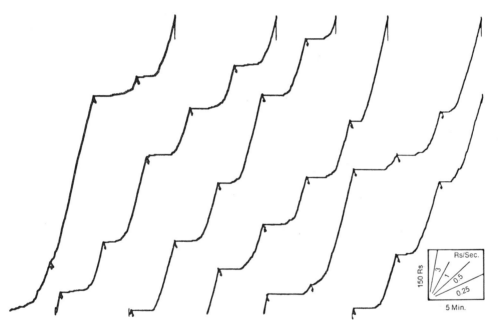

Figure 5–9.   Performance of a pigeon after 66 hours on a FI-4′ schedule. Note the scallops. (From Ferster & Skinner, 1957, by permission of Prentice-Hall.)

behavior it seems quite likely that the subjects form a temporal discrimination with the delivery of reinforcement serving as a cue that another reinforcement will not be forthcoming for some period of time (cf., Trapold, Carlson, & Myers, 1965).

Before leaving the FI schedule, we should note that a scalloping pattern of behavior occurs in many situations in which there is a fixed deadline for some important event such as an examination, or the completion of a paper or a book.

Variable Interval

A variable interval (VI) schedule is similar to a FI schedule except that the length of time between the availability of successive reinforcements is varied rather than fixed. For example, the first reinforcement may be produced by the first response following a one-minute interval, the second reinforcement by the first response following a three-minute interval, the third by the first response following a two-minute interval, etc. Such a schedule with different time intervals occurring in a random order may be designated by the length of the average interval. In the example given just above, if only one-, two- and three-minute intervals were used, and if they were presented in a random order and used equally often, then the schedule could be designated as VI–2′. Thus a VI schedule compares to a FI schedule in the same way that a VR schedule compares to a FR schedule. In the VI, as in the VR schedule, the irregular changes in the availability and/or delivery of reinforcement deprive the subject of any cue that it can reliably use to predict the occurrence of the next reinforcement. And, in the VI as in the VR schedule, the subjects' behavior is less regular; there is no consistent pattern, like scalloping, associated with VI schedules. Instead, the typical steady-state behavior produced by VI schedules is characterized by generally consistent rates of responding as demonstrated in Figure 5–10.

These four basic schedules of intermittent reinforcement include conditions in which the delivery of reinforcement is either directly related to the number of responses (ratio schedules) or depends on

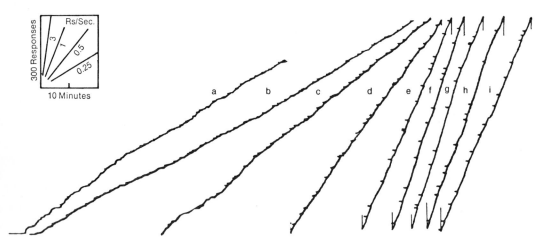

Figure 5–10.   Development of steady-rate responding on a VI-1′ schedule. (From Ferster & Skinner, 1957, by permission of Prentice-Hall.)

the passage of time as well as on a response (interval schedules) and either of these schedules may be regular (fixed) or irregular (varied). In general, ratio schedules produce higher rates of responding than interval schedules and fixed schedules produce more stereotyped and regular behavior patterns than varied schedules. The exact relationship between schedules depends on the parameters of the schedules.

We have only presented the briefest consideration of these simple reinforcement schedules. A more detailed treatment may be found in many sources ranging from the seminal work of Skinner (1938) to a catalogue of schedule effects in pigeons (Ferster & Skinner, 1957) to more recent theoretical analyses (Schoenfeld, 1970; Nevin, 1973). However, even in this brief treatment it should be obvious that these simple schedules have, in general, regular and predictable effects on the behavior of organisms and, therefore, they may be used as important tools in the experimental analysis of behavior. We shall now describe three more schedules of particular interest.

Other Schedules

Differential Reinforcement for Rate

In ratio schedules there is a contingency between rate of responding and reinforcement—the higher the rate, the sooner the subject receives the reinforcement. In interval schedules there is less of a contingency between response rate and the delivery of a reinforcement but, nevertheless, there is some contingency between rate and reinforcement in the sense that subjects responding at a higher rate are more likely to be responding at the end of the criterion interval and are thus more likely to receive reinforcement sooner.

It is possible to directly reinforce rate of responding and to set up contingencies reinforcing either specific high rates or low rates of responding. The key to setting up these contingencies is the concept of *interresponse time (IRT)*, the time between successive responses. In a differential reinforcement for high rates of responding (DRH schedule) the subject will obtain a reinforcement only if it emits a specified number of responses *prior* to the completion of a time interval. For example, the subject may be required to emit 10 responses in a five-second period in order to obtain reinforcement. Each time that this requirement is met a reinforcement is delivered.

Of more interest is the schedule which differentially reinforces low rates of responding (DRL schedule). On this schedule the subject must refrain from responding for a specified period of time. The first response after this time period has elapsed produces a reinforcement; responses prior to the completion of the time period reset the clock so that the time period starts all over again. For example, on a DRL 10-second schedule the subject must allow an IRT of 10 seconds to elapse in order to obtain reinforcement. Performance on a DRL schedule may be assessed by determining the percentage of possible reinforcements that the subject obtains and/or by examining the distribution of IRTs. A typical distribution of IRTs obtained on a DRL 20-second schedule is shown in Figure 5–11. It is apparent that well practiced subjects make most of their responses after the criterion interval has timed out and thus obtain reinforcement. Errors tend to be concentrated in the time intervals just before the criterion interval is timed out and just after the delivery of a reinforcement.

The DRL schedule is particularly interesting in that it may be used as a technique for investigating an organism's time estimation skills and/or an organism's ability to inhibit responding for a specified time. Some variables that have facilitatory effects on other schedules interfere with performance on DRL schedules. For example, larger amounts of reward generally facilitate responding where there is a direct relationship between responding and the

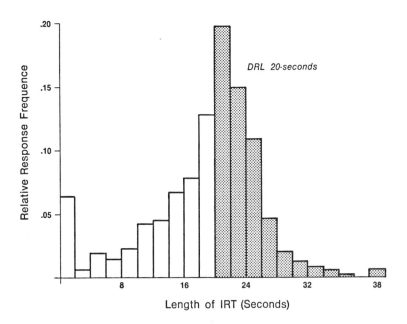

Figure 5–11. Distribution of interresponse times (IRT) on a DRL 20-second schedule. Responses in 2-second class intervals are plotted as a ratio of total responses. The shaded area indicates reinforced IRTs. (Based on Mallot & Cumming, 1964; *see* Nevin, 1973.)

receipt of the reward; e.g., running speeds in a runway are generally faster the greater the reward, and in simple operant schedules, where there is a direct relationship between rate and the receipt of reinforcement, there is also a general facilitating effect in the amount of reward (e.g., Keesey & Kling, 1961; Meltzer & Brahlek, 1968). However, in DRL schedules large rewards interfere with DRL performance (Beer & Trumble, 1965). It is as if the subjects have a more difficult time inhibiting responses with large rewards. Incidentally, this type of result might favor a cognitive or anticipatory response theory of instrumental learning over a simple Thorndikian S–R reinforcement interpretation. It seems that the subjects are somehow anticipating the large reward and responding too soon.

Concurrent Schedules

The final schedule that we shall consider in this chapter concerns the condition where there are actually two different schedules of reward in effect concurrently. In a concurrent schedule the subject has a choice of making either of two separate responses, each of which has its own schedule of reinforcement associated with it. For example, pigeons may be exposed to two response keys, one illuminated by red light and one illuminated by green light. Responding on the red key may be reinforced on a VI–2 minute schedule, and responding on the green key may be reinforced on a VI–4 minute schedule. These schedules are independent of one another, and the subject may respond on either one at any time. Under conditions such as these it has been found that subjects will divide their responses (and time) between the two schedules in direct proportion to the frequency of reinforcement they receive from the two schedules. For example, if subjects are reinforced on a concurrent VI–1, VI–1, then 50 percent of total reinforcements are available from each alternative, and under these conditions subjects make about 50 percent of their responses to each alternative. If the schedules are VI–1, VI–2, then two-thirds of the reinforcements are available in the first alternative, and subjects tend to make about two-thirds of their responses to that alternative. This relationship may be put in terms of a simple equation—

$$\frac{B1}{B1 + B2} = \frac{R1}{R1 + R2}$$

—which states that the proportion of behavior (*B*) emitted to one of two alternatives will equal the proportion of reinforcement (*R*) available from that alternative (*see* Herrnstein, 1970; Baum, 1974).

A graphic example of this direct proportionality that holds between response rate and reinforcement frequency is shown in Figure 5–12. In these data, obtained by Herrnstein over a wide range of interval values in concurrent VI schedules, it is apparent that the proportion of responses made on one component of the concurrent schedule equaled the proportion of reinforcements obtained on that component. Similar results have been obtained with rats and humans as subjects (Shull & Pliskoff, 1967; Schroeder & Holland, 1969; Baum, 1975), as well as with pigeons in a situation in which all of their daily food was acquired (Baum, 1972). This latter experiment is interesting in that, like the experiments mentioned earlier by Collier et al., the animals lived in the experimental apparatus and were never deprived of food by the experimenter. Thus, this type of experiment more closely approximates the natural living

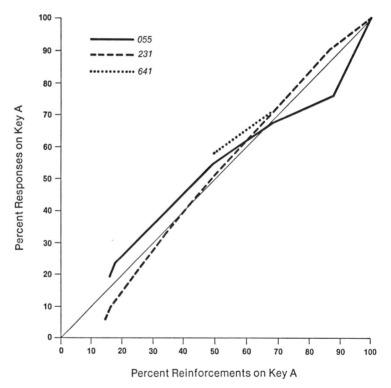

Figure 5–12.   The relative frequency of responding to one alternative in a two-choice procedure for three pigeons as a function of the relative frequency of reinforcement thereon. Variable interval schedules governed reinforcements for both alternatives. The diagonal line shows matching between the relative frequencies. (From Herrnstein, 1961, © Soc. Exp. Anal. Behavior.)

conditions of the animals in the sense that responding is based on normal feeding patterns rather than deprivation imposed by the experimenter. An even closer approximation was obtained in a later study by Baum (1974) in which he found that the matching function was obtained from a flock of free-ranging wild pigeons. The fact that regular effects of reinforcement schedules are still obtained under these conditions is encouraging for the general applicability of other laboratory investigations of reinforcement schedules.

The matching results obtained with concurrent schedules are quite interesting in that they are another example of the relativity of reinforcement. Recall that in our discussion of contrast effects in Chapter 4 we indicated that the occurrence of contrast showed that the rewarding value of a given unit of food or concentration of sucrose was relative in that it could be changed if the subject had an opportunity to compare that unit or concentration with another reward. The matching function obtained with concurrent schedules also indicates relativity in that a subject's response rate to a constant schedule of reinforcement (e.g., a VI–1) will change as a function of changes in the reinforcements available in *other*, comparison, schedules. Or, to put it another way, the matching function indicates that the reinforcing properties of a particular schedule depend on what other schedules the subject is concurrently experiencing.

We shall return to contrast effects in Chapter 10 when we discuss stimulus control, and, in that context, we shall have another occasion to mention the matching law. Before closing the topic now, we should mention that the concept of a concurrent schedule seems to have some face validity for direct application to aspects of human behavior. Much of human behavior could be thought of as involving complex concurrent schedules; we often have a choice of engaging in any one of several enterprises at one time. For example, we may read, or watch TV, or play tennis, or eat, etc. An understanding of how we come to distribute our time among such possibilities may possibly be derived from research on simpler concurrent schedules of reinforcement.

III. SUMMARY

In this chapter we have reviewed some of the research concerned with the effects of intermittent rewards on animal behavior. The material was organized into two major sections; first, those studies concerned with an analysis of how intermittent rewards produce increased resistance to extinction, and, second, those studies concerned with how a long history of intermittent rewards influenced steady-state behavior.

The first series of experiments were primarily discrete-trial studies conducted in runways and involving relatively brief samples of the animal's behavior. In this section we concentrated primarily on two current theories of partial reinforcement; the Amsel Frustration Theory and Capaldi's Sequential Theory. According to the frustration interpretation, the experience of nonreward after an expectancy of reward has been acquired elicits an emotional response of frustration. If this frustration is first experienced in extinction (following a 100 percent reward schedule in acquisition) it should accelerate extinction. The larger the reward expected, the greater frustration there should be, and the faster extinction should be.

However, if the frustration is experienced in acquisition in a context where rewards are also received (acquisition on a partial reinforcement schedule), then the frustration stimuli become associated with the performance of the instrumental response. Now, when the nonrewards of extinction elicit frustration, a group with a history of partial reinforcement is more persistent because it has learned to persist (make the instrumental response) in the face of frustration (frustration-related stimuli occasion the performance of the instrumental response). We reviewed evidence concerning some predictions the frustration theory makes concerning (a) the relationship between amount of reward, percentage reward, and resistance to extinction, (b) the existence of a Frustration Effect (FE), and (c) the aversiveness of stimuli associated with nonreward.

Capaldi's Sequential Theory is of more recent origin than frustration theory, and it emphasizes the importance of the actual sequence of rewards and nonrewards that the animal experiences. In particular, this theory emphasizes the importance of an association formed between the memory of a nonreward and the performance of an instrumental response. This association is formed on NR sequences and is at the basis of the partial reinforcement extinction effect. Sequential theory has shed light on the importance of variables not predicted by a frustration theory. The evidence reviewed indicated the importance of trial sequence effects, the existence of a "small-trials PREE," the possible role played by initial nonrewarded trials, and other predictions derived from sequential theory.

Those studies concerned with the steady-state effects of intermittent reinforcement have demonstrated a relationship between prolonged exposure to a particular schedule of reinforcement and the development of characteristic and predictable patterns of responding. Characteristics associated with six schedules (fixed interval, variable interval, fixed ratio, variable ratio, differential reinforcement for low rate, and concurrent schedules) were examined. The characteristic behaviors associated with these schedules probably reflect the operation of a variety of psychological processes, and the schedule-associated behaviors will be useful in the elucidation of these processes.

Although the data reviewed in this chapter have been derived from a limited number of species (rats and pigeons primarily), the basic phenomena discussed (the PREE, and behaviors associated with schedules) occur across virtually the entire phylogenetic spectrum from fish to man and are very robust phenomena.

Speak, tell us to the end. For sufferers it is sweet to know beforehand clearly the pain that still remains for them.

Aeschylus, *Prometheus Bound*

In the previous chapters we have described some of the variables that influence instrumental learning when the behavior is directed toward approaching some reward. In this chapter we shall examine instrumental behavior in situations in which the environmental object or event is aversive to the organism, something that the organism would withdraw from, given the opportunity.

There are four major patterns of aversively controlled behavior that are studied in the laboratory:

1. *Escape learning* involves the learning of a response that either removes the organism from the vicinity of a noxious stimulus, or terminates the noxious stimulus.
2. *Avoidance learning* involves the learning of a response that prevents the occurrence of an aversive stimulus.
3. *Punishment* involves the presentation of an aversive stimulus contingent upon the occurrence of a particular response.
4. *Conditioned emotional responses* involve those situations in which the organism has no control over the aversive stimulus, but may be able to predict its occurrence.

We shall now consider these procedures in more detail.

I. ESCAPE BEHAVIOR

The study of escape behavior is relatively straightforward. Laboratory investigations typically take the form of placing a rat in a runway apparatus in which the start and middle sections have an electrified floor. The most distant or goal area of the runway is not electrified. If and when the rat runs to this goal section, it escapes the electric shock. Learning in this situation is relatively rapid, requiring only a few trials, and is directly related to the degree of shock reduction accomplished by the escape response (Bower, Fowler, & Trapold, 1959). Other aspects of escape behavior are quite similar to approach behavior in that they are influenced in similar ways by similar variables. For example, escape behavior that terminates shock on only some of the trials (partial reinforcement) is more resistant to extinction than escape behavior that terminates shock on all of the trials (Bower, 1960). Similarly, delaying reinforcement (shock termination) produces decrements in escape behavior, and shifting amount of reinforcement (degree of shock reduction) sometimes leads to contrast effects (Nation, Wrather, & Mellgren, 1975).

The consideration of the effects of amount of reinforcement in escape behavior leads to a distinction that must be made between appetitive and aversive paradigms with regard to the definition of amount of reinforcement. In an appetitive design the subject is typically deprived of a needed substance, and then that substance (e.g., food or water) is used as the reinforcement. In these experiments the degree of deprivation and the amount of the substance used as the reinforcement may be varied independently. However, in experiments using an aversive stimulus as the reinforcement there is no deprivation involved. Instead, the aversive stimulus itself plays a dual role: The onset of this stimulus provides the motivation to engage in behavior, thereby serving a function analogous to deprivation in appetitive experiments, and the termination of this same stimulus then serves as the reinforcement for the response that led to

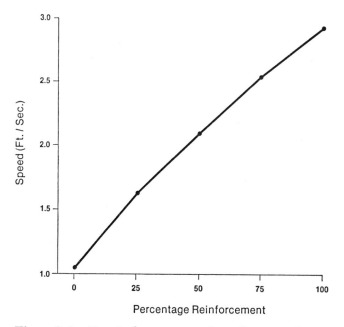

Figure 6–1. Terminal escape speed as a function of percentage of reinforcement. A 20-second delay of shock termination constituted a nonreinforced trial. (From Bower, 1960.)

the termination. Given these conditions, a somewhat different procedure must be used to manipulate amount of aversive reinforcement. This procedure is exemplified in a study by Bower, Fowler, and Trapold (1959).

In the Bower et al. experiment the intensity of the shock in the start box and run section of a straight runway was a constant 250 volts. The shock in the goal section was different for different groups of rats: 50 volts for one group, 150 volts for a second group, and 200 volts for a third. Note that the escape response in none of these groups actually terminated shock, but it did reduce the shock intensity, and the amount of reduction varied with different groups. In the first group the amount of shock reduction (and hence, the amount of reinforcement) was 200 volts; in the second group it was 100 volts; and the third group accomplished a 50-volt reduction in shock by performing the escape response. The performance of the groups in terms of escape speed was directly related to the amount of reinforcement. Thus, amount of reinforcement with initial shock level held constant (analogous to holding degree of deprivation constant) affects escape behavior in a manner similar to the way it affects behavior in a situation using positive reinforcement.

Looking at the other side of this relationship, varying the intensity of the initiating aversive stimulus with amount of reinforcement held constant also influences escape behavior. Within limits, the greater the intensity of the initiating stimulus, the better the escape behavior (e.g., Azrin, Hake, Holz, & Hutchinson, 1965).

One variable that affects escape behavior differently than approach behavior is partial reinforcement. As noted in the last chapter, partial reinforcement does not degrade performance in an instrumental approach task. However, partial reinforcement leads to less rapid escape behavior than does 100 percent reinforcement (Figure 6–1). In this experiment, nonreinforcement was defined as a 20-second delay in the termination of shock once the goal area was reached. These detrimental effects of infrequent reinforcement on escape behavior are not restricted to the runway apparatus or the rat. For example, it has been found that pigeons will cease responding on fixed-ratio escape schedules at ratios lower than those that will maintain responding for positive reinforcers (Hineline & Rachlin, 1969).

II. AVOIDANCE BEHAVIOR

The topic of escape learning merges naturally into the topic of avoidance learning. It would seem to be biologically advantageous for any organism not only to be able to escape from an aversive, and perhaps dangerous, situation but also to be able to avoid potentially hazardous situations. The laboratory study of avoidance behavior has been extensive, and has generated considerable theoretical interest. A typical investigation involves a two-compartment apparatus, called a shuttle box. The subject may be placed in one side of this apparatus, and after a specific time, electric foot-shock is presented through the grid floor. If the subject crosses over to the other side, it escapes the shock and terminates the trial. The subject is returned to the original side of the apparatus on each trial and eventually may cross over to the opposite compartment *before* the shock is presented. Typically the two sides are distinctly different in terms of brightness and/or in terms of the location of a stimulus signaling impending shock. This experimental paradigm is termed a one-way active avoidance design; "one-way" because the subject must *move* in just one direction, and "active avoidance" because the subject must *make* some specified response in order to avoid the shock.

A simple variation on this basic procedure might require the subject to *remain* in the side in which it is placed in order to avoid shock. That is, the subject will get a shock only if it crosses from the side in which it was placed to the other side. In order to avoid shock, the subject must remain in the first side. This paradigm is termed *passive avoidance* since the animal is required to abstain from responding. These two basic laboratory procedures, active and passive avoidance, roughly parallel the two major ways of avoiding aversive consequences in the natural environment, that is, by fleeing or freezing.

There are literally hundreds of studies that have varied the parameters and procedures of avoidance training. Rather than attempting to summarize these results, we will approach the data through a consideration of theories of avoidance learning.

Theories of Avoidance Behavior

The Fear Hypothesis

Avoidance learning presented an interesting problem to advocates of an S–R reinforcement approach to animal learning. The problem had two aspects. First, avoidance behavior implied that animals are somehow "seeing into the future," anticipating an impending event and doing something to prevent its occurrence. Remember that Thorndike's explanation of the behavior of the animals in his puzzle box explicitly excluded the idea that the animals were anticipating the consequences of their actions. Those that followed in the Thorn-dikian position were then confronted with the problem of how to explain avoidance learning, a behavior that, almost by definition, implied anticipation.

The second aspect of this problem was related to the first. What was the reinforcement for avoidance learning? If an animal success-fully avoided, it received no shock. Was the nonoccurrence of shock to be considered a reinforcer? If so, this would again imply that the animal was anticipating future events and obtaining reinforcement from something that did *not* happen because of its behavior. Was there any way of explaining avoidance learning without resorting to such cognitive terms as "expectancy"?

One solution to this problem was developed by Mowrer (1939). Mowrer's explanation was, essentially, that there was no avoidance learning—at least from the animal's point of view, there was only escape behavior. The explanation involved the presumed operation of two factors[1]: One of these factors was the conditioning, by Pav-lovian processes, of an emotional response of fear to the situational stimuli present in the avoidance apparatus. Thus, in the presence of the situational stimuli (the CS), the rat is shocked (the UCS) a number of times. *The pairing of the shock with the apparatus stimuli leads to the conditioned emotional response of fear being elicited by these apparatus stimuli.* The learning is the first factor in Mowrer's theory.

After the fear response has been acquired, the once neutral ap-paratus stimuli are now aversive. But this aversiveness can be reduced by escaping from the section of the apparatus in which these cues are present. For example, in the shuttle box the rat may escape the aversive cues by crossing over to the "safe" side. If this response is made before the shock is presented, it would appear to be an avoidance response, but need not be so from the animal's point of view. In Mowrer's theory, the reinforcement for this escape response was interpreted to be the reduction in fear that occurs as a result of the animal getting away from the aversive stimuli. This is the second factor in the theory—*the reinforcement of escape be-havior by fear reduction.*

Mowrer's theory was an inspired application of known principles to explain apparent avoidance behavior without resorting to the use of cognitive concepts, or the need to assume that the animal's cur-rent behavior was being controlled by events that might take place

---

1. Hence, the theory is sometimes termed the "two-factor theory." We use the term fear hypothesis because the presumed role played by fear is central to the theory, and in addition, there are several versions of the two-factor theory, some of which use the concept of fear, and some of which do not.

in the future. There simply was no avoidance as far as the animal was concerned, only escape.

Support for Mowrer's position comes mainly from evidence that Pavlovian processes can indeed influence avoidance behavior. We shall briefly consider some of this evidence.

PAVLOVIAN PROCESSES IN AVOIDANCE BEHAVIOR

Solomon and Turner (1962) trained restrained dogs to push panels mounted on either side of their heads in order to avoid shock. The impending occurrence of shock was signaled by a light. If the dogs pressed the panel in the 10-second interval between light onset and programmed shock appearance, the light was terminated and the shock was not presented. That is, the dog's response succeeded in avoiding the shock.

After this response was well learned, the dogs were removed from the avoidance situation and given discriminative Pavlovian training (*see* Chapter 2). During this phase of the experiment, two different tones were used as conditioned stimuli. One of these tones (the CS$^+$) regularly preceded shock; the other tone (CS$^-$) was never followed by shock. Since this was a Pavlovian conditioning procedure, the stimuli and shocks were presented without regard to the animal's behavior. As a further guarantee that the animals would not learn any responses during this phase that might be considered instrumental responses, the dogs were exposed to the stimulus-shock contingencies while paralyzed by a d-tubocurarine, a curare-related drug that produces flaccid paralysis.

In the third phase of the experiment, after recovery from the paralytic agent, the dogs were placed back in the avoidance situation, but now under an extinction contingency. That is, no more shocks were presented. But something different was presented—the CS$^+$ and the CS$^-$ that the dogs had experienced in the Pavlovian phase of the experiment. Neither of these stimuli had ever been presented in the avoidance situation before and, of course, the dogs had never learned to associate these stimuli with the performance of an avoidance response. However, Solomon and Turner found that when the CS$^+$ was presented, the dogs pressed the panel quite rapidly. Panel presses were less likely to occur during CS$^-$ presentation.

These data indicated that something the dogs had learned during the Pavlovian conditioning phase *transferred* to the avoidance situation, and influenced the performance of the avoidance response. An interpretation of these data, consistent with Mowrer's theory, would be as follows: During both the avoidance and Pavlovian training, an emotional response of fear had been produced in the dogs by the experience with shock. During the avoidance phase, the dogs had learned a response (panel pushing) which was effective in removing a fear-arousing stimulus (the light). When the CS+ from the Pavlovian phase was presented, it elicited the same emotional response of fear and the dogs did what they had earlier learned to do in the presence of fear—they pressed the panels. Thus, even though the tone stimuli were not present when the dogs learned the avoidance response, they were effective in exerting some control over this response because they elicited an emotion in common with the avoidance situation.

In a similar experiment (Leaf, 1964), the order of the first two experimental treatments was reversed from that used by Solomon and Turner, and the avoidance response was different (a hurdle jump instead of a panel push), but the results were essentially the same.

There are numerous other experiments that support the notion that learning occurring during Pavlovian conditioning can influence avoidance behavior (*see* Chapters 3 and 8 for other examples, and Rescorla & Solomon, 1967, for a review). A crucial factor to remember in interpreting these experiments is that the influence cannot be attributed to overt motor responses in common between the two types of learning. In Pavlovian conditioning the UCS is presented regardless of the subject's response, and in the experiments just described, the dogs were paralyzed during Pavlovian conditioning so there could be no overt motor response learned at all. The transfer, then, is reasonably attributed to some central event, and the idea that it is a learned fear response that is in common between the two paradigms fits in well with Mowrer's original hypothesis. However, it is just this point, that fear is necessary, or even involved, in avoidance learning, that has been a consistent point of attack on Mowrer's two-factor hypothesis.

THE ROLE OF FEAR IN AVOIDANCE BEHAVIOR

If fear is important for avoidance learning, one would expect a strong correlation between measurements of a fear response and avoidance performance. However, there is evidence that fear may increase during the early stages of avoidance learning, but then decline during later stages, just when avoidance performance is at its best (Kamin, Brimer, & Black, 1963). Similarly, observation of animals performing a well practiced avoidance response provides little evidence that the animals are in a state of high arousal or fear (Woodworth & Schlosberg, 1954); to anthropomorphize a bit, the animals appear to be somewhat lackadaisical in responding. Consistent with these observations is the evidence showing that damaging the sympathetic nervous system (which mediates the peripheral manifestations of arousal and emotion) interferes with the acquisition, but not the maintenance, of avoidance behavior (Wynne & Solomon, 1955; DiGiusto & King, 1972).

Thus, the data are not in complete agreement with Mowrer's hypothesis. On present evidence, an emotional response may be important for avoidance learning, but it does not seem to be important for the maintenance of avoidance responding. Introspectively and anthropomorphically, this seems to make some sense; potentially aversive situations lose their aversiveness when they are under control. To cite a common example, there is usually very little fear involved in meeting oncoming traffic on a highway despite the potentially devastating results of an impact. In all but a few cases, the situation is under control.

Consistent with observational and autonomic data are the data on the relationship between shock intensity and the acquisition of an avoidance response. Surprisingly, from the point of view of the fear hypothesis, there seems to be an *inverse* relationship between shock intensity and the rate of acquisition of an active avoidance response. That is, the stronger the shock, the poorer the acquisition. We say, surprisingly, from the point of view of the fear hypothesis, because it would seem reasonable, that the more intense the shock, the stronger the fear should be and, hence, the more reinforcement there should be when an avoidance response is made. However, the data do not agree with this seemingly reasonable extension of the fear hypothesis. What is wrong? Before getting into this question, we have to make a qualification and introduce a few more complexities in the experimental paradigms used to study avoidance behavior.

So far we have confined our discussion to the simple *one-way avoidance* situations. Many investigators have found it convenient to have the rats shuttle back and forth between the two sides of a two compartment box in order to avoid shock (this has the practical advantage of making automation easy). In these *two-way avoidance* experiments, a discriminative stimulus is usually provided on each side of the apparatus to signal when shock is impending on that side. Thus, when a rat crosses from Side A to Side B and successfully avoids shock, after a while a stimulus signaling shock comes on in Side B, and now the rat must cross back to Side A in order to avoid shock. This back-and-forth shuttling behavior must persist for an entire experimental session (usually an hour or so).

It is in these situations (and in situations in which a rat must learn to press a lever in order to avoid shock) that the *inverse relationship* between shock intensity and avoidance learning is typically found (e.g., Moyer & Korn, 1964; D'Amato & Fazzaro, 1966). In the simpler one-way avoidance situation, a direct relationship between shock

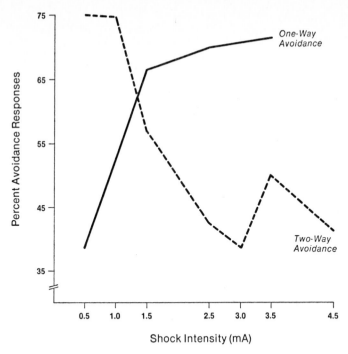

Figure 6–2. Effect of shock intensity on the acquisition of two-way and one-way avoidance responses. (Adapted from Moyer & Korn, 1964, 1966.)

intensity and avoidance learning may be found (Moyer & Korn, 1966). These different effects of shock intensity in one-way and two-way avoidance responding can be seen in Figure 6–2.

The fear hypothesis itself does not tell us to expect differences in the effects of shock intensity as a function of the apparatus used. There must be some other factor important in avoidance learning that relates, perhaps, to the spatial and topographical characteristics of the response and not simply to presumed fear. We will go into this idea below when we consider the role of *species-specific defense responses*. For now, we can see that the data on shock intensity are not entirely consonant with the fear hypothesis and, further, they introduce the idea that the response demands made on the animal may be important for the understanding of avoidance acquisition.

On the other hand, the *maintenance* of a well-learned avoidance response is directly related to shock intensity (D'Amato, Fezzarro, & Etkin, 1967). But, as noted above, it is precisely under these maintenance conditions that fear seems to play an unimportant role.

THE FUNCTION OF CS TERMINATION

Perhaps the point of strongest attack on the fear hypothesis has been concerning the function of CS termination. In the typical avoidance experiment, a stimulus signaling shock is presented to the animal in one compartment. If the subject moves out of the compartment within a specified time period[2], the stimulus signaling shock is terminated and the subject has avoided shock. From the point of view of the fear hypothesis, the termination of the CS should be critical since it is this event that provides the source of reinforcement—fear reduction. The occurrence of fear reduction is, of course, dependent on the CS eliciting fear in the first place. The questions we shall consider now concern these presumed functions of the CS.

Avoidance Learning Without a CS. If the fear-eliciting properties of the CS are critical for avoidance learning, then it should be impossible for avoidance learning to occur without a CS. We shall describe two avoidance learning situations in which there appears to be no CS, but avoidance learning nevertheless occurs. The first of these is termed *free-operant* or *Sidman avoidance.* Sidman (1953) described a procedure in which shocks are programmed to occur at fixed time periods *if a response is not made.* If a response is made, then a timer controlling shock delivery is reset and restarted. For example, if a rat is in Side A of a shuttle box, a brief inescapable shock may be programmed to occur every 20 seconds unless the rat moves over to Side B. If the rat does move over before the 20 seconds has elapsed, the timer is reset and now a shock is programmed to occur in 20 seconds on Side B, unless the rat moves back over to Side A, etc. Thus, the rat can avoid shocks by making the specified response prior to the termination of the temporal period controlling shock delivery (this period is usually termed the shock-shock interval).[3]

Although acquisition is generally slow, most rats can learn this type of avoidance behavior. Does this mean that CS termination is not critical for avoidance learning? Not necessarily; an argument can be made that there is a CS in Sidman avoidance, although this CS is not overtly apparent as it is in other avoidance paradigms. The proposed CS is some neural process associated with the passage

---

2. Often termed the CS–UCS interval, again reflecting the presumed importance of Pavlovian processes in avoidance learning.

3. Another parameter of Sidman avoidance is the response-shock interval—the time between the last response and the next programmed shock. In our example, we are assuming that the response-shock interval is the same as the shock-shock interval.

of time. Evidence for the existence of such a process that could be used as a CS are the following points:

(1)   Temporal factors can apparently exert an influence in Pavlovian conditioning. For example, the presentation of a UCS such as food at regular time intervals can lead to conditioning, conditioning that can be demonstrated by omitting the UCS occasionally with the result that the subject will salivate at approximately the time when the UCS would have been presented (*see* Chapter 2). Note that there is no explicit CS presented in this paradigm. Similarly, the phenomenon of *inhibition of delay* mentioned in Chapter 3 also provides evidence that the passage of time can have stimulus functions in Pavlovian conditioning.

(2)   There are also instrumental learning paradigms that indicate a functional role for the passage of time. For example, the scalloping behavior that occurs on FI schedules (*see* Chapter 5) indicates that subjects are estimating how long it has been since the last reinforcement, or conversely, how close it is to the availability of the next reinforcement. The acquisition of a DRL schedule (*see* Chapter 5) also indicates that rats and other lower organisms can estimate the passage of a short time interval, and this estimation can be used to control overt responses.

(3)   Finally, there is evidence gathered from the Sidman avoidance task itself that suggests quite strongly that the subjects are estimating the passage of time. If no time estimation were involved, one would expect responding to be randomly distributed within the shock-shock interval or response-shock interval. However, examination of the pattern of responding that does occur in Sidman avoidance experiments indicates that responding is not randomly distributed. Instead, there is a tendency for responses to be more likely to occur the longer the time interval since the last response (Anger, 1963). This behavior is much like the behavior that occurs on FI and DRL schedules and indicates that subjects are indeed estimating the passage of time in Sidman avoidance tasks.

Thus, it is possible to imagine an internal process associated with the passage of time (time since last shock and/or time since last response) that may function in a way similar to an externally presented CS. When a response is made, the process is interrupted. This interruption has the same function as CS termination; it reduces fear and thereby reinforces the avoidance response. We can see that, although the evidence is indirect, the occurrence of Sidman avoidance behavior is not greatly damaging to the critical role assigned to CS termination by Mowrer's fear hypothesis.

The second paradigm in which avoidance is apparently learned without a CS is more convincing in demonstrating the nonnecessity of a CS. The procedure in these experiments is quite complicated, but it essentially involves placing a rat in an operant chamber and delivering shocks at random intervals. Responses on either of two levers serve to reduce the probability of a subsequent shock, but these responses do not always directly avoid, or postpone, a shock. In fact, some lever responses may lead to immediate shocks, if a shock happened to be programmed at that time. But, over the long run, pressing the levers will lead to a lower probability of shock than not pressing the lever. It has been found that avoidance learning will occur under these conditions and, further, the rats will learn to press most often on one of two levers that leads to the greatest reduction in shock frequency (Herrnstein & Hineline, 1966; Herrnstein, 1969).

There is no CS involved in the above experiments; there is nothing that accurately predicts the impending presence or absence of an immediate shock. There is only a long-term reduction in the density of shock consequent to pressing the levers. The fact that rats are able to learn the lever-pressing response in this situation argues quite persuasively that rats can be attuned to long-term changes in the probability of shock presentation, and that reduction in the long-run frequency of shock occurrence can serve as a reinforcement in avoidance learning.

However, what these data mean for the fear hypothesis is less clear. We say this because the evidence of avoidance learning in the Herrnstein and Hineline paradigm does not appear until the rats have made thousands of lever-presses. The relevance of this learning to interpreting behavior in situations in which learning is (and must be) several orders of magnitude faster is not clear at the present time (cf., Bolles, 1970). We shall have more to say about this issue below when we discuss Bolles's species specific defense response theory of avoidance learning.

What is clear from a consideration of both the Sidman avoidance and the Herrnstein-Hineline paradigm is that avoidance learning becomes considerably more difficult when the CS is either internal to the organism or totally absent.

Analysis of CS Termination. Another experimental approach used to analyze the mechanisms of avoidance learning has been to manipulate the contingency between the avoidance response and CS termination. At the risk of being redundant, we will say again that the termination of the CS contingent upon the performance of the avoidance response is critical with respect to the fear hypothesis.

The importance of CS termination was investigated by Kamin (1956, 1957). In the first of these experiments Kamin attempted to directly compare the effects of CS termination and UCS avoidance.

Kamin's experiment was a one-way avoidance task conducted in a shuttle box, with a 5-second CS–UCS interval. Four groups of rats were used.

The first group was a standard avoidance group—responses during the CS–UCS interval both terminated the CS and avoided the UCS.

For the second group, responses during the CS–UCS interval served to avoid the UCS, but they did *not* terminate the CS. That is, if the rats crossed over to Side B during the CS–UCS interval, they were not shocked, but this avoidance response did not terminate the CS, which remained on for the duration of the CS–UCS interval. The purpose of this group was to assess the importance of the UCS avoidance contingency without the usually correlated CS termination.

In the third group, response during the CS–UCS interval terminated the CS but did not avoid the shock. In other words, if the animals in this group crossed from Side A to Side B during the CS–UCS interval, the CS was immediately terminated but the shock was delivered as scheduled at the end of the CS–UCS period. The purpose of this group was to assess the effectiveness of the CS termination contingency, without the usually correlated UCS avoidance.

The last group was essentially a Pavlovian conditioning group. Responses made during the CS–UCS interval had no effect either on CS termination or on UCS avoidance.

The results of Kamin's experiment are presented in Figure 6–3. It can be seen that the normal avoidance group performed the best and the Pavlovian group the worst. Such would be expected. The remaining two groups, the groups of interest, were intermediate in their avoidance performance and not much different from each other. It appears that both failure of responses during the CS–UCS interval to avoid shock and failure of such responses to terminate the CS have equally deleterious effects on avoidance behavior.

From this experiment, then, it appears that the CS termination contingency and the UCS avoidance contingency are both important in avoidance learning. However, the results of this experiment, while interesting in themselves, are inconclusive with regard to the fear hypothesis. Consider in particular the performance of the rats whose responses terminated the CS, but did not avoid the UCS. The performance of this group was considerably below the performance level of the normal avoidance group, and the decrement might be taken as evidence against the critical role assigned to CS termination by the fear hypothesis. However, note that this group was also being punished for making the avoidance response! That is, when they crossed from Side A to Side B, the CS was terminated,

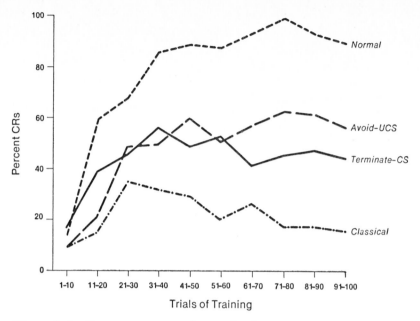

Figure 6–3. Percent responses during the CS–UCS interval as a function of CS and UCS termination contingencies. *See* text for further explanation. (From Kamin, 1956.)

but then, at the end of the programmed CS–UCS interval, a shock was delivered, thus punishing the avoidance response. Therefore, these data cannot be clearly interpreted as providing evidence concerning the relative unimportance of CS termination in reinforcing avoidance behavior. In a later study Kamin (1957) found evidence indicating that the CS termination contingency was indeed important in that the longer the CS termination was delayed after an avoidance response was made, the poorer the final level of avoidance performance.

A Feedback Stimulus.   Another, and more fruitful, approach to the role of CS termination in avoidance learning has come from a series of studies by several investigators in which an extra stimulus, one correlated with the performance of the avoidance response, has been included. The rationale for this treatment is the following: It is possible to think that one of the functions of CS termination in the standard avoidance experiment is to provide information to the animal, that is, to allow the animal to discriminate that it has made the "correct" response. We shall describe two experiments that tested this interpretation of the function of CS termination.

The first of these experiments (D'Amato, Fazzaro, & Etkin,

1968a) was similar in design to the Kamin experiment described above. One group of rats experienced the standard avoidance contingencies, a second group was exposed to Pavlovian contingencies (responses during the CS–UCS interval did not influence the occurrence of the UCS), and a third group for which CS termination was delayed until after the performance of an avoidance response.

The interesting aspect of this study was the inclusion of two additional groups of rats. In these two groups the performance of an avoidance response also did not terminate the CS, but such a response did cause another stimulus, the feedback stimulus, to appear (the two groups differed in whether the feedback stimulus was a light or a noise). The question of interest was whether or not this extra stimulus would support avoidance performance in a manner similar to normal CS termination.

The results of the experiment indicated the following: The group given the standard avoidance contingency performed considerably better (about 65 percent avoidance responses) than the group with the delayed CS termination (about 40 percent avoidance responses), which was in turn better than the group given the Pavlovian contingency (about 20 percent responses during the CS–UCS interval). The final level of performance for the groups given the feedback stimulus was about equal to the group given the standard avoidance contingencies (about 65 percent avoidance responses) and, therefore, considerably superior to the group with the delayed CS termination. This result is interesting because the feedback stimulus was never paired either with shock onset or offset, it occurred only on successful avoidance trials, when there was no shock presented. A similar effect of a feedback stimulus on avoidance learning was found in a second experiment by D'Amato et al. (1968a) in which a trace conditioning paradigm was used.

Taken as a whole, these results support the conclusion that CS termination normally functions as a feedback stimulus, informing the animal that it has made the "correct" response. When another stimulus, a stimulus contingent upon the performance of an avoidance response, is substituted for CS termination, performance is as good as when the CS itself terminates.

Do these results imply that the fear hypothesis is completely wrong? Does CS termination have nothing to do with fear reduction? Such a conclusion would not be entirely warranted on the basis of the present data. It is possible that CS termination serves a dual function of reducing fear and providing information. In this regard it is interesting to note that in the D'Amato et al. (1968a) experiment, the feedback stimulus groups did not reach the performance level of the normal avoidance contingency group until quite late in acquisition training. This could be interpreted to mean that the presumed fear-reducing properties of CS termination are of primary importance early in avoidance learning, but the feedback aspects of CS termination are of primary importance later in training. This interpretation would also be consonant with the observational evidence that we reviewed earlier indicating that overt signs of fear decline in well practiced avoidance tasks.

In summary, the two-factor fear hypothesis enjoys some support in that there is strong evidence that Pavlovian conditioning can influence instrumental avoidance learning via the functions of the CS. It is not, however, clear that these CS functions are entirely related to fear and fear reduction. It seems quite likely that CS onset and termination can have informational value to the animal; value that is separable from its fear-related effects. Other evidence indicates that emotional responses may not be equally important at all stages of avoidance performance. We turn now to a brief look at other theories of avoidance learning, which emphasize other aspects of behavior rather than presuming fear arousal and reduction.

Avoidance Cue Hypotheses

A number of investigators believe that the principal task confronting an animal placed in an avoidance situation is to discriminate that an avoidance contingency exists (Herrnstein, 1969; D'Amato, 1970). That is, we cannot verbally instruct an animal that if it makes such and such a response, it will avoid an aversive event. The animal must discover this for itself. The avoidance-cue interpretation focuses on those aspects of the avoidance task that are necessary for the animal to discover the existence of an avoidance contingency.

We have already considered some of the data relevant to this hypothesis. Specifically, we mentioned that Herrnstein and Hineline (1966) have demonstrated that rats can acquire a lever-pressing response if responses on the lever have the effect of a long-run reduction in shock density. Thus, without the benefit of a CS or a feedback stimulus, rats are able to detect the existence of an avoidance contingency. However, we also mentioned that this learning takes an extraordinarily long time, involving thousands of lever-presses.

On the basis of his experiments with feedback stimuli, D'Amato (1970) reasoned that CS termination may function, in large part, as an avoidance cue. The CS termination (or a feedback stimulus) is effective because it allows the animal to detect that it has made an effective response. Without such a stimulus change, it becomes difficult for the animal to discriminate the effect its response is having on the environment, and we get the poor performance or difficult learning that is characteristic of Sidman avoidance and the Herrn-stein-Hineline procedure.

However, there is another factor involved in the importance of the animal detecting the existence of an avoidance contingency. Specifically, the animal must make a response during the CS–UCS interval and, subsequently, not get shocked. If no such responses occur, the animal will have no basis for detecting that an avoidance contingency exists. In Mowrer's early formulation of the fear hypothesis (Mowrer & Lamoreaux, 1942), he believed that an escape response from the UCS that initially occurred gradually became anticipatory and, thus, the animal eventually made a response *before* the UCS onset. It is these anticipatory responses that allow the animal to discriminate the existence of an avoidance contingency.

Some recent experiments have indicated that prior escape from the UCS may not be necessary for the emergence of avoidance behavior, at least not in all avoidance paradigms (Bolles, 1969). However, emphasis on the role played by responses anticipatory to UCS presentation still seems warranted. Note that in both the Kamin experiment (Figure 6–3) and the D'Amato et al. experiment described earlier (*see* p. 166), a considerable number of responses occurred during the CS–UCS interval in the Pavlovian groups; groups that did not experience the avoidance contingency. D'Amato (1967) has argued that the existence of these responses is necessary for the avoidance contingency to be discriminated and that any treatment which increases the likelihood of these anticipatory responses occurring should facilitate the acquisition of the avoidance response. Treatments that seem to have such an effect include, e.g., injections of magnesium pemoline (Collins & D'Amato, 1968); low as opposed to high intensity shock (D'Amato & Fazzaro, 1966); one-way avoidance, as opposed to two-way avoidance (Theios, Lynch, & Lowe, 1966); discontinuous as opposed to continuous shock (e.g., D'Amato, Keller, & Biederman, 1965); and lesions of the septal area (e.g., Trafton, 1967; Hamilton, 1969).

In summary, the avoidance-cue hypothesis emphasizes that animals must make a response during the CS–UCS interval in order to discover that an avoidance contingency exists. These responses seem to develop even when no avoidance contingency exists, as in Pavlovian conditioning. However, when an avoidance contingency does exist, then the frequency of these responses increases over and above the level found with just Pavlovian training. Experimental conditions that facilitate the development of anticipatory responses seem to facilitate the acquisition of an avoidance response.

Once the avoidance response is made, the course of acquisition appears to be considerably more rapid if there is a stimulus change directly contingent upon the avoidance response. This stimulus may be either immediate termination of the CS itself, or the addition of an extra stimulus, a feedback stimulus. There is some evidence that CS termination may be more effective early in training, but at asymptote there is little difference between these two types of stimulus manipulation. If no external stimulus change is consequent upon the performance of the avoidance response, as in the case of Sidman avoidance or the Herrnstein-Hineline procedure, then avoidance learning is apparently quite difficult.

Relaxation Theory

Another theoretical interpretation of avoidance behavior emphasizes the rewarding effects of stimuli associated with the absence of shock. This theory, termed a relaxation theory (Denny, 1971), postulates that subjects in an avoidance task learn to *approach* stimuli associated with the absence of shock, and the reinforcement for this approach response is relief, or relaxation, that occurs in the presence of these stimuli. The experimental evidence gathered in support of this hypothesis is of the following type: Rats are trained to perform a simple one-way avoidance response or a jump-out avoidance response. Both of these responses are learned relatively rapidly by rats. A specific stimulus (e.g., a flashing light) is presented in the safe compartment. After the avoidance response has been learned, the effects of this stimulus are tested by presenting it in the compartment usually associated with shock. These tests may be of two types; either the stimulus is presented during the extinction of an avoidance response, or during the learning of a new avoidance response. When the stimulus is presented during extinction, it is found that extinction proceeds more rapidly than it would in the absence of this stimulus. When the stimulus is presented during the learning of a new avoidance response, it is found that learning is retarded (Weisman, Denny, Platt, & Zerbolio, 1966; Denny, 1971).

Both of these effects may be explained by assuming that the rats had learned to "relax" in the presence of this stimulus during the learning of the original avoidance response. When this relaxation-inducing stimulus is presented in the shock compartment, it facilitates extinction because relaxation is incompatible with the performance of the avoidance response. Similarly, if the stimulus is presented in the shock compartment during the acquisition of a new avoidance response, it retards acquisition for the same reason—it promotes relaxation which is incompatible with the performance of the avoidance response. However, if such a stimulus is presented in the safe region of the apparatus during the learning of a new avoidance response, then it facilitates acquisition (*see* Denny, 1971). This result is also consistent with relaxation theory; the interpretation is that the stimulus previously associated with the safe region provides an approach stimulus for the animal during the learning of the new avoidance response.

Some other data that may be interpreted as supporting relaxation theory are the following: One-way avoidance learning is considerably easier if the two compartments of a shuttle box are distinct and heterogeneous (Knapp, 1965). However, in a two-way avoidance task, distinctive compartments *retard* the acquisition of the avoidance task (Denny, Zerbolio & Weisman, 1969). The interpretation of these data from the relaxation viewpoint is that in a one-way avoidance the animal can learn to approach a safe compartment, and the more distinct the compartments the easier this response is to learn. However, in a two-way avoidance task there is no safe *compartment*, the animal may get shocked in either compartment, and there is only a safe *time period*. Thus, in a two-way avoidance task the animal must learn that place or location cues are irrelevant to its safety; only temporal cues are important. Each compartment is only temporarily safe, safe until the next CS onset. Learning that location cues are irrelevant is assumed to proceed more quickly when the compartments are less distinctive than when they are heterogeneous.

The reader will note that stimuli associated with safe areas are conceptually quite similar to feedback stimuli. The difference in theoretical interpretation of these two stimuli appears to be the following: The safety or relaxation approach assumes an emotional component to these stimuli, one that would elicit approach responses. Those that emphasize the avoidance cue approach have directed their attention more to the discriminative or informational aspects of the feedback stimuli, rather than towards possible emotion-related effects of these stimuli. The two approaches do not seem incompatible, and further research is likely to tell us which is the more useful interpretation, or perhaps, how they may be combined.

One further difference between feedback stimuli and relaxation stimuli is operational. That is, relaxation stimuli are typically there before the animal makes its response and the animal approaches these stimuli, whereas feedback stimuli are introduced contingent upon the animal's response. This distinction seems to parallel a distinction between incentive stimuli and secondary reinforcing stimuli (cf., Dinsmoor, 1950).

Species-Specific Defense Reactions

Another dimension was added to the study of avoidance behavior by Bolles (1970), who argued that previous theories of avoidance learning had been amiss for not taking into account how animals deal with potentially dangerous situations in their natural environment. In Bolles' words:

> . . . no real life predator is going to present cues just before it attacks. No owl hoots or whistles 5 seconds before pouncing on a mouse. And no owl terminates his hoots or whistles just as the mouse gets away so as to reinforce the avoidance response. Nor will the owl give the mouse enough trials for the necessary learning to occur (1970, p. 32).

Bolles's point is that each species has innate ways of dealing with dangerous situations, and consideration of these factors might provide a clearer understanding of avoidance behavior and, perhaps, add direction to the further laboratory analysis of the phenomenon.

In the natural environment the animals' defense reactions generally take one of three forms—freezing, fleeing, or fighting. These reactions are likely to be invoked whenever the animal encounters a novel stimulus or a sudden stimulus change. Bolles argues that in the laboratory study of avoidance the occurrence of an electrical shock in the experimental apparatus temporarily converts the domesticated animal into a wild animal by activating species-specific defense responses (SSDRs). How well the animal then learns the avoidance task depends on how closely the response the experimenter requires of the animal matches its SSDR. If there is a close match, "learning" should proceed rapidly; if the required response is greatly different from the SSDR, then learning should take place very gradually, if at all.

Few studies have been conducted which directly compare avoidance learning rates with different response requirements. However, an examination of the extensive literature available on avoidance behavior indicates that learning takes place much more rapidly with some paradigms than with others. This evidence should be interpreted with caution because differences in learning rates may depend on a host of parametric differences, such as shock intensity, type of shock, CS–USC interval, etc. With these cautions in mind, apparatus differences still seem to exist. For example, if the response required of the animal is to jump out of a box to avoid shock or run down a runway to avoid shock, then learning takes place rapidly, in just a few trials (Maatsch, 1959; Theios, 1963). If the paradigm requires the rat to turn a wheel in order to avoid shock, then learning takes longer, but all rats are reported to learn the response within approximately 40 trials (Bolles, Stokes, & Younger, 1966).

We have already had occasion to mention that the two-way shuttle avoidance response is quite difficult for rats to learn—some rats never learn this task (Brush, 1966). Similarly, requiring the rat to press a bar to avoid shock leads to a very long acquisition sequence, and again, some rats apparently cannot learn this response [e.g., D'Amato & Schiff, 1964; also the data reported previously from the D'Amato et al., (1968a) experiment were from a bar-press task; note the low levels of asymptotic avoidance responses after hundreds of training trials (*see* p. 167)].

According to Bolles, these differences in learning rates that are correlated with differences in the apparatus occur because of the relationship of the response required of the animal to its natural SSDR. In the jump-out apparatus, the straight runway, or the one-way avoidance chamber the rat can very easily leave the situation, or flee. Other SSDRs such as freezing or fighting are not successful in terminating or avoiding the shock, thus they are "suppressed." Learning occurs rapidly in these tasks, because one of the animal's SSDRs is effective in extracting the animal from the vicinity of the noxious event.

In the two-way shuttle box, however, the animal cannot totally flee the situation. It can only move back and forth between compartments, both of which are shocked. Other defense responses such as freezing or fleeing are even less effective in avoiding the shock, thus eventually most animals learn to shuttle back and forth. But this learning is slow, and usually a high level of proficiency is not obtained because, according to Bolles's analysis, the constraints of the apparatus do not allow for the expression of an SSDR.

An experiment by Bolles and Grossen (1969) provides some interesting data relevant to apparatus effects in avoidance learning. In this experiment separate groups of rats were trained to avoid shock in three different apparatuses: One group was trained on a one-way avoidance; another group on a two-way shuttle response; and a third group was required to run in a running wheel. Bolles and Grossen also manipulated another variable orthogonally to the avoidance task itself. That is, within each task, separate groups of rats experienced either a CS termination contingency, a feedback stimulus, or neither. The results of this experiment are presented in Figure 6–4. Note that rats in the different avoidance paradigms received a different number of training trials. The amount of acquisition training given in the different tasks was selected on the basis of other data from Bolles's laboratory, showing when asymptotic responding would be reached for each task. The amount of training given was approximately enough to carry each group to asymptote.

There are several facts apparent in the results of the Bolles and Grossen study. First of all, the one-way avoidance was apparently easier than the running wheel which, in turn, was easier than the two-way shuttle. This ordering of apparatus-difficulty is consistent with the SSDR hypothesis; the one-way task allows the subject to

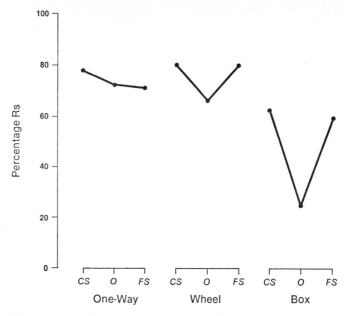

Figure 6–4. Mean percentage of avoidance responses for rats trained with either CS termination (CS), Feedback Stimulus presentation (FS), or neither (O). Training consisted of 20 trials in the one-way avoidance situation, 40 trials in the running wheel, and 80 trials in the two-way shuttle box. (From Bolles, 1970.)

flee from a particular location that is always associated with shock. The two-way shuttle and wheel tasks are not compatible with any SSDR and are also more difficult to learn. Why the running wheel task should be easier than the two-way shuttle task is not entirely clear, but may have something to do with the rat's being able to run continuously in the wheel (as if it were covering a lot of ground!), but not in the shuttle box.

A second interesting aspect of these results is that CS termination and a feedback stimulus were about equally effective in supporting avoidance behavior. A third, and related aspect, is that the importance of these stimuli clearly depended upon the task used. In one-way avoidance there was little difference among the three stimulus conditions. In other words, learning was just as good with neither CS termination nor a feedback stimulus as it was with either of them. However, in the two-way shuttle and wheel-turning task, both stimulus contingencies produced better learning than the absence of a stimulus contingency, and further, the effectiveness of the stimulus contingency was greatest in the two-way avoidance, the most difficult task.

The relative effectiveness of the stimulus contingencies in these three tasks may reflect the degree to which SSDRs are involved in the avoidance performance. In the one-way task avoidance is primarily determined by the operation of an SSDR of fleeing, thus relatively little learning is involved and the stimulus contingencies are not very important. However, SSDRs are ineffective in the wheel-turn and two-way task, requiring that learning play a more important role. As a result, the stimulus contingencies have more of an effect on avoidance performance.

Bolles's theory has focused attention on the importance of the response required of the animal. A good case can be made that the single best predictor of how well an animal is going to perform in an avoidance task is the nature of the response requirement. It is certainly reasonable to think that rats come into an experimental situation predisposed to respond in certain ways to aversive events. However, whether the SSDR hypothesis will be the best way to conceptualize these predispositions must await more research, particularly more extensive research with species other than the rat and more research on animals' responses to natural predators (cf., Blanchard & Blanchard, 1972).

Another direction that future research is likely to take is an analysis of genetic contributions to avoidance learning. For example, one recent behavior genetic study (Wilcock & Fulker, 1973) has indicated that there seem to be genetically controlled processes of freezing and fleeing that occur in the two-way shuttle box behavior of rats. During the early stages of training rats tend to freeze, and later they develop a more active approach to the problem. The indicated genetic basis of the behavior patterns is a point in favor of the SSDR approach. We shall have more to say about genetic influences on avoidance learning and other types of behavior in Chapter 9.

In considering the idea that animals may come into an experimental situation predisposed to perform in certain ways which may be compatible or incompatible with the avoidance task, one might think that these predispositions could be altered experimentally prior to introducing the animal to the avoidance task. For example, consider bar-pressing. We have seen that this is quite difficult for rats to learn as an avoidance response. In the SSDR analysis this difficulty might be traced to the absence of any relationship between the response requirements of lever-pressing and such SSDRs as fleeing or freezing. Suppose, however, that rats are trained to press a lever for a food reward prior to introducing them to the shock avoidance contingency. Will a well established lever-pressing response for food make it easier for the rat to learn lever-pressing as an avoidance response? Giulian and Schmaltz (1973) have con-

ducted such an experiment and found that rats so trained performed
very well on a bar-press avoidance task. Apparently it is reasonable
to assume that predispositions to respond in particular ways may be
experientially based, as well as genetically based.

An Overview of Avoidance Behavior

We have covered quite a bit of data and speculation concerning
avoidance behavior, and yet we have only scratched the surface of
the available research. We shall now briefly review what we have
covered, organizing the material around the factors which reliably
influence avoidance behavior.

1. The Nature of the Response.   The type of response required
of an animal is an important predictor of the adequacy of the avoidance behavior that will develop. If the response is a simple one that
allows the animal to leave the situation in which it is shocked, then
avoidance behavior will develop rapidly and to a high level. However, if the task includes a response that requires the animal to
shuttle back and forth between two locations that are both sometimes associated with shock (as in two-way avoidance), or is one that
does not allow the animal to leave the situation (as in wheel-turn or
bar-press) then avoidance performance will be slow to develop, and
be relatively poor at asymptote.

2. Shock Intensity and Type.   Shock intensity seems to be in-
versely related to the acquisition of an active avoidance response,
but directly related to the maintenance of the avoidance response. It
is possible that the inverse relationship is due to a greater tendency
for higher shock to produce freezing responses that would then
interfere with the development of an active avoidance response. The
plausibility of this interpretation is supported by data indicating that
freezing tendencies predominate early in avoidance learning, and
by other data indicating that *passive* avoidance learning (where
freezing is adaptive) is directly related to shock intensity (e.g., Azrin,
1960).

Another aspect of shock that is important is whether the shock is
continuous or discontinuous. It has been found that discontinuous
shock (e.g., brief bursts) produces superior avoidance learning, at
least in some tasks (e.g., D'Amato & Fazzaro, 1966). It seems likely
that discontinuous shock is superior because it tends to "break up"
the freezing response, thus leading to the rapid acquisition of the
active avoidance response.

3. *The Escape Contingency.* It seems quite natural to think that when an organism learns to escape from an aversive situation that it will, in the future, avoid that situation. This ready way of thinking, perhaps, led early researchers to assume that an escape contingency was necessary for the development of an avoidance response. That is, animals first learned to escape from shock by making a particular response, and then the escape response began occurring sooner and sooner until, eventually, it preceded shock onset and became an avoidance response. This is indeed how learning seems to occur in most avoidance situations. However, research has demonstrated that the escape contingency is *not necessary* (Mowrer & Lamoreaux, 1942; Bolles, 1969). That is, animals can learn an avoidance response without the presence of an escape contingency, and they can learn one response as an avoidance response when a different response is actually effective in escaping from shock but not effective in avoiding shock (Bolles, 1969). What the presence of an escape contingency does contribute, it seems, is a tendency toward making responses anticipatory to the presentation of the shock, and these anticipatory responses may serve an important function.

4. *Anticipatory Responses.* It is the occurrence of anticipatory responses that allows an animal to detect the presence of an avoidance contingency. In other words, unless an animal responds prior to shock onset, it will never detect that it is possible for it to avoid shock by responding at a specified time. Anticipatory responses seem to be related to Pavlovian processes in that such responses occur even when there are no instrumental avoidance contingencies in effect (Kamin, 1956, *see* Figure 6–3; D'Amato, Fazzaro, & Etkin, 1968a, b). As discussed earlier, any experimental condition that increases the likelihood of anticipatory responses should facilitate the acquisition of an active avoidance response.

5. *Stimulus Effects.* Once an anticipatory response occurs, the stabilization of that response as an avoidance response seems to be facilitated if the response produces a distinctive stimulus change. It does not seem to make too much difference whether this stimulus change is the termination of a stimulus (CS) signaling the impending occurrence of shock, or the onset of a feedback stimulus—a stimulus correlated with the performance of the avoidance response. These stimulus changes are more important and more effective when the task is difficult to learn. It is possible that the apparent unimportance of CS termination and/or feedback stimuli in the one-way avoidance task (Bolles & Grossen, 1969) is due to the already great stimulus change that occurs when the animal runs from one compartment to another. Under these conditions, CS termination and feedback stimuli may simply be redundant stimulus changes, perhaps not as potent or effective as the larger stimulus change associated with the different compartments. In this regard, it has been found that one-way avoidance is facilitated if the two compartments of an avoidance chamber are heterogeneous (Knapp, 1965).

It is possible that CS termination results in fear reduction which reinforces avoidance learning early in training, but, as acquisition proceeds, the function of CS termination shifts primarily to an informational one. This change is CS termination function might, in turn, be correlated with the overt signs of a decline in fear during the performance of a well learned avoidance response. Other support, not previously mentioned, for an informational interpretation of the CS comes from studies in which an explicit CS was introduced into Sidman avoidance tasks at a time close to the end of a response-shock period. When this is done (cf., Keehn, 1959), rats tend to delay the performance of their avoidance response *until* the CS is presented. In other words, the rats take advantage of the signaling properties of the CS. If one were thinking entirely in terms of a CS eliciting fear, then the response of rats "holding back" their avoidance response until a CS was presented would seem strange. However, if one is willing to admit that a CS can also have informational (or predictive) value, then such behavior on the part of rats is not strange at all.

Another (but not incompatible) way of interpreting the apparently different time courses taken in the development of effectiveness by CS termination and by feedback stimuli is as follows: The effectiveness of both stimulus contingencies depends upon learning. The CS is directly paired with shock and thus comes quickly to elicit fear (or function as a danger signal as Bolles, 1970, terms it). However, the functions of a feedback stimulus which occur after a successful avoidance response has been made might be more difficult to learn because the stimulus is not directly associated with a primary reinforcer.

Bolles (1970) and others have argued that the feedback stimulus might be interpreted as a *safety signal* (just as the CS functions as a danger signal). The learning of the safety value of this stimulus might be expected to take some time because the "meaning" of safety depends on some prior established danger (just as the frustrative effects of nonreward depend upon the prior establishment of an expectancy of reward, *see* Chapter 5, pp. 120–22). Since this learned safety is derived, and dependent on the establishment of the aversiveness of the situation, it would be expected that it would take longer for the feedback stimulus to become effective than it does for the CS to become effective.

It will be noted that this safety signal interpretation of the feedback stimulus is also compatible with Denny's relaxation theory. Denny emphasizes the approach learning aspects of the avoidance task, and it would be expected that subjects would approach a "safety signal" when placed in a general context where shock is received. The safety signal interpretation is also compatible with the research presented in connection with Denny's theory regarding the effects of a stimulus associated with relaxation on the acquisition and extinction of avoidance responses.

6. *Pavlovian Processes in Avoidance.*   The term Pavlovian processes refers, of course, to learning in situations in which the presentation of reinforcing events is not contingent upon the subject's response. We have reviewed evidence showing that Pavlovian conditioning can indeed influence avoidance behavior. The presumed mechanism of this influence, according to the fear hypothesis, is the conditioning of fear to the CS. It also seems likely that safety-signal effects can be established by Pavlovian procedures (that is, without a response requirement). Recall that in Chapter 3, pp. 74–76, we described a study by Rescorla in which dogs were first trained on a Sidman avoidance task, then given Pavlovian conditioning. In the Pavlovian conditioning of the experiment one of the groups of dogs was exposed to a backward conditioning paradigm. When the dogs were placed back in the Sidman avoidance situation again, and the CS from the Pavlovian phase was presented to this group, the rate of responding *slowed down*. It was as if this group had learned that the CS predicted a period free of shock, a safe period. In another study, Rescorla (1966) has determined that a safety signal established in Pavlovian conditioning will function like a feedback stimulus in an avoidance task.

It thus appears that the cue values of both the CS and a feedback or safety signal may be established by Pavlovian processes independent of avoidance response requirements. These data strongly indicate that both Pavlovian and instrumental processes play a functional role in normally acquired avoidance responses.[4] The feedback stimulus as suggested by Bolles (1970), may gradually acquire safety signal effects in the usual avoidance task, and this gradual acquisition is why the feedback stimulus effects do not "catch up" to the CS termination effects until late in acquisition.

---

4. Thus, the term "two-factor theory" should not be taken as synonymous with the fear hypothesis. It is not just fear that may be established through Pavlovian conditioning; safety or relaxation stimuli may also be established in this way. It is also possible that nonmotivational (or cognitive) learning may be established by Pavlovian processes and play a role in avoidance behavior.

7. *Instrumental Processes in Avoidance.* Data obtained by Herrnstein and Hineline (1966), and previously described, indicate that long-term reduction in average shock density may serve to reinforce instrumental learning. This reinforcement seems to operate without the presence of a stimulus that acquires motivational significance through Pavlovian processes. It is interesting to note again that learning based on the Herrnstein-Hineline procedure seems to take an extraordinarily long time, requiring thousands of bar-presses and shock.

Extinction of Avoidance Behavior

Extinction in avoidance learning usually means the elimination of the shock for failure to respond. If the subject has become highly efficient at avoidance responding, it might be expected that some time would elapse before the subject would discover that an extinction contingency was in effect, and thus, the avoidance response would be quite resistant to extinction. Such a result has been found with dogs that were trained with very intense shocks in acquisition (Solomon & Wynn, 1954; *also see* Kimble, 1961, for a theoretical discussion of these data). Extinction usually proceeds in a regular fashion, and is affected in a straightforward manner by some familiar independent variables. For example, resistance to extinction seems to be directly related to the intensity of the shock used in acquisition (e.g., D'Amato, Fazzaro, & Etkin, 1967). If partial reinforcement is defined by the percentage of trials on which an avoidance response terminates the CS, then partially reinforced animals are more resistant to extinction than continuously reinforced subjects (Katzev & Enkema, 1973). However, if partial reinforcement is manipulated by shocking subjects on only a small percentage of trials on which they fail to respond during the CS–UCS interval, then both acquisition and extinction performance is poorer in partially reinforced than in continuously reinforced animals (Katzev & Enkema, 1973). It seems that more parametric research will have to be done before the generality of these findings will be understood.

III. PUNISHMENT

Punishment refers to the response-contingent application of an aversive stimulus (D'Amato, 1970). This definition stresses the idea that the aversive event is applied in relation to a specific response. Defined in this way, the term punishment is not synonymous with the term aversive stimulus itself. An aversive stimulus may be used as a punishment (i.e., its application may be made response contingent); or it may be used in some other way so as to promote escape or avoidance learning; or it may be applied independent of the subjects' behavior. This latter use will be considered in the next section of this chapter. In this section we shall be concerned with the response contingent application of an aversive event.

When punishment is used, the purpose of the punishing agent is usually to suppress or eliminate undesired behavior. Is punishment effective in doing this? For some time it was thought that punishment would lead to only a temporary and perhaps slight suppression of behavior (Thorndike, 1932; Estes, 1944; Skinner, 1953). However, now that a great deal more research has been accomplished, the evidence is quite strong that punishment can, under some conditions, produce nearly complete suppression of behavior and, in general, punishment is an effective way of controlling behavior (cf., Solomon, 1964). However, the effectiveness of punishment depends upon the conditions under which it is applied. We shall now review some of the conditions that are known to influence the effectiveness of punishment (for more complete reviews, *see* Campbell & Church, 1969; Fowler, 1971; Fantino, 1973).

Conditions Influencing Punishment

Intensity of Punishment

The more intense the punishment, the greater the suppression. This relationship has now been demonstrated a number of times (e.g., Azrin, 1960; Camp, Raymond, & Church, 1967). In the latter study, virtually total suppression of a bar-press response that was reinforced with food on a VI–1 schedule was found when the subjects (rats) were given a 2.0 milliampere shock for responding. In contrast, a 0.1 milliampere shock produced very little suppression and even this small amount of suppression seemed to go away as the animals had extensive experience with the shock.

Duration of Punishment

A variable that has effects much like intensity is duration of punishment. In general, the longer the duration of a punishment of a given intensity, the greater the suppression (Church, Raymond, & Beauchamp, 1967). In this study it was found that a 0.16 milliampere shock applied for 3.0 seconds led to virtually complete suppression of a bar-press response rewarded with food on a VI–1 minute schedule. Shocks of lesser duration (i.e., 1.0, 0.50, 0.30, and 0.15 seconds) produced less suppression, and in the case of the shorter duration punishments there was a tendency for suppression to recover with experience with the shock.

Degree of Deprivation

In the laboratory punishment is typically administered contingent upon responses that have been learned on the basis of food reward. In the examples mentioned above, we have noted that the punished subjects were responding on VI schedules for food. The question of interest here is, does the degree of food deprivation influence the effectiveness of punishment? In an investigation of this problem Azrin, Holz, and Hake (1963) trained pigeons on a VI–3 minute schedule of reinforcement with a food reward. During training, the subjects were reduced to 85 percent of their free-feeding weight. The suppressive effects of an intense electric shock applied after every hundredth response were examined with the pigeons at a

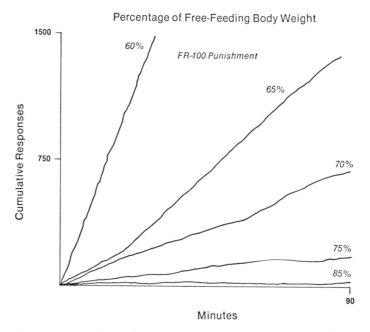

Figure 6–5. Effect of food deprivation (percent free-feeding body weight) on punished responding. The data are from a single pigeon responding on VI–3-minute schedule of food reinforcement and punished by a 160-volt shock on an FR–100 schedule. Delivery of shocks is indicated by the event marks on the cumulative curves. (From Azrin, Holz, & Hake, 1963, © Soc. Exp. Anal. Behavior.)

number of different body weights. It was found that the punishment was intense enough to produce complete suppression when the pigeons were run at the original level of 85 percent of their free-feeding weight. However, when the pigeons were made hungrier by reducing them to lower body weights (e.g., 75, 65, 60 percent) the shock had less suppressive effects; and in fact when the pigeons were at 60 percent of their free-feeding weight, they maintained a very high rate of responding despite the shock (*see* Figure 6–5).

These data indicate that the motivational level of the subject must be taken into account in assessing the suppressive effects of punishment. It appears that the more motivated the subject is, the less suppression will be obtained by a given aversive event. It would be expected that amount of reward would have effects similar to deprivation, only perhaps not to as great a degree.

Strength of Punished Response

Many drugs, such as alcohol or tranquilizers, that normally disrupt a learned task have much less of an effect if the task has been highly practiced. There is some evidence that punishment works in a similar fashion. For example, Miller (1961) found that an electric shock was more effective in disrupting running behavior in the runway if the rats had had relatively few training trials than it was after the rats had more extensive training. However, considerably more research will be needed before any complete understanding of this relationship will be available (cf., Born, 1967).

Schedules of Punishment

In perhaps the majority of punishment experiments the punishment has been administered after every response. However, in the Azrin et al. (1963) experiment described above, the pigeons were shocked after every hundredth response. It will be recognized that this is an FR–100 schedule of punishment. In this same experiment the effects of a number of other FR schedules of punishment were examined, and the results indicated that the more frequently punishment was administered (e.g., FR–1, FR–100, as opposed to FR–500, FR–1000) the greater the suppression. Thus, increasing the frequency of punishment has effects much like increasing the intensity or duration of punishment.

Gradual Introduction of Shock

Miller (1960) demonstrated that the suppressive effects of electric shock are attenuated if the shock is very gradually increased in stages across a large number of trials. After approximately 750 trials in a runway, a group that had experienced no shock was abruptly shifted to a 335-volt shock. A second group was also receiving a 335-volt shock at this time, but the shock had been gradually increased over most of the previous 750 trials. The suppression of running behavior was much greater in the group that had experienced the abrupt introduction to shock (*also see* Terris & Wechkin, 1967).

Delay of Punishment

Shock has much greater suppressive effects if applied immediately than if delayed (e.g., Kamin, 1959; Camp, Raymond, & Church, 1967). In this regard, the effects of punishment are much the same as the effects of reward (*see* Chapter 4, pp. 107–11). For example, Camp et al. (1967) found that the suppression of a lever-press response was only approximately half as great if punishment was delayed 30 seconds, as it was when punishment was administered immediately.

If subjects (apparently both rats and humans) are given a choice between immediate punishment and delayed punishment, they choose immediate punishment (e.g., Renner & Houlihan, 1969; Cook & Barnes, 1964).

There appears to be an interesting discrepancy between the greater suppressive effects of immediate punishment and the choice of immediate punishment. The greater suppressive effects of immediate punishment might be taken to mean that immediate punishment is more aversive than delayed punishment. However, this would not be consistent with the subject's choice for immediate over delayed punishment. How to resolve this discrepancy? D'Amato (1970) has suggested a couple of possible mechanisms. For one thing, there is considerable evidence that organisms prefer predictable to unpredictable aversive events. From this, it might be argued that an immediate shock is more predictable than a delayed shock, and thus preferred.

But, if delayed shock is more aversive (because it is unpredictable) than immediate shock, why does it produce less suppression of behavior? The answer here may be that the delay removes the aversive event from immediate contact with the behavior to be suppressed and allows for other behavior to intervene between the target response and the actual delivery of the shock. Thus, from the subject's point of view, there may be a difficult problem of discriminating exactly what response is being punished. For example, if an electric shock is delivered 30 seconds after the rat presses a lever, the rat may be nowhere in the vicinity of the lever; it may be engaged in some other unrelated behavior such as eating or grooming. These behaviors may be partly suppressed by the shock. The point is that punishment seems to suppress the behavior with which it is most contiguous.

Availability of Alternative Responses

The suppressive effects of punishment may be much greater if the subject has some alternative response to perform, which will also obtain its reward (Whiting & Mowrer, 1943); the animal's behavior simply shifts in the direction of the nonpunished alternative.

Cue Value of Punishment

If a shock is not too intense, it may be used as a cue to signal the availability of a positive reward. Under these conditions then, subjects may be trained to approach an electric shock. For example, electric shock for the correct response (in addition to food) may facilitate learning of a discrimination, and an electric shock may increase resistance to extinction (e.g., Pavlov, 1927; Meunzinger, Bernstone, & Richards, 1938; also Fowler, 1971 for a review of this literature).

Increased Persistence from Intermittent Punishment

If rats are punished on only some of the trials on which they also receive a food reward, their resistance to continuous punishment is enhanced. For example, in an experiment by Banks (1966) rats were first trained to run in a straight runway for a food reward. Following this, the animals were divided into two groups, and one of these groups received a shock on a randomly selected 3 of the 10 daily trials. The 0.32 milliampere footshock applied for 0.1 seconds was delivered just as the rat touched the food reward. The second group of rats never received shock during this stage of the experiment. After 80 trials of such training, all rats were shifted to continuous shock. The results of this experiment are presented in Figure 6–6.

It can be seen that the introduction of intermittent punishment in Stage 2 of the experiment had the effect of temporarily slowing down the shocked rats. However, they seemed to be recovering from this effect as the third stage of the experiment was started. In this third stage, it can be readily seen that the transition to continuous shock had a much greater disruptive effect on the rats without prior experience with intermittent shock. Similar effects of intermittent punishment have been found in other studies, and in some cases this

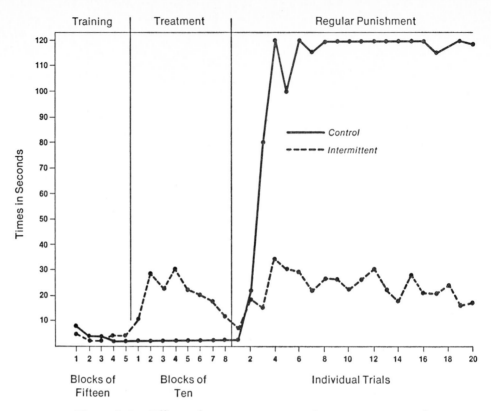

Figure 6–6. Effects of prior experience with intermittent punishment on later exposure to continuous punishment. In the first phase of the experiment (training) both groups are given only food rewards; in the second phase (treatment) the group labeled intermittent was exposed to intermittent punishment; in the third phase of the experiment both groups were exposed to continuous punishment. (From Banks, 1966.)

increased persistence has been found to generalize to aversive stimuli other than the ones used in original training (e.g., Banks & Torney, 1969; Terris & Barnes, 1969).

These effects of intermittent punishment on later experience with continuous punishment are similar to the effects that experience with intermittent reward has on later experience with extinction (continuous nonreward). This similarity is also evident in the results of studies which have directly examined the effects of experience with intermittent punishment on later extinction. These experiments regularly find that such experience with intermittent punishment produces increased resistance to extinction (e.g., Logan, 1960; Fallon, 1968, 1969; Linden, 1974).

If intermittent punishment increases resistance to the effects of both continuous punishment and continuous nonreward, it is reasonable to ask whether the increased persistence also works the other way. That is, will experience with intermittent nonreward produce increased resistance to punishment? This question has also been addressed in several experiments (e.g., Brown & Wagner, 1964; Linden & Hallgren, 1973) and the answer is yes. The performance of rats under conditions of either extinction (Panel A) or continuous punishment (Panel B) after different types of acquisition experience is shown in Figure 6–7. It can be seen that the rats that had experienced continuous reinforcement (CRF) in acquisition were the least resistant to extinction; these were followed by rats that had experienced intermittent punishment (P) in acquisition, and in turn, by rats that had experienced partial reinforcement (N) in acquisition. Thus, experience with intermittent punishment produced increased resistance to extinction, but not as much as direct experience with intermittent nonreward.

Examining Panel B of the figure, we can see that experience with continuous reinforcement (CRF) led to rapid suppression when continuous punishment was introduced, but prior experience with either intermittent reward (N) or intermittent punishment (P) afforded some degree of protection from the effects of continuous punishment. The transfer from intermittent punishment to continuous punishment was greater than the transfer from intermittent nonreward to continuous punishment. Thus, there is a symmetry to the increased persistence produced by intermittent punishment and intermittent nonreward.

What accounts for this relationship between punishment and nonreward? We do not have the space to go into much detail here, but we will mention theoretical considerations offered by Martin (1963) and by Wagner (1969). Basically, it is argued that partial punishment and partial nonreward must have something in common because the effects of one transfer and influence the other. One possible mechanism for explaining the similarity between punishment and nonreward is to assume that both conditions lead to similar emotional responses; frustration in the case of nonreward, and fear or pain in the case of electric-shock punishment. It is the similarity of these emotional responses that accounts for the transfer demonstrated by Brown and Wagner (1964) and by Linden and Hallgren (1973).

As for the persistence effects themselves, we have already covered Amsel's theory of the partial reinforcement extinction effect (*see* Chapter 5, pp. 120–26). Others (e.g., Martin, 1963; Banks, 1966) have suggested that a simple extension of Amsel's theory substituting fear or pain for frustration would be sufficient to handle the

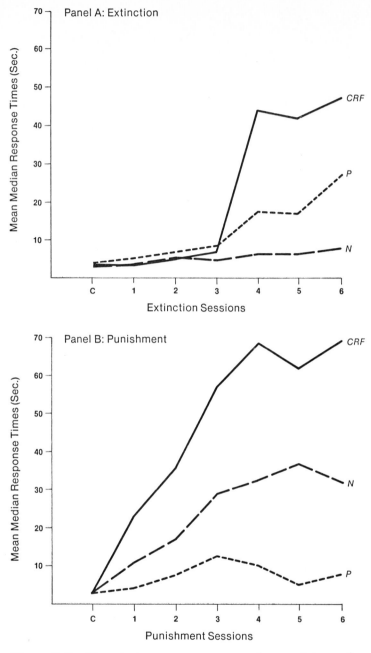

Figure 6–7. Time to traverse a runway under conditions of extinction (Panel A) or punishment (Panel B) for groups of rats differing in their prior experience with intermittent punishment (P), intermittent nonreward (N), or continuous reward (CRF). (From Linden & Hallgren, 1973.)

demonstrated effects of intermittent punishment. For example, the rats that experienced intermittent shock in Figure 6–6 were less influenced by shock on every trial because they had previously associated anticipatory fear with the performance of the instrumental response. Interested readers may refer to Chapter 5 and pursue the articles by Martin and Wagner for further details.

IV. CONDITIONED SUPPRESSION

Under some conditions the presentation of an aversive event that is *not* contingent upon a response may still lead to the suppression of ongoing instrumental behavior. The experimental procedure used to investigate this behavior generally takes the following form: First, rats are trained to press a lever on a schedule of positive reward (usually a VI). Once a stable rate of responding has been established, a stimulus (e.g., a tone or light) that eventually will be used as a CS is presented a couple of times during a training session. The purpose of this procedure is to determine the suppressing effects of the novel stimulus. Typically, the suppressing effects of the stimulus are minor and habituate so that the stimulus presentation has no effect on the rate of responding.

The next step in the procedure is the introduction of the UCS, usually shock. Several times during a training session the CS is presented for a relatively long duration (1–3 minutes) and is immediately followed by the UCS. This procedure regularly leads to a decline in the lever-pressing rate during the CS–UCS interval. It is this decline that gives the paradigm the name of *conditioned suppression*. In interpreting the results of these experiments, it is important to remember that the subjects are not shocked for pressing the lever per se. The shock is presented independently of the subject's behavior—it is this fact that distinguishes this paradigm from punishment (which by definition, is response contingent).

If the subjects are not directly punished for pressing the lever in these experiments, and if the subjects are food deprived and can obtain food rewards by pressing the lever, the question arises as to why they stop pressing the lever when the CS is presented. The prevalent interpretation is that an emotional state of fear is conditioned to the CS by virtue of its contingent presentation with the shock and that this fear state, once aroused by the CS, is incompatible with the regular performance of a food-motivated instrumental response (cf., Maier, Seligman, & Solomon, 1969; McAllister & McAllister, 1971). Thus, the suppression is interpreted to be the result of a Pavlovian conditioned response (fear) interfering with an instrumentally conditioned response (lever-pressing). It is this interpretation that has led to the term *conditioned emotional response* (CER) to be used synonymously with conditioned suppression in describing this paradigm.

Conditioned suppression is influenced in a relatively straightforward way by a number of variables, for example:

1. The greater the shock intensity, the greater the suppression (Annau & Kamin, 1961).
2. A delayed conditioning paradigm produces more suppression than a trace conditioning paradigm, but good conditioning (as measured by suppression) can be obtained with long CS–UCS intervals (Kamin, 1965).
3. The greater the stimulus change associated with CS onset, the greater the suppression (Kamin, 1965).

A more detailed discussion of the variables influencing conditioned suppression may be found in the McAllister and McAllister (1971) paper.

In considering the conditioned fear interpretation of the suppression that occurs in this paradigm, the reader may have wondered about some possible alternative explanations. For example, is it not possible that lever-pressing is suppressed because some of the shocks delivered at the termination of the CS actually come when the subject is pressing the lever and, therefore, actually punish lever-pressing? This interpretation can be ruled out by giving the CS–UCS pairings entirely outside of the lever-pressing situation. When this is done, the CS is then superimposed in the lever-pressing situation, and suppression is still obtained (e.g., Kamin, Brimer, & Black, 1963).

If we can assume that the suppression obtained is not due to the punishment of the instrumental response and is due to fear elicited by the CS, how does this assumed fear response actually influence lever-pressing? One possibility is that the fear state directly elicits responses such as crouching or freezing that interfere with bar-pressing. If the rat is crouching down, it cannot go over and press the lever. It is also possible that the subject adopts behaviors that tend to reduce the impact of the shock, and that these behaviors compete with the response of approaching and pressing the lever. This possibility is consistent with the preparatory response interpretation of Pavlovian conditioning discussed in Chapter 3, (*see* pp. 69–72). The relative contributions of innately elicited competing responses and preparatory competing responses have not yet been determined, but it seems likely that some such combination will account for the conditioned suppression obtained in this paradigm.

V. LEARNED HELPLESSNESS

In Pavlovian conditioning the CS and UCS are presented independently of the subject's behavior. We have just seen that if a CS associated with shock is presented in an appetitive situation, instrumental responding tends to be suppressed. By contrast, the presentation of a discriminative Pavlovian CS for shock enhances instrumental avoidance responding.

There is another research paradigm in which unavoidable and inescapable shocks are found to influence later instrumental behavior. The basic procedure in this paradigm is as follows: Animals (typically dogs) are given a series of intense and long-duration (e.g., 5 seconds) shocks that they can neither escape nor avoid. A day or so after this, the dogs are placed in a two-compartment avoidance apparatus and two-way avoidance training is initiated. The avoidance performance of dogs so treated is very poor compared to animals without the prior experience with inescapable shock. In one experiment (Overmier & Seligman, 1967), it was found that the average escape latency of dogs pretreated with long inescapable shock was 54 seconds, and 5 out of 8 dogs never escaped at all. Comparable figures for dogs without the inescapable shock experience were 22 seconds and 1 out of 8 dogs.

In considering the results over a number of experiments, Seligman, Maier, and Solomon (1971) report that approximately 63 percent of dogs given the uncontrollable shock experience generally fail to escape in later training tasks, whereas in untreated dogs the figure is approximately 6 percent. The failure of the treated dogs to escape is apparently not due to an insensitivity to shock. These dogs have been described as being active on the first presentations of shock in the avoidance apparatus, but on later shock presentations they tend to just "take the shock," sometimes whimpering. This bizarre behavior has been termed "learned helplessness" and we shall describe some of the conditions which seem to influence this behavior and some of the evidence relevant to the interpretation of the behavior. Our presentation will closely follow the review by Seligman et al. (1971).

Learned helplessness is most likely to occur either in two-way avoidance tasks or in situations such as a bar-press avoidance or a wheel-turn where the subject has to manipulate the environment. It does not seem to occur in one-way avoidance tasks. Prior experience with inescapable shock either has no effect on later one-way avoidance training or may actually facilitate it. It is also possible that prior inescapable shock experience may facilitate passive avoidance learning, although the data seem somewhat inconclusive at the present time.

There have been a number of interpretations offered for this effect of prior inescapable shock. For example, it is possible to think that the dogs might somehow get "adapted" to the shock during pretreatment so that it is not as intense and aversive during avoidance learning. However, there is considerable evidence against this interpretation: (1) the pretraining shocks are very intense; (2) Overmier and Seligman (1967) reported that their dogs did not appear to be adapted in that they showed overt signs of emotional behavior such as vocalizations and defecation; (3) increasing the intensity of the shock in the avoidance training phase does not help; (4) prior experience with *escapable* shock does *not* lead to helpless behavior in a two-way avoidance situation as the adaptation interpretation might predict.

Another interpretation is that the dogs may learn certain behaviors when they are given inescapable training, and these behaviors later compete with the performance of escape and avoidance responses. Although plausible, this interpretation seems unlikely in the light of evidence that dogs paralyzed during the inescapable training phase by curare still show the helplessness effect (Overmier & Seligman, 1967). The paralysis would seem to rule out the learning of competing responses.

Another interpretation is that the dogs may be "emotionally exhausted" after the experience with inescapable shock, and thus unable to perform in the avoidance task. Some support for this idea comes from the finding in several early studies that the helpless behavior pattern seems to be transient and that it is not found if a few days are allowed to elapse between a session of inescapable shock training and later avoidance training. However, there is also evidence that argues against this interpretation. For example, if more than one session of inescapable shock experience is given and/or if laboratory-reared dogs are used, then the helplessness effect persists over many days (Seligman & Groves, 1970; Seligman, Rosellini, & Kozak, 1975). Secondly, escape training given prior to the experience with inescapable shock seems to eliminate the helplessness effect. It is not clear why prior escape training should alleviate emotional exhaustion.

Still another interpretation is that learned helplessness may be due to a depletion of brain norepinephrine (a neurotransmitter) as a result of the inescapable shock experience (Weiss, Stone, & Harrel, 1970). While there is evidence that receiving a large number of inescapable shocks does lower brain norepinephrine level (Weiss et al., 1970), it seems unlikely that this would account for learned helplessness or the variables that influence it. For example, there is little reason to think that exposing a "helpless" animal to the avoidance contingency by dragging it through the apparatus would restore norepinephrine levels, yet this treatment "cures" helplessness. Similarly, there is little reason to think that exposing an animal to escapable shock prior to exposing it to inescapable shock would prevent the depletion of norepinephrine, yet this prior treatment serves to "immunize" a rat or dog from the helplessness syndrome (Seligman & Beagley, 1975).

Finally, the interpretation favored by Seligman et al. (1971, 1975) is based on an associative process. Seligman believes that the subjects actually learn that they are helpless in the experimental situation. Some of the evidence in favor of this interpretation is the evidence cited just above. That is, dogs given experience first with escapable shock seem to be protected from the deleterious effects of experience with inescapable shock. Perhaps they are so protected because they learn first that there are situations under which their behavior may have some control over an aversive environment.

A second piece of evidence is that the helplessness may be eventually overcome if the experimenter simply drags the dogs back and forth in the avoidance apparatus, thus exposing them to the existence of the escape and avoidance contingencies (Seligman, Maier, & Geer, 1968). This treatment is reminiscent of our earlier discussion of the importance of the anticipatory response in avoidance learning. At that time we remarked that any treatment that increases the probability of an anticipatory response should enhance avoidance learning. The treatment we are discussing here, prior inescapable shock, appears to have the effect of virtually eliminating anticipatory responses (cf., Anisman & Waller, 1973), and thus the animal is not in a position to detect the existence of an avoidance contingency. However, the failure of anticipatory responses to occur is probably not the only story here, for it has been sometimes observed that a pretreated dog will make an escape response, but it is unlikely to repeat it.

A third piece of evidence is that cage-reared animals, that is, animals without a history of control over their environment, seem to be more susceptible to the helplessness syndrome than noncage-reared animals.

The learned helplessness hypothesis has strong cognitive connotations, and it is also consistent with Rescorla's view of the kind of learning that may take place in Pavlovian conditioning when a truly random control group is used (see Chapter 3, pp. 73–75). Recall that when a CS and UCS are presented independently of one another, animals appear to learn that they are not related—that the

CS does not help predict the occurrence of the UCS. In the learned helplessness situation, the dogs may learn that the occurrence of the shocks is independent of their behavior, that there is nothing that they can do about shock. The hypothesis is interesting and it is tempting to jump from these behaviors of dogs to possibly similar behavior patterns that occur in depressed humans. However, it is recognized that considerably more research must be done before we understand the factors controlling learned helplessness in animals.

VI. SUMMARY

In this chapter we have considered data and theories arising from the study of behavior in situations in which the organism is confronted with an aversive stimulus. We have seen that animals can generally learn to readily escape from a noxious stimulus and this escape behavior is influenced in a relatively straightforward way by a number of variables.

We have also seen that lower animals can apparently learn to avoid the impending occurrence of a noxious event, and this ability of lower animals has generated a good deal of theoretical effort in attempts to explain the behavior. To a large extent the theoretical interest in avoidance learning arose from the apparent incompatibility between this behavior and the dominant behavioristic orientation of explanation in animal behavior, i.e., that animals do not anticipate the outcome of their actions. Current theoretical approaches seem to favor a combination of biological predispositions inherent in different species and the utilization of the informational aspects of stimulus change produced by the performance of a successful avoidance response.

In this chapter we have also reviewed how behavior is suppressed by the response contingent application of a noxious stimulus (punishment) and by the nonresponse contingent application of aversive stimuli (the conditioned suppression paradigm). We have seen that, contrary to some theoretical speculations of the recent past, punishment can be a very effective way of controlling the behavior of organisms. Exactly how effective punishment is depends upon the parameters of its application. Instrumental behavior is also suppressed by the presentation of a Pavlovian CS that had been previously paired with a noxious event. The suppression occurring in this paradigm may be more general than that occurring with punishment and may be due to an emotional response and/or behaviors elicited by the CS that are incompatible with the ongoing instrumental behavior.

Finally, we briefly reviewed the phenomenon of learned helplessness—the experimental paradigm in which the exposure of animals to inescapable shock interferes with their later ability to learn an escape response. This paradigm, like avoidance learning, has generated a good deal of theoretical effort and, at the present time, the data seem to be compatible with Seligman's interpretation that animals so treated may have learned that they have no control over their environment, at least in that situation, so that when the opportunity for control is present they do not profit from it.

CHAPTER *7*

Control of the Internal Environment

*The palate reels like a wronged lover. Was all
that sweetness counterfeit?*

Erica Jong

In the previous chapters we have gone into considerable detail to discuss the basic mechanisms that allow the organism to cope with the outside world. We have noted, in the case of classical conditioning, that the organism has the capability to learn, and hence to anticipate, the relationship between contiguous events in the external environment. Although by definition the organism cannot alter these relationships, this type of learning allows the organism to indulge in two rather basic luxuries, preparedness and prediction.

The second basic type of learning which we considered in detail was instrumental learning. It is in this type of learning that the so-called higher organisms excel, being able to engage in complex *manipulations* of the external world such that the environment can, to a large extent, be controlled to meet the demands or the whims of the organism.

In the present chapter we shall consider the mechanisms by which the organism monitors and manipulates the *internal* environment. We will demonstrate that the naive organism is, under many conditions, capable of rejecting a poison or finding a cure, of selecting a diet or generating a mood. In short, we shall see that the central nervous system of the organism is directing a finely orchestrated interaction between the outside world and the inside world. The mass of data that has been collected during the past decade or so belies the traditional view that the internal environment is strictly (and simply) under the control of reflexes.

I. CONDITIONED AVERSIONS

Ever since man began living in groups and storing foodstuffs, the rat has been considered one of the most dreaded animals. The rat is an omnivore and is capable of gnawing through all but the hardest materials used for containers in which to store food. Once the rat has reached a source of food, the amount which is actually consumed is almost negligible when compared to the amount which he scatters, soils, exposes to the elements, and otherwise damages. Consequently, man and rat have coexisted for centuries despite man's persistent attempts to eradicate the destroyer of food.

In his attempts to eradicate the rat, man has tried countless traps, barriers, and natural enemies, all of which worked effectively against some of the rats. None of them worked against all of the rats, and it has been suggested by Barnett (1963) that those remaining may have passed on to their offspring genetic characteristics which made them innately wary of any strange object in their environment.

Perhaps the most persistent means which man has used in his attempts to place the rat on the endangered species list has been poisoning. If the rat insists upon eating the food that man has stored, then the logical way to eliminate the rat is to place poisoned food in areas where the rat is sure to find it. But poisoning was only effective in reducing the rat population, not in eliminating it. Those rats which escaped death following their first meal of the poisonous substance refused to eat that particular food again, regardless of its palatability. Even modern-day poisons that are lethal in minute quantities are seldom effective in eliminating a population of rats.

This uncanny ability of the rat to avoid sources of poisonous foods has been known for many years and has been given the descriptive name of *bait shyness*. Perhaps because of a reluctance to admit that the rat was not to be outsmarted, the phenomenon of bait shyness traditionally has been considered a challenge to be overcome rather than a lesson from which to learn. The students of behavior who finally recognized the lesson were John Garcia and Robert A. Koelling who, in 1966, published an article which clearly demonstrated that the phenomenon of bait shyness (which is now usually referred to as *conditioned aversion*) is an interesting type of learning. These findings have opened the door to previously unsuspected areas of learning research, have shed light on areas which have been a source of confusion for years, and have seriously challenged some of our fundamental "laws" of learning.

Basic Procedures

A critical observation which greatly facilitated the experimental investigation of the bait-shyness phenomenon was that the poisonous agent itself need not necessarily be a part of the food being ingested. It was found, for example (Haley & Snyder, 1964), that ionizing radiation when paired with flavored but nonpoisonous fluids resulted in a subsequent aversion to that particular flavor.

Similarly, numerous later studies have employed injections of drugs following food or fluid consumption to show similar effects. The results of these experiments suggested a similarity to the more conventional Pavlovian conditioning procedures. According to this analysis, the flavored substance serves as the CS, the irradiation and poisoning serve as the UCS, and the gastrointestinal illness is the UCR. Because of the temporal pairing of these stimuli, subsequent presentations of the CS lead to an avoidance response (i.e., the rat does not consume the substance). But, is this really the same type of conditioning as shown in a standard shock avoidance procedure?

In a series of experiments which has become a landmark in this area of research, Garcia and Koelling (1966) made direct attempts to compare conventional avoidance paradigms with conditioned aversion paradigms. In one of these experiments, the rats were pretested to determine the intake of either flavored (saccharin) water or "bright-noisy" water under standard conditions. The so-called "bright-noisy" water was produced by using a drinkometer circuit such that whenever the rat licked the drinking tube, an electromechanical relay would click and a light would flash. Thus, in one case the CS was impinging upon interoceptive (taste) receptors and in the other case, upon exteroceptive (visual and auditory) receptors. In both instances, the drinking session was followed by X-irradiation. Subsequent tests showed an aversion to drinking the flavored water, but no change in consumption of the water which was accompanied by the audio-visual stimuli.

In a parallel experiment, electric shock to the paws was used as the aversive stimulus and directly opposing results were obtained: The electric shock was quite effective in suppressing the sub-

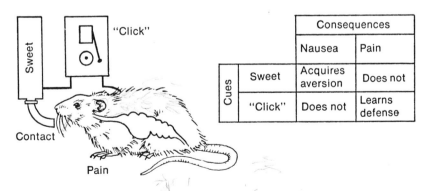

		Consequences	
		Nausea	Pain
Cues	Sweet	Acquires aversion	Does not
	"Click"	Does not	Learns defense

Figure 7–1. The effects of pairing a gustatory cue or an auditory cue with external pain or internal illness. (Based on Garcia & Koelling, 1966, and redrawn from Garcia et al., 1973; courtesy of Plenum Press.)

sequent intake of bright-noisy water, but was ineffective in producing an aversion to flavored water.

The results of these experiments (*see* Figure 7–1) provided a dramatic demonstration that the effectiveness of a stimulus to serve as a CS can depend heavily upon the consequences of the reinforcer. More specifically, stimuli which arise from the external environment may tend to be associated with consequences of the external environment, whereas stimuli arising from the internal environment may tend to be associated with consequences of the internal environment. As Garcia and Koelling (1966) expressed it, natural selection may have favored mechanisms which allow the sick organism to postulate, "It must have been something I ate."

It should be noted at this point that anecdotal data abound to indicate that similar phenomena occur in humans. Nearly everyone has an aversion to some particular food and, in many cases, the onset of the aversion can be related to an ensuing illness. The illness may have been the result of actual contamination of the food or, more commonly, the result of a chance association with the onset of some unrelated malady which produced gastrointestinal disturbance. Interestingly, the conscious knowledge that the food itself was not contaminated has little or no ameliorating effect on the subsequent conditioned aversion (cf., Seligman & Hager, 1972).

Temporal Parameters

One of the difficulties which learning theorists encountered in their attempts to assimilate this conditioned aversion phenomenon into a traditional framework was that the onset of the aversive gastrointestinal consequences (the UCR) frequently does not occur for several hours following the consumption and taste of the food (the CS). How could learning take place with such long delays?[1] Numerous experiments had already shown that in conventional learning situations learning was difficult, if not impossible, to establish with delays of more than a few seconds interposed between the CS and UCS (*see* Chapter 4). In those cases in which learning following delays had been demonstrated, it was always

---

1. It should be noted that the nature of the stimuli in the conditioned aversion paradigm allow the definition of two different delays. The CS–UCS delay is identical to that defined in traditional learning situations; the CS (usually taste) is followed at some later time by the UCS (a procedure that leads to illness). In addition, it is necessary to consider the UCS–UCR interval; there is typically a delay ranging from several minutes to several hours between the time of the treatment and the onset of the visceral disturbance. The only parallel in traditional learning situations is the conduction time (usually a fraction of a second) of the nerve fibers that conduct the impulses for the unconditioned response.

possible to show that some mediating chain of stimuli was available to bridge the gap. Several possible explanations were advanced to account for this apparent exception in the case of conditioned aversion. One plausible explanation was that the taste stimuli associated with the ingested substance have long-lasting aftereffects to bridge the gap between the initial taste and the subsequent gastrointestinal disorder. Another possibility was that the initial stages of the aversive post-ingestive state began within a short time and gradually built up to a peak at some later time. A third possibility, which was not taken seriously by many, was that this type of learning is simply different and can actually occur with very long delays. As we shall see, virtually all the available data support this latter alternative.

The first convincing demonstration that learning could occur after long CS–UCS intervals was again provided by Garcia and his associates (1972). In this experiment, rats consumed a saccharin solution which was followed after delays of 30, 45, 75, 120 or 180 minutes by an injection of apomorphine, a substance which produces severe gastrointestinal symptoms in humans. As shown in Figure 7–2, substantial aversion was produced with delays of up to 75 minutes. Clearly, this delay could not have been bridged by the early cues associated with the onset of the visceral disturbance—the substance which produced the internal malaise was not intro-

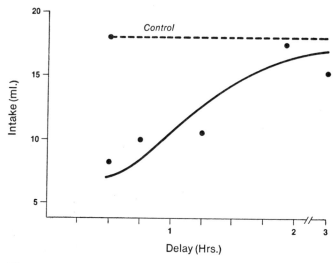

Figure 7–2. Mean fluid intake of saccharin-flavored water on the first extinction day, following five conditioned pairings of saccharin and apomorphine for groups differing in delay of injection. (From Garcia et al., 1973; courtesy of Plenum Press.)

duced until *after* the delay had elapsed. This type of finding has since been reported many times and there is no doubt as to the validity of the phenomenon. But what about the first possibility listed above? Is it not possible that the taste of the substance may have lingered throughout the interval to bridge the gap between the initial taste and the illness?

Those who were skeptical of this type of delayed learning challenged Garcia and his coworkers to provide evidence that the lingering taste was not serving as a mediator. Although this is a more difficult argument to repudiate, there are a number of rather clever experiments which suggest that prolonged taste factors are not essential to this phenomenon, although they could contribute to the phenomenon under some conditions. One experiment (*see* Garcia, McGowan, & Green, 1972) which attempted to answer this question utilized a flavor which does not have the long-lasting aftertastes that are characteristic of the more commonly used saccharin and quinine. The flavor was the slightly sour taste of a dilute hydrochloric acid solution. This dilute HCl solution was, of course, mixed with the much more concentrated secretions of the stomach, so that one cannot argue that the circulating substance was stimulating the taste receptors via the blood stream. Furthermore, the rats had been deprived of food, and after the drinking session they were allowed access to dry food pellets for one hour, which almost certainly would eliminate any residual taste of the solution from the mouth. In spite of all of these precautions to prevent aftertastes, the rats showed a strong aversion to the HCl solution upon subsequent presentation.

Equally convincing evidence has been provided by Rozin (1969) who demonstrated that rats were capable of developing a conditioned aversion to a specific *concentration* of a substance (either higher or lower) even though the injection of the aversive apomorphine followed 30 minutes later. Since the same substance was involved in both cases, it is difficult to argue that differing aftertastes were involved. Thus, we are left with the almost inescapable conclusion that this type of learning can be established with real delays of up to several hours interposed between the CS and UCS. As Garcia, McGowan, and Green (1972) have stated:

> Admittedly, the notion that ingestion produces a chain of stimulus events which bridge the long CS–UCS interval is one that is difficult to exclude with complete conviction. But even if this were the case, gustatory-visceral conditioning would still be difficult to understand in S–R terms. No one would expect to establish avoidance responses in a few trials if a tone was turned on (and left on) and electric shock was delivered hours later; not even if a symphony of tones were used to bridge the CS–UCS interval (p. 15).

The clear implication here is that some *central* mediating event is used to bridge the delay. In other words, we can think of the CS as initiating some process which later allows the organism to pair this information with the postingestive consequences. We will now consider some of the parameters which determine the effectiveness of the CS in initiating this process.

It should be noted that some recent evidence suggests that foot-shock can be associated with flavors under certain carefully controlled conditions. Krane and Wagner (1975) found that footshock presented immediately after a novel taste was ineffective, but if presented several minutes later, led to some conditioned aversion to the taste. If these initial findings are confirmed, it may mean that the apparent dichotomy is not between visceral learning with internal cues and exteroceptive learning with external cues as suggested by Garcia and his associates. Rather, the implication would be that internal cues are more readily associated with events that occur following relatively long intervals, whereas external cues are more readily associated with events that follow immediately. In view of the bulk of the data that have been collected to date, it seems likely that Krane and Wagner's data will only place some limitations on the cue-to-consequences notion, rather than replacing it.

CS Parameters

In the last section we have seen strong evidence that conditioned aversions can be established with long intervals interposed between the CS and the UCS. In this respect, the ability to associate two temporally disparate stimuli seems superior to the more conventional learning processes which are drastically impaired by intervals of even a few seconds between stimuli. We are tempted to ask what sort of evolutionary pressures have been active to place such severe temporal limitations on the conventional learning mechanism. The answer, as Garcia has pointed out repeatedly, is rather obvious. In the external environment, events which are causally related and of importance to the organism almost always occur in a close temporal sequence. The snap of the twig signals only the immediate presence of an intruder, not the presence of an intruder scheduled to appear several hours later. Similarly, the sting of the bee, a very potent UCS, is associated only with the immediately preceding buzzing noise and not with some equally distinct noise such as the roar of the lion which was heard two hours earlier. If these signals were associated retroactively to stimuli which had been present minutes or hours earlier, virtually all of the associations would be meaningless, and the organism would have no valid information about the relationships of the components of the external environment.

By contrast, the events of the internal environment tend to proceed much more slowly. Virtually none of the poisonous substances in the natural habitat of the organism act immediately, only a few act within seconds, and most require several minutes or hours before they produce noticeable internal distress. Given these limitations, it is clear that a mechanism which did not span these intervals would be of virtually no value to the organism. But this mechanism is not without its liabilities.

For the omnivorous organism which spends much of its time searching for and consuming various types of food, it is almost inevitable that poisonous substances will occasionally be encountered. Given the long intervals over which the ensuing illness can be associated with tastes, would we not expect aversions to be established toward all of the foods which had been consumed during the previous several hours? Pushing this point even further, would we not expect the organism to eventually develop aversions to virtually all of the foodstuffs in its environments because of chance associations with poisonous substances or naturally occurring illnesses? The development of such nonspecific associations would be clearly maladaptive, and it should come as no surprise that safeguards against such occurrences have been built into this learning mechanism. The specificity of the associations formed seems to be based primarily upon the characteristics of the taste, or CS.

The ability of a particular foodstuff to serve as the CS in a conditioned aversion paradigm does not seem to be related to particular classes of tastes per se; a large variety of different tastes have been utilized successfully in this paradigm. A much more crucial variable seems to be the novelty of the substance being consumed. In general, the more novel the substance (i.e., the less experience the organism has had with the substance), the easier it is to demonstrate a conditioned aversion to that substance (*see* Table 7–1). This novelty effect seems to easily overpower recency. For example, if a rat is given a novel substance to eat, then one hour later given access to its regular diet, which is followed by the injection of a poisonous substance, subsequent tests will show that a strong conditioned aversion to the novel substance has been developed, while the intake of the regular diet will remain unchanged (cf., Revusky and Bedarf, 1967, for specific examples).

We are reminded once again of what Cannon (1932) has referred to as the "wisdom of the body." Under most naturalistic circumstances it is much more probable that illness will be the result of a novel food rather than the regular diet. In fact, wild rats show a rather interesting phenomenon known as *neophobia*, or a fear of new things (*see* Barnett, 1963). Not only are they generally reluctant to approach new objects in their environment (e.g., traps), but they show considerable caution in the consumption of a new food substance which becomes available. Upon the first encounter with a new substance, they will consume only a small amount and wait several hours before consuming more of the substance. It is as though the rat were waiting to see if the small sample of the substance produced an illness before making it part of the regular diet.

*Table 7–1. Proportion of Rats Requiring More Time to Drink the Novel Fluid Than the Familiar Fluid on the Day of Conditioning (both experiments)**

Novel Food	Familiar Food	Proportion
Sucrose	Milk	0.417
Milk	Sucrose	.958
Grape juice	Milk	.958
Milk	Grape juice	.917

*Except when sucrose was novel, each proportion shown was reliably greater than the chance level of .500 ($p < .001$, sign test). (Adapted from Revusky and Bedarf, 1967, © Am. Assoc. Adv. Science.)

Given this selective attention to the consequences of novel food substances, what happens if the regular diet somehow becomes contaminated? Will the rat then fail to show a conditioned aversion and perish? The answer is usually no. Although the technique of initially providing unpoisoned bait has been used with some success in attempts to increase the probability of consuming an overdose, once the poison has been added, sublethal dosages are still followed by conditioned aversion, especially if no novel foods have been consumed during the interim. Perhaps the best way to convey both the ability to establish conditioned aversions to a common substance and the exquisite discriminations of taste which can be established is to review the initial observations of Garcia, Ervin, and Koelling (1966) which led to their investigation of the phenomenon of conditioned aversion.

As is frequently the case in scientific discovery, the crucial observations were made in the context of a relatively unrelated set of experiments. In this case, Garcia was investigating the physiological effects of various dosages of X-irradiation. Because the animals were required to spend a considerable amount of time in the X-ray chamber each day, food and water were supplied in both the experimental chamber and the home cage. A peculiar effect was observed—over the course of the experiment, the rats that received substantial dosages of X-irradiation began to show a large decrease in food and water intake while in the test chamber; but they consumed more than normal amounts in the home cage, even though the temporal parameters of the illness are such that the peak of the disturbance occurred in the home cage.

The effects of novelty and indeed the more general implications of conditioned aversion were not known at that time, but the appropriate conclusion was reached that conditioned aversion was involved. Somewhat later, the detailed basis of this effect was discovered. Because of size limitations in the test chamber, a small plastic centrifuge tube was used instead of the standard glass water bottle. Later, informal tests showed that the rats had actually learned to discriminate between water which had been allowed to sit in a plastic container overnight and water which had been stored in a glass container. The very subtle taste of plastic in the common substance water had been associated with the illness produced by the X-irradiation. (Although there is obviously the possibility that the rats learned not to drink in a particular place, more recent data do not support this view.)

This discussion has emphasized the important role of taste cues because of their importance to mammalian species. It should be noted, however, that other organisms may be especially adapted to utilize other sensory modalities. The principal dietary selections of grain-eating birds are encased in a hard outer shell that is usually not broken down until it reaches the crop, and therefore such seeds provide little information via taste factors. Accordingly, it would be more advantageous to utilize visual cues. Consistent with this notion is the observation that the quail will acquire a stronger conditioned aversion to colored water than to water having a particular taste; rats show the opposite pattern (Wilcoxin, Dragoin & Kral, 1971).

UCS Parameters

On the basis of the preceding discussion, one might speculate that any substance which produces a visceral disturbance could be used as the UCS in a conditioned aversion paradigm. In general, this would appear to be an appropriate conclusion. As we have mentioned, X-irradiation produces nausea and general gastric disturbances and is a very effective UCS. One of the most potent compounds which has been used in the investigation of conditioned aversions is the poisonous salt, lithium chloride. If it is either ingested voluntarily or injected into the organism, the lithium ions appear to displace sodium ions (obtained from sodium chloride, or table salt) which are involved in numerous physiological mechanisms. The result is a very generalized symptomology and, if taken in sufficient dosages, death may result. For the purposes of conditioned aversion experiments, the dosages employed are typically far below the lethal threshold.

In spite of the effectiveness of the techniques outlined above, it may not be safe to conclude that the UCS *necessarily* must be a poison which leads to aversive visceral states. A wide range of compounds, including barbiturates, tranquilizers, amphetamines, and even belladonna alkaloids (which are often used clinically to *relieve* gastric distress), have been found to be more or less effective in producing conditioned aversion. It is perhaps safer to conclude that any substance which produces an unusual visceral effect is likely to have the potential to serve as the UCS for conditioned aversion, even though the substances are not poisonous, in the traditional sense.

Although there have been no formal attempts to order these compounds in terms of their effectiveness, it is clear that certain of these compounds are less effective than others. In general, the basis for stating that some compounds are less effective than others is related to the number of pairings of the taste with the aversive agent which are required to produce a certain amount of suppression of intake. Only those compounds which induce severe illness are capable of producing a near-total suppression after only one pairing with a particular substance. Those which produce only marginal disturbances may require numerous pairings before the intake of the substance is substantially reduced. These relationships are further complicated by the novelty of the foodstuffs which are offered; the pairing of a regular component of the diet with even a powerful UCS may not result in conditioned aversion until after several pairings.

Some Peculiarities of Conditioned Aversion

We have discussed the phenomenon of conditioned aversion as a somewhat specialized type of learning which shares many of the characteristics of conventional learning while retaining some rather major differences. The similarities include the importance of having a relatively mild, novel stimulus (the CS) followed by an unconditioned stimulus. The important parameters of the CS and the UCS, as well as the importance of repetition, are also characteristic of more conventional learning. By contrast, the conditioned aversion paradigm is operational under conditions of long interstimulus intervals, whereas attempts to demonstrate conventional learning under such conditions fail.

In addition to the differing temporal characteristics, there are several other sources of data which suggest that we are dealing with a special type of learning. One source of such data has come from physiological experiments that have shown that certain types of brain damage which impair conventional passive-avoidance acquisition actually facilitate the acquisition of conditioned aversion (McGowan, Hankins, & Garcia, 1972; Weisman, Hamilton, & Carlton, 1972).

Another indication that conditioned aversion may be a separate type of learning comes from the anecdotal observations that cognitive awareness of the phenomenon is of little or no value in terms of reducing the aversion. As indicated earlier, the knowledge that the conditioned aversion which one has developed **was** based upon the chance pairing with a viral illness has little or no effect on the aversive quality of the food; the reaction is still as though the food itself had been poisonous. Animal data have provided further support for the noncognitive nature of this type of learning. In a fascinating series of experiments conducted by Roll and Smith (1972), rats were given access to a novel food, then deeply anesthetized over a period of several hours. During the time in which the animals were unconscious, one group was X-irradiated and another group received sham exposure. Subsequent tests showed that conditioned aversion had developed, even though the animals were deeply anesthetized at the time of the onset of illness, and had remained anesthetized for a period of eight hours. In other words, conscious awareness of the visceral disturbance is not essential to establish the conditioned aversion, nor is it effective in eliminating the conditioned aversion.

II. SPECIFIC APPETITES

The maintenance of the *internal milieu* is a complicated and multifaceted set of processes which apparently includes learned and unlearned (reflexive) neural activity. In the first section of this chapter, we have concentrated on the mechanisms which help the animal to survive in the face of a variety of foodstuffs, some of which may induce gastrointestinal illness or outright poisoning. It is obvious, however, that there is more to survival than avoiding the possibility of being poisoned; the organism must also consume those foodstuffs which contain appropriate quantities of fats, proteins, carbohydrates, vitamins, and trace elements. In some very simple organisms which have both a limited behavioral repertoire and a limited environmental niche, the problem of obtaining an adequate diet has been nicely inserted into the life cycle of the organism.

As described in Chapter 1, certain types of moths lay their eggs on the leaf of the hackberry plant where they hatch out and have available an appropriate source of nutrients (the leaves). When the larvae are transformed into the adult stage, this adult will lay the eggs on the hackberry leaf. This behavior gave rise to a controversy as to whether the behavior was genetically determined or the result of some environmental influences. Later experimental evidence revealed that if the eggs were transported from the hackberry leaf to the leaves of an apple tree, the larvae would hatch out, eat this new type of leaf, and the resulting adult organism would lay the eggs on the leaf of the new species host. In other words, the diet which was first available to the hatching larvae determined the location in which the adult organism would lay the eggs.

Some of the more complicated organisms, such as the jawless fishes (cyclostomes) which obtain food by straining microorganisms from the water, occupy such a narrow ecological niche that there are seldom any alternatives to the available diet.

Most mammals, and especially omnivorous animals such as the rat, do not enjoy the luxury of either of these mechanisms which essentially relieves the organism of the need to choose an appropriate diet on a daily basis. Because the consumption of particular types of foodstuffs that are selected from a large variety of potential foodstuffs involves a great deal of overt behavior, psychologists have asked the question: Which aspects of this behavior are learned, and which are the result of such things as genetically controlled mechanisms (e.g., taste factors)?

One of the earliest investigations of this phenomenon was undertaken by Harris, Clay, Hargreaves, and Ward (1933) who found that rats which had been deprived of some essential aspect of their diet would, when given the opportunity, selectively choose a diet which contained this essential component. They termed this a "specific hunger." These findings were extended by Richter, Holt, and Barelare (1938) who provided rats with a smorgasbord, each item containing only a limited portion of the spectrum of required nutrients. In spite of differences in palatability among the diets, rats given a free choice of dietary nutrients chose the foodstuffs in such a manner that their overall intake reflected an adequately balanced diet. Richter postulated that deficiencies in the diet produced altered taste reactivity such that diets containing the essential elements became more highly preferred. This notion was later challenged by electrophysiological evidence that the responsiveness of taste fibers remained unchanged following depletion (Pfaffman & Bare, 1950) and by later studies showing that rats would choose a diet containing an essential component which had no taste, so long as some specific (though unrelated) taste was associated with the diet containing the missing dietary component (Rozin, 1967).

Gradually, psychologists began to favor the view that the specific hunger phenomenon represented a type of learning. It was argued (Richter, 1943) that the taste of a particular diet which contained a needed component was associated with the general improvement of health which was to follow. The major force which acted against the general acceptance of this notion was the fact that long delays were involved. It was not until the conditioned aversion experiments had rather convincingly demonstrated that such delays could be tolerated in visceral learning that this view became more acceptable.

Interestingly, the conditioned aversion data which set the stage for the acceptance of specific appetite as a learning phenomenon also set the stage for the research which was to discredit the notion—at least as it was originally formulated. Recent data and speculation (Revusky & Bedarf, 1967; Rozin & Kalat, 1972) have suggested an interesting alternative to the notion of associating a particular taste with a later improvement in one's general feeling of well-being. The suggestion is that the organism is not learning a preference for the diet which contains the needed component, but rather is learning a conditioned aversion to the food that is missing the essential component. Although this appears to be a somewhat roundabout way of selecting a diet, experiments involving the establishment of relative preferences for various tastes before, during, and after a particular period of dietary deficiency tend to support this view.

As shown in Figure 7–3, thiamine-deficient rats show a significant increase in the preference for a novel diet. If the novel diet contains thiamine, they continue to select this substance; if the thiamine has been added to the familiar diet, the preference for novelty disappears within a few days. Such an effect could be either the result of neophilia produced by deficiency or by an aversion to the familiar diet that was deficient in thiamine. Rozin and Kalat observed that the deficient rats scooped out and spilled the familiar diet in much the same way that normal rats treat a quinine-adulterated diet.

In fairness to the original view of learning to associate a taste with an improvement in the feedback from the *internal milieu,* we

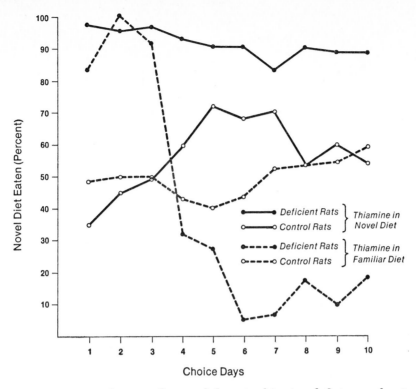

Figure 7–3. Preferences for novel diets in thiamine-deficient and pair-weighed control rats. (From Rozin & Kalat, 1972, by permission of Prentice-Hall.)

should point out that recent experiments have provided some support for this notion. One of the more intriguing examples of this is an experiment (Green & Garcia, 1971) which involved the injection of apomorphine into rats. The administration of apomorphine induces a rather complicated sequence of events: Following an initial period of rather severe visceral disturbances, there is a rapid improvement leading to elation or the "kick" which is, at least in part, responsible for the addictive potential of the drug. If the rats were exposed to a novel taste prior to the administration of the drug, a strong conditioned aversion was exhibited on subsequent exposures to the taste. By contrast, exposure to a novel taste after injection of the drug, but timed to anticipate the "kick" of the drug, led to an enhanced preference for the taste (*see* Figure 7–4). In a somewhat different vein, it has been found that rats that are allowed to rehydrate after severe water deprivation by drinking flavored water will show a preference for that flavor even though the deprivation conditions have long since passed (Revusky, 1968). It is not difficult to conjecture that associations such as these may be responsible for the discovery of real or superstitious sources of folk medicine. Fortunately, most maladies run their course and improvement occurs with no treatment. If some treatment is interposed between the onset of the illness and the recovery, mechanisms are available for what we might call a "conditioned medication" effect.

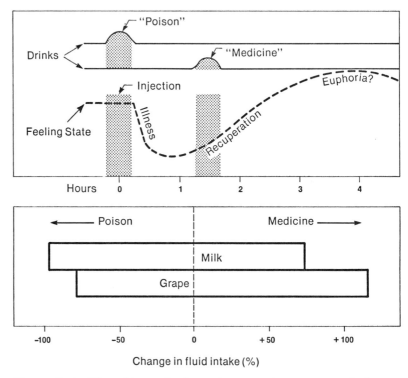

Figure 7–4. The effects of arbitrarily presenting one taste before illness (poison) and another taste before recuperation (medicine) resulting from emetic injections. These data indicate that the reputed efficacy of both medicines and placebos may be due to gustatory-visceral conditioning. (Based on Green & Garcia, 1971, and from Garcia et al., 1974, © Am. Assoc. Adv. Science.)

Finally, a brief outline of some of the developmental factors which influence dietary selection should be noted. Recent studies of the rat have indicated that social factors play an important role in the development of the dietary habits of the young rat (Bronstein, 1975; Galef & Clark, 1971). The results of these studies indicate that weanling rats will eat only those foods which they observe the adult rats consuming. Although the determinants of this behavior are not yet known, the result is that a summary of the knowledge which the adult rats have gained through conditioned aversions and preference are, in a sense, transmitted to the next generation. Although we tend to verbalize the selection of diets for human infants, the fact that baby food manufacturers add ingredients to make them palatable to adults suggests that much of this behavior may also be at a noncognitive, visceral level.

In summary, research has shown that organisms utilize (in varying degrees) genetic programming, learned aversions, learned preferences, and social (cultural) factors to perform the very important task of maintaining an appropriate internal environment in terms of nutrition. In the succeeding sections of this chapter, we will discuss the voluntary or learned control which the organism can exercise over other aspects of the internal environment.

III. CONTROL OF VISCERAL RESPONSES

The ability of organisms to select specific foods on the basis of the changes induced in the internal environment has been and continues to be of particular interest to students of learning. In fact, the degree of interest in this phenomenon is, in some aspects, rather surprising. After all, it has been known for centuries that both man and beast respond to the needs of the internal environment by seeking and consuming food when they become "hungry." The digestion of the food returns the internal environment to a more or less nominal condition, and the organism is free to engage in alternative behaviors for a while. The interest which has been generated by the phenomena of conditioned aversion and specific appetites has been based primarily on the precision (selectivity) of these mechanisms and the fact that the temporal limitations of this type of learning are dramatically different from those of the more conventional types of learning.

Although the behavior associated with these types of learning leads to the control of the internal environment, it should be emphasized that this control is somewhat indirect. The organism monitors the internal environment, engages in some overt behavior (i.e., an interaction with the external environment), then monitors the internal environment again. The changes in the internal environment are used only as a source of information, rather than as the target of directed activity. The question arises, "Does the organism have the capabilities for a more direct control over the internal environment?"

In the discussion of Pavlovian conditioning (Chapters 2 and 3), we have cited numerous examples of the control of the internal environment through learning. This control comes in the form of changes in heart rate, blood pressure, skin conductance, gastrointestinal secretions, etc. But once again, there is a strong link to the external environment—the internal changes are, for the most part, related to the organism's response (frequently an emotional response) to the relationship between the external CS and the external UCS. We have seen (cf., Chapter 3), in the case of so-called interoceptive conditioning, that the CS and UCS need not impinge upon exteroceptors, but can be equally effective when directed upon interoceptors. (In this regard, the phenomena of conditioned aversion and specific appetites may be special cases of interoceptive classical conditioning.) In all of these instances the resulting change in the internal environment is apparently the result of an involuntary response to some external event—even though the attempts to seek out or to avoid the external event may have been quite voluntary.

This distinction between voluntary and involuntary responding was once used as one of the defining characteristics of Pavlovian and Thorndikian conditioning—the former involving primarily autonomic responses, the latter somatic responses. Accordingly, the prevailing assumption has been that direct voluntary control of the internal environment was not possible. In fact, Kimble (1961) has stated that insofar as these autonomic (visceral) responses are concerned, ". . . the evidence points unequivocally to the conclusion that such responses can be modified by classical, but not by instrumental, training methods (p. 100)."

In spite of the general agreement among psychologists that the conclusion expressed by Kimble was correct, there were those who believed that voluntary control of autonomic activity (often referred to as involuntary activity) was possible, at least under some circumstances. Most of the evidence for this alternative point of view was anecdotal in nature and surrounded by mystique. Specifically, much of the evidence supporting the notion of voluntary autonomic control came from those who practiced the art of yoga. The practitioners of this art were said to be able to slow, or even stop, the beating of the heart for extended periods of time, to stop breathing for long periods, and even to perspire at will.

The major difficulty in accepting these demonstrations as evidence for the voluntary control of the autonomic nervous system was that these states can be controlled (and, in some cases, obviously were controlled) either by somatic manipulations such as building up pressure in the chest to conceal the heartbeat, or by some mediational imagery such as imagining it was very hot to induce sweating. In other words, the question was not whether these responses could be controlled, but whether they could be controlled *directly*, without some mediating imagery or somatic muscle involvement. The very difficult experimental question was, how can these mediating behaviors be circumvented to allow the straightforward demonstration of the ability (or inability) to directly control autonomic responses?

One of the most rigorous attempts to meet this challenge was undertaken by Neal Miller and his associates in the mid-1960s (Miller, DiCara, Solomon, Weiss, & Dworkin, 1970). We will consider the rationale and procedures of these experiments in some detail both because they are critical to the interpretation of the results and because they can serve as a model for the experimental approach to a very difficult problem.

One of the first problems which required a solution was that of somatic muscle involvement. How could the possibility of such involvement be eliminated? One obvious solution to the problem would be to paralyze the somatic musculature by injecting a drug called curare. This drug paralyzes the somatic muscles, including the intercostal muscles and the diaphragm, making artificial respiration necessary to support the organism.

Although the administration of curare solves the problem of somatic muscle involvement, it creates a second problem: How is it possible to induce a rat to control some autonomic response if it is paralyzed and maintained on artificial respiration? As we have seen in earlier chapters, instrumental conditioning of a response requires that a reinforcer be delivered within a brief interval after the response has been performed. The administration of a conventional reinforcer such as food or water to a paralyzed organism is out of the question. Miller and his associates solved this problem by using electrical brain stimulation as the reinforcer. Using a modification of the technique discovered by Olds and Milner (1954), they implanted electrodes in the brains of the rats, then allowed them to voluntarily (by pressing a lever) administer the electrical stimuli to the brain. In this way, they could verify that stimulation of a particular portion of the brain could sustain an operant response. Once these parameters had been established, they could then be used for reinforcement of an immobilized animal because no somatic response is required to "consume" the reinforcement.

With these two major problems solved, the only remaining difficulty was to make the delivery of the brain stimulation contingent upon the performance of some autonomic response. The response chosen for these early experiments was a change in heart rate. The heart rate was monitored by electrodes and fed into electronic equipment which monitored the frequency of the train of heartbeats. The experimenter chose an arbitrary level of heart rate above or below the normal rate and set the recording equipment to automatically deliver an electrical stimulus to the brain on each occasion that the momentary heart rate went beyond the prescribed boundary. The question was, "Can the rat learn to voluntarily increase or decrease its heart rate in order to obtain the rewarding brain stimulations?"

As shown in Figure 7–5, the rats in this experiment showed a rather impressive ability to learn either to increase or to decrease their heart rate. Although this was an encouraging first step toward demonstrating the voluntary control of autonomic responses, it certainly was not compelling enough to reverse the longstanding belief that such responses were strictly involuntary. The most critical

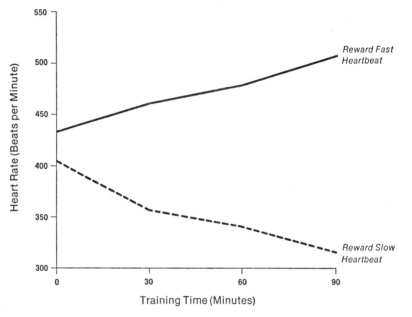

Figure 7–5. Heart-rate changes are shown for rats rewarded for increasing the rate (solid line) and for decreasing it (broken line). Animals were curarized and rewarded with brain stimulation. (From DiCara, 1970; © Scientific American, Inc.)

problem remaining was one of mediating imagery. It is somewhat difficult to accept the notion that a rat is thinking about a narrow escape from a cat in order to increase its heart rate, or about lounging in a cheese bin to reduce its heart rate when the alternative is to change a long-held view of learning. The possibility of such ideation (even if it involves something as "simple" as a change in arousal) cannot be ignored.

In an effort to provide evidence against the notion of mediating emotional responses, Miller and his associates took advantage of one of the characteristics of the autonomic nervous system. Autonomic responses, and especially those which result from activity of the sympathetic division of the autonomic nervous system, tend to occur in clusters rather than singly. As an example, a fear reaction may involve increases in heart rate, blood pressure, respiration, and skin conductance, along with a decrease in gastric motility and a shift of the blood supply from the viscera to the somatic muscles—to list a few. Given this characteristic of a concert of responses, it is possible that the increase in heart rate which Miller recorded was simply one of many changes which was occurring as a result of learning to initiate a fear reaction (this would also be of some interest). In order to convincingly demonstrate that the changes in heart rate per se were being conditioned, it was necessary to show that this response was specific and occurred in the absence of some general pattern of autonomic responses.

The data which are summarized in Figure 7–6 are representative of the experiments which Miller performed to counter the argument that a generalized emotional response was being conditioned. In these experiments, both heart rate and intestinal contractions were monitored. During the course of these experiments, some rats received rewarding brain stimulation for changes in heart rate while others received rewarding brain stimulation for changes in intestinal contractions. As shown in the left panel of the figure, when intestinal contractions were reinforced, the heart rate remained unchanged. However, when changes in heart rate were reinforced in these animals, the heart rate (but not the intestinal contractions) showed the appropriate changes (*see* right panel). In other words, the data support the notion of specific control rather than secondary changes due to a more general emotional response.

The specificity of these changes has been verified in a number of different experiments using these same basic procedures. Not only can the organism learn to control heart rate and intestinal contractions, but also blood pressure, skin conductance, and even urinary output of the kidneys. Perhaps the most impressive example of selectivity involved the voluntary control of blood flow through the ears, as measured by the change in amount of light passing through the ear onto a photocell. Not only was it possible to train the rat to control the flow of blood to the ear, but also to train the rat to increase the blood flow in one ear while decreasing it in the other ear—a feat that could hardly be the result of a general emotional reaction.

In the words of a television comedian, behind every silver lining there is a dark cloud. Miller and his associates spent several

218

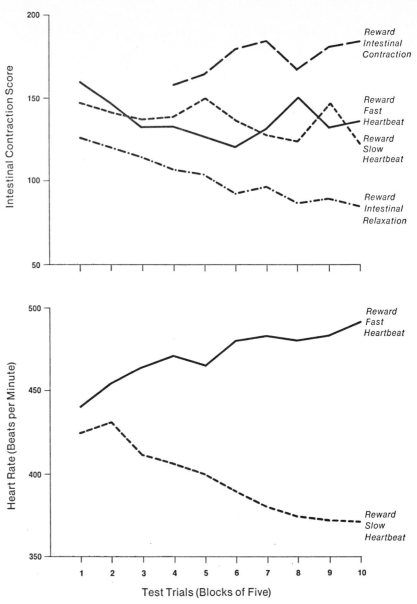

Figure 7–6. Intestinal contraction is learned independently of heart-rate changes. In the graph above, contractions are increased by rats rewarded for increases (dashed line) and decreased by rats rewarded for decreases (dotted line). The intestinal-contraction score does not change appreciably, however, in rats rewarded for increasing or decreasing heart rate (solid lines in top panel). Specificity of learning is shown by this graph and the one on the bottom. Here the results for heart rate rather than intestinal contraction are shown for the same animals. Rats rewarded for changing their heart rate, change it in the appropriate direction. Rats rewarded for intestinal changes did not change heart rate. (Based on DiCara, 1970; © Scientific American, Inc.)

years amassing evidence which challenged our basic concepts of boundaries of instrumental learning. These efforts were met with great skepticism, but gradually the results became more and more difficult to attribute to some procedural artifact. Researchers began to think seriously about the potential implications of these findings for the control of health problems, e.g., the reduction of abnormally high blood pressure through conditioning rather than medication. However, the initial attempts to apply these techniques in the clinic proved to be painstakingly slow and only marginally effective. Obviously, it is not practical to paralyze a patient, implant electrodes and maintain the patient on artificial respiration in order to reduce blood pressure. Instead, the blood pressure is monitored by a plethysmograph cuff and feedback is provided by the onset of an external stimulus, e.g., a light, each time the blood pressure changes in the appropriate direction. Using these techniques, it was possible to demonstrate a statistically significant amount of voluntary control of blood pressure, but the magnitude of the effect was disappointingly small. It was suggested that the effects were more difficult to obtain in humans because of the lack of controls that are possible with animal subjects (cf., Figure 7–7).

This is a reasonable hypothesis but, as the years went by, it has

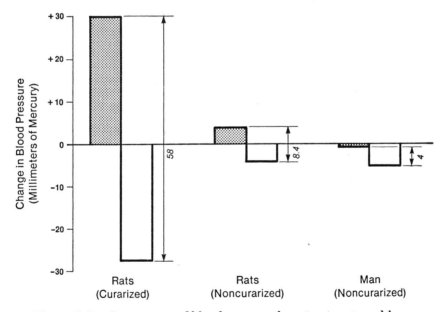

Figure 7–7. Comparison of blood-pressure learning in rats and humans. Those rewarded for increasing (hachured bars) and for decreasing (open bars) blood pressure show that the difference between curarized and noncurarized subjects is greater than the difference between species. (Based on DiCara, 1970; © Scientific American, Inc.)

become more and more difficult for Miller and his coworkers to demonstrate the phenomenon in laboratory animals. The reasons are not known; a likely explanation is that some procedural details that are crucial to this phenomenon have been inadvertently omitted from the experimental protocol, but attempts to precisely replicate the early studies have proven difficult. At this time the issue remains unresolved, but many laboratories are actively pursuing the problem (*see,* for example, DiCara, 1970). That voluntary autonomic control is possible continues to stimulate a considerable amount of research, but it is clear that we have a great deal to learn about these phenomena before they fulfill their initial promise.

IV. VOLUNTARY CONTROL OF BRAIN ACTIVITY

In 1929 a German physiologist named Hans Berger discovered that electrodes placed on the surface of the scalp could monitor electrical activity from the brain. He called this the electroencephalogram, or the EEG. Since that time a great deal of effort has been directed toward improved methods of recording and analysis of the EEG, with the hope that the sophisticated analysis of the EEG could unlock some of the mysteries of brain functions. Although the information gained from this area of research has not fulfilled the original expectations, it has nonetheless provided a considerable amount of useful information and interesting data. Of particular interest to our present considerations are the recent findings which indicate that at least some aspects of the electrical activity of the brain can be brought under voluntary control.

Before considering the evidence for the voluntary control of the EEG, we should very briefly outline the major characteristics of the EEG under differing conditions. The most salient variable which changes the characteristics of the EEG is the general state of arousal of the organism. The EEG patterns characterized in Figure 7–8 show the changes that accompany the behavioral processes of going from wakefulness to deep sleep. As it describes, the primary changes which occur in the EEG as the organism goes from a state of arousal to a state of deep sleep is a progressive increase in the amplitude and decrease in the frequency of the waveform.[2]

---

2. There is actually an exception to this general statement in the case of so-called "paradoxical sleep." This refers to a stage of deep sleep (as defined by responsiveness to environmental stimuli) that is accompanied by a low-voltage, high frequency pattern of activity (i.e., a pattern similar to that seen during arousal!). The paradoxical sleep stage typically appears several times during a normal sleeping period and has been correlated with reports of dreaming.

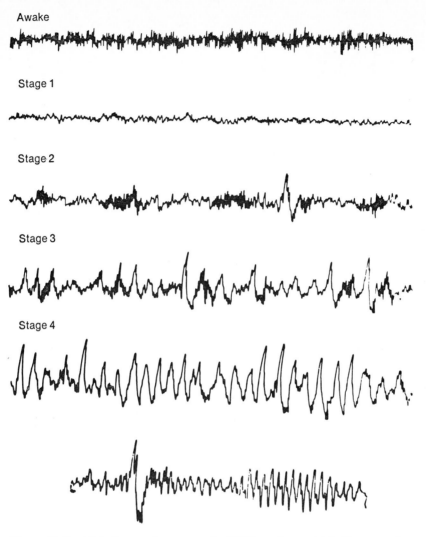

Figure 7–8. This figure shows sample EEG tracings which illustrate the typical patterns seen in wakefulness, the four non-REM EEG stages, and REM sleep. The top five lines represent thirty seconds of brain wave recording while the bottom line, REM sleep, is eight seconds. (From Dement, 1972; courtesy of the San Francisco Book Company.)

Within a few years after the discovery of the EEG it was observed that the onset of a stimulus, especially a visual stimulus, could produce a sudden desynchronization of the alpha-wave, a phenomenon which was termed an "alpha-block." While investigating this phenomenon Durup and Fesard (1935) observed that the alpha-block was exhibited during a trial in which an equipment failure resulted in the omission of the light stimulus. This malfunction led to the discovery that the alpha-block could be conditioned, the typical procedure being to use a low-level click (which had no direct effect on the alpha activity) as the CS and a light as the UCS (*see* Figure 7–9). More systematic studies were carried out later (e.g., Jasper & Shagass, 1941) showing that in trace conditioning, the onset of the alpha-block was more accurate than the subjects' estimates of the interval between the CS and UCS; this latter finding suggested that the effect may not be consciously mediated.

Although the conditioned alpha-block is an interesting

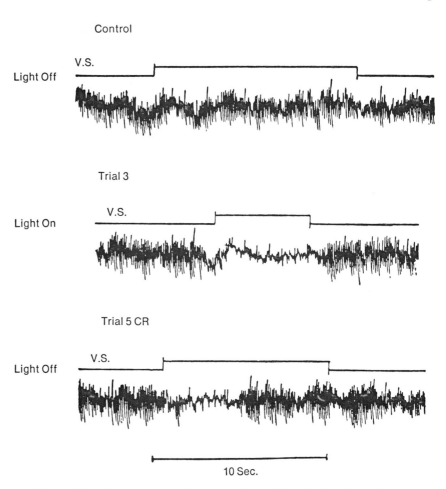

Figure 7–9. Voluntary conditioning of the alpha rhythm. First line shows lack of effect of voluntary signal (V.S.) before conditioning. Second line is the conditioning trial with light. Third line shows conditioned voluntary response with no light stimulus. Note short duration of alpha block in voluntary CR relative to duration in UCR. (From Jasper & Shagass, 1941.)

phenomenon, it is perhaps not too surprising that the brain, which controls the processes of learning, should also exhibit measurable changes which reflect these processes. Perhaps a more interesting question is, "Can the electrical activity of the brain be voluntarily controlled?" The answer to this question had to await the development of rather sophisticated technology, including on-line computer analysis of the frequency and amplitude characteristics of the EEG wave.

Much of the early work which attempted to answer this question was done by Fox (Fox & Rudell, 1968; Rosenfield & Fox, 1971) who placed electrodes in the brains of cats and fed the electrical signals into a computer. The computer was programmed so that it could monitor the voltage and frequency characteristics of the EEG as the information arrived. The typical procedure was to choose some characteristic of the EEG that had a low probability of occurrence and program the computer to automatically deliver a milk reward each time this electrical event occurred. Cats that were tested under these conditions readily learned to control the EEG as can humans with electrodes that are placed on the scalp.

It is somewhat difficult to imagine the direct value of being able to exercise control over the EEG; these minute electrical signals are almost certainly incapable of producing any significant changes in the external environment. It is more likely that the subjects are simply engaging in a recurrent thought pattern or mood which is reflected by the "appropriate" change in electrical activity in the portion of the brain being monitored by the electrode. It is important to emphasize that this control, just as in the case of voluntary control of heart rate or blood pressure, is indirect. If the subject is simply instructed to produce a certain change in one of these measures, the attempts are totally unsuccessful. The critical feature is that the subjects must be given some sort of *feedback* from the response to indicate when the appropriate response is occurring (we normally have little or no feedback from these internal responses). Given this informative feedback, it appears as though the subjects can be very successful in manipulating the EEG and at least moderately successful in manipulating autonomic responses.

Even though the subject may be generating the change in neural activity, the process may be so subtle that the subjects do not realize it. Kimmel (1974) points out that virtually all of their subjects report no awareness that the delivery of reinforcement was in any way related to their behavior. This is even true in the case of reinforcement being contingent upon striated or voluntary muscle contractions. In one such study (Hefferline, Keenan, & Harford, 1959), subjects were reinforced for muscle contractions of the thumb. Surprisingly, the resulting thumb cramps were attributed to other factors (e.g., "the electrodes were too tight") rather than to voluntary contractions.

One additional type of experiment requires mention because of its inherent interest and because it has frequently been misinterpreted. The experiment involves the demonstration of the conditioning of a single brain cell. In these experiments (Olds, 1969), a microelectrode was lowered into the brain to enable the recording of the action potentials of a single neuron. In most cases, such cells exhibit a characteristic baseline rate of firing. It was found that if this electrical activity was monitored by computer, that the rate of firing of the cell could be increased or decreased by making the presentation of rewarding brain stimulation (through another electrode) contingent upon this change in firing rate. Although this would appear at first glance to represent a rather incredible degree of control over the brain, it is probably no more or less impressive than control of the gross EEG—the mere fact that only one cell is monitored does not imply that only one cell is changing. In all likelihood tens of thousands of cells are changing in some more or less consistent pattern along with the cell being monitored. (The interested reader is referred to both a technical book (Sheer, 1961) and a recent novel (Crichton, 1972), which consider in more detail the technical and social implications of these studies, respectively.)

During recent years, there has been a great deal of interest expressed by some segments of society in the ability to control particular patterns of brain-wave activity. The rationale is that such control might enable the subject to voluntarily initiate periods of exceptional creativity or exceptional feelings of well-being. One of the more popular (though somewhat costly) attempts to acquire this ability has been to purchase a portable EEG analyzer which is programmed to present a tone whenever the predominant frequency of the EEG is 10 Hz. (i.e., alpha activity). Many users of this device find that they can train themselves to produce the relaxed and pleasant feeling of the alpha-state, a state which can also be reached without training or equipment simply by closing the eyes, relaxing, and avoiding visual imagery.

Another EEG pattern which has enjoyed some interest is the somewhat irregular 3–5 Hz. theta activity that typically occurs during the transition from wakefulness into sleep. There are numerous anecdotal reports of unusually high incidence of creative ideas at this time, perhaps because of a lowering of the boundaries between those areas which, in the more alert state, are assumed to be logically separate. In any event, one of the difficulties of supporting this notion is that the state is very transient; if the subject either progresses into sleep, or returns to the waking state, the ideas are

frequently lost completely or become too fragmented to piece together again. There is, of course, the real possibility that this state is
not associated with creativity, but with the *feeling* that one is being
creative.

These somewhat altered states of consciousness are of some
interest, but it is much too early to know whether they can provide
us with either a happier or a more productive existence. It must be
recognized that in spite of the impressive sophistication of the
computer analysis technology, that the EEG represents a very
crude and restricted measure of the intricate workings of the brain;
the computer cannot extract more information from the EEG than
was present initially, and the subject who is linked to this computer
has no contingencies which reinforce a degree of control which is
finer than the feedback provided by the computer. These
techniques are certainly worth investigating for the limited information which they can provide regarding central nervous system
functions. However, it is probably unrealistic to expect more than a
trickle of information from this very complex area.

V. SUMMARY

All organisms must interact with two separate environments—the
external environment and the internal environment. Obviously
these two domains are not independent of each other. The *internal
milieu* depends upon the success of the organism in finding food,
avoiding danger and, in general, upon the organism's interaction
with and interpretation of the external world. The first eight chapters of this text are primarily devoted to an analysis of the organism's response to the contingencies of the external environment. This amount of coverage reflects the emphasis that characterized much of the research that was conducted prior to the mid-
1960s. Indeed, some theorists (e.g., Skinner, 1938) have adopted
the stance that the internal environment of the organism need not
even be considered, that the behavior of the organism can be predicted and controlled strictly on the basis of the organism's response to the external environment. This somewhat extreme view
is simply an exaggerated form of a more general tendency to down-
grade the importance of internal factors, perhaps because of a tendency to associate internal phenomena with introspection. But the
organism *is* the internal environment, and it should come as no
surprise that the organism has the capabilities to manipulate inter-

nal events. It is this domain of behavior that has been considered in the present chapter.

Mechanisms for the control of the internal environment exist at several levels. In Chapter 1 we reviewed examples of genetically programmed and inflexible interactions with the external world. The same types of mechanisms exist for the internal environment. Many of the "simple" digestive and metabolic processes operate continuously with no direct volitional control exerted by the organism. In mammals, for example, certain areas of the brainstem monitor the levels of carbon dioxide in the blood to control the rate of breathing. Conscious control of this mechanism is unnecessary and, in fact, the amount of conscious control that can be exerted over this mechanism is rather limited.

A somewhat more complicated level of internal control involves the regulation of the energy requirements of the organism. In some species this is almost as simple as breathing; nutrients are filtered from the surrounding seawater. Broader ranging organisms such as birds and mammals have more complicated systems that control the intake of nutrients. This type of system is typically referred to as a motivational system because deprivation of food enhances the activity of the organism that is directed toward obtaining food. The implication, of course, is that the organism somehow monitors the status of its nutrient stores and engages in behaviors that are appropriate for the replenishment of needed substances. But, this is a complex task. Only a limited portion of the objects in the external environment are edible and, of these, some contain essential nutrients and others do not. The organism must, to a larger extent, select an appropriate diet. This selection is aided by certain innate propensities, e.g., most humans do not like the taste of bluegrass and most horses (we suspect) do not like the taste of sirloin steak. Such differences in the chemical senses provide a first-order guidance system for the selection of appropriate foods.

Despite the restricted environmental niche of the organism and the innate differences in the processing of information in the chemical senses, the organism must still *learn* a great deal about the selection of food. Simply stated, the organism must learn which food sources contain essential nutrients, which do not, and which contain poisonous substances. We have discussed two basic learning phenomena that are involved in this selection, specific appetite and conditioned aversion.

These two phenomena are clearly interrelated and may even lie along a continuum of a single process. The conditioned aversion phenomenon has recently received a great deal of attention because it was this phenomenon that demonstrated that the temporal characteristics of learned aversion are different from the temporal characteristics exhibited in more traditional experiments involving instrumental or classical conditioning. A summary of the major variables that influence conditioned aversion is shown in Figure 7–10. As indicated by the figure, the degree of conditioned aversion is increased as a result of increasing either the intensity of the flavor of the test solution or the intensity of the illness that follows ingestion. The degree of conditioned aversion declines as a function of

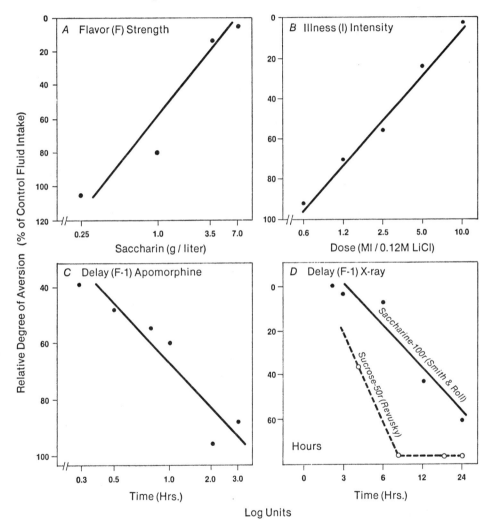

Figure 7–10. The effect of varying intensity and time parameters upon aversions induced by agents producing illness. (Based on Garcia et al., 1974, by permission of Am. Assoc. Adv. Science.)

the length of the CS–UCS interval, but the delays that can be toler-ated are several orders of magnitude longer than those exhibited in Pavlovian and instrumental learning situations.

In addition to the implications of the conditioned aversion phenomenon as it relates to learning theories, it has considerable ecological and practical significance. For example, a group of inves-tigators (Gustavson, Garcia, Hankins, & Rusiniak, 1974) have initi-ated a program of conditioned aversion in the open range to reduce the killing of sheep by coyotes. Packets of ground lamb meat con-taining poison are distributed across the range. The coyotes that eat these bait packets become ill and develop a learned aversion for the taste of lamb, thereby reducing the frequency of lamb killings in the area.

Another aspect of the control of the internal environment in-volves the autonomic nervous system which controls such things as heart rate, blood pressure, vasodilatation, etc. The long-held view that this division of the nervous system was strictly involuntary was challenged in the mid-1960s by Neal Miller and his associates. Although more recent efforts in this area have been only moder-ately successful in demonstrating the voluntary control of au-tonomic responses, there is a considerable body of evidence that such control is possible. The important question is whether or not this type of control can be developed to the point of having medical significance.

The brain is known to exert control over both involuntary and voluntary responses, so it might be expected that it is possible to exert some control over the activity of the brain. Experiments in-volving both humans with scalp electrodes and experimental ani-mals with implanted electrodes have demonstrated that specific patterns of activity can be conditioned either as an instrumental response or as a conditioned response in a classical conditioning paradigm.

The ability to exert voluntary control over the activity of the autonomic nervous system and in the brain has been recognized only during recent years and the question arises: Why were these abilities not recognized earlier? The primary reason is that it is only during the last few years that technological development has taken place to allow the monitoring and on-line analysis of bioelectric activity. This allows the experimenter to give the subject feedback (e.g., the onset of a light) indicating that the appropriate response is being made. Without this feedback there is little or no control of the response. The importance of feedback should not convey the im-pression that external information is *essential* for the control of activity in the brain or the autonomic nervous system—it is not likely that evolutionary pressures have anticipated the technological developments that allow these experiments to be conducted. Rather, the feedback is probably essential to define the nature of the response that is required by the experimental situation.

Under more natural conditions, the control of the internal environment seems to be involved with the selection of a battery of responses that prepare the *internal milieu* for the occurrence of some impending event. For example, Pavlov noted that the anticipatory "psychic secretions" of his dogs reflected not only the arrival of food but also the type of food—the gastric secretions were appropriate for the digestion of the particular foodstuff that was proffered. Although the data are less clear-cut, a similar degree of control is probably present in other situations. For example, the pattern of activity in the brain and autonomic nervous system probably differs greatly depending on whether an athlete is anticipating an important tennis match or anticipating a television interview; the two states of increased arousal are different. The recent experimental efforts to selectively control such responses are analogous to the early experiments of Pavlov; a very complicated system is placed under an artificially simple set of control procedures. The resulting simplification of the system allows the experimenter to begin an analysis of the important relationships that characterize the overall system.

Theoretical Interpretations of Learning

To adapt to its world an organism
must learn relations of two sorts:
(1) the meaning of stimuli, external or
internal, and (2) the consequences
of its own response.

J.P. Seward

In this chapter we shall consider some theoretical views of the elements that make up instrumental learning. We shall consider again the three broad theoretical positions presented in Chapter 4, i.e., S–R theory, cognitive theory, and anticipatory response theory; we shall consider what function Pavlovian conditioning processes may have in instrumental behavior; and we shall consider possible biological constraints imposed on simple conditioning and learning processes.

I. WHAT IS LEARNED IN INSTRUMENTAL LEARNING

S–R Theory

Let us consider again the basic instrumental learning task. An animal is placed in an apparatus such as an operant chamber, and if it presses a lever, a pellet of food is delivered. As we described in Chapter 4, this situation may be thought of as possessing three elements; a stimulus (the lever), a response (moving the lever), and an outcome (the presentation of food). When we place a food-deprived animal in a situation such as this (or a Thorndikian puzzle box, or a runway, etc.), we find that its rate of making the response increases with repeated experience in the situation. We term this increase in response rate (or in response probability) learning. Thorndike's view as to the nature of this learning was that the animal formed an association between the stimulus (S) and the response (R). Remember that in Chapter 4 we stated that Thorndike's interpretation of learning explicitly ruled out the explanation that the animal was learning to anticipate the outcome (O) of its response. The association formed was between the stimulus and response;

there was, in Thorndike's view, no association formed between the stimulus and outcome or between the response and the outcome. The function of the outcome (food pellet in our example) was to "stamp-in" or reinforce the S–R association.

In one form or another, the S–R view of simple learning dominated theoretical interpretations of animal learning throughout most of this century (e.g., Skinner, 1938; Hull, 1943; Miller, 1959; Estes, 1959; Skinner, 1961). Central to all these formulations was the idea that stimuli present in the instrumental learning situation came to exert control over behavior because they became associated with the performance of an overt response. We shall now consider evidence which indicates that an association between a stimulus and a response is not the only thing, perhaps not even the major thing, that animals learn.

Transfer of Control Experiments

We have, in several places in this text, cited evidence that training with Pavlovian contingencies will later influence instrumental behavior. For example, in both Chapters 3 and 6, we mentioned an experiment by Rescorla in which stimuli paired with shock in a Pavlovian paradigm led to an increase in rate of responding in a Sidman avoidance task; whereas stimuli paired with the absence of shock led to a decrease in the rate of avoidance responding (*see* pp. 74 and 159).

We mention this experiment again because it, and others, show that a stimulus that has been paired with a common consequence in both Pavlovian and instrumental training (e.g., shock) can exert control over the instrumental behavior without ever having been paired with the specific instrumental response. Results such as those obtained by Rescorla imply that something other than S–R relationship is learned in the normal course of instrumental learning. More specifically, these transfer of control experiments indicate that an association is learned between two environmental stimuli; the predictive stimulus (i.e., the CS) and the contingent stimulus (e.g., the reinforcement). Let us now consider the evidence from transfer of control experiments that supports this conclusion.

The basic rationale of a non-S–R interpretation of the transfer of control experiments is that, in the Pavlovian conditioning paradigm, the reinforcement is delivered independently of the subjects' responses, and thus, the transfer demonstrated must be due to something other than a commonality in responses between the Pavlovian and instrumental training. However, one stumbling block for this interpretation is that, despite the lack of contingency between response and reinforcement that is programmed into Pavlovian conditioning, the subject may still be making some sort of preparatory or approach response and the transfer demonstrated may be due to these instrumental contingencies that "contaminate" the Pavlovian conditioning (*see* Chapter 3). One way to rule out this possibility is to prevent the subject from responding in the Pavlovian conditioning phase of the experiment. We have already seen examples of this strategy. Recall the experiments by Solomon and Turner (1962) and by Leaf (1964) mentioned in Chapter 6 (*see* p. 159).

In the Solomon and Turner and the Leaf experiments the subjects (dogs) were paralyzed during the Pavlovian conditioning phase and thus could make no responses at all. And yet, it was still found that CSs from the Pavlovian training influenced instrumental avoidance behavior. These and other similar experiments (e.g., Overmier & Leaf, 1965) indicate strongly that the transfer demonstrated was not due to a commonality between the subjects' responses in the Pavlovian and instrumental training, and therefore, indirectly support the hypothesis that the transfer is due to a learned relation between the predictive (CS) and contingent (shock) stimuli.

Definitive evidence ruling out transfer on the basis of responses has been more difficult to obtain in the case of experiments with appetitive reinforcements since some response on the part of the subject is usually required to consume the reward. However, transfer from appetitive Pavlovian to appetitive instrumental training has been obtained in such a wide variety of situations that transfer of specific responses seems to be an unlikely explanation. For example, appetitive transfer of control experiments have shown the following: (a) a tone paired with the presentation of food will later enhance rate of bar-pressing in extinction even though the tone was never presented when the subjects were learning to press the lever for a food reward (Estes, 1944); (b) the acquisition of a discrimination between stimuli signaling reward and nonreward (or two different amounts of reward) is facilitated by prior Pavlovian experience with these stimuli (Bower & Grusec, 1964; Flaherty & Davenport, 1968, 1969); (c) the reversal of an instrumental discrimination may be facilitated by prior Pavlovian experience with the stimulus reinforcement contingencies reversed (e.g., Trapold, 1966); (d) extinction of an instrumental response may be facilitated by prior exposure of the animals to unrewarded goal-box stimuli (Seward & Levy, 1949; Moltz, 1957); (e) the development of a scalloping pattern of response rate on an FI schedule is facilitated by prior regular, nonresponse contingent, delivery of food pellets (Trapold, Carlson, & Myers, 1965); and (f) that prior experience with stimuli paired with the delivery of water increases the incidence of locomotor and exploratory behavior when these stimuli are presented in an open field apparatus (Bindra & Palfai, 1967).

These experiments, and others (*see* Rescorla & Solomon, 1967; Bolles & Grossen, 1970) amply demonstrate that positive transfer from Pavlovian training to instrumental training is found in a wide variety of situations. The very generality of the finding casts doubt upon the possibility that the transfer effects are due to responses learned in the Pavlovian stage of training. As further evidence, we shall describe in some detail a recent experiment by Hearst and Peterson (1973) that set out specifically to investigate the possibility that the transfer demonstrated in these experiments was due to the transfer of a learned response.

The Hearst and Peterson experiment involved four separate stages of training. In the first stage, the subjects (rats) were trained to perform a discriminated instrumental response. That is, the subjects were reinforced for making an instrumental response only in the presence of a flashing light (a stimulus that is correlated with the availability or reinforcement is termed an S^+ or sometimes an S^D, or discriminative stimulus). The response required was a chain-pulling response and, while the S^+ was on, the subjects were reinforced on a FI–30-second schedule. The rats were not reinforced for chain pulling when the light was off.

In the second stage of this experiment the chain was removed from the apparatus, a lever was inserted, and the subjects were reinforced for lever-pressing. During this stage the subjects were divided into three groups that differed in how a new stimulus, a tone, was related to the reinforcement contingency. For one group the tone was correlated with availability of reinforcement (tone was an S^+). For this group, lever-pressing was reinforced on a VI–30-second schedule when the tone was sounding. Lever-pressing was not reinforced in the absence of the tone. In the second group the tone served as an S^-, they were *not* reinforced for lever-pressing when the tone was sounding, but were reinforced in the absence of the tone. In the third group, the presence of the tone was uncorrelated with the availability of reinforcement for lever-pressing (cf., Rescorla's truly random control). In this group the tone was designated an S^0.

In the third stage the lever was removed, the chain reinserted, and the subjects were reinforced for chain-pulling with the flashing light as an S^+ and darkness as S^-.

In the final stage of the experiment the chain-pulling response was extinguished. During extinction, the rats received some presentations of the light alone and some presentations of a compound stimulus (cf., Chapter 3) of the light plus the tone. The purpose of these presentations was to determine how the tone interacted with the light in controlling the chain-pulling response. In considering the possible outcomes of this compound stimulus test, remember two things: (a) the tone had never been presented with the chain-pulling response before; and, (b) there were three groups of rats for which the tone should have different functions, an S^+ group, an S^- group, and an S^0 group.

The degree to which presentation of the compound tone and light altered the chain-pulling response (in comparison with presentation of the light alone) is shown in Table 8–1. It is apparent that addition of the tone as an S^+ to the light considerably enhanced the rate of chain-pulling, whereas the addition of the tone that had served as an S^- to the light produced a substantial decrease in the rate of responding. The addition of the tone as an uncorrelated stimulus produced a small drop in the rate of responding.

Table 8–1. Median Percentage Change in Response Output Produced by Tone in Each Group During an Extinction Test*

Stimulus Condition	Change in Chain-Pulling Response
Tone as S^+ added to light as S^+ (Conditioned Excitation)	+76.0%
Tone as S^- added to light as S^+ (Conditioned Inhibition)	−35.5%
Tone as S^0 added to light as S^+ (Uncorrelated)	−14.2%

*From Hearst & Peterson, 1973.

Hearst and Peterson obtained very similar results when the lever-press was used as response 1, and the chain-pulling response as the second response, and when a nose-poke response was used as response 1 and the lever-press as response 2. Thus, the response enhancing and depressing effects of stimuli correlated with the availability or nonavailability of reward do not depend on the type of responses used and do not depend on the pairing of the stimuli with specific responses. To emphasize again, the tone influenced responses that had never previously been performed in its presence. What seems to be important is the correlation between the tone and the availability of a reward.

These data reviewed above are clearly incompatible with a simple S–R view of learning. Rats learn something other than just the attachment of responses to stimuli; they learn something about the relationship between environmental stimuli and the availability of rewards, and this learning is sufficient to influence a number of different responses.

Anticipatory Response Theory

The development of anticipatory response theory was based directly on the idea that we have been discussing so far in this chapter—the idea that Pavlovian processes are involved in instrumental behavior. Recall from our discussions in Chapters 4 and 5 that Hull, Spence, and others assumed that Pavlovian responses are conditioned, become anticipatory, and influence instrumental behavior. In its more recent applications, anticipatory response theory has become essentially a theory of incentive motivation and it is this approach to which we now turn.

Hull-Spence Incentive Theory

In his systematic treatment of behavior, Hull (1943) assumed that three major factors were necessary to account for behavior: (a) *Habit*, which reflected associations between stimuli and responses and accounted for the influence of learning on behavior; (b) *Drive*, which reflected the subject's state of deprivation and accounted for the influence of motivation on behavior; and (c) *Inhibition*, which reflected primarily the amount of work involved in making a response and accounted for decrements in behavior such as extinction. The interaction among these three processes was assumed to account for behavior—*Habit* giving behavior direction, determining what would be done; *Drive* giving it energy, determining how vigorous the behavior would be; and *Inhibition*, providing a restraining influence.

Experimental data quickly pointed out several inconsistencies in Hull's theory, which was subsequently revised by both Hull (1952) and Spence (1956). The principal alteration in the theory that will concern us here was the addition of an extra factor—*Incentive Motivation*. Hull, in his earlier theory, had assumed that amount of reward influenced *Habit*; the greater the reward, the stronger the S–R association. However, Crespi's results (*see* Chapter 4) were not consistent with this assumption. In Crespi's experiment, the performance changed abruptly subsequent to a shift in reward—those rats for which the reward had been shifted upward increased their running speed within a trial or two following the shift, and those rats for which the reward had been shifted downward decreased their running speed within a trial or two. The rapidity with which these changes in behavior occurred was not consistent with the idea that S–R associations (Habit) were relatively permanent and resistant to change. In order to account for results like Crespi's, Spence assumed that reward did not influence Habit, but instead influenced the new and added factor of incentive motivation—the larger the reward the greater the incentive motivation.

Thus, in Spence's (1956) theory, four factors were included to account for behavior; *Habit,* the strength of which was determined primarily by the number of training trials (the number of occasions S and R occurred contiguously); *Incentive Motivation,* the strength of which was determined by reward variables such as amount and delay; and *Drive and Inhibition,* as described above. The addition of incentive motivation meant that there were two motivational factors that possessed a certain degree of complimentarity: Drive, which was based on internal deprivation states and energized behavior; and Incentive, which was based on learning about external stimuli and guided approach behavior.

It was through the incentive mechanism that Pavlovian conditioning was assumed to play its role. The Pavlovian conditioning of fractional anticipatory responses (r_g–s_g) was assumed to be the basis of incentive motivation. All of the transfer of control experiments that we have mentioned thus far could be taken as support for the incentive viewpoint. It appears that nearly all reward-related variables may be manipulated without a response contingency (i.e., by a Pavlovian paradigm), and yet the stimuli will influence behavior in which there is a response contingency. These results are consistent with Spence's model in which reward variables influence incentive motivation which is a factor independent of response learning itself (Habit).

The Hull-Spence anticipatory response theory has been extremely influential. We have seen numerous examples where extensions of the theory have been used to explain the effects of partial reinforcement (Amsel's theory), of intermittent punishment (Martin's adaptation of Amsel's theory, *see* Chapter 6), and reward contrast effects (Bower, 1961). The theory has been extended to explain more complex behavior (Logan & Wagner, 1965), and a theory by Mowrer (1960) is in principle quite similar, at least in regard to the heavy emphasis placed on the role of Pavlovian conditioning in instrumental behavior.

However, in recent years, the general Hull-Spence approach has encountered considerable difficulty. There have been four major problems that we shall consider. The first concerns the necessity of a construct such as Drive to explain instrumental behavior. Bolles (1967) has compiled a considerable amount of evidence indicating that deprivation does not have the range of effects on behavior that was assumed by the Hull-Spence theory. Accordingly, a source of motivation attributed to Drive may not be necessary. We do not have the space to present this considerable evidence here, and the reader is urged to consult Bolles (1967). Suffice it to say that the evidence has convinced contemporary theorists that incentive motivation is the only motivational construct needed to account for behavior (e.g., Mendelson & Chorover, 1965; Bindra, 1972, 1974). We shall examine Bindra's theory later.

The second problem with anticipatory response theory concerns the status of the anticipatory response. If r_g–s_g represents some fractional component of the consummatory response that has been conditioned to environmental stimuli (*see* Chapters 4 and 5) then it should be possible to measure these responses. Furthermore, if r_g–s_g is the mechanism by which incentive motivation is provided for the performance of the instrumental response, then the r_g–s_g response should precede the performance of the instrumental response itself. There have been a large number of studies seeking a correlation between the occurrence of responses presumably reflecting Pavlovian conditioning (e.g., salivation) and the performance of instrumental responses (e.g., lever-pressing).

These experiments show that salivation and instrumental behavior generally covary, but sometimes the instrumental response is performed prior to the initiation of salivation. This is not what would be expected if salivation reflected r_g–s_g and if r_g–s_g provided the source of incentive motivation for the performance of the instrumental response. For example, salivation generally precedes bar-pressing on FI schedules (as would be expected from r_g–s_g theory), but on FR schedules salivation generally lags behind the initiation of lever-pressing (Shapiro, 1962; Kintsch & Witte, 1962; Williams, 1965). Many other experiments, involving both appetitive and aversive reinforcements, have failed to find a correlation between instrumental behavior and peripheral responses presumably classically conditioned (e.g., heart rate, licking) high enough to support the idea that these peripheral responses reflect the anticipation of reward which is learned via Pavlovian conditioning processes.

Even faced with data such as these, it is still possible to retain r_g–s_g as a theoretical mechanism by assuming either that it still may be a useful explanatory construct even without the possibility of measurement or by assuming that the critical anticipatory goal response occurs in the central nervous system, not in the periphery, and that the technology and skills are just not available at the present time to allow for the measurement of this central response. However, many current theorists have chosen theoretical explanations of instrumental behavior that do without r_g–s_g. We shall see examples of these below.

The third problem with the Hull-Spence approach is also related to the r_g–s_g mechanism. Recall that r_g stands for a fractional anticipatory *goal* response; incentive motivation was assumed to be derived from the Pavlovian conditioning of aspects of the goal or consummatory response. The Hull-Spence theory places considerable emphasis on the importance of the consummatory response (as do other theories, e.g., Sheffield, 1966). For example, Spence assumed that the more vigorous the consummatory response the more vigorous the instrumental response should be.

Although few experiments have dealt with the relationship between consummatory and instrumental responses, evidence indicates that the correlation between these responses is not as high as one would expect from the assumptions of Hull-Spence theory. For example, Knarr and Collier (1962) and Collier, Knarr, and Marx (1961) found little correlation between the rate of licking for a sucrose reward and the speed of running in a runway for the sucrose solution.

In addition, the Collier et al. (1961) study was one of many that has failed to obtain a negative contrast effect when rats are shifted from a high concentration to a low concentration of a sucrose solution (e.g., Rosen & Ison, 1965; Flaherty, Riley, & Spear, 1973). That is, these experiments failed to find a contrast effect when measures of instrumental responding were taken. And yet, negative contrast effects subsequent to a decrease in the concentration of sucrose solutions occur with extreme regularity when the consummatory response itself is measured (e.g., Vogel, Mikulka, & Spear, 1968; Flaherty, Capobianco, & Hamilton, 1973). Thus, at least in terms of the probability of detecting a negative contrast effect, there is quite a disparity between measures of consummatory behavior and measures of instrumental behavior—a disparity not consistent with the role assigned to the consummatory response in the Hull-Spence theoretical approach.

The fourth problem with the Hull-Spence theory that we will discuss is related to the general completeness of motivational interpretations of the influence of Pavlovian conditioning on instrumental behavior. But we shall delay the discussion of this point, and the relevant evidence, until we have considered a more recent incentive motivation theory.

Bindra's Incentive Motivation Theory

Bindra (1972, 1974) has developed a theory that continues the trend away from S–R habits and drive, and toward incentive motivation interpretations of behavior that was apparent in the evolution of the Hull-Spence theory. It is because of this relationship that we are placing Bindra's theory at this point in the chapter, under the general heading of anticipatory response theory, although, in Bindra's theory, the role of response learning is greatly deemphasized. In fact, Bindra wholly dispenses with the Hull-Spence concepts of Drive and Habit, maintains the concept of incentive motivation, but does not base it on the learning of an r_g–s_g anticipatory response mechanism.

In Bindra's theory, an organism learns a correlation or contingency relationship between two stimuli S_1:S_2; if S_1 occurs, then S_2 is likely to occur (cf., Rescorla's view of Pavlovian conditioning presented in Chapter 3). If S_1 and S_2 occur together in a predictive relationship often enough, then the central representation of S_1 (termed s_1) will come to produce a "surrogate" of S_2 (termed s_2). Bindra diagrams this relationship as $S_1 \rightarrow S_2$ to indicate that given the environmental stimulus S_1, the central representation of this stimulus, S_1, will immediately produce S_2 prior to the actual occurrence of S_2 in the environment. In other words, the subject will anticipate the occurrence of the predicted second environmental stimulus. Thus, this mechanism accomplishes for Bindra what the r_g–s_g mechanism did for Spence, but does so without postulating an actual response.

The importance of this learned contingency depends upon the characteristics of S_2. If S_2 is a "nonincentive" stimulus, then the major behavioral change that will occur is habituation of the orienting response (*see* Chapter 2). However, if S_2 is an incentive stimulus then the organism may engage in a number of behaviors. In order to explain these behaviors in Bindra's terms, we shall have to go a little more into the theory.

In order for an incentive stimulus to be effective in altering behavior, the organism must be in the appropriate physiological state. Bindra assumes that level of motivation is a function of a *Central Motive State,* which is, in turn, controlled by both the organism's physiological condition (e.g., degree of food or water deprivation, level of specific hormones, etc.) *and* the presence of an incentive stimulus. In other words, in Bindra's system, there is no general motivator comparable to Hull's Drive, there are only specific motivational states directed toward specific incentive stimuli. Once a Central Motive State is active, it functions to selectively excite or inhibit sensory-motor coordinations existing within the central nervous system.

Bindra further assumes that there are three major classes of these sensory-motor relationships: *regulatory* mechanisms, *consummatory* mechanisms, and *instrumental* mechanisms (*see* Figure 8–1). We shall briefly consider examples of each of these.

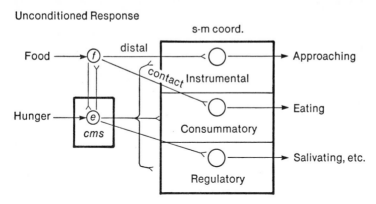

Figure 8–1. A schematic plan of the hypothetical motivational process and its influence on three aspects of response. Abbreviations: cms, central motive state; e, eating central motive state; f, central representation of food; s-m coord., sensory-motor coordinations. (From Bindra, 1974.)

REGULATORY MECHANISMS

When food is presented to a hungry animal, it salivates, digestive juices start flowing, and other physiological reactions (e.g., the release of insulin) may take place. We have seen in Chapter 2 that all of these reactions may take place if a stimulus signaling the impending occurrence of food is presented to a hungry animal. All of these occurrences, and likely many more, are set off by the activation of the central motive state by the incentive stimulus.

CONSUMMATORY MECHANISMS

If the food (or whatever is appropriate to the physiological state) is present, then the organism will make contact with it and consume it. If, however, the actual incentive object is not present, but instead an S_1 signaling the impending occurrence or availability of an incentive object, then *the organism will behave toward the S_1 much as it would toward the actual incentive stimulus.* This point of Bindra's theory bears directly on some recent observations that have been termed *autoshaping.* We shall digress a little at this point to consider this literature. The reader should bear in mind the relevance of the data to Bindra's theory as we have presented it so far.

Autoshaping.   Making a food reward contingent upon the pecking of a lighted disc has been the most frequently used instrumental task with pigeons. Often, the pigeons have been gradually "shaped" to this task by the experimenter reinforcing responses that were successively more like the desired response of key pecking (e.g., orientation toward the key, head movements in the direction of the key, etc.) until, in the end, the pigeons were reliably responding on the key. However, in 1968, Brown and Jenkins showed that pigeons would develop key-pecking responses with *no instrumental response contingency involved at all!* In the Brown and Jenkins experiment, 36 pigeons were given 160 *pairings* of an 8-second white key light followed by a 4-second presentation of a food hopper. Between trials the key was unlighted. The pigeons did not have to peck the key in order to make the food tray available.

The reader will recognize that this procedure is an example of a Pavlovian delay conditioning paradigm. There was no response-reinforcer contingency involved, the food tray was presented regardless of the pigeons' behavior. However, despite this lack of response-contingency, every pigeon eventually pecked the lighted disc during the 8-second interval before the food hopper became available. Brown and Jenkins termed this phenomenon *autoshaping.* The pigeons had apparently shaped themselves *without* a response-reinforcer contingency. Brown and Jenkins further demonstrated that with a backward conditioning paradigm (food hopper presentation followed by lighted disc for 8 seconds), very few key pecks occurred.

In examining the behavior of their pigeons in detail, Brown and Jenkins were able to note three stages in the development of the autoshaped key peck. First, there was a general increase in the pigeons' activity, particularly during a trial; then there was a progressive centering of movements around the area of the key when it was lighted; and, finally, the pigeons began to peck at the key.

Other experiments on autoshaping have shown the following: (a) pigeons will peck the key in the basic autoshaping procedure even if such pecks *prevent* the delivery of reinforcement (Williams & Williams, 1969); (b) autoshaping occurs even when the illumination of the disc signals only an increase (above zero) in the probability that food will be available, but autoshaping does occur when food is equally likely to be available when the key is lighted or unlighted (Gamzu & Williams, 1971, 1973); (c) that the characteristics of the pigeons' key peck in autoshaping differ with different rewards; the pecks on the key are characterized as hard, straight pecks when grain is the reinforcer, but shallow scooping motions against the key when water is the reinforcer (Jenkins & Moore, 1973); (d) that rats autoshaped with a lever tend to lick and gnaw the lever when food is the reinforcer, but tend to sniff, paw, or explore the lever when the reinforcer was direct stimulation of the brain (Peterson, Ackil, Frommer, & Hearst, 1972); (e) that autoshaping occurs in chicks when heat, a reinforcer which requires no approach behavior for its reception, is used (Wasserman, 1973).

All of these autoshaping experiments indicate that approach behavior to stimuli correlated with the availability of reinforcement is under the control of Pavlovian contingencies. In other words, the law of effect is apparently not necessary for the development of instrumental-like behavior. These data also indicate that the approach behavior directed toward the CS is generally like the behavior elicited by the UCS itself. However, this may not always be the case. In the Wasserman (1973) study mentioned above, the chicks pecked a key that preceded the delivery of a heat reinforcement, a UCS that did not elicit pecking. However, Wasserman noted that the form of the autoshaped response changed during the course of the experiment so that eventually the chicks began "snuggling" the key.

According to Konrad Lorenz, a phenomenon related to autoshaping was apparently noticed in Pavlov's laboratory long ago, only its significance was not appreciated at the time. According to Lorenz' story, the American neurologist Lidell, working in Pavlov's laboratory, wondered what would happen if a dog was released from the harness usually used as a restraint during the course of conditioning. The dog that Lidell chose to test had already been conditioned to salivate with the beating of a metronome serving as the CS. When the dog was released, it ran directly to the metronome, began salivating, wagging its tail, and *pushed the metronome with its nose* (Lorenz, 1970)!

Given the existing data on autoshaping, the reasonableness of Bindra's assumption that an animal will direct behavior generally characteristic of the consummatory response toward a conditioned incentive stimulus is apparent. It is also apparent that, at least in simple response situations, there is little or no difference between what is termed a Pavlovian conditioned response and an instrumental response. The same or similar behaviors may result from Pavlovian contingencies (CS–UCS programmed independent of the subject) or from instrumental contingencies (law of effect, *response-dependent* reinforcement). Bindra takes note of this similarity in describing his third class of sensory-motor relationships, instrumental mechanisms

INSTRUMENTAL MECHANISMS

Bindra makes a distinction between two subcategories of instrumental mechanisms: instrumental locomotion and instrumental skill.

Instrumental locomotion involves approach or withdrawal from a location. The behavior is initially guided by stimuli with increasingly greater incentive properties as the goal is neared. If the incentive is appetitive, then the organism's tendency to approach is greater the closer it is to the goal; if the incentive is aversive, then the tendency of the organism to withdraw is greater the closer the organism is to the aversive stimulus. This aspect of Bindra's theory is, of course, very similar to Hull's goal gradient. The difference is that Bindra does not describe the proposed process in terms of anticipatory responses, but rather in terms of approach guided by spatially distributed incentive stimuli. Both theories seem to be similar in that the mechanism is presumed to be learned on the basis of Pavlovian conditioning, or in Bindra's terms, $S_1:S_2$ contingencies. Bindra has the advantage of the autoshaping literature, and he is able to describe instrumental approach behavior as essentially a form of autoshaping. In Bindra's terms:

> Orientation, approach and withdrawal, reaching, and other actions directed at spatially differentiated stimuli are a feature of both classical and operant procedures, though they are made more noticeable in the latter (Bindra, 1972, p. 474).

Instrumental skills such as lever-pressing, chain-pulling, etc., appear to be a little more difficult to explain in Bindra's system. Essentially, Bindra treats stimuli arising from the manipulandum (e.g., lever) as stimuli that are likely, eventually, to acquire greater incentive strength than stimuli lying more in line with a direct approach to the food (e.g., stimuli from the food cup in an operant chamber). Thus, the subject learns a contingency between the stimuli emanating from the manipulandum and the stimuli associated with the reinforcer. This learned contingency results in approach and contact behaviors with the manipulandum, behaviors that are usually sufficient to complete the response requirements. Bindra also recognizes that a second learned contingency may be involved in instrumental skill behavior. This second contingency is between proprioceptive stimuli arising from the performance of the response and the stimuli associated with the reinforcement. In this way muscular movements may also acquire incentive value because of a contingency formed between the feed back stimuli associated with the performance of these movements and the incentive stimuli. This aspect of Bindra's theory is similar to a theory offered by Mowrer (1960) and also similar to the r_g–s_g mechanism except that all associations in Bindra's theory are assumed to be between stimuli, not between stimuli and responses.

In summary, Bindra's theory states that learned modifications of behavior come about *not* by new stimulus-response associations, but rather by learned contingencies between stimuli— contingencies that reflect the correlations between these stimuli in the environment. If S_2 is an incentive stimulus (e.g., food for a hungry organism), then the organism will eventually, as a function of training, anticipate the occurrence of S_2 when S_1 occurs and the organism will begin to behave towards the conditioned incentive stimulus, S_1, much as it would to the true incentive stimulus. The exact form that this behavior assumes depends upon the spatial location of the incentive stimulus and the nature of the incentive. The incentive stimulus and the conditioned incentive stimulus both arouse a motivational state (if the appropriate physiological conditions exist) and direct the organism's behavior toward (or away from) the incentive stimulus. The central motive state activated by the incentive stimulus facilitates or inhibits activity in already existing sensory-motor coordinations. Bindra recognizes little distinction between Pavlovian and instrumental learning in regard to simple learning situations.

Transfer of Control Experiments and Incentive Motivation

We have seen that Anticipatory response theory assumed that Pavlovian processes play an important role in instrumental behavior. But, at the same time that data were being amassed in support of this contention, theoretical emphasis was moving away from anticipatory responses per se and towards incentive theories based on stimulus-stimulus associations. We shall now briefly examine the relevance of the transfer of control experiments for incentive motivation theories of behavior.

The transfer of control experiments that we have had occasion to mention so far in this text are certainly consistent with the notion that conditioned stimuli acquire incentive value in the Pavlovian phase and, through this incentive value, influence instrumental behavior. For example, we have seen at various places in this text that a stimulus paired with a shock in a Pavlovian paradigm will facilitate instrumental avoidance behavior, and, conversely, a stimulus paired with the absence of shock will lead to a decrement in instrumental avoidance behavior. We have mentioned examples of similar effects in the transfer from appetitive Pavlovian conditioning to appetitive instrumental behavior.

A summary of the presumed emotional states elicited by signaling the impending occurrence or absence of appetitive or aversive UCSs is presented in Table 8–2. This table summarizes the work-

Table 8–2. A Basis for Predicting the Results of Transfer of Control Experiments in Terms of Common Incentive Motivational States*

Instrumental Training

		APPETITIVE	AVERSIVE
Pavlovian Conditioning — APPETITIVE	CS⁺	1. ↑ "hope"	5. ↓ "hope"
	CS⁻	2. ↓ "disappointment" "frustration"	6. ↑ "disappointment" "frustration"
Pavlovian Conditioning — AVERSIVE	CS⁺	3. ↓ "fear"	7. ↑ "fear"
	CS⁻	4. ↑ "relief"	8. ↓ "relief"

*The arrows in each box indicate whether prior Pavlovian Conditioning should facilitate (↑) or interfere with (↓) subsequent instrumental behavior. Also included are labels for hypothetical emotional states elicited by the Pavlovian CSs. Cells 1, 2, 7 & 8 of the table are concerned with transfer from Pavlovian to instrumental training with similarly valenced reinforcers; cells 3, 4, 5 & 6 are concerned with transfer from Pavlovian to instrumental training with differently valenced reinforcers.

ing hypotheses of many incentive theorists (e.g., Mowrer, 1960; Rescorla & Solomon, 1967; McAllister & McAllister, 1971; Denny, 1971), and can be used to predict transfer from Pavlovian conditioning to instrumental behavior, based on the presumed emotional state elicited by the CSs and the relevance of these motivational states for instrumental behavior.

Earlier in this chapter we reviewed many experiments that are consistent with the predictions made in cells 1, 2, 7 and 8 of Table 8–2 (see pp. 232–36), but what happens if stimuli are introduced across motivational systems, say from appetitive Pavlovian to aversive instrumental? Although few such experiments have been attempted, most of the results that are available are consistent with a motivational interpretation. For example, Grossen, Kostansek, and Bolles (1969) found that a stimulus paired with food in a Pavlovian paradigm *reduced* avoidance behavior when presented in an instrumental avoidance situation; and, conversely, a stimulus associated with the absence of food in a Pavlovian paradigm facilitated avoidance responding when presented in an instrumental avoidance situation (cf., cells 5 and 6 of Table 8–2). Similar results were obtained by Overmier and Bull (1970). A plausible interpretation of these results is that contrary motivation states (e.g., fear and food expectancy) may interact subtractively. Thus, when a stimulus signaling food is presented in an avoidance situation, the incentive motivational state aroused by this stimulus interferes with the fear motivation state aroused by the stimulus signaling shock in the avoidance situation.

Although this interpretation is plausible and may be a reasonable way to interpret the transfer of control experiments (*see* Rescorla & Solomon, 1967), there are other data indicating that transfer of incentive motivation may not be the entire story. Specifically, there seem to be transfer effects that occur regardless of the incentive motivation conditions that may be prevailing. In order to see a demonstration of this effect, we shall examine another experiment by Overmier and Bull (1970).

In the first stage of this experiment, dogs were trained to *escape* shock by jumping over a hurdle. No stimuli signaling the impending occurrence of shock were used. In the second stage of the experiment the dogs were given *appetitive* Pavlovian conditioning with a food reinforcer. In this second stage of the experiment there were three groups of dogs that differed in the predictive relationships between the CS and food. In one group a tone was paired with the presentation of food (CS$^+$); in a second group the tone was paired with the absence of food (CS$^-$); and in a third group there was no correlation between the tone and presentation of food (CS^0). Finally, in the last stage of the experiment the dogs were given instrumental avoidance training in a shuttle box. The CS used in the Pavlovian phase of training was used to signal shock in the avoidance training. Overmier and Bull found, to their surprise, that the group for which the CS had been paired with the presentation of food (CS$^+$) learned the avoidance response *faster* than the other two groups.

If transfer was due simply to the elicitation of a motivational state by the CS that was appropriate for both the Pavlovian conditioning and for instrumental learning, then these results should not have occurred. Instead, a CS paired with food should hinder the acquisition of an avoidance response just as it produced a decrement in well learned avoidance behavior in the Overmier and Bull (1970) and Grossen et al. (1969) studies mentioned earlier.

However, as paradoxical as these results seem to be from a motivational interpretation, similar effects were found in two other experiments by Overmier and Bull (1970) and in a different paradigm in a recent study by Fowler, Fago, Domber, and Hochhauser (1973). In the Fowler et al. study, the final phase of the experiment involved the acquisition of a brightness discrimination in a T-maze. The reinforcer in the T-maze was food. Prior to the acquisition of the T-maze discrimination, the rats had experience in a Pavlovian conditioning situation with a shock UCS. In the acquisition of the appetitively reinforced brightness discrimination, the CS used in the Pavlovian training was presented contingent upon a correct response, i.e., when the rats chose the correct arm of the T-maze, the CS (a 70 db burst of white noise) was presented. Fowler et al. found that a stimulus that had signaled shock in the Pavlovian phase produced faster learning of the brightness discrimination than a stimulus that had signaled the absence of shock (CS^-) or a stimulus uncorrelated with shock presentation (CS^0). Again, these results seem paradoxical from a motivational point of view (cf., cells 3 and 4 of Table 8–2). Why should a stimulus that signals the impending occurrence of shock promote faster learning of a discrimination based on food reward?

An interpretation of these data offered by Fowler et al. (1973) is as follows: During the course of Pavlovian conditioning the CS acquires two separable properties; a *signaling* property and an *affective* (emotion-eliciting) property. The signaling property reflects the correlation between the CS and the UCS. A CS^+ predicts the impending occurrence of a UCS, a CS^- predicts the absence of a UCS. The affective properties acquired by the CS reflect the aversive and appetitive characteristics of the UCS. The presumed emotional states elicited by the CS are those summarized in Table 8–2.

In order to explain the positive transfer effects obtained in their experiment and in the Overmier and Bull experiments, Fowler et al. assume that, at least under some conditions, the signaling properties of the CS take precedence over the affective properties. That is, a CS^+ from Pavlovian aversive conditioning can facilitate learning when presented with the correct response in an appetitive instrumental task because the predictive properties of the CS are still valid—it is still functioning as a CS^+, still predicting the occurrence of a reinforcer. Similarly, Overmier and Bull interpret their data to indicate that once a stimulus has been established as a signaling stimulus for one type of reinforcer, then it is relatively easy to make that stimulus a signal for a different type of reinforcer, even those that cut across motivational systems. This commonality of signaling properties (CS^+ to CS^+) is sufficient to produce positive transfer despite motivational conditions that indicate negative transfer should occur (e.g., Pavlovian appetitive to instrumental aversive).

These few experiments show that it is possible to obtain and explain positive transfer from Pavlovian conditioning to instrumental behavior on a basis other than a commonality of motivational states. When transfer will occur on the basis of signaling function and when it will occur on the basis of motivational states (as it apparently did in the Grossen et al. experiment mentioned earlier), we are not able to say at the present time. It is possible that transfer on the basis of signaling properties is most likely to occur when the transfer test involves the *learning* of a *new* task rather than when transfer to an already well learned task is examined. However, considerably more research will apparently be needed before the dynamics of transfer from Pavlovian conditioning to instrumental behavior is clearly understood.

In any case, these experiments indicate that cognitive explanations of instrumental behavior may serve as a useful supplement to, or perhaps even replace, incentive motivational explanations.

Cognitive Psychology

Cognitive psychology, as applied to lower animals, represents an attempt to explain behavior in terms other than stimulus-response associations or in terms other than just motivational properties of stimuli. We saw in Chapter 4 that Tolman's explanation of animal behavior was quite different from Thorndike's. Rather than assuming that S–R associations are automatically "stamped-in" by reinforcement, Tolman assumed that animals formed *expectancies* concerning what goal objects are likely to be encountered in a particular situation. These expectancies were thought to be in the form of associations between stimuli (S–S associations). For example, Tolman's interpretation of Pavlovian conditioning was that animals learned that "waiting" in the presence of one signal (the CS) would result in the presentation of food (the UCS). Thus, the association learned was between two stimuli (the signal and the food) and the association was characterized as an expectancy (an expectancy that, in the presence of the signal, food would occur).

Similarly, in the case of instrumental learning, Tolman wrote:

> Correct stimulus-response connections do not get "stamped-in" and incorrect ones do not get "stamped-out." Rather learning consists in the organism's "discovering" or "refining" what all the respective alternative responses lead to (Tolman, 1932, p. 364).

This discovery of what the responses lead to could again be characterized as an expectancy, an expectancy that, in Chapter 4, we termed S–R–O learning. That is, learning that in a given stimulus situation (S) the performance of a particular response (e.g., left turn in a maze, lever-press in a Skinner box) will lead to a particular outcome (e.g., food). Tolman and others also thought that the occurrence of the UCS in Pavlovian conditioning or the reward in instrumental learning was important not because it reinforced an S–R association, but because such an occurrence of the UCS or reward served to confirm (and thereby strengthen) an expectancy.

However, Tolman also felt that expectancies could be learned without the presence of a reward, and these expectancies might then become manifest when a reward was made available. The evidence Tolman used to support this contention was the now classic *latent learning* experiment by Blodgett (1929).

In this experiment, Blodgett trained several groups of rats in a complex maze. One of the groups was given a reward for the correct response from the start of training. The other groups were not rewarded. The rewarded group showed a gradual decline in errors over a number of trials. The nonrewarded groups gave only the slightest evidence of learning; however, when reward was introduced for these groups after different numbers of "acquisition" trials, they then showed a precipitous drop in errors, quickly reaching the level of the group that had been rewarded from the beginning of the experiment. Tolman's interpretation, of course, was that the nonrewarded groups had developed expectancies or formed "cognitive maps" of the maze, and once the reward was first encountered they knew how to get to it on the next trial. It is apparent how the latent learning experiment would lead to the formation of the distinction between learning and performance that we discussed in Chapter 4 (*see* Kimble, 1961 and Mackintosh, 1974, for a review of the latent learning literature).

Tolman's interpretation of animal behavior, while interesting, was certainly not persuasive to most investigators. Responses could be seen and measured. Expectancies were unseen, could not be directly measured, and somehow seemed vague. Thus, the S–R and anticipatory response interpretations dominated experimental and theoretical activity. However, with the accumulating evidence that traditional S–R theories cannot explain a good deal of animal behavior and, in addition, with the apparent inability of incentive motivation theories to completely fill the gap, there has been a recent resurgence of interest in the cognitive approach. For example, in the past few years we have had new cognitive theories offered by Irwin (1971), Bolles (1972), Seligman and Johnston (1973) and Boneau (1974). All these theories have in common the use, in some form, of the term expectancies to explain animal behavior. Let us now briefly examine what some of these recent cognitive theories have to say about instrumental learning.

Bolles's Theory

According to Bolles, what animals learn is that some stimuli (S) predict the occurrence of other biologically important stimuli or events (S*). The animals learn an expectancy that is congruent with the environmental S–S* contingency. The acquisition of these

S–S* expectancies is the principal learning that occurs in both Pavlovian and instrumental learning situations. The term expectancy itself means to Bolles simply the availability of stored information about these environmental contingencies.

The similarity of this type of expectancy to Bindra's S_1–S_2 association is apparent. However, Bolles adds a second type of expectancy that may be learned, an expectancy that corresponds to the predictive relationship that exists between an animal's own behavior (R) and the consequences of the behavior (S*).

Both Pavlovian conditioning and instrumental learning paradigms involve S–S* expectancies, and perhaps both involve R–S* expectancies, but the latter should be clearly more prominent in the instrumental situation in which the subject's response is much more effective in altering the environment. In fact, except for the differential importance of these two expectancies, Bolles now makes little distinction between Pavlovian conditioning and instrumental learning; there should be transfer between the two situations. Thus, the results of all of the transfer of control experiments previously discussed are clearly consistent with Bolles's assumptions.

Bolles' theory shares similarities with Tolman's earlier cognitive account, but there are also differences. The principal difference that we shall mention here concerns the nature of the expectancies learned. Recall that Tolman assumed that animals learned S–R–O expectancies, but Bolles makes no such assumption. Instead, Bolles assumes that the S–S* and R–S* contingencies are translated into behavior by the subject "synthesizing" the two in a "psychological syllogism" so that when stimulus (S) is present the subject engages in response (R) in order to obtain outcome (S*).

Another aspect of Bolles's theory is his assumption that animals may come into an experimental situation with previously learned or *innate* S–S* and R–S* expectancies. The existence of these prior expectancies may impose constraints upon what an animal may learn.

For example, we saw in the last chapter how Bolles uses the concept of a species-specific defense response (SSDR) to help explain avoidance learning. The SSDR may be considered a type of innate R–S* expectancy, an expectancy that freezing or fleeing will produce safety. If the experiment is such that some other response is required as the avoidance response, then the innate R–S* expectancy would interfere with avoidance learning. We will have more to say concerning biological constraints on learning later in this chapter.

Motivation comes into play in Bolles's theory through the value of S*. Bolles assumes that the probability of a response occurring is a function of three factors: the *value* of S* (motivational properties of S*); the strength of an S–S* expectancy; and the strength of an R–S* expectancy. Although Bolles has not yet specifically defined these functions, it may be assumed that the traditional variables that we have mentioned in the previous chapters are all important in determining these relationships.

Seligman and Johnston's Theory

Seligman and Johnston (1973) have developed a cognitive theory of avoidance learning. In their theory it is assumed that an organism retains information concerning contingencies between responses and outcomes in a given situation. The reader will recognize that this is again the S–R–O learning that typically characterizes the cognitive approach. It is the acquisition of information concerning the S–R–O contingencies that Seligman and Johnston refer to as an expectancy. It is also assumed in this theory that an animal has preferences. For example, in an avoidance situation it is assumed that an animal prefers no shock to shock. Given the capability of learning S–R–O contingencies and the existence of preferences, the behavior of an animal in an avoidance situation could be explained in the following way. As a function of its experience in the avoidance task, the animal develops an expectancy that if it responds within a given time period after the onset of a signal (or after the last response or shock in a Sidman paradigm), then it will not receive a shock. The animal may also learn the converse expectancy, that is, if it does not respond within a given time period, then shock will occur. Given the acquisition of these expectancies *plus* the preference for the no-shock outcome, the animal will perform the correct avoidance response. It is assumed that expectancies of either type are strengthened when they are confirmed and weakened when they are disconfirmed.

The cognitive theory of Seligman and Johnston does not rule out the possibility that an emotional response of fear is also involved in avoidance learning. In fact, the theory assumes that the CS does acquire the capacity to elicit fear. However, the theory denies that fear reduction has any reinforcing role in the acquisition of an avoidance response. Learning is on the basis of S–R–O expectancies, not on the basis of responses reinforced by fear reduction. If fear does have a role to play, it is through responses that may be elicited by the fear state, responses such as crouching or fleeing (cf., Blanchard & Blanchard, 1972).

One of the principal advantages of the cognitive account of avoidance learning is in the explanation of extinction. Extinction often takes place quite slowly when the standard extinction procedure of omitting shock is used. In terms of cognitive theory, this is to be expected if the animal is performing the avoidance response at a reasonable rate. This is so because the expectancy of receiving no shock if the response is made will continue to be confirmed, and the expectancy of receiving a shock if the response is not made will have little opportunity to be unconfirmed because the animal rarely fails to make the appropriate response in a well learned avoidance task (at least signaled avoidance tasks).

Other cognitive theories of animal behavior are similar in form to those discussed here, but make a greater use of logical expressions, particularly the logic of conditional probabilities. For a more detailed example of current cognitive theory, the reader should consult Irwin (1971). The flavor of Irwin's theory in its simplest form may be obtained from the Seligman and Johnston theory of avoidance learning; a cognitive theory that was modeled after Irwin's more comprehensive theory.

How much the new emphasis on cognitive processes will contribute to our understanding of elementary animal behavior remains to be seen. The renewed interest in this approach has come primarily from an inability of other approaches to adequately handle all of the available data rather than from any positive contributions from cognitive theory itself. A decision as to whether cognitive terminology or some modification or combinations of S–R and incentive theories will be able to provide the best account of "simple" animal behavior must await more research and more comprehensive theoretical efforts.

For now it may be said that cognitive accounts of behavior do not seem to have the depth nor would have been likely to generate as much research as the more traditional accounts. For example, to explain avoidance behavior in terms of expectancies seems much simpler than trying to account for all the factors that we did in Chapter 6. Is the complexity apparent in Chapter 6 misleading, is avoidance learning to be explained in much simpler terms as cognitive theory seems to imply, or is the apparent simplicity of the cognitive account misleading? At this stage of our knowledge we cannot say. However, the dangers of anthropomorphism seem to be greatest when the cognitive terminology is used, less when anticipatory response terminology is chosen, and least of all when animal behavior is described in S–R terms.

II. BIOLOGICAL PREDISPOSITIONS AND LEARNING

In the remainder of this chapter we shall consider some possible influences of inherent biological predispositions on learning in different species. It is well known that different species of animals differ in their sensory capacities—bats are capable of hearing very high frequency sounds, bees perceive ultraviolet light and polarizations in light, moths are able to detect olfactory stimuli in minute amounts, etc. Similarly, it is obvious that animals differ in their response repertoires—rats may swim, but not as well as fish, and rats are able to grasp objects but they do not have the dexterity of monkeys. These sensory and motor abilities place limits on what an organism may be able to do. However, in the laboratory investigation of animal learning it has often been assumed, at least implicitly, that once these sensory-motor differences were circumvented by selecting perceivable stimuli and responses within the capabilities of the organism, then the fundamental laws of *learning* discovered would be similar for all species investigated. Seligman and Hager (1972) have termed this general assumption the *equipotentiality premise:* the premise that, in Pavlovian conditioning, it matters little what stimuli are selected for the CS and UCS, that all CSs and UCSs are associated with more or less equal facility; and the premise that in instrumental learning ". . . all emitted responses and reinforcers can be associated about equally well . . . . (Seligman & Hager, 1972, p. 2)."

Recently, there has been a convergence of data from both ethological investigations and laboratory research challenging the equipotentiality principle—data which indicate that more attention must be given to biological constraints operating on the organism in the learning situation. In a way, this new emphasis on biological constraints is really another version of the nature-nurture issue. The present framework views the interaction between nature and nurture in terms of innate predispositions that the organism brings into the learning situation. These predispositions influence the ease with which the organism is able to learn the various tasks and associations posed by the experimenter.

Before going into Seligman's theoretical analysis of innate predispositions (Seligman, 1970; Seligman & Hager, 1972), let us first examine some of the experimental evidence that has required the consideration of biological influences on the associative process. We shall mention evidence from a number of experimental situations, some of which we have discussed at other places in this text.

Learning with Long Delays of Reinforcement

Evidence presented in the previous chapter showed clearly that animals are able to associate gastrointestinal disturbances with substances they had tasted several hours previously. The delays over which learning will occur in the conditioned aversion paradigm appear to be sharply different from the delays that will support learning in standard laboratory paradigms involving operant or choice chambers. This difference in the delay of reward function (cf., Figure 4–9, and 7–10, on pp. 109 and 227) has led to the hypothesis that associations important for the survival of the animal in its natural environment may show different temporal characteristics depending upon the nature of the stimuli to be associated.

Stimulus Salience

Conditioned aversion experiments have provided an especially good example of species differences in stimulus salience. Recall (from Chapter 7) that rats are far more likely to associate gastrointestinal disturbances with taste stimuli than with visual or auditory stimuli, whereas quail are more likely to associate such disturbances with visual stimuli than with taste stimuli. These differential likelihoods of stimuli entering into associations seem to be related to the ecological niche and sensory biases of the organisms.

There are other data showing stimulus selection in animal learning, data which clearly indicate that not all stimuli are equally likely to be associated with a given event in a given species. For example, Shettleworth (1972) paired a compound light-noise stimulus with a shock delivered to chicks when they drank quinine-flavored water. After a number of training trials with the compound, the single stimulus elements (light and noise) were presented separately to the chicks. The data showed that only the visual component of the compound had acquired suppressive properties over drinking. Control experiments indicated that this difference was probably not related to perceptual effects of the stimuli in that the chickens appeared to notice the auditory stimuli as much as the visual stimuli.

In another experiment by Shettleworth separate groups of chicks were exposed to the punishment paradigm described above; one group of these chicks had a visual cue paired with the shock, and another group had an auditory cue paired with the shock. Again, only the visual cue acquired suppressive properties over drinking behavior.

Thus, with stimuli presented either singly or in compound, chicks seem to more readily associate visual than auditory cues with the receipt of a shock for drinking. These differences appeared in the absence of any apparent attentional differences related to the two stimulus modalities. Shettleworth's interpretation of these data was that ". . . chicks are *prepared* to associate visual stimuli with some immediate consequence of drinking or pecking (Shettle-worth, 1972, p. 232, italics added)."

A similar example of stimulus selection has been shown in experiments using dogs as subjects (Dodrzecka, Szwejkowska, & Konorski, 1966). In this experiment, the subjects were exposed to auditory discriminative stimuli that differed in quality (buzzer versus metronome) or in directionality (source in front or behind the dog) and trained on different tasks. When the dogs could obtain rewards by placing the left paw on a platform as a response to one stimulus and the right paw on a platform as a response to a second stimulus, they seemed to be able to learn the task only when the stimuli differed in directionality. Differences were less clear when the task was a go–no–go paradigm (respond in the presence of stimulus A, do not respond in the presence of stimulus B); under these conditions most dogs seemed to selectively attend to qualitative differences in the stimuli rather than directionality differences, although some animals learned about both types of stimuli.

As a final example of stimulus selectivity in learning we will briefly mention some data concerning bird-song. Some species of birds sing innately. That is, they do not need to be exposed to the song of their species—even if raised in isolation, they will sing the species-typical song at maturation. However, other species must have some exposure to bird-song during a sensitive period during their early life if they are to make other than rudimentary sounds in adulthood. Of particular interest here is the behavior some birds (e.g., chaffinches and white crowned sparrows) which, if exposed to the song of their own species and the songs of other species, seem to selectively learn the song of their own species (cf., Thorpe, 1963; Marler, 1970; Eibl-Eibesfeldt, 1970). In these birds a learning experience is necessary, but there appears to be a preparedness to learn a particular thing.

These examples of stimulus salience indicate that not all stimuli are equipotential as far as associative learning is concerned. Some stimuli are more readily associated with certain events, and this differential ease of associability appears to be related to the ecological niche of the organism.

Response Predispositions

Earlier in this chapter we described how birds exposed to a Pavlovian contingency of response-disc illumination followed by grain delivery will learn to peck at the key even though no instrumental contingency is involved. This phenomenon of *autoshaping* has indicated that the key-peck response of pigeons is not the arbitrarily selected operant response parallel to the lever-press response of rats, as it has often been assumed to be. Instead it appears that there is a "... species-specific tendency of the pigeon to peck at the things it looks at (Brown & Jenkins, 1968, p. 7)." Autoshaping is important in the present context because there is evidence that some of the principles or laws of reinforcement discovered with the key-peck response in pigeons may not be applicable to more arbitrarily selected instrumental responses (e.g., Hemmes, 1973; Williams & Williams, 1969).

Other data concerning the relationship between the effects of reinforcement and the animal's natural response repertoire were recently obtained by Shettleworth (1975). Shettleworth observed the behavior of golden hamsters (*Mesocricetus auratus*) in an open field under conditions of both ad-libitum food availability and food deprivation. She found that some behaviors such as rearing up on the hind legs, scratching on the wall, and walking around or standing still and sniffing were increased by food deprivation, whereas other behaviors such as face-washing, scratching the body, and scent-marking were decreased by food deprivation. She then selected some of these responses for instrumental reinforcement with a food reward. She found that those responses that were increased in frequency by food deprivation were much more sensitive to the reinforcing effects of a food reward. Responses such as face-washing or scent-marking showed virtually no increase in frequency when a food reward was made contingent on their performance.

These data clearly indicate again that not all responses in the repertoire of an animal are equally sensitive to the effects of a reinforcer. Shettleworth's interpretation of these data is consistent with our presentation of Bindra's theory earlier in this chapter. That is, she suggests that behaviors that would normally occur in a hungry animal in anticipation of food may also be released by presentation of a conditioned incentive stimulus. Of particular relevance to the present topic is that not all behaviors are equally facilitated, there is a strong bias toward the facilitation of those responses the animal is predisposed to make when food deprived.

These data and their interpretation are reminiscent of some earlier observations of Breland and Breland (1961) derived from their experiences in training assorted animals for commercial television productions, department store displays, etc. The Brelands trained animals with food reinforcement to engage in arbitrary but entertaining behaviors such as raccoons "saving" money in a piggy bank, or chickens playing baseball. Although somewhat successful in instigating these behaviors into the animals' repertoire, the Brelands had trouble maintaining the responses because of interference from "natural food-getting behaviors of the different species." For example, the raccoons, instead of engaging in the rewarded be- havior of depositing coins in the piggy bank, began to spend inor- dinate amounts of time rubbing the coins together. The chickens, instead of manipulating the bat as they had been trained to do, began chasing and pecking at the moving baseball.

Interestingly, in the light of Shettleworth's data, the Brelands found that increasing the deprivation of the animals only increased the intensity of the interfering behavior, behavior that actually pre- vented them from obtaining reinforcement (this effect is quite similar to the results of Williams & Williams on negative auto- maintenance, 1969). As a result of their attempts at the operant training of a variety of responses, the Brelands concluded that ". . . the behavior of any species cannot be adequately understood, predicted, or controlled without knowledge of its instinctive patterns, evolutionary history, and ecological niche (Breland & Breland, 1961, p. 684)."

Other data consistent with the importance of response reper- toires come from the realm of avoidance learning. As we saw in Chapter 6, Bolles's interpretation of avoidance learning is that we must take into account any species-specific defense responses (SSDRs) in the repertoire of the animal being investigated if we are to understand its avoidance performance. Thus, rats may do well on passive avoidance, jump-out avoidance, or one-way shuttle avoid- ance because such laboratory paradigms are consistent with the SSDRs of freezing or fleeing. Other avoidance paradigms not con- sistent with the inherent predispositions of the rat take much longer to learn. If Bolles's interpretation is correct, then avoidance behavior, like autoshaping, reminds us that statements about gen- eral rates of learning cannot be made without some consideration of response predispositions that the animal brings into the laboratory situation.

Thus, contrary to Skinner's statement that "the general topog- raphy of operant behavior is not important . . . . (Skinner, 1938, p. 45)," the data briefly reviewed here indicate that response topog- raphy is quite important for the interpretation of apparently learned behavior.

Preparedness

Seligman's interpretation of these and other data indicating biolog- ical influences in the learning paradigm revolves around a concept of *preparedness* (Seligman, 1970; Seligman & Hager, 1972). Be- cause of the evolutionary history of its species, argues Seligman, an organism may enter an experimental situation more or less prepared to associate the contingencies between stimuli or the contingencies between responses and outcomes required by that particular experimental paradigm. If the organism is prepared to make the required associations, then learning will proceed rapidly; if the organism is unprepared, then learning will be slow; if the organism is contraprepared by its evolutionary history, then learning will be very slow or impossible.

For the most part, the concept of a continuum of preparedness is clearly post hoc. However, it provides a potentially useful framework for further investigations into biological influences on learning. For example, Seligman argues that we may want to consider whether or not different laws of learning covary with the dimension of preparedness (ease of conditionability). The data on delay of reinforcement suggest that this may be the case (*but see* Krane & Wagner, 1975, for other interpretations). Seligman suggests that we may also want to consider whether different physiological mechanisms may underlie the dimension of preparedness, or whether different cognitive mechanisms may covary with the dimension. The idea of a continuum of preparedness in animal learning may also be consonant with approaches to language learning in humans (cf., Lenneberg, 1969), with an approach to the understanding of the functions of human cognition as a mechanism for dealing with unprepared contingencies (*see* Furth, 1969), and as an approach to phobic neurosis (Seligman, 1971).

Whether or not a dimension of preparedness turns out to be the best way to conceptualize biological influences on behavior, the data that we have reviewed in this section make it clear that such influences exist and must be taken into account if we are to develop a full understanding of the mechanisms of learning (*see* Seligman & Hager, 1972; and Hinde & Stevenson-Hinde, 1973, for more complete reviews of biological influences on learning).

In the next chapter we shall cover in some detail the effects of differential early experience on later performance in learning situations as well as some of the results obtained with behavior genetic studies and imprinting experiments. All of these manipulations represent other ways of examining the relationship between biological factors and the effects of experience.

III. SUMMARY

In this chapter we have examined some of the historically prominent theoretical interpretations of instrumental learning. We have seen that the stimulus-response interpretation is not consistent with much of the recent data, particularly the transfer of control experiments. These latter experiments have demonstrated that the contingency learning that takes place in the Pavlovian conditioning paradigm has clear influences on instrumental behavior. The implication of the transfer of control experiments is that such Pavlovian conditioning normally occurs in the context of all instrumental learning situations and is an important part of instrumental behavior.

This relationship between Pavlovian conditioning and instrumental learning is consistent with some of the assumptions of the Hull-Spence version of the S–R approach; however, other data have indicated that an incentive motivational theory based on learned contingencies between stimuli may be the more fruitful approach at the present time. Many of the results of transfer of control experiments can be explained by assuming that the transfer demonstrated in these experiments is due to complementary or contrary incentive motivational states present in the Pavlovian and instrumental phases of such experiments.

The experiments that cannot be so explained seem to demand a cognitive approach, at least in the sense that a Pavlovian CS may have signaling properties that go beyond the specific affective qualities of the UCS it signals. That is, animals may learn the more abstract concept that the CS^+ signals an impending occurrence of something and a CS^- signals the absence of something. Because of this possibility and because of the apparent failure of S–R theory to handle recent data, cognitive interpretations of animal behavior are becoming increasingly popular.

Another recent development has been the realization that the evolutionary history of the organism being investigated may importantly determine its performance in a learning situation. Different species may find it easier to *associate* some stimuli than other stimuli, despite the fact that all the stimuli involved are perceivable. Similarly, some responses, although they are in the animals' repertoire, are much less susceptible to the effects of food reinforcers than other responses. These data have indicated that inferences concerning fundamental learning process obtained with "unprepared" or "contraprepared" relationships may not apply to the learning of relationships for which the organism is "prepared."

CHAPTER 9

Developmental and Genetic Influences on Instrumental Behavior

---

... all aspects of an organism may be thought of as 100 percent genetic but not 100 percent determined.

B.E. Ginsburg

In the preceding chapters, we have analyzed behavioral data for the purpose of developing principles concerning the nature of learning. These principles can be viewed as being analogous to themes in a musical composition in that they provide the underlying structure upon which variations are imposed. The variations of a musical theme could consist of modulations in tempo and key while variations upon a learning principle could involve modulations in the topography, vigor, and persistance of a behavior. Thus, although the principles which underlie learning may be shared by all organisms, there will be variability in the manner in which learning is manifested.

Psychologists generally attempt to reduce or limit the variability between subjects of an experiment by holding constant those factors which may contribute to individual differences. Some widely used methods for limiting what has been termed *between subjects variability* consist of using subjects of the same species, age, and sex that have been housed under identical conditions. However, there are a host of other factors, some being quite subtle, that can also contribute to individual differences. These factors can include, for example, an organism's genetic endowment, the type of environment in which it is raised, the amount of stimulation it receives when an infant, and particular characteristics of its mother.

This chapter will consider a number of factors that contribute to individual differences, and thus may influence behavior in situations designed to assess learning. The discussion will show that behavior may be influenced by events occurring prior to and throughout an organism's life. We hope to demonstrate that a study of learning must include an appreciation of the forces acting upon an organism throughout its existence. The development of this appreciation requires a survey of developmental variables, which should provide insights into the type of control procedures that must be considered in experiments dealing with the analysis of behavior.

I. PRENATAL FACTORS
Species-Specific Behavior

The genetic makeup or *genotype* determines, to a great extent, the structure and function of bodily tissue. Given a particular genotype, an animal's fur may be of a certain color and texture; the animal may have a degenerated retina, its brain may lack a corpus callosum, or it may be deficient with respect to certain biochemical constituents of the central nervous system. Observable characteristics that result from the action of genes are known as *phenotypes*.

In addition to controlling the elaboration of structure and function of tissue or perhaps because of such control, genes are involved in the elaboration of particular behaviors that are specific to a given species. These behaviors are considered by many *not* to be a result of learning, but rather the manifestation of a "prewired" or "preprogrammed" disposition to respond in a particular fashion to particular stimuli. Recall the example given in Chapter 1. The male stickleback will display courtship activities only toward a stimulus approximating the swollen abdomen of a gravid female. One can say, then, that the male stickleback is endowed with a predisposition to respond to a certain stimulus. Put another way, the male is *prepared* to respond to the stimulus without prior training.

Although there are a multitude of species-specific behaviors that are amenable to laboratory investigation, one such behavior has received a great deal of attention. Newly hatched birds of certain precocial species (i.e., birds that are relatively mature at hatching) will follow, within the first few days of life, the first moving object to which they are exposed. The normal result of this process known as *imprinting* is that the hatchling will follow an adult member of its own species, usually the mother. However, the hatchling will follow other moving objects should they be the first such objects encountered immediately following hatching. These objects can include such things as a moving replica of an adult of its species, a human, cardboard boxes, balls, etc.

Heinroth (1910) has decribed the behavior of goslings hatched in an incubator and exposed initially only to humans:

> They look at you without betraying any signs of fear; and, if you handle them briefly, you can hardly shake them off. They peep pitifully if you walk away, and soon will follow you about religiously. I have known such a little creature to be content if it could squat under the chair on which I sat, a few hours after I had taken it from the

incubator. If you then take such a gosling to a goose family with young of the same age, the situation usually develops as follows: Goose and gander look suspiciously at the approaching person, and both try to get themselves and their young into the water as quickly as they can. If you walk towards them very rapidly, so that the young have no chance to escape, the parents, of course, put up a spirited defense. This is the time to place the small orphan among the brood and leave in a hurry. In the excitement, the parents at first regard the newcomer as their own and show an inclination to defend it as soon as they see and hear it in human hands. But the worst is yet to come. It does not even occur to the young gosling to treat the two birds as geese. It runs away, peeping loudly and, if a human being happens to pass by, it follows him: it simply looks upon humans as its parents (Heinroth, 1910, p. 594).

Konrad Lorenz (1937) has tried to draw a sharp dichotomy between imprinting and what he terms "associative learning" on the basis of three tenets: (1) Imprinting can be established only during a restricted period in an animal's life, encompassing the first few posthatching days. (Learning, on the other hand, can occur at any stage of development, given that the organism is capable of performing the desired response and that the reward is appropriate.)

(2) Once imprinting occurs it is irreversible. "Once their instinctive social reactions are transposed to a human being, their behavior does not change in the least even if they are kept for years with other members of their own species and without human company (Lorenz, 1957, p. 105)." (Yet we have seen that behavior resulting from a process of learning is far from irreversible; it can be altered by changing the reinforcement contingency or extinguished by withholding reinforcement.) Lorenz also states that many aspects of adult behavior that are not functional when imprinting takes place are exhibited when the organism reaches maturity. For example, the male parakeet can be imprinted to a human soon after hatching. However, it will display courtship activities toward the human only at a much later time, after having attained sexual maturity. (A comparable example cannot be offered for a behavior considered to be learned.)

(3) Imprinting differs from associative learning in that the former involves a response (following) directed not toward the particular imprinting object but rather toward a class of such objects, e.g., if a bird is imprinted to its mother, it will also follow other adult birds of that species. (Apparently Lorenz believed that such a phenomenon does not exist for learned behaviors, yet it is obvious that the principle of stimulus generalization makes this distinction between imprinting and learning rather tenuous.)

Given that certain behaviors such as the following-response of birds and the courtship activities of the male stickleback have been classified as being innate, one can ask whether this precludes the study of such behavior within the framework of learning principles. That is, do those principles which have been formulated to describe learning have any bearing upon innate behaviors? Apparently, for certain behaviors, the answer is yes. A male Siamese fighting fish will display a rather complex series of activities in response to the sight of another male or to its own image in a mirror. This sequence of acts, consisting of approaches, undulating movements, and the erection of fins and gill covers, is known as *aggressive-display*.

As you recall from Chapter 2, Thompson and Sturm (1965) have demonstrated that aggressive-display can be classically conditioned to a formerly neutral stimulus. Their procedure was a simple one. The onset of a light (CS) was paired with the presentation of a mirror (UCS). After a number of such pairings, aggressive-display was exhibited in response to the light. Furthermore, a stimulus that can elicit aggressive-display can function as a reinforcer for instrumental behavior (Thompson, 1963). The fish learned the correct path through an underwater maze when the correct response was reinforced by the sight of its mirror image or of a moving model of a male in an aggressive-display posture. The possibility should be noted that the *exhibition* of aggressive-display, rather than the sight of a male, may have served as the reward for the instrumental response.

Imprinting has also been studied in relationship to principles of learning. Moltz (1968) asked why birds will *continue* to follow the imprinting object after the critical period for the establishment of imprinting has terminated. It was proposed that the birds continue to follow because the imprinting object serves to reduce fear which normally is generated by the imprinting situation, perhaps because of its novelty. Thus, fear reduction reinforces the *instrumental response* of following. Moltz's proposal led to the prediction that the amount of following should be directly related to the amount of fear produced by the imprinting situation.

This prediction was tested in two ways. First, fear of the imprinting apparatus was manipulated by subjecting ducklings to painful electric shock after they had been imprinted to a cardboard cube (Moltz, Rosenblum, & Halikas, 1959). One group received shock in the imprinting apparatus (the imprinting object had been removed), while the other was shocked in a discriminably different apparatus. Two additional groups were treated similarly except that they never received shock. The results showed that the birds that received shock in the imprinting apparatus exhibited more following than did any of the other three groups.

A second prediction based upon the fear reduction proposal was that a decrease in the fear-arousing property of the imprinting situation should produce a decrease in the following response. This was tested by permitting one group of ducklings to explore the imprinting apparatus prior to the introduction of the imprinting object (Moltz & Rosenblum, 1958). This procedure essentially let the ducklings habituate to the apparatus, ostensibly reducing the fear evoked by novelty. A second group of ducklings had no such experience. The results of this experiment showed that the animals given pre-imprinting exposure to the apparatus spent less time following the imprinting object than did the animals not given such exposure.

It is apparent that certain behaviors may be termed *innate* because of the spontaneity with which they are initially displayed. Siamese fighting fish exhibit aggressive-display the first time they see another fighting fish, while certain avian species will tend to follow the first moving object to which they are exposed. Although the *initiation* of such behavior is fixed prior to hatching by the animal's genetic makeup, the *maintenance* of the behaviors may involve, in part, processes that have been shown to be related to learned behavior. As such, it may be best not to categorize behavior in terms of an "innate" versus "learned" dichotomy but rather in terms of those aspects of the behavior that *may be* innate and those aspects that *may be* learned. In any event, it is apparent that a number of behaviors are present within an organism's repertoire as a result of its genetic endowment and that these behaviors initially do not possess the plasticity associated with behaviors that are said to be learned.

Learning Ability as a Phenotype

During the early part of this century researchers began to ask whether learning ability is a phenotype. That is, is the observable capacity to learn determined by one's genotype? Perhaps the earliest data bearing upon this question are those of Bagg (1916). He used mice of various strains, the strains being differentiated by coat color. The number of errors made in learning a complex maze were compared between the strains. It was found that mice with yellow coats made an average of 2.0 errors for the last 15 trials, whereas mice of the other strains made an average of 0.9 errors.

Much work has since been devoted to elucidating the possible role that heredity may play in influencing learning ability. Two procedures typically have been used to make such an assessment: *selective breeding* and *strain comparison.*

The selective breeding procedure consists of separating a group

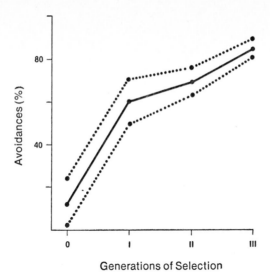

Figure 9–1. Selective breeding for avoidance learning in the mouse (Swiss Webster strain). Each point represents the performance reached at the end of five 100-trial sessions (solid line). Dotted lines show the variability about each point. (From Bovet et al., 1969, © Am. Assoc. Adv. Science.)

of animals into subgroups on the basis of their performance on a particular task. The animals of each subgroup are then bred amongst themselves with the progeny subsequently tested on the task used to differentiate the subgroups. The oldest and probably best known example of the selective breeding procedure comes from the work of Tryon (1929, 1940). A group of rats was separated into subgroups on the basis of the number of errors they made in learning a complex 17-unit maze for food reinforcement. The subgroups consisted of rats that made relatively few errors and rats that made relatively many errors. The "high-error" animals were then bred with one another as were the "low-error" animals. This procedure was repeated generation after generation. It was found that by the 22nd generation there was little overlap between the error scores of the two subgroups. The progeny of the original low-error animals made few errors while those of the high-error animals made many errors in the 17-unit maze. These subgroups, which are still available, are known as Maze Bright (designated S_1) and Maze Dull (S_3) rats.

In an attempt to determine the factors which mediated the difference in performance between the S_1 and S_3 animals, Tryon asked whether they differed in sensory capacity. He rearranged the various units of the maze, interchanged parts, etc. The results provided no support for the sensory hypothesis in that the Dulls continued to make significantly more errors. Tryon then analyzed the error patterns of individual animals. From this analysis he concluded that the Brights were superior to the Dulls in generalizing patterns of the maze. That is, Brights could learn general patterns of direction better than could the Dulls.

A finding similar to Tryon's was presented by Heron (1941) who also selected for errors in a complex maze and then, through selective breeding, generated bright and dull animals. By the 16th generation they made an average of 46.9 and 116.0 errors in the complex maze, respectively. Similarly, Bovet, Bovet-Nitti, and Oliverio (1969) showed that through a selective breeding procedure the number of errors mice made in an avoidance learning situation could be reduced. The results of their experiment are shown in Figure 9–1.

The strain comparison procedure has been used more often than has the selective breeding procedure to study the relationship of genotype to learning. The strain comparison procedure consists of comparing the behavior of animals that are already known to differ genotypically. It should be noted that strains are established and maintained by a procedure known as *inbreeding*, consisting of mating brothers and sisters for a number of generations. The mouse is an extremely useful species for such comparisons because of the wide variety of available strains.

Results obtained from the strain comparison procedure generally have shown that animals of different genotypes may differ in what has been interpreted to be learning ability. For example, Bovet et al. (1969) placed mice of nine different strains into a shuttle box apparatus. Avoidance of electric shock required an animal to run to the other side of the chamber within 5 seconds after the onset of a light. The results are shown in Figure 9–2. As can be seen, three strains were quite poor in acquiring the avoidance response, four strains were intermediate, and two others acquired the response relatively rapidly.

In an additional experiment, other mice of the same nine strains were tested in a complex maze. The results of this experiment are presented in Figure 9–3. Again it is apparent that there are differences in the number of errors made as a function of strain. Interestingly, there seems to be a relationship between avoidance learning and maze learning in that mice of strains that made relatively few errors in the active avoidance situation also made fewer errors in the complex maze task.

Results obtained from studies using both the selective breeding and strain comparison procedure have shown that organisms do

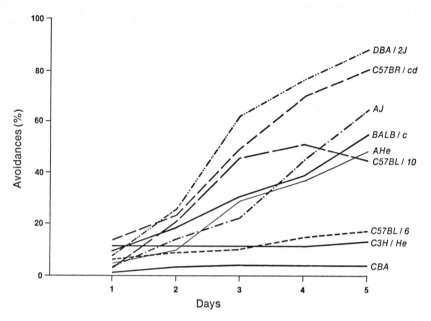

Figure 9–2. Avoidance conditioning of nine strains of inbred mice during five consecutive daily sessions of 100 trials. (From Bovet et al., 1969, © Am. Assoc. Adv. Science.)

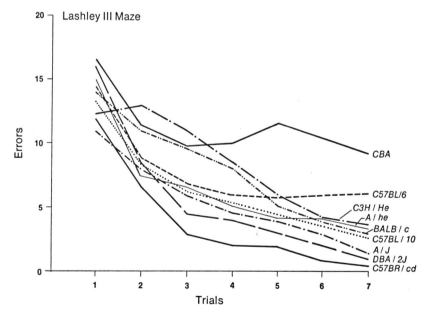

Figure 9–3. Maze learning in nine strains of inbred mice. Each point represents the mean errors of sixteen mice given one daily trial for ten consecutive days. (From Bovet et al., 1969, © Am. Assoc. Adv. Science.)

differ with respect to particular aspects of behavior displayed in learning situations, and that this difference can be attributed in part to genotype. These data have been used to support the notion that learning ability is genetically determined. However, the results of other experiments suggest that an interpretation of the role of genes based solely upon *learning ability* may have to be qualified.

Instead of (or in addition to) affecting one's ability to learn, genes may influence the way in which one reacts to the environment and in so doing may affect *performance*. You will recall that learning has been defined as a relatively permanent change in behavior resulting from practice. By exclusion, then, other changes in behavior will reflect performance. The influence of genes also can be dealt with in terms of learning and performance factors. For example, if the ability to learn is directly related to the number of cells in the cerebral cortex, and if a particular genotype leads to the differentiation of fewer of such cells, one could conclude that that genotype does affect learning (i.e., a learning variable).

But if a certain genotype is responsible for altering the way in which an organism perceived its environment, one could conclude that the genes have affected performance. For example, suppose that animals of one genotype do not see as well as do animals of another genotype. This could certainly affect performance in a learning situation without at all affecting learning ability or, in a global sense, intellectual capacity. As another example, suppose animals of a particular genotype are more fearful of novel learning situations than are genotypically dissimilar animals. Given the characteristics of the learning situation, the increased fearfulness or emotionality may enhance or retard behavior by influencing performance rather than learning. It is quite common to be approached by a student claiming that because of nervousness the performance on an examination was not a reflection of what had been learned. Frequently, this is indeed the case, but one should not ignore the possibility that the degree of nervousness is related to the amount of learning.

Searle (1949) compared Maze Bright and Maze Dull rats in a variety of learning situations. In one such comparison it was found that the Dulls actually made fewer errors than did the Brights in learning to escape from a maze that was partially submerged in water. It was also found that the number of errors made by Dulls in a complex maze could be reduced by altering a characteristic of the maze itself. In order to automatically record an animal's response at a choice point in the 17-unit maze, Tryon used switches in the floor that were activated by an animal's weight. Thus, at many points in the maze the floor was unstable. Searle reported that the Dulls made fewer errors when tested in a complex maze that did not make use of floor switches. As a result of these and of other findings, Searle concluded:

> No evidence was found that a difference exists between Brights and Dulls in the learning capacity per se. A detailed study of the behavior profiles indicated that Brights are characteristically food-driven, economical of distance, low in motivation to escape from water, and timid in response to open spaces. Dulls are relatively distinterested in food, average or better in water motivation, and timid of mechanical apparatus features. It is concluded that brightness and dullness in the original Tryon Maze may be accounted for in large part by such motivational and emotional patterns (Searle, 1949, p. 323).

The results of studies employing the strain comparison procedure also have shown that a difference in reactivity to the test situation may account, in part, for observed differences between strains of animals. Carran, Yeudall, and Royce (1964) reported that mice of strain C_3H learned to actively avoid electric shock more quickly than did mice of strain C58. However, as the intensity of the shock was increased, differences in the rate of learning between the strains decreased. This finding led the investigators to ask whether the basis for the differential learning rate might be due to differential reactivity to shock. To test this possibility, the resistance of the skin was used as a measure of reactivity; the greater the change in resistance in response to shock, the more reactive or emotional the animal. The rapid avoidance learners exhibited a greater change in skin resistance than did the slower learners. It was concluded that C_3H animals learned more quickly because to them the situation was perceived as being more aversive. This explanation also agrees with the finding that an improvement of the avoidance performance of the "slow learners" was obtained following an increase in the intensity of the shock.

Duncan, Grossen, and Hunt (1971) also have performed a study that bears upon the question of whether genotype affects performance or learning. In one experiment, mice of strains C_3H and DBA were placed in an apparatus that provided an electric shock *contingent* upon the animal's response of stepping off a platform. After receiving one such shock, the mouse was returned to its home cage and tested later. A test consisted of again placing the animal in the apparatus and recording the amount of time taken to step off the platform. Presumably, the longer an animal stayed on the platform the more it had learned or remembered about the initial experience. An additional group of C_3H and DBA mice were also used. Mice of this group were treated identically *except* that their initial exposure to the avoidance apparatus consisted of being placed directly upon the electrified floor rather than upon the platform. Thus, the receipt of shock for these animals was *not* contingent upon the response of stepping off the platform.

The data from animals in the contingent condition (initial receipt of shock given as a consequence of stepping off the platform) revealed that the C_3H mice stayed on the platform longer than did the DBAs. However, C_3H mice in the noncontingent condition (initially placed directly upon the electrified floor) also stayed on the platform longer than did the DBA mice. If the noncontingent condition had not been incorporated into the experimental design, one would have concluded that the C_3H animals are better passive avoidance learners than are mice of strain DBA. However, the results obtained from animals in the noncontingent condition make this conclusion only partially justified.

The fact that C_3H animals that were exposed to a noncontingent situation, a situation that should not have produced learning, also spent more time on the platform during the test than did DBA mice (although less time than did mice of the contingent condition) suggests that differential reactivity to the fear-evoking stimulus (shock) also may be a factor mediating differences in passive avoidance behavior between the two strains. That is, the punishment and thus the avoidance learning situation may be more aversive to the C_3H mice; hence, these mice may be more emotional during the avoidance test. It is known that rats and mice will tend to remain motionless when frightened. This, of course, would be beneficial in the passive avoidance situation since it would serve to keep the animals on the platform. By the same logic, increased emotionality should be detrimental to active avoidance behavior. Indeed, although C_3H mice are superior to DBA mice on a passive avoidance task, they are inferior to DBAs on an active avoidance task.

The results of the experiments cited above demonstrate that genetic makeup can exert a profound influence upon certain behaviors assessed in learning situations. At this time, however, the mechanism through which genes exert their influence is unknown. It may be that genes actually modulate the *learning ability* of organisms. In that sense, an organism's genetic makeup may set a limit upon the amount that can be learned. On the other hand, genes may not influence intellectual capacity per se, but rather the manner in which the organism reacts to its environment. This means, then, that as a result of its genotype an animal might perform better or worse in a learning situation as a function of the nature of the task. If this is the case, one would not use global terms such as "bright" or "dull" to describe an animal, but rather one would describe the animal with respect to how it performs in par ticular situations (e.g., a slow passive avoidance learner, etc.). This approach also implies that one should be able to enhance or retard an animal's performance by manipulating certain aspects of the learning situation.

Regardless of how genes exert their influence, one thing is certain—the evolutionary legacy embodied in an organism's genetic inheritance can profoundly affect behavior. Since, under natural conditions, organisms are rarely genotypically identical, it follows that genes contribute to the variability commonly observed in the behavior of animals. In the final analysis, the selection pressures that act upon the gene pool will depend upon the performance of the organism within the prevailing environmental niche. Performance that enhances the probability of survival will be selected whether it be based upon greater learning capacity, enhanced sensory reactivity, or improved motor systems.

Prenatal Maternal Influences

Although the relationship between the mother and her offspring is an intimate one, an even more intimate relationship exists between a pregnant animal and its fetus. This is so because the pregnant animal provides virtually everything necessary for the maintenance of the fetus in addition to comprising the fetus' external environment. This intimacy suggests that the pregnant animal, under certain circumstances, may influence the fetus with this influence manifesting itself in the expression of postnatal behavior.

In order to study the influences that the adult may exert upon her progeny prior to their birth, one must deal with the question of *how* these influences can be assessed. How can one be certain that an independent variable actually is exerting its effect prior to, rather than subsequent to, birth? Suppose you discover that the administration of a certain drug to pregnant animals leads to a reduction in exploratory behavior of their offspring when the offspring are themselves adult. Could you then conclude that the drug exerted its influence prenatally upon the fetus? The answer is no because it is equally plausible that the drug exerted its effect postnatally.

For example, the drug may have produced long-term effects upon the physiology of the adult female causing a reduction in its milk yield. Thus, an alteration in the *postnatal* nutritional state of the young may have mediated the effect of the drug. The drug may have produced long-term effects upon the adult's behavior, manifesting itself in an alteration of maternal behavior. In that case, the effects of the drug may be mediated through a change in the interaction between the mother and its young—a postnatal effect. Therefore, to conclude that a variable has produced its effect prenatally, one must eliminate the possibility that the variable led to long-term consequences which ultimately produced postnatal effects.

One method that has been used to differentiate between pre- and postnatal effects of a variable is referred to as *cross-fostering*. Cross-fostering consists of removing the offspring at birth from some of the experimental mothers (i.e., those administered the variable during pregnancy) and replacing them with young removed at birth from the control mothers (i.e., those not administered the variable in question). In addition young from some of the control mothers are removed and replaced by young from experimental mothers. And finally, young are removed from some of the experimental mothers and replaced by young from other experimental mothers; and young removed from some of the control mothers are replaced by young from other control mothers. The cross-fostering procedure is summarized in Table 9–1.

If the variable in question is exerting its effect prenatally, the offspring born of control mothers and reared by experimental mothers (Group 6) should not differ from young born of *and* reared by control mothers (Group 4 and 5). Moreover, offspring born of and reared by experimental adults (Groups 1 and 2) should not differ from young born of experimental animals and reared by controls (Group 3). Thus, if a prenatal effect does exist, one would expect that Groups 1, 2 and 3 should differ from 4, 5 and 6. If, however, the independent variable affected the offspring postnatally, Groups 1, 2 and 6 should not differ from one another but should differ from Groups 3, 4, and 5.

The cross-fostering procedure poses one problem, that of assessing the effect of cross-fostering itself. It is possible that cross-

Table 9–1. *Cross-Fostering Procedure*

Group Number	Prenatal Environment	Postnatal Environment
1	born of experimental animal	reared by experimental animal
2	born of experimental animal	cross-fostered to experimental animal
3	born of experimental animal	cross-fostered to control animal
4	born of control animal	reared by control animal
5	born of control animal	cross-fostered to control animal
6	born of control animal	cross-fostered to experimental animal

fostering young between any two adults regardless of treatment will affect the later behavior of the offspring. This possibility can be assessed by comparing Group 1 to Group 2. Even though both of these groups of young were born of and reared by experimental mothers, the offspring of Group 2 were fostered to other experimental animals. Thus, if fostering itself does produce an effect, Group 1 and Group 2 animals should differ. The same type of comparison can be made between Groups 4 and 5. In many cases an experiment will employ more than one independent variable and a control condition (e.g., two different drugs and one placebo). To better understand the cross-fostering procedure, it may be useful for you to construct a table based upon three major treatment groups.

Typical of the data demonstrating prenatal maternal influences upon the offsprings' later behavior are those of Thompson (1957), who asked whether prenatal maternal "anxiety" could lead to an alteration of emotional reactivity of the progeny. Adult female rats were trained to avoid a footshock by running from one side of a compartment to another at the onset of a buzzer. Each animal was then mated after it had reached a pre-established level of avoidance performance. Three times a day throughout pregnancy each rat was put into the avoidance chamber, the buzzer was sounded, but the animal was not permitted to cross to the safe side. Although the animals were forced to remain in the section of the chamber in which they previously had received shock, they did *not* receive shock during this portion of the experiment. According to Thompson, this procedure produces anxiety since the animal is prevented from performing a response which it had learned would cope with the aversive situation. Other similar experiments have shown that such procedures lead to ulceration of the stomach lining.

A control group of rats was left undisturbed both prior to and during pregnancy. A cross-fostering design was used and, when 30–40 and 130–140 days of age, the progeny of the experimental and control mothers were tested for *emergence*. As mentioned previously, rats tend to exhibit little activity when they are frightened. One way to assess this fearfulness or emotional reactivity is to record the amount of time it takes a hungry animal to emerge from its home territory and enter a novel environment that contains food. Thompson found that at both test ages the animals born of prenatally stressed adults required more time to reach the food than did the animals born of the nonstressed mothers.

Another way to assess emotional reactivity is by placing an animal in an arena and recording the amount of activity (i.e., how far it walks) and the time it takes to initiate such activity. This is known as an *open field test*. Presumably, the more activity an animal exhibits the less emotional it is. Thompson reported that at both ages the offspring born of stressed animals exhibited a lesser amount of activity than did the offspring of controls. Furthermore, the former took longer to initiate the activity. That maternal anxiety exerted its effect prenatally was shown by the fact that offspring of controls that were fostered at birth to experimental mothers did not differ from animals born of and reared by control mothers. It is not known how prenatal "anxiety" exerts effects upon the fetus. It may be that a change in the hormone levels (e.g., adrenal corticoid hormones) of the adult as a result of exposure to the anxiety- or stress-provoking stimulus somehow affects the fetuses.

Ader and Conklin (1963) also have shown that handling of pregnant rats for 10 minutes, 3 times a day, throughout the course of the 22-day gestation period can affect the emotional reactivity of the offspring. Handling consisted of holding the adult loosely in the hand. The offspring of the handled rats generally exhibited less emotional reactivity as assessed in the open field test.

Ottinger and Simmons (1964) presented data which suggest that a relationship may exist between prenatal anxiety and postnatal behavior in the human. Pregnant women scoring high on a test that

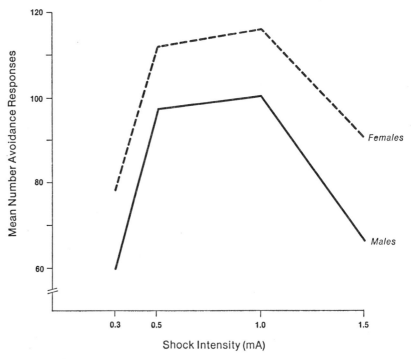

Figure 9–4.   Mean avoidance performance (out of 150 trials) by males and females at different shock intensities. (From Beatty & Beatty, 1970.)

presumably measured anxiety gave birth to infants that cried more than did the offspring of woman rated as "low-anxious." Although follow-up data were not reported, it is possible that the differences between infants of women rated as being high and low in anxiety may be maintained throughout development.

Hormones and Sexual Differentiation of Behavior

An organism's genetic makeup determines, among other things, whether its gonadal organs differentiate into ovaries or testes. The hormones produced and released by the gonads have been shown to act upon peripheral tissue leading to the development of secondary sexual characteristics such as distribution of body hair, muscle tone, fat deposits, etc. In addition to influencing the development of the physical characteristics of "femaleness" and "maleness," gonadal hormones also produce differences between the sexes with respect to particular behaviors. In addition to the obvious differences between males and females in sexual behavior, other, less obvious, differences between the sexes can be found for such di-

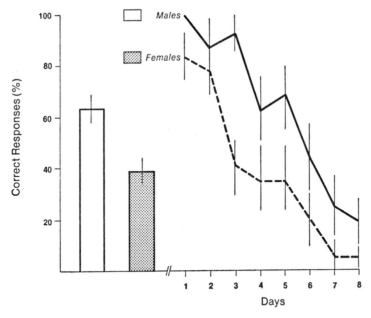

Figure 9-5. Passive-avoidance conditioning by males and females. The bars in the histogram represent the percentage correct responses (out of total trials). The curves on the right show retention of the passive avoidance behavior over days. The vertical bars indicate the standard error. (From Denti & Epstein, 1972.)

verse behaviors as aggression (Edwards, 1969), activity (Levine & Broadhurst, 1963), and the preference for sweet and salty tastes (Valenstein, Kakolewski, & Cox, 1967; Krecek, Novakova, & Stibral, 1972), among others. This section will be concerned with the sexual differentiation of avoidance behavior as an example of the procedures that can be used to assess sex differences in a learned behavior.

Levine and Broadhurst (1963) compared male and female rats on a variety of measures and reported that for one of the strains tested the females made more active avoidance responses than did the males. In a study designed specifically to investigate avoidance behavior, Beatty and Beatty (1970) compared the performance of adult male and female rats. The animals were required to learn an active avoidance task in order to avoid electric shock of various intensities. The results of this experiment revealed that the females made more avoidance responses than did the males at each of the four shock intensities (*see* Figure 9–4).

Superior performance of females on an active avoidance task also has been demonstrated by Denti and Epstein (1972). They reported, in addition, that male rats showed better performance on a *passive avoidance* task than did the females. These results are depicted in Figure 9–5. Thus, females appear to be superior on an active avoidance task whereas males are superior on a passive avoidance task.

One procedure for determining whether a sex difference in a morphological or behavioral characteristic is mediated by gonadal hormones is to administer, for example, the gonadal hormone principally released by the testes to females in the hope of modifying them in the direction of the male. This general procedure was followed by Beatty and Beatty (1970). They injected three-day-old female rats with testosterone, the principal hormone released by the testes, or with a placebo. At 90–105 days of age either the ovaries were surgically removed or an animal was subjected to a sham operation. Following the operations the animals were again administered gonadal hormones. Some of them received daily injections of testosterone, some received injections of estrogen, one of the principal hormones released by the ovaries, others were treated with the placebo. During the course of these injections the animals were given training in an active avoidance apparatus. The experimental design is summarized in Table 9–2, and the results are presented in Figure 9–6.

It can be seen that ovariectimized females that received testosterone during both infancy and adulthood (Group TOT) made fewer avoidance responses than did the animals of any other group.

Table 9–2. Treatments Administered to Groups of Female Rats

Group	n	Infant hormone treatment	Adult surgery	Adult hormone treatment
PCP	11	oil placebo	sham operation	oil placebo
POE	10	oil placebo	ovariectomy	estradiol
POP	10	oil placebo	ovariectomy	oil placebo
POT	11	oil placebo	ovariectomy	testosterone
TCP	9	testosterone	sham operation	oil placebo
TOE	9	testosterone	ovariectomy	estradiol
TOP	8	testosterone	ovariectomy	oil placebo
TOT	10	testosterone	ovariectomy	testosterone

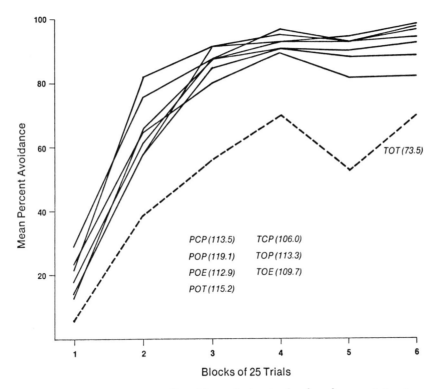

Figure 9–6. Acquisition of avoidance behavior by females receiving testosterone or oil neonatally and estradiol, testosterone, or oil in adulthood, as shown in Table 9–2. Only the ovariectomized females that received testosterone during infancy and adulthood (**TOT**) performed like males. (All other groups were equivalent and are drawn with the same symbols.) Figures in parentheses are mean number of avoidance responses out of 150 trials. (From Beatty & Beatty, 1970.)

Thus, females exposed to testosterone in a manner resembling the exposure normally received by males exhibited "masculinized" active avoidance responding. One would predict from these data that similar testosterone treatment should *facilitate* the passive avoidance behavior of females.

It is not as yet known how the presence or absence of the testicular hormone affects avoidance behavior. There are some data that suggest that the hormonal involvement in avoidance behavior may be mediated by a primary effect upon overall activity. It has been demonstrated that female rats are more active in an open field test than are males (cf., Denenberg et al., 1968) and that the administration of testosterone to females can reduce such activity (Rosenberg et al., 1971). A general increase in activity level could account for a facilitation of active and a retardation of passive avoidance responding.

II. POSTNATAL FACTORS

Postnatal Maternal Influence

The mother typically plays a dominant role in the rather limited world of the infant. Intuitively, then, one would expect that the mother could influence certain aspects of the behavior of her progeny. In order to determine whether the mother does exert such an influence, one must systematically "alter" particular characteristics of the mother, and observe the behavior of the offspring at a later time.

One such technique for changing the characteristics of the mother is known as *cross species fostering*. The technique is very simple, consisting of removing the natural mother and replacing her with a lactating animal of another species. Since the foster mother is of another species, her behavior toward the young should differ from that of the natural mother and may lead to certain alterations in the behavior of the young. Specifically, mice reared by rat mothers were compared to mice reared by mouse mothers (Denenberg, Hudgens, & Zarrow, 1964). It was found, in part, that rat-reared mice were less aggressive toward other mice and exhibited less activity in the open field test of emotional reactivity in adulthood than did mouse-reared mice. To determine whether the effects of cross species fostering were mediated through an altered nutritional state of the young (rat-reared mice were nourished on rat milk, whereas the controls were nourished on mouse milk), the procedure was changed to one euphemistically called the "rat aunt" procedure in which a nonlactating rat was housed with a lactating mouse and her brood (Rosenberg, Denenberg, and Zarrow, 1970). (Nonlactating rats can be induced to exhibit maternal activities by exposing them continuously to young for about six days. In this situation the rat will exhibit maternal behavior toward the young mice and even toward the mouse mother.) Since the young were now kept with a lactating mouse and a nonlactating rat, their nutritional state did not differ from that of young reared only in the presence of an adult mouse. The results obtained with this procedure are essentially the same as those obtained by using the rat mother preparation. Thus, altering the characteristics of a mother by substituting for the natural mother a lactating animal of another species can affect the offspring's later exhibition of social behavior and activity as assessed in an open field test.

Another way to study the influence of a mother on her offspring is to alter the mother without substituting another animal for her as was the case for cross species fostering. This type of approach has been taken to investigate the influence the mother may exert upon dietary selection of the young. Galef and Henderson (1972) tested the possibility that the mother can influence the food its offspring will choose to consume when they begin to ingest solid food. Lactating rats were removed from their young for three daily 1-hour periods, during which the adults were fed. Half of them were given a standard laboratory diet while the others were provided with a tastier food, one that is normally preferred over the standard diet. The young were subsequently tested for their preference by placing them in an apparatus that contained both diets. The tests, which lasted for 20 minutes, were given on postnatal days 17–23. It was found that the young whose mothers had consumed the standard, less preferred diet, ate more of it during the preference tests than did those whose mothers were fed the more preferred food during lactation. After eliminating the possibilities that the young learned something about the diets of their mothers by ingesting particles of food that may have clung to the adults following the daily feeding sessions or that information may have been conveyed to the young by the eating of fecal matter from the adult, Galef and Henderson concluded that whatever the nature of the information conveyed from the lactating animal to its brood, it is likely "transmitted" in the milk itself.[1]

The preceding discussion has shown that a lactating animal can influence certain types of behavior of its offspring. Although the lactating animal does represent the dominant force in the environ-

---

1. This cross-generational transfer of information may be a rather general phenomenon. Recall, for example, the dietary selection of moths described in Chapter 1.

ment of the infant, there are other components of the environment that also can influence behavior. The following section will consider the relationship between the environment and certain aspects of behavior.

Environmental Stimuli

The behavior of pregnant and lactating animals involves a number of species-specific activities that serve to promote the survival of the young. The pregnant rabbit, for example, will line its nest with hair plucked from its own body. Lactating animals typically will spend many hours hovering over their young in order to nurse them and to keep them warm. It is apparent, then, that the environments of infants, especially those of the same species, are relatively similar. However, it is also true that the quality and quantity of stimuli impinging upon young of similar species may differ from nest site to nest site and even within a given nest. These differences can result from temperature fluctuations, the number of young present, the size and complexity of the nest itself, the availability of food (the less food in the immediate vicinity the more time the mother must spend away from the young), the availability of other adults, the amount of territory that can be safely explored, and so forth. The rather obvious fact that animals of a given species are not bombarded by identical types of stimulation has prompted researchers to consider whether differential experience with qualitatively and quantitatively different forms of stimulation may in itself modify behavior.

Two general methods can be used to provide the organism with stimulation. It can be provided directly by the experimenter or indirectly by certain aspects of the environment. We will begin the discussion by considering the effects produced by directly subjecting the organism to stimulation.

Handling

The most widely used method of providing stimulation to the organism directly is known as "handling." Handling, however, is an inaccurate designation because the animals are not fondled or caressed but rather are removed from the mother, placed individually into separate containers for 3–5 minutes, and returned to the mother. This procedure is usually carried out some time prior to weaning and is performed over the course of a number of days, sometimes throughout the entire lactation period. Other procedures which have been used to stimulate young include subjecting them to heat, cold, electric shock, and shaking. These procedures essentially produce the same effects as does handling.

It has been reported that animals handled during infancy are less reactive to novel situations than are nonhandled animals. Specifically, handled rats will engage in more activity in an open field and will emerge from their home cages into a novel environment sooner than will their nonhandled counterparts (cf., Denenberg & Smith, 1963). In addition to affecting activity, handling produces effects upon a number of physiological processes. For example, handled male and female rats will reach sexual maturity earlier than will nonhandled animals (Morton, Denenberg, & Zarrow, 1963). Ader (1969) reported that handling advances the age at which certain endogenous biological rhythms first occur; handled animals begin to exhibit a 24-hour rhythm in the release of corticoid hormones from the adrenal gland at 16 days of age, whereas nonhandled animals do not display such rhythmicity until 21–25 days of age. One of the effects of early handling, then, is an advancement of maturation. This has been put to good use with respect to premature human infants for whom it has been shown that early stimulation (e.g., a rocking incubator) can lead to a more rapid physical advancement as compared to the "normal" premature infant who essentially spends the first few weeks of life in the restrictive environment of the incubator.

Returning to emotional reactivity, handling not only alters behavior (open field and home cage emergence) but concomitantly affects the hormonal response to emotion-provoking stimulation. Within minutes following exposure to a stressful stimulus, the adrenal gland releases a hormone called corticosterone (for humans and a few other species the hormone differs slightly and is called cortisol). Corticosterone plays an important role in the mobilization of certain physiological responses to stress such as protein catabolism and gluconeogenesis as well as in reducing muscular fatigue. It has been reported that rats handled in infancy will give a lesser adrenal corticosterone response to the relatively mild stress of a novel environment (Levine, Haltmeyer, Karas, & Denenberg, 1967). However, handled animals will exhibit a more rapid corticosterone response when subjected to a distinctly stressful stimulus such as electric shock (Haltmeyer, Denenberg, & Zarrow, 1967).

These data have been interpreted as indicating that the handled animal is better able to adapt to its environment since it may be beneficial not to release large amounts of corticosterone in mildly stressful situations that may pose little threat to the organism's survival, whereas it is to the organism's advantage to quickly release large amounts of the adrenal hormone in situations that clearly threaten survival. It is not known whether the relationship between the change in behavior and in adrenal activity as a function of handling is a causal one (the adrenal change causes the change in behavior, or vice versa) or just a correlative one (although occurring at the same time, adrenal changes and behavioral changes are causally unrelated).

Since handling affects an organism's behavioral and physiological reactivity to stressful situations, it would be expected that handling should also affect particular behaviors exhibited within the context of a learning situation. Handled rats do not differ from non-handled rats with respect to the ability to solve a complex maze for a food reward (Schaefer, 1963). However, handled rats have been shown to make more active avoidance responses than nonhandled rats (*see* review by Denenberg, 1968). This follows from the fact that handled animals are more active when confronted with a novel, stress-provoking situation. It appears, then, that early stimulation may effect behaviors displayed in situations involving aversive stimulation or stress. Handled animals may react and thus respond to the aversive properties of the situation in a manner different from that of nonhandled animals.

Enriched Environment

Another procedure for manipulating the stimulation received by an organism consists of changing particular aspects of its environment so that those living in one environment receive stimulation differing from that received by the inhabitants of another environment. Psychologists have been concerned with determining whether particular attributes of the environment can affect behavior and physiology. A research team headed by David Krech and Mark Rosenzweig has presented some interesting relationships between the environment, the brain, and behavior. Their procedure was basically quite simple (for a review, *see* Rosenzweig, Krech, Bennet, & Diamond, 1968). One group of rats was assigned to a condition known as an enriched environment. Beginning on the 25th day of life, 10 rats were placed in a large cage equipped with "toys" (small, manipulable objects, ladders, tunnels, etc.). Every day each rat was permitted to explore an open field, and about 30 days into the treatment the animals were given training in a variety of mazes for a sugar reward. (Answering an anticipated question, the handling that occurred in transporting the animals to and from the open field and mazes does not in itself lead to the effects summarized below). A second group of animals was assigned to a "restricted" environment which consisted of housing them separately in cages that prevented them from seeing or touching another animal. This environment did not contain playthings.

Following its stay in one of these housing conditions, an animal was either given a behavioral test or it was sacrificed and the brain removed, dissected, weighed, and assayed for levels of certain biochemicals. It was predicted that as a result of living in an enriched environment the brain should be more active and this increased activity would be reflected by higher levels of a neurotransmitter, acetylcholine. The results of a number of experiments tend to support the prediction. For example, acetylcholine levels were higher in areas of the brain lying beneath the cortex in those animals kept in an enriched environment. The weight of the brain was also influenced. The cerebral cortices of the rats maintained in the enriched condition were approximately 4.5 percent heavier than were those of the animals kept in the restricted environment. Furthermore, the portion of the cortex involved with vision underwent the greatest change in weight as a function of the enriched environment.

Additional experiments were performed to delineate the factors necessary for bringing about the changes in levels of acetylcholine and weight. It was shown that the effects could be produced irrespective of the training portion of the treatment. That is, neither the daily exposure to the open field nor to the various mazes were necessary in order to produce the effects. The social stimulation (animals in the enriched condition were housed 10 per cage) also was shown to be unnecessary. Through elimination, then, it appears that the size of the environment and the objects within the environment are the necessary ingredients for inducing the modifications of the brain.

Experiments were also performed to determine the length of time required to produce the brain changes. Although the original procedure involved maintaining the animals in the enriched condition for 80 days, it has since been shown that the effects can be obtained following 30 days of exposure to the enriched environment. Also, animals need not be kept in the enriched environment for 24 hours a day; as little as 2 hours a day of exposure can yield the effects. Finally, there does not appear to be a critical period in the life of the animal subsequent to which the enrichment procedure will be without effect. Changes of the brain can be produced by housing *adult* rats in the enriched environment.

An enriched housing condition also has been shown to affect behavior (Krech, Rosenzweig, & Bennet, 1962). After having learned the correct path through a complex maze based upon visual discrimination between two stimuli (doors were either white or black), the animals were given reversal training. The correct stimulus was made incorrect and the formerly incorrect stimulus was correct. The reversal procedure was repeated a number of times. Animals maintained in the enriched condition, although they did not differ from the animals kept in the restricted condition with respect to initial learning, learned the reversal task more quickly.

An earlier experiment by Forgays and Forgays (1952) also showed that environmental enrichment can affect maze-learning behavior. Weanling rats (26 days old) were housed in different types of cages for approximately 64 days. Some of them were kept in large cages with and without playthings while others were housed in smaller cages without playthings. Following the differential treatments, the animals were tested in the complex Hebb-Williams maze. Animals that lived in the large cages with playthings made fewer errors than did the animals of the other conditions. Furthermore, the animals that were maintained in the large cage without playthings, although inferior to the animals similarly housed but with playthings, were superior to the animals housed in the small cages. The authors suggested that as a result of living in a large environment the animals used visual distance cues to a greater extent than did the animals living in the small cages. The practice in using distance cues would facilitate the animals' later maze-learning behavior. The authors did not speculate as to why the presence of playthings produced effects over and above those produced by the large living cage. It may be that the presence of additional objects in the environment further promoted the use of distance cues.

Exposure of an organism to a relatively large environment containing objects that can be manipulated and which can serve as stimuli for activity can affect its behavior and physiology. As is the case for handling, it is not known whether the changes of the brain cause the change in behavior or whether the two events, although occurring following the same antecedent condition, are independent of one another.

The early handling and environmental enrichment studies have demonstrated that the postnatal environment can exert a marked influence upon the behavior and physiology of the organism. Although we have dealt with both handling and enrichment within the context of stimulation, the two manipulations do differ in one important respect. The concept of critical period does apply to handling since it will not be effective when administered to the adult (at least with respect to the tests commonly employed). However, environmental enrichment is effective when administered to the adult or even to "elderly" animals (Cummins, Walsh, Budtz-Olser, Konstantinas, & Honfall, 1973). This means that the brain retains a certain amount of plasticity which once was considered to be characteristic only of the brain of the infant.

The question of how the effects of handling and enrichment are produced remains unanswered. It has been demonstrated that handling is itself a stressor in that it elicits a rapid increase in levels of corticosterone in infant rats (Denenberg et al., 1967). This finding has led to the hypothesis that the high levels of corticosterone resulting from handling act upon and permanently modify the brain of the infant, thus permanently altering its reactivity to stress in the direction of better adaptability. This formulation leads to the provocative idea that early stress is beneficial to the organism—a notion directly in opposition to the long-held psychoanalytic view that early trauma will produce long-term deleterious effects.

III. PRENATAL-POSTNATAL INTERACTION

A number of factors operative during the prenatal and postnatal periods of an organism's existence can influence its behavior. Although these factors have been considered separately in order to simplify our discussion, one should not be misled into believing that these factors (and many others that, because of limitations of space, have been omitted from the discussion) necessarily operate separately. To what extent and in what direction a postnatal factor will influence behavior in most cases will depend upon the operation of a prenatal factor. It can be said, then, that particular pre- and postnatal variables *interact* with one another. There are innumerable examples of this, and we have chosen the following as being illustrative of the principle of interaction.

Cooper and Zubek (1958) reared Maze Bright and Maze Dull rats (they had been established using the selective breeding procedure) in an enriched or restricted environment from the 25th to the 65th day of life. At the end of that period they were tested in a complex maze and their performance was compared to that of animals maintained under normal laboratory conditions. Environmental enrichment had no effect upon the maze performance of the Brights but did improve the performance of the Dulls. Conversely, the restricted environment impaired the performance of the Brights but had little effect upon that of the Dulls. Here we have an example of the way in which a postnatal condition (housing condition) interacts with a prenatal condition (genotype). Depending upon the genotype and the housing condition, performance in the complex maze may either be facilitated, impaired, or unaffected.

Levine and Wetzel (1963) handled rats of two strains for 3 minutes a day for the first 21 days postnatally. The animals were given active avoidance training upon reaching adulthood. A significant Handling X Strain interaction was noted in that the avoidance scores of one strain of rats that had been handled were higher than those of the other strain/treatment groups. Again we have an example of an interaction between a prenatal (genotype) and postnatal condition (handling).

Prenatal and postnatal factors may interact with one another with the result of such interaction determining many characteristics of the organism's behavior. Such interaction has one very important implication—namely, that behavioral variability should almost always exist between individuals. The fact that under natural conditions two organisms will rarely be of an identical genotype means that even if they are from the same environment (which in itself does not mean that they are exposed to *identical* environmental forces) they may differ upon a number of behavioral characteristics, a result of the interaction between genotype and postnatal factors.

IV. SUMMARY

In this chapter we have considered a number of factors or variables which have been shown to influence behavior. These factors are considered developmental in nature since they can appear throughout the life of the organism.

We have seen that behavior can be affected by factors occurring prenatally as well as postnatally. One such factor is the elaboration of the organism's genes. Genes can exert almost as much influence upon an organism's behavior as they can upon physical morphology. One class of behavior that is heavily influenced by an organism's genotype is termed innate or species typical behavior. These behaviors are initially exhibited spontaneously, ostensibly in the absence of practice. However, we have seen that the maintenance of such behavior may be influenced by learning processes.

We also have seen that genes may influence behavior in situations designed to assess learning. It is believed by some that the genotype determines the organism's intellectual capacity. Experiments were discussed which indicate that rather than modulating intellectual capacity, genes may influence the manner in which the organism responds to its environment.

One process that genes control is the differentiation of the reproductive and endocrine systems. We have seen how the early hormonal environment can markedly affect a variety of behaviors such as avoidance responding.

And finally, we have seen that the pregnant animal can exert an influence over its offspring with such an influence manifested long after birth. For example, rats that are stressed during pregnancy will tend to produce offspring that are more "emotional" than those of nonstressed animals.

We also considered a number of developmental factors which exert their influences postnatally. The quality and quantity of environmental stimulation can exert effects upon both physiology and behavior, the former concerning the biochemistry of the brain and responsiveness of the adrenal gland to stress, and the latter dealing with behaviors which have been used to assess emotionality. It also was shown that the mother can influence behavior postnatally. These behaviors can include such basics as feeding and aggression.

In short, this chapter has dealt with a number of factors which can affect the organism's behavior. These factors can "prepare" an entire species to respond in a particular manner to a certain stimulus, as well as contribute to individual differences in behavior within a species. In order to understand behavior and to deal effectively with learning processes, one must gain insights into the role played by developmental variables.

CHAPTER 10

Stimulus Control: Generalization, Discrimination, and Contrast

Then I went for some Ziffs, They're exactly like Zuffs,
But the Ziffs live on cliffs and the Zuffs live on Bluffs.
And, seeing how bluffs are exactly like cliffs,
It's mighty hard telling the Zuffs from the Ziffs.

Dr. Seuss

I. GENERALIZATION

In Chapter 2, we saw that training animals with a given stimulus as the CS (e.g., a 1 khz tone) does not strictly limit conditioning to that CS (*see* pp. 37–39). If stimuli of different frequencies (e.g., 0.8 khz or 1.2 khz) are presented, they are likely to elicit the CR even though they were never explicitly paired with the CS. This tendency of stimuli that are physically similar to the conditioned stimulus to elicit the CR is termed *generalization*. We also saw in Chapter 2 that the more dissimilar the new stimulus was from the CS, the less likely it was to elicit the CR. We termed this decreasing likelihood of eliciting the CR a *generalization gradient*.

Generalization and the generalization gradient are also obtained when instrumental training procedures are used. For example, the data presented in Figure 10–1 were obtained from pigeons trained to peck a key on an intermittent schedule of reinforcement (Guttman & Kalish, 1956). For different groups, the discs on which the pigeons pecked to obtain reinforcement were illuminated with different colors. The wavelengths of the impinging light for the various groups were 530, 550, 580 and 600 nanometers (nm). For humans, these wavelengths range from yellowish-green to red. During training 60-second periods in which the response key was illuminated were alternated with 10-second periods of no illumination. Reinforcement was never available during these latter periods.

Generalization testing was begun after the key-pecking response was well acquired. The procedure consisted of illuminating the response key with wavelengths other than those used as the discriminative stimulus during training. For example, the pigeons

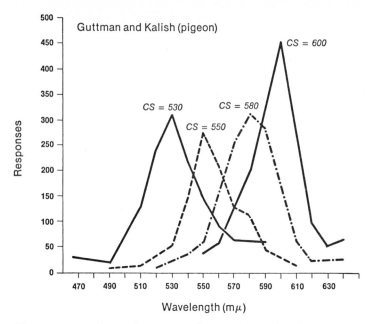

Figure 10–1. Generalization gradients obtained with separate groups of pigeons trained to key peck with the key illuminated at the indicated wavelengths. (From Guttman & Kalish, 1956.)

trained with a 580 nm discriminative stimulus were presented with the key illuminated at wavelengths of 520, 540, 550, 560, 570, 580, 590, 600, 610, 620, and 640 nm. These stimuli were presented in a random order. The generalization gradients shown in Figure 10–1 were plotted by determining how many responses the pigeons made in a given time period to each of these test stimuli. As is apparent in Figure 10–1, most responses were made to the stimulus associated with reinforcement during training.

However, responses were made to other stimuli and the greater the physical difference (in nm) between these stimuli and the discriminative stimulus, the fewer the responses made in their presence. It is also apparent that the general symmetrical shape of the generalization gradient was similar in the four groups given different wavelengths as the discriminative stimuli. However, some statistical departures from symmetry were noted in that the right halves (longer wavelengths) of the 550-nm and 600-nm groups were different from the left halves in slope and different in slope from the other two groups. These differences have some theoretical significance that we shall come to later in this chapter, (*see* p. 299) but for now the general shape and similarity of the generalization gradients are the important points to remember.

Another important aspect of the Guttman and Kalish experiment is that generalization testing is carried out in *extinction*. In investigating generalization, we are asking how likely it is that an animal will respond in a stimulus context different from the one in which it was trained. This question is most clearly answerable when the animal is not also reinforced for responding in the new stimulus context. One of the advantages of the Guttman and Kalish procedure of training the animals initially on an intermittent schedule of reinforcement is that extensive generalization testing may be conducted because of the greater resistance to extinction produced by such intermittent schedules (cf., Chapter 5). However, extinction does eventually occur as a function of the generalization testing procedure and the occurrence of extinction seems to alter the shape of the generalization gradient. The data presented in Figure 10–2 depict the generalization gradient obtained at four stages of the testing procedure.

In the later test series (10–12), it is apparent from the decline in response rate to the discriminative stimulus that extinction is occurring. It is also apparent that this decline in response rate is relatively greater at the discriminative stimulus than at other stimulus values and, as a result, the generalization gradient becomes broader. That

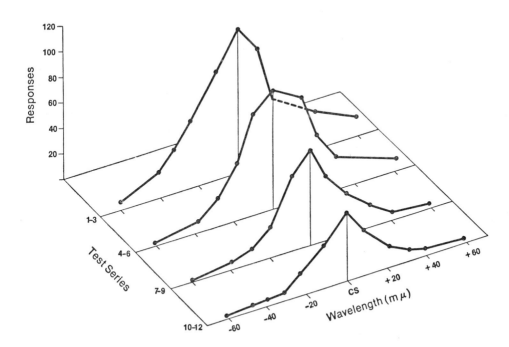

Figure 10–2.   Mean generalization gradients obtained at several stages of extinction. (From Guttman & Kalish, 1956.)

is, as extinction proceeded, the pigeons tended to make a relatively greater proportion of their responses at stimuli other than the discriminative stimulus.

This tendency for the generalization gradient to be broader when the response rate to the training stimulus is relatively low seems to be characteristic of generalization. A similar effect was found when Guttman and Kalish examined generalization in terms of individual pigeon's response rates to the discriminative stimulus. That is, pigeons that demonstrated a high rate of responding to the discriminative stimulus tended to show steeper generalization gradients than pigeons demonstrating a relatively low rate of responding to the discriminative stimulus.

Before continuing with this analysis, we should consider terminological difficulties that may be beginning to puzzle the reader. We have just examined two cases in which generalization gradients are broader when response rates are low. It is tempting to suggest that generalization increases when response rates are low. But this notion immediately encounters some conceptual difficulties—how can we say that generalization is greater when response rates are

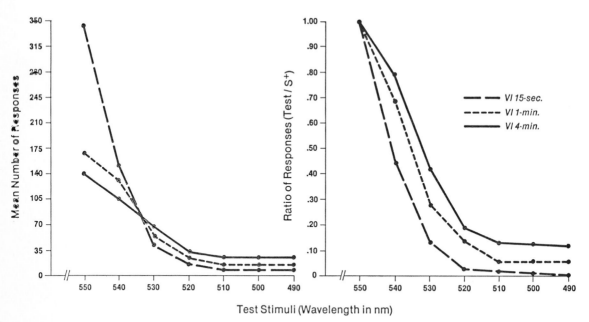

Figure 10–3.   Generalization gradient as a function of schedule of reinforcement. Presented in the left panel are the absolute number of responses made to each test stimulus following training with a 550 nm light. Presented in the right panel is the ratio of responses made to the test stimuli as a function of responses made to the training stimuli. (Modified from Haber & Kalish, 1963, © Am. Assoc. Adv. Science.)

low if the animals are actually responding less to a generalization stimulus under low response rate conditions than under high response rate conditions? The answer is, of course, that we are speaking in terms of relative generalization, not absolute generalization. That is, generalization is greater if we think in terms of the ratio or proportion of responses made, rather than in terms of the absolute responses made to the test stimulus.

This difference may become clear if we examine another case in which degree of generalization seems to be related to rate of responding. Haber and Kalish (1963) examined how generalization was related to the schedule of reinforcement used in acquisition. In particular, generalization was examined following training on VI–15-second, VI–1-minute, and VI–4-minute schedules of reinforcement. Training was carried out with a 550-nm light as the discriminative stimulus and generalization was examined by presenting a number of different wavelengths towards the short end of the spectrum. Two ways of looking at the degree of generalization obtained are presented in Figure 10–3. The absolute number of responses made to each stimulus is presented in the left-hand panel. This method of presentation indicates that there were only minor differences in the degree of generalization as a function of schedule of reinforcement.

However, when the data are plotted in terms of the ratio of responses made to the test stimulus as a function of the response made to the training stimulus, a completely different picture emerges. These data, plotted in the right-hand portion of Figure 10–3, show that more generalization occurred following training on the VI–4-minute schedule than occurred following training on the other two schedules. But now, when we use the term generalization in this way, it must be clear that it is a relative measure of generalization: *The amount of responding made to the test stimulus in comparison to the amount of responding made to the training stimulus.* So, when we stated that generalization was greater in the Guttman and Kalish experiment when response rates were low, we were stating a measure of relative generalization. The concept of relative generalization can be expressed in terms of either the steepness of the slopes of the generalization gradients (cf., the Guttman & Kalish experiment) or by describing the data in terms of response ratios (cf., the Haber & Kalish experiment). Each of these reflects the same idea.

There is another consistency between the Guttman and Kalish and the Haber and Kalish experiments that is worth noting. That is, conditions that led to a lower rate of responding led to more relative generalization (note the lower rate of responding to the test stimulus after VI–4-minute training in Figure 10–3).

Other investigators have also found a consistent relationship between acquisition training schedule and degree of generalization. For example, Hearst, Koresko, and Poppen (1964) found that, in general, the less dense the reinforcement frequency the greater the generalization and that generalization is greater following training on DRL schedules than following training on VI schedules having comparable reinforcement densities. These results are compatible with the ideas concerning the relationship between rate of responding and generalization that were developed above. Response rates generally decline as VI schedules increase in length and, of course, response rate on DRL schedules is, by necessity, low.

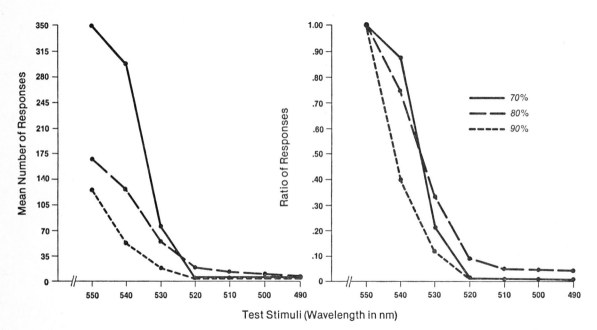

Figure 10–4. Generalization as a function of deprivation level. The manner of presentation is the same as in Figure 10–3. (Modified from Kalish & Haber, 1965.)

However, despite the seeming regularities encountered between generalization and response rate, this relationship does not hold over all conditions investigated. For example, Thomas and Switalski (1966) compared generalization following training on comparable VR and VI schedules. They found that generalization was greater following training on the VR schedule (the schedule that produced the higher response rate) than following training on the VI schedule.

Clearly, the effects of schedules of reinforcement on generalization have not been explored enough to permit any definitive statement concerning their effects. Although there seems to be a relationship between response rate and generalization in a number of situations, it is not known whether this relationship is just coincidental or reflects the operation of a common underlying process.

A number of other variables have also been shown to influence generalization, but the exact nature of the influence is not clear. For example, deprivation state appears to affect degree of generalization. The results of one study (Kalish & Haber, 1965) are presented in Figure 10–4. The data are again plotted in terms of both absolute responding and relative response rates (as in Figure 10–3). It is apparent from the figure that degree of relative generalization was not greatly affected by the deprivation conditions. This effect is, in some sense, puzzling. Intuitively, one might expect that the more deprived an animal is the more likely it would be to respond to stimuli that differed from those present during training. This is true if we look at absolute response rates but not if we look at relative steepness of generalization slopes.

Other studies have found more complex nonmonotonic relationships between degree of deprivation and generalization; and still other studies have found little or no relationship between deprivation and generalization (*see* Kalish, 1969; and Nevin, 1973, for other studies). It is apparent that the effect of deprivation on generalization probably depends upon a number of other variables operating at the same time, variables such as method of testing, schedule of reinforcement, whether the reinforcer is appetitive or aversive, etc. Until the nature and degree of these interactions are explored, there can be little in the way of a definitive statement on how deprivation influences generalization.

A similar state of affairs exists for other issues concerning generalization. For example, it has often been assumed, for theoretical reasons, that gradients of approach to appetitive reinforcers are less steep than gradients of avoidance associated with aversive reinforcers (e.g., Miller, 1944, 1961). Indeed, a number of studies conducted in the runway apparatus supported this theoretical speculation (cf., Miller, 1959, 1961). However, a series of studies by Hearst (1969), investigating parameters such as we have been describing, and others has indicated that any broad statement concerning critical differences in the steepness of approach and avoidance gradients must await more parametric research. In Hearst's words:

> By proper manipulation of certain experimental conditions, one can produce a steep approach gradient or a flat approach gradient, a steep avoidance gradient or a flat avoidance gradient (1969, p. 263).

There are, however, enough data to consider some of the many theoretical issues concerning the nature of generalization and the relationship between generalization and discrimination. We turn now to a brief discussion of these issues.

II. GENERALIZATION AND DISCRIMINATION

We saw in Chapter 2 that presentation of a UCS following one CS (CS⁺) but not after another CS (the CS⁻) leads to the formation of a discrimination. That is, after some training, the CR would be elicited by the CS⁺ but not by the CS⁻.

The data in Figure 10–5 show the effects of specific discrimination training on the generalization gradient. The data were obtained by Hoffman (1969) in a CER paradigm, a procedure that has characteristics of both instrumental training and Pavlovian conditioning (*see* Chapter 6).

The left-hand portion of Figure 10–5 illustrates the generalization of suppression obtained following training with a single stimulus associated with shock. The right-hand portion of the figure shows a gradient obtained over an identical range of stimuli but, in this case, a discrimination procedure was used in training; one stimulus, the 1-khz tone, was always followed by shock, whereas another stimulus, a 0.9-khz tone, was never followed by shock. It is

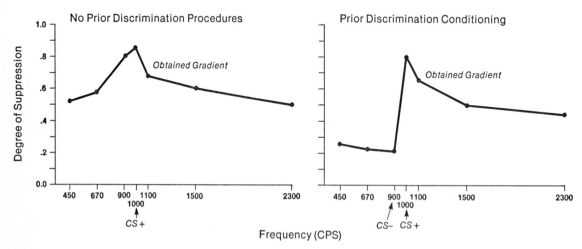

Figure 10–5. Generalization gradients obtained in a CER paradigm after training with a single CS value (left panel) and following discrimination training (right panel). (From Hoffman, 1969, by permission of Prentice-Hall.)

apparent that the animals showed little suppression when the 0.9-khz tone or any tone below it in frequency was presented.

Thus, the effects of discrimination training, explicitly pairing one stimulus with reinforcement and another stimulus with non-reinforcement, was to establish a sharper degree of *stimulus control* than was obtained without such differential reinforcement. By stimulus control it is meant that the animals' behavior—suppression in this case—comes under the influence of specific stimuli in the environment, the behavior being considerably more likely to occur when that particular stimulus is present than when it is not present. It should be noted that in the Hoffman experiments the differential behavior established by discrimination training itself seemed to generalize to stimuli similar to the CS$^+$ and CS$^-$. That is, suppression occurred to the CS$^+$ and to stimuli of higher frequency, whereas little suppression occurred to the CS$^-$ and stimuli of lower frequency. We shall return to an examination of the characteristics of generalization gradients obtained following discrimination training below (*see* p. 306). But now let us consider one of the theoretical issues of historical importance in the area of generalization and stimulus control.

Is Differential Reinforcement Necessary for Stimulus Control?

One view of generalization, a view associated with Hull (1943) and Spence (1936) is, essentially, that generalization is due to common elements possessed by the training stimulus and the test stimulus. These common elements may be overlapping environmental stimuli or characteristics of the sensory and neural apparatus itself. For example, when an animal is trained with a 550-nm light as the discriminative stimulus, this light may activate some sensory and neural processes that are also activated by a 530-nm light. As a result of this common activation, both stimuli acquire, in Hullian terms (*see* Chapter 8), "habit strength." Therefore, when the 530-nm light is presented as a generalization stimulus, it has some tendency to promote responding even though it was never explicitly paired with the reinforcement.

Again, this tendency is due to the sharing of elements between the original training stimulus and the test stimulus. This interpretation implies that a generalization gradient should occur and that extended training might serve to sharpen that gradient to the extent that some of the elements held in common between the training and test stimuli were distinctive features of the external environment. A further implication of the Hull-Spence approach is that extended training might serve to steepen the generalization gradient while not leading to complete stimulus control. Such a lack of complete stimulus control would be expected to the extent that the elements possessed in common by the training and test stimuli were internal to the animal, such as those involved in sensory-neural processes.

A number of studies have been conducted to investigate the influence of extended acquisition training on the generalization gradient but, unfortunately, these studies have not led to any definitive conclusions. Many studies (e.g., Hoveland, 1937; Hearst & Koresko, 1968) indicate that the height of the generalization gradient increases with extended acquisition training. Thus, in terms of absolute responses made, more responding generally occurs to test stimuli after extensive training than after less training. However, when relative generalization gradients are examined, the effects are once again not so clear. Sometimes broader gradients have been found with extended training (e.g., Margolius, 1955) but other studies, using quite different procedures, have found steeper gradients with extended training (e.g., Hearst & Koresko, 1968).

However, even when the steeper gradients were observed following extended training, there was little indication that any sharp degree of stimulus control could be established by simply extended training with one reinforced stimulus. Other research extending from that done in Pavlov's laboratory (Pavlov, 1927) until the present is also consistent with this conclusion. It appears that some degree of differential reinforcement is necessary in order to establish a sharp degree of differential responding between physically similar stimuli.

As consistent as the Hull-Spence theoretical approach seems to be with the data reviewed thus far, it has not been accepted by all. In particular, Lashley and Wade (1946) have taken a quite different position. They have argued that a stimulus dimension does not exist as such for an organism until it has had an opportunity to compare at least two points on that dimension. In other words, Lashley and Wade have stated that without some form of differential conditioning there will be no stimulus control at all; there will be no generalization gradient; there will be apparent complete generalization resulting from the organism's complete lack of "attention" to that stimulus dimension.

The Lashley and Wade position appears, at first glance, to be completely contradicted by the data. We have had occasion to mention a number of studies in which no specific differential reinforcement has been given and yet a gradient of generalization has been obtained. For example, in the Guttman and Kalish study described at the beginning of this chapter, the pigeons in any particular group were reinforced only in the presence of one wavelength; no specific differential reinforcement was given and yet a generalization gradient was obtained. However, these results and all others described thus far are not as critical of the Lashley-Wade position as they appear to be. To see why, we must again consider the procedure employed in the Guttman and Kalish experiment and typically employed in generalization studies.

Recall that, in the Guttman and Kalish research, during training the 1-minute periods in which the key was illuminated were interspersed with 10-second periods in which the key and the chamber were not illuminated and in which pecks were not reinforced. This procedure itself may be thought to constitute a differential reinforcement treatment. Moreover, the discriminative stimulus itself was discretely localized, and therefore pecks at other portions of the apparatus, in the vicinity of the key or elsewhere, might also be considered differential reinforcement training on a wavelength dimension. In addition to this, one must consider the prior history of the animals being tested. In the wild or in the laboratory it would seem that the subjects might have had some opportunity to experience and be differentially reinforced for responding on a wavelength dimension.

Thus, if these speculations concerning possibilities for unintended differential reinforcement are correct, the standard generalization experiment cannot be considered to provide critical data against the Lashley-Wade interpretation of generalization. There are indications from other experiments that some importance should be attached to the opportunities for differential reinforcement to occur in the standard generalization experiment. For example, Jenkins and Harrison (1960) trained pigeons to peck on a key for reinforcement, using a 1.0-khz tone as the discriminative stimulus. When other tones were presented in a generalization test, no generalization gradient was found. That is, the pigeons were just as likely to peck at the key when tones of 0.3 khz or 3.5 khz were presented as when the discriminative stimulus was presented. The marked difference between these results and others might be due to the lack of opportunity for differential reinforcement to occur in the Jenkins and Harrison experiment. That is, since the stimulus was not localized, there would be no opportunity to peck at stimuli similar to the discriminative stimulus and be nonreinforced for such pecking, an opportunity that does exist when localized wavelength presentations are used as discriminative stimuli.

Further support for this possibility was obtained in an experiment by Heinemann and Rudolph (1963). In this study, a spatially localized stimulus was used, but the size of this stimulus was varied in different groups of pigeons. In one group the discriminative stimulus consisted of an illumination of a small area just around the outside of the response key; in a second group, the discriminative stimulus consisted of the illumination of virtually the entire wall of the operant chamber in which the response key was contained; the discriminative stimulus for the third group was intermediate between these two. Subsequent to acquisition, generalization was tested along a dimension of illumination intensity. A typical symmetrical generalization gradient was obtained with the small and medium area discriminative stimuli; however, the group with the large area stimulus showed a flat gradient (complete generalization) along the brightness dimension.

The results of the Jenkins and Harrison (1960) and the Heinemann and Rudolph (1963) experiments then support the idea that unintended differential reinforcement may occur when spatially localized stimuli are used and, thus, such experiments cannot be considered critical for deciding between opposing theoretical positions of Hull-Spence and Lashley-Wade.

Another factor that must be considered in any attempts to come to grips with a theoretical understanding of generalization has been highlighted in a series of experiments by Thomas and his colleagues (e.g., Thomas, Burr, & Eck, 1970; Eck & Thomas, 1970). Until this point in our discussion, we have been considering problems imposed by unintended differential reinforcement relating in particular to the stimulus dimension that is later involved in generalization testing. However, the experiments by Thomas and his colleagues indicate that there should perhaps be another concern—that is, previous experience with differential reinforcement on stimulus dimensions other than those subject to immediate generalization testing. In particular, what the Thomas experiments have shown is that experience with discrimination learning in one stimulus dimension transfers and facilitates learning a discrimination on a different stimulus dimension. For example, if pigeons are first trained to respond differentially to lines of two different orientations (e.g., 90° and 60°) and subsequently trained to discriminate between two different wavelengths, it is found that the pigeons with prior discrimination experience, even though it was on a different dimension, learn the second discrimination faster than birds without such prior training.

This indicates that a generalization gradient might be obtained following nondifferential reinforcement training on one stimulus dimension *if* the subjects had had prior experience with differential reinforcement on a *different stimulus dimension.*

With all these potential control problems is it at all possible to critically examine the Lashley-Wade position? One other mode of attack on this problem that we shall consider at the present time is exemplified by an experiment of Peterson (1962). Peterson raised ducklings in a monochromatic environment; from the moment of hatching the ducklings were raised in a chamber illuminated with a 589 nm light. During this time the ducklings were also trained to peck on a response key also illuminated with the same 589 nm

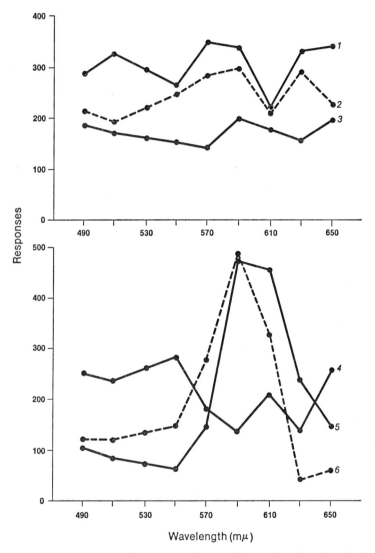

Figure 10–6. Generalization gradients obtained with individual ducklings following differential rearing experience. Ducks 1–3 were raised in a monochromatic environment; ducks 4–6 were raised in white light. (From Peterson, 1962, © Am. Assoc. Adv. Science.)

light. After this differential-rearing experience, the ducklings were given a generalization test with the response key illuminated by a number of different wavelengths. The results of this experiment, presented in the top panel of Figure 10–6, show that the ducklings that had experienced only one wavelength until the time of testing showed complete generalization to all other wavelengths. Thus, these ducklings that had no experience with wavelengths other than 589 nm, and therefore no opportunity for differential reinforcement, behaved as if wavelength did not exist as a dimension. In contrast, ducklings that were raised in a similar fashion but in an environment illuminated by a white light showed a standard generalization gradient. The data from these ducklings are presented in the bottom panel of Figure 10–6.

The difference between these two groups of ducklings is presumably related to the lighting in their environment. Ducklings reared in white light had the opportunity to experience different colors in their environment. Presumably these ducklings also received differential reinforcement as a function of wavelength since only pecking on the 589 nm stimulus was reinforced. Similar, although often not as striking, effects of restricted early visual experience have been found in another experiment with ducklings (Tracy, 1970), in an experiment with monkeys (Ganz & Riesen, 1962) and in observations of congenitally blind humans (Ganz, 1968). These results tend to offer support for the Lashley-Wade position that some degree of differential reinforcement to a stimulus dimension is necessary if that stimulus continuum is to become an effective dimension for the organism. Exactly what type of differential reinforcement, how much, and by what mechanism such differential reinforcement operates to produce an effective stimulus dimension is not yet known.

Is Generalization a Failure of Discrimination?

When stimulus control is not established, is this complete generalization due simply to a failure to discriminate between the different stimuli? In other words, are generalization and discrimination really different ways of looking at the same phenomena, opposite sides of the same coin? This would appear to be a common sense way of looking at generalization and discrimination. However, this has not been easy to show experimentally. Fox example, one early study indicated that there was no relation between degree of generalization along a wavelength dimension and the ability to perceive differences along that dimension (Guttman & Kalish, 1956). However, a later study (Marsh, 1967) indicated that this result might have been due to some of the experimental procedures employed in that experiment. In support of this possibility is the fact that other studies (e.g., Kalish, 1958) have found very close agreement between ability to discriminate differences and degree of generalization.

We do not have the space in this text to go into an extensive discussion of this issue (*see* Kalish, 1969, and Mostofsky, 1965, for a more thorough treatment). However, we can say that the close relationship, if not identity, between degree of generalization and subsequent discriminability between two stimuli is clearly indicated in experiments by Haber and Kalish (1963) and Kalish and Haber (1965). These experimenters used the generalization gradient to predict the degree of stimulus control that would be established when two stimuli on the visual wavelength continuum were differentially reinforced.

The generalization gradients relevant to these studies are those already presented in Figures 10–3 and 10–4. In the experiment of interest here, Haber and Kalish trained one group of pigeons in a discrimination paradigm with a 550 nm light as S$^+$ and a 540 nm light as S$^-$. A second group of pigeons was trained with a 540 nm light as S$^+$ and a 530 nm light as S$^-$. The rationale for these procedures can be appreciated by examining, for example, the generalization gradient for the 70 percent deprivation group in Figure 10–4 (p. 296). The generalization curve indicates that the difference between 540 nm and 530 nm was greater for this group than the difference between 550 nm and 540 nm. This difference in generalization may be expressed by obtaining ratios of response to the two stimuli (i.e., responses to 540 nm/responses to 550 nm, and responses to 530 nm/responses to 540 nm). Kalish and Haber found that such ratios obtained from the generalization gradient were essentially the same as those obtained in the discrimination with one of the stimuli as S$^+$ and the other as S$^-$. In other words, the greater the difference between stimuli obtained on a generalization test the easier it was to establish stimulus control by differentially reinforcing those stimuli. Similar results have been found in other contexts (e.g., Jaynes, 1958) and such results indicate quite strongly the virtual identity of these two processes.

Postdiscrimination Gradients

We have seen in Figure 10–5 that gradients of generalization obtained after discrimination training are different from those obtained when there has been no discrimination training. In the example given in Figure 10–5, obtained in a CER paradigm, the

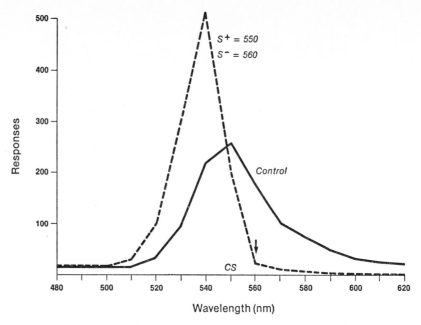

Figure 10–7. Generalization gradients obtained following discrimination training with an S+ at 550 nm and an S− at 560 nm; and following nondiscriminative training with the 550 nm stimulus. (Modified from Hanson, 1959.)

chief difference between the generalization and postdiscrimination gradients was the failure to obtain generalization in the region of the S− stimulus following discrimination training. In this section we shall consider the differences between postdiscrimination and generalization gradients in more detail, particularly those differences found in appetitive tasks.

Shown in Figure 10–7 is a portion of the data obtained in an experiment by Hanson (1959). The group labeled "control" was given training with a response key illuminated with a 550-nm light and then given standard generalization tests in extinction. The other group was intermittently reinforced for responding when the response key was illuminated with the 550-nm light (the S+) and not reinforced for responding when the key was illuminated with a 560 nm light (the S−). Following discrimination training, this group was also given a generalization test over the same range of stimuli as the control group. Differences between the two groups in the results of this generalization testing are apparent in the figure. These differences consist of three aspects: (1) The postdiscrimination gradient is steeper than the generalization gradient, (2) the peak level of responding is shifted away from the S+ (i.e., more responses were made to stimuli of shorter wavelength than S⁺ even though they were never experienced in training), and (3) level of responding is considerably higher in the postdiscrimination gradient than in the generalization gradient.

These three differences between postdiscrimination gradients were also found with other stimuli as S⁻ in the Hanson study and in numerous experiments since Hanson (*see* Purtle, 1973, for a review). What is it about discrimination training that produces these differences in generalization? What is it that serves to sharpen the gradient of generalization, moves the point of responding from S⁺ to another stimulus in a direction away from the S⁻, and raises the overall level of responding? We shall now examine some theoretical accounts of discrimination learning and some data that relate to these characteristics of the postdiscrimination gradients.

Gradients of Excitation and Inhibition

Spence (1937) assumed that discriminative responding reflected the combined influence of excitatory tendencies acquired by the S⁺ as a result of having been paired with reinforcement and inhibitory tendencies acquired by the S⁻ as a result of having been paired with nonreinforcement. That is, S⁻ comes to control a tendency not to respond during the course of discrimination learning. Spence further assumed that this inhibitory tendency, like the excitatory tendency, would generalize to similar stimuli. Such hypothetical gradients of excitatory and inhibitory tendencies are shown in Figure 10–8. The stimulus dimension illustrated in the

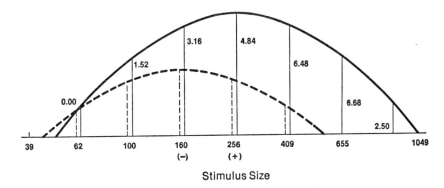

Stimulus Size

Figure 10–8. Hypothetical gradients of excitation (solid line) and inhibition (dashed line) obtained following discrimination training with a 256 CM² figure as S⁺ and a 160 CM² figure as S⁻. Differences between the S⁺ and S⁻ in excitatory potential are shown within the figure. (From Spence, 1937.)

figure is one of stimulus size (area) and the gradients presented are those hypothesized to exist following discrimination training with a 256 cm² figure as S⁺ and a 160 cm² figure as S⁻. A further assumption of Spence's was that these gradients of excitation and inhibition combined algebraically. Response tendencies (habit strengths) that should exist at each stimulus value following such algebraic combination are indicated within the gradients.

Examination of Spence's model indicates that it accounts quite readily for the peak shift obtained in a postdiscrimination gradient. The prediction of peak shift may be seen in the net excitatory tendencies existing after the algebraic combination of the excitatory and inhibitory gradients. Note that the greatest tendencies to respond should exist not at the original S⁺ stimulus but at stimuli different from S⁺, stimuli different in the direction of being *further removed from* S⁻. This is, of course, the effect found in the Hanson experiment and many other experiments.

Spence's explanation of the peak shift assumes the existence of gradients of inhibition and excitation. Independent evidence for the existence of a gradient of excitation exists in the form of the standard generalization curve. That is, the typical generalization gradient may be thought of as representing gradients of excitation or tendencies to respond to the presented stimulus.

There is also evidence supporting the existence of gradients of inhibition. An example of such a gradient is presented in Figure 10–9. In this experiment Terrace (1972) trained pigeons on a discrimination task in which the S⁺ was a homogeneous field of white light and the S⁻ was a homogeneous field of light with a 570 nm wavelength. It is apparent that the three pigeons tested were least likely to respond at the S⁻ wavelength and showed increasing response rates as the wavelength of the test stimuli diverged from the S⁻ value. It is plausible to assume that this gradient of nonresponding reflects an underlying gradient of inhibition (we will consider the three curves presented in the lower right-hand portion of the figure below). Evidence indicating the generalization of inhibition has also been obtained by others (e.g., Bass & Hull, 1934; Honig, Boneau, Burstein, & Pennypacker, 1963; and Hearst, Besley, & Farthing, 1970).

Thus, it is reasonable to think in terms of gradients of both excitation (tendencies to respond) and inhibition (tendencies to not respond); however, the exact shape of these gradients and, more importantly, how they interact is not really known at this time. It is, of course, just these points, the shape and manner of interaction of the two gradients, that would be crucial for determining the precise adequacy of the Spencian model in explaining the peak-shift phenomenon. For now, all we can say is that it still represents a useful model in some situations (e.g., Klein & Rilling, 1974), but the degree of precision with which it can predict peak-shift must await further data on inhibition (*see* Hearst et al., 1970) and gradient interactions.

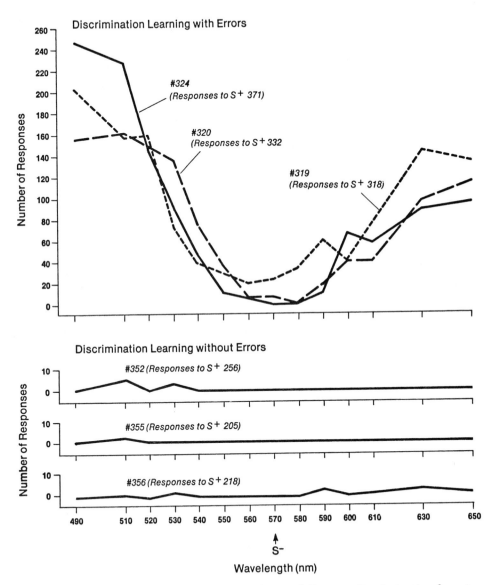

Figure 10–9. Gradients of inhibition following discrimination learning with and without errors. (From Terrace, 1972.)

Inhibition, Peak Shift, and the Aversiveness of S⁻

Many investigators have assumed the existence of another factor in the relationship between the inhibitory properties of the S⁻ and the peak shift. That is, as a result of being associated with non-reinforcement, the S⁻ acquires aversive motivational properties, properties often linked with the concept of frustration (cf., Chapter 4). Much of the systematic research in this area has been conducted by Terrace (1966a) and has been very well summarized in a number of sources (e.g., D'Amato, 1970), in addition to Terrace's own writings. Accordingly, we will briefly describe the apparent relationship but not dwell too long on it.

Terrace (1963a, b) developed a procedure whereby it is possible to train pigeons on a discrimination without these pigeons making many responses to the S⁻ stimulus during the course of acquisition. Considering responses to the S⁻ stimulus to be errors, Terrace termed the results of training pigeons with his technique to be errorless discrimination learning. Pigeons so trained would respond at high rates to S⁺ and virtually not at all to S⁻. Of particular relevance to the present discussion is the fact that post-discrimination gradients of pigeons trained with Terrace's errorless procedure are not characterized by a peak shift. That is, the peak of responding generally occurs to the S⁺ stimulus and is not shifted in a direction away from the S⁻.

Another difference between pigeons trained in the errorless fashion and pigeons that have acquired a discrimination with standard training techniques is revealed by the administration of certain drugs. Terrace (1963b) has found that response rates to the S⁻ stimulus are markedly increased in pigeons trained in the standard way following the administration of chlorpromazine or imipramine. However, pigeons trained with the errorless procedure show no change from their zero rate of responding to the S⁻ when administered these drugs.

On the basis of these and other data, Terrace reasoned that pigeons normally actively inhibit responding to S⁻ because such responses are aversive (perhaps because they are "frustrating"). Under the influence of some drugs such responding is less aversive and thus more responses are made. However, for pigeons trained without errors, S⁻ is not an aversive stimulus, but rather a neutral stimulus and, thus, the administration of these drugs produces no increase in responding in pigeons so trained. There is no increase in responding because they have not been actively inhibiting responding to S⁻ in the first place.

If this explanation is accepted, then it is but a small step to go back to the first difference found between pigeons trained with and without errors, the absence of the peak shift in the latter trained animals, and to reason that the peak shift might be due to the aversiveness of the S⁻. That is, it is the aversiveness associated with responding to S⁻ that directs responses further "down" the stimulus continuum away from S⁻ in birds trained in the standard manner. Since S⁻ is not aversive in pigeons trained without errors, no peak shift occurs.

Further support for this line of reasoning is provided by data showing: (a) that animals will learn a response to escape momentarily from an S⁻ stimulus, thereby indicating its aversiveness (Terrace, 1971b); (b) that U-shaped gradients of inhibitory control around S⁻ obtained after standard discrimination training are not obtained after errorless discrimination training (*see* lower curves of Figure 10–9); and by the absence of peak shift in normally trained animals when they are tested under the influence of a drug that serves to reduce the aversiveness of S⁻ (Lyons, Klipec, & Steinsultz, 1973). Terrace (1974) has also obtained evidence of active inhibitory responses in the sense that responses antagonistic to the response required to S⁺ are made by humans in a simple stimulus control experiment.

Thus, there is considerable evidence supporting the conclusion that the nonreinforced stimulus in a standard discrimination experiment develops inhibitory and aversive properties and that these properties are perhaps causally related to the occurrence of peak shift (*see* Purtle, 1973; Nevin, 1973; D'Amato, 1970; and Kalish, 1969 for further discussions of this issue).

Enhanced Responding in the Postdiscrimination Gradient

The characteristic of the postdiscrimination gradient that we turn to now is the elevation in response rate that is normally found in the postdiscrimination gradient in comparison to the generalization gradient (cf., Figure 10–7, *see* p. 306). If Spence's model of discrimination learning is a reasonably adequate account of the peak shift phenomenon, it is readily apparent that it is a totally inadequate explanation of response enhancement following discrimination training. The Spence model predicts that the peak of responding should be *less* following discrimination training than following nondiscriminative training. This prediction derives from the assumed summation of excitatory and inhibitory gradients; the subtraction of the inhibitory tendencies should result in less responding to S⁺ and related stimuli following discrimination training than comparable responding when no S⁻ has been involved in original training. In some situations this prediction has been verified (e.g., Gynther, 1957). However, in most experiments that have been conducted, response rate is enhanced following discrimination learning. This enhancement in response rate has come to be a topic of study in its own right and we shall turn to it before attempting to directly relate such enhancement to other characteristics of the postdiscrimination gradient.

Behavioral Contrast

In the typical discrimination experiment that we have been discussing thus far in this chapter, the reinforced and nonreinforced stimuli are presented in some alternating fashion. Such a procedure is often termed a *successive discrimination procedure* or, when there are schedules of reinforcement associated with the S⁺ and S⁻, a *multiple schedule.* In other words, a multiple schedule consists of the alternation of two stimuli, each signaling the presence of a different schedule of reinforcement. Often, as in the case of most experiments mentioned thus far in this chapter, one of the schedules, the schedule associated with S⁻, is extinction. But this need not always be the case.

Reynolds (1961), working with multiple schedules, noticed an interesting effect, an effect that can be readily appreciated if we describe Reynolds' procedure. Pigeons were trained to peck a response key on a VI–3-minute schedule of reinforcement. The key was sometimes illuminated red and sometimes green, but differential reinforcement was not initially correlated with these different colors. After a stable response rate had been established, Reynolds shifted his birds to a multiple schedule; a VI–3-minute schedule remained in effect when the key was illuminated one color but, in the presence of the other color, the reinforcement schedule was shifted to extinction.

Subsequent to the shift there was a decline in response rate to the stimulus signaling the extinction schedule. So much would be expected. But the interesting result was obtained with the unshifted component. Response rate to the stimulus that continued to signal the VI–3-minute schedule *increased.* It is this increase in response rate above baseline (or above unshifted controls) that is termed *behavioral contrast.* In general, then, behavioral contrast may be obtained by holding the reinforcement schedule constant in one component of a multiple schedule and decreasing the density of reinforcement in the other component.

It is clear that this increase in response rate to the unshifted component is not predicted by Spence's theory of discrimination learning. In fact, because of the assumed subtraction of the inhibitory gradient from the excitatory gradient, quite the opposite should occur; response rate to the unshifted component should decrease. But behavioral contrast is a well established phenomenon; it occurs over a wide range of conditions when both multiple and concurrent schedules of reinforcement are used (cf., Freeman, 1971; Rachlin, 1973), and it is apparently this phenomenon that accounts for the response enhancement that occurs in post-discrimination gradients. As to why behavioral contrast itself occurs is not at all clear at the present time, but a number of conditions that contribute to its occurrence are known. Since many of these conditions also apparently contribute to the occurrence of the peak shift effect, we will discuss them together in the context of the relationship between peak shift and behavioral contrast.

Variables Influencing Peak Shift and Behavioral Contrast

Both peak shift and behavioral contrast tend to occur under conditions where response rates in one component of a multiple schedule are reduced by conditions that are, in some sense, unfavorable to the animal. For example, in general, the greater the difference in reinforcement density between the S^+ and S^- component of a multiple schedule, the greater the peak shift (Dysart, Marx, McLean, & Nelson, 1974) and the greater the behavioral contrast (Reynolds, 1961b; Keller, 1970; McSweeney, 1975). Similarly, the more difficult the discrimination the greater the peak shift (Farthing, 1974) and also the greater the behavioral contrast (Bloomfield, 1972).

Further support for this similarity comes from many other studies showing, for example, that (a) drugs which eliminate the peak shift also eliminate behavioral contrast (Terrace, 1963b; Bloomfield, 1972), (b) penalizing S^- responses increases behavioral contrast (Bloomfield, 1972) and peak shift (Grusec, 1968), (c) some types of errorless discrimination training eliminates behavioral contrast and also eliminates the peak shift (Terrace, 1966, 1972), and (d) making reinforcement in the S^- component contingent upon the animals *not* making a response (differential reinforcement of other behavior or *DRO schedule*) eliminates both the peak shift (Yarczower, Gollub, & Dickson, 1968) and behavioral contrast (Nevin, 1968).

In sum, the conditions that produce peak shift are also likely to produce behavioral contrast. But what are these phenomena due to? All of the conditions we have reviewed above that led to peak shift and contrast also produce a reduction in response rate to the S^- component. This might lead to the conclusion that a reduction in response rate to the S^- component is a necessary and sufficient condition for the occurrence of contrast (e.g., Terrace, 1966a). However, other investigators have reasoned that contrast (and possibly peak shift) is due to a decline in the frequency of reinforcement in S⁻ and not to the decline in response rate per se (e.g., Reynolds, 1961; Herrnstein, 1970). Normally these two events, decline in reinforcement frequency and decline in response rate, covary and it has proven difficult to determine whether either one is uniquely responsible for contrast and peak shift (cf., Freeman, 1971; Purtle, 1973).

Recently, a number of experiments have provided evidence relevant to the foregoing question, and we shall now briefly examine these experiments and attempt to sort out the conditions that determine whether or not peak shift and behavioral contrast will occur. The majority of these experiments have examined behavioral contrast and not peak shift. Thus, we will generally confine the rest of this discussion to behavioral contrast, but keeping in mind that these two phenomena seem to be closely linked in that the conditions that produce one are also likely to produce the other.

The hypothesis that reduction in reinforcement frequency is a necessary condition for behavioral contrast seems not to be supported by the following experiments. If an animal is trained with a VI schedule in S⁺ and a DRL schedule in S⁻, but the DRL is adjusted so that reinforcement frequency is equated, behavioral contrast is still obtained (Terrace, 1968). Recall that in a DRL schedule (cf., Chapter 5) an animal must *withhold responding* for a specified time after each reinforcement. In the experiment just described, responding in S⁻ was reduced, reinforcement frequency was maintained, and behavioral contrast occurred. This indicates that it is the reduction in response rate that is important for the occurrence of behavioral contrast.

Similar results are obtained with schedules that differentially reinforce behavior other than that involved in making the instrumental response. For example, a pigeon may be given access to food if it *does not* peck at the key for a certain period of time. Such a schedule is termed a DRO schedule (differential reinforcement of other behavior) and when a schedule of this type is employed as the S⁻ component of a multiple schedule, behavioral contrast is obtained. The contrast effect occurs despite the equalization of reinforcement frequency between the S⁺ and S⁻ components (Weissman, 1970).

Thus, the experiments with both DRL and DRO schedules indicate that reduction of response rate is more important than reduction in reinforcement frequency in determining the occurrence of behavioral contrast. However, it turns out that things are not that simple.

Evidence was obtained by Halliday and Boakes (1972) showing that a decline in response rate to S⁻ will not always lead to a behavioral contrast effect. The evidence was obtained through the use of a schedule termed a multiple VI–1-minute, Free VI–1-minute. In this schedule, the animal must respond on a VI schedule during S⁺ to obtain food but during S⁻ the food is presented at the same rate without the animal having to respond for it.[1] When this schedule is employed, there is typically a decline in response rate to S⁻, but there is no evidence of behavioral contrast in the response rate to S⁺. In fact, response rate to S⁺ itself often declines, a result opposite to behavioral contrast.

We have already mentioned another instance in which there is little or no responding to S⁻ and yet no behavioral contrast occurs [i.e., after errorless discrimination training (Terrace, 1966), *see* pp. 310–11].

Thus, we now have two examples in which there is a decline in response rate, but no behavioral contrast. What does this say for the hypothesis that a decline in response rate is a necessary and sufficient condition for contrast? One thing that it might say is that the hypothesis must be modified. This is just what Terrace (1972) did. On the basis of the evidence then available, Terrace concluded that a decline in response rate will produce behavioral contrast if that decline resulted from "active inhibition" of the response. If the decline in response rate to S⁻ occurs for some other, perhaps passive, reason, as may be the case after errorless discrimination training or on a free schedule of food in S⁻, then contrast will not occur. It is the active inhibition that is important for the occurrence of contrast. Halliday and Boakes (1972) had a similar idea—explaining behavioral contrast in terms of a rebound (when S⁺ was presented) from inhibition. These revised hypotheses imply that a decline in response rate is a necessary condition for contrast, but it is not a sufficient condition. Contrast occurs only if the decline is due to an active process.

However, once again, it appears that this cannot be the entire story. Halliday and Boakes (1974) have gathered evidence indicating that contrast may occur in some conditions without a decline in response rate to S⁻. This evidence was obtained with the use of the multiple VI Free VI schedule as the first stage in a somewhat complex experiment. The general procedure of this experiment was as follows: Pigeons were first trained to peck at a response key, il-

---

1. In schedules of this type, the use of the symbols S⁺ and S⁻ tend to lose their meaning and, therefore, many investigators turn to using S_1 and S_2 to indicate the stimuli associated with the two components of the multiple schedule. For the sake of continuity, we will continue to use S⁺ and S⁻.

luminated by white light, on a VI–1-minute schedule. The birds were then divided into two groups. One group was shifted to a *multiple* VI–1-minute, Free VI–1-minute schedule with a red illumination indicating S⁺ and green illumination indicating S⁻ (the free component). As we mentioned in the earlier discussion of this schedule, there is a decline in response rate to S⁻ but there is no evidence of contrast. During this stage of the experiment, the second group of pigeons was maintained on a VI–1-minute schedule when the keys were illuminated both red and green.

Comparison of the two groups when responses had stabilized in this stage of the experiment showed that, in the group with the free component, responses to S⁻ had declined almost to zero and the response rate to S⁺ was somewhat *lower* than the average response rate of the group maintained on the VI–1-minute schedule for both red and green stimuli (*see* Figure 10–10 for a comparison of one typical bird from each group).

In the next, and most interesting, stage of the experiment both groups were shifted to a *multiple* VI–1-minute extinction schedule with the red illumination as S⁺. Examination of response rates to S⁺ showed that behavioral contrast occurred in both groups.

The occurrence of contrast is not surprising in the group given standard training. However, note that in the group shifted from the *multiple* VI Free VI schedule the contrast occurred *without a decline in responding*. Another way of putting this result is that contrast was produced by a decline in reinforcement frequency without the usually correlated decline in response rate.

Thus, a reduction in response rate is neither a necessary nor sufficient condition to produce contrast. But, a decline in reinforcement frequency is also not necessary to produce contrast (remember the DRL and DRO schedules). Can we make any general statement as to the conditions likely to produce contrast? The following seems to be plausible at the present time. There is still some merit to the Halliday and Boakes (1972) and Terrace (1972) idea that active response inhibition is important and a condition that, in and of itself, may produce contrast. However, we have just seen that contrast will also occur in a situation where there is no further decline in response rate, but where there is a reduction in reinforcement frequency. Thus, reinforcement frequency reduction also, in and of itself, appears to be capable of producing contrast (*see also* Thomas & Cameron, 1974).

Conditions that lead to active response inhibition and conditions that otherwise involve the reduction in reinforcement frequency might both be thought of as aversive. Indeed, an animal will readily learn to terminate an S⁻ stimulus (e.g., Terrace, 1971b; Dickinson, 1972). Therefore, it could be concluded that behavioral contrast will occur in situations in which the S⁻ is aversive. Thus, we are brought back to the position originally taken by Terrace in regard to peak shift—that is, peak shift is due, in some fashion, to the aversiveness of the S⁻. We are brought to that same conclusion in regard to behavioral contrast; a conclusion that is consistent with the general close correspondence between conditions that produce contrast and the conditions that produce peak shift.

We do not want to conclude this area leaving the impression that all is known about behavioral contrast and peak shift. There are many facets to these phenomena that we have not touched on, and many facets that are still not clearly understood. We can only list some of these other interesting topics and leave them to the pursuit of the interested reader. For example, we still do not understand the conditions that will produce response inhibition and how this inhibition, when it is generated, will interact with tendencies to

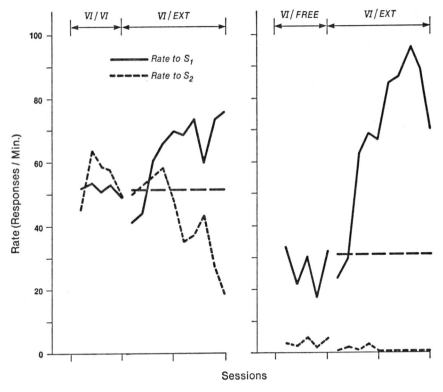

Figure 10–10.   Response rates to S⁺ and S⁻ of selected pigeons exposed to the schedules described in the text. Contrast in the S⁺ component is apparent in both birds even though a decline in response rate to S⁻ occurred only in the VI/VI bird. (Modified from Halliday & Boakes, 1974, © Soc. Exp. Anal. Behavior.)

respond. Why do we get behavioral contrast rather than the seemingly reasonable subtractive processes proposed by Spence? Under what conditions are such tendencies to not respond aversive to the organism? Why, under some conditions, can contrast and peak shift apparently be dissociated (Yarczower, Dickson & Gollub, 1966; Rosen & Terrace, 1975)?

We have also not been able to spend any time on the close relationship between behavioral contrast and Herrnstein's matching law (cf., Chapter 5), or the relationship between behavioral contrast and the discrete trial contrast effects mentioned in Chapter 4. In regard to the latter, it should be recalled that the concept of frustration was prominent in attempts to explain both discrete trials contrast and the aversiveness of the S⁻ in multiple schedules (*see* Terrace, 1966; D'Amato, 1970; Scull, Davies, & Amsel, 1970; Scull, 1973; Mackintosh, Little, & Lord, 1972; Mackintosh, 1974 for further information on this topic). Other topics that may be pursued further include the relationship between behavioral contrast in the pigeon and autoshaping (e.g., Keller, 1974; Gamzu & Schwartz, 1973), or conditions that may differentially affect contrast in different species (e.g., Pert & Gonzalez, 1974; Gonzalez & Powers, 1973; Mackintosh et al., 1972).

III. SUMMARY

Animals trained to make an instrumental response in the presence of a particular discriminative stimulus will tend to make that response in the presence of other, similar, stimuli. The shape of such a gradient of generalization is subject to the influence of a number of variables such as the schedule of reinforcement in effect during training and degree of deprivation.

Differential reinforcement of two points on a stimulus dimension will produce a gradient of responding that has characteristics different from a generalization gradient. Such a postdiscrimination gradient differs from a generalization gradient in having a steeper slope, particularly in the region of S⁻, and in having an elevated peak of responding shifted from the value of S⁺ in a direction away from S⁻. A theory of discrimination learning based on the assumed summation of excitatory and inhibitory gradients can explain some, but not all of these effects of discrimination training.

The peak shift and the elevated rate of responding to the S⁺ (behavioral contrast) appear to be closely related phenomena and both seem to be produced by conditions that contribute to the aversiveness of the S⁻.

Stimulus Control: Acquisition Processes

. . . without selective interest,
experience is an utter chaos.

W. James

I. CONTINUITY AND NONCONTINUITY THEORY

We shall turn now to a consideration of the processes involved in the acquisition of a discrimination. Historically, there have been two generally opposing views of discrimination learning, views that we have already considered to some extent in our discussion of generalization. As we mentioned in the last chapter, Spence (1936, 1937) and Hull (1943) assumed that discrimination involved the gradual acquisition of excitatory and inhibitory tendencies to the S+ and S− stimuli, respectively. This position is termed the *continuity* theory because it assumes that the acquisition of a discrimination is a continuous, gradual process. It is further assumed in this theory that all stimuli perceived when a reinforcement is presented acquire some excitatory strength (increase in the probability of eliciting the response) and, similarly, all stimuli present when a response is not reinforced acquire some inhibitory tendencies. The stimuli designated as S+ and S− in an experiment eventually come to acquire relatively specific control over behavior because they are the stimuli most reliably present when behavior is reinforced or not reinforced.

Quite another view of discrimination learning was taken by Lashley (1929) and by Krechevsky (1932). Again, a considerable portion of this theoretical position was presented when we considered generalization. For now, two basic assumptions are important. First, Lashley and Krechevsky both assumed, quite contrary to Spence and Hull, that discrimination learning is *not* a gradual process of the accumulation of excitatory and inhibitory tendencies to all stimuli present when reinforcement is delivered or omitted. Instead, Krechevsky argued that an animal learns something about only those stimuli to which it is attending at a given moment. About other stimuli, it learns nothing. Krechevsky viewed discrimination learning as a considerably more dynamic process than did Hull and

Spence. Lashley and Krechevsky hypothesized that the animal, in a sense, actively attacks the discrimination problem by forming "hypotheses" as to which stimulus is associated with the reward. While it is behaving on the basis of a hypothesis and attending to the stimuli consistent with its hypothesis, it learns nothing about any other stimuli that may be present when reward is delivered or omitted.

The flavor of these two opposing views may be gathered from the following example. Suppose that an animal is allowed to run in a T-maze in which one arm is white, the other is black, and the remainder of the maze is a neutral brightness. Suppose further that the black arm has been designated as correct (S^+) and that, therefore, there is always a reward at the end of the black arm and never a reward at the end of the white arm. As one further refinement, suppose that the location of the black and white arms are randomly varied from trial-to-trial to ensure that the animal will learn a brightness discrimination, and not simply learn to turn left or right.

According to Spence's theory, each time the rat encounters the reward in the black arm, black and all other stimuli present gain an added degree of excitatory tendency, and each time the rat enters the white arm and encounters no reward, the white stimulus, and all other stimuli present, gain an added degree of inhibitory tendency. The "all other stimuli present" may include such things as odors from the apparatus or from previous rats, visual or auditory cues present in a particular part of the test room or apparatus, stimuli deriving from muscular movements used in running or making a particular turn, etc. Over the long run, the white and black stimuli should gradually gain control over the animals' behavior because they are always correlated with reward. The other stimuli may be less correlated with the location of reward.

Krechevsky postulated that discrimination of this type is learned in quite a different manner. When first placed in the maze, the rat may attend to only a limited number of the stimuli present, say, for example, just olfactory cues. While attending to these cues ("working on an olfactory hypothesis"), the animal will learn nothing of the relationship between the brightness cues and reward. Similarly, as long as the animal attends to any cue other than brightness, it will learn nothing about the correlation between brightness and reward. But once the animal does attend to the brightness stimulus dimension, then learning will be very rapid. This view of Krechevsky's is termed the *noncontinuity* theory because it assumes that learning of a discrimination is not a gradual continuous process, but rather it is abrupt once attention is focused on the right cues. This abrupt learning had the characteristics of *insightful* behavior.

The opposition of the continuity and noncontinuity views of discrimination learning generated considerable discussion in the literature of the 1930s and 1940s as various experiments were conducted in an attempt to show one or the other view to be the "correct" interpretation of discrimination learning. The principal type of experiment that we shall mention here is the *presolution reversal* experiment. Taken at face value, the early versions of the noncontinuity theory would predict that reversing the reward values of two stimuli in a discrimination learning experiment prior to the time the subject began to attend to these stimuli should have no effect on the ultimate time required to solve the discrimination. In our example of the black and white T-maze, if the reward was correlated with black for a few trials but then switched to white *before* the animal began attending to the brightness cues, the number of trials that it takes the animal to solve the discrimination should not be increased.

Spence's position, however, predicts that such presolution reversals should retard the development of discrimination learning because the animal learns something on every trial, and what it learned over the first few trials in such an experiment would not be consistent with the response tendencies appropriate for correct performance in the final form of the problem.

Without going into the details of such experiments, we can say that the weight of the evidence at the end of the 1940s seemed to favor the continuity position of Spence and Hull. The presolution reversal experiments generally showed that the reversal of S^+ and S^- after a few acquisition trials interfered with the development of appropriate performance on the discrimination problem (e.g., McCulloch & Pratt, 1934; Spence, 1945; Goodrich, Ross, & Wagner, 1961).

However, there were still some nagging problems. Some experiments did indicate that presolution reversal might not have an effect as long as there were not too many reversed trials (Krechevsky, 1938), or if the discriminative stimuli were located in a place where the animals were unlikely to look (Ehrenfreund, 1948). The phrase "unlikely to look" in the previous sentence relates to the heart of the difficulty in deciding between continuity and noncontinuity interpretations of discrimination learning. In order to make any such decision, it would be necessary to know what stimuli the animals were attending to, and when they were attending to these stimuli. In the absence of any clear way of measuring this attention, the weight of the evidence from the presolution reversal experiments seemed to favor the continuity position of Spence; most often, presolution reversal interfered with discrimination acquisition.

In the late 1940s and early 1950s, however, a series of experiments reopened the continuity-noncontinuity issue from a slightly different point of view. These experiments are of three types (*see* Riley, 1968), the overlearning-reversal experiment, the acquired distinctiveness of cues experiment, and the learning-set experiment. We shall describe each of these experimental situations and their relevance for the continuity-noncontinuity issue, and then go on to some more recent data on the topic of selective attention.

The Overlearning-Reversal Experiment

Reid (1953) trained three groups of rats in a T-maze brightness discrimination to a criterion of 18/20 correct choices. After the criterion was reached, one group was given training with the reward values of the discriminada reversed, the former S$^+$ was now incorrect and the former S$^-$ was now rewarded. One of the remaining two groups was given an additional 50 trials in the original problem before reversal, and the final group was given 150 additional trials on the original problem before reversal. Surprisingly, the result of the experiment was that the latter group, the group given 150 overtraining trials on the original experiment, learned the reversal faster than the other two groups.

In order to explain this finding, Reid adopted a two-stage hypothesis. He assumed that the acquisition of a task such as a T-maze brightness discrimination actually involves two kinds of learning. At the same time that the animal is learning to make a response of approaching the correct stimulus and not approaching the incorrect stimulus, it is also learning to attend to the stimulus dimension from which the S$^+$ and S$^-$ were drawn. For example, if black and white maze arms are the S$^+$ and S$^-$ stimuli, at the same time that the rat is learning to approach black and not white, it is learning to attend to brightness cues. A second assumption that Reid made in order to explain his data was that this second type of learning, learning to attend to a stimulus dimension, develops more slowly than the approach response learning.

The two-stage hypothesis may be used to explain Reid's data in the following way. The animals that were reversed after reaching criterion and after 50 overtraining trials had not yet learned the attending response to any great degree and thus, when the correct and incorrect stimuli were reversed they had to relearn which of the various stimuli in the apparatus to approach and which to avoid. However, in the animals given the 150 overtraining trials, the attentional response had been well learned so, when the S$^+$ and S$^-$ were reversed, the animals learned this reversal relatively quickly because the brightness dimension was still relevant (i.e., the correct and incorrect stimuli were still on the brightness dimension) and, by attending to this stimulus dimension, the animals could quickly learn which aspect to approach (i.e., white).

Now, this explanation, as applied to Reid's data, was post hoc. Was it necessary to have such a complicated explanation for the data? Before looking into this question we would like to indicate the relevance of this type of experiment for the continuity-noncontinuity issue. The reader will have noticed the similarity between Reid's two-stage hypothesis and certain aspects of the Lashley-Krechevsky position. At the risk of being too obvious, we will simply point out that the concept of attention can be used to explain his data and used in a way similar to the Lashley-Krechevsky usage—viz., the animals attend to a stimulus dimension and once they are attending to the relevant dimension (have adopted the correct hypothesis), then learning is relatively rapid.

The surprising finding of faster reversal learning by animals given extra training on the original task led to an explosive growth in the number of experiments conducted to investigate this phenomenon. For some time the results of these experiments were quite confusing; many replicated Reid's findings, but many others did not (cf., Sperling, 1965a). Eventually, the following conclusion seems to have emerged from the mass of experimentation; the overlearning reversal effect (ORE) is likely to be obtained if the discrimination is a relatively difficult one, and if the amount of the reward given for the correct response is large (Theios & Blosser, 1965; Mackintosh, 1965a, 1969; Sperling, 1965b).

The importance of the difficulty aspect for attentional theories is the following. It may be assumed that in a simple discrimination there is a high probability that the animal attends to the relevant dimension from the beginning of training and, thus, there is little or no learning of an attentional response involved (cf., Lovejoy, 1966). Under these conditions, overtraining would not be expected to facilitate reversal. In the rat, a spatial discrimination (learning to go left or right in a T-maze) appears to be a relatively easy discrimination (Mackintosh, 1965b, 1969) and the ORE is unlikely to occur in a spatial discrimination with rats (Mackintosh, 1965a, 1969). However, in a difficult discrimination the animal is likely, at the beginning of the experiment, to be attending to the wrong stimuli. Thus, in a difficult discrimination, the learning of the correct attentional response plays a more important role, and it is under these conditions that overtraining is likely to facilitate reversal. For the rat, a brightness discrimination appears to be relatively difficult (Mackintosh, 1965b), and it is in a brightness discrimination that the ORE is most likely to occur (Mackintosh, 1969).

Evidence in regard to this interpretation has been provided by Mackintosh (1965b) who found that overtraining facilitated the reversal of a brightness discrimination in rats but not in chicks. It would appear that in birds a brightness discrimination is not difficult per se, since birds may be thought to have a higher probability of attending to visual stimuli than rats (cf., the data on conditioned aversions in Chapter 7). Thus, overtraining a chicken on a brightness discrimination is like overtraining a rat on a spatial discrimination. Further evidence in support of this idea was found in another experiment by Mackintosh (1965b) in which it was shown that overtraining would facilitate the reversal of a brightness discrimination in chickens if the discrimination was made difficult enough.

There are other possible explanations for the ORE but, at the present time, it appears that an explanation involving the concept of attention is most consistent with the data (cf., Mackintosh, 1969; Lovejoy, 1966). In this regard it is interesting to note the results of experiments that provide an opportunity to present for brief observation periods the stimuli involved in a discrimination. In both humans and monkeys, the number of times (and duration) the subjects choose to produce these stimuli before making a response to one of them increases with problem difficulty (Premack & Collier, 1966), and with changes in the experimental situation such as reversal of the discrimination (D'Amato, Etkin, & Fazzaro, 1968). It is as if the more complex the discrimination, the more attention to the stimuli that is required.

Why a large reward magnitude should be necessary to produce the ORE in rats (Mackintosh, 1969) is not clear at the present time. It may be that the large reward is more likely to lead to frustration and thus faster extinction to the formerly correct stimulus (cf., Chapter 4), or it may be that the large reward is itself involved in directing attention. Mackintosh (1969) seems to favor the latter alternative.

In any event, it is apparent why the ORE experiment is one of several experimental situations that has led to a resurgence of interest in the concept of attention and a reexamination of the continuity-noncontinuity issue, this time with a more favorable outcome for the noncontinuity interpretation of discrimination learning (Mackintosh, 1965a).

Acquired Distinctiveness of Cues

A second line of evidence reviving interest in the concept of attention came from the research of Lawrence (1949, 1950). Lawrence trained rats in a simultaneous discrimination task in which they had to learn to approach one stimulus, say a black card, and not another stimulus, say a white card. After this discrimination was well learned (90 percent correct), the animals were trained in a *conditional* discrimination task. In a conditional discrimination the correct choice response depends upon which stimuli are present. For example, if both left and right choices are covered with a white card, then a left choice is correct, whereas if both are covered with a black card, then going to the right-hand side would be rewarded. The important aspect of a conditional discrimination is that the animal is not rewarded for approaching or avoiding a particular stimulus; the stimulus serves as a cue for a choice response which is based on something other than direct approach or avoidance of that cue.

Lawrence found that groups given training similar to that described above learned the conditional discrimination faster than groups in which the conditional cues in the transfer test were different from the approach cues used in the initial simultaneous discrimination task. In particular, animals for which the conditional cue was present but irrelevant (not correlated with reward) during the simultaneous discrimination task did not learn the conditional task as fast as animals for which the conditional cue was the relevant cue (correlated with reward) during the simultaneous task.

How are these results related to the continuity-noncontinuity issue? Lawrence argued that the positive transfer shown between the two tasks could not be accounted for on the basis of excitatory tendencies associated with S^+ and inhibitory tendencies associated with S^-. A stimulus that served to direct an approach response in the simultaneous task did not serve that function in the conditional task; that is, approaching the black stimulus in the conditional task could not lead to good performance since both choice alternatives were half the time black and half the time white.

If commonality of an approach response could not account for the transfer, what did? Lawrence argued that it was a process of *learning to attend* to the relevant cues that accounted for the transfer. Note that even though the black and white stimulus cards of our example do not direct an approach response in the conditional discrimination, they are still relevant for the solution of the discrimination. Lawrence argued that if the animal learns to attend to the relevant stimulus dimension (e.g., brightness) in the simultaneous discrimination, then the solution of the conditional discrimination should be faster if this same dimension is still relevant. The experiment we have described, as well as others conducted by Lawrence and other investigators, bears out this hypothesis. Thus, the heading for this section comes from Lawrence's idea that the relevant cues acquire distinctiveness in the simultaneous discrimination and this distinctiveness aids in the solution of the conditional discrimination as long as the same stimulus dimension is relevant for the solution of the conditional problem. The similarity of this interpretation to the Lashley-Krechevsky view of discrimination learning is evident; animals must learn to attend to the stimulus dimension relevant for the solution of the discrimination problem, and once this is done, the solution of the problem, in terms of making the rewarded response, comes fairly rapidly (*see* Riley, 1968, for a more complete analysis of the acquired distinctiveness of cue experiments).

Learning Set

The third set of data important for bringing renewed interest to the continuity-noncontinuity issue came from Harlow's investigations of discrimination learning in Rhesus monkeys (Harlow, 1949, 1959). In the typical experiment of Harlow's, monkeys were trained on a simultaneous discrimination problem in an apparatus similar to that illustrated in Figure 11–1. Harlow's procedure was interesting in that the number of trials given with any particular pair of stimuli was small (e.g., 6–14), but the monkeys were given experience with a large number of stimulus pairs. That is, after six trials

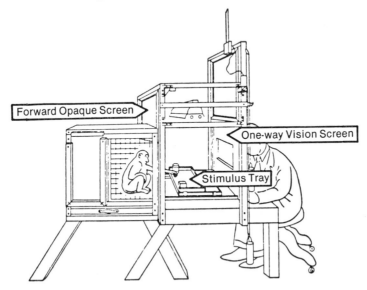

Figure 11–1. The 1949 version of the Wisconsin General Test Apparatus (WGTA). (After Harlow, 1951.)

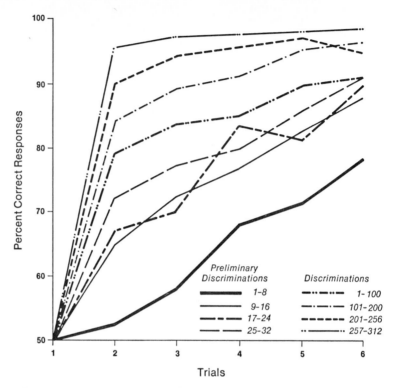

Figure 11–2. Discrimination learning curves presented as a function of problem blocks experienced. (Modified from Harlow, 1949.)

with a triangle as S⁺ and a circle as S⁻, there would be another six trials with a square as S⁺ and a toy fire engine as S⁻, etc. Proceeding in this fashion, the monkeys would eventually be given experience with several hundred different stimulus pairs.

The results of such an experiment may be examined in two ways: The improvement in performance across the six trials with a given pair of stimuli (termed *intraproblem* learning), and the improvement in rate of learning as a function of the number of different stimulus pairs experienced (termed *interproblem* learning). Both of these effects may be seen in Figure 11–2. The curve labeled 1–8 represents average intraproblem improvement in the first eight discrimination problems presented to the monkeys. Performance on Trial 1 should be at chance (50 percent correct), since the monkeys have no way of determining which of the two stimuli is to be rewarded. Performance gradually improves from Trial 1 through Trial 6 as the monkeys learn which stimulus is rewarded within each pair presented to them.

The remaining curves in the figure also designate intraproblem improvement across the six trials of each problem. But, in addition, these curves also represent average performance after the monkeys have had experience with more and more different pairs of stimuli. It is evident that the additional experience leads to better performance on the part of the monkeys. This better performance is apparent in the ever improving (approaching 100 percent) correct responses from Trial 2 through Trial 6. It is this improved performance correlated with the number of discriminations solved that is termed *interproblem learning,* and it is this interproblem learning that makes the learning-set data relevant for the continuity-noncontinuity issue.

Looking back at Figure 11–2 again, we can see that learning is characterized by gradual improvement early in training, but later, after experience with a number of problems, the solution to a problem becomes abrupt (see the curve labeled 257–312) in Figure 11–2. That is, the animal solves the problem after the first trial; performance on Trial 2 is virtually 100 percent. What is it about experience with a large number of discrimination problems that changes the course of learning from one of gradual improvement to one of sudden solution after one trial?

One possibility is that, through extensive training, the animal learns to attend to a stimulus dimension relevant for the solution of all the discrimination problems. But what could this dimension be? The discriminative stimuli themselves change every few trials, so it couldn't be anything related to these stimuli per se that serves as the relevant dimension. However, one factor that is constant across all problems is this: The stimulus rewarded on the first trial of every problem is also rewarded on the remaining five trials. If the monkeys learned this, they could obtain the information needed to solve all problems on the first trial. That is, if they select one stimulus, say a triangle, and it is rewarded, then they can select that stimulus on the remaining five trials and it will also be rewarded. If, on the first trial, they select a stimulus that was not rewarded, they still have all the information needed to solve the problem on Trial 2, that is, they can select the stimulus not chosen on Trial 1.

Thus, the stimulus relevant for the solution of any problem is not associated with the discriminative stimuli per se, but rather is an abstract stimulus correlated with the outcome of the animals' response on Trial 1. If that outcome is a reward, then choosing that stimulus for the remaining trials will always lead to a reward; if the outcome is the absence of reward, then shifting to the alternative stimulus for the remaining trials will always lead to a reward. Another way of stating this is that the animal eventually adopts a hypothesis of *win-stay, lose-shift* ("win" meaning a rewarded response, "lose" meaning a nonrewarded response). The adoption of such a hypothesis would lead to the solution of every problem on Trial 2.

The importance of these experiments for the continuity-noncontinuity issue is now clear. They show that learning can be abrupt, discontinuous, and apparently insightful, but this type of learning is itself dependent on extensive earlier experience with a large number of discrimination problems, the solution of each of which is initially a gradual process. The transfer from the slow, gradual type of learning to the abrupt solution apparently comes after the animal has adopted a win-stay, lose-shift hypothesis or, in other words, after the animal has learned to attend to the relevant dimension. During the course of its extensive experience with the discrimination problems the animal is, at one and the same time, learning to solve each problem and learning how to solve a *class* of problems. This latter learning is what gives this experimental paradigm its name of learning-set or learning-to-learn.

Once again we find it convenient to describe a set of experimental results with phrases like "attending to the relevant dimension," and "adopting the correct hypothesis," phrases that are clearly compatible with Lashley and Krechevsky's interpretation of discrimination learning. But is there any evidence these phrases are more than descriptive? Is there any supporting evidence or analysis indicating that such processes do occur in monkeys or other animals? There is, and we shall briefly consider it now.

Error Factors

Harlow (1959) has shown that it is possible to analyze learning-set behavior in a way that shows that the errors made by monkeys during the course of learning-set acquisition are not simply random errors but are, most often, instances of systematic response patterns that are inappropriate for the solution of the problem. For example, on the first trial of a problem a monkey may be presented with a triangle as S^+ on the left side and a circle as S^- on the right side. Let us say that the monkey chooses the triangle on this trial. Now, on Trial 2, the monkey may be presented with the triangle (still S^+) on the right and the circle on the left. If the monkey chooses the circle on this trial, it may not be due to a random process, instead, it may be due to the fact that the reward on Trial 1 was actually ambiguous (cf., Spence, 1956). That is, the monkey has no way of determining whether the reward received on Trial 1 was for choosing the triangle or for choosing the stimulus on the left side. If the monkey responds to the left side on Trial 2 because that is where the reward was on Trial 1, then that is a systematic error, an error that Harlow called a *differential cue* error factor. Harlow showed that the percentage of these errors declines as the animal becomes experienced in the learning set task.

Stimulus perseveration is another error factor that Harlow has shown declines during the course of learning-set experience. This error factor is due to persisting with an incorrect stimulus through a series of trials, perhaps because the monkeys have some preference for that particular object (Harlow, 1959). Figure 11–3 shows the decline in stimulus perseveration errors as a function of learning-set experience.

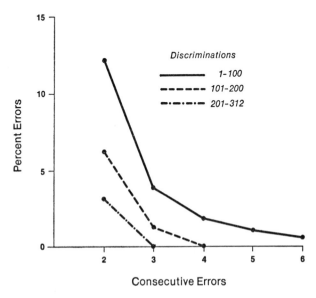

Figure 11–3. Decrease in stimulus-perseveration errors during the course of learning-set formation. (After Harlow, 1959, by permission of McGraw-Hill.)

In a similar fashion, Harlow has shown that responding primarily on the basis of position (*position habit* error factor) and the tendency to shift from a rewarded to the nonrewarded stimulus, perhaps because of curiosity (*response-shift* error factor), also decline during the course of learning-set experience. Indeed, the process of learning-set formation may be thought of as the gradual elimination of these error factors (Harlow & Hicks, 1957). But now notice how similar this analysis is to Lashley's ideas about discrimination learning in general. That is, if error factors are considered as incorrect hypotheses adopted by the monkeys, then we can say that learning-set acquisition involves, among other things, the discarding of incorrect hypotheses (*see also*, Miles, 1965, pp. 68–70).

Successive Reversals

If the win-stay, lose-shift strategy is presumed to be at the basis of learning-set proficiency, it would be useful to determine whether animals could be trained to adopt such a response strategy independent of the learning-set situation, and then see if this strategy transferred to learning-set behavior. In one investigation of this question, Schusterman (1962) trained chimpanzees on a long series of successive reversal problems with just a few stimuli. That is, the chimps were presented with two stimuli, one of which was correct. After the subjects had made the correct choice on 12 consecutive trials, the reward values were reversed, the formerly S+ was now S−, and training was continued until the animal again made the correct choice on 12 consecutive trials, whereupon the stimuli were reversed again, etc. After extensive training in this task, the chimps were shifted to a learning-set situation where they received training with large numbers of different stimuli in the standard learning-set procedure. Schusterman found that it did not require extensive training for these chimps to show the typical learning-set behavior of virtually 100 percent correct on Trial 2. In fact, the chimps showed such behavior within the first block of 30 problems.

How can such a degree of positive transfer between successive reversal experience and learning-set behavior be explained? One possibility is that the same strategy is involved in both. That is, in the successive reversal task the animal may learn to stay with one stimulus as long as it is rewarded. After the first occurrence of nonreward, the animal will then shift to the other stimulus (which is now rewarded), and so on. But this is the same win-shift, lose-stay strategy that is assumed to be important for learning-set formation. The occurrence of positive transfer between the two tasks thus supports the interpretation of learning-set behavior in terms of this hypothesis.

A similar interpretation was applied to slightly different experimental procedures by Warren (1954) and by Riopelle (1955). Again, these experiments indicated that the function of a reward changes during the course of learning-set experience from one of differentially strengthening response tendencies (as Spence thought) to one of primarily providing information as to what response will be correct on the next trial.

Other Hypotheses

If a win-stay, lose-shift hypothesis is normally involved in the development of learning-set, it might be asked if it is possible to train monkeys with procedures that make other hypotheses relevant and then see if a learning-set develops on the basis of these other hypotheses. Brown and McDowell (1963) undertook such an experiment. They attempted to capitalize on the response-shift tendencies demonstrated by monkeys and train this, not as an error factor, but as the hypothesis necessary for solution of a special discrimination problem, the response-shift problem. In this experiment the monkeys received only two trials with each pair of stimuli. On the first trial, choice of either stimulus was rewarded. But, in order to receive a reward on the second trial, the monkeys had to choose the stimulus that was not chosen on the first trial. In other words, the monkeys had to learn to shift responses between Trials 1 and 2. Brown and McDowell found that there was a systematic decline in errors as a function of experience in this task so that after 960 problems the percentage of errors on Trial 2 had declined from the 70 percent present early in training to approximately 10 percent. Apparently, the monkeys had adopted a response-shift strategy. Note that this strategy would be expected to produce negative transfer to a learning-set situation.

Other experiments have demonstrated that monkeys can learn to respond to "concepts" of novelty and familiarity, to oddity in color or form, and to use the color of the tray on which the objects are presented as a cue indicating which of two strategies will be correct on that trial (*see* Miles, 1965; French, 1965; Levine, 1965; and Harlow, 1959, for reviews).

Retention

Further support for the hypothesis analysis of learning-set behavior comes from investigations of retention. Bessemer (1967; Bessemer & Stollnitz, 1971) has found that learning-set experienced monkeys show virtual complete forgetting, within a few minutes to an hour, of which two stimuli presented within a problem were not rewarded. This surprisingly rapid forgetting will be analyzed in more detail later in the text (*see* p. 403), but we mention it now because Bessemer's interpretation is consistent with the point we are making in this section. Bessemer argues that the rapid forgetting of stimulus-reward correlations indicates that the learning (and remembering) of differential approach or avoidance tendencies to specific stimuli is not important for the high performance levels demonstrated by experienced monkeys. Rather, what is important is a hypothesis which is based on short-term memory for relatively recent events, i.e., the outcome of the previous trial. The outcome (reward or nonreward) acts as a conditional cue allowing the animal to use the win-stay, lose-shift hypothesis and be correct on all trials after Trial 1. When an animal is removed from the testing situation, even for a few minutes, and then brought back and presented with a problem it has just solved, it acts as if it is a new problem and responds on the basis of some hypothesis (or error factor such as stimulus preference) on the first trial. After this trial, it operates on the basis of the win-stay, lose-shift hypothesis.

The rapid forgetting of *intraproblem* learning by learning-set experienced monkeys is more compatible with a hypothesis-analysis of learning set behavior than with an analysis based on differential approach-avoidance tendencies, as would be implied by the continuity view of learning.

We have now covered three sets of experimental results: over-learning reversal, acquired distinctiveness of cues, and learning-set, all of which can apparently best be explained with the aid of concepts coming from the noncontinuity view of discrimination learning; *viz.*, attention to relevant stimulus dimensions and the use of hypotheses or attempted solutions to discrimination problems. It should also be noted that, in some of these situations, some of the assumptions of continuity theory also apply and thus the two views may not be mutually exclusive. For example, intraproblem learning during the early stages of learning-set training appears to be a gradual and continuous process. It is only after some experience that the discontinuities associated with Trial 2 solution begin to appear. Similarly, the overlearning reversal effect does not always occur. It may be that selective attention does not play a critical role in all simple discrimination learning, but as the task becomes more difficult, the role of selective attention and hypothesis behavior becomes more important (*see* Mackintosh, 1965a).

We turn now to a direct demonstration of selective attention in animals and a consideration of some experiments designed to investigate the conditions leading to selective attention.

II. SELECTIVE ATTENTION, BLOCKING, AND SURPRISE

Selective Attention

We shall first describe two experiments that, using similar techniques, clearly demonstrated the existence of selective attention in animals. The first was performed by Lashley (1938) with rats in the Lashley jumping stand. The rats were first trained on a simultaneous discrimination with forms (square and triangle) as the relevant stimulus dimension. After the rats were performing well on the discrimination task, the stimuli were altered so that animals

were presented with either the bottom halves *or* the top halves of
the square and triangle. Lashley found that the presentation of only
the bottom halves of the figures still occasioned nearly perfect responding. But the presentation of the top halves led to 50 percent
random responding. In other words, the breaking down of the
square and triangle into component parts indicated that the animals

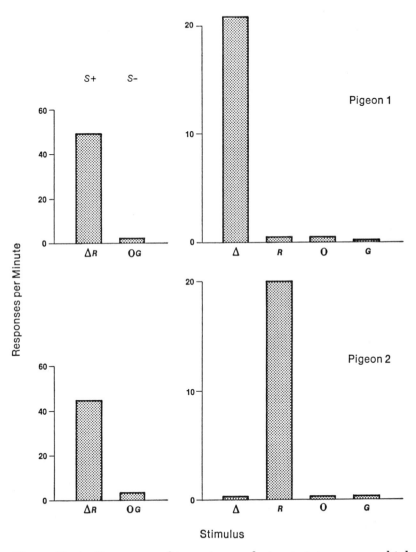

Figure 11–4. Responses of two pigeons during training on a multiple
schedule with compound stimuli (left panel) and during tests with the
compound stimuli broken down into their components. *See* text for explanation. (After Reynolds, 1961, © Soc. Exp. Anal. Behavior.)

had only been attending to part of the figures all along and had solved the discrimination problem on the basis of attending to the lower sections. They had apparently learned nothing about the upper halves of the figures.

A conceptually similar experiment with equally clear results was conducted by Reynolds (1961). Reynolds trained pigeons on a multiple VI–3-minute extinction schedule. The S^+ and S^- during discrimination training were both compound stimuli; a white triangle on a red background was used as S^+ and a white circle on a green background was used as S^-. After the birds were exhibiting many responses in the presence of S^+ and virtually none in the presence of S^- (*see* left half of Figure 11–4), the pigeons were shifted to an extinction schedule. In extinction the compound stimuli that had been present during acquisition were "broken down" into their components. That is, sometimes the response key was illuminated red, sometimes green, sometimes just the triangle was presented, and sometimes just the circle. The purpose of this phase of the experiment was, of course, to determine whether the pigeons had selectively attended to any aspect of the compound stimuli present during acquisition. The results of this test are presented in the right half of Figure 11–4. Clearly, pigeon #1 had learned the discrimination primarily on the basis of responding to the white triangle; the red color had no tendency to control its responding. Pigeon #2, however, had learned the discrimination primarily on the basis of attending to color; the triangle in this bird had little control over responding.

These two experiments clearly demonstrate that animals do not learn equally about all aspects of the stimuli present in a discrimination situation. They may select some specific aspect of the stimuli present and use that to respond appropriately. It is important to note that in both of these experiments the animals came into close contact with the compound discriminative stimuli during training; in the Lashley experiment the rats had to jump right at the cards in order to get to the reward; in the Reynolds experiment the birds pecked directly on the place where the stimuli were projected. It is also interesting to note that in the Reynolds experiment one of the birds attended to form, whereas the other attended to color (cf., the stimulus preference error factor mentioned in the learning-set discussion).

What are the conditions controlling such selective attention in animals? Ethologists have been describing for some time instances of selective attention (and/or selective perception) in animals. That is, in many situations the behavior of lower animals seems to be controlled by only a small part of the total stimulus array available from a species mate (e.g., robin's red breast, stickleback's red underside). However, these stimuli (termed *releasing stimuli*) are apparently responded to on an innate basis (cf., Tinbergen, 1967; Eibel-Eibesfeldt, 1970) and are not the topic of concern for this text. We are concerned with the conditions that control selective attention within an individual, not within a species. Some recent experiments by Kamin (1969) have been addressed to just this question.

Blocking

Kamin's experiments were conducted with rats utilizing the CER paradigm (*see* Chapter 6). The general procedure involved training the rats to bar-press for a food reward on a VI–2.5-minute schedule in test sessions that lasted two hours. During this two-hour period, 4 CS–UCS sequences occurred independently of the animals' behavior. The CS was typically 3 minutes long and was followed immediately by a 1 mA, 0.5-second electric shock as the UCS. The dependent variable was an index of how much the rat suppressed its bar-pressing during the CS. The CS itself was either a white noise (N), a light (L), or a compound stimulus made up of both the noise and the light (LN).

Kamin's experimental approach was to determine whether prior experience with one element of a compound CS would prevent the second element from acquiring control over behavior when it was subsequently presented in a compound with the first element. A typical experimental design and results are illustrated in Table 11–1. There were four groups in the experiment illustrated. Group 1 was first given 16 CS–UCS pairings with the noise alone as CS, then 8 pairings with the light-noise compound as the CS and, finally, were given a test trial with the light alone as the CS. As is apparent from the suppression ratios presented in Table 11–1, the light did not function as an effective CS for this group. However, in Group 2, which received only the 8 LN compound trials, the presentation of the light alone in the test phase led to virtual complete suppression of responding. Thus, the comparison of Group 1 and Group 2 shows that prior experience with one element of the compound stimulus *blocked* the other element from acquiring stimulus control over the animals' behavior.

The extent of this blocking is evident in the comparison of Groups 1 and 3. Group 1, which had 8 trials with the light paired with shock in a compound, showed a lack of suppression equivalent to Group 3, which never experienced the light. Thus, the light was not functionally present in Group 1. The comparison of Groups 1 and 4, both of which received the same number and kind of condi-

Table 11–1. Suppression Ratios (SR) Obtained in Four Groups of Rats Given the Indicated Training in a CER Paradigm*

	PHASE I	PHASE II	TEST	SR
Group 1	N (16)	LN (8)	L	.45
Group 2	—	LN (8)	L	.05
Group 3	—	N (24)	L	.44
Group 4	LN (8)	N (16)	L	.25

*Suppression ratios close to .50 indicate no suppression (equal responding before and during the CS), suppression ratios close to 0.0 indicate a lack of responding during the CS. See text for further explanation. (Modified from Kamin, 1969, by permission of Prentice-Hall.)

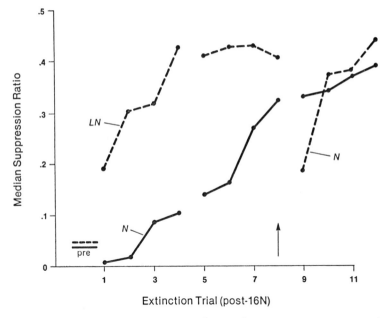

Figure 11–5. Suppression ratios obtained in extinction in a group in which a light was superimposed on the noise CS (LN) and in a noise alone group (N). *See* text for further explanation. (After Kamin, 1969, by permission of Prentice-Hall.)

tioning trials, shows that the effect of training with a single element is greater if that training precedes conditioning with the compound stimulus. Group 4 does, however, show less suppression than Group 2, indicating that there is some retroactive (or recency) effect of the training with the single element.

In other experiments Kamin demonstrated that the blocking effect is specific to pretraining with one of the stimuli, and it does not make much difference whether the light or the noise is used as the pretraining stimulus, either one blocks the acquisition of stimulus control by the other stimulus. If only the compound training is given, and then each stimulus is presented separately, each is found to have acquired some degree of stimulus control. Thus, in Kamin's experiments it is clearly the pretraining that produces the blocking (the reader may recall that a similar effect was demonstrated in Pavlov's laboratory; *see* Chapter 3).

To what is this blocking due? One possibility entertained by Kamin was that the animal does not notice or perceive the second stimulus in the compound because its "attention is focused" on the first element. A second possibility is that the animal does notice the second element, but does not condition to it because it is redundant. In terms of Rescorla's theory of Pavlovian conditioning that we described in Chapter 3, we might say that the animal does not condition to the superimposed element of the compound because it has already learned a contingency between the first element and the UCS and this contingency is sufficient to predict the occurrence of shock. In other words, the second element is redundant, it does not provide any new information (cf., Egger & Miller, 1962).

In order to distinguish between these two possible interpretations (lack of perception or lack of conditioning because of redundancy), Kamin performed the following experiment. Two groups of rats were given 16 conditioning trials with the noise alone as the CS. Following this, one group was given 8 *extinction* trials with an LN compound as the CS, whereas the second group was given 12 *extinction* trials with the noise alone as the CS. Finally, the first group (the LN group) was given 4 more *extinction* trials with the noise alone as the CS. The purpose of this experiment was to determine whether the added element (the light) would be noticed if it predicted something new, *viz.*, nonreinforcement. The results of the experiment are shown in Figure 11–5.

The degree of suppression after 16 trials was the same in the two groups. The presentation of the compound stimulus on the first trials of extinction to group LN decreased the amount of suppression. The group presented with the usual noise alone on the first extinction trial showed no change in suppression.[1] The interesting aspect of the data on the first extinction trial is that the difference between these two groups appeared before the nonoccurrence of the UCS. That is, the suppression measure is taken during the CS and before the scheduled occurrence of the UCS. Thus, the differ-

---

1. The difference between the two groups was not statistically significant but, as Kamin pointed out, highly suggestive.

ence between the two groups on Trial 1 of extinction indicates that the rats did indeed notice the superimposed element even before it predicted the occurrence of something new, nonreinforcement.

Thinking back to the first experiment of Kamin's that we described (*see* pp. 337–38), we can now tentatively rule out the first interpretation presented above; that is, that the animals do not perceive the added stimulus because their attention is focused on the single element. By inference, these data mean that the animals do notice the superimposed element but do not condition to it if it predicts nothing different from the single element.

Looking again at Figure 11–5, we can see that on the second extinction trial, there was a continued decrease in the suppression of group LN, but little change in the noise alone group. This difference indicates that a single nonreinforced trial to the compound was sufficient for the rats to detect a difference between the LN compound, which was not reinforced, and the noise alone, which always had been reinforced. The difference in rates of extinction between the two groups again indicates clearly that the added element was perceived in the compound group.

On extinction Trial 9, the stimulus for the LN group was changed back to the noise alone. It is apparent in Figure 11–5 that this change led to an *increase* in suppression. This effect indicated that, to some degree, the extinction trials with the compound stimulus had preserved the N element from extinction. In other words, the animals had learned, to some extent, that it was the *compound* of LN that was nonreinforced.

Other studies by Kamin have shown that increasing the number of compound training trials from 8 to 24 (in the Group 1, Table 1 design) does not attenuate the blocking effect at all. Blocking is, however, reduced if the amount of prior training with the single element is reduced or if the prior training with the single element is extinguished prior to the introduction of the compound stimulus. These latter two results again support the idea that it is something about the CS being an adequate predictor of the UCS that is at the basis of blocking. If the adequacy of the single element is reduced by not giving sufficient conditioning trials or by extinguishing it first, then the added element of the compound acquires some control over behavior.

Further evidence on this relationship was provided by a study of eyelid conditioning by Wagner and Saavedra (reported in Rescorla & Wagner, 1972). The conditions experienced by the three groups of rabbits in this experiment, as well as the results, are summarized in Figure 11–6. Group 1 received 200 conditioning trials with a compound CS consisting of a light (L) and a tone (T) paired with a cheek-shock UCS. In addition, this group received an

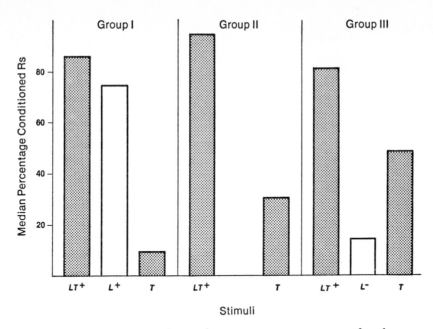

Figure 11–6. Percent conditioned responses in groups trained with compound, or compound and component stimuli, and tested with one of the component stimuli (L = Light, T = Tone). *See* text for further explanation. (Adapted from Wagner & Saavedra as presented in Rescorla & Wagner, 1972, by permission of Prentice-Hall.)

additional 200 trials in which the L alone was paired with the UCS. These latter trials were intermixed with the compound CS trials. Group 2 received just the 200 trials with the LT compound. Group 3 also received 200 trials with the LT compound and, in addition, 200 trials with the L alone that were *not* followed by the UCS. Thus, both Groups 1 and 3 received extra trials with the L alone. In Group 1 these extra trials were reinforced; in Group 3 they were nonreinforced.

The results of these differential acquisition treatments were tested by presenting the T alone. Note that all groups had received an equal number of trials with the T in compound with the light. The results of these test trials, summarized in Figure 11–6, showed the following: The T had acquired the least control over behavior in Group 1, more in Group 2, and most in Group 3. What accounted for these differences among groups that had all equal experience with the tone? The answer is apparently the additional experience with the light given to Groups 1 and 3.

In Group 1 both the compound trials and the single element

trials reinforced the L as a predictor of the UCS, thus the T, being redundant, acquired little control over behavior. In Group 3 the L alone trials were nonreinforced, thus, perhaps, increasing the predictability of the T in the LT compound, leading to the acquisition of relatively greater control by this stimulus. In Group 2, in the absence of any specific experimental treatment, both elements of the compound apparently acquired some control over behavior. These latter results are consistent with those reported by Kamin in the CER task. Thus, the results of the Wagner and Saavedra experiment can perhaps be summarized as showing that the more the light predicted shock, the less the likelihood that anything would be learned about the relationship between tone and shock.

If redundancy on the part of the superimposed element is at the basis of the lack of conditioning to this element, then a different set of results should be obtained if the compound predicts something different than the prior trained single element. That is, blocking should not be obtained if the redundancy can be eliminated. We have already considered one approach to this problem in Kamin's experiment in which the compound cue predicted extinction. This experiment indicated that something indeed was learned about the compound when it predicted something new, the absence of a UCS.

Surprise

Another approach to this hypothesis is illustrated by the experiment outlined in Table 11–2. There were three groups of rats in this experiment by Kamin. The first group received 16 conditioning trials with the N alone followed by 8 trials with the LN compound, and then the test with the L alone. The shock level for all the conditioning trials was 1 mA. Group 2 received identical treatment except that the shock level was increased from 1 mA to 4 mA, when

Table 11–2. Suppression Ratios (SR) in Three Groups of Rats Given the Indicated Experimental Treatments*

	PHASE I	PHASE II	TEST	SR
Group 1	N 1-mA (16)	LN 1-mA (8)	L	.45
Group 2	N 1-mA (16)	LN 4-mA (8)	L	.14
Group 3	N 4-mA (8)	LN 4-mA (8)	L	.36

*Group 1 received a constant low intensity shock, Group 3 a constant high intensity shock, and in Group 2 the shock was changed from low-to-high intensity when the compound stimulus was introduced. (Modified from Kamin, 1969, by permission of Prentice-Hall.)

the compound CS was first introduced. Group 3 received the high intensity shock in all of its conditioning trials. The suppression ratios (*see* Table 11–2) indicate the following. The standard blocking effect was obtained in Group 1 (cf., Group 1 in Table 11–1). However, the blocking effect was considerably attenuated if the shock intensity was increased when the compound cue was introduced. The data from Group 3 indicate that the reduced suppression obtained in Group 2 could not be entirely attributed to the effects of the more intense UCS per se, but rather must be related to the *change* in shock intensity when the compound was introduced.

Again, we see that these results indicate that conditioning to the superimposed element does not occur *unless* the added element is correlated with a different consequence for the animal than is the single, prior trained, element. Or, as Kamin (1969) expressed it, conditioning may not occur unless the UCS surprises the animal. Such conditions of surprise may include a change to extinction, an increase in UCS intensity, and extra added shock as part of the UCS (which eliminates blocking; Kamin, 1969), a reversing of the usual consequences of a CS^+ and a CS^- (Wagner, Rudy, & Whitlow, 1973); or presentation of a brief stimulus 3–5 seconds after the occurrence of the UCS (Gray & Appignanesi, 1973).

Rescorla & Wagner's interpretation of data such as these is the following:

> ...organisms only learn when events violate their expectations. Certain expectations are built up about the events following a stimulus complex: expectations initiated by that complex and its component stimuli are then only modified when consequent events disagree with the composite expectation (Rescorla & Wagner, 1972, p. 75).

III. MODIFIED NONCONTINUITY AND CONTINUITY THEORY

We started this chapter by describing two historically important versions of discrimination learning. The continuity theory of Spence and Hull assumed that animals learn something about all stimuli perceived when a reward is delivered and that learning was gradual and continuous. The noncontinuity theory of Lashley and Krechevsky assumed that animals selectively attend to only one stimulus at a time, learn nothing about stimuli not attended to, form hypotheses about what stimuli are relevant (predictive of reward), and that learning occurs abruptly once the relevant stimuli are discovered. The mass of data that has accumulated since (only a very small portion of which we have presented) has led to modifications in both positions.

First of all, it is clear that the original version of continuity theory is not correct. Attention and hypotheses have served as very useful theoretical concepts in explaining a wide variety of simple discrimination learning experiments (e.g., the ORE, acquired distinctiveness of cues, learning-set). In addition, it is clear that simply exposing animals to a stimulus situation and presenting reinforcement does not guarantee that all stimuli present are going to be associated with the reward (e.g., the experiments of Lashley, Reynolds, Kamin; and Wagner & Saavedra), not even if these stimuli are clearly perceived (the experiments of Kamin on blocking). It is also clear that learning in some situations can be abrupt (learning-set) and that sometimes increased training does not apparently lead to increased "habit-strength" (ORE experiments).

However, the original version of noncontinuity theory is also too simple. There are some situations in which learning does occur gradually, the ORE does not always occur, under some conditions increased training does seem to lead to increased habit strength, and animals do not learn about *only* one stimulus at a time; rather, in some situations the amount learned about each stimulus in a multidimensional stimulus display seems to be additive, so that the more stimuli that are present, the better the performance (e.g., McGonigle, 1967).

The failure of the simple versions of both noncontinuity and continuity theory has led to modified versions of both, with the result that both approaches have become considerably less extreme and closer together. Modified noncontinuity theory has taken many forms, but basically this approach takes the position that animals may learn about more than one stimulus at a time, but they do not learn equal amounts about all stimuli present. Some stimuli are attended to *more* than others and this differential attention leads to differential learning. Sometimes it is also assumed that the more that is learned about one stimulus, the less that is learned about other stimuli (Mackintosh, 1965; Sutherland & Mackintosh, 1971).

Some evidence seems to support this idea. For example, the Reynolds experiment discussed earlier (*see* p. 335) and the blocking studies of Kamin and Wagner and Saavedra, also discussed earlier (*see* p. 337) are compatible with this idea. Other experiments mentioned in Mackintosh (1965) are also consistent with the idea that attention to one stimulus may reduce the amount learned about other stimuli. However, the specific conditions under which this relationship applies are still not known (cf., Warren & McGonigle, 1969), but it is clear that pretraining with one stimulus is one effective experimental method of reducing the control acquired over

behavior by subsequently introducing other perceivable, but redundant, stimuli.

In a recent mathematical model of attentional theory, Lovejoy
(1968) has assumed that the degree of control over behavior acquired by a reinforced stimulus is in part a function of the distinctiveness of that stimulus. Distinctiveness in turn depends upon
structural factors (cf., biological factors discussed in Chapters 7 and
8), and on prior experience (e.g., Lawrence's experiment, the blocking experiments).

Continuity theory has also been modified to account for the data
demonstrating stimulus selection. The chief difference between
modified continuity theory and modified noncontinuity theory is
that the former still attempts to explain stimulus selection (not
equal amounts are learned about all stimuli) without the concept of
attention itself. This theory has been described in a number of
papers (e.g., Wagner, 1969; Rescorla & Wagner, 1972; Wagner &
Rescorla, 1972), and it is based principally on Pavlovian conditioning events. The basic premise of the Wagner-Rescorla model is that
the reinforcing effect of a UCS is greater the less it is predicted by
the CS complex. This premise is clearly related to Kamin's idea of
surprising UCSs and to both Rescorla's contingency view of
Pavlovian conditioning and the preparedness view of Pavlovian
conditioning presented in Chapter 3. We shall very briefly present
and describe some of the formal properties of the model.

The basis of the model is contained in the following simple
equation utilized in many mathematical models of learning (cf.,
Estes, 1959):

$$\Delta p_{n+1} = \beta(\lambda - p_n).$$

This equation states that the change in the probability of a response
after any given trial (p_{n+1}) depends upon how fast learning occurs
(the learning rate parameter, β) and the difference between the
probability of a response on the previous trial (p_n) and the
maximum possible response probability in that situation (the
asymptote of learning, λ). That is, the amount learned on any one
trial is a function of the amount already learned at the start of that
trial and of the total amount of learning that will occur with the
UCS used. This equation states that learning should be gradual and
continuous; the continuity position.

The Wagner-Rescorla model changes the basic linear model to
account for the effects observed in experiments such as those of
Kamin and Wagner and Saavedra. Specifically, these changes relate
to the amount of "associative strength" that will be acquired by
each element of a compound stimulus on a given trial. In formal
terms:

$$\Delta V_A = \alpha_A \beta_1 (\lambda_1 - V_{AX})$$
$$\text{and}$$
$$\Delta V_X = \alpha_X \beta_1 (\lambda_1 - V_{AX}).$$

These two equations describe the change in associative strength (V) that will take place in *each* component of a compound stimulus (AX) when that compound is followed by a reinforcement. These changes depend upon the learning rates associated with each stimulus (α), learning rate parameters related to the specific UCSs employed (β), and the asymptotic level of associative strength that will be supported by each UCS (λ). An additional assumption made by the model is that the associative strength of a compound stimulus (V_{AX}) is a simple additive function of the associative strengths of the component stimuli

$$V_{AX} = V_A + V_X.$$

Now, let us briefly examine how this model handles some of the data that we have covered. What should be the effect of pretraining with one element of a compound? Such pretraining should increase the total associative strength of the compound (because $V_{AX} = V_A + V_X$) close to the asymptote (λ). Thus, when the second element is added to the compound, as in the Kamin experiments, it should acquire little associative strength because the compound is already close to the maximum possible. Furthermore, extra training with the compound alone should not help. However, reducing the amount of pretraining, or extinguishing the training already given to the compound, should increase the associative strength acquired by the superimposed element. Of course, these are results we have already presented in the Kamin studies and in the Wagner and Saavedra experiment. Notice that the Wagner-Rescorla model explains these results without the concept of attention.

What about Kamin's finding concerning the effect of increasing shock intensity when the compound is introduced? This result can be handled by the model by assuming that more intense shock will lead to a greater asymptote of associative strength, and thus, there will be more "room" for the superimposed element to acquire associative strength.

Further data relating to implications of the Wagner-Rescorla model were obtained in a study of Marchant and Moore (1973). The design of this experiment was similar to Kamin's studies, but in an eyelid conditioning paradigm with rabbits as subjects. In one experiment it was found that conditioning to light in a light-tone compound could be blocked by prior training with the tone alone. This would be expected. But in a second experiment it was found that prior training with the light over an equivalent number of trials did not produce blocking of conditioning to the tone when the tone and light were compounded. This result would be compatible with the model only if it could be shown the light was less of a salient stimulus than the tone, and thus would have a lower learning rate parameter.

Evidence that this was true was adduced by Marchant and Moore by examining data from their laboratory that showed that conditioning was less to a light CS than to a tone CS when an equivalent amount of training was given. As a further check on this possibility, an additional experiment was run in which an extra amount of training with the light CS was given in order to "make up" for the apparent lower learning rate. It was found that, after this treatment, blocking of tone was obtained by prior conditioning with the light. Other data that also support the model can be obtained in the previously cited Wagner and Rescorla articles.

Recent attempts to extend the model more directly to instrumental learning situations have not been completely successful (Feldman, 1971; Neely & Wagner, 1974). These studies have indicated that there may be a difference between presenting an equivalent number of single element trials before compound training as opposed to intermixed with compound training. Specifically, these experiments have indicated that blocking may be lessened if the magnitude of the reward or the percentage of the reward is shifted when the compound stimulus is presented provided that the single stimulus pretraining has preceded the compound training. These results are compatible with Kamin's findings that blocking is attenuated when the compound predicts something new. However, the same manipulations do not have as much of an attenuating effect if single stimulus training and compound training are intermixed (as in the Wagner & Saavedra experiment described earlier).

At this point the reader may have the "here-we-go-again" feeling. Neither modified noncontinuity theory nor modified continuity theory has yet captured the whole story. The Wagner-Rescorla model is a very interesting attempt to explain data seemingly demanding the concept of attention without using that concept. Their model has been applied in a relatively limited area, primarily Pavlovian conditioning phenomena, but it has given a reasonably good account of the data in that area and has generated a good deal of interesting research and some rethinking of some old concepts. On the other hand, the model has little to say, as yet, about more complex situations, such as learning-set, where attention and hypothesis behavior seem firmly rooted.

Modified noncontinuity theory has been applied with some

success to a different set of data, primarily complex discrimination learning tasks such as the ORE and other kinds of shift experiments; and, in particular, it seems applicable when humans are the subjects. Both attention theory and hypothesis behavior have been put in mathematical model form (Lovejoy, 1968; Levine, 1969) with some successes that are beyond the scope of this book.

In any case, it is clear that the weight of the experimental evidence since the pioneering efforts of Spence and Lashley have shifted the direction of theorizing more in the direction of noncontinuity theory. There is no question that associations formed to stimuli may be selective. Furthermore, this intervening research has indicated a number of experimental procedures that may be employed to produce stimulus selection. But, the specification of how best to conceptualize this stimulus selection, exactly how much will occur, the mechanism of such selection, and how other variables and experimental paradigms may interact with selection, all are yet to be determined.

IV. SUMMARY

In this chapter we have examined two general theoretical interpretations of discrimination learning. One approach has assumed that the acquisition of stimulus control is a gradual and continuous process of acquiring approach tendencies to S^+ and inhibition of approach to S^-. In addition, this viewpoint has also assumed that all perceivable stimuli present acquire associative connections with these differential approach tendencies.

The second major theoretical interpretation of discrimination that we reviewed has assumed that the acquisition of stimulus control is a discontinuous process that involves the animal selectively attending to only portions of the stimulus array present in its environment. Only those stimuli attended to were assumed to acquire associative tendencies to control behavior.

We have described experimental evidence relevant to these two viewpoints, evidence from presolution reversal experiments, overlearning reversal experiments, acquired-distinctiveness of cue experiments, learning-set experiments, and direct studies of selective attention. The data from these experiments have required modifications in both viewpoints. Noncontinuity theories have been generally modified to assume that animals may learn something about more than one stimulus at a time, but different stimuli have different degrees of associative tendencies perhaps because of structural characteristics of the organism and/or because of the past experience of the organism. Various models of differential attention have been proposed.

Continuity theory has been modified to account for data clearly indicating stimulus selection in animal learning. However, the model proposed by Wagner and Rescorla accounts for such in conditioning principles without requiring the concept of attention. The model has generated a good deal of research and has met with some success, particularly in terms of accounting for data in the Pavlovian conditioning paradigm.

Memory: History and Basic Phenomena

Mehmed Ali Halici of Ankara, Turkey, on October 14, 1967, recited 6,666 verses of the Koran from memory in six hours.

Guinness Book of World Records

I. SOME EARLY VIEWS OF MEMORY

The importance of memory retrieval was well recognized by the orators of ancient Greece and Rome. At that time the spoken word was the major form of communication; legislators, businessmen, and theologians had to present their messages in speech form, "from memory," and the accuracy of their reproduction was very important. Thus pressured, the orators clearly realized how it was one thing to recite a speech just reviewed in the privacy of one's own home, but quite another problem to deliver this speech within a context different from that in which the speech was originally constructed and studied—especially if the time between studying and reciting the speech included a long interval occupied by interfering verbal activities. Such difficulties resulted in the development of techniques for accurate recall, the discipline of mnemonics taught within the general study of rhetoric.

The Origin of Mnemonics

Mnemonics concerns the application of special techniques to assist memory processing. One basic technique is to systematically place different items that are to be remembered in well-known environmental locations. This technique was supposedly originated by a Greek poet named Simonides. According to one historian, Simonides was reciting his poems in front of a large crowd at a banquet hall. He was called out of the building for a brief period, which was to his good fortune, because at that moment the roof collapsed killing everyone inside. Further compounding the tragedy, the victims were smashed quite beyond recognition by the heavy stonework used in the buildings of those days. When asked to help identify the victims for their respective families, Simonides found, to his surprise, that he could identify all of the names in accord with the previous seating arrangement.

This technique of pairing names with discrete geographical locations was then applied under less macabre circumstances to pairing basic ideas with discrete geographical locations. Thus, to permit efficient retrieval of the appropriate sequential order of points to be made in a speech, an orator first would imagine himself walking through a path in some familiar building like his home. At specific locations along these paths, concrete objects would be imagined for representing the points of his speech. For example, if his first point was to insist on a cleaner bathhouse, he might imagine a huge cleaning brush inside a tiny bathtub, all resting on the doorknob of his front door; if his second point was to urge assignment of more slaves to this job, he might imagine his foyer crowded with slaves, and so forth. At the time of the speech the orator would then imagine retracing his path and, in effect, "pick up" each point as he reached its location.

A variety of versions of this technique were employed and much polemical energy spent (e.g., on whether, for a long speech requiring more "locations," it was better to imagine two separate houses or a single larger house). The application of such mnemonic techniques was passed on from teacher to student for thousands of years. Even as Bacon and Descartes were establishing a scientific revolution, memory was maintained by them as an art to be practiced rather than as an object of scientific study (for further discussion of these issues, *see* Yates, 1966).

The Art of Memory Processing

Memory processing as a topic of art, entertainment, or applied technique is clearly distinguishable from memory as a topic of scientific investigation. We still see a little of the former today, although the application of mnemonic techniques has been relatively deemphasized by the educational methods used in the United States during the past 50 or 60 years, in comparison with previous methods and those of some European countries.

Individuals having extremely facile mnemonic skills have always been viewed with some fascination. One such individual named Salo Finkelstein was hired by the American Broadcasting Company to compute returns from the 1932 presidential election. In those precomputer days Finkelstein was supposed to calculate faster than any machine available (Bousfield & Barry, 1933; Hunter, 1964). Another individual with these sorts of skills was a Russian named Shereshevskii, who applied his memory processes primarily as an entertainer. This man actually suffered from an inability to carry on normal conversation and, indeed, he had general difficulty in adjustment because of an inability to forget unnecessary details. This remarkable case was studied for a number of years by the Russian psychologist Luria (1968). Still another man, identified as "VP" by Hunt and Love (1972), also was studied as a special case of exceptional mnemonic skill. It is perhaps notable that the latter two cases, Shereshevskii and VP, both received their early schooling in a locale in eastern Europe where memorization was emphasized for its own sake and viewed as a skill worthy of a great deal of effort.

Such case histories are indeed fascinating. But these studies become science only when they are sufficiently systematic and when the behavioral phenomena studied, or the processes that may underlie this behavior, are related to other systematically acquired knowledge of memorial behavior. It was not until the late nineteenth century that questions and assertions about the nature of memory processing became sufficiently systematic to qualify as a science.

The Science of Memory Processing

Among the earliest persons to consider memory processing as an object of scientific analysis was the great Russian physiologist, Sechenov. Sechenov analyzed topics that we now consider psychology, and provided a model for Pavlov. To a limited extent, Sechenov was concerned with processes underlying retention and forgetting, and he suggested some mechanisms by which acquired information might be maintained following learning for use in subsequent modification of behavior (Sechenov, 1863, reproduced 1965, p. 70).

American psychologists were well represented among the early scholars of memory processing by William James (1890). James had few established facts at his disposal but nevertheless wrote about the nature of memory with extraordinary insight and eventual influence. He was concerned with a variety of issues that are still with us, such as whether or not a memory ever leaves an individual once it is acquired (e.g., James, 1890, p. 127).

Imagine yourself in the late nineteenth century surrounded by philosophical acclamations of how the memory process functions. At this time many scholars were becoming more clearly aware that introspections about behavior were unlikely to lead to systematic knowledge. How then would you objectively measure the product of memory processing? How would you assess the characteristics of memory behavior? And, how would you determine those factors which cause forgetting and those which do not?

The first man to tackle this problem with sufficient tenacity and ingenuity as to influence other scholars was a young German named Herman Ebbinghaus. Ebbinghaus decided that the best way to study memory processing objectively was to teach himself discrete bits of new knowledge under standardized conditions. Then, at some later time, he would test how well he remembered under the same standardized conditions. To force himself to learn "from scratch" insofar as possible, Ebbinghaus constructed non-words, combinations of three letters termed "nonsense syllables" (*see* Figure 12–1). Being well acquainted with the writings of the British associationists, Ebbinghaus was interested in questions about how our minds seem to emit ideas in associated strings. So, he decided to learn 10 or 12 of these nonsense syllables in a list,

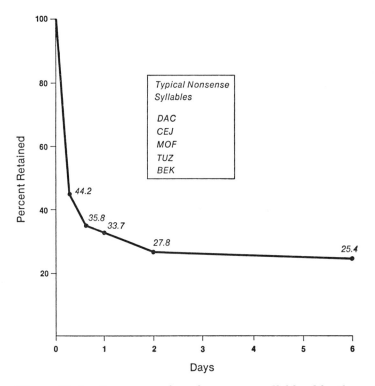

Figure 12–1. Some examples of nonsense syllables like those invented by Ebbinghaus along with a graph showing the course of forgetting. Later studies revealed that these data exaggerate the amount of forgetting owing to the fact that Ebbinghaus had learned many interfering lists.

always maintaining their same serial order. These lists of nonsense syllables were considered analogous to strings of associated ideas.

When Ebbinghaus was able to recite a list without an error, he would put it aside, doggedly proceed with other lists, and then come back to the list in question after a prespecified interval. He then compared the number of trials needed to relearn the list with the number required during original learning. The number of repetitions that were thus "saved" by having undergone original learning were recorded as an index of retention. What Ebbinghaus found was that his retention dropped with frightening speed. After a day or so, he often lost as much as 75 percent of the information that he had acquired (*see* Figure 12–1). This 75 percent figure has limited generality, however, a problem we shall return to later (*see* pp. 365–66).

The empirical study of memory thus originated with concern for retention of verbal materials. This source of information about memory continues to be of fundamental importance today. Indeed, a large number of the important advances, conceptual and empirical, have evolved from the study of human verbal memory. Consideration of human verbal memory in appropriate detail would, however, require an extensive background of rather esoteric material concerning methods of study and phenomena of human learning. We do not feel this is warranted here, although the importance of such material for a general understanding of memory processing should not be underestimated. With the possible exception of processes concerned exclusively with linguistic memories—if such processes indeed exist—we may expect to find memories to be processed in similar fashion by humans and animals. Accordingly, we shall have occasion to cite evidence from both human and infrahuman species. Additional material relating to the study of human learning and retention may be found elsewhere (e.g., Hall, 1971; Kausler, 1974; Jung, 1968; Spear, 1970; Underwood, 1966).

In one sense there is reason to prefer animals for the study of memory processing because of the wider scope of experimental manipulations that are possible. Of particular importance are three kinds of manipulations that simply cannot be accomplished in experiments with humans. The first is the extreme experiential control that may be exerted over animals from the time of birth, including the opportunity to test after retention intervals that may vary from a few seconds to a lifetime. The second is the opportunity to compare animals of selected genetic history. The third is the experimental modification of physiological systems that may be linked to memory processes.

We shall see that each of these classes of variables—environmental, subject, and physiological—has been shown to have important effects on memory processing. But to acquire some perspective of what we now know about memory and what we can expect to discover in the future, we turn next to a brief history, first in terms of the ideological orientation and methods used to study retention and forgetting, and then to the facts and theories that have resulted. We shall focus upon the study of animal memory with supplementary reference to human memory.

Trends in the Study of Memory Processing Prior to 1950

Hunter's Delayed-Response Task

Paths of interest in science often have their direction influenced by innovative techniques. So it was that W. L. Hunter helped to develop two topics that were to occupy a great deal of the research energy devoted to animal memory during the first half of the twentieth century. The technique, the *delayed-response task*, was studied by Hunter at the University of Chicago between 1910 and 1912. Like many important technical innovations, the delayed-response task is quite simple conceptually. This task also is simple to instrument, although Hunter did it the hard way for his first publication. Hunter exposed a confined animal to three doorways, behind each of which was a light bulb (*see* Figure 12–2). He tested rats, dogs, or raccoons (and also children) with this task.

First, Hunter trained the subjects to walk through the single doorway where the bulb was lighted. The hungry animal received food when this was accomplished. Hunter laboriously trained each animal on this signaled approach task until flawless performance was achieved, which required between 150 and 500 trials. At this point he began to turn the light off *before* the animal arrived at the doorway. After the animal had adjusted to this modification and again was performing flawlessly, Hunter began to introduce periods of delay between the time the bulb was turned off and release of the animal from his cage.

The critical question was this: How long a delay could the animal tolerate between exposure to the light (which indicated the correct doorway) and the opportunity to choose among the doorways? In later studies Hunter eliminated some of the tedium from the training procedure by simply exposing the reward object until he thought the animal noticed it (obviously a weak link in this technique). Then he hid it again until the animal had made its choice. This later version was termed the "direct" method of delayed-response task and has been the procedure most often followed in subsequent experiments.

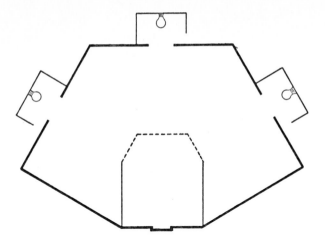

Figure 12–2. A diagram of the apparatus Hunter used to investigate delayed responding. The light above one of the doors would be turned *on* to indicate the location of the reward, then turned *off* for a period of time before allowing the subject to select one of the doors.

The Significance of Hunter's Study

In addition to the technique itself, Hunter's monograph in 1913 offered three points of potential interest to many psychologists. The first, his interpretation of possible mechanisms underlying delayed responding, was largely ignored. But the other two—the extent to which delayed responding depended upon "cognitive" behaviors and the phylogenetic ordering of animals in terms of their capacity for delayed responding—became objects of intense study by many comparative psychologists throughout the remainder of the first half of the twentieth century. As we shall see, progress might have been better served if instead the first point had been expanded and the latter two ignored.

Hunter's work was conducted at the time of the important behavioristic revolution, and Hunter himself was a leader in this movement. Accordingly, he was reluctant to interpret delayed responding as simply a consequence of the sorts of cognitive ideation that humans were supposed to possess. Instead, Hunter considered essentially three classes of behavior that might account for delayed responding. At one extreme was the "overt orienting attitudes" that he observed being employed by rats and dogs. An exaggerated case would be the pointing behavior of a bird dog. Here, the animal would remain physically positioned, aimed at the correct alternative throughout the retention interval. At the other extreme, the highest level of cognitive capacity, Hunter considered "thought" that included imagery. Between the extremes, to account for the behavior of raccoons and young children who seemed to be able to tolerate long delays without using overt physical orientation, he suggested the use of "intra-organic cues, sensory thought" which did not include imagery.

At the time of Hunter's first monograph people were even more aware of the memory capacities of animals than they are today. For example, horses were still used widely for transportation, and it was well known that a horse could follow a familiar path back home without guidance and that its behavior changed detectably as more familiar objects were encountered nearer home. Among psychologists like Hunter, however, the tendency was to account for these behaviors in terms of "sensory recognition": The horse may *recognize* a particular turn in the road as "correct" when encountered, but did not necessarily have a stored representation of that turn which would permit its *recall* when the horse arrived at the stable. Although the conceptual separation of an animal's capacity for "sensory recognition" from that of something called "recall" is beneficial with respect to deriving the most parsimonious explanation of observable events, the separation, unfortunately, resulted from a prejudice about the distinction between recognition and recall in human behavior. In fact, the foundation for the latter separation was more shifting of sand than rock, and still is. Even today it is not at all clear whether the processes underlying recall and recognition are very different, and many apparent functional distinctions are not well understood. For example, human recall is *not* always poorer than recognition, and sometimes it is a good deal better (*see* Tulving & Thomson, 1973).

The point is that scientists were misled by such distinctions between hypothetical memory processes, misled because the distinctions had no substance. The observable and hypothetical properties of overt (pointer-like) behavior and internal representations were, of course, substantially different in the extreme cases, but these cases were largely trivial. Extreme pointing behavior could easily be excluded by a variety of such techniques as rotating the cage relative to the door, by shifting the position of the discriminanda (that may not have been actual doors but perhaps simply different food dishes with covers), or by taking the animal from the room during the delay period.

There arose nevertheless an extended flood of studies, some conducted by otherwise ingenious scientists, toward the misdirected aim of determining whether lower animals such as rats could tolerate any delay without maintaining their physical position. We now know that positioning is not the only device that animals might use to physically bridge a retention interval (*see* Blough, 1959, discussed below). Moreover, the current easing of pressure toward strict behavioristic orientation, together with general empirical advances in the study of memory processes, make internal memory representations both useful for theory and plausible in fact.

A second unfortunate offspring from Hunter's original study was the pursuit of a phylogenetic ordering of memory capacities. Based in large part upon a superficial understanding of evolution, a number of experiments were conducted to determine essentially "which animals remember best." With the advantage of hindsight, we see that such studies were misdirected. Different species of animals have, for example, quite different predispositions to attend to certain stimuli and to respond for certain reinforcers. Such differences make it difficult to compare directly different species within a single experimental procedure.

In summary, we see in retrospect that one consequence of Hunter's influential pioneering study of animal memory was to divert valuable research energy into the study of unproductive questions. However, the importance of the technique cannot be denied. There have been two major benefits: The delayed-response task has been a very valuable clinical technique, a behavioral assay which, as Fletcher (1965) noted, "... reveals phylogenetic, ontogenetic, and sex differences; it detects, where other tests fail to detect, the effects of brain lesions, drugs, radiation, and deprivation (p. 129)." Furthermore, while the delayed-response task may not keep memory processes as cleanly separated from performance effects as one might like, it has led to the development of a more efficient instrument, the delayed-matching-to-sample task. Together these tasks have added a great deal to our knowledge of memory processes in animals, as we shall observe in our later consideration of short-term retention.

Early Studies of Long-Term Memory in Animals

Long-term memory may be distinguished from short-term memory solely on operational grounds. For long-term memory retention is tested after longer intervals (usually more than a day) and original learning is acquired to a higher degree of achievement than for tests of short-term memory. We shall return to the implications of these definitions later. For now we use this operational distinction to keep separate the short-term memory work initiated by Hunter from other studies of retention in animals.

Studies of long-term memory in animals were of little importance during the first half of the twentieth century. There was little evidence of forgetting in these studies, and this surprising *retention* in "dumb" animals was so interesting that the basis of *forgetting* did not seem worth studying. Moreover, such studies were conducted with little or no theoretical orientation, so there was no pressure for clear experimental questions and design. We turn next to illustrations of these two reasons and an analysis of their foundation in fact.

Magnitude of Forgetting in Early Studies of Animal Memory

Perhaps the major impact of the meager forgetting found in laboratory animals was to direct the attention of behavior theorists toward the study of motivation as an apparently more important determinant of learned behavior. In effect, the definition of learning as a "relatively permanent" change in behavior resulting from practice was read as "essentially permanent." This was an unfortunate misconception. We can illustrate this point by careful examination of two of the studies most often cited as evidence that "negligible" forgetting occurs in laboratory animals, one by Wendt (1938), the other by Skinner (1950).

Wendt conditioned a dog to withdraw its foot upon the presentation of a tone which had been paired with a painful stimulus. The dog was then given considerable overtraining, including four times as many training trials as were necessary for original learning. During the last training session the dog responded appropriately on 97 percent of the trials; after a two-and-a-half-year retention interval, foot withdrawal occurred on 80 percent of the test trials. This indicated that some forgetting had occurred, albeit remarkably little. However, the retention becomes rather less remarkable and the forgetting still more apparent in view of the initial overtraining and two other circumstances: First, the retention test was preceded by three footshocks, a treatment known to reduce forgetting in a variety of circumstances, as we shall see; second, a test given seven months after the first retention test yielded *no* conditioned foot withdrawals at all in response to the tone—effectively, maximal forgetting, although relearning subsequently did occur rapidly.

Similarly, the retention that Skinner demonstrated for pigeons after an interval of five years was truly remarkable in terms of one measure, the rapidity with which the birds responded when initially presented the discriminative stimulus (a pattern presented on a previously dark key). Nevertheless, even the best performer among these birds showed 50 percent to 75 percent forgetting in terms of the total number of responses emitted.

Absence of Theory Concerning Retention and Forgetting

The lack of theoretical orientation and the consequently non-analytical data gathering that absorbed some of the efforts in this area may be illustrated by an experiment published by Corey (1931). Corey carefully ran 186 rats in a multiple-choice maze until they made no errors on five consecutive trials. Then 14 days later, the rats were retrained on the same task. This describes Corey's entire study; it was not an experiment because there was only one condition. Yet, the energy and financial expense to Corey must have been quite costly. It is interesting that such dull experiments were performed in the study of memory at a time when extremely exciting ideas were being exchanged about learning processes by some of the most creative scientists who have ever worked in the science of behavior, such as Pavlov, Lashley, Tolman, and Hull. Were these theorists unconcerned about forgetting?

Pavlov may be a special case: He seldom measured long-term retention in his dogs (but, *see* Pavlov, 1928, p. 350), he performed no analytical experiments concerning long-term retention, and he did not theorize about long-term retention. We might speculate that Pavlov was uninterested in studying forgetting simply because he did so little of it himself. Apparently his own memory capacities approached what is popularly termed "total recall." In spite of a huge research program involving numerous coworkers, Pavlov was reported to remember vividly the details of most of the individual protocols of his various experiments, and he constantly amazed people by remembering their names even though he may have seen them for only a brief single meeting 20 or 30 years earlier.

Lashley, one of the most influential psychobiologists of the first half of the twentieth century, was deeply involved in understanding how memories are stored, both in terms of what is learned and how and where this storage occurs in the central nervous system. But although he was concerned with how these memories became manifested in behavior (e.g., Lashley, 1950), he rarely theorized directly about the processes responsible for forgetting, nor did he test such ideas in normal animals.

Tolman, Hull, Guthrie, and other learning systematists of the 1930s and 1940s directed their theories at the necessary and sufficient conditions for learning. They gave special emphasis to motivational determinants and the prediction of general performance.

However, experimentally viable ideas about retention and forgetting were developing in the 1930s and 1940s, primarily by McGeoch and two of his students, Melton and Underwood. These studies were addressed primarily to local, functional issues of human verbal learning, but this work provided a firm foundation for later developments of general, profound importance to understanding memory processing. A brief sketch of this activity is presented next.

Key Developments in the Study of Human Memory

McGeoch wrote a theoretical paper in 1932 which may be said in retrospect to have been pivotal in the study of retention and forgetting. In this paper, McGeoch argued convincingly against the prevailing view that forgetting was interpretable in terms of a fundamental weakening, a "decaying," of learned associations that progressed spontaneously from the time of original learning. A similarly effective argument was made against an alternative interpretation. This view, suggested 30 years earlier by Müller and Pilzecker, was that events occurring shortly after learning caused forgetting because they interrupted the perseverating neural activity initiated by the learning. This disruption presumably prevented consolidation of the memory trace.

McGeoch argued instead that forgetting was a consequence of either of two factors, the acquisition of competing associations between original learning and the retention test, or changes in the stimulus context which occurred between learning and the retention test. His theoretical and empirical focus, however, was clearly upon the former factor, the role of interference in forgetting and, specifically, *retroactive interference*.

"Retroactive interference" simply means that new information or stimuli can interfere with previous learning. For example, consider a person on his way to a grocery store without a shopping list to purchase milk, bread, flour, eggs, and butter who meets a friend who says, "I am also going to the store. I have to buy milk, jelly, donuts, bacon, and flour." The first person who had to memorize his own list of items may now tend to forget some of the items as a result of hearing another list of items. Thus, new learning can interfere with retention of prior learning.

Within the next 20 years, three guiding principles became established empirically. The first concerned retroactive interference. McGeoch saw that in order to understand the precise mechanisms through which learning of new verbal associations impaired retention of previously learned ones, it would be necessary first to understand how learning of the interfering associations themselves was affected by the previous learning. In other words, because the fundamental determinant of interference presumably was the degree of similarity between two conflicting tasks, it was necessary to first understand how the learning of one such task transferred to the learning of another.

A second guiding principle was discovered by Melton and Irwin (1940) and can be termed *covert interference*. Experimental evidence revealed that the interfering effects on retention could not inevitably be measured in terms of mixups between the alternative verbal associations. In other words interference in retention could occur covertly, quite apart from those more obvious instances in which the subject simply said the wrong word at the wrong time. It became clear that more subtle behavioral aberrations were involved which would require more subtle techniques of assessment.

The third principle was the establishment of *proactive interference* as a source of forgetting, equally or more important than retroactive interference. Underwood (1945, 1957) demonstrated this principle with a convincing flair, showing that conflicting associations acquired even before original learning could contribute dramatically to subsequent forgetting. As an example, the memory of last week's shopping list may make it more difficult to remember this week's list. Clearly, for forgetting to occur the interfering learning need not take place between original learning and the retention test.

A parallel line of analysis, which unfortunately did not receive equal empirical attention, was initiated by Bartlett (1932). Sir Bartlett's book, initiated as part of his Ph.D. dissertation in 1916, has continued to be read to this day because of its consideration of a more complex case of forgetting than that dealt with by McGeoch; namely, the forgetting of entire sentences or stories. Bartlett and later Koffka were particularly concerned with the way in which perceptual principles might account for forgetting. Similarly, they were interested in the influence of general techniques or cognitive frameworks—"schemata"—used by subjects at the time of original learning in comparison with those applied at the retention test. Perhaps it is because of the complexity of this topic that it was difficult to frame testable questions from this loose theoretical framework. This may account for the lesser influence of these ideas at that point in the history of the science of memory.

II. THE MODERN ERA (1950 TO THE PRESENT)

Several events converged about 1950 to renew concentrated effort on the study of animal memory. These events took two forms. On the one hand, there were technical advances in physiological analysis which permitted new approaches to the study of memory storage processes; and on the other hand, there were scholarly advances in memory theory and research.

Memory Storage Processes ("Consolidation")

World War II resulted in techniques of physiological measurement and in massive clinical evidence of some relevance to the study of memory. This information was placed at the disposal of scientists just prior to 1950. An example of the clinical knowledge applicable to the study of memory may be found in Russell and Nathan's (1946) review of the amnesic consequences of head injury. Among 1,029 cases examined, 87 percent of the victims of head injury reported some amnesia, the basis of which was fundamentally unknown. Similarly, new knowledge that resulted directly or indirectly from the war effort helped generate a flourishing pharmaceutical industry. Soon to become available were a wide variety of drugs which had profound effects on behavior including, perhaps, the processing of memories.

In 1950, Lashley was reaching the conclusion of his most extensive research effort, the identification of the locus of memory storage in the brain. His failure to discover such a locus, and his facetious conclusion that learning just must not be possible, are classic. The implication was that it was time for some new, more dynamic models of memory and its physiological basis.

Toward such a model, one of Lashley's many successful students, D. O. Hebb, published an influential book, *Organization of Behavior* (1949). In this book, Hebb suggested that the memory (i.e., the internal representation of an episode) did not directly enter a stable state; rather, the memory was initially in a labile, fragile form. In this labile state, the memory was subject to disruption, or destruction, by events like traumatic head injury. This was not all new. Similar ideas had been suggested as long ago as 1900 by Müller and Pilzecker and had been dismissed, for human verbal learning at least, by McGeoch (1932). But, Hebb's treatment of these issues was particularly elegant and his examples were convincing. Before long, psychologists began to capitalize on the broad range of experimental manipulations possible in the study of animal memory and developed evidence which seemed beautifully consistent with Hebb's model.

In the same year that Hebb's book appeared, C. P. Duncan (1949) published the results of research he had been conducting for several years previously, showing that retention could be impaired in rats if a learning trial were followed by an electroconvulsive shock in which the basic path of the electrical current was through the brain. Moreover, the sooner the electroconvulsive shock followed a trial, the more detrimental was the effect. We shall return to further consideration of this work later. For now, the point is that the general effect was exactly as predicted from Hebb's conception of an initially labile stage of memory.

There followed a decade of scattered effort directed at the effects of disrupting memory processing prior to the time of its conversion to a more stable form—i.e., prior to "consolidation"—by electroconvulsive shock or other modification of the central nervous system. About 1960, work on this consolidation concept was revived by a variety of sources: An instructive review of the topic by Glickman (1961); new information regarding the chemical basis of neural transmission and the possibility that memory might be stored in protein form (see, for example, Katz and Halstead, 1950); and the beginning of what was to be a most thorough and skillful study of the characteristics of "consolidation" by one of Tolman's students, James L. McGaugh.

Developments in the Study of Human Memory

The period from 1950 to 1960 found four exciting developments of special significance for advancing our understanding of human retention.

First, toward analyzing the determinants of retention, Underwood and his associates (see, for example, Underwood; 1966, 1967) found that previous conclusions concerning variables which purportedly affected retention had been quite incorrect because of a methodological error. Earlier studies of learning and retention had failed to control *degree of original learning* prior to the retention interval. With final degree of learning precisely controlled, several factors which previously had seemed to influence forgetting—such as whether the materials to be remembered consisted of words or nonwords and whether the subjects had been slow or fast learners—were shown, in fact, to have no influence whatsoever on forgetting.

A second discovery by Underwood also concerned a methodological oversight that had occurred in earlier studies of forgetting. Most earlier studies had tested retention with subjects who were well practiced in learning and recalling verbal material in the laboratory. These studies, like the classic experiments of Ebbinghaus, had led to the conclusion that humans forget about 75 percent of learning after 24 hours. Underwood demonstrated, however, that if one considers only the retention scores of subjects who had *not* previously learned a number of similar verbal associations in the laboratory, forgetting after 24 hours was more likely to be about 25 percent instead of the previously accepted estimate of about 75 percent. This discovery also emphasized again the importance of proactive interference for forgetting because *proactive interference* had caused the 50 percent greater forgetting by the well-practiced subjects.

A third development initiated by Underwood was the analysis of the mechanisms of *retroactive interference*. Realizing that interference was unlikely to be a unitary factor, Underwood and his associates began to develop techniques for analyzing the separable effects induced by interfering learning.

The fourth critical development between 1950 and 1960 originated almost simultaneously in England and in the United States. This was the introduction of a technique for studying the retention of a single verbal item over very short retention intervals. The technique, consisting of the presentation of a single verbal item along with instructions that served to prevent rehearsal of that item, was simple, efficient, and easily applied. It was not long before the psychological journals were bursting at their seams with new studies of retention, this time concerning "short-term memory."

Throughout the 1960s and 1970s, the spectrum of developments concerning human memory broadened. Some of the more basic features of this era, both conceptual and technical, may be listed briefly:

1. The interference theory of forgetting matured into a very testable version presented by Postman and Underwood (1973), and a series of tests soon revealed that the theory needed shoring up as do all good theories eventually.
2. The analysis of short-term retention became increasingly refined with the increased use of computerized techniques for presenting materials and for assessing behavioral data against mathematical models.
3. The use of computers also permitted new innovative means for learning about human information processing through the behavioral technique of measuring reaction times, a procedure which, somewhat ironically, had been largely abandoned in experimental psychology as being old-fashioned. By further understanding information processing, certain time-dependent features of perception were uncovered which made the distinction between perception and certain cases of "short-term memory" somewhat blurred.
4. The importance of rehearsal by humans and their amazing capacity for accomplishing rehearsal under adverse circumstances became increasingly clear. Indeed, the general realization that the human subject was a good deal more than

a learning machine and operated on his materials in a direct yet complicated fashion was seen in another line of research—that of organizational processes. The means through which humans covertly organize material to be learned became a topic of a great deal of research activity throughout the 1960s, leading ultimately to the general study of mnemonic techniques. Paralleling this study and the increased understanding of computers was a widespread distinction between memory storage and memory retrieval.

Despite these and other developments, however, little was added to the general conclusion about what factors influence retention once the degree of original learning is equated. A good deal was learned, of course, about how learning becomes established and how it is retained in the face of other activities. And there is surely a good deal more to be learned about memory through the use of normal human subjects. However, restrictions in the use of human subjects, mentioned above, suggest that we can expect to learn a good deal of otherwise unattainable information about memory processing from psychobiological research with animals. Nevertheless, as we progress through this material, we shall have occasion to point out parallel or otherwise related information concerning memory processing by normal humans.

What is the present state of knowledge in psychobiology concerning retention and forgetting, i.e., concerning the relationship between storage and retrieval of memories? There are two classes of such knowledge. First, we know something about the functional relationships between memory processes and experiential or environmental variables. Second, we have begun to integrate these facts under general principles, pretheoretical ideas and theories. Linked to both of these classes of knowledge is information about the physiological basis of memory.

To fully understand and appreciate what has become known about the retention and forgetting of memories, it is necessary to keep a sharp analytical eye on the meaning of these terms and their relationship to preceding material in this book concerning learning. We turn next to a brief consideration of how the relationship between learning and retention may be conceptualized.

Relationships Between Learning and Retention

Retention and forgetting are closely related to the degree of original learning. This relationship is not perfect, however. In a trivial sense, of course, if learning has not occurred, neither can retention. On the other hand, there is no doubt that some factors may influence learning without affecting retention and vice versa. To clarify and support this statement, we shall consider three questions: (1) Will more information ever be evidenced at a retention test than during original training? (2) Does equivalent learning always imply equivalent retention? (3) How does degree of original learning affect retention?

Additional Information During Retention Tests

Through the use of inference, which implies previously stored information, more information may be held by a subject in memory than was provided to him during the formal training session. For example, suppose you learned that one alligator is two feet long and a second is four feet long. Asked to describe these alligators at a retention test, you may give not only their respective lengths but, if you knew that alligators grow about a foot a year for their first six or seven years, you might reply in addition that the second alligator was two years older than the first. This sort of information processing has been linked to "semantic memory," possibly a class of memory processing unique to humans, but certainly involving only a fraction of the memories processed.

Relatively little is known about semantic memory in reference to general behavior, so we will be concerned primarily with "episodic memory" (cf., Tulving, 1972). The term episodic memory, as the name implies, refers to the representation of episodes that can be temporally coded. As an example, the recollection of the sequence of events, observations, and conversations that took place before lunch yesterday would involve episodic memory: the integration of these events with more general information that is not temporally coded (e.g., the fried eggs I had for breakfast contained high levels of cholesterol) involves semantic memory. Although there is little evidence to date which demands these two classifications, it may be useful to maintain the distinction because of the possibility that semantic memory may be unique to humans.

Relationship Between Degree of Learning and Retention

If equal learning always led to equal retention, the concepts of retention and forgetting would be unnecessary. We know that equally learned episodes may be forgotten at different rates, and it does not help at all to say simply that if they were forgotten at different rates, they were not learned equally. The fact is that independent operations can be used to define learning and retention, as we shall see.

The degree of original learning can be assessed in any number of different ways. Measures of the subsequent retention have indicated generally that retention is better with higher degrees of learning. But this conclusion is mitigated by the second difficulty, which is that it is not at all clear what is meant by "degree of learning." We shall have occasion to return to this problem later. For now, we shall consider three ways in which a distinction is drawn between learning and retention.

Operational Distinction Between Learning and Retention

Traditionally, the following distinction has been made: "Retention" is measured whenever the interval since the last learning trial exceeds the interval that had elapsed between prior learning trials. In other words, a "retention interval" is any duration longer than the intertrial interval. But, if learning requires only one trial, the problem is obviously different. Now the task is to identify the point during that trial at which learning occurred and, as yet, this can be accomplished only on some theoretical basis. Once the point of "learning" is established, the retention interval can be any length at all.

There are two, more subtle, aspects to the operational definition of retention:

1. Retention always is assumed to be a consequence of prior learning. Accordingly, retention must be defined by the difference between the behaviors of organisms that have learned and those that have not. This comparison typically is only implicit. Humans tested for retention of a list of nonsense syllables are unlikely to respond correctly if they have not learned the items. On the other hand, a rat may run rapidly during a retention test whether or not he previously has learned to do so. Therefore, such a comparison between trained and untrained organisms may become explicit and even critical for interpreting certain treatments of memory.

2. The second point concerns conclusions about the causal properties of the retention interval. For such conclusions it is necessary to compare performance on two independent tests of retention, one after a short interval, one after a longer interval. The short interval or "immediate" test usually is necessary to establish the baseline of terminal degree of learning. Also, the circumstances of the retention test itself may provide quite different retrieval cues than were provided by the last learning trial. Therefore, retrieval of

the memory may be affected by the test, and this influence must be controlled experimentally (e.g., Spear, 1971, 1973). Consequently, it is necessary to use performance on a test given shortly after training as the baseline from which further retention decrement is compared.

Conceptual Distinction Between Learning and Retention

The concept "retention" is concerned with previously acquired information that is manifested in behavior at some time *after* an organism has been removed from the physical or symbolic presence of that information. Implicit here is that, within the animal, active recycling of information representing the episode has been interrupted. Before the interruption is learning; after the interruption is retention.

Functional Distinction Between Learning and Retention

If a variable produces differences in retention which do not correspond to the effects that variable has on learning, we say that learning and retention differ *functionally*. Perhaps the clearest examples of such functional differences may be found in the context of human verbal learning as follows:

1. A list of verbal items having a high degree of "meaningfulness" is learned a good deal more rapidly than a list of less meaningful items ("meaningfulness" has been defined in many different ways, but all would agree that, e.g., DOG, PAD and TOP have higher meaningfulness than DZG, PLD and TFP). Meaningfulness, however, has little or no influence on retention.

2. Intralist similarity has profound effects on rate of learning. A list of similar single items like DOG, CAT, HORSE and COW are learned more rapidly than less similar items like DOG, CAR, PENCIL and APPLE. Intralist similarity, however, has no apparent influence on retention.

3. There is no doubt that some people learn very rapidly and others more slowly. However, once equivalent degrees of learning are attained, no differences are found in rate of forgetting.

4. Increasing the distribution of practice has little effect on ability to associate one word with another (paired-associate

learning). However, there are certain conditions under which increases in distribution of practice may greatly facilitate retention (Keppel, 1964; Wickelgren, 1972). (For more information concerning these and similar effects in verbal learning, see reviews by Jung, 1968; Keppel, 1972; Spear, 1970; Underwood, 1964, 1966, 1972.)

With animals, too, there are cases of functional differences between learning and retention. For example, there are a variety of tasks that may be learned equally rapidly by immature and mature animals but which, after long retention intervals, are forgotten more rapidly by animals that had learned during immaturity (Campbell & Spear, 1972). A variable which may influence learning but not retention is intensity of shock in avoidance learning (Feigley & Spear, 1970).

That there are functional differences between learning and retention is not surprising. A wide variety of processes have been postulated to determine retention quite independently of the circumstances of learning. Such processes include the following: Interference from previous or subsequent learning; simple decay of the physiological underpinnings of memory; a "consolidation" process occurring subsequent to learning to facilitate storage of the memory; or changes in stimuli (whether subtle or obvious and whether external or internal to the organism) from those which had been present during original learning.

III. SUMMARY

This chapter has traced some of the major developments in memory research. The early Greeks and Romans were more interested in the application of techniques than in the actual study of memory.

The first systematic attempt to study memory was undertaken by Ebbinghaus, who contributed several key ideas: (a) He introduced the nonsense syllable, indicating his appreciation of the concept of *meaningfulness;* (b) he introduced experimental procedures for the analysis of learning and retention in a systematic and orderly fashion; and (c) he demonstrated, unwittingly, the importance of interference.

At about the same time that Ebbinghaus was conducting his studies, Hunter and other workers began to develop procedures for the study of retention in animals. Most important in this regard was the development of so-called delayed-response task for the study of short-term memory.

Perhaps the most important development in the history of memory research was the concept of interference. Work by Underwood and others has shown that the retention of certain materials can be reduced by learning that has taken place previously (proactive interference) or by learning that has taken place subsequently (retroactive interference). These concepts have been fruitfully applied to both human verbal learning and to animal learning.

More recently, experimental procedures have been devised to reduce the covert process of rehearsal, providing a foundation for studies that may eventually clarify the nature and importance of this process which apparently extends the opportunity for learning beyond the temporal boundaries established by the external environment.

The Dynamics of Memory

Its a poor sort of memory that only works backwards.

Lewis Carrol, *Through the Looking Glass*

In this chapter we will consider the conditions under which information previously acquired by an organism comes to influence its present behavior. We find it convenient to approach this problem in terms of three major issues.

The first issue concerns a description of the basic effect of forgetting: As time passes from the point of learning, is the decline in retention likely to take a regularly decreasing path? Might this path not sometimes increase? Can retention ever improve by simply waiting out a longer interval? Or does retention fluctuate rhythmically, first decreasing, then increasing, then decreasing again and so on? We realize, of course, that forgetting cannot be assessed in a vacuum. When we say that we want to discuss the course of forgetting as a function of time, we really mean "time" only descriptively because it is the events taking place during that period of time that really determine forgetting; time is not causal.

The second issue concerns alternative ways of thinking of retention. Is long-term retention different from short-term retention? Is it a consequence of several stages of processing or a single stage?

The third issue involves the physiological structure of memories, which will be considered in Chapter 15.

I. THE COURSE OF FORGETTING

A Steady Decline

The typical course of forgetting, which also has the most intuitive appeal, is a simple decline in retention over time; the longer the interval since initial learning, the less likely the task is to be remembered. Moreover, the decline is thought to be most rapid immediately following learning, gradually approaching some baseline level of retention (*see* Figure 12–1, p. 354).

Reminiscence

The monotonically decreasing function is by no means the only retention curve reported. The term "reminiscence" has been used for many years in psychology to refer operationally to cases in which performance on a retention test is better after long than after short intervals. This effect may be seen clearly in humans given a tedious motor task such as trying to keep one's finger on a dot that moves irregularly and unpredictably across a television screen. It has been known for years that with such motor tasks, reminiscence is more apparent with massed practice (i.e., practice uninterrupted by rests). If instead the person is given distributed practice with frequent periods of rest interspersed between periods of practice, less reminiscence occurs. In other words, with distributed practice less "spontaneous" improvement occurs after a long retention interval.

Because of such characteristics, reminiscence typically has been explained in terms of the buildup of some negative factor like "inhibition" or "error tendencies" so long as practice continues. Over a longer retention interval there is more opportunity for the dissipation of such inhibition or error tendencies. Thus, while *performance* is undeniably better after a long retention interval, there is no implication that the memory has somehow gained in "strength" during the retention interval.

Such a facilitation in memory strength would be both interesting and desirable. Imagine studying hard for a relatively brief period and then sitting back to rest in the knowledge that, by resting, you are somehow facilitating the processing of the memories you have just acquired. Unfortunately, the evidence for reminiscence in human verbal learning is limited. This is also the case with animal learning, at least in terms of methodologically sound measures of retention that do not include a heavy component of motor performance. But even so, the existing literature includes more firm examples of reminiscence with animal subjects than in terms of human verbal memory. In the 1930s a number of examples of reminiscence in human verbal learning were published, but they have never been satisfactorily replicated. In the past 25 years only two clear cases of reminiscence in human verbal memory have appeared, and in these the retention intervals over which retention performance improved was on the order of seconds (Keppel & Underwood, 1967; Peterson, 1966).

Perhaps this apparent inconsistency may be attributed to subtle differences in the verbal materials employed. For example, potential instances of reminiscence have been reported with words characterized as inducing a relatively high level of arousal (Kleinsmith & Kaplan, 1963, 1964). An equally interesting possibility has arisen in terms of reminiscence for items presented in the form of simple pictures, with recall measured in terms of the labels for those pictures. Shapiro and Erdelyi (1974) presented subjects with a list of 60 simple sketches of discrete objects (e.g., fish, key, table, football, etc.). The subjects wrote the names of as many of the items as they could, beginning either 30 seconds or 5 minutes after their presentation. Subjects tested 5 minutes after presentation of the pictures were 12 percent more accurate in their recall than were subjects tested 30 seconds after presentation. This increase was of only borderline statistical significance, but it did agree with previous data gathered by Erderlyi and Becker (1974). In the latter study accuracy in the recall of picture labels also increased over time, although in this case successive opportunities to recall intervened. For example, in two experiments in which, following an initial recall attempt, subjects were permitted a 7-minute interval to sit quietly and think about the stimulus items (the "think" condition in these experiments), improvement in recall after the interval was 13 percent and 10 percent for Experiments 1 and 2, respectively (Erdelyi & Becker, 1974). Apparently, a slight increase in recall of picture labels occurs over time whether repeated opportunities to recall are given or not. Finally, it is of some interest that this increase in recall was not found for items presented as words and recalled as words, in any of three experiments (Erdelyi & Becker, 1974; Shapiro & Erdelyi, 1974). Erdelyi and his colleagues have suggested that the use of visual imagery may be responsible for the apparent increase in recall with the passage of time. It is as yet unclear whether reminiscence effects will prove to be robust under these circumstances.

Incubation

The notion of incubation is similar to that of reminiscence in that it refers to an increase in learned performance during a retention interval. The major difference is that incubation has been applied exclusively to instances involving an emotional response like fear. Because of the emotional context of the resultant memory, and because the term "incubation" has been applied widely both in studies of human and animal memory, separate consideration is warranted.

Incubation is really an old concept insofar as it has been used for humans. Consider the admonition to a person who falls off a horse: Get right back up in the saddle or else it will become more difficult to do so with the passing of time.

Incubation is in some ways an unfortunate choice of terms since it implies that a "seed of fear" is somehow planted and grows spontaneously in an organism over time. This tempts one to use incubation as an explanatory concept when it is intended only to be descriptive, in the same way that we have used "retention" and "forgetting."

Incubation in humans typically has been assessed through the measurement of responses of the autonomic nervous system such as heart rate and GSR. A standard experiment consists of pairing a neutral stimulus such as a letter, word, or light with the occurrence of a mild but uncomfortable electrical shock (UCS) that elicits changes in the autonomic response in question (e.g., a decrease in skin resistance). As we would expect from our knowledge of classical conditioning, the neutral stimulus, as a result of the pairings with the UCS, will come to elicit the change in the autonomic response. With respect to incubation, it is sometimes observed that

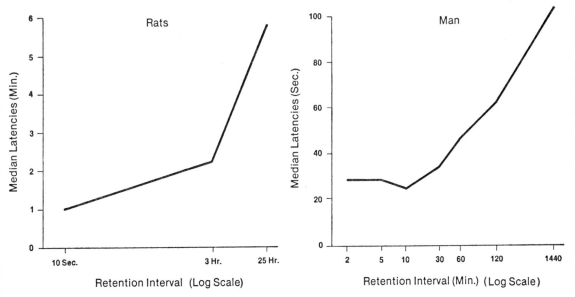

Figure 13–1. Representative incubation functions are shown. In each curve the change is shown, with increasing length of retention interval, in the tendency for rats (left panel) or mice (right panel) to withhold a punished response; the longer the interval since punishment of the response, the greater the tendency to withhold the response. It should be noted that such incubation functions are not an inevitable occurrence in the processing of memories involving punishment. (From Pinel & Cooper, 1966; Geller & Jarvik, 1970, courtesy of Plenum Press.)

the autonomic response is greater the longer the retention interval (i.e., the longer the time between acquisition and testing).

Following instrumental aversive conditioning with animals, there are clear instances of incubation in terms of instrumental behavior. Rats and mice show more avoidance a day or so later than immediately after training under certain conditions of one-trial passive avoidance conditioning. An example may be seen in Figure 13–1, in which the top portion shows the latency of rats to lick a water spout at differing intervals after they had been shocked while licking it, and the lower portion the performance of mice in terms of their latency to cross over into a compartment in which they have been shocked during original training. Incubation also may be found following multitrial active avoidance conditioning in rabbits, guinea pigs, or rats (e.g., Gabriel, 1972).

Why should instrumental avoidance performance improve with longer retention intervals if there is no corresponding increase in the aversiveness ("fear") of the stimulus being avoided? Three reasons seem plausible. The first applies primarily to the retention of one-trial passive avoidance learning and concerns a point mentioned before. Under some conditions, footshock given to rats or mice results in initial hyperactivity which then decreases progressively with the passage of time. If one outlet for the increased activity happens to be the compartment in which the animal previously was shocked, this will be recorded after short intervals as "poor retention." This hyperactivity will have dissipated after longer intervals and retention will seem, therefore, to have "improved."

Another mechanism which may account for incubation concerns the indirect effects of the aversive stimuli; those consequences which influence the stimulus context of the organism. For example, in a one-trial passive avoidance situation the animal receives a strong electrical shock when it leaves the arbitrarily defined safe compartment. This noxious stimulus induces a variety of transient autonomic changes including the release of epinephrine, adrenal corticoids, etc. The resulting feedback to the organism may change the perception of the environment sufficiently to make the results of a short-term retention test (i.e., while these changes are still in effect) different than the results of a long-term retention test.

A third explanation of incubation has been applied to data gathered from both humans and animals. The idea underlying this explanation is based upon the contention, largely supported, that generalization increases over a retention interval (see Chapter 10). The generalization of particular interest involves stimuli that are similar to those initially associated with the aversive event. Using the example of the person falling off a horse, an immediate test

might show very little fear of other horses. But given time to develop, a more generalized fear reaction could occur such that a later
test would reveal a considerable increase in the fear of all horses.
Such an explanation has been applied successfully to incubation
found in terms of human classical conditioning (Saltz & Asdourian,
1962), classical conditioning with animals (McAllister & McAllister, 1967) and instrumental conditioning with animals (Gabriel,
1972).

Temporarily Impaired Retention—The Kamin Effect

The Kamin Effect is the only nonmonotonic retention function that
has received significant theoretical attention. It may be described
fairly simply: Following aversive conditioning, retention is quite
good after a few minutes as well as a day or two later, but retention
is relatively poor after intermediate intervals of an hour or so in
length. An example of the Kamin Effect is shown in Figure 13–2.

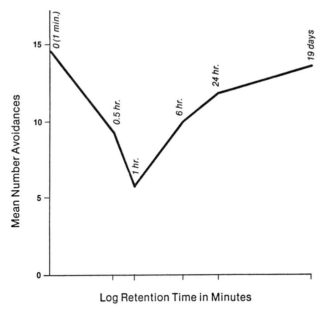

Figure 13–2.   Mean number of avoidances emitted by
rats given 25 opportunities to avoid at differing intervals following limited initial training (25 trials) on a
relatively difficult, shuttle-box avoidance task. This
function—exaggerated forgetting after retention intervals of intermediate length—has been termed the
"Kamin Effect." (From Kamin, 1957.)

This unusual retention function was initially viewed largely as an anomaly, and for several years the Kamin Effect was not the object of much research, aside from some additional work by Kamin and by Brush (e.g., Brush, 1971). Subsequently, however, the Kamin Effect was recognized more widely as having some theoretical importance. It proved to be a reliable phenomenon which could not be traced to artifactual consequences of procedure or to simple changes in the general activity levels in the animals. Furthermore, the intermediate-length retention intervals which yield poorest retention were found to correspond with temporally dependent,

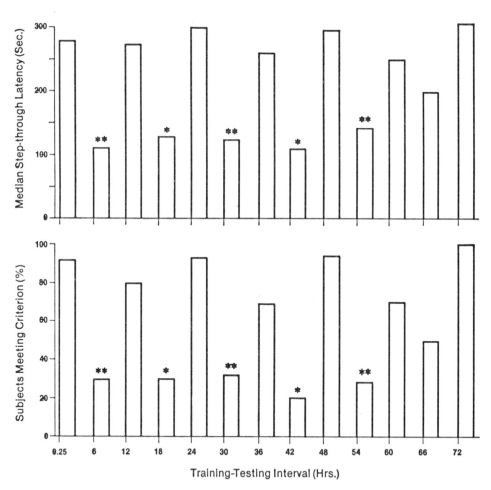

Figure 13–3. Retention scores for subjects given one trial of passive avoidance training are shown for separate groups of rats, each of which was tested after one of 13 multiples of 6 hours following training. In both the upper and lower curves, the higher the number, the better the retention. (From Holloway & Wansley, 1973, © Am. Assoc. Adv. Science.)

physiological effects induced by stress, such as hormonal and neurotransmitter activity.

Several peculiarities and limitations of the Kamin Effect deserve mention. A critical limitation is that this phenomenon appears to occur *only* with aversive conditioning; no studies to our knowledge, either published or unpublished, have convincingly demonstrated the Kamin Effect with appetitive conditioning. Even in aversive situations, this lapse of retention becomes evident only after the first few retraining trials, and it can be eliminated completely by exposing the animal to aversive events just prior to the retention test. Finally, Brush (1971) has shown that the greater the degree of original learning, the shorter is the retention interval at which the poorest retention occurs.

Current explanations of the Kamin Effect center around motivational and memory factors. In general terms the motivational explanation says that because of a change in the autonomic nervous system the animal simply is unable to cope as effectively with a new bout of aversive conditioning at intermediate retention intervals. For example, the animal may be less capable, physiologically, of entering a state of arousal, or state of emotion that is appropriate to the performance of an avoidance response.

The memory explanation also focuses upon the internal changes that follow aversive conditioning. But for this explanation, these processes are believed to modify potential internal retrieval cues such that retrieval of the memory of original conditioning is impaired. In simplest terms, then, the motivational interpretation suggests the animal recognizes the relationship between the CS and UCS but cannot become fearful, or otherwise behave in such a way as to help himself; the memory interpretation suggests that the information about the relationship is not accessible to the animal.

Multiphasic Retention Functions—
Repeated Fluctuations in Retention

Following the initial demonstration by Kamin that there could be a decline in retention followed by a return to previous levels, researchers began to be alert for the possibility of other types of fluctuations in memory processes. If the potential exists for such a change to occur during one time period, it seems reasonable that the change could repeat itself, perhaps on a regular temporal basis. In other words, the time course of retention may be multiphasic, with peaks and troughs in the level of retention. An example of such multiphasic retention is shown in Figure 13–3.

The question arises: How do we account for such multiphasic

retention? One possibility is that the actual physical process of memory storage (whatever it may be) is such that different stages of the process are less accessible than others for retrieval. A more likely possibility is that some regularly changing physiological function may interact with retention. As indicated in the figure, the cyclic nature of retention can be quite regular and may be related to the well-established circadian rhythm (which involves fluctuations in activity and hormonal levels). The resulting changes in the internal and external environment may provide a sufficiently large shift in contextual cues to make retrieval much easier if the memory test corresponds to the same conditions as were present during training. However, the form of the function in Figure 13–3 has not inevitably taken this particular multiphasic form under all circumstances tested (e.g., Caul, Barrett, Thune, & Osborne, 1974). But on the other hand, Holloway, Wansley, and their associates have published considerable evidence of such multiphasic functions obtained under a variety of conditions of both aversive and appetitive conditioning (Wansley & Holloway, 1975a & b; Hunsicker, 1974). Further research is needed to determine the generality of these initial findings.

II. ANALYSIS OF LONG-TERM RETENTION

Is Retention Assayed or Assessed?

The term "assay" technically refers to a test intended to discover the existence or nonexistence of some component. For example, you might have your morning coffee *assayed* to determine whether or not it contained arsenic. On the other hand, if you were sure that it contained arsenic, it would be of some interest to know how much in order to determine how rapidly you should be rushed to the hospital. In that case you would want someone to *assess* the quantity of arsenic.

When we analyze the results of memory experiments, it is tempting to do so as if retention were subject to assay. Certainly, it is more dramatic to say that a particular treatment "eliminated" memory retrieval or "completely obliterated" the memory representation of an episode, or to conclude that "total recall" occurred. Also, such all-or-none statements are more adaptable to our Aristotelian logic; it simply is easier for us to think about retention that way.

Unfortunately, science is not prepared to assay retention. We mislead ourselves whenever we think of memory retrieval as total or nonexistent. Most tests of memory processing measure only one representation of an episode that may be stored by the organism, and at most, two or three may be measured. In assessing an animal's memory of a discrimination episode, we measure how often the animal responds to the stimulus that previously signaled reward; we do not measure the animal's representation of the amount of food reward he had received, how cold the apparatus was, what sorts of odors and incidental objects were to be found elsewhere in the apparatus, etc. In this case, the "etc." is significant. It is used to illustrate that not only do we not measure many aspects of a memory representation, we ordinarily do not know what they are.

We are somewhat better off in assessing memories of humans because we can simply ask them what they remember about a particular episode. But this would carry us only a bit further; we know from a long history of psychological study that asking people how they behave may not tell us much about how they behave in fact.

The point here is not to complain about the measuring instruments available to us in the study of memory processing. The science improves constantly in this respect, and it could well be asserted that measurement in this area of study is more advanced than that found in most other areas of behavioral science. Instead, the point is to induce caution in the conclusions we draw from any single study. We learn about memory processing only from what we measure, and what we measure often is quite arbitrary. And surely, we *assess* a memory representation, we do not *assay* it.

Retention May Be Influenced By How It Is Measured

All areas of behavioral science must deal with the following fact: By measuring behavior, we may alter it. This problem has been dealt with at length philosophically, and it is particularly relevant to disciplines such as social psychology. The problem arises in the study of memory processing, too, with direct relevance for understanding memory processing.

Retrieval Cues Provided By a Retention Test

We know that a critical step in memory processing is memory retrieval. Also, we can be fairly certain that memory retrieval is determined in part by the presence of events at the retention test which might serve as retrieval cues because of their similarity with events stored as attributes of the original memory. Such retrieval cues may be thought of as "reminders" if you like. Some techniques for measuring retention as a test requiring that an animal *relearn* a task involves the re-presentation of a number of elements and events that occurred when the memory was acquired originally, including the reward used, the motor response emitted or elicited, the sequence of events between each trial, and so forth. In contrast, other measurement techniques provide a minimum of potential retrieval cues, as when a single test trial is given, or when several test trials are given but without, e.g., re-presenting the conditions of reinforcement previously used.

The result has been that some retention phenomena, the Kamin Effect for example, are more likely to occur when retention is tested with a relearning measure. Other effects, such as proactive interference, are more likely to influence retention when measurement is completed before a large number of retrieval cues are re-presented to the subject. This is precisely what one would expect if some retention phenomena depend upon an extensive, persistent discrepancy between events at the retention test and the stored memory attributes, while others are due to a more transient failure to discriminate between conflicting memories which share many memory attributes. Further discussion of such effects may be found elsewhere (e.g., Spear, 1971, 1973).

Recognition and Recall

The study of human memory also encounters instances in which estimates of retention may depend upon how it is measured. A common comparison is retention measured by recognition versus recall. In one sense this comparison is similar to that above where the reference was to animal experiments. For the typical recognition test a person is asked to identify items that he previously has been asked to learn from among a group of other items. As when relearning is the test of retention, a number of potential retrieval cues are presented in a recognition test, including the precise items that are to be remembered. On the other hand, some circumstances of the recognition test are quite different from those of original learning, including especially the spatial and temporal arrangements of the critical items. When recall is tested, the subject is simply asked to give as many items as he can remember, so that relatively few potential retrieval cues are presented; alternatively, cues may be provided systematically for "cued recall."

The question of whether there is a fundamental difference in the memory processing undergone during recognition and recall is an important issue. Tulving (1972) has argued that the same processes are involved in both cases. One of the reasons for expecting a difference in processes underlying recognition and recall is that recognition has been believed to be always superior to recall. Tulving and others have shown that this is not so. Rather, argues Tulving, the critical determinant of both recognition and recall is whether the retrieval cues provided at the retention test correspond to attributes encoded when the material was first presented for study. To illustrate, subjects were presented with three 5-letter units (e.g., ACCOU, HIDEO, AMNES) and then asked to associate each of these, respectively, with the 2-letter units NT, UT, and IC. For the test of recall, each 5-letter unit was presented as before and subjects were asked to give the associated 2-letter unit. In one such test, accuracy in recall of the appropriate 2 letters was about 70 percent; but when asked to recognize the 2-letter units, accuracy was only about 10 percent (Watkins, 1974).

The point to be made here is that under some circumstances recognition is not better than recall and can be a good deal worse. Furthermore, many other circumstances have been found in which cued recall is better than recognition (assuming that the cues which accompany recall are not provided for the recognition test). This finding has been important for evaluating theories of recall (Tulving & Thompson, 1973; Watkins & Tulving, 1975; Wiseman & Tulving, 1976.)

For example, a predominant general model of the recall process has assumed two stages: first, generation by an individual of a pool of items which conceivably might be the correct items to be recalled, and second, recognition of the actual (correct) items from among the items in this pool. According to this "generation-recognition" model, if all correct items always were generated, then recall through this model might be equal to recognition (as measured from among a set of alternatives generated by the experimenter); but if any error occurs in the generation stage, then recall always will be poorer than recognition. Clearly, however, this model never would expect recognition to be better than recall. Thus the established finding that recall may be better than recognition calls into question the generation-recognition model of the recall process and, in addition, demonstrates the value of certain retrieval cues or aspects of the semantic context for determining recall. In fact, the recognition process also is known to be influenced by these factors (though not always), in accord with the view of Tulving and his associates that common processes are involved in recognition and recall.

Underwood (e.g., 1972) has taken an opposing view. He argues that recognition and recall involve different memory processes in that recognition may not require the retrieval process. Underwood's view is that recognition of items previously presented from among items not presented requires only that they be discriminated. Therefore, the recognition process may proceed with the use of only discriminative attributes of a memory. The recall process, however, requires memory attributes of an associative nature for retrieval of the target memory attribute. As further support for the different-processes view, Underwood has cited a number of functional differences between recognition and recall. For example, recognition appears to be a good deal more resistant than recall to the detrimental effects of interfering learning. It will be interesting to see how these opposing views fare in light of future research.

Additional Determinants of Memory Retrieval

We will now deal with the influence of environmental events occurring after memory storage that facilitate subsequent memory retrieval. Reference here is to what is sometimes termed "reminders." Reminders are familiar to us as those mnemonic aids we all use in an effort to alleviate or prevent forgetting. A reminder may be as remote as a string around one's finger or as specific as a word or sentence jotted down somewhere to help us "reconstruct" some more extensive literature or episode. Descriptively, a reminder boils down to being some portion of a previous episode represented in memory, in particular a portion of the episode sufficiently significant to have been noticed by the organism and represented as one or more memory attributes.

A reactivation treatment is a potential reminder, and is described here because of its apparent significance in the memory representation of an animal. A reactivation treatment may consist of re-exposing the animal to elements of the previous learning task such as the training apparatus, the reinforcer (e.g., food pellet or footshock) or the animal's motivational state during learning. If the reactivation treatment evokes attributes otherwise unlikely to be aroused (retrieved), then it may be termed an effective reminder. The effectiveness of reactivation treatments is easily understood at a descriptive level, but the details of their action remain somewhat of a mystery.

While we cannot know at this time the precise mechanism through which reactivation treatments may alleviate forgetting, we do know that they "work." One example of the effectiveness of reactivation treatments involves the alleviation of the forgetting that normally occurs as a result of electroconvulsive shock. As will be discussed in Chapters 14 and 15, the administration of electroconvulsive shock (ECS) immediately after learning leads to almost complete forgetting of a passive avoidance response (usually, the response to be avoided is stepping off a platform onto an electrified grid). However, if re-exposed to certain elements of the original task, such as the footshock previously received as punishment, the rat shows good retention of the passive avoidance response (e.g., Lewis, 1969). Thus, it cannot be said that the ECS treatment prevented the storage of the memory, rather it impaired the animal's ability to retrieve the memory.

Another example involves a phenomenon that has been called "infantile amnesia," the forgetting that occurs for events and relationships learned at an early age. Campbell and Jaynes (1966) found that rats trained to passively avoid an electric grid shock at 25 days of age showed little retention when tested at 53 days of age. But a separate group of rats received shocks 7, 14 and 21 days after original training to "reactivate" the memory of the original learning, and these animals showed excellent retention at 53 days of age. A control group that received only the reactivation treatments showed no evidence of "retention," which tends to indicate that additional learning which took place during the reactivation treatments was not sufficient in itself to account for the retention effect. This phenomenon is best described by the following quote: "Indeed, what objects does the child remember? It remembers only those which are often before its eyes; the infant soon forgets even its mother, should she die" (Sechenov, 1863; cited in Campbell & Spear, 1972).

The efficacy of reactivation treatments has also been shown in other situations that need not be detailed here (*see* Spear, 1973, 1976). Examples of these include:

1. Reduction or elimination of "warm-up decrement," the decrement in retention that occurs after a 24-hour interval relative to instrumental performance prior to the interval.
2. Reduction in forgetting induced by the acquisition of conflicting memories, i.e., retroactive and proactive interference.
3. Reduction or elimination of "simple forgetting," i.e., the retention decrement found after several weeks relative to that found soon after original training.

In retention by humans there is similar evidence that forgetting of verbal materials may be alleviated if they are presented either with verbal items that actually appeared on the list to be learned or with items which did not actually appear but were probably represented as attributes of the original memory nevertheless. For example, if words like APPLE, PEACH, PEAR, DOG, CAT, and HORSE were to have been learned for later recall, forgetting is reduced if subjects are presented the category names, *fruit* and *animal.*

Recent evidence has indicated that a reactivated memory may have properties similar to those of a recently acquired memory. For example, electroconvulsive shock induces amnesia if it follows learning by a few seconds, but not if it follows initial learning by 24 hours. However, if a reactivation treatment is given 24 hours, or even longer after learning, and if this reactivation treatment is followed within seconds by an electroconvulsive shock, amnesia for that learning does occur. In other words electroconvulsive shock has the same effect on a recently reactivated memory as if that memory has just been acquired (Lewis, 1969; Miller & Springer, 1973; Spear, 1973).

A similar phenomenon has been found with memory-enhancing "hypermnesic" agents such as strychnine. Under certain conditions, strychnine appears to facilitate retention if it is administered soon after acquisition of a memory, but not if presented after a longer interval. However, the application of strychnine may be delayed for as long as three days after learning and still have the effect of facilitating later retention, provided that a reactivation treatment was given just prior to the strychnine (Gordon & Spear, 1973).

The point of these experiments is simple: when an animal is treated to reactivate a previously acquired memory, the animal behaves as if that memory had, instead, just been acquired. One can guess as to why this should be the case, but at this point the guesses cannot be very specific. Generally, it would appear that for a memory to be retrieved or for a specific target attribute of the memory to be retrieved, a certain number or a certain kind of other attributes of that memory must be aroused. Probably a memory attribute is aroused whenever the animal notices an event sufficiently similar to that originally represented by the memory attributes. Undoubtedly, the conditions necessary for memory retrieval will be found to be a good deal more complicated than this. In the meantime, this conceptualization can serve as a rough pretheoretical framework for the development of appropriate experiments.

III. PROCESSING MEMORIES AFTER SHORT VERSUS LONG INTERVALS

Is There Only One Kind of Memory Storage Process?

It should be clear that we do not know precisely what memory processing is. By appropriate research we can make inferences about memory processing, and we can certainly observe its product. But we cannot at this time specify what biological steps occur to permit information "fed" into an organism to be integrated with information already stored in the organism and then ultimately to influence the organism's behavior.

We can, for example, place a hungry rat in a Skinner box and make food pellets contingent upon the animal's pressing a lever. We can then infer that this information has been somehow absorbed by the rat because after it has been exposed to this contingency for some time, it comes to behave differently. Furthermore, this altered behavior is likely to be maintained for days, weeks, or years whether or not the animal is to be exposed to the box in the interim, and this strengthens our inference. What we do not know is whether this information—about how a food pellet may appear when the lever is pressed—is processed any differently than is the rat's "recognition" of which is the more comfortable corner of his cage in which to sleep.

We know even less about the relationship between the processes that control memories representing learned behaviors and other biological processes having similar characteristics. Consider physiological immunization for example. Here, organisms are treated in such a way as to be resistant, for a limited interval of time, to injurious biological interaction with toxic agents. Like a stored memory, however, the effects of immunization do not last indefinitely—the duration of the effects depend upon variables such as the intensity or quality of the original treatment, and the effects may be modified by interpolated treatments or experiences. Do common biological processes underlie immunization and memory storage?

Are There Separate Processes for Short-Term and Long-Term Retention?

A much more fruitful approach to elucidating possible differences in memory storage processes has emphasized the temporal aspects of memory rather than the content of memory. The possibility of separate storage processes for short-term and long-term memory has been a topic of considerable interest. We turn now to a brief consideration of this issue.

A variety of theories view two separate stages of memory processing roughly as follows: First, the organism's representation of events is thought to pass through a short-term memory process. At this point the representation is fragile in the sense that if the associated physiological systems were disrupted, the memory would be lost. Certain time-dependent processes are believed to operate on the memory during this stage, so that the representation would effectively "die away" unless maintained by some form of repetition. Humans may do this symbolically through rehearsal; animals may need to depend upon re-exposure to some approximation of the original event. If the memory survives this ephemeral, short-term memory stage, then it may be transferred to a more permanent state, the long-term memory store. The nature of processing in this store has been largely ignored except that the memory is believed now to be more immune to either physiological disruption or some time-dependent "decay" process.

The above characteristics may be found in a surprising majority of the models of memory posed during the 1950s and 1960s. What sorts of evidence may be used to support such ideas? To properly compare short-term and long-term memory processing, all factors other than retention interval—especially degree of original learning—must be held constant. With this scientifically obvious qualification, we can now consider evidence bearing on the distinction between short-term and long-term memory processing.

Introspective Evidence

Introspection may be dismissed as nonscientific because it cannot be observed publicly. However, such evidence may be important to the extent that it serves as a fruitful source of hypotheses that can be systematically investigated.

It may seem obvious that remembering the phone number of an obscure pizzeria from the moment you close the phone book until the number is dialed is fundamentally different from remembering a phone number that you have dialed every day or so. Surely the likelihood of retention an hour later is quite different, and so seem the mental gymnastics we go through in remembering the two numbers. But this does not demand different kinds of processing.

First, it is not sufficient to claim a difference in processes just because retention is better after short than long intervals. Declining retention could be a property of a single memory process. To establish separate processes we must, at a minimum, establish functional differences. That is, we must show that with certain manipulations of procedure, the environment or the materials to be remembered, retention after short intervals is influenced differently than that after long intervals. To do so introspectively requires that we maintain strict internal criteria for what are thought to be different procedures or materials, and that we attend closely to the control of our internal thought processes. We know that humans are unlikely to accomplish the first and notoriously unreliable in accomplishing the second.

Second, it may appear that we rehearse during short intervals (while "holding" the pizzeria number) but not during long intervals. But this, too, is difficult to assess introspectively as well as any other way. For example, what constitutes rehearsal? Is it necessary to repeat covertly, but explicitly, all materials to be remembered, precisely as they are presented? If not, might not exposure during a long interval to events similar to those represented by the critical memory set off the same sorts of "rehearsal" mechanisms as those found during the short-term retention?

It would not be difficult to go on complaining about introspection as a research technique, and probably few people today would argue in favor of it. However, the possibility that there are different processes for short- and long-term memory, as implied in the introspective evidence, has led to research tactics based on these distinctions. The widespread use of such tactics justifies separate consideration of retention after short and long intervals. We shall now consider relevant experimental data.

Retention After Short Intervals in Humans

Brief Retention of Sensory Images

Retention after short intervals has been considered separately from retention after long intervals for nearly a century of psychological investigation. When considered long ago by writers such as William James (1890), however, reference was to a much shorter-term memory than is generally considered today. James discussed a relatively short-lived "primary" memory often referred to in the present literature as *iconic memory,* a topic that requires elaboration.

Our sensory systems are wired to permit us to maintain a sensory impression for a brief period after direct receptor contact with an environmental event. For humans, the most useful case of this is in terms of vision. A visual "trace" of an object persists for about 200 milliseconds. This permits us to see, for example, a movie as a continuous stream of events rather than as a sequence of discrete pictures and the light from a fluorescent bulb as constant when, in fact, it flickers. This sensory impression could be considered a kind of memory (iconic memory). For example, if a similar visual stimulus is presented within 50 milliseconds or so after the first, humans will report that they have not seen the first, a phenomenon termed *backward masking.*

How can we measure retention of information over intervals in the range of milliseconds? An example is provided in a classical experiment by Sperling (1960). For this experiment, humans were presented with two or three rows of letters and numbers, usually arranged with four items per row. Presentation was very brief, about 50 milliseconds. It was known that the most that could be recalled from such a presentation was about four items. Sperling found that if subjects were properly signaled as to which row of items they were to concentrate upon, they were fairly accurate in repeating the items. The signals used were tones, a very high tone for the top row, a very low tone for the bottom row, and so forth. By presenting the tones *after* exposure to the items, Sperling could infer how long the subjects "held" the image of the items. Or in other words, Sperling could estimate the span of iconic memory for these very familiar items. He found that, in general, the longer the subjects had to wait after exposure to the display of items before being signaled as to which they should repeat, the less accurate they were. Moreover, even with familiar items like numbers and letters, subjects were reasonably accurate only if signaled within a few hundred milliseconds; and the signal was no help at all if not presented well within one second after the display.

It is not clear how iconic memory is related to retention over intervals in the range between seconds and years, but some interesting possibilities exist. For example, individuals appear to differ rather widely in sensory memory of this sort, and some children in particular have been cited for a capacity to retain exact visual images intact for a relatively long period, a capacity sometimes termed *eidetic imagery*. For example, one study reported that some children can "see" a vivid image for as long as four minutes after a visual presentation has been removed. It should be emphasized that these children were not reporting what they *had seen*, but what they could still *see*. Such a capacity was found in approximately 8 percent of elementary school children tested, (Haber & Haber, 1964). Mr. Shereshevskii, the mnemonist with a superior long-term memory (Luria, 1968), also seemed to have an unusual capacity for such imagery.

Retention of Verbal Materials After Short Intervals

If humans are presented a single verbal item and asked 15 or 20 seconds later to recall it, they almost certainly will do so without error. Accuracy may be impaired by two major factors—a failure in the initial perception of the item or by preventing the subject from rehearsing the item during the retention interval. Perception can be manipulated quite easily, but the control of rehearsal is something else again. Rehearsal by humans, whether a species-specific behavior or not, is a topic of some interest in itself in terms of how it acts to alleviate forgetting. But in order to test the properties of short-term retention, it is necessary to first work under circumstances in which short-term *forgetting* occurred. And for that, rehearsal must be retarded if not prevented.

There are several ways in which rehearsal can be retarded. One is by applying the "Brown-Peterson paradigm" wherein, to prevent rehearsal during the retention interval, subjects are given some distracting task that includes materials which are not formally similar to those to be remembered. For example, if the item to be recalled is a trigram such as DKG, a number such as 873 may be presented immediately after the trigram, and the subject asked to count backwards from that number by three's until the time for recall. This procedure produces rapid forgetting. Another method of assessing short-term retention involves the "probe technique." During the retention interval, items that the subject is instructed to learn are continually being presented. After a certain retention interval, defined also in terms of a certain number of interpolated items, a probe or signal is presented to the subject indicating which of the previous items is to be recalled. In the example shown in Table 13–1 the subject sees the items listed. When the word "moon" is presented the second time, it is accompanied by a signal and the subject must respond by saying "chair," the word that followed "moon" when it was previously presented.

Table 13–1. ***Example of the Probe Technique for Studying Memory***

Stimuli	
Coat	
List	
Truck	
Moon	
Chair	
Cup	*Recall* = Subject should
Foot	respond to probe
Book	by saying "chair"
|	
|	
|	
|	
|	
Board	
Moon (plus probe)	

A third widely used technique for measuring short-term memory is to equate it with the "recency effect" in free recall of words. In the free-recall task, a subject is simply presented with a list of 15 to 20 words and immediately asked to repeat as many as he can. The items most likely to be given correctly are those presented during the first part of the list (the "primacy effect") and the last part of the list ("recency effect"). The recency effect is attributed to the human's capacity for short-term memory, because the effect does not occur if a long interval elapses between presentation of the last items in the list and the opportunity for recall (the primacy effect is still present after long intervals). Accordingly, the characteristics of this recency effect have been studied to understand the characteristics of short-term memory. The techniques that have been used to control rehearsal in the study of short-term memory probably do not eliminate it, if only because there is now good evidence that humans can process information in parallel, i.e., separate items of information may be processed simultaneously. Therefore, while it is certainly of value to understand the characteristics of rehearsal, rehearsal is a somewhat different problem than is ordinarily considered under the heading "memory."

Retention After Short Intervals in Animals

Delayed Matching to Sample

The task called *delayed matching to sample* has come to be preferred over delayed responding as a test of short-term memory in animals. Delayed matching to sample is descriptively titled; for this task, the animal is required to select (match) between two or more alternatives the stimulus (sample) which previously had appeared alone. For example, a triangle may be projected briefly on a screen, then, after a delay of 10 seconds, the *triangle* will reappear together with a *square*. If the animal responds to the *triangle*, it will receive a food reward. Otherwise, all stimuli disappear and a new trial begins.

The delayed matching to sample technique has the advantage of being more readily automated than delayed responding, thus reducing human error. This task also allows position to be eliminated as a discriminative cue by randomly presenting the stimuli on either side. This is important because if the animal can determine the correct alternative by its position, then accurate responding could be accomplished simply by physical orientation toward the correct alternative during the delay. The contribution of memory processes, if any, could not be determined in such a case.

This is not to say that all forms of mediation by physical activity during the retention interval may be eliminated a priori, even with the delayed matching task.

Blough (1959) tested four pigeons on a delayed matching to sample task with delays of either 0, 2, 5, or 10 seconds. At the beginning of a trial, either a flickering light or a steady light was presented to the pigeon through a vertical aperture located between two identical discs which served as response keys. Following the appropriate delay, both samples were presented, one on each disc. When the hungry pigeons pecked the disc that was illuminated in the same way as the sample had been, grain was presented for the bird to eat.

Two of the pigeons were extremely efficient regardless of the retention interval. They exhibited some remarkable behavior: Depending upon which stimulus had been presented as a sample, the birds performed in predictable, ritualistic ways during the retention interval. One pigeon stepped back from the keys and slowly waved its head back and forth if the sample had been flickering light; but if the steady light had been the sample, this bird pecked at the top of the vertical aperture during the retention interval. The other bird spent the retention interval biting at the top of the vertical aperture when the flickering light was presented as the sample; after the steady light had appeared as the sample, this bird pecked directly at the center of the aperture.

Thus, Blough's birds behaved as if they had selected certain idiosyncratic, overt mediating behaviors to symbolize the particular sample that had been presented. The mediating behavior then served to direct the pigeons' behavior at the matching test. This interpretation seemed to be verified by other evidence. For example, these mediating behaviors were disturbed when Blough attempted to take pictures of these behaviors; as the alternative mediating behaviors became less distinctive for each bird, their retention performance declined in accuracy.

The possibility of such mediating behavior suggests that caution should be used in interpreting the results of the delayed matching to sample memory task; the possibility exists that motor behavior may serve a mediating function in this task just as it may in delayed responding. The dangers of the sorts of mediation observed by Blough can be reduced by increasing the number of alternative samples employed for a single bird or animal. But whenever only a very few samples are employed, one should be wary of possible contamination by some subtle mediating devices. The mediation behavior is interesting in its own right, but it is merely bothersome if one is primarily concerned with memory.

Assuming the absence of mediating devices in delayed matching and delayed responding, we can address ourselves to three kinds of questions. First, what are the variables that facilitate or impair retention? Second, how might short-term memory capacities enter into other sorts of behaviors studied with similar methods? Third, what attributes are most likely to be forgotten in this task?

Treatments Influencing Animal Retention in Delay Tasks

Delayed Response

Analysis of delayed responding has been surprisingly unsuccessful in identifying factors that influence memory processes after initial storage of the memory is accomplished (for a review of some relatively early experiments analyzing delayed responding, *see* Fletcher, 1965). For example, the more spatially separated the alternatives are prior to the retention interval, the better is retention. But this variable probably has its effect on discrimination learning, leading to a higher level of learning, hence influencing memory storage rather than retrieval of the animals' activity level or distractions during the delay interval. It may influence retention, but this probably is due to an effect on performance rather than memory (Fletcher, 1965). There is some indication that retention may be better when training trials on delayed responding are more widely distributed. But while this may be a genuine memory effect, it also may be a simple consequence of "boredom" (Gleitman, Wilson, Herman, & Rescorla, 1963).

The delayed matching to sample task, described previously, has been especially useful in analyzing variables that may influence retention independent of their effects on either perception or original storage of the memory. The analytical value of this is obvious, as we can see, in the following brief review of some of these variables.

Distraction During the Retention Interval

Retention of a visual sample by monkeys can be dramatically enhanced by simply turning out the lights during the retention interval. This effect has been shown in both the delayed response task (Malmo, 1942), and in the delayed matching to sample task (D'Amato, 1973). The magnitude of this effect is illustrated by two examples. The first example consists of a disparity between two estimates of retention capacities of monkeys in the delayed matching to sample test. Mello (1971) reported that monkeys consistently responded correctly after intervals of nearly 4 minutes, which was about 15 times longer than the corresponding estimate by Jarrard and Moise (1971). Among the procedural differences probably responsible for this discrepancy was the fact that Mello's animals spent their retention intervals in darkness, while in Jarrard and Moise's study the light in the test chamber was left on between presentation of the sample and the matching test. The second example is found in a study by D'Amato and O'Neill (1971). All

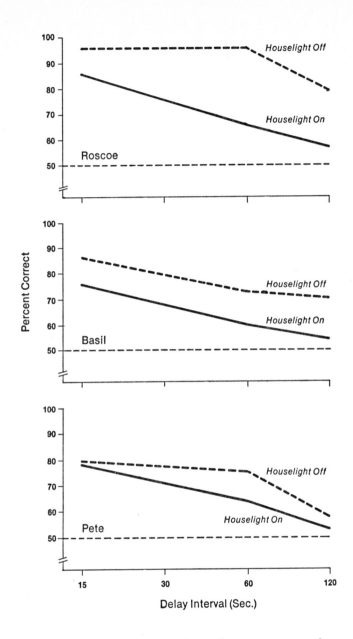

Figure 13–4. Accuracy of matching a previously presented stimulus is shown for increasing retention intervals during which the apparatus containing the monkey was either lighted or dark. Data for each of three monkeys are shown. (From D'Amato & O'Neill, 1971, © Soc. Exp. Anal. Behavior.)

three of the monkeys tested in this study failed to perform at better than chance levels when exposed to illumination during a 2-minute retention interval, but retention was significantly better than chance if the two minutes were spent in darkness (*see* Figure 13–4). Overall, darkness during the retention interval reduced errors by about one-third.

Why illumination affects retention in this way is not yet clear. It does not seem to matter whether darkness occurs soon after presentation of the sample, just prior to the matching test, or in the middle of the retention interval. Generally, however, the more darkness during the retention interval, the better the retention (Etkin, 1972). Relative illumination during the retention interval, in comparison to that during presentation of the sample, presentation of the test stimulus, or between trials, seems to be unimportant. Rather, the effect is a consequence of the absolute illumination during the retention interval; less forgetting occurs if the monkey is kept in darkness during the retention interval, regardless of illumination at other times (D'Amato & O'Neill, 1971). The effect does not seem to be due to the occurrence of more distracting stimuli during the retention interval when the lights are on, because presenting auditory stimulation, either white noise or tapes of monkeys chattering, has no effect on delayed matching performance (Worsham & D'Amato, 1973). It should be noted, however, that all of these studies used visual cues and distractions were produced by other visual stimuli. The possibility exists that discrimination based on auditory cues would be impaired by other auditory cues, but not by visual stimuli.

Gradual Improvement in Retention Over Long Retention Intervals

Improvement in retention with general practice is particularly interesting if the improvement is more pronounced after longer intervals. Although it has long been clear that animals may become more efficient *learners* with practice, there previously has been no good evidence that either humans or animals could learn to show better retention independent of better learning. However, D'Amato (1973) has reported that at least a few monkeys, after thousands of trials of exposure to the delayed-matching-to-sample task stretching over several years, have come to improve their retention performance after long intervals to a greater degree than after short intervals. It is not yet clear whether this improved retention is caused by an increased effectiveness in combating proactive or retroactive interference, learning to better estimate the relative lengths of retention intervals, or some improved system of "encod-

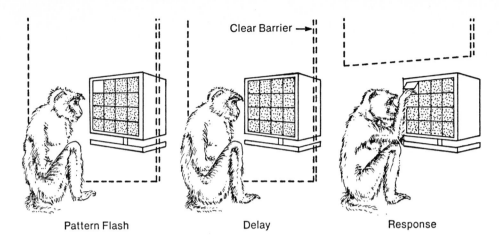

Figure 13–5. Schematic illustration of the sequence of stages (progressing temporally, from left to right) in the delayed multiple-response task devised by Medin. In this illustration the upper left corner panel is lighted, then turned off during the delay, and finally the monkey makes the correct response for which he will find a preferred food in the pigeonhole. (From Medin & Davis, 1974.)

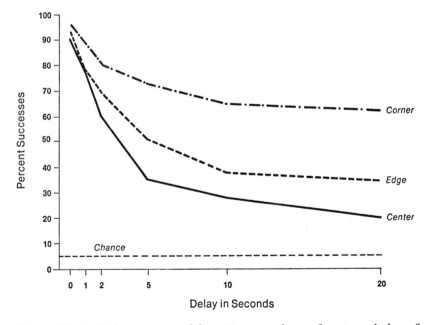

Figure 13–6. Relative rates of forgetting are shown for pigeonholes of differing location. *Also see* the apparatus illustrated in Figure 13–5. (From Medin, 1969.)

ing" the stimuli by the monkey. What is clear is that the effect is related to memory processing and not perception, because the degree of improvement is most pronounced at the longer intervals.

An Influence of Stimulus Redundancy on Forgetting

Forgetting of a stimulus in a delayed response task may be affected by the number of features which characterize that stimulus beyond its fundamental definition (Medin, 1969). To study this problem, Medin employed a delayed response task which was unusual. A monkey was presented a 4–X–4 matrix of 16 covered pigeonholes, any one of which might contain a preferred food (e.g., a raisin). The baited pigeonhole was illuminated, then darkened during the retention interval and the test when the monkey finally was permitted a single opportunity to select one of the pigeonholes (*see* Figure 13–5). In other words, the monkey's task was to remember which of the pigeonholes had been illuminated before the retention interval.

Medin tested the relative rates with which the location of a given pigeonhole would be forgotten when it was in the corner, on the edge, or in the center of the matrix. As one can see from glancing at Figure 13–5, these locations are surrounded by 3, 5, or 8 neighboring cells. Medin reasoned that "when the arbitrarily correct cell is surrounded by a large number of adjacent cells, the probability of a successful guess will be lowered (1969, p. 413)." The results shown in Figure 13–6 indicated that this prediction was verified and that the effect increased as the retention interval lengthened. The latter relationship, in combination with the equivalent performance for these stimuli when no delay was imposed, indicates that this variable influenced rate of forgetting and not initial perception or degree of original learning. It is not yet clear how this effect may be understood, but we may expect it to have some significance for understanding memory processing, if only because so few variables have been found to influence rate of forgetting in such a clear manner.

Other Variables of Potential Importance

Four other variables are worth mentioning because there are good reasons to expect that they influence retention. So far, none of these variables has been shown indisputably to affect retention after long intervals any differently than on an immediate test or after short intervals; yet, it is probably too early to conclude they are ineffective in this respect.

(1)   We have mentioned that the *number of alternative samples*

may influence performance in delayed matching to sample. If only two possible samples are used, the animals may form overt representational responses for bridging the retention interval and thus show inflated retention scores. On the other hand, the use of a small number of alternative samples may impair retention performance by increasing the probability of confusion at the retention test because the subject can't remember which of the two stimuli was last used as a sample. Perhaps the greater effect of this variable will occur at the longer retention interval. Such an impairment effect is suggested by the better retention performance obtained by Mello (1971, *see* above) over that of Jarrard and Moise (1971), which may be attributed in part to the use of 21 possible samples by Mello compared to only 2 by Jarrard and Moise. In a direct test of the effect of number of alternative samples, Etkin and D'Amato (1969) found no differences in retention when the sample pool included 2, 3, or 4 possible stimuli. However, experiments manipulating a greater number of alternative stimuli will be needed before a definite answer to this question will be available.

(2) One might expect that increasing the *duration of exposure* to the sample would facilitate retention. D'Amato and Worsham (1972) varied sample duration systematically, as part of an attempt to understand the excellent retention shown by their monkeys. They found that retention remained unimpaired even when sample duration was as brief as .06 seconds and concluded that this was not an important variable in the short-term memory processing of monkeys.

Experiments using humans as subjects have provided evidence both for and against this notion (Shaffer & Shiffrin, 1972; Sperling, 1960). The conditions under which increased duration facilitates subsequent retention in humans may be limited to the use of highly complex visual materials. Otherwise the postexposure time given human subjects for processing (e.g., rehearsal) of the item seems more important for subsequent retention.

(3) To what extent will retention be impaired by *generally distracting activities that occur during the retention interval?* If animals do indeed use physical mediating devices such as those used by Blough's pigeons in delayed matching, or if simple physical orientation is relevant during delayed responding, interpolated competing activities should impair retention. Other sources of impaired retention, such as disruption of some covert attentional processes, also may result from interpolated activities.

Using a delayed-response task, Fletcher (1965) found a positive correlation between general activity during the retention interval and number of errors made by the monkey at the test. Of course, it cannot be clear what is causing what in this case. Perhaps if monkeys fail to learn, they do not remember the correct alternative, and they become more active during the retention interval. This could account for the positive correlation as easily as the possibility that animals retain more poorly if they are more active. Moreover, Etkin (1972) measured the activity of monkeys during the retention interval in delayed matching and found no relationship between activity and retention.

However interesting, such correlational evidence can be only suggestive. The proper way to determine whether general interpolated activity impairs retention is with experimental tests. This has been accomplished in two studies.

In the first such test, Jarrard and Moise (1970) compared delayed matching in monkeys. One group of monkeys was allowed to roam about the experimental chamber during the retention interval, while monkeys in the other group were confined to a chair during the entire interval. The latter treatment was intended to enhance the animal's attention or to decrease distractibility. Nevertheless, retention by the confined animals was no better than that of the freely moving animals.

The second study (Moise, 1970) was similar to the first in that monkeys were tested on delayed matching with variation in the potential for distraction during the retention interval. However, in this study interpolated activity was manipulated in terms of the number of occasions on which a white light was presented to the monkey and the point during the retention interval at which this light was presented. The critical feature of the white light was that it was a discriminative stimulus; the monkeys had been trained to respond rapidly in the presence of this light in order to obtain a food pellet. If they responded too slowly, no pellet was given. Throughout the experiment, if these animals did not respond to the white light in less than 1.25 seconds, the trial was automatically terminated and a new trial initiated.

The appearance of the white light caused some impairment of retention, but in view of the importance of the light to the monkey, the small magnitude of the effect probably is more interesting than the fact of its statistical significance. The difference amounted to only about 9 points in terms of percentage correct responding. Moreover, the specific time during the retention interval at which the distracting stimulus was interpolated made no difference in retention.

(4)   Several studies have shown better retention with longer *intertrial intervals* (Gleitman et al., 1963; Waugh & Norman, 1965). Jarrard and Moise (1971) used intertrial intervals of 5, 15, 30, or 60 seconds in a delayed matching to sample task. Matching perfor-

mance over a delay was clearly better with the longer intertrial intervals (15–60 seconds).

Short-Term Memory in Learning-Set Behavior

Learning-set has sometimes been called "learning-to-learn," and refers to the observation that animals may increase their *rate* of learning with extensive practice on discrimination problems.

This phenomenon can be readily demonstrated in a variety of species when the subjects are given many problems in which they must discriminate between two objects. For example, a food pellet may be obtained if the "correct" object is moved by the monkey, but not when the alternative object is chosen. Each discrimination problem is given for a prescribed number of trials, often 6. After many such problems, the monkey achieves a "learning-set" such that essentially it obtains all the information it needs for solution on the first trial of each problem. Thus, performance on trial two is virtually 100 percent correct. The question is, how does the monkey accomplish this?

Intuitively, the answer is simple enough: the monkey learns that only one stimulus is correct for each problem. Hence, if the object selected is rewarded on the first trial, the animal will continue choosing that object; conversely, if it is not rewarded, the alternative stimulus will be selected on the remaining trials.[1]

Such an explanation is reasonably descriptive, but it does little to explain the fundamental basis of the monkey's behavior. Left unanswered is the fundamental question, how does the monkey come to appreciate, and to apply, the information presented on the first trial? For many years attempts were made to understand this phenomenon is terms of reinforcement and other principles used in theories of learning (*see* Harlow, 1959). More recently, an analysis of learning-set in terms of memory processes has been made (Bessemer, 1967; Bessemer & Stollnitz, 1971).

Bessemer suggested that lower primates also may acquire an "hypothesis," which may be stated for the case of typical learning-set procedures as "win-stay, lose-shift." The use of such an hypothesis would be expected to be accompanied by the following characteristics of retention: (a) If correct responding is to occur on Trial 2, the monkey must retain information representing the object

---

1. Although most studies of learning-set have involved primates as subjects, the phenomenon is not restricted to such species. Rats can acquire a learning-set as readily as primates if olfactory (rather than visual) stimuli are used as the cues (e.g., Slotnick & Katz, 1974).

chosen on Trial 1, whether or not that choice was rewarded; (b) As more problems are experienced, retention for the objects presented on earlier problems need not occur; indeed, such retention would be maladaptive because it might interfere with the solution of new problems; (c) We would expect, on the other hand, that the win-stay, lose-shift hypothesis itself should be retained over very long intervals. The existence of these three characteristics is supported by the following data.

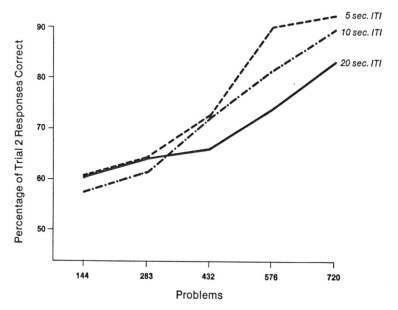

Figure 13–7. This figure shows the mean percentage of correct responses given on the second trial of a discrimination problem as a function of the number of problems experienced and the interval between Trial 1 and Trial 2. The results indicate the acquisition of learning-set with increasing numbers of problems, and in addition that the longer the interval (ITI) between Trial 1 and Trial 2, the less successful is the monkey in utilizing the information acquired on Trial 1. (From Deets, Harlow, & Blomquist, 1970.)

The first characteristic suggests that Trial 2 performance requires the memory of Trial 1, thus it should be very sensitive to the interval between Trial 1 and Trial 2 or, more generally, to any manipulation that affects retention of information acquired on Trial 1. Deets, Harlow, and Blomquist (1970) have shown that after learning-set is well established, Trial 2 performance is good with a 5-second interval, but becomes progressively worse with 10- and 20-second intervals (*see* Figure 13–7).

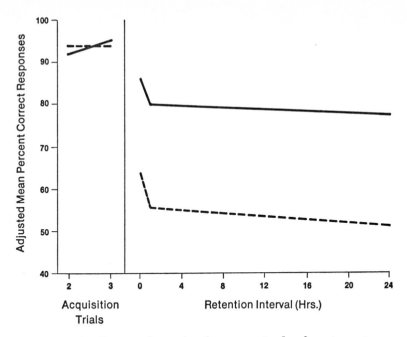

Figure 13–8. For monkeys that have acquired a learning-set percentage correct responses is shown following three acquisition trials
(on which, as indicated, solution was attained by the monkeys) by
intervals of either 2–3 minutes, 1 hour, or 24 hours. Very rapid forgetting is indicated during the first hour of the retention interval.
The upper line indicates performance on problems for which the
monkeys' choice on the first acquisition trial had been correct and
rewarded, and the lower line indicates performance on problems in
which their first choice had been incorrect and nonrewarded. (From
Bessemer & Stollnitz, 1971.)

The second characteristic suggests that there should be rapid
forgetting of the specific stimulus-reward relationships experienced in earlier problems. Consistent with this, Bessemer and
Stollnitz (1971) found very rapid onset of forgetting of specific problems. They gave a series of problems, and measured retention after
intervals of either 2–3 minutes, 1 hour, or 24 hours. What they
found was a good deal of retention decrement after 2–3 minutes,
and nearly maximum decrement after 1 hour (*see* Figure 13–8).
This indicates that as a consequence of information processed
about learning-set tasks, the monkey does not allow specific contingencies of reinforcement to influence its behavior for very long.

This does not necessarily imply that the loss of memory is complete. Other experiments have shown that the animals may recall
that specific stimuli have been seen, even though the specific
stimulus-reward relationships are forgotten.

The third characteristic suggests that the learning-set itself—the "hypothesis" of win-stay, lose-shift—is retained over long periods. Most tests given after intervals of months or a few years have shown essentially no loss in learning efficiency. After longer periods learning-set may be partially forgotten, however. Stollnitz (1970) tested monkeys after a 6-year interval during which they experienced only a few discrimination problems. He found a general loss in retention of learning-set performance, including an average decline of 23 percent in accuracy on Trial 2.

The point of this section has been to show how the study of retention and forgetting may have value beyond the specific retention phenomena being tested. Bessemer has added insight into an established phenomenon of behavior, learning-set, by analyzing the characteristic changes in short-term memory that accompany the development of this phenomenon. In doing so, he has added to our understanding of both learning-set and short-term memory.

Indirect Evidence for Special Memory Processing Soon After Learning

Short-term memory has been studied with another method which is quite different from the direct assessment of retention after short intervals. Very generally, this method involves two steps. The first is to apply, shortly after learning, treatments intended to alter memory processing. The second step is to test net retention, but not until the side effects of the treatment have dissipated. Treatments that have been most often applied in this context are those that decrease retention, but some treatments that facilitate retention also have been studied.

We have mentioned how some traumatic events, such as a blow to the head, may impair retention for immediately preceding events. This is called "retrograde amnesia"—"amnesia" because of the retention loss (although literally amnesia refers to the complete absence of memory) and "retrograde" because the trauma acts on the memories of past events. A number of treatments which can cause retrograde amnesia have been identified, and we know to some extent how far backward in time they may be effective. Other treatments have been used experimentally to produce or enhance memory (sometimes referred to as "hypermnesia"). Such an effect may be produced by appropriate doses of strychnine and other central nervous system stimulants.

In principle, we should be able to experimentally manipulate retrograde amnesia to provide inferences about memory processes that occur shortly after learning. An assessment of the memory processing that occurred during learning may be found by introducing an amnesic treatment at various intervals after learning. The inference about short-term memory processes requires two simple assumptions. First, we assume that memory processing is halted or otherwise disrupted by an amnesic treatment. Next, we assume that the memory processing that occurs between learning and the time of the amnesic treatment contributes somehow to later behavior. On this basis, we should be able to assess indirectly the memory processing that occurs between learning and the amnesic treatment just as we assess directly such memory processing by simply measuring retention after short intervals following learning.

Importance of Retrograde Effects on Memory

The effect of independent variables on memory processes, especially memory retrieval, may be most clearly assessed when the variation is imposed long after acquisition of the memory. But the fact is that the most dramatic effects of amnesic or hypermnesic treatments are obtained when they are applied just prior to, or immediately following, training. Experiments of this kind are likely to be relatively uninteresting for understanding learning and memory, however. For example, amnesic treatments prior to training or very shortly thereafter (say, 500 milliseconds, or less) may impair perceptual processes. To take an extreme case, it would be trivial to show that amnesia results when electroconvulsive shock (ECS) is delivered to an animal just prior to a training trial, because we know that little or none of the world is perceived just after an ECS. We also know that backward masking of perception may occur. As we have seen above, backward masking is defined when events that follow very soon after a stimulus prevent or alter perception of that stimulus.

The clearest interpretation may be obtained when a *retrograde amnesia gradient* is measured. A retrograde amnesia gradient, for our purposes, is the critical relationship indicating that an amnesic agent is more effective if it is introduced soon after training than if it is introduced at a later time (*see* Figure 13–9).

A gradient of retrograde amnesia implies characteristics of an amnesic agent that are particularly important. First, by showing that an effect caused soon after training is not also produced by a later application of the treatment, one can be reasonably certain the amnesia is not a consequence of having permanently impaired the animal's capacity to perform at the retention test. To take an extreme example, assume that the amnesic treatment produced blindness; the same low retention score would occur no matter when the treatment is given, i.e., there would be no gradient. Even if the blindness were only temporary, it could not account for the retrograde amnesia gradient, because in this gradient the greatest effects occur at the point most removed from the retention test, and this would allow more time for recovery. Therefore, one can safely assume that the effects produced by an amnesic treatment are on retention and not on perceptual or motivational variables.

Post-training memory processes are very important theoretically. It has been assumed that memory storage requires the operation of a "consolidation" process that accounts for the manner in which an internal representation of external events is established in the central nervous system. The occurrence of the retrograde amnesia gradient shows that this consolidation process takes longer than the time involved in the perception per se of the external event. We turn now to specific agents which, when introduced shortly after learning, impair subsequent retention.

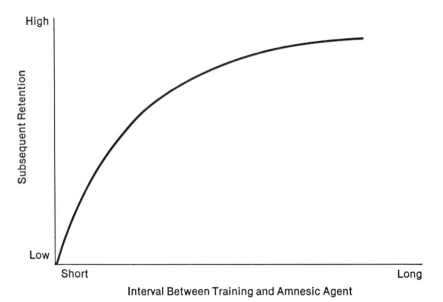

Figure 13–9. Idealized gradient of retrograde amnesia. The curve represents the progressively decreasing influence of amnesic agent on subsequent retention the longer the interval between training and administration of the amnesic agent.

Sources of Retrograde Amnesia

A wide variety of techniques have been used to produce retrograde amnesia, thereby supporting the notion of special processing soon after learning.

(1)   One of the most widely used techniques for producing re-trograde amnesia is the administration of *electroconvulsive shock* (ECS). This treatment involves the passage of a relatively powerful electric current through the brain via electrodes attached to the ears, the cornea, or the scalp. These treatments have been used experimentally as well as clinically. In the latter case, the treatment is used most often to treat severely depressed human patients. Both the experimental data and the clinical data agree that this treatment produces a severe impairment of retention for the events that im-mediately preceded the administration of the ECS, but not for events that were learned at earlier times.

(2)   A variation of the ECS treatment involves the *direct stimu-lation of the brain* via implanted electrodes. The use of this treat-ment has been almost exclusively limited to experimental pur-poses, and the results are generally consistent with those of exper-iments involving ECS—the major difference is in terms of the current parameters. One advantage of this technique is that it may help eventually to identify the structures of the brain that are criti-cally involved in memory processing.

(3)   The retrograde gradient has also been produced by the drastic lowering of body temperature, *hypothermia*, immediately following learning. This procedure has been used quite success-fully by Riccio et al. (1968) who used the procedure of dunking the rats in cold water to lower the body temperature by about 30 de-grees within a few minutes.

(4)   The ability of the brain to function normally is rapidly im-paired by *hypoxia*, or lowered level of oxygen. This can be induced experimentally by placing the animal in a small enclosed capsule or in a chamber that is devoid of oxygen.

(5)   An interesting source of retrograde amnesia has been termed *psychological incongruity*. An ingenious study of Pavlovian conditioning in the rabbit by Wagner, Rudy, and Whitlow (1973), has indicated that an "unexpected" combination of environmental events shortly after a learning trial may disrupt subsequent reten-tion. The unexpected or incongruous pairing of events consisted of presenting a stimulus (e.g., a clicking noise) followed immediately by a mild electrical shock to the eyelid when, in the animal's past, that clicking noise always signaled that *no* shock would occur. Another incongruous event would be presentation of a flashing light which previously had consistently predicted the occurrence of shock, but now was *not* followed by shock.

Wagner et al. found that if such incongruous events follow shortly after a learning trial, learning is impaired. As with the amnesic agents mentioned above, impairment did not occur if a sufficient duration elapsed between a learning trial and presentation of the incongruous event. This suggested that the retarded learning was not a consequence of conflicting information acquired from aspects of the incongruous events but rather, in accord with Wagner's theory, it was the incongruity per se which resulted in a sort of retrograde amnesia.

(6)   Finally, a wide variety of drugs have been used to induce amnesia, and if properly administered, the retrograde gradient. Two classes of compounds are of particular importance in this regard. Anesthetics are quite effective in inducing retrograde amnesia, as might be expected. Another class of compounds, protein synthesis inhibitors, also produce retrograde amnesia—a finding that has attracted considerable theoretical interest.

IV. SUMMARY

This chapter has focused upon the changes in retention which occur with the passage of time. The relationship between retention and length of the retention interval was shown to vary markedly, depending upon such factors as the conditions of learning and the task to be learned, together with other factors. Consideration was given the circumstances responsible for some cases of progressively improving retention, temporarily impaired retention, and multiphasic retention functions of various forms.

Particularly the course of retention is likely to be modified by explicit events which occur during the retention interval, especially those occurring in close proximity to the retention test. In considering this point, it was noted that neither total recall of, nor complete failure to recall, events of learning were likely to be detected with any known techniques of measurement if such behavior is probable or even possible.

It was suggested that a variety of events, including structure of the retention test itself, could influence retention, perhaps through an influence on the memory-retrieval process. An example was provided in considerations of recognition-versus-recall tests of retention. Finally, a set of events occurring during the retention interval, termed "reactivation treatments," were discussed in terms of their influence in alleviating forgetting and their apparent modification of the accessibility of memories in other ways as well.

The separate consideration of retention after short and after long intervals was considered. Although evidence does not appear to demand that the processing of memories manifested shortly after learning be different from that of memories not required for much longer periods, characteristics of the former were considered separately primarily because the empirical study of short-term retention has been separate from that of long-term retention.

Techniques for studying short-term retention in normal humans and animals were discussed, followed by a review of a variety of factors tested as possible determinants of the rate at which unitary stimuli are forgotten over short intervals. Few factors were found to influence forgetting (independent of degree of original learning) under these circumstances. Those which do appear to do so include the degree of illumination during the retention interval (when visual stimuli are processed as memories), degree and kind of experience with similar problems of short-term retention, and perhaps some aspects of the content of the memory including degree of stimulus redundancy. Finally, the study of retrograde amnesia was discussed as one experimental technique useful for understanding the processing of memories during short intervals following learning.

Sources of Forgetting

---

*Pictures hanging in a hallway
and the fragment of a song,
Half-remembered names and faces,
but to whom do they belong?*

Berger & Berger, *The Windmills of Your Mind*

We have seen that acquired memories are not inevitably accessible. In a word, forgetting occurs. We have seen something of the circumstances under which forgetting is more or less likely to occur. But we have not, as yet, considered in any detail just *why* forgetting sometimes occurs and sometimes does not. The purpose of this chapter is to consider *why*.

In this chapter we shall consider the progress that has been made in understanding the bases of two general sorts of forgetting. One is the most typical forgetting that occurs in the day-to-day "normal" processing of memories. The other concerns forgetting that arises under relatively abnormal circumstances, typically involving some general malfunction or specific insult of the organism's neurophysiological system.

I. FORGETTING IN THE NORMAL PROCESSING OF MEMORIES

Throughout this section, it is well to keep in mind that forgetting is not entirely maladaptive. Although it is frustrating to find acquired information inaccessible to our use, we also can appreciate the intolerable confusion that would result if, whenever we began to dial a telephone, we retrieved simultaneously all possible numbers we have ever learned.

Given that forgetting is an adaptive psychological activity, we may expect to find its occurrence rather universal and its sources more natural than mysterious. Indeed, even in ancient Greece the inclination was not to invoke demons as the cause of forgetting, but rather to relate it to what was then known about nature. For example, forgetting was once attributed to a disruption in the distribution of light, dark, heat, and cold in the body. Another suggestion was that forgetting was a consequence of the unequal distribution of air throughout the body, inspired apparently by people who exhaled (sighed) in relief upon retrieval of an important memory.

There is reason to believe that our theorizing has advanced somewhat from that of ancient Greece. More recently, suggested causes of forgetting have involved relatively concrete testable factors like interference from conflicting memories. Unlike theorizing about motivation, in which we often find explanations in the form "the devil [or some other motivational force] made me do it," the field of memory is relatively free of theories of the analogous form "the devil made me forget it." One proposed source of forgetting is dangerously close, however. This is "decay," to which we now turn.

Decay Theory

A retention curve which declines in time may be said to be a "decaying function." In this descriptive sense the use of the term "decay" is quite innocuous; but then it also lacks explanatory power. Historically, the unfortunate custom has been to slip into the use of "decay" to *explain* a decreasing retention curve. Unless decay itself can be tied to something observable in nature, it does not really help scientifically to say "the retention decrement was due to the decay of the memory," because this translates as "the retention decrement was due to the retention decrement of the memory" (the term "forgetting" sometimes has been used in a similarly inappropriate fashion). Decay, as McGeoch (1932) has emphasized, must be related meaningfully to concrete events that occur in time if it is to be of scientific benefit. Time alone explains nothing.

One should not get the impression that decay is inevitably useless for explaining forgetting, because it is not. Suppose the biological substrate of a memory were explicitly identified as, say, a clump of cells somewhere in the brain. Suppose further that some progressive changes in these cells, such as their death or general metabolic turnover, coincided with the rate of forgetting of that memory. Under these circumstances, one surely would be justified in referring to those biological changes collectively as "decay" and then proceeding to apply the term for explanation.

Equally, one would be justified in using decay as an intervening variable. As such, the term might summarize a common effect resulting from, say, various ways of varying the metabolism of the brain in combination with various ways of assessing forgetting (if forgetting were indeed found to depend upon the rate of metabolism in the brain).

As yet, we do not appear to be in a position to apply decay for explanation in such a meaningful way. And even if we could, if the above conditions were met, we would need to remain cautious. We must recognize that changes—even deterioration—in the composition of a physiological substrate of memory, do not necessarily imply disintegration of a memory. Such changes might instead imply development of the memory, storage of new information rather than destruction of old. This may be seen by analogy with the construction of a computer. Electronic parts used to process or represent information may ordinarily be integrated by making the appropriate connections with wire; but, theoretically, one could accomplish the same end by beginning with all components wired in all possible ways and then selectively snipping the inappropriate connections. Similarly, the death of cells or reduced connections in the physiological substrate of a memory could represent newly acquired information, and there is some evidence for this possibility (Rosenzweig, Mollgaard, Diamond, & Bennett, 1972).

Interference Theory

There is virtually no disagreement about the fact that one source of forgetting is the acquisition of conflicting memories. The influence of interference on retention has been analyzed systematically. The result is general agreement upon certain processes underlying the effect. So, it is quite proper to speak of an "Interference Theory" within which interference-induced forgetting may be evaluated and analyzed. For a more thorough history and description of the basic content of Interference Theory, two excellent sources dealing with verbal learning are papers by Postman (1971) and Postman and Underwood (1973).

Our present interest concerns Interference Theory in a broad sense and how its principles might apply toward understanding forgetting generally, beyond verbal learning.

The Cornerstone of Interference Theory

Interference theory rests on this notion: interference in retention depends upon the similarity between the materials to be retained and the interfering materials. Specifying what we mean by similarity is another matter, however. It is here that the complexity arises.

We can be fairly certain that acquiring the proper motion for the forehand and backhand in tennis is unlikely to interfere with retention of the words to your favorite popular song. But what about the effect of learning the tennis motions on remembering the best movement in squash or handball, or the effect of learning one new song on remembering another? From here, the questions get progressively more complex. For example, if you are to remember a list of words like PEAR, LION and MATCH, each paired uniquely with a specific stimulus, will the subsequent learning of a list including PEER, LINE, and MASK be more likely to cause forgetting than a list like APPLE, TIGER and LIGHTER? In other words, is acoustical similarity more important than semantic similarity for determining interference in retention?

Such complexities may be dealt with, however, while maintaining the general tenet of interference theory: This is, generally, that if the respective contents of two memories are not at all similar, there is no reason to expect the learning of one will influence the retention of the other.

Basic Mechanisms of Interference

The basic mechanisms of Interference Theory can best be appreciated if we remember that it was developed to account for the forgetting of lists of paired verbal units. The items had been learned according to these sorts of instructions: "When a word appears, try to say the word previously paired with it." A sound argument can be made that such a list is the prototype of much learning undergone by humans. In any case, this probably was the most analytical procedure with which to begin.

The questions to be answered by the mechanisms of interference come about when subjects learn two similar lists, say, in which the first member of each pair of words is the same, but the second member is different (*see* Table 14–1). One question is, why is retention of the first list impaired by having learned the second (i.e., why does retroactive interference occur)? The other question is why is retention of the second list impaired by having learned the first (i.e., why does proactive interference occur)?

There are two sets of interference mechanisms. The first set is addressed, essentially, to considerations of how an organism might get "mixed-up" about which environmental event belongs to which memory. In the case of humans having learned two lists of the kind

Table 14–1. *Mechanism of Interference*

List 1	List 2	Test
cup / desk	cup / lock	cup / ?
box / card	box / shelf	door / ?
door / soup	door / home	door / ?

Learn List 1	Interval	Learn List 2	Interval	Test either List 1 or List 2

just described, this mix-up might occur as "response competition." Although two responses have been paired with the same stimulus words, one pairing occurring in the first list and another in the second list, only one response can be given if only one list is tested for retention. So, if the incorrect response happens to be dominant at the moment of the test, forgetting is inferred.

This conception was thought initially to have a great advantage in that one could actually observe this mechanism at work. It first appeared that the extent of response competition could be measured directly in terms of the number of times the incorrect response was given, as an objective measure of forgetting. But it was soon discovered that, under such circumstances, subjects most often give no response at all when forgetting occurs, and anyway, the number of incorrect responses given (i.e., intrusions) is not a very good indicator of the actual amount of forgetting.

A specific example of the mix-up mechanism is "list differentiation." Forgetting may be attributed to a failure in list differentiation when a human recalls an item "correctly" in that he had learned it within the context of the experiment, but recalls it with reference to the inappropriate list of items. In other words, when the learning of one list interferes with retention of the other, one of the memory attributes lost is identification to which list the particular item belongs. This mechanism has been important for explaining proactive interference. It has the advantage of being directly testable, which permits better understanding of its characteristics. There can be no doubt that Interference Theory explains thoroughly and accurately a variety of phenomena concerning human retention, but complexity arises from a number of sources when considering animal memory:

(1) Humans may be instructed about *what* to remember; animals, however, are not so instructed. If an organism has acquired two or more conflicting memories in succession, it is one thing to test retention of a particular memory the subject is instructed to remember and quite another to simply "test retention," without reference to which memory is being tested. The latter, of course, is precisely what must be done with lower animals. Thus for animals, far more than for humans, the consequences of interference in retention are tied closely to the organism's disposition to do the last thing learned, together with the similarity between the context of testing and the contexts associated with either of the previous episodes of learning.

(2) An equally obvious difference is the content of memories tested in animals and humans. Most memories tested in animals involve a single discrete response signaled by a single stimulus, whereas those with humans more typically involve sets of stimuli

and responses. Some of the more important concepts of Interference Theory, such as list differentiation, are intended to deal with sets of stimuli and responses. Obviously, these mechanisms cannot be applied readily to many cases of animal memory.

Changes in Contextual Stimuli

The theoretical mechanisms of Interference Theory have evolved primarily for tests of human memory. What is needed is the evolution of a set of mechanisms to account for the effects of interference and retention in animals. One possibility is in terms of the influence of contextual stimuli.

An animal may respond to any of three classes of stimuli during a retention test. The first class are those stimuli which formed the critical contingencies of training, including perhaps a conditioned or discriminative stimulus and some sort of reinforcer as a food pellet or a footshock. A second class of stimuli—possibly of equal importance for retrieval of a memory—may be termed "contextual stimuli." These are stimuli which, while not an essential component of the reinforcement contingencies of training, are nevertheless closely correlated with the occurrence of those reinforcement contingencies. In other words, certain stimuli like the particular room that contains the training apparatus may be called contextual stimuli because, for the most part, the animal is exposed to this room only when he is also exposed to a particular set of training conditions. Probably, the animal notices a good number of contextual stimuli during training and such contextual stimuli are likely to be represented as attributes of the memory of training. A third class of stimuli are novel events to which the animal has not previously been exposed during training. Modification of any of these three classes of stimuli may influence retention *performance*, but for differing reasons.

Alteration of the first class of stimuli need not be considered here. Stimuli such as the CS and UCS which define the reinforcement contingencies must not be changed, because it is the assessment of the permanence of these contingencies that is the fundamental purpose of the retention test. If the CS is changed, we are studying stimulus generalization rather than retention; if the UCS changes, we are studying shifts in reinforcement conditions, not retention.

Contextual stimuli, however, are very susceptible to change between memory acquisition and the retention test. Contextual stimuli may include both the internal physiological conditions of the animal and the external environment, and changes in these are likely from either uncontrolled or experimentally controlled sources. The removal or disappearance of contextual stimuli is likely to impair retention by decreasing the number of potential retrieval cues to which the animal is exposed. If a contextual stimulus is not only removed but also replaced by a stimulus represented in a conflicting memory, the conflicting memory may be retrieved. Given such an "interference" effect, a retention deficit will be recorded. These cases represent the fundamental sources of failure in memory retrieval.

If a novel stimulus appears at the retention test, performance may be impaired for reasons unrelated to memory processing. Animals, and humans too, respond in very particular ways to unexpected (novel) stimuli. A common example is when your dog perks up its ears and raises its head in response to an unusual sound. Such responses are called "orienting responses." When they occur, the animal's attention may be diverted from the conditioned, discriminative or contextual stimuli present. Novel stimuli may thus provoke unconditioned exploratory responding which interferes with the expression of the learned behavior. We should be aware of how performance on a retention test may be impaired by novel stimuli in order to control them and avoid contamination of our analysis of memory processing.

These details aside, we turn now to a few brief examples of how memory retrieval may be controlled by contextual stimuli.

External Contextual Stimuli

A phenomenon termed "switching" has been studied by the Russian psychologist Asratian and his colleagues (Asratian, 1965). "Switching" may be exemplified as follows: (1) A dog is given several presentations of a bell followed by a mild footshock and becomes conditioned to withdraw its foot upon the occurrence of the bell. Pairings of the bell and footshock are given each morning by a particular experimenter. (2) Each afternoon, a different experimenter conditions the same dog by presenting the identical bell, but instead of a subsequent footshock, this time the bell is followed by food placed into the mouth of the dog, and the aim is to induce conditioned salivation.

Before long, whenever the test is given in the morning by the first experimenter, the dog responds to the bell by withdrawing its foot but not salivating; in the afternoon, when tested by the second experimenter, the dog responds to the same bell by salivating, but does not withdraw its foot. If some aspect of the context is changed —for example, if the second experimenter should test the dog in the morning or the first experimenter test it in the afternoon—then the animal is likely to both salivate and withdraw its foot in response to the bell.

Such an effect may be interpreted in several ways. Generally, though, the implication is that the contextual stimuli, the experimenter, and time of day were important discriminative attributes of otherwise conflicting memories.

Stimulus context also has been shown to control memory retrieval under circumstances in which the experiments are less susceptible to alternative interpretation than are Asratian's. For example, if rats are given a single session of training to turn right for food in a T-maze and then are given a session of learning to turn left, but in a different experimental room, alternative retrieval of the memories to turn right or to turn left appears to be determined by the room in which the animal is tested (Chiszar & Spear, 1969).

A similar instance is found if rats are trained first to remain in a small compartment and not jump over a hurdle into an alternative compartment; and next, in a different room but with identical apparatus, they are trained to jump rapidly over the hurdle. Subsequently, responding is controlled by the room in which they are tested. If tested in the first room, most of the rats don't jump the hurdle at all on most of the test trials; if tested in the second room, most of the rats jump the hurdle very rapidly (less than 5 seconds) on most of the test trials. The implication is that retrieval of a particular target memory attribute (representing "not jumping" or "jumping fast") was selectively aroused by exposure to the contextual stimuli represented by attributes of that same memory.

It is true, of course, that animals which have acquired two or more conflicting memories must depend upon stimulus context for "instructions" about what it is they are to remember. This provides part of the function of the retrieval cues, but not all. Retention by animals also may be influenced by changes in stimulus context when they have undergone only a single session of learning in the laboratory. Furthermore, retention by humans (who obviously *can* be instructed about what to remember) may be influenced considerably by apparently trivial changes in the environment. For example, if humans learn a list of words while they are lying down, they may be better able later to recall those words when lying down than when they are standing up (Rand & Wapner, 1967).

Internal Contextual Stimuli

Retention may be controlled dramatically by drug-induced alteration of an animal's internal environment. An animal trained while under the influence of a particular drug may show little evidence of retention after the effect of that drug has worn off, or if a different drug is injected. But if the animal is tested while under the influence of the same drug as during training, retention will be about as good as if the animal had not been drugged during either training or testing (i.e., the drug state functions as a retrieval cue). It is as if expression of learning depends upon the state of the animal during testing relative to that during training. Accordingly, such effects have been termed "state-dependent learning."

Animals will readily learn that a particular drug state indicates which of two alternative behaviors is more appropriate. This may be interpreted to imply that a particular drug state becomes an attribute of the same memory as a particular behavior, and that the probability of retrieving that memory is increased whenever that drug state occurs. In terms of specific examples, rats can readily learn that if they have been injected with a particular drug, they must turn right in a T-maze in order to escape shock, but if injected with a different drug, they must turn left. Monkeys will learn which of two visual patterns they should select in order to receive food when under the influence of a particular drug and that, when under the other drug, the food can be obtained only by selecting the alternative pattern.

The critical point about such cases is that these animals come to respond appropriately *before* the presence of reward signals which alternative is correct. Accurate responding is therefore possible only on the basis of their drug state.

Aging

Aging has appeared to influence retention in two ways. First, there appears to be a deficit in retention after short intervals for both very young organisms and very old organisms. At this time it is unclear whether the basis of this apparent deficit is due to impaired perception, learning or memory-storage processes, or if this represents a genuine deficit in retention. Perhaps a clearer effect of aging on retention per se is a phenomenon sometimes termed "infantile amnesia." Reference here is to the common inability for adult humans to recall events occurring in their life before about the age of three.

It should be clear that aging itself is not an especially satisfactory explanatory device for understanding memory processing. As a causal factor, aging is rather like the concept "time." It is best defined in terms of correlated events, in this case the behavioral and physiological changes that take place as the organism grows older.

We have implied a difficulty in precisely assessing the basis of the apparent short-term retention deficit in very old organisms.

This difficulty may be traced to some general problems in conducting research with aged beings. For instance, there is really no sound basis for assessing motivational differences between aged and younger humans or animals. Also, the use of very old animals is an expensive matter because of the long period of maintenance required. Finally, there is the inevitable difficulty of pathology associated with old age and of subject selection—might not organisms that die at younger ages differ from those having greater longevity in terms of their capacity for memory processing? Old organisms are very susceptible to disease and general physiological malfunction. These afflictions might contribute to a deficit in memory processing and yet go unnoticed as a causal factor. To take an extreme, and somewhat morbid example, there are indications that a declining capacity for short-term retention in humans is a good predictor of death within a year's time, at least for certain, mainly institutionalized, populations. It seems unlikely that such retention deficits reflect the typical consequences of aging in any general sense; rather these deficits are more probably linked to whatever pathology is responsible for imminent death.

Knowledge of the retention deficit at the other extreme, very young ages, is likely to progress more rapidly. The neurophysiological development of certain animals, from birth to adulthood, is rapidly becoming identified and understood. This should facilitate research concerning the contribution of neurophysiological systems to the ontogeny of memory processing. Also, techniques for studying learning and retention in human infants, even those only a day or two old, are becoming perfected.

It must be admitted, though, that behavioral techniques for studying retention in neonates still leave a good deal to be desired. There is no problem in studying precocial animals, like the guinea pig, which are born with a nearly fully developed central nervous system, and a capacity to learn within an hour or so of birth at rates comparable to adults of the species. The technical difficulties lie in the testing of altricial animals like the rat and mouse, and in most ways these are the more interesting animals to study. Such altricial animals show clear changes in cognitive behaviors as the animal matures, and we should remember also that the human is an altricial organism.

What we do know is that with the rat and mouse there are gross deficiencies in acquiring new information from the time of birth until at least the time of weaning, about 21 days of age in most laboratories. Within the first week of life, there is little indication of any capacity for learning in the rat. Fortunately for the rat population, survival during this time doesn't depend on new learning, assuming the rat's mother is reasonably competent. The newborn rat is an amazingly robust organism, capable of surviving deprivation of oxygen for almost an hour, and the lowering of temperatures to 1 degree centigrade (the adult rat is rendered unconscious after a few seconds of oxygen deprivation and will die if his temperature drops below 15 degrees centigrade).

Beginning at about 8 or 9 days of age, there is good evidence that new information may be acquired and retained over at least several hours. By the age of 15 or 16 days, after the rat's eyes have opened and mobility is more adultlike, learning can be demonstrated in a variety of situations. However, a problem arises for researchers interested in retention because it is very difficult to equate the level of original learning by these very young infants with that of older animals. And, in addition to the usual controls necessary to separate maturation from learning, we must also worry about how certain tasks might be especially influenced by maturation of specific capacities. For example, at age 8 or 9 days when the rat has appeared to begin showing a capacity for retention over several hours, the rat also leaps forward in his capacity for processing olfactory information. So, we must ask to what extent the retention we measure might be simply a reflection of this newly acquired olfactory skill.

The capacities for acquisition of information and the short-term retention of this information may be impossible to separate in very young organisms; these two capacities are linked closely, even in adults. However, current research is being conducted with the assumption that it will be possible to demonstrate a deficit in short-term retrieval that is not dependent on a deficit in original acquisition.

When humans have reached the age of 2 years or so, and rats the age of 20 days or so, their capacity for some kinds of memory processing can be said to be adultlike. We know that toddlers readily learn and retain a good deal of information, such as the location of their toys and the names of their relatives and playmates. Rats between the ages of 20 and 25 days learn and retain over short periods with an efficiency often indistinguishable from that of adults. But after long intervals—several years in the case of humans, several weeks in the case of rats—these young humans and animals show more forgetting than their adult counterparts. This long-term retention deficit by infants is what has been termed "infantile amnesia."

The evidence for infantile amnesia in humans cannot really be said to be impressive because it has not been demonstrated experimentally in a convincing fashion. Among five of the more extensive studies of this sort, the average age of the earliest memory recalled varied between 3 and 3.8 years. On only about 4 percent of the occasions were memories recalled that were acquired before the age of one year. Women tended to recall earlier memories than men, and usually included more detail in their early memories. Also, women were more likely to recall memories involving joy, while men more often recalled memories involving fear.

It is difficult, of course, to put much credence in this sort of evidence. The problems of validity are enormous. So, however entertaining this sort of evidence might be, this is one of those frequent occasions in which one must turn to research will lower animals for solid answers with any sort of analytical potential.

We have mentioned that beginning about the age of 20 days, some tasks may be learned as rapidly by immature rats as by adults. This fact, together with some very careful considerations of how motivational factors may be equated (*see* Campbell, 1967), has permitted the study of retention differences in immature and mature rats independent of learning and motivational differences. Even under these circumstances, numerous studies have shown that retention after long intervals is poorer by the immature than the mature animals. Reviews of these studies may be examined for more detail (Campbell & Spear, 1972).

Potential explanations for infantile amnesia are easy enough to generate. Much of the emphasis for the early investigations of human infantile amnesia may be traced to Freud's explanation of such forgetting as a consequence of the repression of infantile sexuality. Three other explanations of the day were summarized by Allport (1937) as the following: (1) Human infants are deficient verbally and so memories of events occurring before about the age of 3 do not reach the state of "conscious conceptualization"; (2) the context of the infant's existence, sleeping in a crib on the floor, being patted on the head or spanked, are so different from that of adulthood that expression of infant memories is unlikely in adulthood; and (3) in terms of the limited physiological knowledge of the day, the long-recognized deficiency of myelin in the brain of infants was thought to limit the infant's capacity to store memory traces.

While it now seems unlikely that myelin has much to do directly with the storage of memories, and while the scientific value of the concept "repression" is questionable, the remaining two alternatives remain plausible explanations today, in one form or another. The problem is that any number of other explanations are about equally plausible, and relatively little hard evidence exists on which to base a decision. In attempting to explain, Campbell and Spear (1972) found it useful to consider separately those factors which are primarily experiential and behavioral on the one hand, and neurophysiological on the other. In the growing organism, the onset of certain species-specific behaviors (imprinting, for example) or the acquisition of conflicting memories may interfere with early memories. Similarly, maturation-induced changes in information processing (such as perceptual learning) may impair retrieval of early memories or their translation into adultlike behaviors.

On the physiological side, developmental changes of potential importance for memory processing include the dramatic increase in the number of neural synapses that occurs as neural cells develop a full set of dendritic branches. As illustrated in Figure 14–1, the number of interconnections, synapses, between cells increases astronomically in maturing animals. In the rat, for example, the number of synaptic junctions increases about tenfold between the ages of 15 and 30 days. This is pertinent because synaptic junctions have long been considered a critical site for memory storage, and because it is within this age range of 15–30 days that the capacity for long-term retention appears to increase dramatically.

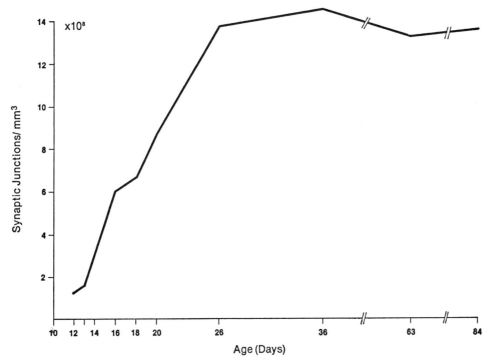

Figure 14–1. The rapid increase in the number of synapses in the brain of the developing rat is shown to be especially marked between the postnatal ages of about 15 and 25 days. The number of synapses at each age are based upon actual counts from thin layers of the parietal cortex and derived on a basis of a mathematical model. (From Aghajanian & Bloom, 1967.)

It is intriguing to speculate on the possible significance of this relationship. For example, perhaps memories may ordinarily be sorted in a number of different places in the brain ("redundant representation"). This would provide a general protective advantage and should facilitate later retrieval. In the immature rat, then, memories may be stored with less redundancy, which may limit the effectiveness of subsequent retrieval of these memories. Also, the subsequent addition of new synaptic connections in the maturing rat may make earlier memorial representations less accessible as more intricate circuits overlay the earlier ones. Hence, the early memories may be retrieved less effectively as adults. Further suggestions of this sort may be found in the paper by Campbell and Spear, although at this point, again, there is little hard evidence on which to base theoretical decisions.

II. FORGETTING IN THE ABNORMAL PROCESSING OF MEMORY

We are concerned in this section with the consequences of physiological trauma. Types of trauma of special importance for memory processing are severe brain concussion and, of course, direct cellular damage or lesions in the brain itself. Accidents are the typical source of these sorts of trauma. Damage to the side of the head is particularly significant for our purposes because it is here, in the temporal region, where damage seems to alter memory processing dramatically.

In dealing with the effects of trauma, there are two general considerations to be kept in mind. The first is whether physiological trauma ever affects memories that were stored for a long period prior to the trauma. We already have seen the retrograde amnesia gradient and how it clearly shows that memories acquired just prior to a physiological insult are disrupted more than those acquired in the distant past.

What is not clear in these situations is whether old memories are affected at all. What we are concerned with here are memories that were acquired months or years prior to physiological trauma, so that available studies of the retrograde amnesia gradient do not really apply. This is a difficult problem with which to deal experimentally. Accordingly, little systematic evidence is available for deciding this issue. There is evidence that certain brain lesions in monkeys may disrupt memories acquired days before (Iverson, 1973), but again, this does not reach into the past as far as one might like.

Fortunately, some preliminary studies have been conducted on retention of very old memories in brain-damaged humans by Elizabeth Warrington and her colleagues. These investigators devised questionnaires to test the recall or recognition of events to which their patients should have been exposed in the past. Included were questions concerning events or pictures of individuals that have appeared in the news during the 1930s, 40s, 50s, 60s and 70s. The question was whether human amnesics, whose brain damage had occurred relatively recently, were as deficient in processing these old memories as in processing more recent ones. In comparison with nonamnesic but otherwise comparable patients, the amnesic patients were found to be quite deficient for memories presumably acquired in the distant past, prior to their affliction. Surprisingly, these results indicated that the amnesics' deficiencies for old memories were about as great as that for more recent memories.

The second general consideration concerns the importance of where in the brain the physiological damage or disruption occurs. This implies the possibility that some portions of the brain may be more important for the storage of memories than others. Lashley's famous conclusion, circa 1950, was that such a discrete storehouse of memories does not exist, at least not in the cortex of the brain. This generalization is no longer useful, however. It now appears that previously acquired memories may be disrupted by lesions in some areas of the cortex but not in others, and this occurs independently of sensory disruption. This is not to say that we can identify where particular memories are actually stored, but only to assert that the precise localization of insult to the brain is an important determinant of the extent to which memory processing may be disrupted.

Analysis of Amnesia in Humans

The range of mental dysfunction in humans which may be said to involve a deficit in memory processing is astounding, and so the difficulty of analyzing these cases is equally astounding. It would be hard to find a deficit in "memory processing" that has not already been recorded in medical history. Furthermore, each case includes idiosyncrasies which defy classification on any reasonably broad and useful diagnostic scale. As in other areas of medicine, complaints about the inadequacy of diagnostic classifications are not difficult to develop and support with "exceptional" cases.

We restrict the present discussion by first considering only those cases of amnesia concerned with retention of particular "episodes," a discrete set of events which occurred at a particular time in the person's history. This excludes other deficiencies in the application of stored memories, other gaps in previously acquired dispositions such as an inability to recognize and apply common words (aphasia) or more commonly when the deficit is relatively restricted (disphasia), a loss in retention of how certain learned movements are accomplished (apraxia), and so forth.

Some Case Histories

The specialized nature and subtlety of apparent gaps in stored memories of a nonepisodic nature may be illustrated by certain consequences of damage to the frontal portions of the brain. As Barbizet (1970) has noted, memory deficits in such victims are not at all obvious; these patients readily recognize objects, people and locations with which they have been exposed in the past; they can acquire new information, and are generally unconcerned about the possibility that their memory processing may be deficient. A case of this type has been described by Barbizet: a thirty-five-year-old man (Roger), who had been working as head storekeeper of a large factory at the time he suffered a trauma to the right frontal portion of the brain. Within three months this man had no obvious signs of abnormality, as determined by routine neurological tests, in his speech and his general ability to take care of himself. However, upon more thorough psychological testing, certain disorders of a memory-processing nature became apparent. His retention after shorter intervals was variable in accuracy, sometimes strikingly poor, and he showed unusual difficulty with certain tasks of a concept-formation nature, especially those which required retention of previous information to permit formation of a conceptual rule. The inability to hold new information for the purpose of problem-solving is exemplified in the following portion of an interview with Roger (from Barbizet, 1970, pp. 84–85):

Q. What is the length of one quarter of the Eiffel Tower?
A. After long hesitation, he said that he did not know.
Q. What is the height of the Eiffel Tower?
A. 300 meters
Q. What is half of 300?
A. 150
Q. What is half of 150?
A. 75
Q. What is the length of one quarter of the Eiffel Tower, which measures 300 meters?
A. (After long cogitation) . . . 200 meters (and despite many attempts he failed each time).[1]

---

1. From *Human Memory and Its Pathology*, by Jacques Barbizet. W. H. Freeman and Company. Copyright © 1970.

The point of this case is to show that deficits in memory processing from brain damage may be quite subtle and may go undetected in normal, everyday conversation. In addition, with this particular affliction (damage to the frontal area of the brain) there was a particular fluctuation in the quality of Roger's memory processing which may be characterized as susceptibility to distraction by certain immediate stimuli, such as a gesture by the examiner or a noise outside the room. Such distractibility is characteristic of the behavior of monkeys subjected to lesions in a similar location of the brain.

Such cases are particularly interesting within the context of the psychobiology of memory processing because monkeys given systematic lesions of this same portion of the brain not only are recognized as especially distractable but also have been suspected as suffering from a deficit in memory processing (albeit quite different from that described above).

Even within our restricted consideration of amnesia, the complexity can be staggering. A deficit in retention is only one of a number of symptoms of mental dysfunction, often occurring in combination with delirium, epilepsy, diffuse intellectual impairment, or stupor. The range of deficits in processing memories of episodes is extensive, including simple retention loss of an unusual amount due to deficient original learning and also, perhaps, ". . . a severe inability to recall or record all current events, with preservation of more distant memories; a limited, but complete, amnesia for a sharply defined period; repeated episodes of such amnesia; or a period of partial amnesia with hazy and inaccurate recollection (Whitty & Lishman, 1966, pp. 72–73)."

Finally, the general sources of amnesia may include not only those linked to neurological malfunction but also what has been termed psychogenic or hysterical amnesia. Often such "nonorganic" amnesia is defined simply by exclusion of identifiable sources of neurological malfunction, although in all fairness it should be recognized that such a diagnosis usually involves more intricate reasoning. An example has been reported by Stengel (1966, pp. 183–84):

> A 37-year old woman had a car accident in October, 1962. She was admitted to the hospital unconscious and it took her two weeks to recover clear consciousness. Neurological examination was negative. X-ray of the skull immediately after the accident revealed a fracture of the left parietal bone, but there was no indication of a localized injury to the brain. When examined in February, 1965, she still had a retrograde amnesia of a similar duration. She was referred to a psychiatrist because of a dull headache and other pains, which were regarded as neurotic. The neurologist regarded the amnesia as

largely psychogenic. Psychological testing failed to reveal memory impairment apart from the amnesia.

This patient had probably suffered a transient brain damage which caused unconsciousness, but in the absence of localizing symptoms and a general memory impairment, excluded serious organic lesion. Retrograde amnesia due to brain injury, however severe, does not exceed one week (Russell, 1935) and a post-traumatic amnesia rarely covers a period of more than four weeks. This patient's extensive amnesias were out of proportion to the degree of the brain injury suffered and had to be regarded as largely psychogenic. She had shown hysterical reactions to her father's death 10 years before the accident. In her case, brain damage had precipitated psychogenic amnesia which was superimposed on an "organic" amnesia. Psychotherapeutic exploration revealed profound bitterness against the husband who drove the car when the accident happened. The patient's hostility against him may have played a part among the psychogenic factors which determined the character of the amnesia in this case.

Perhaps the most analytical story that has evolved concerning human amnesia is that linked to damage in the temporal lobe of the brain, as mentioned above. This rather remarkable type of amnesia is best described by a summary of another proto-typical case (Barbizet, 1970, p. 59):

> At the age of 16, HM, who had been normal up to then, began to suffer from epileptic attacks, which, on account of their intensity and frequency, made all normal activity impossible for him. At the age of 27, he submitted to a mesial temporal bilateral resection performed by Scoville. This operation, which spared the entire temporal neocortex, consisted of a total excision of the internal part of the temporal lobe, beginning at the apex of the temporal lobe and destroying the anterior two-thirds of the hippocampus, the uncus, and the amygdaloid nuclei of both sides. After a period of confusion, a very severe memory disorder became established and had remained practically unchanged ever since. This intelligent patient had no troubles of praxognosis; his language was normal and so was his verbal span. He suffered, however, from such a gradual forgetting that he retained practically nothing of the events of his current life. For instance, 6 months after his operation, his family moved into another house on the same street; he could never remember the new address and always returned to the old house. His parents moved again a few years later, and, although he seemed to know that he had moved, he could not remember the address. He could not remember where things belonged; he mowed the lawn regularly, but had to ask his mother each time where the mower was kept. He did the same puzzles day after day and reread the same magazines. He did not recognize or know the names of his neighbors, and invariably treated them as strangers. He managed to retain three figures for about fifteen minutes, provided he was not interrupted by anything and was able to repeat them mentally.

He had a retrograde amnesia covering approximately the year prior to his operation; on the other hand, 12 years after the latter he had preserved almost intact his store of earlier memories, and was inclined to repeat the same anecdote several times to the same person without being aware of the repetition.[2]

Experimental Analysis of Memory Processing Capacity in Amnesic Humans

Cases such as that of HM presented a paradox. On the one hand, there was good reason to suspect that the temporal-hippocampal region of the brain was an important substratum of memory processing: patients with neural damage in the region of the hippocampus had striking deficits in memory processing; the famous demonstrations by Penfield and his colleagues indicated that memories of past events are evocable by stimulation in the region of the hippocampus; and it began to make a great deal of sense in terms of certain tangential behavioral evidence, anatomical evidence, and theory to view this part of the brain as perhaps the primary locus of memory processing, perhaps that evasive storehouse of memory.

Yet, on the other hand, experimental analysis of this possibility through systematic brain lesions in animals did not yield the sort of retention deficit expected. Rather, the consequences of such lesions appeared better characterized as a deficit in something like "inhibition," a general failure to withhold inappropriate responding. Partly for this reason, a more fine-grained analysis of human amnesia was desirable.

One of the first steps in this analysis tested an implication of the amnesic's normal capacity for light conversation, that is, that no marked deficiency was evident in short-term retention. Generally, amnesics seemed quite capable of accurately recalling items just presented them, so long as the number of items to be recalled did not exceed the normal memory span of about 6 items or so, regardless of whether the materials were presented visually or acoustically. The patient HM, in a test of recognition, exhibited retention after short intervals that was well within the range of normal subjects.

Six amnesic patients having the same symptoms as HM were compared systematically with nonamnesic control patients in short-term retention of sets of 3 words. The Brown-Peterson testing para-

---

2. From *Human Memory and Its Pathology,* by Jacques Barbizet. W. H. Freeman and Company. Copyright © 1970.

digm, which reduces or prevents rehearsal by presenting a distracting task during the retention interval, was used. The investigators (Baddeley & Warrington, 1970) found that over a 60-second interval, retention was essentially the same for the amnesic and nonamnesic patients.

Baddeley and Warrington also compared the short-term retention of these two kinds of subjects in terms of the recency effect in free recall. The recency effect, you will remember, is the tendency for people to recall more efficiently the two or three items most recently presented. This effect has been viewed by some as representing short-term memory processing. Although the amnesic patients were clearly inferior in recalling items that had appeared earlier in the list, they did not differ from the controls in recalling the terminal items of a list of words.

Thus, although some conflicting results have been obtained with certain materials, one can feel fairly safe in concluding that the mnemonic difficulty in amnesics does not reside in their capacity for processing information after short intervals. We have noted above that a similar claim—essentially normal retention by amnesics—has been made regarding information acquired prior to the onset of amnesia [although in view of the data by Warrington & Sanders (1971), some doubt about this conclusion must exist].

The victims of the sorts of amnesia under consideration here cannot be trusted to travel from their homes to the hospital, because they simply cannot remember the locations of the bus stop, nor their homes, nor the hospital; and even after long periods of hospitalization, they may not remember where the hospital bathroom is. Obviously, a mnemonic deficiency exists; what is it?

These cases of human amnesia were attributed widely to a general failure to acquire new information. The apparently normal retention in amnesics for very recent or very remote events was combined with the then-popular assumption that for information to be acquired, it must pass through short-term memory processing before entering the "storehouse" of long-term memories. The common supposition developed that the key defect in amnesics was in their transfer from short-term to long-term memory processing. It was further supposed that the mechanism for such transfer must therefore lie, anatomically, in or about the hippocampus.

Such a formulation was viewed by Weiskrantz as both dramatic and surprising. "It is dramatic because one knows so little about the physiological foundations of LTM (long-term memory) that any lead as to where to concentrate one's efforts is welcome. It is surprising because past efforts to locate the 'engram' have merely confirmed its elusiveness; if it is so difficult to locate the engram, it is surprising that one can so easily locate the gate that controls entry into it (Weiskrantz, 1971, p. 26)." Weiskrantz's skepticism was, as we shall see, entirely appropriate.

Milner (1962) had found that over a three-day period the amnesic patient HM showed significant improvement on a motor learning task, a finding later substantiated with a variety of motor tasks by Corkin (1968). Then, in 1968, Warrington and Weiskrantz found with a verbal learning task that a significant number of the errors made by amnesics were intrusions, items that had been correct on some other verbal learning task that had been presented a day or two before.

What emerged from these findings was the suspicion that more capacity for the relatively permanent acquisition of new information existed in amnesics than was previously estimated, perhaps because the rough tests commonly applied did not perfectly assess memory capacity to the exclusion of other behavioral malfunctions suffered by amnesics. We shall see that one such behavioral malfunction was a difficulty in withholding incorrect verbal responses. To more properly assess retention by amnesics, what was needed was a different technique for teaching and for assessing the acquisition of new information in amnesics. Such a technique was applied by Warrington and Weiskrantz.

The Warrington-Weiskrantz Experiments

Warrington and Weiskrantz began with the modest intention of assessing retention by amnesics and normals whose learning had reached approximately equivalent levels. Such an experiment could not be completed with the conventional procedure of presenting a list of 10 words to be studied for various numbers of trials, simply because amnesics were unable to attain the same level of learning as that of normal control subjects when this procedure was used. Warrington and Weiskrantz recognized nevertheless that without equivalent learning, meaningful comparison of retention deficits was impossible.

The search began for a task which could be learned to perfection by amnesics, but at the same time would not be learned so rapidly by control subjects as to be immediately overlearned by them. Such a task was found in a paper by Gollin (1960) concerning visual recognition in children. For this task pictures or words are presented in fragmented form, as shown in Figure 14–2. This fragmented form appears as if the word or pictures were drawn in pencil and then a thin eraser run through the drawing. With this analogy, degree of fragmentation could be progressively increased by increasing the number of times the "eraser" was run through the drawing in approximately random direction. For the learning task

Figure 14–2. Example of the variation in degree of fragmentation of items employed in the fragmented-word task of Warrington and Weiskrantz. In order to learn a list of words, subjects are shown progressively more complete forms of the word until they are able to identify it accurately on the basis of the most fragmented form. (From Warrington & Weiskrantz, 1970.)

itself the subject is presented with three versions of a word, in its most fragmented, lesser fragmented or whole form. On each trial the subject is presented first the most fragmented form, then the lesser fragmented, and finally the whole form until a correct identification is made. The objective, of course, is to be able to identify the object in its most fragmented form. An error is counted each time either one of the fragmented forms is incorrectly identified.

This procedure had two special advantages for the purposes of Warrington and Weiskrantz. First, the task could be learned by amnesics in a relatively short time, yet was not immediately overlearned by normal control subjects. Second, errors in this task were unlikely to take the form of incorrect responses. Nearly all errors were omissions, the "I don't know the answer" variety. This latter advantage was somewhat serendipitous, but nevertheless provided a clue for further analysis of amnesia, as we shall see.

When retention by amnesic and nonamnesic patients was compared after they had achieved approximately equal learning of these materials, a striking result occurred; the amnesics showed quite good retention, not only after 24 hours, but also after a 72-hour interval had elapsed between learning and retention. After 72 hours, moreover, retention by the amnesic patients did not differ statistically from that shown by nonamnesic control subjects.

These results were so remarkable that they prompted immediate questions as to whether this task was really representative of "learning" in any general sense. Perhaps what was acquired in this task was not information about the specific items, but rather some general perceptual skill for improved recognition of *any* object presented in fragmented form. In other words, perhaps the "retention" shown by the amnesics did not result from the formation of memories involving specific words or pictures previously seen, but was due instead to a modification of the perceptual process which would have permitted them to more effectively "solve" fragmented pictures whether or not they previously had seen these particular fragmented pictures.

To guard against this possibility, Warrington and Weiskrantz performed similar tests on amnesics with different kinds of materials. Instead of using the fragmented versions of words or pictures described above, five-letter words were presented in partial form by simply omitting certain letters. Initially, only the first two letters were presented, then the first three, and finally all five letters. In other words, if PORCH were the word to be learned, the subject would first be shown PO, then POR, then PORCH, the objective being to learn to say PORCH when only PO was shown.

With either this procedure or the fragmented-item procedure, certain circumstances were identified in which retention by amnesics was no different than that of normals. These circumstances are particularly important for analytical reasons, because they suggest that the special benefit to amnesics of this "fragmented" or of "partial information" procedure was not due to more effective storage of the memory, but rather that it permitted more efficient retrieval. This critical point was derived from comparison of the following two experiments.

Warrington and Weiskrantz (1970) compared retention of amnesics and normals when either of three methods was used to assess retention. One method was to measure recall—the subjects simply spoke as many of the words from the list that they could. The second method was to measure recognition—subjects were presented words to be learned, then asked to identify these words from among an equal number of alternative words. As the third type of retention test, the words were presented in fragmented form and were to be identified.

Subjects in the first experiment learned the words under the fragmented-word procedure described above. Retention was tested after 1 minute, during which time each subject was instructed to count backwards from 100. When tested with the same fragmented-word procedure used during learning, retention of the amnesics and nonamnesics did not differ. The retention of the amnesics was

Figure 14–3.   **Figure 14–4.**

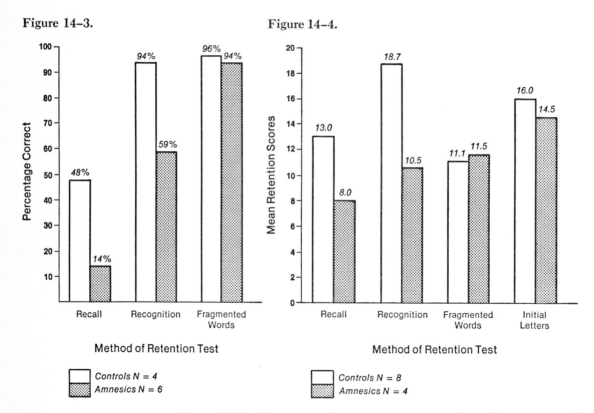

Figure 14–3. Percentage of correct responses is shown for amnesic and control subjects following their learning of words by the fragmented-word technique (described in the text; *also see* Figure 14–2). Results are shown separately for each of three methods of testing retention. (Based on Warrington & Weiskrantz, 1970.)

Figure 14–4. Mean number of correct responses is shown for amnesic and control subjects. All subjects were tested with one of four methods, following conventional presentation of only the complete form of each word. (Based on Warrington & Weiskrantz, 1970.)

a good deal poorer, however, when assessed in terms of performance on the recognition or recall tests (*see* Figure 14–3). Whether or not similar retention performance was given by amnesics and nonamnesic controls seemed to depend upon how retention was tested.

To pursue this possibility further in the second experiment, conventional presentation of materials was used. Here, the subjects were simply presented a list of words in their usual, unfragmented form, and asked to read them aloud. Amnesics are, of course, known to be deficient in terms of learning under these procedures; could this deficiency be removed by the appropriate type of retention test? As can be seen in Figure 14–4, the answer is "yes."

The results of this second experiment showed that if retention is tested by the fragmented-word technique, retention deficits in the amnesic subjects may be decreased; in this case, moreover, the deficit was completely eliminated. Taken together, these two experiments imply that it does not matter so much how the materials were presented during original learning; the critical feature is how retention is tested.

Warrington and Weiskrantz's preliminary interpretation of amnesia is derived from the inference that the basis of this affliction is in the act of memory retrieval. The amnesic's deficit in memory retrieval may be alleviated by presenting partial information, additional retrieval cues, at the time retention is measured. Without these additional retrieval cues—and this is the critical link—amnesic individuals are relatively ineffective in preventing the retrieval and expression of inappropriate, incorrect information. Amnesics are not primarily deficient in the transfer of information from the short-term to the long-term "memory store." Amnesics do not suffer inadequate "memory consolidation." Rather, the sorts of amnesia considered here reflect a deficit in those processes ordinarily employed to dissipate, inhibit, or otherwise prevent the retrieval of inaccurate information. This interpretation of amnesia is consistent with the following facts about amnesia:

1. A considerable number of intrusions (inappropriate information) from prior learning appears in the retention responses of amnesics.
2. Amnesics have shown significant learning and effective retention over long intervals in terms of motor learning, and motor learning is particularly resistant to interference (the expression of previously acquired, but now inappropriate and inaccurate information) from prior conflicting learning.
3. Amnesics have sometimes seemed even more deficient in terms of recognition than in recall. Certainly, in terms of the

number of overt errors. One may reasonably assume that simply replying "yes" or "no" incorrectly **is** more probable than responding with an incorrect word.

4. Cues about the semantic content of words to be recalled appear to benefit amnesics more than normals (Warrington & Weiskrantz, 1971).

5. When rats and monkeys are subjected to brain damage similar to that of these amnesics, a dominant characteristic of their behavior is an inability to withhold inappropriate responses.

The studies of Warrington and Weiskrantz constitute a significant advance in the analysis of human amnesia. The idea that these cases of amnesia reflect a deficiency in controlling interfering memories not only can explain much of what is known about amnesia but, equally important, suggests a useful framework within which further research on amnesia may be conducted. This idea is especially promising analytically because so much is known already about how interfering memories are controlled in the normal processing of memories.

Nevertheless, we must cautiously recognize the boundaries of this analysis of amnesia. While the work by Warrington, Weiskrantz, and their colleagues probably is the best to date on this topic, research with human amnesics is for the most part rather inconclusive, even at best. One obvious problem is diagnosis and classification. We have mentioned that the abnormal processing of memories rarely is an isolated symptom. Even with those special cases of unimpaired general intelligence and perception, amnesics may differ from normals, even normal hospitalized patients, in a number of ways. If the amnesia is due to advanced alcoholism or severe senility any number of associated pathologies may be found, some undiagnosed; if the amnesia is due to brain damage, it is most unlikely that the subjects can be equated on all capacities except the amnesia if only because the precise site of the lesion can rarely be determined until (or unless) a postmortem examination is completed. This emphasizes again the advantage of testing these problems with animal subjects because of the infinitely more precise control that may be obtained over the nature of the brain damage.

An elaboration of these and similar problems in this difficult area of research is not needed here. One further point is worth considering, however. This is the problem of how difficulties in one phase of memory processing might indirectly impair other phases, whether the initial difficulties are recognized realistically by the patient or only realized through labels assigned by a physician. There is a classical example of a psychiatrist performing a rather crude examination of an amnesic patient. The psychiatrist hid a sharp pin in his fingers and shook hands with the patient. Subsequently, the patient was reluctant to shake hands with this psychiatrist although unable, or perhaps unwilling, to report why. It is not difficult to imagine why an institutionalized patient, especially one experiencing daily difficulties in keeping separate and well-classified the occurrence of different events, would be somewhat reluctant to suggest that such a preposterous event as being stuck with a pin by her doctor would actually have occurred.

The point is that we know very little about how variables like "confidence" or "plausibility" influence the retrieval of certain memories. It is undoubtedly true that the retention or general knowledge exhibited by some individuals may be underestimated because these individuals may find it easier to say "I don't remember" or because their internal criteria for confidence that they do remember may be especially rigorous. Simply, some people are more reluctant to make an overt error than others. Consideration of the criteria subjects may use to determine when they should or should not emit a particular response has long played an important role in assessing perceptual behaviors such as signal detection; and it has only begun to be considered in the analysis of normal memory processing. When this factor is systematically assessed in studies of abnormal processing, it may be found more important than has been suspected.

Analysis of Acute, Experimentally Induced Amnesia

In the last chapter we considered the topic of experimentally induced amnesia as one means for studying short-term retention process. At this point we shall consider how retrograde amnesia may be understood. One step is to determine whether the effect is primarily upon memory storage or upon memory retrieval. But the traditional path toward this understanding (one familiar generally to science) is to ask how retrograde amnesia may be modified. When we discover what treatments make a difference in retrograde amnesia, we reach a better position from which to construct and test hypotheses about the ultimate basis of retrograde amnesia. We turn now to a consideration of the facts and hypotheses that have evolved in taking this path.

Degree of Amnesia

Experimentally induced amnesia is not an all-or-none matter; retention loss rarely is complete even in operational terms. It is more appropriate to think in terms of *degree* of amnesia.

Among the most carefully analyzed factors determining degree of amnesia are quantifiable properties of the amnesic agent. Intensity of various kinds of amnesic agents, such as flurothyl or carbon dioxide, has been found to determine degree of amnesia. Probably because electroshock is more conveniently varied in intensity than are other amnesic agents, more is known about the effects of variation in intensity of electroshock.

Degree of amnesia increases in correspondence with the intensity of the electroshock used as an amnesic agent; quite a simple relationship. One of the more obvious correlates of increasing current passing through the brain is an increasing frequency of behavioral seizures. The correlation between degree of amnesia and the occurrence of behavioral seizures has influenced some theorists to suggest a causal relationship. It has been suggested, for example, that competing responses acquired during the behavioral seizure interfere with retention.

However, there is good evidence that behavioral seizures are not at all necessary for amnesia. First, a large number of experiments have shown that retrograde amnesia may be caused by applying low intensities of current to discrete areas of the brain, especially the subcortical, limbic system. This sort of electrical stimulation usually does not result in a behavioral seizure. Second, a number of studies of the influence of peripherally induced electroconvulsive shock have found that the minimal current levels needed to produce amnesia are lower than those needed for certain forms of behavioral convulsion.

Further reason for discounting a causal relationship between behavioral convulsions and amnesia may be found in a series of studies by McGaugh, Zornetzer, and their colleagues. These studies were fairly successful in manipulating independently the intensity of electroshock applied to the brain and the probability of a behavioral convulsion. This was accomplished by subjecting the animal to an anticonvulsant drug (ether) immediately before the electroshock was delivered to the brain. They found considerable amnesia in spite of the absence of behavioral convulsions. Next, they conducted a very systematic analysis of this fact. The results of one of their major experiments (Zornetzer & McGaugh, 1971) is shown in Figure 14–5. This figure shows the probability (degree) of amnesia occurring with mice subjected, just after a training trial, to differing intensities of electroshock to the brain.

The resulting relationship, shown for mice made resistant to behavioral seizures and mice normally susceptible to behavioral seizures, illustrates a number of important points. First, amnesia is more likely, the higher the stimulating current. Second, the etherized animals did not have behavioral seizures (the "seizures" indicated on the figures refer to *brain* seizures); yet, the increase in the probability of amnesia with increased current occurred for these animals very much like that found in animals which did have behavioral seizures (the "no-ether condition").

Figure 14–5 shows, however, that amnesia *is* related to *brain* seizures. The threshold for brain seizure—the current intensity necessary to induce brain seizures in at least 50 percent of the mice —differed markedly (13.2 mA for the etherized mice, 2.8 mA for the nonetherized mice). Yet, when the probability of a brain seizure

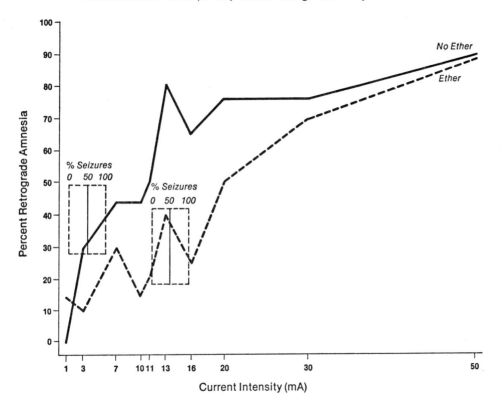

Figure 14–5. Percentage of mice judged (on the basis of a rigid response criterion) to be amnesic as a function of the intensity of electrical shock presented transcorneally to each mouse following training. Animals exposed to ether prior to training (lower line) gave no behavioral convulsions. The threshold for brain seizure is indicated in terms of current intensity, both for animals previously exposed to ether and those not so exposed. It should be noted that amnesia does not depend upon behavioral convulsions and that the extent of amnesia increases with increasing current intensity, well beyond the point at which all animals exhibit a brain seizure, indicating that the mere occurrence of a brain seizure is not the sole determinant of retrograde amnesia. (From Zornetzer & McGaugh, 1971.)

was equated for these two groups, amnesia did not differ.

One final point made by Figure 14–5 is that amnesia apparently is determined by something over and above the simple occurrence of a brain seizure. Well beyond the point at which all mice exhibited brain seizures, further increases in current intensity produced an increase in the probability of amnesia. Perhaps the production of certain kinds of electrical activity in the brain, as a consequence of the increasing electroshock, may be the fundamental determinants of amnesia. Alternatively, perhaps as current intensity increases, the number of discrete areas in the brain affected may also increase. Or perhaps certain ongoing patterns of electrical activity in the brain may be disrupted only by very severe electrical currents. Of course, it is possible that intensity of electrical current per se—the number of coulombs passing through a cell—is the fundamental determinant of amnesia. Conclusions at this level of analysis have yet to be decided.

Degree of Learning Prior to the Amnesic Treatment

A thread of evidence running through several research areas suggests that high degrees of learning may protect organisms against amnesia. Although the fundamental determinants of "degree of learning" are debatable, it is common practice to assume that higher degrees of learning are indicated by higher probabilities of a correct learned response. The latter may be achieved by continuing training until progressively more stringent criteria of performance are met, or by continuing training beyond the point at which performance is normally perfect.

Drugs that inhibit protein synthesis in the brain may cause amnesia if a low-to-moderate degree of learning was achieved under the drug's influence. The drug is less likely to cause amnesia, however, if higher degrees of learning were attained. This evidence has been verified by studies with rodents, birds, and fish, so it has considerable generality. Moreover, a similar relationship has been found for amnesia caused by the application of potassium chloride to the cerebral cortex. The primary consequence of this treatment is to cause a cessation of electrical activity in the cerebral cortex. Burešová and Bureš (1972) found that this treatment induced retrograde amnesia if rats had received only three daily sessions of training on a discrimination task, but not if 12 days of training had been given.

When learning is established by a single training trial, degree of learning may vary, with the variation in the magnitude of the reinforcer, such as intensity of footshock in a passive avoidance task.

Increases in such footshock yield corresponding increases in the probability of a passive avoidance. When electroconvulsive shock is applied following a single passive avoidance training trial, amnesia is less likely to result the more intensive punishment is used during training.

With humans, it is known that overlearned sensorimotor acts are unaffected by drugs which markedly affect behaviors that are not so well established. Also, humans suffering any of a variety of forms of relatively chronic amnesia may go unnoticed in public because overlearned behaviors such as "small talk" and common gestures are relatively unaffected.

The reason for this "protective" action of high degrees of learning is unclear. Perhaps high degrees of learning are accompanied by multiple sites and modes of representation of the memory in the brain, and so a given drug may be correspondingly less likely to affect all of them. A related possibility is suggested by evidence that even with high degrees of original learning, amnesia may be detected if retention is measured after sufficiently long retention intervals. Perhaps it is *access* to the memory that is impaired in many cases of amnesic patients and the deficit will be detected only if alternative routes of access to the memory are impaired by other causes, such as long retention intervals. Of course, this is just speculation. More certain answers may be anticipated as we learn more about the processes that underlie higher degrees of learning.

Scope of Amnesia

Just as amnesia may vary in degree, there also appears to be variation in precisely how the amnesia is shown in an animal's behavior. Most studies of experimentally induced amnesia measured only one aspect of an animal's behavior, so the generality of the amnesic effects in terms of other behavior could not always be detected. When additional response measures began to be used, the results were surprising. We have seen that a rat which steps off a platform and receives a footshock on the floor will ordinarily not step off again the next day. However, if the footshock were immediately followed by an electroconvulsive shock, amnesia "occurs" in that the animal is not at all reluctant to step off the next day. It was discovered, however, that animals rendered amnesic in these terms were not necessarily amnesic for the particular *location* of the floor on which they had received the footshock. Rather, they avoided that location. This showed that at least one portion of the animal's memory for the avoidance training was still accessible to influence behavior.

A good deal of evidence has indicated that in spite of amnesia for "skeletal responding" (such as withholding a response of stepping down or stepping through) evidence for retention may nevertheless be found in terms of autonomic responding (such as the animal's heart rate or defecation). Experimenters often express the subjective opinion that although their animals are undeniably amnesic in terms of the objective measure of skeletal responding, the animals seem nevertheless quite frightened to be returned to the experimental apparatus. Accordingly, changes in heart rate of the sort that might index fear often have been found to be relatively unaffected by the same amnesic treatments which clearly impair retention of instrumental responding.

Is autonomic responding inevitably protected from amnesia? The answer is no. Such autonomic responding does often appear to be more resistant to the effects of amnesic treatments, but with the proper manipulations, amnesia for autonomic responding may be found just as for instrumental responding. Springer (1973) has established convincing evidence for this conclusion.

Springer (1973) presented rats with a white noise followed immediately by a severe footshock. When these rats subsequently were presented the white noise (the CS), they would stop drinking, their heartbeats would be altered, and their defecation increased as if the noise had acquired aversive properties. In a word, the rats became afraid of the CS. The question was this: if the pairing of the white noise and the footshock were followed by an electroconvulsive shock, would the animal be amnesic for the significance of the white noise?

As expected, Springer initially found amnesia in terms of cessation of drinking but not in terms of changes in heart rate or defecation. However, Springer found that by increasing the intensity of the electroconvulsive shock, amnesia could be found in terms of the autonomic measures as well as in terms of drinking behavior. Moreover, he also found that the retrograde amnesia gradient differed for these responses. When retention was measured in terms of interruption of drinking, amnesia occurred even when the electroconvulsive shock was delayed as long as 15 seconds following training. Amnesia in terms of defecation, however, occurred only if the electroconvulsive shock occurred within 3.5 seconds after training, and amnesia in terms of heart rate occurred only if the amnesic agent was presented immediately after training.

We are far from complete understanding of these results. What is clear, however, is that different attributes of a memory may undergo different rates or kinds of processing; we should be continually aware of this point of complexity as we try to understand memory processing in general.

Amnesia Changes With Retention Interval

Like most other activities, the pursuit of science is governed to a surprising extent by practical considerations. So it is that when the modification or observation of behavior requires an interval between experimental sessions—between training and a retention test, in particular—that interval typically has been 24 hours, for obvious practical reasons. We have seen that most amnesic treatments are accompanied by side effects which obviously would contaminate tests of retention. By and large, such aftereffects dissipate quickly (although not all do) and so a 24-hour interval between the amnesic treatment and the retention test seemed reasonable as well as practical.

In one sense it is fortunate that the use of the 24-hour interval was so widespread as to be nearly unanimous. The fact is that this interval is a very important determinant of the amount of amnesia measured. So, if the length of this interval had differed capriciously across studies, the resulting chaos would have thwarted understanding in this area. On the other hand, because this interval was held at 24 hours for so long, a very important determinant of amnesia went unrecognized, and understanding of the fundamental character of amnesia was correspondingly impaired anyway. Nevertheless, the choice of 24 hours as the interval between the amnesic treatment and the retention test is somewhat ironic because amnesia appears to increase gradually from the time the amnesic agent is delivered to a point about 24 hours later, and then gradually declines thereafter. It is convenient to consider separately the change that occurs between delivery of the amnesic agent and 24 hours later and the change occurring thereafter.

Increases in Amnesia During the First 24 Hours

Some amnesic treatments, such as electroconvulsive shock, cause temporary debilitation in the animal (or person). Suppose that the animal is in fact unconscious for a few minutes and then is tested for retention of passive avoidance. Good retention of passive avoidance is defined when, for example, the animal does not enter a compartment in which it previously was shocked. Under these circumstances we may expect that the retention of this unconscious animal would be objectively assessed as good; unconscious animals are unlikely to move from one compartment into another. Such an effect is not interesting to us, and a number of very careful tests have been conducted to discount this sort of trivial artifact. Still, the result following electroconvulsive shock has been better retention for the first hour or so than 24 hours later. This effect has been found in several different laboratories, with several amnesic agents, and using mice, rats, and chickens, so it is not likely a chance result.

While a number of amnesic agents have been accompanied by an increase in amnesia during the first 24 hours, the effect is linked most closely to drugs that act to reduce protein synthesis in the brain. These drugs, including acytoxycycloheximide, cycloheximide, and puromycin, were first tested as amnesic agents in terms of retention of discrimination learning by mice. With drug doses that markedly reduce protein synthesis in the brain during learning, subsequent retention was found to be quite good up to 3 hours after learning, but significant amnesia was found after 6 or 24 hours. The basic effect subsequently was found under a number of other circumstances with the precise time course apparently depending upon a variety of factors. These factors seem to include not only degree of original learning but also the particular task that was learned, magnitude of reinforcer, species (whether fish, rats, or mice) and perhaps a strain of mouse as well.

A full explanation as to why amnesia often increases during the first 24 hours following amnesic treatment is not likely to appear for some time. When it does, however, we may expect to see a great leap forward in our understanding of amnesia in general.

Further Changes in Amnesia After 24 Hours

When retrograde amnesia has been detected in humans following accidental brain trauma, it is commonly observed that, with time, increasingly more of the forgotten memories may be retrieved. Similarly, in a dramatic study by Bickford, Molder, Dodge, Svien, and Rome (1958), retrograde amnesia induced in humans by direct stimulation of the brain through deeply implanted electrodes resulted in amnesia that was not permanent, but rather, after a day or so retrieval of the forgotten memories occurred.

What has been accomplished toward understanding such "spontaneous" recovery from amnesia in systematic studies with animals? This issue has been studied, but it is a complex one with no definite answers as yet. Such "spontaneous" recovery from amnesia regularly occurs with certain amnesic agents such as potassium chloride and antibiotics. With electroconvulsive shock as the amnesic agent, eventual recovery from amnesia sometimes has been found, but about an equal number of experiments have not found this effect (and occasionally amnesia has been found to increase rather than decrease over a period of many days following treatment).

A resolution of this issue would seem to require that the notion of "spontaneous" be addressed. There are two concrete factors which may cause recovery: the dissipation of factors produced by the amnesic agent which act to retard expression of the memory, or the occurrence of environmental events which facilitate expression of the memory. A good deal of progress has been made in the latter respect. It is now quite clear that recovery from amnesia may be induced by the proper environmental conditions. We turn next to a brief look at the evidence for such stimulus-induced recovery from amnesia.

Stimulus-Induced Recovery from Amnesia

Recovery from acute amnesia may be facilitated by re-exposure to some events of the episode to be remembered. The success of psychotherapeutic techniques in reducing the scope of a patient's amnesia following a traumatic experience may depend in part upon the therapist's skill in presenting effective "reminder" cues to the patient and leading the patient to produce his own reminder cues. Experimental verification of this would be difficult. What can be established, however, is the effectiveness of certain "reminder" stimuli in alleviating amnesia that has been induced experimentally.

The establishment of treatments that effectively alleviate amnesia has important theoretical implications. Acute amnesia may be attributed to either of two general sources, destruction of the memory or impairment of its retrieval. We already have discussed the first possibility as following from the view that a memory representation takes a labile, fragile stage shortly after learning. In this view, an amnesic agent delivered shortly after learning is expected to destroy the memory or at least terminate its further development. If, however, amnesia could later be alleviated—the memory "reactivated"—then it would be impossible logically to maintain that the memory had been destroyed and difficult to assert that its complete development had been impeded. Furthermore, if reactivation of the memory were contingent upon the presentation of events associated with the episode originally learned, one would be led to suspect that such events functioned as retrieval cues to alleviate what had been, fundamentally, a deficit in memory retrieval.

Retrograde amnesia for avoidance learning may be alleviated by re-presenting the animal with the aversive stimulus associated with that learning. There is further evidence that amnesia for appetitive conditioning may be alleviated by re-presenting the appetitive reinforcer, although this procedure has not been widely used.

The typical procedure has been to train rats on a passive avoidance task, and then immediately subject them to an electrocon-vulsive shock sufficient to induce amnesia. Prior to the retention test some animals are given a footshock of the kind experienced during original learning. Usually the circumstances of this "re-activating" footshock are different from those of original learning. Animals given such a footshock show little or no amnesia. So far, it has not seemed to matter *when* the reactivating footshock is given, so long as it occurs some time between delivery of the amnesic treatment and the retention test. Moreover, alleviation of the am-nesia seems to be relatively permanent; retention of the original avoidance learning is maintained solidly for some time following delivery of the reactivating footshock.

There is indication that the success of a reactivation treatment in alleviating amnesia may depend upon both the strength of original learning and the severity of the amnesic treatment. These facts have been used by some theorists to argue that the reactivation treatment (e.g., the footshock) merely adds to original learning and that recovery from amnesia will occur only if the amnesia was in-complete originally. This is a plausible argument but it seems un-likely for these three reasons: (1) the typically wide disparity between the conditions of original learning and those of the re-activating treatment; (2) the fact that the amnesia alleviated by such treatments has seemed otherwise quite thorough; and (3) the wide variety of circumstances under which reactivation treatments are effective.

Reactivation treatments have taken several different forms such as re-presentation of various conditions of reinforcement and simple re-exposure to the training apparatus. These treatments have been effective over a wide range of amnesic agents and vari-ation in training procedures. Furthermore, as mentioned previ-ously, such reactivation treatments also have been found to alleviate forgetting induced by sources other than amnesic agents, such as that caused by interference or long retention intervals (Spear, 1973, 1976; Spear & Parsons, 1976).

We have suggested before that the basic effect of reactivation treatments is to return the memory to a state of activation com-parable to that found immediately following original learning. This interpretation has been confirmed by a phenomenon which may be termed "indirect reactivation."

We have seen that if the delivery of an amnesic agent is delayed for too long following learning, amnesia for that learning does not occur. Lewis and his colleagues (e.g., Lewis, 1969, Misanin, Miller, & Lewis, 1968) suggested, however, that the critical interval was between the time a memory is *active* and delivery of the amnesic agent rather than the interval between original training and the amnesic agent. Thus, if delivery of the amnesic agent were immediately preceded by reactivation of the memory, one should be able to induce amnesia long after original learning. This is precisely the result obtained by Lewis and by others.

Furthermore, this effect has been found under various circumstances, including memories concerning classical conditioning, instrumental aversive conditioning, and complex discrimination learning of both an appetitive and aversive character. Also, several reactivation treatments have been effective under these circumstances, including presentation of the CS of original conditioning, re-exposure to the apparatus, re-presentation of the aversive stimulus, re-establishment of the motivational conditions of original learning, and re-exposure to certain specific cues associated with the learning apparatus.

It would be a drastic overstatement to assert that these cases of memory reactivation—stimulus-induced recovery from amnesia— are well understood. Any number of unanswered questions remain (*see* Spear, 1976, for further discussion of this topic). Does a reactivated memory have precisely the same characteristics as a recently acquired memory? To what extent are changes in general arousal produced by the reactivation treatment important for the reactivation effect? When a memory is reactivated, it must acquire new attributes by association with contemporary events; is this modified memory stored separately from the original or are stored memories inherently unstable, essentially dynamic, and continuously modified during further processing? These are examples of questions that must be answered if we are to understand such cases of memory processing, and the answers should have vast implications for memory processing in general.

III. SUMMARY

Following a brief consideration of the utility of forgetting, four sources of forgetting normally encountered by animals and humans were emphasized. The first, decay, was seen to be of primarily descriptive value, having little importance as an explanatory concept as yet, even at the level of biochemical neurophysiology. Interference, the second source of forgetting, was shown to have a long history of application and analytical development in terms of human verbal memory processing, on both the empirical and theoretical level. Application of these interference concepts and data at a more general level has been initiated to a limited extent, although some difficulties were noted in applying them to the behavior of animals.

The third source of forgetting discussed was changes in contextual stimuli, both external and internal. A rule of potentially great importance for understanding retention and forgetting, and a rule which has a long history of application in psychology, is that retention will occur (i.e., learning will be manifested) to the extent that events noticed during the retention test correspond to those noticed (and presumably stored as the memory) during original learning.

The final source of forgetting discussed was aging. While there are some indications that forgetting of recently acquired events may increase as organisms reach ages describable as elderly, this is not yet clear. Various methodological difficulties in this research were noted. Perhaps a clearer effect of aging is the forgetting that occurs for events learned prior to physiological maturity. This effect ("infantile amnesia") long has been suspected in human subjects, but is difficult to test in that context. More recently, infantile amnesia has been substantiated experimentally with animal subjects.

Abnormal sources of forgetting of two general types were discussed. The first was the chronic amnesia often observed in humans following particular types of brain damage. The second was acute, retrograde amnesia, of which the most carefully controlled experiments have employed animal subjects. Brief consideration was given the scope of the deficits in memory processing which might arise from brain damage to humans, and some case histories were presented. Emphasis was given the drastic deficits in long-term retention found among humans with damage to the temporal regions of the brain. Experimentally deduced characteristics of the latter cases of amnesia were shown to be, in some respects, different from the clinical caricature of this deficit. Recent analyses of this affliction have suggested that its locus may reside in a deficit in memory retrieval, rather than in memory storage.

With regard to experimentally induced retrograde amnesia, we reviewed several variables which serve to determine the extent of the induced amnesia. Because a variety of techniques have been found which alleviate induced amnesia, it is apparent that the occurrence of retrograde amnesia does not automatically imply a failure in memory storage or permanent destruction of a memory already stored.

Physiological Correlates of Memory

She talked about her life, the present and the past, about things she remembered. She had a lot to tell because her memory was good—and she was more than 130 years old.

A. Leaf (1973)

The brain is a remarkable biological organ that can store information for more than a century, or lose it within seconds. The elderly Russian woman described in the quote above talked freely about her marriage at age sixteen, apparently utilizing information that had first been stored more than 114 years earlier. Using what is presumably a similar, though somewhat less antiquated storage system, each of the authors of this volume has occasionally walked down two flights of stairs to the departmental office only to find that the purpose of the mission has been forgotten. The disparity between these two examples raises several questions: In what form are memories stored? Are there different types of storage for different types of memories? Where are memories stored? Are different memories stored in different places? How are memories retrieved from storage, and do different memories require differing retrieval mechanisms? It should be immediately pointed out that the answers to these questions are not entirely known. This chapter will describe a variety of different experimental approaches to these questions and will summarize some of the known phenomena regarding the physical bases of memory.

I. THE NATURE OF THE ENGRAM

Sustained Electrical Activity

One of the fundamental assumptions that has to be made is that our perceptions and our experiences produce changes in the central nervous system that represent these events. In other words, there must be some *trace* of the past experience that is stored in a relatively permanent form. This trace, whatever it may be physically, has been termed the *engram*. It should be noted at the outset that the ability to store information does not necessarily imply a high degree of complexity. Examples of physical memory storage are ubiquitous: A bent wire stores information about the previous application of a force; a photographic emulsion stores information about a previous pattern of light; a depression in the muddy bank of a stream stores information about the species and size of an animal that has paused to drink. Although it is probably unrealistic to expect the storage system of the brain to be as simple as any of these examples, it is important to realize that the storage of information need not be based upon some mystical set of events, but can be represented by relatively simple physical changes. Accordingly, most of the theories of memory that have been proposed during the past century have been based upon one or more of the fundamental characteristics of the nervous system (cf., Chapter 1).

One of the earliest observations of the nervous system was that the excitation of neural tissue was accompanied by electrical activity (*action potentials*). A single neuron exhibits an action potential upon stimulation and can transfer this electrical activity to an adjacent neuron via a chemical mediator, the neurotransmitter substance. The amplitude and time course of the electrical activity can be accurately described on the basis of the physical dimensions of the neuron and the parameters of the applied stimulus. Reasonably accurate predictions and descriptions can even be made for the electrical activity of a few neurons interconnected in simple circuit. But as the number of neurons increases (i.e., as the complexity of the circuit increases), the ability to precisely describe the electrical response to a stimulus becomes impossible.

It seems reasonable to assume, however, that in a system as complicated as the brain (i.e., several billion neurons), each stimulus complex produces a different and highly complex pattern of electrical activity. If one accepts this notion of differential activity patterns, then one of the most straightforward models of memory storage is that the actual *pattern* of electrical activity *is* the memory trace. But we know that this activity follows, to a certain degree, the temporal characteristics of the applied stimulus. How is it stored after the stimulus is terminated? One possibility is that the entire complex need not be stored, but that the essential aspects of the stimulus can be maintained through a so-called *reverberating circuit* (*see* Figure 15–1). A reverberating circuit involves a series of neurons that constitute a feedback loop such that the activity, once initiated, is sustained. One of the most highly formalized theories based upon the notion of sustained electrical activity is that of Hebb (1949), who called these self-sustaining circuits *cell assemblies*.

Although the notion of memory storage by sustained activity has considerable face validity, there are at least two major problems.

One problem involves the storage capacity of the brain: Is it possible, for example, to provide enough active circuits for all of the memories of an adult? The answer to this question is extremely complex because we do not know how many cells are necessary for each circuit or, for that matter, how many different memories a person may have in storage. If the order of magnitude for the number of cells in a memory circuit is about 10^2 to 10^4 and if we can store 10^6 to 10^8 different memories, it would begin to put a strain on our 10^9 neurons—especially since many of these are involved with strict input and output functions and may not be involved with memory processes. Even if this capacity exists, is it reasonable to assume that a greater and greater portion of the brain becomes electrically active as more and more information is acquired? There is no evidence for such a phenomenon.

A related and more serious problem encountered by this theoretical viewpoint is the duration of the sustained electrical activity. There is direct electrophysiological evidence that such activity can be sustained for several seconds, and it is reasonable to assume that it could be maintained for several minutes, perhaps even hours. But can it be sustained for a week? For a year? For 114 years? Almost certainly not—the metabolic cost of such long-term maintenance seems totally unreasonable. For this type of long-term storage we need to consider an alternative mode of storage that cannot only withstand years of exposure to a constantly changing environment, but which can do so with a minimum of metabolic expense.

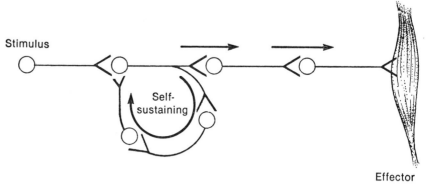

Figure 15–1. Simple model of a reverberating circuit.

Enhanced Synaptic Efficiency

A number of different physiological theories have been proposed to account for long-term storage of information. Although these theories differ considerably in terms of the proposed mechanism, virtually all of them share a single basic principle: The end result of the storage process is to (permanently) increase the efficiency of a set of synapses. Referring back to Figure 15–1, these theories would propose that the critical aspects of the circuit would not maintain the electrical activity per se, but rather would maintain an enhanced *susceptibility* to being activated. This enhanced sensitivity could be the end result of the relatively short-lived electrical activity of the reverberating circuit, so the two mechanisms should be considered to be complementary rather than opposing. We will now consider some of the proposed mechanisms of permanent storage.

Growth of Synaptic Terminals

During the course of embryological development, the long fibers of neurons grow out to establish synaptic connections with other neurons or with effector cells. There is some evidence that a certain amount of this outgrowth may continue in particular parts of the brain well into adulthood. Is it possible that the precise nature of this growth is determined by the experience of the organism, thereby serving as a mechanism for permanent storage? Going even further, is it possible that connections that are already physically formed become more efficient as a function of use?

Traditionally, the answers to the questions posed above have been either negative or guardedly positive, the reason being that the central nervous system appears to be relatively unchanging in some respects. Unlike all other organs and structures of the body, the central nervous system maintains the same population of cells throughout the life of the organism; these cells do not undergo mitotic division and, therefore, do not replicate themselves. Consequently, it was assumed that the connections formed in the central nervous system were stable. The most extreme view of this would propose that the organism is given a mosaic of genetically determined connections that can be used in differing combinations depending upon the experiences of the organism.

Recent evidence has indicated that the central nervous system is static only with respect to the cell *population*, but can change considerably with respect to the *connections* among the cells. It should be emphasized that the number of cells in the central nervous system (CNS) is greatly outweighed by the number of connections. Each cell receives many inputs (as many as 16,000 in some spinal cells) and, in turn, contributes inputs to many other cells. It is precisely these synaptic connections that recently have been shown to have the ability to change (e.g., Raisman, 1969). Although

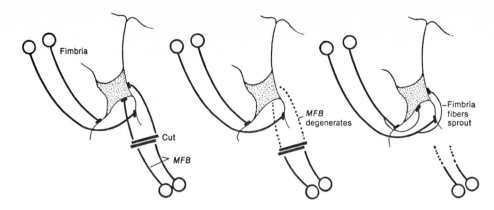

Figure 15–2. Simplified diagram of sprouting, events that take place following CNS damage. If one set of fibers is cut, the fibers that synapse on the cell body degenerate. Then, the fibers of another system produce "sprouts" that move in to occupy these vacated positions. (Schematic illustration of the results of Raisman, 1969.)

there is little or no evidence for actual regeneration of damaged neural tissue, such damage does induce the formation of *new* connections in adjacent regions, a phenomenon called *sprouting (see* Figure 15–2). It is important to note that this sprouting does not duplicate the original circuitry, but rather allows undamaged fibers to occupy vacated synaptic sites. These new connections, which could account for some of the observed recovery of function, are established more readily in the presence of a naturally occurring substance known as *nerve growth factor.* Although the importance of this substance in the central nervous system is not known, it has been credited with reducing recovery time in peripheral nerve damage (cf., Frazier, Angeletti, & Bradshaw, 1972).

Given the ability to establish new connections in response to surgical damage, it is unreasonable to assume that similar changes may take place under normal conditions in response to changes in activity levels of the cells? In other words, it is now conceivable that totally new connections can be formed in the adult organism as a function of experience; such a change would seem to be tailor-made for the storage of information.

Changes in Macromolecules

The theory of memory storage that has received the most attention is the so-called *nucleotide rearrangement theory.* This theory (actually, a number of related theories) has met with considerable skepticism, but has stimulated a great deal of research and theorizing.

The development of the nucleotide rearrangement theory has paralleled rather closely the development of genetic research in the fields of chemistry and biology. These latter fields of research have shown rather convincingly that all of the characteristics of the organism are encoded by the internal arrangement of the component parts of DNA molecules. During the development of the embryo, the genetic information is translated into a related structure, RNA, which, in turn, determines the amino acid sequences of the protein structures that make up the specialized cells of the body. Since all cells contain both DNA and RNA, it has been suggested that these molecules, which are specialized in information storage, may in some way be susceptible to changes such that *acquired* or learned information could be stored. The implicit assumption is that this change in molecular structure could somehow be translated into rather specific neural activity during the process of retrieval.

The evidence for this notion has been more spectacular than convincing. One of the first studies related to this theory involved the planaria, a simple flatworm (McConnell, 1962, McConnell & Shelby, 1970). After training the worms in a Pavlovian conditioning situation, the worms were cut in half and the two halves were allowed to regenerate new head and tail sections, respectively. The startling finding was that both types of worms (those with new tails and, surprisingly, those with new *heads*) acquired the conditioned response faster than did naïve controls. McConnell attributed this to the presence of some chemical trace that contained the code for this learning experience. The possibility that the RNA molecule might be involved was supported by the finding that worms allowed to regenerate in the presence of a substance that partially blocked RNA synthesis did not show the improved ability to learn. Even more surprising was the report that worms that had eaten the crushed remains of trained worms showed a faster rate of learning than worms that had eaten untrained worms.

As might be expected, these reports were met with more than a little skepticism. The most compelling argument against these results is the possibility that the planaria is not capable of learning the conditioned avoidance response, but is simply *sensitized* to the presentation of the CS (a bright light). In this case, it would be argued that the response to the light is not the result of CS–UCS pairing, but rather a type of "startle" response to the CS as a result of previous exposure to shock. If this argument is valid, then arguments about memory storage in half of a worm or transfer of memory to a naïve worm must be altered to emphasize transferred sensitivity to environmental change rather than transferred associations. Clearly, the acceptance of the transfer of learned information from one organism to another required the demonstration of similar phenomena in higher organisms.

The attempt to demonstrate these phenomena in higher organisms was soon to follow by a group of Danish workers (Nissen, Roigaard-Peterson, & Fjerdingstadt, 1965; Fjerdingstadt, Nissen, & Roigaard-Peterson, 1965). RNA extracts were obtained from rats that had been trained in a maze task. Those extracts, as well as extracts from untrained rats, were injected into naïve subjects. The rats that received the extract from trained donors acquired the maze task faster than those that received the extract from untrained rats. Shortly thereafter, a group of researchers from the United States (Babich, Jacobson, Bubash, & Jacobson, 1965) reported that they too could transfer a learned response to a naïve organism by injecting RNA extract obtained from the brain of a trained rat. These reports were viewed with tremendous interest and excitement, tempered by skepticism. The statistical magnitude of the effects were marginal at best. These researchers did not really assess the facilitation of learning in terms of an operant response, but simply recorded approaches to a lever—and this in the presence of food powder sprinkled around the lever to "keep the animal active!" Finally, a host of other researchers reported that they had repeatedly tried and failed to replicate the results (Byrne et al., 1966).

Perhaps the most convincing results for the macromolecular storage of information came from the laboratory of Ungar (e.g., 1966, 1972). For many years prior to the startling reports of McConnell and the Fjerdingstadt group, Ungar's laboratory had been involved in the investigation of tolerance to certain drugs, especially morphine. The term tolerance refers to the fact that a constant amount of a drug may produce smaller and smaller effects with repeated dosages. Ungar reported that the tolerance to the drug could be transferred to a normal mouse by the injection of an extract from the brain of the tolerant mouse. Although an interesting finding, most researchers were understandably reluctant to make the leap from drug tolerance to memory storage.

In an attempt to extend these findings, Ungar adopted a habituation procedure, exposing the subjects to repeated presentations of either a loud noise or a strong puff of air; either of these stimuli elicited a startle response which gradually waned as a function of repeated presentations. Following habituation to one of the stimuli, the brains of the rats were homogenized and various extracts were injected into naïve recipients. The results clearly showed more rapid habituation to the stimulus to which the donor had been habituated, but not to the other stimulus. More recently, Ungar (1970) has reported the isolation of an extract from the brains of mice that have been trained to avoid shock by promptly leaving a darkened compartment. This extract, which he calls *scotophobin* from the Greek words meaning darkness and fear, reportedly will cause naïve mice to leave a normally preferred dark chamber in the absence of electrical shock.

In spite of the tremendous interest and investment in this area of research since the early 1960s, it has not fulfilled its initial promise. Clearly lacking is the demonstration of the transfer of a discrete, learned response such as a lever-press, a sequence of turns in a maze, or the choice of a particular cue such as a square versus a circle. The effects that have been convincingly demonstrated cannot be characterized as specific examples of learning; rather, they seem to be more akin to changes in arousal level, or a rather general shift in the sensitivity of a particular sensory system (e.g., auditory or tactile). Although such changes may contribute to memory, they do not represent the degree of specificity that is shown behaviorally.

Perhaps the breaking of the genetic code by Watson and Crick (cf., Watson, 1968) was nothing more than a cruel temptation for memory researchers. The DNA/RNA model is a beautifully simple mechanism for the storage and transmission of genetic information. But this information, by most standards, is permanent—being susceptible only to occasional changes known as mutations. Can this be the same mechanism that is being used for the storage of acquired information? Could such a model account for a system that is both permanent and flexible? If so, is it reasonable to expect that *all* of the memories stored in one individual can be transferred to another (why stop with the specific task that the investigator used to train the animal)? Is it possible to change the structure of these macromolecules by nervous activity? If so, could this change be translated back into nervous activity for retrieval purposes?

The answer to these questions is probably no (cf., Briggs & Kitto, 1962). The requirements for storage of genetic information are probably radically different from those for the storage of learned information. Although the data are far from compelling, the notion that reverberating electrical activity holds memory in storage for short intervals, while the growth of synaptic terminals mediates long-term storage, seems more likely. The possibility of an intermediate mechanism cannot be ruled out. Like Tantalus, the memory researchers may be condemned to watch, but never reach the fruits of the DNA/RNA model of information storage.

II. THE LOCATION OF THE ENGRAM

The Role of the Cortex

The preceding section of this chapter has been primarily concerned with a discussion of the possible mechanisms for the storage of information at the level of the individual neuron or synapse. Another way of approaching the problem of memory storage is to essentially ignore the actual mechanism of memory storage and search for the anatomical location of memory storage within the brain as a whole.

By the time Pavlov began his conditioning studies in the early part of the century, there already was a considerable backlog of knowledge concerning the functions of various subdivisions of the cortex. It was known, for example, that the precentral gyrus of the brain was organized in a point-to-point manner in the control of muscular movement. Immediately posterior to this region, the postcentral gyrus was similarly organized into a point-to-point relationship for the input of somesthetic information. The occipital lobes subserved the visual sense, while the temporal lobes were involved with taste, olfaction, and hearing. The rather extensive remaining areas to which specific functions could not be readily ascribed were thought to be association areas (*see* Figure 15–3).

The notion of association areas in the cortex being involved with higher mental functions was quite compatible with the major theoretical viewpoints that were present during the early 1900s. Pavlovian theory, for example, assumed that learning took place in the cortex according to the following scheme: Sensory information reached the cortex by the classical sensory pathways and produced local areas of excitation. These areas of excitation radiated or spread to other areas that were concurrently under excitation. Conditioning was attributed to the formation of pathways between the area excited by the CS and the area excited (concurrently) by the UCS and the motor output systems of the organism.

This notion of essentially straight-line relationships between incoming stimuli and the output of responses was perfectly compatible with the strict behavioristic notions that were being set forth by Watson and his followers. Equally compatible with Pavlov's cortical theory of learning were the Freudian views that placed the cortex in charge of the higher cognitive processes of the organism. However, during a 30-year period beginning in the early 1920s, a single investigator, Karl Lashley, amassed a tremendous body of data arguing against the notion of specific cortical pathways that subserve learning and memory functions.

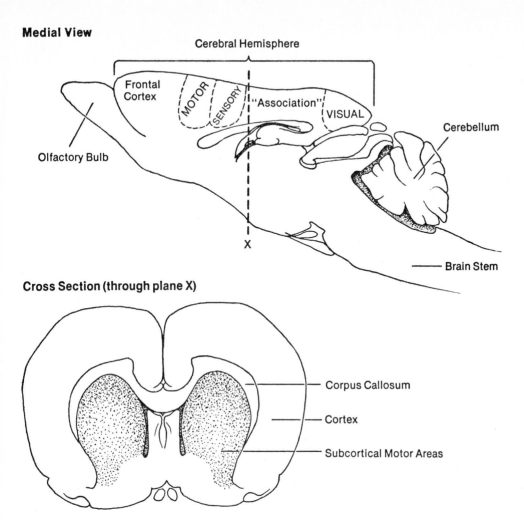

Medial View

Cerebral Hemisphere

Frontal Cortex

MOTOR

SENSORY

"Association"

VISUAL

Olfactory Bulb

Cerebellum

X

Brain Stem

Cross Section (through plane X)

Corpus Callosum

Cortex

Subcortical Motor Areas

Figure 15–3. Highly schematized drawing showing the major functional regions of the rat brain.

One of the clear predictions derived from the notion that particular areas of the cortex mediate learning and memory was that destruction of the motor regions of the cortex should eliminate the conditioned response. Lashley showed that this clearly was not the case (*see* Lashley, 1950). In one of these experiments, rats were trained to make a differential motor response to light. This habit remained intact even following complete destruction of the motor areas of the cortex and the frontal poles (in rats, this operation produces motor impairment, but not paralysis).

The permanence of the memory of learned motor responses was even more dramatic in an experiment involving monkeys. They were initially trained to unlatch a box to obtain food, the latches being designed to require a high degree of both manual and spatial skills. After learning this task, the motor cortex was surgically destroyed (in monkeys, this operation results in severe motor deficits, including partial paralysis). Over the course of several weeks or months, they regained much of their motor abilities. Following this partial recovery, they immediately performed the complicated learned response even though they had never been exposed to the training boxes during the recovery period.

It is difficult to imagine how a learned motor response could survive in either of the experiments outlined above if the response was in some way stored in the motor areas.

Another prediction that could be made is that the cortical areas of the sensory systems are critically involved in the establishment and storage of learned responses. In this context, Lashley found that the learned response remained intact so long as the animal was left with some sensory abilities. For example, massive destruction of the visual association areas along with substantial damage to the visual cortex could be tolerated without loss of a learned visual response, provided the animal was still capable of seeing the relevant stimuli. Finally, Lashley investigated the possibility that cortical connections may be involved in complex multisensory responses but not in simpler responses. The apparatus chosen for these experiments was a complicated maze, the mastery of which almost certainly involves visual, olfactory, kinesthetic, and tactile cues. After training in this task, deep slices were made through the cortex in a number of different planes. This damage, which would certainly destroy any long interregion connections existing in the cortex, had no effect on the performance or initial acquisition of this task.

On the basis of these studies, Lashley concluded the following:

> It is difficult to interpret such findings, but I think they point to the conclusion that the associative connections or memory traces of the conditioned reflex do not extend across the cortex as well-defined arcs or paths. Such arcs are either diffused through all parts of the cortex, pass by relay through lower centers, or do not exist (Lashley, 1950, p. 500).

The Role of Subcortical Relays
Sensory Relays

The compelling results of Lashley's experiments involving cortical lesions directed attention to subcortical structures. Again, the logic of these experiments was fairly simple: If the original learning and storage of habits is not mediated by direct interconnections in the cortex, then perhaps connections are being made via subcortical relay stations. (The reader should keep in mind that the assessment of the role of these structures was technically difficult at that time because the stereotaxic procedures for reaching deep brain structures were not yet in widespread use.) The two areas that were thought to be the most likely sites of subcortical relays were the thalamus (in the case of sensory relays) and the subcortical motor areas (basal ganglia). Several types of experiments bear on this issue; the experiments chosen for discussion below are representative of the rationale and conclusions of a large number of such studies.

One of the basic assumptions of these experiments was that the removal of the cortical projection area of a sensory system would force the subject to function on the basis of subcortical structures, a logic that is difficult to refute. In one such experiment, Lashley (1950) trained normal rats to perform a discrimination based upon the presence or the absence of a light. Removal of the visual cortex resulted in a total loss of retention, but the rats were able to relearn the task. The number of trials required to reach criterion was virtually the same for normal rats, rats that were retrained following removal of the visual cortex, and rats that initially acquired the task after removal of the visual cortex. It appeared, therefore, that the subcortical visual regions (the optic tectum) had the neuronal capability to acquire and store the visual habit, but did not do this as long as the visual cortex was intact.

A similar state of affairs seems to exist in the auditory system: In a classical series of experiments, Diamond and Neff (1957) showed that cats did not retain an auditory discrimination following removal of the auditory cortex, but were normal with respect to either relearning or original acquisition.

In general, this type of study has been interpreted as supporting the notion that at least the primary projection areas of the cortex are importantly (but not *essentially*) involved in the acquisition and storage of sensory-motor habits. It is possible, however, to account for these results without attributing any storage functions to the cortex. Consider, for example, the visual system. Damage inflicted upon the primary projection area most certainly produces a profound change in the visual perception of the organism (in man, but not lower organisms, it results in blindness). Let us say, for example, that a normal rat has been trained to discriminate a triangle from a circle. Following damage to the visual projection area, these two stimuli may still be perceived as being different, but because of the disruption of the visual system, they may bear little or no perceptual resemblance to original stimuli. Thus, the subject essentially would be required to learn a totally new discrimination. In conclusion, the strongest statement that can be supported is that the sensory cortex has been *implicated* in storage processes under normal conditions.

Motor Relays

The data from experiments investigating the role of subcortical *motor* relays will not even support the notion of involvement in storage under normal circumstances. Lesions of the major subcortical motor areas—the basal ganglia and the cerebellum—produce profound motor impairment from which recovery proceeds slowly and usually is incomplete. The data from a number of Lashley's

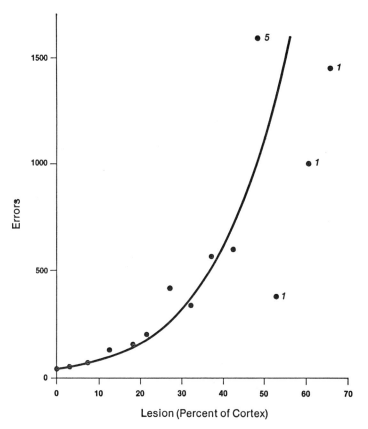

Figure 15–4.   The relation of errors in maze learning to the extent of cerebral damage in the rat. The extent of brain injury is expressed as the percentage of the surface area of the isocortex destroyed. (After Lashley, 1957.)

experiments are clear: If the organism has the physical capability of performing the task, there is no loss of performance. In some of these experiments, the rats had such profound motor disabilities that they practically rolled through the complex mazes, but they did not enter the wrong alleys. It seems likely that the motor responses are learned in terms of the effects upon the environment, rather than in terms of a discrete series of muscular contractions that lead to a specific response topography.

One of the more interesting experiments demonstrating this principle involves the anticipatory response of lifting one's index finger from an electrode in response to the presentation of a tone that precedes the delivery of electrical shock. There is virtually no change in the level of performance if the hand is turned over so that a directly *opposing* response, finger flexion, is required. The subject learns to remove the finger from the electrode, rather than to contract a specific set of muscles (Wickens, 1938).

Before continuing with the next section, we should briefly review the state of affairs following the investigations by Lashley and others. It was clear that the so-called "association areas" of the cortex or, for that matter, any long cortical-to-cortical connections are not the basis of the memory of learned responses. Equally clear is the lack of involvement of the subcortical motor areas and the subcortical sensory areas, at least under normal circumstances. It was on this basis that Lashley (1950) made his famous tongue-in-cheek statement that learning may not be possible. In partial disclamation of this statement, Lashley adopted the *mass action* principle of cortical function. Simply stated, this principle suggests that the cortex is involved in memory processes, but that it functions en masse rather than in terms of discrete sensory or motor areas. The evidence for this seemingly strange notion was that the degree of impairment of a complex maze learning task was closely related to the *total amount* of cortical damage, rather than to the locus of the damage (*see* Figure 15–4).

Interestingly, notions closely related to the mass action principle have received considerable attention recently because of the development of holographic techniques. A hologram can be produced by exposing a photographic plate with the reflection of two or more laser beams from an object. This plate, when developed and viewed with the laser beams in the same positions, has compelling three-dimensional characteristics. It is possible, for example, to move from one side to the other of the photograph and actually see *around* the pictured objects. The comparison of holography to the principle of *mass action* is based upon yet another interesting characteristic of the hologram. If the photographic plate is shattered, each of the fragments contains the *entire* image of the object, although it is smaller and less detailed. The analogy is obvious—the entire cortex may be involved with the storage of a memory, but any significant subdivision of the cortex may possess all of the essential elements of that memory. Until we know a great deal more about both the cortex and the hologram, the validity of this analogy will remain unknown.

Hippocampus

The results of the experiments of Lashley and many others during the early decades of this century were so convincing that by 1950 all but the very stubborn and the very optimistic had long since abandoned the hope of finding a specific region of the brain that was primarily responsible for the storage of memory. Then, in the early 1950s, a series of reports began to appear which were based upon the effects of electrical stimulation or surgical removal of the hippocampus (e.g., Penfield, 1954; Scoville & Milner, 1957). The medical problem of these particular patients was epilepsy, resulting from a so-called *seizure focus* in the temporal lobe. It is not uncommon in such cases for the seizure focus to spread to adjacent areas and, more importantly, to the same region of the opposite hemisphere; the result of such a spread is often a rather dramatic exacerbation of the severity of epileptic seizures.

The spread of the seizure focus and the resulting debilitation can frequently be prevented by surgical removal of the affected area. To do this, a section of the skull was removed to expose the temporal cortex. Then electrical stimulation of the area in question was carried out while the patients were awake. (Local anesthesia was used to prevent pain from the wound edge.) The feedback from this stimulation, as reported by the patient, was utilized by the surgeon to determine, insofar as possible, which areas of the brain were to be removed.

The effects of this stimulation were quite different for the temporal lobe (specifically, the hippocampus) than for other regions of the brain. Whereas stimulation of other areas typically produced either a motor movement or a report of a sensory input (e.g., a finger movement or a tingling in the left arm), the stimulation of the temporal lobe would sometimes elicit a report of a vivid recollection of a past experience. As long as the electrical current was applied, the train of events would continue at the appropriate tempo and in an extraordinarily vivid fashion; the patients reported that the experience was much more vivid than normal recall. Rather than simply remembering a conversation with a particular person, it was as though they actually saw and heard the person. Since they were also conscious and aware of the operating room environment, this was reported as a strange sort of dual consciousness. Because of the surgical requirements, the location of each of the stimulus points was carefully marked. If stimulation was reapplied to a particular point, the same memory would usually be elicited again, beginning in the same temporal location as when initially elicited. The vivid nature of these recollections along with the strict localization of different recollections quite obviously suggests that the hippocampus may be involved with permanent memory storage.

Additional evidence for hippocampal involvement in memory processing comes from case histories involving damage to this structure. Several of the early patients had rather large portions of the hippocampus removed bilaterally, as a result of the seizure focus already having spread to both hemispheres. Postsurgical observations revealed a severe disruption of certain types of memory processes (*see* Scoville & Milner, 1957). Specifically, these patients appeared to have normal recall of past events ranging as far back as childhood. They also had normal digit spans, a task which is similar to looking up a telephone number and remembering it for a few seconds in order to dial it. But these patients had a severe impairment in the ability to acquire and store new information for more than a few minutes. If introduced to a member of the hospital staff, the patient would greet the stranger normally and even carry on a normal conversation with the person. However, if the staff member left and returned a few minutes later, the patient not only failed to recall the name, but had no recollection of having seen the person before. This sequence of introduction, briefly leaving, and reintroduction could be repeated over and over within a short period of time, the patient never showing any sign of recollection. The unexpected severity of this disturbance obviously limited the use of this surgical procedure for the treatment of epilepsy.

Although the hippocampus has clearly been implicated in the memory processes of humans, one of the disturbing sequels to Penfield's reports has been the inability to duplicate a deficit of comparable magnitude in a laboratory animal. In addition to limiting the generality of the phenomenon, this state of affairs makes it virtually impossible to learn more about the nature of the memory deficit, perhaps even to find ways of ameliorating the effect.

A possible clue to the difference between the human cases and the animal studies comes from a study by Milner (1962). Normal subjects and patients with hippocampal damage were given the task of tracing a star in a device which prevented them from seeing their hand or the star, except through a mirror. Because of the reversed image, this is initially a difficult task, but one which shows rather rapid learning. The brain-damaged patients acquired this task at the same rate as normal subjects. On the following day, the normal subjects showed full retention of the acquired skill. The patients with hippocampal damage had no recollection of prior participation in the experiment and had to receive complete instructions before beginning. But, when they began the task (on what they considered to be the first trial), the performance was *equal to that of the normal subjects* (*see* Figure 15–5).

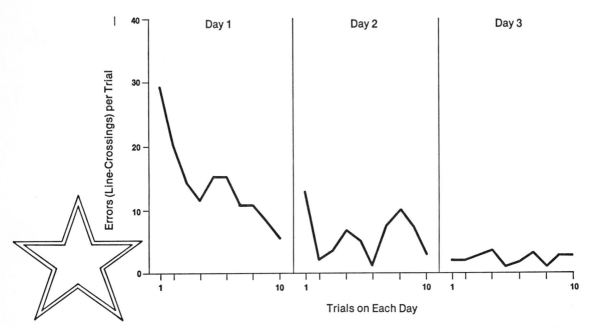

Figure 15–5. At left, the star used in the mirror-drawing test. The subject had to trace a complete path between the lines while watching his hand only through a mirror. At right, a learning curve for a patient with bilateral ablation of the medial temporal lobe. (After Milner, 1962, © Litton Educational Publishing, reprinted by permission of Van Nostrand Reinhold.)

Apparently the subjects had forgotten all of the verbal and conceptual elements of the experimental situation, but showed full retention of the complicated motor skill. It may be that the experiments that have been done with laboratory animals are more akin to the mirror-tracing response than to the instructions associated with the task. In any event, it seems clear that the processing and storage of memory *involves* the hippocampus, although there is still some question as to both the *generality of the effect* and the *precise nature* of the role of the hippocampus.

III. INFORMATION PROCESSING IN A DUAL BRAIN

The Split Brain

One of the major characteristics of the morphology of mammals that extends all the way back to very simple multicelled organisms is bilateral symmetry; i.e., both the internal and external structures of the body tend to be present in pairs, each being a mirror image of the other. The brain is no exception to this rule. The cerebral hemispheres of mammals are separated by a deep midline fissure that completely separates the two cortical mantles. If this fissure is spread apart, one can easily see a broad, flat band of fibers, the corpus callossum, that connect the two hemispheres of the brain. Detailed anatomical studies have shown that this bundle represents some 200 million fibers in man, each of which appears to travel from a particular point within one hemisphere to the corresponding point within the other hemisphere. This anatomical arrangement raises a number of questions: Is this fiber bundle strictly a messenger system that gives each hemisphere the same information to allow essentially duplicate processing, or does the corpus callossum act as a coordinating system that allows one hemisphere to perform one class of functions while the other performs a different class of functions?

The corpus callossum is not, of course, the only system of fibers interconnecting the two halves of the brain. All of the major sensory systems have crossed components, as do the motor systems. These systems are organized such that the left half of the brain mediates the perception of the right half of the external environment and controls the movements of the right half of the body. The reason, if any, for the development of this crossed organization remains a mystery.

In an attempt to assess the role of the corpus callossum and other fiber bundles that connect the two halves of the brain, Myers and Sperry (1953) cut the crossed projections of the visual system as well as the corpus callossum in cats. Subsequent behavioral tests of these animals revealed two rather intriguing findings: Perhaps the most surprising finding was that the transection of the largest fiber bundle of the brain, the corpus callossum, had no observable effect on the general mental faculties of the animal. In a typical experiment, the crossed fibers of the visual system were also transected so that the visual input from one eye would be restricted to one

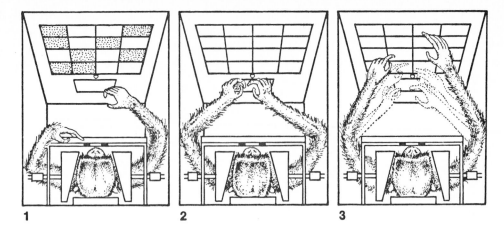

Figure 15–6. Split-brain monkeys can handle more visual information than normal animals. When the monkey pulls a knob (1), 8 of 16 panels light momentarily. The monkey must then start at the bottom and punch the lights that were lighted and no others (2). With the panels lighted for 600 milliseconds normal monkeys get up to the third row from the bottom before forgetting which panels were lighted (3). Split-brain monkeys complete the entire task with the panels lighted only 200 milliseconds. The monkeys look at the panels through filters; since the optic chiasm is cut in these animals, the filters allow each hemisphere to see the colored panels on one side only. (From Gazzaniga, 1967, © Scientific American, Inc.)

side of the brain. With one eye blindfolded, the cat could learn a discrimination on the basis of visual cues as rapidly as do normal cats, even though only one-half of the brain was in use for the acquisition of the task (*see* Gazzaniga, 1967).

A second finding was that the two halves of the brain, when separated, could independently and simultaneously learn different tasks. In the experiment just outlined, for example, switching the blindfold to the opposite eye revealed that the other side of the brain was completely naïve; as many trials were required to learn the task with the opposite eye as were required initially (*see* Gazzaniga, 1967). Further experiments with monkeys revealed that it was possible for an organism to perform *simultaneously* two separate tasks at the same rate that a normal animal could perform a single task (*see* Figure 15–6). In other words, it is possible (at least under some conditions) for the organism with a split brain to process information at twice the rate of a normal animal.

Later studies revealed, as one might expect, that there was a price attached to this apparent superiority following the split-brain operation. The details of the rather subtle changes that accompany such damage are best exemplified by the results of studies involving human patients in whom the corpus callossum has been transected. The medical reason for these operations was essentially the same as that described previously in the case of temporal lobe lesions. The spread of epileptic seizures from one hemisphere to the other could, presumably, be prevented by the transection of

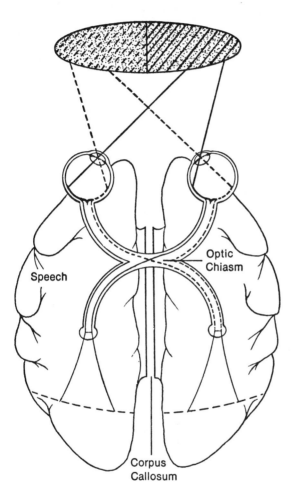

Figure 15–7. Visual input to a bisected brain is limited to one hemisphere by presenting information only in one visual field. The right and left fields of view are projected, via the optic chiasm, to the left and right hemispheres of the brain respectively. If a person fixes his gaze on a point, information to the left of the point goes only to the right hemisphere and information to the right of the point goes to the left hemisphere. Stimuli in the left visual field cannot be described by a split-brain patient because of the disconnection between the right hemisphere and the speech center, which is in the left hemisphere. (From Gazzaniga, 1967, © Scientific American, Inc.)

the fibers that travel between the two areas. Because of the lack of any easily observable behavioral change following transection of the corpus callossum in experimental animals, this seemed to be a particularly promising technique for the treatment of epilepsy. As a result of detailed behavioral studies of a number of patients who have undergone this operation, Sperry and his associates have revealed important findings with respect to the functions of the two hemispheres and the interconnecting corpus callossum.

When Sperry and his associates began to make detailed observations of the behavior of patients with corpus callossum transection, it became apparent that certain abnormalities were present, even outside of formal testing situations (cf., Gazzanniga, 1967). The patients typically performed virtually all tasks with the right hand, while ignoring the left hand. This failure to respond to the left side of the body was sometimes rather dramatic, to the point of not noticing when objects were bumped into, or even failing to put the left arm into a coat sleeve. This was not the result of any specific sensory deficit or motor paralysis, but rather represented a perceptual deficit.

Specifically designed tests revealed that the two hemispheres process different types of information in rather different fashions. It is obviously unethical to cut the crossed fibers of the visual system for the purpose of conducting an experiment in humans, but the same results can be obtained by either flashing the visual stimulus briefly into one visual field, or by using special polarized lenses (*see* Figure 15–7). Using either of these methods, the visual information can be presented so that it reaches only the left hemisphere or only the right hemisphere.

Such tests revealed that the left hemisphere responded normally to verbal information and could be used to provide accurate verbal descriptions of objects presented in the right visual field (this visual field projects to the left hemisphere). This finding is, of course, related to the fact that the area that controls speech is typically located in the left (dominant) hemisphere.

The right hemisphere has much more limited verbal abilities. Objects that are presented in the left visual field cannot be described verbally but, curiously, the subjects can match the written names of common objects by picking up the appropriate object. They can even arrange letters to form words, but are then unable to *name* the words just formed! These findings should not, however, be taken to mean that the right hemisphere is inferior to the left. In tasks that involve spatial manipulation, temporal sequences such as melodies, the utilization of environmental sounds and others, the right hemisphere is clearly superior to the left.

The Reversible Split Brain (Spreading Depression)

In the early 1940s, several investigators (e.g., Dusser de Barenne & McCulloch, 1941; Leao, 1944) reported that the application of KCl crystals to the cortex produced a depression of electrical activity that spread from the point of the stimulation until large areas of the cortex were involved. Following removal of the stimulation, the cortical electroencephalogram returned to apparently normal parameters over the course of several hours.

Since the electrical activity reflects the functioning of neurons, the temporary electrical silence is presumed to reflect a temporary loss of function of the affected area. The depression of electrical activity spreads until it reaches a deep fissure in the surface of the cortex, which it will not cross. In the rat brain, the only deep fissure is the midline fissure separating the two hemispheres, so the application of KCl to one hemisphere results in the loss of function in the entire cortical mantel of that hemisphere, while the opposite hemisphere shows no signs of electrical depression. Bures and Buresova (1960) saw the promise of this phenomenon as a technique for the investigation of memory processes and developed an imaginative series of experiments that have provided some important additional insights regarding the normal interaction between the two hemispheres.

In the first series of experiments they trained normal rats to turn either left or right to escape electrical shock. Twenty-four hours later, the rats were treated with KCl on one hemisphere only and trained to turn in the opposite direction. On the following day, the animals were retested, some with no spreading depression, some with spreading depression on the same side, and some with spreading depression on the opposite side. The animals in the first two groups consistently chose the side that had been correct during the reversal training. By contrast, the rats with spreading depression in the opposite hemisphere showed no apparent retention of the intervening reversal training and chose the side that had been correct during initial acquisition (*see* Figure 15–8). In other words, the information acquired while one hemisphere was nonfunctional was not automatically transferred to the opposite hemisphere during the intervening period of time when both hemispheres were intact.

Although it seemed highly unlikely, these investigators considered the possibility that rats may normally use only one hemisphere or the other to acquire such a task, and that the information stayed on that side. To rule out this possibility, they trained a large

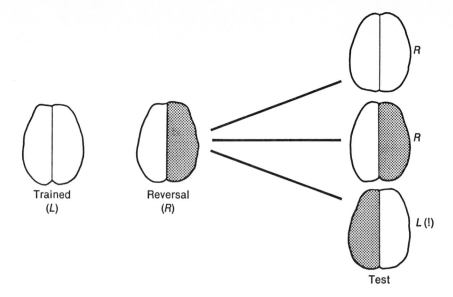

Figure 15-8. The unmarked surface of the brain diagram at the extreme left indicates that all rats were trained to turn in one direction (e.g., left) with no treatment. Then the rats received reversal training with one hemisphere (hachured) treated with KCl. When tested with either no treatment or with the same hemisphere treated with KCl, the reversed habit was shown. But, when tested with the opposite hemisphere depressed, the original habit was shown. Thus, the reversal training had not been transferred to the hemisphere that was depressed during the reversal training. (Based on the results of Bures & Buresova, 1960.)

number of rats under normal conditions, then tested one-half of the rats with the left side depressed and the other half with the right side depressed. Without exception, all rats showed retention of the previously learned task. The probability of randomly selecting the "correct" side for each rat is negligibly small—hence, the conclusion that under normal conditions, *each* hemisphere has all the information necessary to perform the task.

If the information normally crosses from one hemisphere to the other (presumably via the corpus callossum), then why had it not crossed during the hours in which both hemispheres were functional? One possibility is that the transfer may take longer than the interval used in these experiments. To test this possibility, Russell and Ochs (1963) trained rats with one hemisphere depressed, then allowed them to recover for periods ranging up to several weeks. The results were the same—the information was not transferred to the opposite hemisphere as indicated by tests in which the originally functional hemisphere was treated with KCl.

These investigators then set about to determine the requirements for effecting the transfer from one cortex to the other. The answer was at once simple and intriguing: The presentation of a single *reinforced* trial during the period when both hemispheres were functional was sufficient to transfer the learned information from the originally functional hemisphere to the originally depressed hemisphere. Thus, there appears to be some triggering mechanism that can produce the rapid transfer of all the information, even though there appears to be no *passive* transfer over the course of several weeks in the absence of this triggering event.

Dissociated States

In the previous sections of this chapter we have discussed various types of experimental procedures that essentially force the organism to function with only part of the central nervous system: In the case of lesions, the organism is obviously functioning without the tissue that has been removed (and it should also be noted that the lesion produces a variety of secondary effects in the remaining tissue). In the case of KCl-induced spreading depression, the organism is temporarily forced to function without one (or both) of the cerebral cortices. In the case of the transection of the corpus callossum, the organism is forced to function without the interaction between the two hemispheres (except via long, polysynaptic pathways through the subcortex). In each of these cases, it has been shown that a loss of memory can occur but subsequent relearning and retention is possible. We will now consider another method of limiting brain functions—by the injection of drugs that act upon certain chemically defined populations of neurons.

There is, of course, a long history of interest in the effects of drugs upon mental functions. Long before the days of modern neuropharmacology, the medicine men, religious shamans, and other practitioners had discovered that derivatives of certain plants could lead to altered mental states. With the advent of modern pharmacology that was based upon the chemical mediators of neural activity, there developed an interest in drugs that could improve or impair mental abilities. To outline even the major successes and failures of these attempts would go well beyond the scope of this treatment; suffice it to say that the problem of producing specific effects that could not be attributed to changes in sensory, motor, or general arousal functions has remained a persistent, perhaps insoluble problem.

In the course of investigating the effects of drugs on performance, Overton (1964) detected a very important flaw in the design of virtually all of the experiments that were being conducted in this area. A typical experiment at that time went as follows: The subjects would first be trained to perform a particular task. Then, either a drug injection or a saline injection would be administered during the test session. Any resulting impairment associated with the drug would be attributed to the direct effect of that drug upon the neural systems that are involved with memory functions (assuming, of course, that sensory and motor impairments could be shown to be minimal).

The experimental design used by Overton to point out the inappropriateness of this conclusion was quite simple: As shown in Table 15–1, one-half of the animals were trained following the injection of a drug, while the remaining half were trained following the injection of saline. Then, each of these groups was subdivided so that one subgroup was tested with saline and the other tested with the drug. The results were quite clear. The rats that were *trained with the drug, then tested with saline* showed severe impairment, as did the rats that were trained with saline, then tested with the drug. By contrast, those rats that received saline during both sessions *or the drug during both sessions* showed complete retention. In other words, the effect apparently was not specific to the action of the drug upon some substrate of memory, but rather was dependent upon the *difference* in treatment between the training session and the testing session. Overton referred to this as *dissociated learning* or *state dependent learning,* the implication

Table 15–1.   State-Dependent Learning Design*

		TESTING	
		DRUG	*NO DRUG*
TRAINING	*DRUG*	Good Retention	Poor Retention
	NO DRUG	Poor Retention	Good Retention

*Shaded areas = Conditions the same during both training and testing.
(Based on results of Overton, 1964.)

being that in order to retrieve a particular set of information it is necessary for the central nervous system to be in essentially the same physiological state as during acquisition.

There are two, somewhat different, theoretical accounts of this phenomenon:

One explanation of the dissociated learning is essentially a *stimulus generalization decrement model.* It is a well-known fact that many drugs are capable of producing an array of symptoms that include such things as nausea, dizziness, drowsiness, blurred vision, ringing of the ears, heart palpitations, flushing of the skin, etc. Different classes of drugs (and to a certain extent, different drugs within a class) produce different patterns of symptoms. The stimulus generalization decrement model essentially postulates that the altered perceptions of both the external and internal environments create a sufficient difference between the drug state and the nondrug state to prevent the retrieval of information that was acquired while in the opposite state.

The alternate view of state dependent learning can be termed a *subsystem replacement model.* The drugs that are active in the central nervous system (and they must be to produce state dependent learning) are typically rather selective with respect to the population of neurons that they influence. For example, a class of compounds termed anticholinergics (e.g., scopolamine) act by blocking the action of the neurotransmitter acetylcholine. Another class of compounds known as adrenergic blockers (e.g., dibenzyline) act by blocking the activity of neurons that utilize norepinephrine as a transmitter substance. Although no drugs are truly specific, the effects upon other populations of neurons are typically much less dramatic, and are sometimes called "side-effects." According to this model, the failure to retrieve while in different functional states is analogous to the failure to retrieve when first one hemisphere, then the other is inactivated by KCl-induced spreading depression—the organism is essentially naïve because the currently functional population of neurons was never exposed to the learning situation. On the surface this notion may seem less likely than the stimulus generalization model, but there is some evidence that weighs rather heavily in favor of the subsystem replacement model.

The earliest study favoring the notion of separate systems being utilized while in different functional states was actually done several decades prior to Overton's findings. The problem being investigated was whether or not the actual performance of the response is necessary in order to learn an appropriate conditioned response. Girden and Culler (1937) administered a drug called curare that paralyzes skeletal muscles, then paired a conditioned stimulus with electrical shock to the foot. When tested later without the paralyzing drug, the animals did not perform the response, thus supporting the notion that the performance of the response was essential. But about the same time, several other lines of evidence had shown rather convincingly that the response was *not* essential.

In an effort to account for these conflicting results, Black, Carlson, and Solomon (1962) suggested that curare may have an action on the central nervous system in addition to the peripheral paralyzing effects. Support for this notion came from their finding that animals that had been trained while paralyzed with curare performed the conditioned response when tested following decortication, but not if tested normally. They suggested that curare may block cortical functions, thereby forcing the learning to take place in subcortical circuits. When tested in the normal state, the essentially untrained cortex would dominate. The removal of the cortex may allow the subcortical circuits to express the prior learning.[1]

The types of drugs that lead to dissociable states provide further clues as to the nature of the phenomenon. Several classes of drugs are highly effective in producing dissociable states while others are ineffective. The question arises: Is this due to stimulus generalization or to functionally separate systems? Both notions predict the same results for the drugs that are effective. But what about the drugs that are relatively ineffective? A case in point involves the compound scopolamine, which is available in two slightly different chemical forms: The chemical structure of scopolamine methyl bromide prevents it from leaving the bloodstream in the brain, so it acts only in the peripheral nervous system; scopolamine hydrobromide freely enters the brain and thus influences both the peripheral and the central nervous system. Thus, both compounds produce peripheral symptoms including blurred vision, increased heart rate, heart palpitations and a dry-mouth sensation. It might be expected that both compounds would lead to dissociated states as predicted by the generalization decrement model. But only the *centrally* active form of the compound is effective in producing dissociated learning. This could, of course, be attributed to a greater change in the sensorium of the organism, but the fact that the peripherally active form is virtually ineffective rather than less effective casts doubt upon this explanation.

---

1. For the sake of accuracy, it should be pointed out that the results of later studies involving curare have not always been consistent with the dissociation notion. This may be attributable, in part at least, to the fact that curare was not available as a pharmaceutically pure compound, but rather as a crude extract—a situation that has led to similar inconsistencies in other areas of research. The studies cited in the text are, however, of historical importance in setting the stage for more recent experimentation.

A further analysis of the types of compounds that produce dissociated states also favors the subsystem replacement notion rather than stimulus generalization. A number of compounds, including scopolamine methyl bromide and lithium chloride, produce their major effects in the periphery and are quite effective in producing conditioned aversion with only one or a few pairings (*see* Chapter 7). These same compounds that produce gastric disturbances do not lead to dissociated states. The stimulus generalization model is placed in the somewhat embarrassing position of agreeing that the alteration in the organism's sensorium is sufficient to mediate conditioned aversion while being ineffective (even at much higher dosages) in mediating the dissociation phenomenon. The subsystem replacement model would not predict dissociation with these compounds because they would not be expected to interfere with the normal circuitry of the brain.

The basic tenets of the subsystem replacement notion may be summarized by referring to the highly schematized model shown in Figure 15–9. Assume that there are separate *populations of neurons* that are capable of mediating the acquisition of a particular task. Under normal conditions, Population I would dominate and exercise the greatest control over the behavior of the subject. But, if this population of neurons is blocked by a drug, the next higher order of circuits, Population II, would mediate the acquisition of

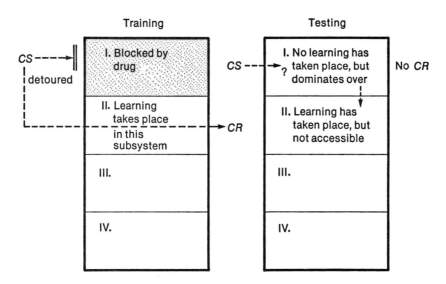

Figure 15–9. Hierarchy of systems that *can* be used for a particular task. The higher-order system will always dominate (subsystem replacement model), so that behavior which is normally controlled by System I becomes controlled by System II during drugged states.

the task. Testing under the influence of the drug would be expected to show good retention. But, if tested in a nondrugged state, the behavior would be controlled primarily by Population I, and a retention deficit would be indicated since this part of the neural circuitry was inactivated during initial acquisition. These notions may be easier to comprehend by considering the analogy of an administrative hierarchy. Decisions may be made by subordinates while the boss is on vacation (drugged). Without this information the boss may not function properly upon his return to normal duties.

The arguments outlined above were not designed to provide compelling proof against the notion of generalization decrement, but rather to provide an alternative view that reflects the multiplicity of memory processing. In the experiments involving KCl-induced spreading depression or split-brain preparations, it would be easy to suggest that the dissociation of behavior is due to stimulus generalization decrement. However, it has been more fruitful to view these results as evidence that different subdivisions of the brain (i.e., the left and right hemispheres) have the capability of functioning independently under the appropriate experimental conditions. It is also easy to suggest that the injection of certain drugs produces dissociation through stimulus generalization decrement. But it may be more appropriate to view these results as evidence that different subdivisions of the brain (i.e., pharmacologically defined populations of neurons) have the capability of functioning independently under the appropriate experimental conditions.

The fact that there are a number of different classes of drugs that produce dissociation, apparently through their actions on several different populations of neurons, suggests that it is possible to go a step beyond the split brain to what we could refer to as a segmented brain. Each class of drugs may leave the organism with an arrangement of inactive and active populations of cells that is different from that which exists in the nondrugged state.

IV. A GENERAL SUMMARY

The series of chapters just completed has examined memory and retrieval from a number of different perspectives. Among these have been historical accounts of mnemonic devices and case histories of persons having exceptionally good or exceptionally impaired abilities to recall information. We have examined laboratory studies ranging from human verbal learning to simple one-trial learning in rats. We have examined techniques ranging from psychosurgery to electron microscopy. The question arises: What can we say about memory that could not have been said by the early Greeks? Despite the controversial nature of much of the data described in these chapters, there are certain generalities that most investigators find acceptable.

In an earlier chapter, it was pointed out that the only reason for studying memory is the fact that forgetting occurs; if it did not, it would only be necessary to know the prior training that had taken place to know what memories were still intact. The simplest and most common-sensical notion of forgetting is that the strength of the memory simply fades with time due to some unknown process. Despite the face validity of this notion, relevant experimental evidence has been difficult to obtain. Memories may not be lost through the ravages of time like a pebble is worn down by the rushing waters of a stream. Rather, it would appear that memories are lost through interference in much the same way as a particular pebble is lost among the many similar pebbles of the stream bed. In the case of memory retrieval, it has been shown that particular associations can interfere either with associations that are learned at a later time (proactive interference) or with associations that were learned earlier (retroactive interference). The more closely related these interfering associations, the more easily they disrupt the other association.

There is also considerable evidence that forgetting occurs not so much as a result of the actual loss of an association, but rather from an inability to retrieve that association. Tulving (1974) has pointed out that a memory consists of two sets of information, the information that has been stored in the organism and the information that is currently present in the external environment. If these external stimuli, called retrieval cues, are appropriate to the situation, then the previously learned information can be retrieved and used. If not, there is a failure to retrieve, and it is concluded that forgetting has occurred.

One of the most common day-to-day experiences is the occurrence of forgetting of previously acquired information. In most cases, this can be attributed to interfering associations or to a relative lack of appropriate retrieval cues. But in a disturbing number of cases, the forgetting seems to occur almost instantaneously. The recently dialed telephone number must be looked up again, or the name of the person just introduced fades before the handshake is complete. Interference mechanisms probably play an important role in this type of forgetting as well as in forgetting during longer intervals, but this was not known until recently.

Consequently, there have developed notions that there may be different processes for laying down memories—short-term and long-term mechanisms. Although the initial reasons for suspecting multiple processes of memory storage were based on somewhat shaky assumptions, the resulting experimental evidence has provided some general support. Short-term memories may be based on electrical activity, while longer-term memories may be based on physiological or metabolic changes. Various types of physiological trauma produce severe disruption of the ability to retrieve short-term memories, while memories that have been established earlier remain intact. In other words, the older memories appear to be more firmly entrenched than those that were recently acquired.

In the present chapter, we have discussed a variety of mechanisms that could account for both the short-term and the long-term storage of memories. Anatomical studies have been hard pressed to demonstrate an area of the brain that is critical for the processing of memories, although there is a considerable body of evidence that the hippocampus may be of importance. The search for the biochemical bases of memory has also been fraught with disappointment, there being little evidence to convincingly support any of the various notions that have been proposed. The hundreds of studies that were devoted to these problems were not, however, done in vain.

Although these studies often failed to support a particular theory, the resulting data have been very useful in adding to our information about memory and retrieval in general. We have learned, for example, that internal cues are of considerable importance in the retrieval of certain types of memories, that newly retrieved memories may be as temporarily unstable as newly acquired memories, and that the memory traces (whatever they are) appear to be duplicated in some respects and deposited in numerous regions of the brain under normal circumstances. Under specific conditions (e.g., drug injections or surgery), it is possible to temporarily restrict the regions in which this can occur and later demonstrate that these multiple storage sites are not the result of the "passive" transfer of information at later times. Rather, the multiple representations appear to be laid down at the time of learning when the information is still undergoing "active" processing.

An important concept that has been developed in conjunction with the notions of short-term and long-term memory is consolidation. Regardless of the theoretical viewpoint, there must be some process to translate the relationships of various sensory inputs into permanent storage. Experimental efforts to describe this process have been reasonably successful in determining the temporal characteristics of this process, but the physical basis of this storage mechanism has remained elusive.

Reference List

Ader, R. Early experience accelerates maturation of the 24-hour adrenocortical rhythm. *Science*, 1969, **163**, 1225–26.

Ader, R., & Conklin, P.M. Handling of pregnant rats: Effects on emotionality of their offspring. *Science*, 1963, **142**, 411–12.

Aghajanian, G.K. & Bloom, F.E. The formation of synaptic junctions in developing rat brain: a quantitative electron microscopic study. *Brain Research*, 1967, **6**, 716–27.

Ainslie, G.W. Impulse control in pigeons. *Journal of the Experimental Analysis of Behavior*, 1974, **21**, 485–89.

Allport, G.W. *Personality: A psychological interpretation*. New York: Holt, 1937.

Amsel, A. The role of frustrative nonreward in noncontinuous reward situations. *Psychological Bulletin*, 1958, **55**, 102–18.

Amsel, A. Frustrative nonreward in partial reinforcement and discrimination learning. *Psychological Review*, 1962, **69**, 306–28.

Amsel, A., & Roussel, J. Motivational properties of frustration. *Journal of Experimental Psychology*, 1952, **43**, 363–68.

Anger, D. The role of temporal discriminations in reinforcement of Sidman avoidance behavior. *Journal of the Experimental Analysis of Behavior*, 1963, **6**, 477–506.

Anisman, H., & Waller, T.G. Effects of inescapable shock on subsequent avoidance performance: Role of response repertoire changes. *Journal of Behavioral Biology*, 1973, **9**, 331–35.

Annau, Z., & Kamin, L.J. The conditioned emotional response as a function of intensity of the US. *Journal of Comparative and Physiological Psychology*, 1961, **54**, 428–32.

Armus, H.L. Effect of magnitude of reinforcement on acquisition and extinction of a running response. *Journal of Experimental Psychology*, 1959. **58**, 61–63.

Asratian, E.A. *Compensatory adaptation, reflex activity in the brain*. Oxford: Pergamon Press, 1965.

Ayres, J.J.B., Benedict, J.O., & Witcher, E. Systematic manipulation of individual events in a truly random control in rats. *Journal of Comparative and Physiological Psychology*, 1975, **88**, 97–103.

Azrin, N.H. Sequential effects of punishment. *Science*, 1960, **131**, 605–6.

Azrin, N.H., Holz, W.C., & Hake, D.F. Fixed-ratio punishment. *Journal of the Experimental Analysis of Behavior*, 1963, **6**, 141–48.

Azrin, N.H., Hake, D.F., Holz, W.C., & Hutchinson, R.R. Motivational aspects of escape from punishment. *Journal of the Experimental Analysis of Behavior*, 1965, **8**, 31–44.

Babich, F.R., Jacobson, A.L., Bubash, S., & Jacobson, A. Transfer of a response to naive rats by injection of ribonucleic acid extracted from trained rats. *Science*, 1965, **149**, 656–57.

Baddeley, A.D., & Warrington, E.K. Amnesia and the distinction between long and short-term memory. *Journal of Verbal Learning and Verbal Behavior*, 1970, **9**, 176–89.

Bagg, H.J., Individual differences and family resemblances in animal behavior. *American Naturalist*, 1916, **50**, 222–36.

Baker, T.W. Component strength in a compound CS as a function of number of acquisition trials. *Journal of Experimental Psychology*, 1968, **79**, 347–52.

Banks, R.K. Persistence to continuous punishment and nonreward following training with intermittent punishment and nonreward. *Psychonomic Science*, 1966b, **5**, 105–6.

Banks, R.K. Persistence to continuous punishment following intermittent punishment training. *Journal of Experimental Psychology,* 1966b, **71**, 373–77.

Banks, R.K., & Torney, D. Generalization of persistence: The transfer of approach behavior to differing aversive stimuli. *Canadian Journal of Psychology,* 1969, **23**, 268–73.

Barbizet, J. *Human memory and its pathology.* San Francisco: W.H. Freeman, 1970.

Barnett, S.A. *The rat: A study in behavior.* Chicago: Aldine, 1963.

Barry, H., III. Effects of strength of drive on learning and on extinction. *Journal of Experimental Psychology,* 1958, **55**, 473–81.

Barry, H., III. Effects of drive strength on extinction and spontaneous recovery. *Journal of Experimental Psychology,* 1967, **73**, 419–21.

Bartlett, S.C. *Remembering: A study in experimental and social psychology.* Cambridge: Cambridge University Press, 1932.

Bass, M.J., & Hull, C.L. The irradiation of a tactile conditioned reflex in man. *Journal of Comparative Psychology,* 1934, **17**, 47–65.

Baum, W.M. Choice in a continuous procedure. *Psychonomic Science,* 1972, **28**, 263–64.

Baum, W.M. On two types of deviation from the matching law: bias and undermatching. *Journal of the Experimental Analysis of Behavior,* 1974, **22**, 91–101.

Baum, W.M. Time allocation in human vigilance. *Journal of the Experimental Analysis of Behavior,* 1975, **23**, 45–53.

Beach, F.A. The descent of instinct. *Psychological Review,* 1955, **62**, 401–10.

Beatty, W.W., & Beatty, P.A. Hormonal determinants of sex differences in avoidance behavior and reactivity to electric shock in the rat. *Journal of Comparative and Physiological Psychology,* 1970, **73**, 446–55.

Beecroft, R.S. *Classical conditioning.* Goleta, Calif.: Psychonomic Press, 1966.

Beer, B., & Trumble, G. Timing behavior as a function of amount of reinforcement. *Psychonomic Science,* 1965, **2**, 71–72.

Benedict, J.O., & Ayres, J.J.B. Factors affecting conditioning in the truly random control procedure in the rat. *Journal of Comparative and Physiological Psychology,* 1972, **78**, 323–30.

Berger, H. Uber das Elektroenkephalogram das Menschen. I. *Archives of Psychiatric Nervenky,* 1929, **87**, 527–70.

Bessemer, D.W. Retention of object discriminations by learning-set experienced monkeys (Doctoral dissertation, University of Wisconsin, 1967). (University Microfilms, Ann Arbor, Michigan. No. 67-16, 893).

Bessemer, D.W., & Stollnitz, F. Retention of discriminations and an analysis of learning set. In M. Schrier & F. Stollnitz (Eds.), *Behavior of nonhuman primates: Modern research trends* (Vol. IV). New York: Academic Press, 1971.

Bevan, W. An adaptation level interpretation of reinforcement. *Perceptual and Motor Skills,* 1966, **23**, 511–31.

Bevan, W. The contextual basis of behavior. *American Psychologist,* 1968, **23**, 701–13.

Bickford, R.G., Molder, D.W., Dodge, H.W., Jr., Svien, H.J., & Rome, H.P. Changes in memory function produced by electrical stimulation of the temporal lobe in man. *Research Publications of the Association for Research in Nervous and Mental Diseases,* 1958, **36**, 227–43.

Bindra, D. A unified account of classical conditioning and operant training. In A.H. Black & W.F. Prokasy (Eds.), *Classical conditioning II.* New York: Appleton-Century-Crofts, 1972.

Bindra, D. A motivational view of learning performance and behavior modification. *Psychological Review,* 1974, **81**, 199–213.

Bindra, D., & Palfai, T. The nature of positive and negative incentive-motivational effects on general activity. *Journal of Comparative and Physiological Psychology,* 1967, **63**, 288–92.

Bitterman, M.E. Animal learning. In J.B. Sidowski (Ed.), *Experimental methods and instrumentation in psychology.* New York: McGraw-Hill, 1966.

Bitterman, M.E. Thorndike and the problem of animal intelligence. *American Psychologist,* 1969, **24**, 4.

Black, A.H., Carlson, N.J., & Solomon, R.C. Exploratory studies of the conditioning of automatic responses in curarized dogs. *Psychological Monographs,* 1962, **76** (1, Whole No. 29).

Black, R.W. Shifts in magnitude of reward and effects in instrumental and selective learning: A reinterpretation. *Psychological Review,* 1968, **75**, 114–26.

Blanchard, D.C., & Blanchard, R.J. Innate and

conditioned reactions to threat in rats with amygdaloid lesions. *Journal of Comparative and Physiological Psychology,* 1972, **81,** 281–90.

Blodgett, H.C.   The effect of the introduction of reward upon the maze performance of rats. *University of California Publication in Psychology,* 1929, 4, 113–34.

Bloomfield, T.M.   Contrast and inhibition in discrimination learning by the pigeon: Analysis through drug effects. *Learning and Motivation,* 1972, 3, 162–78.

Blough, D.S.   Delayed matching in the pigeon. *Journal of the American Analysis of Behavior,* 1959, 2, 151–60.

Bolles, R.C.   *A theory of motivation.* New York: Harper, 1967.

Bolles, R.C.   Avoidance and escape learning: simultaneous acquisition of different responses. *Journal of Comparative and Physiological Psychology,* 1969, **68,** 355–58.

Bolles, R.C.   Species-specific defense reactions and avoidance learning. *Psychological Review,* 1970, 77, 32–48.

Bolles, R.C.   Reinforcement, expectancy and learning. *Psychological Review,* 1972, **79,** 394–409.

Bolles, R.C., & Grossen, N.E.   Effects of an informational stimulus on the acquisition of avoidance behavior in rats. *Journal of Comparative and Physiological Psychology,* 1969, 68, 90–99.

Bolles, R.C., & Grossen, N.E.   The noncontingent manipulation of incentive motivation. In J.H. Reynierse (Ed.), *Current issues in animal learning.* Lincoln: University of Nebraska Press, 1970.

Bolles, R.C., Stokes, L.W., & Younger, M.S.   Does CS termination reinforce avoidance behavior? *Journal of Comparative and Physiological Psychology,* 1966, **62,** 201–7.

Boneau, C.A.   Paradigm regained? Cognitive behaviors restated. *American Psychologist,* 1974, 29, 297–309.

Booth, J.H., & Hammond, J.L.   Configural conditioning: Greater fear in rats to compound than component through overtraining of the compound. *Journal of Experimental Psychology,* 1971, 87, 255–62.

Boring, E.G.   *A history of experimental psychology.* New York: Appleton-Century-Crofts, 1957.

Born, D.G.   Resistance of a free operant to extinction and suppression with punishment as a function of amount of training. *Psychonomic Science,* 1967, 8, 21–22.

Bousfield, W.A., & Barry, H.   The visual imagery of a lightning calculator. *American Journal of Psychology,* 1933, 45, 353–58.

Bovet, D., Bovet-Nitti, F., & Oliverio, A.   Genetic aspects of learning and memory in mice. *Science,* 1969, **163,** 139–49.

Bowen, J., & McCain, G.   Occurrence of the partial reinforcement extinction effect after only one NRNR sequence of trials. *Psychonomic Science,* 1967, 9, 15–16.

Bower, G.H.   Partial and correlated reward in escape conditioning. *Journal of Experimental Psychology,* 1960, 59, 126–30.

Bower, G.H.   A contrast effect in differential conditioning. *Journal of Experimental Psychology,* 1961, **62,** 196–99.

Bower, G.H., Fowler, H., & Trapold, M.A.   Escape learning as a function of amount of shock reduction. *Journal of Experimental Psychology,* 1959, **58,** 482–84.

Bower, G.H., & Grusec, T.   Effect of prior Pavlovian discrimination training upon learning an operant discrimination. *Journal of the Experimental Analysis of Behavior,* 1964, **7,** 401–4.

Breland, K., & Breland, M.   The misbehavior of organisms. *American Psychologist,* 1961, **61,** 681–84.

Briggs, M.H., & Kitto, G.B.   The molecular basis of memory and learning. *Psychological Review,* 1962, **69,** 537–41.

Brogden, W.J.   Sensory preconditioning. *Journal of Experimental Psychology,* 1939, **25,** 323–32.

Bronstein, P.M., Levine, M.J., & Marcus, M.   A rat's first bite: The nongenetic, cross-generational transfer of information. *Journal of Comparative and Physiological Psychology,* 1975, 89, 295–98.

Brown, P.L., & Jenkins, H.M.   Autoshaping of the pigeon's key peck. *Journal of the Experimental Analysis of Behavoir,* 1968, **11,** 1–8.

Brown, R.T., & Wagner, A.R.   Resistance to punishment and extinction following training with shock or nonreinforcement. *Journal of Experimental Psychology,* 1964, **68,** 503–7.

Brown, W.L., & McDowell, A.A.   Response shift learning in rhesus monkeys. *Journal of Comparative and Physiological Psychology,* 1963,

56, 335–36.

Brush, F.R. On the differences between animals that learn and do not learn to avoid electric shock. *Psychonomic Science*, 1966, **5**, 123–24.

Brush, F.R. Retention of aversively motivated behavior. In F.R. Brush (Ed.), *Aversive conditioning and learning*. New York: Academic Press, 1971.

Bures, J., & Buresova, O. The use of Leao's spreading depression in the study of interhemispheric transfer of memory traces. *Journal of Comparative and Physiological Psychology*, 1960, **53**, 558–65.

Buresova, O., & Bures, J. The effect of prolonged cortical spreading depression on learning and memory in rats. *Journal of Neurobiology*, 1961, **2**, 135–46.

Byrne, W.L., Samuel D., Bennet, E.L., Rosenzweig, M.R., Wasserman, E., Wagner, A.R., Gardner, F., Galambos, R., Berger, B.D., Margules, D.L., Fenichel, R.L., Stein, L., Corson, J.A., Enesco, H.E., Chorover, S.L., Holt, C.E., III, Schiller, P.H., Chiappetta, L., Jarvik, M.E., Leaf, R.C., Dutcher, J.D., Horovitz, Z.P., & Carlton, P.L. Memory transfer. *Science*, 1966, **153**, 658–59.

Camp, D.C., Raymond, G.A., & Church, R.M. Temporal relationship between response and punishment. *Journal of Experimental Psychology*, 1967, **74**, 114–23.

Campbell, B.A. Developmental studies of learning and motivation in infraprimate mammals. In H.W. Stevenson, E.H. Hess, & H.L. Rheingold (Eds.), *Early behavior: Comparative and developmental approaches*. New York: Wiley, 1967.

Campbell, B.A., & Church, P.M. *Punishment and aversive behavior*. New York: Appleton-Century-Crofts, 1969.

Campbell, B.A., & Jaynes, J. Reinstatement. *Psychological Review*, 1966, **73**, 478–80.

Campbell, B.A., & Sheffield, F.D. Relation of random activity to food deprivation. *Journal of Comparative and Physiological Psychology*, 1953, **46**, 320–22.

Campbell, B.A., & Spear, N.E. Ontongeny of memory. *Psychological Review*, 1972, **79**, 215–36.

Campbell, P.E., Batsche, C.J., & Batsche, G.M. Spaced trials reward magnitude effects in the rat: Single versus multiple food pellets. *Journal of Comparative and Physiological Psychology*, 1972, **81**, 360–64.

Campbell, P.E., Knouse, S.B., & Wroten, J.D. Resistance to extinction in the rat following regular and irregular schedules of partial reinforcement. *Journal of Comparative and Physiological Psychology*, 1970, **72**, 210–15.

Cannon, W.B. *The wisdom of the body*. New York: Norton, 1932.

Capaldi, E.D. Resistance to extinction in rats as a function of deprivation level and schedule of reward in acquisition. *Journal of Comparative Physiological Psychology*, 1972, **79**, 90–98.

Capaldi, E.D., & Singh, R. Percentage body weight and the successive negative contrast effect in rats. *Learning and Motivation*, 1973, **4**, 405–16.

Capaldi, E.J. Partial reinforcement: A hypothesis of sequential effects. *Psychological Review*, 1966, **73**, 459–79.

Capaldi, E.J. A sequential hypothesis of instrumental learning. In K.W. Spence & J.T. Spence (Eds.), *The psychology of learning and motivation* (Vol. 1). New York: Academic Press, 1967.

Capaldi, E.J. Memory and learning: A sequential viewpoint. In W.K. Honig & P.H.R. James (Eds.), *Animal memory* (Ch. 3). New York: Academic Press, 1971.

Capaldi, E.J. Successive negative contrast effect: Intertrial interval type of shift and four sources of generalization decrement. *Journal of Experimental Psychology*, 1972, **96**, 433–38.

Capaldi, E.J. Partial reward either following or preceding consistent reward: A case of reinforcement level. *Journal of Experimental Psychology*, 1974, **102**, 954–62.

Capaldi, E.J., Hart, D., & Stanley, L.R. Effect of intertrial reinforcement on the aftereffect of nonreinforcement and resistance to extinction. *Journal of Experimental Psychology*, 1963, **65**, 70–74.

Capaldi, E.J., & Lynch, D. Repeated shifts in reward magnitude: Evidence in favor of an associational and absolute (noncontextual) interpretation. *Journal of Experimental Psychology*, 1967, **75**, 226–35.

Capaldi, E.J., & Spivey, J.E. Stimulus consequences of reinforcement and nonreinforcement: Stimulus traces or memory. *Psychonomic Science*, 1964, **1**, 403–4.

Carlton, P.L. The interacting effects of deprivation and reinforcement schedule. *Journal of Experimental Analysis of Behavior*, 1961, **4**, 379–81.

Carran, A.B., Yeudall, L.T., & Royce, J.R. Voltage level and skin resistance in avoidance conditioning in inbred strains of mice. *Journal of Comparative and Physiological Psychology*, 1964, **58**, 427–30.

Caul, W.F., Barrett, R.J., Thune, G.E., & Osborne, G.L. Avoidance decrement as a function of training-test interval: Single cycle or multi-phasic? *Behavioral Biology*, 1974, **11**, 409–14.

Champion, R.A. Stimulus intensity effects in response evocation. *Psychological Review*, 1962, **69**, 429–49.

Chiszar, D.A., & Spear, N.E. Stimulus change, reversal learning and retention in the rat. *Journal of Comparative and Physiological Psychology*, 1969, **69**, 190–95.

Church, R.M, & Black, A.H. Latency of the conditioned heart rate as a function of CS–UCS interval. *Journal of Comparative and Physiological Psychology*, 1958, **51**, 478–82.

Church, R.M., Raymond, G.A., & Beauchamp, R.D. Response suppression as a function of intensity and duration of a punishment. *Journal of Comparative and Physiological Psychology*, 1967, **63**, 39–44.

Collier, G. Consummatory and instrumental responding as functions of deprivation. *Journal of Experimental Psychology*, 1962, **64**, 410–14.

Collier, G. Body weight loss as a measure of motivation in hunger and thirst. *Annals of the New York Academy of Science*, 1969, **157**, 594–609.

Collier, G., Hirsch, E., & Hamlin, P.H. The ecological determinants of reinforcement in the rat. *Physiology of Behavior*, 1972, **9**, 705–16.

Collier, G., Knarr, F.A., & Marx, M.H. Some relations between the intensive properties of the consummatory response and reinforcement. *Journal of Experimental Psychology*, 1961, **62**, 484–95.

Collier, G., & Squibb, R.L. Diet and activity. *Journal of Comparative and Physiological Psychology*, 1967, **64**, 409–13.

Collins, J., & D'Amato, M.R. Magnesium pemoline: Effects on avoidance conditioning mediated by anticipatory responses. *Psycho-nomic Science*, 1968, **12**, 115–16.

Cook, J.O., & Barnes, L.W., Jr. Choice of delay of inevitable shock. *Journal of Abnormal and Social Psychology*, 1964, **68**, 669–72.

Cooper, R.M., & Zubek, J.P. Effects of enriched and restricted early environments on the learning ability of bright and dull rats. *Canadian Journal of Psychology*, 1958, **12**, 159–64.

Coppock, H.W., & Chambers, R.M. GSR conditioning: An illustration of useless distinctions between "type" of conditioning. *Psychological Reports*, 1959, **6**, 171–77.

Corey, S.M. An experimental study of retention in the white rat. *Journal of Experimental Psychology*, 1931, **14**, 252–59.

Corkin, S. Acquisition of motor skill after bilateral medial temporal excision. *Neuropsychologia*, 1968, **6**, 255–65.

Craig, W. Appetites and aversions as constituents of instincts. *Biological Bulletin*, 1918, **34**, 91–107.

Crespi, L.P. Quantitative variation of incentive and performance in the white rat. *American Journal of Psychology*, 1942, **55**, 467–517.

Crespi, L.P. Amount of reinforcement and level of performance. *Psychological Review*, 1944, **51**, 341–57.

Crichton, M. *The terminal man.* New York: Bantam Books, 1972.

Culbertson, J.L. Effects of brief reinforcement delays on acquisition and extinction of brightness discriminations in rats. *Journal of Comparative and Physiological Psychology*, 1970, **70**, 317–25.

Culler, E.A. Recent advances in some concepts of conditioning. *Psychological Review*, 1938, **45**, 134–53.

Cummins, R.A., Walsh, R.N., Budtz-Olsen, O.E., Konstantinas, T., & Hórsfall, C.R. Environmentally induced changes in the brains of elderly rats. *Nature*, 1973, **243**, 516–18.

Daly, H.B. Excitatory and inhibitory effects of complete and incomplete reward reduction in the double runway. *Journal of Experimental Psychology*, 1968, **76**, 430–38.

Daly, H.B. Learning of a hurdle-jump response to escape cues paired with reduced reward or frustrative nonreward. *Journal of Experimental Psychology*, 1969a, **79**, 146–57.

Daly, H.B. Is instrumental responding necessary for nonreward following reward to be frustrated? *Journal of Experimental Psychology*, 1969b, **80**, 186–87.

D'Amato, M.R. Role of anticipatory responses in avoidance conditioning: An important control. *Psychonomic Science*, 1967, **8**, 191–92.

D'Amato, M.R. Experimental psychology: Methodology, psychophysics, and learning. New York: McGraw-Hill, 1970.

D'Amato, M.R. Delayed matching and short-term memory in monkeys. In G.H. Bower (Ed.), *The psychology in learning and motivation: Advances in research and theory* (Vol. VII). New York: Academic Press, 1973.

D'Amato, M.R., & Cox, J.K. Delay of consequences and short term memory in monkeys. In D. Medin, R. Davis, & W. Roberts (Eds.), *Coding processes in animal memory.* New York: Erlbaum, 1976.

D'Amato, M.R., Etkin, M., & Fazzaro, J. Cue producing behavior in the Capuchin monkey during reversal, extinction, acquisition, and overtraining. *Journal of the Experimental Analysis of Behavior*, 1968, **11**, 425–33.

D'Amato, M.R., & Fazzaro, J. Discriminated lever press avoidance learning as a function of type and intensity of shock. *Journal of Comparative and Physiological Psychology*, 1966, **61**, 313–15.

D'Amato, M.R., Fazzaro, J., & Etkin, M. Discriminated bar press avoidance maintenance and extinction in rats as a function of shock intensity. *Journal of Comparative and Physiological Psychology*, 1967, **63**, 351–54.

D'Amato, M.R., Fazzaro, J., & Etkin, M. Anticipatory responding and avoidance discrimination as factors in avoidance conditioning. *Journal of Experimental Psychology*, 1968a, **77**, 41–47.

D'Amato, M.R., Fazzaro, J., & Etkin, M. Effects of shock type and intensity on anticipatory responses. *Journal of Comparative and Physiological Psychology*, 1968b, **66**, 527–29.

D'Amato, M.R., Keller, D., & Biederman, G. Discriminated avoidance learning as a function of parameters of discontinuous shock. *Journal of Experimental Psychology*, 1965, **70**, 543–48.

D'Amato, M.R., & O'Neill, W. Effects of delay-interval illumination on matching behavior in the Capuchin monkey. *Journal of the Experimental Analysis of Behavior*, 1971, **15**, 327–33.

D'Amato, M.R., & Schiff, D. Long-term discriminated avoidance performance in the rat. *Journal of Comparative and Physiological Psychology*, 1964, **57**, 123–26.

D'Amato, M.R., & Worsham, R.W. Delayed matching in the Capuchin monkey with brief sample durations. *Learning and Motivation*, 1972, **3**, 304–12.

Davenport, J.W. The interaction of magnitude and delay of reinforcement in spatial discrimination. *Journal of Comparative and Physiological Psychology*, 1962, **55**, 267–73.

Dawkins, R. Selective neuron death as a possible memory mechanism. *Nature*, 1971, **229**, 118–19.

Debold, R.D., Miller, N.E., & Jensen, D.D. Effect of strength of drive determined by a new technique for appetitive classical conditioning of rats. *Journal of Comparative and Physiological Psychology*, 1965, **59**, 102–8.

Deets, A.C., Harlow, H.F., & Blomquist, A.J. Effects of intertrial interval and trial 1 reward during acquisition of an object-discrimination learning set in monkeys. *Journal of Comparative and Physiological Psychology*, 1970, **73**, 501–5.

Dement, W.C. *Some must watch, while some must sleep.* San Francisco: Freeman, 1972.

Denenberg, V.H. A consideration of the usefulness of the critical period hypothesis as applied to the stimulation of rodents in infancy. In G. Newton & S. Levine (Eds.), *Early experience and behavior.* Springfield, Ill.: Charles C Thomas, 1968.

Denenberg, V.H., Brumaghin, J.T., Haltmeyer, G.C., & Zarrow, M.X. Increased adrenocortical activity in the neonatal rat following handling. *Endocrinology*, 1967, **81**, 1047–52.

Denenberg, V.H., Hudgens, G.A., & Zarrow, M.X. Mice reared with rats: Modification of behavior by early experience with another species. *Science*, 1964, **143**, 380–81.

Denenberg, V.H., Karas, G.G., Rosenberg, K.M., & Schell, F. Programming life histories: An experimental design and initial results. *Developmental Psychobiology*, 1968, **1**, 3–9.

Denenberg, V.H., & Smith, S.A. Effects of handling stimulation and age upon behavior. *Journal of Comparative and Physiological Psychology*, 1963, **56**, 307–12.

Denny, M.R. Relaxation theory and experiments. In F.R. Brush (Ed.), *Aversive conditioning and learning.* New York: Academic Press, 1971.

Denny, M.R., Zerbolio, D.J., & Weisman, R.G. Avoidance behavior as a function of the length of nonshock confinement. *Journal of Comparative Physiological Psychology,* 1969, **58,** 252–57.

Denti, A., & Epstein, A. Sex differences in the acquisition of two kinds of avoidance behavior in rats. *Physiology and Behavior,* 1972, **8,** 611–15.

Deutsch, R. Conditioned hypoglycemia: A mechanism for saccharin-induced sensitivity to insulin in the rat. *Journal of Comparative and Physiological Psychology,* 1974, **86,** 350–58.

Diamond, I.T., & Neff, W.D. Ablation of the temporal cortex and discrimination of auditory patterns. *Journal of Neurophysiology,* 1957, **20,** 300–15.

DiCara, L. Learning and the autonomic nervous system. *Scientific American,* 1970, **222,** 30–39.

DiGiusto, E.L., & King, M.G. Chemical sympathectomy and avoidance learning in the rat. *Journal of Comparative and Physiological Psychology,* 1972, **81,** 491–500.

DiLollo, V., & Beez, V. Negative contrast effect as a function of magnitude of reward decrement. *Psychonomic Science,* 1966, **5,** 99–100.

Dinsmoor, J.A. A quantitative comparison between the discriminative and reinforcing functions of a stimulus. *Journal of Experimental Psychology,* 1950, **40,** 458–72.

Dodrzecka, C., Szwejkowska, G., & Konorski, J. Qualitative versus directional cues in two forms of differentiation. *Science,* 1966, **153,** 87–89.

Doty, R.W., & Rutledge, L.T. "Generalization" between cortically and peripherally applied stimuli eliciting conditioned reflexes. *Journal of Neurophysiology,* 1959, **22,** 428–35.

Duncan, C.P. The retroactive effect of electroshock on learning. *Journal of Comparative and Physiological Psychology,* 1949, **42,** 32–44.

Duncan, N.C., Grossen, N.E., & Hunt, E.B. Apparent memory differences in inbred mice produced by differential reaction to stress. *Journal of Comparative and Physiological Psychology,* 1971, **74,** 383–89.

Dunham, P.J. Contrasted conditions of reinforcement: A selective critique. *Psychological Bulletin,* 1968, **69,** 295–315.

Dunlap, W.P., & Frates, S.B. Influence of deprivation on the frustration effect. *Psychonomic Science,* 1970, **21,** 1–2.

Durup, G. & Fesard, A. L'électroencephalogramme de l'homme. *Année Psychologie,* 1935, **36,** 1–32.

Dusser de Barrene, J.C., & McCullock, W.S. Suppression of a motor response obtained from area 4 by stimulation of area 4s. *Journal of Neurophysiology,* 1941, **4,** 311–23.

Dysart, J., Marx, M.H., McLean, J., & Nelson, J.A. Peak-shift as a function of multiple schedules of reinforcement. *Journal of the Experimental Analysis of Behavior,* 1974, **22,** 463–70.

Ebbinghaus, H. *Memory.* (Written in 1885; Translated by H.A. Ruger & C.E. Bussenius). New York: Teachers' College, Columbia University, 1913.

Eck, K.O., & Thomas, D.R. Discrimination learning as a function of prior discrimination and nondifferential training: A replication. *Journal of Experimental Psychology,* 1970, **83,** 511–13.

Edwards, D.A. Early androgen stimulation and aggressive behavior in male and female mice. *Physiology and Behavior,* 1969, **4,** 333–38.

Egger, M.D., & Miller, N.E. Secondary reinforcement in rats as a function of informational value and reliability of the stimulus. *Journal of Experimental Psychology,* 1962, **64,** 97–104.

Ehrenfreund, D. An experimental test of the contiguity theory of discrimination learning with pattern vision. *Journal of Comparative and Physiological Psychology,* 1948, **41,** 408–22.

Ehrenfreund, D. Effect of drive on successive magnitude shift in rats. *Journal of Comparative and Physiological Psychology,* 1971, **76,** 418–23.

Eibl-Eibesfeldt, I. *Ethology: The biology of behavior.* New York: Holt, Rinehart & Winston, 1970.

Elliott, M.H. The effect of change of reward on the maze performance of rats. *University of California Publications in Psychology,* 1928, **4,** 19–30.

Ellison, G.D. Differential salivary conditioning to traces. *Journal of Comparative and Physiological Psychology,* 1964, **57,** 373–80.

Erdelyi, M.H., & Becker, J. Hypermnesia for pictures: Incremental memory for pictures but not words in multiple recall trials. *Cognitive Psychology,* 1974, **6,** 159–71.

Estes, W.K. An experimental study of punishment. *Psychological Monographs*, 1944, **57** (3, Whole No. 263).

Estes, W.K. Stimulus response theory of drive. In M.R. Jones (Ed.), *Nebraska symposium on motivation*. Lincoln: University of Nebraska Press, 1958.

Estes, W.K. The statistical approach to learning theory. In S. Koch (Ed.), *Psychology: A study of a science* (Vol. 2). New York: McGraw-Hill, 1959.

Etkin, M. Light induced interference in a delayed matching task with Capuchin monkeys. *Learning and Motivation*, 1972, *3*, 317–24.

Etkin, M.W., & D'Amato, M.R. Delayed matching-to-sample in short-term memory in the Capuchin monkey. *Journal of Comparative and Physiological Psychology*, 1969, *59*, 544–49.

Fallon, D. Resistance to extinction following learning with punishment of reinforced and nonreinforced licking. *Journal of Experimental Psychology*, 1968, *76*, 550–57.

Fallon, D. Resistance to extinction following partial punishment of reinforced and/or nonreinforced responses during learning. *Journal of Experimental Psychology*, 1969, *79*, 183–85.

Fantino, E. Aversive control. In J.A. Nevin & G.S. Reynolds (Eds.), *The study of behavior*. Glenview, Ill.: Scott, Foresman, 1973.

Farthing, G.W. Behavioral contrast with multiple positive and negative stimuli on a continuum. *Journal of the Experimental Analysis of Behavior*, 1974, *22*, 419–25.

Feather, B.W. Semantic generalization of classically conditioned responses: A review. *Psychological Bulletin*, 1965, *63*, 425–41.

Fehrer, E. Effects of amount of reinforcement and of pre- and post-reinforcement delays on learning and extinction. *Journal of Experimental Psychology*, 1956, *52*, 167–76.

Feigley, D.A., & Spear, N.E. Effect of age and punishment condition on long-term retention by the rat of active and passive avoidance learning. *Journal of Comparative and Physiological Psychology*, 1970, *73*, 514–26.

Feldman, J.M. Added cue control as a function of reinforcement predictability. *Journal of Experimental Psychology*, 1971, *91*, 318–25.

Ferster, C.B., & Skinner, B.F. *Schedules of reinforcement*. New York: Appleton-Century-Crofts, 1957.

Fitzgerald, R.D. Effects of partial reinforcement with acid on the classically conditioned salivary response in dogs. *Journal of Comparative and Physiological Psychology*, 1963, **56,** 1056–60.

Fitzgerald, R.D., Martin, G.K., & O'Brien, J.H. Influence of vagal activity of classically conditioned heart rate in rats. *Journal of Comparative and Physiological Psychology*, 1973, *83*, 485–91.

Fitzgerald, R.D., Vardaris, R.M., & Teyler, T.J. Effects of partial reinforcement followed by continuous reinforcement on classically conditioned heart rate in the dog. *Journal of Comparative and Physiological Psychology*, 1966, *62*, 483–86.

Fjerdingstud, E.J., Nissen, T., & Røigaard-Petersen, H.H. Effect of ribonucleic acid (RNA) extracted from the brain of trained animals on learning in rats. *Scandinavian Journal of Psychology*, 1965, *6*, 1–6.

Flaherty, C.F., Capobianco, S., & Hamilton, L.W. Effect of septal lesions on retention of negative contrast. *Physiology and Behavior*, 1973, *11*, 625–31.

Flaherty, C.F., & Davenport, J.W. Noncontingent pretraining in instrumental discrimination between amounts of reinforcement. *Journal of Comparative and Physiological Psychology*, 1968, *66*, 707–11.

Flaherty, C.F., & Davenport, J.W. Effect of instrumental response pretraining in classical-to-instrumental transfer of a differential reward magnitude discrimination. *Psychonomic Science*, 1969, *15*, 235–37.

Flaherty, C.F., & Davenport, J.W. Successive brightness discrimination in rats following regular versus random intermittent reinforcement. *Journal of Experimental Psychology*, 1972, *96*, 1–9.

Flaherty, C.F., & Kelly, J. Effect of deprivation state on successive negative contrast. *Bulletin of the Psychonomic Society*, 1973, *1*, 365–67.

Flaherty, C.F., & Largen, J. Within subjects positive and negative contrast effects in rats. *Journal of Comparative and Physiological Psychology*, 1975, *88*, 653–64.

Flaherty, C.F., Riley, E.P., & Spear, N.E. Effect of sucrose concentration and goal units on runway behavior in the rat. *Learning and Motivation*, 1973, 4, 163–75.

Flaherty, C.F., & Sepanak, S. Bidirectional contrast effects as a function of sucrose concentration disparity. Paper presented at the Psychonomic Society meetings, Boston, 1974.

Fleming, R.A., Grant, D.A., North, J.A., & Levy, M. Arithmetic correctness as the discriminadum in classical and differential eyelid conditioning. *Journal of Experimental Psychology*, 1968, **77**, 286–94.

Fleming, R.A., Grant, D.A., & North, J.A. Truth and falsity of verbal statements as conditioned stimuli in classical and differential eyelid conditioning. *Journal of Experimental Psychology*, 1968, **78**, 178–80.

Fletcher, H.J. The delayed response problem. In A.M. Schrier, H.F. Harlow, & F. Stollnitz (Eds.), *Behavior of nonhuman primates: Modern research trends* (Vol. 1). New York: Academic Press, 1965.

Forgays, D.G., & Forgays, J.W. The nature of the effect of free environment experience in the rat. *Journal of Comparative and Physiological Psychology*, 1952, **45**, 322–28.

Fowler, H. Suppression and facilitation by response contingent shock. In F.R. Brush (Ed.), *Aversive conditioning and learning*. New York: Academic Press, 1971.

Fowler, H., Fago, G.C., Domber, E.A., & Hochhauser, M. Signaling and affective functions in Pavlovian conditioning. *Animal Learning and Behavior*, 1973, **1**, 81–89.

Fox, S.S., & Rudell, A.P. The operant controlled neural event: A formal and systematic approach to electrical coding of behavior in the brain. *Science*, 1968, **162**, 1299–1302.

Franchina, J.J., & Brown, J.S. Reward magnitude shift effects in rats with hippocampal lesion. *Journal of Comparative and Physiological Psychology*, 1971, **76**, 365–70.

Frazier, W.A., Angeletti, R.H., & Bradshaw, R.A. Nerve growth factor and insulin. *Science*, 1972, **176**, 482–88.

Freeman, B.J. Behavioral contrast: Reinforcement frequency or response suppression. *Psychological Bulletin*, 1971, **75**, 347–56.

French, G.M. Associative problems. In A.M. Schrier, H.F. Harlow & F. Stollnitz (Eds.), *Behavior of nonhuman primates: Modern research trends*. New York: Academic Press, 1965.

Frey, P.W., & Butler, C.S. Rabbit eyelid conditioning as a function of unconditioned stimulus duration. *Journal of Comparative and Physiological Psychology*, 1973, **85**, 289–94.

Frey, P.W., & Ross, L.E. Classical conditioning of the rabbit eyelid response as a function of interstimulus interval. *Journal of Comparative and Physiological Psychology*, 1968, **65**, 246–50.

Furth, H.G. *Piaget and knowledge: Theoretical foundation*. Englewood Cliffs, N.J.: Prentice-Hall, 1969. Section reprinted in *Biological boundaries of learning*. New York: Appleton-Century-Crofts, 1972.

Gabriel, M. Incubation of avoidance produced by generalization to stimuli of the conditioning apparatus. *Topics in learning and performance*. New York: Academic Press, 1972.

Galef, B.G., Jr., & Clark, M.M. Social factors in the poison avoidance and feeding behavior of wild and domesticated rat pups. *Journal of Comparative and Physiological Psychology*, 1971, **75**, 341–57.

Galef, B.G., & Henderson, P.W. Mother's milk: A determinant of the feeding preferences of weaning rat pups. *Journal of Comparative and Physiological Psychology*, 1972, **78**, 213–19.

Gamzu, E., & Schwartz, B. The maintenance of key pecking by stimulus-contingent and response-independent food presentation. *Journal of the Experimental Analysis of Behavior*, 1973, **19**, 65–72.

Gamzu, E., & Williams, D.R. Classical conditioning of a complex skeletal response. *Science*, 1971, **171**, 923–25.

Gamzu, E.R., & Williams, D.R. Associative factors underlying the pigeon's key pecking in autoshaping procedures. *Journal of the Experimental Analysis of Behavior*, 1973, **19**, 225–32.

Gantt, W.H. The nervous secretion of saliva: The relation of the conditioned reflex to the intensity of the unconditioned stimulus. *American Journal of Physiology*, 1938, **123**, 74.

Ganz, L. An analysis of generalization behavior in the stimulus deprived organism. In G. Newton & S. Levine (Eds.), *Early experience and behavior*. Springfield, Ill.: Charles C Thomas, 1968.

Ganz, L., & Riesen, A.H. Stimulus generalization to hue in the dark-reared macaque. *Journal of Comparative and Physiological Psychology*, 1962, **55**, 92–99.

Garcia, J., Clark, J.C., & Hankins, W.G. Natural responses to scheduled rewards. In P.P.G. Bateson & P.H. Klopfer (Eds.), *Perspectives in ethology.* New York: Plenum Press, 1973, pp. 1–43.

Garcia, J., Ervin, F.R., & Koelling, R.A. Learning with prolonged delay of reinforcement. *Psychonomic Science,* 1966, **5,** 121–22.

Garcia, J., Hankins, W.G., & Rusiniak, K.W. Behavioral regulation of the milieu interne in man and rat. *Science,* 1974, **185,** 824–31.

Garcia, J., & Koelling, R.A. The relation of cue to consequence in avoidance learning. *Psychonomic Science,* 1966, **4,** 123–24.

Garcia, J., McGowan, B.K., Ervin, F.R., & Koelling, R.A. Cues: Their relative effectiveness as a function of the reinforcer. *Science,* 1968, **160,** 794–95.

Garcia, J., McGowan, B.K. & Green, K.F. Biological constraints on conditioning. In M.E.P. Seligman & J.L. Hager (Eds.), *Biological boundaries of learning.* New York: Appleton-Century-Crofts, 1972.

Gazzaniga, M.S. The split brain in man. *Scientific American,* 1967, **217,** 24–29.

Geller, A., & Jarvik, M.E. The role of consolidation in memory. In R.E. Bowman & S.P. Datta (Eds.), *Biochemistry of brain and behavior.* New York: Plenum Press, 1970.

Girden, E., & Culler, E. Conditioned responses in curarized striate muscle in dogs. *Journal of Comparative and Physiological Psychology,* 1937, **23,** 261–74.

Giulian, D., & Schmaltz, L.W. Enhanced discriminated bar press avoidance in rat through appetitive preconditioning. *Journal of Comparative and Physiological Psychology,* 1973, **83,** 106–12.

Glazer, H.I. Instrumental conditioning of hippocampal theta and subsequent response persistence. *Journal of Comparative and Physiological Psychology,* 1974. **86,** 267–73.

Gleitman, H., Wilson, W.A., Herman, M.M., & Rescorla, R.A. Massing and within-delay position as factors in delayed-response performance. *Journal of Comparative and Physiological Psychology,* 1963, **56,** 445-51.

Glickman, S.E. Perseverative neural processes and consolidation of the memory trace. *Psychological Bulletin,* 1961, **58,** 218–33.

Goldman, L., Coover, G.D., & Levine, S. Bidirectional effects of reinforcement shifts on pituitary adrenal activity. *Physiology and Behavior,* 1973, **10,** 209–14.

Gollon, E.S. Developmental studies: A visual recognition of incomplete objects. *Perceptual and Motor Skills,* 1960, **11,** 289–98.

Gonzalez, R.C., Fernhoff, D., & David, F.G. Contrast, resistance to extinction, and forgetting in rats. *Journal of Comparative and Physiological Psychology,* 1973, **84,** 563–71.

Gonzalez, R.C., & Powers, A.S. Simultaneous contrast in goldfish. *Animal Learning and Behavior,* 1973, **1,** 96–98.

Goodrich, K.P. Performance in different segments of an instrumental response chain as a function of reinforcement schedule. *Journal of Experimental Psychology,* 1959, **57,** 57–63.

Goodrich, K.P., Ross, L.E., & Wagner, A.R. An examination of selected aspects of the continuity and noncontinuity positions in discrimination learning. *The Psychological Record,* 1961, **11,** 105–17.

Gordon, W.C. *Time-dependent memory processes occurring after reactivation or retrieval of a memory.* Unpublished doctoral dissertation, Rutgers University, 1973.

Gordon, W.C., & Spear, N.E. The effects of strychnine on recently acquired and reactivated passive avoidance memories. *Physiology and Behavior,* 1973, **10,** 1071–75.

Gormezano, I. Investigations of defense and reward conditioning in the rabbit. In A.H. Black & W.F. Prokasy (Eds.), *Classical conditioning II: Current research and theory.* New York: Appleton-Century-Crofts, 1972.

Gormezano, I., & Coleman, S.R. Effects of partial reinforcement on conditioning, conditional probabilities, asymptotic performance, and extinction of the rabbits nictitating membrane response. *Pavlovian Journal of Biological Science,* 1975, **10,** 13–22.

Gormezano, I., Schneiderman, N., Deaux, E., & Fuentes, I. Nictitating membrane: Classical conditioning and extinction in the albino rabbit. *Science,* 1962, **138,** 33–34.

Grant, D.A. A preliminary model for processing information conveyed by verbal conditioned stimuli in classical conditioning. In A.H. Black & W.F. Prokasy (Eds.), *Classical conditioning II: Current research and theory.* New York: Appleton-Century-Crofts, 1972.

Grant, D.A., & Schipper, L.M. The acquisition and extinction of conditioned eyelid responses as a function of the percentage of fixed ratio random reinforcement. *Journal of Experimental Psychology,* 1952, **43,** 313–20.

Grant, D.A., & Schneider, D.E. Intensity of the conditioned stimulus and strength of conditioning. II. The conditioned galvanic skin response to an auditory stimulus. *Journal of Experimental Psychology*, 1949, **39**, 35–40.

Gray, S.A. Sodium amobarbital, the hippocampal theta rhythm and the partial reinforcement extinction effect. *Psychological Review*, 1970, **77**, 465–80.

Gray, T., & Appignanesi, A.A. Compound conditioning: Elimination of the blocking effect. *Learning and Motivation*, 1973, **4**, 374–80.

Green, K.F., & Garcia, J. Recuperation from illness: Flavor enhancement for rats. *Science*, 1971, **173**, 749–51.

Grice, G.R. The relation of secondary reinforcement to delayed reward in visual discrimination learning. *Journal of Experimental Psychology*, 1948, **38**, 1–16.

Grice, G.R., & Hunter, J.J. Stimulus intensity effects depend upon the type of experimental design. *Psychological Review*, 1964, **71**, 247–56.

Grindley, G.C. Experiments on the influence of the amount of reward on learning in young chickens. *British Journal of Psychology*, 1929, **20**, 173–80.

Grings, W.W. Cognitive factors in electrodermal conditioning. *Psychological Bulletin*, 1973, **79**, 200–210.

Grossen, N.E., Kostanek, D.J., & Bolles, R.C. Effects of appetitive discriminative stimuli on avoidance behavior. *Journal of Experimental Psychology*, 1969, **81**, 340–43.

Grusec, T. The peak shift in stimulus generalization: Equivalent effects of errors and noncontingent shock. *Journal of the Experimental Analysis of Behavior*, 1968, **11**, 239–49.

Gustavson, C.R., Garcia, J., Hankins, W.G., & Rusiniak, K.W. Coyote predation: Control by conditioned aversion. *Science*, 1974, **184**, 581–83.

Guttman, N. Equal reinforcement values for sucrose and glucose solutions as compared with equal sweetness values. *Journal of Experimental Psychology*, 1954, **47**, 358–61.

Guttman, N., & Kalish, H.I. Discriminability and stimulus generalization. *Journal of Experimental Psychology*, 1956, **51**, 79–88.

Gynther, M.D. Differential eyelid conditioning as a function of stimulus similarity and strength of response to the CS. *Journal of Experimental Psychology*, 1957, **53**, 408–16.

Haber, R.N., & Haber, R.B. Eidetic imagery: 1. Frequency. *Perceptual Motor Skills*, 1964, 19, 131–38.

Haber, A. & Kalish, H.I. Prediction of discrimination from generalization after variation in schedule of reinforcement. *Science*, 1963, **142**, 412–13.

Haley, T.J., & Snyder, R.S. (Eds.), *The response of the nervous system to ionizing radiation*. Boston: Little, Brown, 1964.

Hall, J.L. *Verbal learning and retention*. Philadelphia: Lippincott, 1971.

Halliday, M.S., & Boakes, R.A. Discrimination involving response-independent reinforcements: Implications for behavioral contrast. In R.A. Boakes & M.S. Halliday (Eds.), *Inhibition and learning*. London: Academic Press, 1972.

Halliday, M.S., & Boakes, R.A. Behavioral contrast without response-rate reduction. *Journal of the Experimental Analysis of Behavior*, 1974, **22**, 453–62.

Haltmeyer, G.C., Denenberg, V.H. & Zarrow, M.X. Modification of the plasma corticosterone response as a function of infantile stimulation and electric shock parameters. *Physiology and Behavior*, 1967, **2**, 61–63.

Hamilton, L.W. Active avoidance impairment following septal lesions in cats. *Journal of Comparative and Physiological Psychology*, 1969, **69**, 420–31.

Hanson, H.M. Effects of discrimination training on stimulus generalization. *Journal of Experimental Psychology*, 1959, **58**, 321–34.

Harlow, H.F. The formation of learning sets. *Psychological Review*, 1949, **56**, 51–65.

Harlow, H.F. Learning set and error factor theory. In S. Koch (Ed.), *Psychology: A study of a science* (Vol. 2). New York: McGraw-Hill, 1959.

Harlow, H.F. Primate learning. In C.P. Stone (Ed.), *Comparative psychology*. New York: Prentice-Hall, 1951.

Harlow, H.F., & Hicks, L.H. Discrimination learning theory: Uni process vs. duo process. *Psychological Review*, 1957, **64**, 104–9.

Harris, L.J., Clay, J., Hargreaves, F.J., & Ward, A. Appetite and choice of diet. The ability of Vitamin B deficient rats to discriminate between diets containing and lacking the vitamins. *Proceedings of the Royal Society of London*, 1933, **113**, 161–90.

Hartman, T.F. Dynamic transmission, elective generalization and semantic conditioning. In W.F. Prokasy (Ed.), *Classical conditioning*.

New York: Appleton-Century-Crofts, 1965.

Hearst, E. Aversive conditioning and external stimulus control. In B.A. Campbell & R.M. Church (Eds.), *Punishment and aversive behavior*. New York: Appleton-Century-Crofts, 1969.

Hearst, E., Besley, S., & Farthing, G.W. Inhibition and the stimulus control of operant behavior. *Journal of the Experimental Analysis of Behavior*, 1970, **14**, 373–409.

Hearst, E., & Koresko, M.B. Stimulus generalization and amount of prior training on variable interval reinforcement. *Journal of Comparative and Physiological Psychology*, 1968, **66**, 133–38.

Hearst, E., Koresko, M.B., & Poppen, R. Stimulus generalization and the response reinforcement contingency. *Journal of the Experimental Analysis of Behavior*, 1964, **7**, 369–80.

Hearst, E., & Peterson, G.B. Transfer of conditioned excitation and inhibition from one operant response to another. *Journal of Experimental Psychology*, 1973, **99**, 360–68.

Hebb, D.O. *The organization of behavior*. New York: Wiley, 1949.

Hefferline, R.F., Keenan, B., & Harford, A. Escape and avoidance by human subjects without their observation of the response. *Science*, 1959, **130**, 1338–39.

Heinemann, E.G., & Rudolph, R.L. The effect of discriminative training on the gradient of stimulus generalization. *American Journal of Psychology*, 1963, **76**, 653–58.

Heinroth, O. Beitrage zur Biologie, nämentlich Ethologie und Physiologie der Anatiden. *Proceedings of the 5th International Ornithological Congress*, 1910, 589–702.

Helson, H. *Adaption-level theory: An experiment and systematic approach to behavior*. New York: Harper, 1964.

Hemmes, N.S. Behavioral contrast in pigeons depends upon the operant. *Journal of Comparative and Physiological Psychology*, 1973, **85**, 171–78.

Henke, P.G. Persistence of runway performance after septal lesions in the rat. *Journal of Comparative and Physiological Psychology*, 1974, **86**, 760–67.

Heron, W.T. The inheritance of brightness and dullness in maze learning ability in the rat. *Journal of Genetic Psychology*, 1941, **59**, 41–49.

Herrnstein, R.J. Relative and absolute strength of response as a function of frequency of reinforcement. *Journal of the Experimental Analysis of Behavior*, 1961, **4**, 267–72.

Herrnstein, R.J. Method and theory in the study of avoidance. *Psychological Review*, 1969, **76**, 49–69.

Herrnstein, R.J. On the law of effect. *Journal of the Experimental Analysis of Behavior*, 1970, **13**, 243–66.

Herrnstein, R.J., & Hineline, P.N. Negative reinforcement as shock frequency reduction. *Journal of the Experimental Analysis of Behavior*, 1966, **9**, 421–30.

Hess, E.H. The relationship between imprinting and motivation. In M.R. Jones (Ed.), *Nebraska Symposium on Motivation*, 1959, 44–77.

Hilgard, E.R., & Marquis, D.G. *Conditioning and learning*. New York: Appleton-Century-Crofts, 1940.

Hill, W.F., & Spear, N.E. Resistance to extinction as a joint function of reward magnitude and the spacing of extinction trials. *Journal of Experimental Psychology*, 1962, **64**, 636–39.

Hinde, R.A., & Stevenson-Hinde, J. *Constraints on learning*. London: Academic Press, 1973.

Hineline, P.N., & Rachlin, H. Notes on fixed-ratio and fixed-interval escape responding in the pigeon. *Journal of the Experimental Analysis of Behavior*, 1969, **12**, 397–401.

Hirsch, E., & Collier, G. The ecological determinants of reinforcement in the guinea pig. *Physiology and Behavior*, 1974, **12**, 239–49.

Hoffman, H.S. Stimulus factors in conditioned suppression. In B.A. Campbell & R.M. Church (Eds.), *Punishment and aversive behavior*. New York: Appleton-Century-Crofts, 1969.

Holloway, F.D., & Wansley, R.W. Multiphasic retention deficits at periodic intervals after passive-avoidance learning. *Science*, 1973, **180**, 208–10.

Honig, W.K., Boneau, C.A., Burstein, K.R., & Pennypacker, H.S. Positive and negative generalization gradients obtained after equivalent training conditions. *Journal of Comparative and Physiological Psychology*, 1963, **56**, 111–16.

Hoveland, C.I. The generalization of conditioned responses. IV. The effects of varying amounts of reinforcement upon the degree of generalization of conditioned responses.

Journal of Experimental Psychology, 1937, **21,** 261–76.

Huang, I.N. Successive contrast effects as a function of type and magnitude of reward. *Journal of Experimental Psychology,* 1969, **82,** 64–69.

Hughes, L.F., & Dachowski, L. The role of reinforcement and nonreinforcement in an operant frustration effect. *Animal Learning and Behavior,* 1973, **1,** 68–72.

Hulicka, I.M., Capehart, J., & Viney, W. The effect of stimulus variation on response probability during extinction. *Journal of Comparative and Physiological Psychology,* 1960, **53,** 79–82.

Hull, C.L. The goal gradient hypothesis and maze learning. *Psychological Review,* 1932, **39,** 25–43.

Hull, C.L. The rat's speed-of-locomotion gradient in the approach to food. *Journal of Comparative and Physiological Psychology,* 1934, **17,** 393–422.

Hull, C.L. *Principles of behavior.* New York: Appleton-Century-Crofts, 1943.

Hull, C.L. *Essentials of behavior.* New Haven: Yale University Press, 1951.

Hull, C.L. *A behavior system.* New Haven: Yale University Press, 1952.

Hulse, S.H., Jr. Amount and percentage of reinforcement and duration of goal confinement in conditioning and extinction. *Journal of Experimental Psychology,* 1958, **56,** 48–57.

Humphreys, L.G. Acquisition and extinction of verbal expectations in a situation analogous to conditioning. *Journal of Experimental Psychology,* 1939, **25,** 294–301.

Hunsicker, J.R. *The retention function for appetitive responding in rats.* Unpublished master's thesis, University of Oklahoma, Norman, Oklahoma, 1974.

Hunt, E., & Love, T. How good can memory be? In A.W. Nelson & E. Martin (Eds.), *Coding processes in human memory.* Washington, D.C.: V.H. Winston & Sons, 1972.

Hunter, I.M.L. *Memory.* Baltimore: Penguin Books, Inc., 1964.

Hunter, W.S. The delayed reaction in animals and children. *Behavior Monographs,* 1913, **2.** Serial #6.

Irwin, F.W. *Intentional behavior and motivation.* New York: Lippincott, 1971.

Ison, J.R., & Cook, P.E. Extinction performance as a function of incentive magnitude and number of acquisition trials. *Psychonomic Science,* 1964, **1,** 245–46.

Iverson, S.D. Brain lesions and memory in animals. In J.A. Deutsch (Ed.), *The physiological basis of memory.* New York: Academic Press, 1973.

James, W. *The principles of psychology.* New York: Henry Holt, 1890.

Jarrard, L.E., & Moise, S.L. Short-term memory in the stump tail (*Macaca speciosa*): Effect of physical restraint of behavior on performance. *Learning and Motivation,* 1970, **1,** 267–75.

Jarrard, L.E., & Moise, S.L. Short-term memory in the monkey. In L.E. Jarrard (Ed.), *Cognitive processes of nonhuman primates.* New York: Academic Press, 1971.

Jasper, H.H., & Shagass, C. Conscious time judgments related to conditioned time intervals and voluntary control of the alpha rhythm. *Journal of Experimental Psychology,* 1941, **28,** 503–8.

Jaynes, J. Imprinting: The interaction of learned and innate behavior. IV. Generalization and emergent discrimination. *Journal of Comparative and Physiological Psychology,* 1958, **51,** 238–42.

Jenkins, H.M. Resistance to extinction when partial reinforcement is followed by regular reinforcement. *Journal of Experimental Psychology,* 1962, **64,** 441–50.

Jenkins, H.M., & Harrison, R.H. Effect of discrimination training on auditory generalization. *Journal of Experimental Psychology,* 1960, **59,** 246–53.

Jenkins, H.M., & Moore, B.R. The form of the autoshaped response with food or water reinforcers. *Journal of the Experimental Analysis of Behavior,* 1973, **20,** 163–81.

Jones, J.E. Contiguity and reinforcement in relation to CS-UCS intervals in classical aversive conditioning. *Psychological Review,* 1962, **69,** 176–86.

Jung, J. *Verbal learning.* New York: Holt, Reinhart & Winston, 1968.

Kalish, H.I. The relationship between discriminability and generalization: A reevaluation. *Journal of Experimental Psychology,* 1958, **55,** 637–44.

Kalish, H.I. Stimulus generalization. In M.H. Mary (Ed.), *Learning: Processes.* London: The Macmillan Co., 1969.

Kalish, H.I., & Haber, A. Prediction of discrimination from generalization following variations in deprivation level. *Journal of Comparative and Physiological Psychology,* 1965, **60**, 125–28.

Kamin, L.J. The effects of termination of the CS and avoidance of the US on avoidance learning. *Journal of Comparative and Physiological Psychology,* 1956, **49**, 420–24.

Kamin, L.J. The retention of an incompletely learned avoidance response. *Journal of Comparative and Physiological Psychology,* 1957a, **50**, 457–60.

Kamin, L.J. The gradient of delay of secondary reward in avoidance learning. *Journal of Comparative and Physiological Psychology,* 1957b, **50**, 445–49.

Kamin, L.J. The delay-of-punishment gradient. *Journal of Comparative and Physiological Psychology,* 1959, **52**, 434–37.

Kamin, L.J. Temporal and intensity characteristics of the conditioned stimulus. In W.F. Prokasy (Ed.), *Classical conditioning: A symposium.* New York: Appleton-Century-Crofts, 1965.

Kamin, L.J. Predictability, surprise, attention and conditioning. In B.A. Campbell & R.M. Church (Eds.), *Punishment and aversive behavior.* New York: Appleton-Century-Crofts, 1969.

Kamin, L.J., Brimer, C.J., & Black, A.H. Conditioned suppression as a monitor of fear of the CS in the course of avoidance training. *Journal of Comparative and Physiological Psychology,* 1963, **56**, 497–501.

Kanarek, R.B. *The energetics of meal patterns.* Unpublished doctoral dissertation, Rutgers —The State University, 1974.

Katz, J.J., & Halstead, W.C. Protein organization and mental function. *Comparative Psychological Monographs,* 1950, **20**, 1–39.

Katzev, R.D., & Enkema, S.J. Acquisition and extinction of signaled avoidance as a function of intermittent reinforcement. *Learning and Motivation,* 1973, **4**, 176–96.

Kausler, D.H. *Psychology of verbal learning and memory.* New York: Academic Press, 1974.

Keehn, J.D. The effect of a warning signal on unrestricted avoidance behavior. *British Journal of Psychology,* 1959, **50**, 125–35.

Keesey, R.E. Intracranial reward delay and the acquisition of a brightness discrimination. *Science,* 1964, **143**, 700–701.

Keesey, R.E., & Kling, J.W. Amount of reinforcement and free operant responding. *Journal of the Experimental Analysis of Behavior,* 1961, 4, 125–32.

Keller, J.V. Behavioral contrast under multiple delays of reinforcement. *Psychonomic Science,* 1970, **20**, 257–58.

Keller, K. The role of elicited responding in behavioral contrast. *Journal of the Experimental Analysis of Behavior,* 1974, **21**, 249–57.

Keppel, G. Facilitation in short- and long-term retention of paired associates following distributed practice in learning. *Journal of Verbal Learning and Verbal Behavior,* 1964, **3**, 91–111.

Keppel, G. Forgetting. In L. Sechrist, C.P. Duncan, & A.W. Melton (Eds.), *Human memory: Festschrift for Benton J. Underwood.* New York: Appleton-Century-Crofts, 1972.

Keppel, G., & Underwood, B.J. Reminiscence in the short-term retention of paired-associate lists. *Journal of Verbal Learning and Verbal Behavior,* 1967, **6**, 375–82.

Kimble, G.A. *Hilgard and Marquis' conditioning and learning.* New York: Appleton-Century-Crofts, 1961.

Kimble, G.A. Attitudinal factors in eyelid conditioning. In G.A. Kimble (Ed.), *Foundations of conditioning and learning.* New York: Appleton-Century-Crofts, 1967.

Kimble, G.A. Cognitive inhibition in classical conditioning. In H.H. Kender, & J.T. Spence (Eds.), *Essays in neobehaviorism.* New York: Appleton-Century-Crofts, 1971.

Kimble, G.A., & Ost, J.W.P. A conditioned inhibitory process in eyelid conditioning. *Journal of Experimental Psychology,* 1961, **61**, 150–56.

Kimble, G.A., & Reynolds, B. Eyelid conditioning as a function of the interval between conditioned and unconditioned stimuli. In G.A. Kimble (Ed.), *Foundations of conditioning and learning.* New York: Appleton-Century-Crofts, 1967.

Kimmel, E. Judgments of UCS intensity and diminution of the UCR in classical GSR conditioning. *Journal of Experimental Psychology,* 1967, **73**, 532–43.

Kimmel, H.D. Adaption of the GSR under repeated applications of a visual stimulus. *Journal of Experimental Psychology,* 1964, **68**, 421–22.

Kimmel, H.D. Further analysis of GSR conditioning: A reply to Stewart, Stein, Winokur, Friedman. *Psychological Review*, 1964, **71**, 160–66.

Kimmel, H.D. Instrumental inhibitory factors in classical conditioning. In W.F. Prokasy (Ed.), *Classical conditioning: A symposium.* New York: Appleton-Century-Crofts, 1965.

Kimmel, H.D. Instrumental conditioning of autonomically mediated responses in human beings. *American Psychologist*, 1974, **29**, 325–35.

Kimmel, H.D., & Pennypacker, H.S. Differential GSR conditioning as a function of the CS-UCS interval. *Journal of Experimental Psychology*, 1963, **65**, 559–63.

Kintsch, W., & Witte, R.S. Concurrent conditioning of bar-press and salivation responses. *Journal of Comparative and Physiological Psychology*, 1962, **55**, 963–68.

Klein, M., & Rilling, M. Generalization of free operant avoidance behavior in pigeons. *Journal of the Experimental Analysis of Behavior*, 1974, **21**, 75–88.

Kleinsmith, L.J., & Kaplan, S. Paired-associate learning as a function of arousal and interpolated interval. *Journal of Experimental Psychology*, 1963, **65**, 190–93.

Kleinsmith, L.J., & Kaplan, S. Interaction of arousal and recall interval in nonsense syllable paired-associate learning. *Journal of Experimental Psychology*, 1964, **67**, 124–26.

Knapp, R.K. Acquisition and extinction of avoidance with similar and different shock and escape situations. *Journal of Comparative and Physiological Psychology*, 1965, **60**, 272–73.

Knarr, F.A., & Collier, G.H. Taste and consummatory activity in amount and gradient of reinforcement functions. *Journal of Experimental Psychology*, 1962, **63**, 579–88.

Krane, R.V., & Wagner, A.R. Taste aversion learning with a delayed shock US: Implications for the "generality of the laws of learning." *Journal of Comparative and Physiological Psychology*, 1975, **88**, 882–89.

Krecek, J., Novakova, V., & Stibral, K. Sex differences in the taste preference for a salt solution in the rat. *Physiology and Behavior*, 1972, **8**, 183–88.

Krech, D., Rosenzweig, M.R., & Bennet, E.L. Relations between brain chemistry and problem-solving among rats raised in enriched and impoverished environments. *Journal of Comparative and Physiological Psychology*, 1962, **55**, 801–7.

Krechevsky, I. "Hypotheses" in rats. *Psychological Review*, 1932, **39**, 516–32.

Krechevsky, I. A study of the continuity of the problem-solving process. *Psychological Review*, 1938, **45**, 107–34.

Kremer, E.F., & Kamin, L.J. The truly random control procedure: Associative or nonassociative effects in rats. *Journal of Comparative and Physiological Psychology*, 1971, **74**, 203–10.

Krippner, R.A., Endsley, R.C., & Tacker, R.S. Magnitude of G_1 reward and the frustration effect in a between subjects design. *Psychonomic Science*, 1967, **9**, 385–86.

Lashley, K.S. *Brain mechanisms and intelligence.* Chicago: University of Chicago Press, 1929.

Lashley, K.S. The mechanism of vision: I. A method for rapid analysis of pattern-vision in the rat. *Journal of Genetic Psychology*, 1930, **37**, 353–460.

Lashley, K.S. The mechanism of vision: XV. Preliminary studies of the rat's capacity for detail vision. *Journal of Genetic Psychology*, 1938, **18**, 123–93.

Lashley, K.S. In search of the engram. *Symposia of the Society for Experimental Biology*, 1950, **4**, 454–582.

Lashley, K.S., & Wade, M. The Pavlovian theory of generalization. *Psychological Review*, 1946, **53**, 72–87.

Lawrence, D.H. Acquired distinctiveness of cues: I. Transfer between discriminations on the basis of familiarity with the stimulus. *Journal of Experimental Psychology*, 1949, **39**, 770–84.

Lawrence, D.H. Acquired distinctiveness of cues: II. Selective association in a constant stimulus situation. *Journal of Experimental Psychology*, 1950, **40**, 175–88.

Leaf, A. Every day is a gift when you are over 100. *National Geographic*, 1973, **143**, 92–119.

Leaf, R.C. Avoidance response evocation as a function of prior discrimination fear conditioning under curare. *Journal of Comparative and Physiological Psychology*, 1964, **58**, 446–49.

Leão, A.A.P. Spreading depression of activity in the cerebral cortex. *Journal of Neurophysiology*, 1944, **7**, 359–90.

Lenneberg, E.H. On explaining language. *Science*, 1969, **164**, 635–43.

Levey, A.B., & Martin, I. Shape of the conditioned eyelid response. *Psychological Review*, 1968, **75**, 398–408.

Levine, M. Hypothesis behavior. In A.M. Schrier, H.F. Harlow, & F. Stollnitz (Eds.), *Behavior of nonhuman primates: Modern research trends*. New York: Academic Press, 1965.

Levine, M. Neo-noncontinuity theory. In G. Bower & J.T. Spence (Eds.), *The Psychology of Learning and Motivation* (Vol. 3). New York: Academic Press, 1969.

Levine, S., & Broadhurst, P.L. Genetic and ontogenetic determinants of adult behavior in the rat. *Journal of Comparative and Physiological Psychology*, 1963, **56**, 423–28.

Levine, S., Haltmeyer, G.C., Karas, G.G., & Denenberg, V.H. Physiological and behavioral effects of infantile stimulation. *Physiology and Behavior*, 1967, **2**, 55–59.

Levine, S., & Wetzel, A. Infantile experiences, strain differences, and avoidance learning. *Journal of Comparative and Physiological Psychology*, 1963, **56**, 879–81.

Lewis, D.J. Sources of experimental amnesia. *Psychological Review*, 1969, **76**, 461–72.

Linden, D.R. The effect of intensity of intermittent punishment in acquisition on resistance to extinction of an approach response. *Animal Learning and Behavior*, 1974, **2**, 9–12.

Linden, D.R., & Hallgren, S.O. Transfer of approach responding between punishment and frustrative nonreward sustained through continuous reinforcement. *Learning and Motivation*, 1973, **4**, 207–17.

Liu, I. A theory of classical conditioning. *Psychological Review*, 1964, **71**, 408–11.

Liu, S.S. Differential conditioning and stimulus generalization of the rabbit's nictitating membrane response. *Journal of Comparative and Physiological Psychology*, 1971, **77**, 136–42.

Logan, F.A. *Incentive*. New Haven: Yale University Press, 1960.

Logan, F.A. Decision making by rats: Delay versus amount of reward. *Journal of Comparative and Physiological Psychology*, 1965, **59**, 1–12.

Logan, F.A., Beier, E.M., & Kincaid, W.D. Extinction following partial and varied reinforcement. *Journal of Experimental Psychology*, 1956, **52**, 65–70.

Logan, F.A., & Wagner, A.R. *Reward and punishment*. Boston: Allyn & Bacon, 1965.

Longo, N., Milstein, S., & Bitterman, M.E. Classical conditioning in the pigeon: Exploratory studies of partial reinforcement. *Journal of Comparative and Physiological Psychology*, 1962, **55**, 983–86.

Lorenz, K. The companion in the bird's world. *Auk*, 1937, **54**, 245–73.

Lorenz, K. Companionship in bird life. In C.H. Schiller (Ed.), *Instinctive behavior: The development of a modern concept*. New York: International University Press, 1957.

Lorenz, K. A talk with Konrad Lorenz. *New York Times Magazine*, July 5, 1970.

Lovejoy, E. Analysis of the overlearning reversal effect. *Psychological Review*, 1966, **73**, 87–103.

Lovejoy, E. *Attention in discrimination learning*. San Francisco: Holden-Day, 1968.

Ludvigson, H.W., & Gay, S.E. Differential reward conditioning, S^- contrast as a function of the magnitude of S^+. *Psychonomic Science*, 1966, **5**, 289–90.

Luria, A.R. *The mind of a mnemonist*. New York: Basic Books, 1968.

Lyons, J., Klipec, W.D., & Steinsultz, G. The effect of chlorpromazine on discrimination performance and the peak shift. *Physiological Psychology*, 1973, **1** (2), 121–24.

Maatsch, J.L. Learning and fixation after a single shock trial. *Journal of Comparative and Physiological Psychology*, 1959, **52**, 408–10.

Mackintosh, N.J. Selective attention in animal discrimination learning. *Psychological Bulletin*, 1965a, **64**, 124–50.

Mackintosh, N.J. Overtraining, extinction, and reversal in rats and chicks. *Journal of Comparative and Physiological Psychology*, 1965b, **59**, 31–36.

Mackintosh, N.J. Further analysis of the overtraining reversal effect. *Journal of Comparative and Physiological Psychology*, 1969, **67**, 1–18.

Mackintosh, N.J. Distribution of trials and the partial reinforcement effect in the rat. *Journal of Comparative and Physiological Psychology*, 1970, **73**, 341–48.

Mackintosh, N.J. *The psychology of animal learning*. London: Academic Press, 1974.

Mackintosh, N.J., Little, L., & Lord, J. Some determinants of behavioral contrast in pigeons and rats. *Learning and Motivation*, 1972, **3**, 148–61.

Mackintosh, N.J., & Lord, J. Simultaneous and successive contrast with delay of reward. *Animal Learning and Behavior*, 1973, **1**, 283–86.

Maier, S.F., Seligman, M.E.P., & Solomon, R.L. Pavlovian fear conditioning and learned helplessness: Effects on escape and avoidance behavior of (a) the CS–US contingency, and (b) the independence of the US and voluntary responding. In B.A. Campbell & R.M. Church (Eds.), *Punishment and aversive behavior*. New York: Appleton-Century-Crofts, 1969.

Mallott, R.W., & Cumming, W.W. Schedules of interresponse time reinforcement. *Psychological Record*, 1964, **14**, 211–52. In J.A. Nevin (Ed.), *The study of behavior: Learning, motivation, emotion and instinct*. Glenview, Ill.: Scott, Foresman, 1973.

Malmo, R.B. Interference factors in delayed response in monkeys after removal of frontal lobe. *Journal of Neurophysiology*, 1942, **5**, 295–308.

Manning, A.A., Schniederman, N., & Lordahl, D.S. Delay versus trace heart rate: Classical discriminative conditioning in rabbits as a function of interstimulus interval. *Journal of Experimental Psychology*, 1969, **80**, 225–30.

Marchant, H.G., III, & Moore, J.W. Blocking of the rabbits' conditioned nictitating membrane response in Kamin's two-stage paradigm. *Journal of Experimental Psychology*, 1973, **101**, 155–58.

Margolius, G. Stimulus generalization of an instrumental response as a function of the number of reinforced trials. *Journal of Experimental Psychology*, 1955, **49**, 105–11.

Marler, P. A comparative approach to vocal learning: Song development in white-crowned sparrows. *Journal of Comparative and Physiological Psychology*, 1970, **71**, 1–25.

Marsh, G.D. Inverse relationship between discriminability and stimulus generalization as a function of number of test stimuli. *Journal of Comparative and Physiological Psychology*, 1967, **64**, 284–89.

Martin, B. Reward and punishment associated with the same goal response: A factor in the learning of motives. *Psychological Bulletin*, 1963, **60**, 441–51.

McAllister, W.R., & McAllister, D.E. Incubation of fear: An examination of the concept. *Journal of Experimental Research and Personality*, 1967, **3**, 80–90.

McAllister, W.R., & McAllister, D.E. Behavioral measurement of conditioned fear. In F.R. Brush (Ed.), *Aversive conditioning and learning*. New York: Academic Press, 1971.

McCain, G. Partial reinforcement with a small number of acquisition trials: Modified extinction procedures. *Psychonomic Science*, 1965, **2**, 133–34.

McCain, G. Partial reinforcement effects following a small number of acquisition trials. *Psychological Monographs*, 1966, Suppl. **1**, (1, Whole No. 12), 251–70.

McCain, G. The partial reinforcement effect after minimal acquisition: Single pellet reward, spaced trials. *Psychonomic Science*, 1969, **15**, 146.

McConnell, J.V. Memory transfer through cannibalism in planarians. *Journal of Neuropsychiatry*, 1962, **3**, 542–48.

McConnell, J.V., & Shelby, J.M. Memory transfer experiments in invertebrates. In G. Ungar (Ed.), *Molecular mechanisms in memory and learning*. New York: Plenum Press, 1970.

McCullock, T.L., & Pratt, J.C. A study of the presolution period in weight discrimination by white rats. *Journal of Comparative Psychology*, 1934, **18**, 271–90.

McGeoch, J.A. Forgetting and the law of disuse. *Psychological Review*, 1932, **39**, 352–70.

McGonigle, B. Stimulus additivity and dominance in visual discrimination performance by rats. *Journal of Comparative and Physiological Psychology*, 1967, **64**, 110–13.

McGowan, B.K., Hankins, W.G., & Garcia, J. Limbic lesions and control of the internal and external environment. *Behavioral Biology*, 1972, **7**, 841–52.

McHose, J.H., & Ludvigson, H.W. Role of reward magnitude and incomplete reduction of reward magnitude in the frustration effect. *Journal of Experimental Psychology*, 1965, **70**, 490–95.

McSweeney, F.K. Matching and contrast on several concurrent treadle press schedules. *Journal of the Experimental Analysis of Behavior*, 1975, **23**, 193–98.

Medin, D.L. Form perception and pattern reproduction by monkeys. *Journal of Comparative and Physiological Psychology*, 1969, **68**, 412–19.

Medin, D.L., & Davis, R.T. Memory. In A.M. Schrier & F. Stollnitz (Eds.), *Behavior of nonhuman primates: Modern research trends* (Vol. V). New York: Academic Press, 1974.

Mellgren, R.L. Positive and negative contrast effects using delayed reinforcement. *Learning and Motivation*, 1972, **3**, 185–93.

Mello, N. Alcohol effects on delayed matching-to-sample performance by Rhesus monkeys. *Physiology and Behavior*, 1971, **7**, 77–101.

Melton, A.W., & Irwin, J.M. The influence of degree of interpolated learning on retroactive inhibition and the overt transfer of specific responses. *American Journal of Psychology*, 1940, **53**, 173–203.

Meltzer, D., & Brahlek, J.A. Quantity of reinforcement and fixed-interval performance. *Psychonomic Science*, 1968, **12**, 207–8.

Mendelson, J., & Chorover, S.L. Lateral hypothalamic stimulation in satiated rats: T-maze learning for food. *Science*, 1965, **149**, 559–61.

Meredith, A.L., & Schneiderman, N. Heart rate and nictitating membrane: Classical discrimination conditioning in rabbits under delay versus trace procedures. *Psychonomic Science*, 1967, **9**, 139–40.

Miles, R.C. Discrimination learning sets. In A.M. Schrier, H.F. Harlow, & F. Stollnitz (Eds.), *Behavior of nonhuman primates: Modern research trends.* New York: Academic Press, 1965.

Miller, N.E. A reply to "sign gestalt or conditioned reflex?" *Psychological Review*, 1935, **42**, 280–92.

Miller, N.E. Experimental studies in conflict. In J. McHunt (Ed.), *Personality and behavior disorders.* New York: Ronald, 1944.

Miller, N.E. Liberalization of basic S–R concepts: Extensions to conflict, behavior, motivation, and social learning. In S. Koch (Ed.), *Psychology: A Study of a science* (Vol. II). New York: McGraw-Hill, 1959.

Miller, N.E. Learning resistance to pain and fear. Effects of overlearning, exposure and rewarded exposure in context. *Journal of Experimental Psychology*, 1960, **60**, 137–45.

Miller, N.E. Some recent studies of conflict, behavior and drugs. *American Psychologist*,
1961, **16**, 12–14.

Miller, N.E. Learning of visceral and glandular responses. *Science*, 1969, **163**, 434.

Miller, N.E., DiCara, L.V., Soloman, H., Weiss, J.M., & Dworkin, B. Learned modification of autonomic functions. In T.X. Barber, L.V. DiCara, J. Kamiya, N.E. Miller, D. Shapiro, & J. Stoyra (Eds.), *Biofeedback and self-control.* New York: Aldine-Atherton, 1970.

Miller, R.R., & Springer, A.D. Amnesia, consolidation, and retrieval. *Psychological Review*, 1973, **80**, 69–79.

Milner, B. Les troubles de la mémoire accompagnant des lésions hippocampiques bilatérales. In P. Passouant (Ed.), *Physiologie de l'hippocampe.* Paris: Centre Nationale de Recherche Scientifique, 1962. Translated by the author: In P.M. Milner & S.E. Glickman (Eds.), *Cognitive processes and the brain.* Princeton, N.J.: Van Nostrand, 1962.

Milner, B., Corkin, S., & Teuber, H.L. Further analysis of the hippocampal-amnesic syndrome: 14-year followup study of H.M. *Neuropsychologia*, 1968, **6**, 215–34.

Misanin, J.R., Miller, R.R., & Lewis, D.J. Retrograde amnesia produced by electroconvulsive shock after reactivation of a consolidated memory trace. *Science*, 1968, **160**, 554–55.

Moise, S.L. Short-term retention in *Macaca speciosa* following interpolated activity during delayed matching from sample. *Journal of Comparative and Physiological Psychology*, 1970, **73**, 506–14.

Moltz, H. Latent extinction and the fractional anticipatory response mechanism. *Psychological Review*, 1957, **64**, 229–41.

Moltz, H. An epigenetic interpretation of the imprinting phenomenon. In G. Newton & S. Levine (Eds.), *Early experience and behavior.* Springfield, Ill.: Charles C Thomas, 1968.

Moltz, H., & Rosenblum, L.A. The relationship between habituation and the stability of the following response. *Journal of Comparative and Physiological Psychology*, 1958, **51**, 658–61.

Moltz, H., Rosenblum, L.A., & Halikas, N. Imprinting and level of anxiety. *Journal of Comparative and Physiological Psychology*, 1959, **52**, 240–44.

Morton, J.R.C., Denenberg, V.H., & Zarrow, M.X. Modification of sexual development through stimulation in infancy. *Endocrinology*, 1963, **72**, 439–42.

Mostofsky, D.I. *Stimulus generalization.* Stanford: Stanford University Press, 1965.

Mowrer, O.H. A stimulus-response analysis and its role as a reinforcing agent. *Psychological Review*, 1939, **46**, 553–65.

Mowrer, O.H. *Learning theory and behavior.* New York: Wiley, 1960.

Mowrer, O.H., & Lamoreaux, R.R. Avoidance conditioning and signal duration: A study of secondary motivation and reward. *Psychological Monographs*, 1942, **54** (5, Whole No. 247).

Moyer, K.E., & Korn, J.H. Effect of UCS intensity on the acquisition and extinction of an avoidance response. *Journal of Experimental Psychology*, 1964, **67**, 352–59.

Moyer, K.E., & Korn, J.H. Effect of UCS intensity on the acquisition and extinction of a one-way avoidance response. *Psychonomic Science*, 1966, **4**, 121–22.

Muenziger, K.F., Bernstone, A.H., & Richards, L. Motivation in learning: VIII. Equivalent amounts of electric shock for right and wrong responses in a visual discrimination habit. *Journal of Comparative and Physiological Psychology*, 1938, **26**, 177–186.

Myers, R.E., & Sperry, R.W. Interoculary transfer of a visual form discrimination habit in cats after section of the optic chiasma and corpus callosum. *Anatomical Record*, 1953, **115**, 351–52.

Nation, J.R., Wrather, D.M., & Mellgren, R.L. Contrast effects in escape conditioning of rats. *Journal of Comparative and Physiological Psychology*, 1974, **86**, 69–73.

Nation, J.R., Wrather, D.M., & Mellgren, R.L. Contrast effects with shifts in punishment level. *Bulletin of the Psychonomic Society*, 1975, **5**, 167–69.

Neely, J.H., & Wagner, A.R. Attenuation of blocking with shifts in reward: The involvement of schedule-generated contextual cues. *Journal of Experimental Psychology*, 1974, **102**, 751–63.

Nevin, J.A. Differential reinforcement and stimulus control of not responding. *Journal of the Experimental Analysis of Behavior*, 1968, **11**, 715–26.

Nevin, J.A. The maintenance of behavior. In J.A. Nevin (Ed.), *The study of behavior: Learning, motivation, emotion, and instinct.* Glenview, Ill.: Scott, Foresman, 1973.

Nevin, J.A. Stimulus control. In J.A. Nevin (Ed.), *The study of behavior: Learning, motivation, emotion, and instinct.* Glenview, Ill.: Scott, Foresman, 1973.

Nissen, T., Rϕigaard-Petersen, H.H., & Fjerdingstad, E.J. Effect of ribonucleic acid (RNA) extracted from the brain of trained animals on learning in rats. II: Dependence of RNA effect on training conditions prior to RNA extraction. *Scandinavian Journal of Psychology*, 1965, **6**, 265–72.

Noble, M., & Harding, G.E. Conditioning in Rhesus monkeys as a function of the interval between CS and US. *Journal of Comparative and Physiological Psychology*, 1963, **56**, 220–24.

Olds, J. Conditioned responses to hippocampal and other neurons. *Electroencephalography and Clinical Neurophysiology*, 1969, **26**, 159–66.

Olds, J., & Milner, P. Positive reinforcement produced by electrical stimulation of septal area and other regions of rat brain. *Journal of Comparative and Physiological Psychology*, 1954, **47**, 419–27.

Olsen, O.W. *Animal parasites: Their biology and life cycle.* Minneapolis: Burgess Publishing Co., 1962.

Olsen, O.W. *Animal parasites: Their life cycles and ecology.* Baltimore: University Park Press, 1973.

Osgood, C.E. *Method and theory in experimental psychology.* New York: Oxford University Press, 1953.

Ottinger, D.R., & Simmons, J.E. Behavior of human neonates and prenatal maternal anxiety. *Psychological Reports*, 1964, **14**, 391–94.

Overmier, J.B., & Bull, J.A., III. Influences of appetitive Pavlovian conditioning upon avoidance behavior. In J.H. Reynierse (Ed.), *Current issues in animal learning: A colloquium*, 1970.

Overmier, J.B., & Leaf, R.C. Effects of discriminative Pavlovian fear conditioning upon previously or subsequently acquired avoidance responding. *Journal of Comparative and Physiological Psychology*, 1965, **60**, 213–17.

Overmier, J.B., & Seligman, M.E.P. Effects of inescapable shock upon subsequent escape and avoidance responding. *Journal of Comparative and Physiological Psychology*,

1967, **63**, 28–33.

Overton, D.A. State dependent or "dissociated" learning produced with pentobarbital. *Journal of Comparative and Physiological Psychology*, 1964, **57**, 3–12.

Patten, R.L. Frustrative facilitation effects of nonzero reward magnitude reduction on goal box activity and runway locomotion. *Journal of Experimental Psychology*, 1971, **90**, 160–62.

Patten, R.L. Facilitation effect of incomplete reward reduction in discrimination: Comparison of within-subject and between-subject methods. *Journal of Experimental Psychology*, 1973, **100**, 185–94.

Pavlik, W.B., & Reynolds, W.F. Effects of deprivation schedule and reward magnitude on acquisition and extinction performance. *Journal of Comparative and Physiological Psychology*, 1963, **56**, 452–55.

Pavlov, I.P. *Conditioned reflexes*. London: Oxford University Press, 1927.

Penfield, W. The permanent record of the stream of consciousness. *Proceedings of the 14th International Congress of Psychology*, 1954, 47–69.

Pennypacker, H.S. A magnitude measure of the conditioned eyelid response. In G. Kimble (Ed.), *Foundations of conditioning and learning*. New York: Appleton-Century-Crofts, 1967.

Perkins, C.C., Jr. The relation of secondary reward to gradients of reinforcement. *Journal of Experimental Psychology*, 1947, **37**, 377–92.

Perry, S.L., & Moore, J.W. The partial reinforcement effect sustained through blocks of continuous reinforcement in classical eyelid conditioning. *Journal of Experimental Psychology*, 1965, **69**, 158–61.

Pert, A., & Gonzalez, R.C. Behavior of the turtle (*chrysemys picta picta*) in simultaneous, successive, and behavioral contrast situations. *Journal of Comparative and Physiological Psychology*, 1974, **87**, 526–38.

Peterson, G.B., Ackil, J.E., Frommer, G.P., & Hearst, E.S. Conditioned approach and contact behavior toward signals for food or brain stimulation reinforcement. *Science*, 1972, **177**, 1009–11.

Peterson, L.R. Remininscence in short term memory. *Journal of Experimental Psychology*, 1966, **71**, 115–18.

Peterson, N. Effect of monochromatic rearing on the control of responding by wavelength. *Science*, 1962, **136**, 774–75.

Pfaffman, C. The pleasures of sensation. *Psychological Review*, 1960, **67**, 253–68.

Pfaffman, C., & Bare, J.K. Gustatory nerve discharges in normal and adrenalectomized rats. *Journal of Comparative and Physiological Psychology*, 1950, **43**, 320–24.

Pinel, J.P.J., & Cooper, R.N. Incubation and its implications for interpretations of the ECS gradient effect. *Psychonomic Science*, 1966, **6**, 123–24.

Porter, J.J., Madison, H.L., & Senkowski, P.C. Runway performance and competing responses as functions of drive level and method of drive measurement. *Journal of Experimental Psychology*, 1968, **78**, 281–84.

Postman, L. Transfer, interference and forgetting. In J.W. Kling & L.A. Riggs (Eds.), *Woodworth and Schlosberg's experimental psychology*. New York: Holt, Rinehart & Winston, 1971.

Postman, L., & Underwood, B.J. Critical issues in interference theory. *Memory and Cognition*, 1973, **1**, 19–40.

Premack, D., & Collier, G. Duration of looking and number of brief looks as dependent variables. *Psychonomic Science*, 1966, **4**, 81–82.

Prokasy, W.F., Grant, D.A., & Meyers, N.A. Eyelid conditioning as a function of unconditioned stimulus intensity and intertrial interval. *Journal of Experimental Psychology*, 1958, **55**, 242–46.

Pubols, B.H., Jr. Incentive magnitude, learning and performance in animals. *Psychological Bulletin*, 1960, **51**, 89–115.

Purtle, R.B. Peak shift: A review. *Psychological Bulletin*, 1973, **80**, 408–21.

Rachlin, H. Contrast and matching. *Psychological Review*, 1973, **80**, 217–34.

Raisman, G. Neuronal plasticity in the septal nuclei of the adult rat. *Brain Research*, 1969, **14**, 25–48.

Rand, G., & Wapner, S. Postural status as a factor in memory. *Journal of Verbal Learning and Verbal Behavior*, 1967, **6**, 268–71.

Razran, G. Empirical codifications and specific theoretical implications of compound stimulus condition: Perception. In W.F. Prokasy (Ed.), *Classical conditioning: A symposium*. New York: Appleton-Century-Crofts, 1965.

Razran, G. The observable unconscious and

inferable conscious in current Soviet psycho-physiology: Interoceptive conditioning, semantic conditioning, and the orienting reflex. *Psychological Review,* 1961, **68**, 81–147.

Razran, G.A. A quantitative study of meaning by a conditioned salivary technique (semantic conditioning). *Science,* 1939, **90**, 89–91.

Redford, M.E., & Perkins, C.C., Jr. The role of autopecking in behavioral contrast. *Journal of the Experimental Analysis of Behavior,* 1974, **21**, 145–50.

Reid, L.S. Development of noncontinuity behavior through continuity learning. *Journal of Experimental Psychology,* 1953, **46**, 107–12.

Renner, K.E. Influence of deprivation and availability of goal box cues on the temporal gradient of reinforcement. *Journal of Comparative and Physiological Psychology,* 1963, **56**, 101–4.

Renner, K.E. Delay of reinforcement: A historical review. *Psychological Bulletin,* 1964, **61**, 341–61.

Renner, K.E., & Houlihan, J. Conditioning affecting the relative aversiveness of immediate and delayed punishment. *Journal of Experimental Psychology,* 1969, **81**, 411–20.

Rescorla, R.A. Predictability and number of pairings in Pavlovian fear conditioning. *Psychonomic Science,* 1966, **4**, 383–84.

Rescorla, R.A. Pavlovian conditioning and its proper control procedures. *Psychological Review,* 1967, **74**, 71–80.

Rescorla, R.A. Informational variables in Pavlovian conditioning. In G.H. Bower & J.T. Spence (Eds.), *The psychology of learning and motivation* (Vol. 6). New York: Academic Press, 1972.

Rescorla, R.A. Effect of US habituation following conditioning. *Journal of Comparative and Physiological Psychology,* 1973a, **82**, 137–43.

Rescorla, R.A. Evidence for "unique stimulus" account of configural conditioning. *Journal of Comparative and Physiological Psychology,* 1973b, **85**, 331–38.

Rescorla, R.A., & LoLordo, V.M. Inhibition of avoidance behavior. *Journal of Comparative and Physiological Psychology,* 1965, **59**, 406–12.

Rescorla, R.A., & Solomon, R.L. Two-process learning theory: Relationships between Pavlovian conditioning and instrumental learning. *Psychological Review,* 1967, **74**, 151–82.

Rescorla, R.A., & Wagner, A.R. A theory of Pavlovian conditioning: Variations in the effectiveness of reinforcement and nonreinforcement. In A.H. Black & W.F. Prokasy (Eds.), *Classical conditioning. II: Current research and theory.* New York: Appleton-Century-Crofts, 1972.

Revusky, S.H. Effects of thirst level during consumption of flavored water on subsequent preference. *Journal of Comparative and Physiological Psychology,* 1968, **66**, 777–79.

Revusky, S., & Bedarf, E.W. Association of illness with ingestion of novel foods. *Science,* 1967, **155**, 219–20.

Reynolds, G.S. Attention in the pigeon. *Journal of the Experimental Analysis of Behavior,* 1961a, **4**, 203–8.

Reynolds, G.S. An analysis of interactions in a multiple schedule. *Journal of the Experimental Analysis of Behavior,* 1961b, **4**, 107–17.

Riccio, D.C., Hodges, L.A., & Randall, P.K. Retrograde amnesia produced by hypothermia in rats. *Journal of Comparative and Physiological Psychology,* 1968, **66**, 618–22.

Richter, C.P. Total self-regulatory functions in animals and human beings. *The Harvey Lectures,* 1943, **38**, 63–103.

Richter, C.P., Holt, L.E., & Barelare, B., Jr. Nutritional requirements for normal growth and reproduction in rats studied by the self-selection method. *American Journal of Physiology,* 1938, **22**, 734–44.

Riley, D.A. *Discrimination learning.* Boston: Allyn & Bacon, 1968.

Riopelle, A.J. Learning sets from minimum stimuli. *Journal of Experimental Psychology,* 1955, **49**, 28.

Rizley, R.C., & Rescorla, R.A. Associations in second-order conditioning and sensory preconditioning. *Journal of Comparative and Physiological Psychology,* 1972, **81**, 1–11.

Robbins, D. Partial reinforcement: A selective review of the alleyway literature since 1960. *Psychological Bulletin,* 1971, **76**, 415–31.

Roll, D.L., & Smith, J.C. Conditioned taste aversion in anesthetized rats. In M.E.P. Seligman & J.L. Hager (Eds.), *Biological boundaries of learning.* New York: Appleton-Century-Crofts, 1972.

Rosen, A.J., Glass, D.H., & Ison, J.R. Amobarbital sodium and instrumental performance changes following reward reduction. *Psychonomic Science*, 1967, **9**, 129–30.

Rosen, A.J., & Ison, J.R. Runway performance following changes in sucrose rewards. *Psychonomic Science*, 1965, **2**, 335–36.

Rosen, A.J., & Tessell, R.E. Chlorpromazine, Chlordiazepoxide, and incentive-shift performance in the rat. *Journal of Comparative and Physiological Psychology*, 1970, **72**, 257–62.

Rosen, A.P., & Terrace, H.S. On the minimal conditions for the development of a peakshift and inhibitory stimulus control. *Journal of the Experimental Analysis of Behavior*, 1975, **23**, 385–414.

Rosenberg, K.M., Denenberg, V.H., & Zarrow, M.X. Mice *(mus musculus)* reared with rat aunts: The role of rat-mouse contact in mediating behavioral and physiological changes in the mouse. *Animal Behavior*, 1970, **18**, 138–43.

Rosenberg, K.M., Denenberg, V.H., Zarrow, M.X., & Frank, B.L. Effects of neonatal castrations and testosterone on the rats' pupkilling behavior and activity. *Physiology and Behavior*, 1971, **7**, 363–68.

Rosenfield, J.P., & Fox, S.S. Operant control of a brain potential evoked by a behavior. *Physiology and Behavior*, 1971, **7**, 489–93.

Rosenzweig, M.R., Krech, D., Bennet, E.L., & Diamond, M.C. Modifying brain chemistry and anatomy by enrichment or impoverishment of experience. In G. Newton & S. Levine (Eds.), *Early experience and behavior*. Springfield, Ill.: Charles C Thomas, 1968.

Rosenzweig, M.R., Mollgaard, K., Diamond, M.C., & Bennet, E.L. Negative as well as positive synaptic changes may store memory. *Psychological Review*, 1972, **79**, 93–96.

Ross, L.E. The decremental effects of partial reinforcement during acquisition of the conditioned eyelid response. *Journal of Experimental Psychology*, 1959, **57**, 74–82.

Ross, L.E., & Spence, K.W. Eyelid conditioning under partial reinforcement as a function of UCS intensity. *Journal of Experimental Psychology*, 1960, **59**. 379–82.

Rozin, P. Specific aversions as a component of specific hungers. *Journal of Comparative and Physiological Psychology*, 1967, **64**, 237–42.

Rozin, P. Central or peripheral mediation of learning with long CS–US intervals in the feeding system. *Journal of Comparative and Physiological Psychology*, 1969, **67**, 421–29.

Rozin, P., & Kalat, J.W. Learning as a situation specific adaptation. In M.E.P. Seligman & J.L. Hager (Eds.), *Biological boundaries of learning*. New York: Appleton-Century-Crofts, 1972.

Runquist, W.N., & Spence, K.W. Performance in eyelid conditioning as a function of UCS duration. *Journal of Experimental Psychology*, 1959, **57**, 249–52.

Russel, R. Amnesia following head injuries. *Lancet*, 1935, **2**, 762–75.

Russell, I.S., & Ochs, S. Localization of a memory trace in one cortical hemisphere and transfer to the other hemisphere. *Brain*, 1963, **86**, 37–54.

Russell, W.R., & Nathan, P. Traumatic amnesia. *Brain*, 1946, **69**, 28–300.

Saltz, E., & Azdurian, D. Incubation of anxiety as a function of cognitive differentiation. *Journal of Experimental Psychology*, 1963, **66**, 17–22.

Schaefer, T. Early "experience" and its effects on later behavioral process in rats: II. A critical factor in the early handling phenomenon. *Transactions of the New York Academy of Sciences*, 1963, **25**, 871–89.

Schlesinger, K., & Wimer, R. Genotype and conditioned avoidance learning in the mouse. *Journal of Comparative and Physiological Psychology*, 1967, **63**, 139–41.

Schneiderman, N. Response system divergencies in aversive classical conditioning. In A.H. Black & W.F. Prokasy (Eds.), *Classical conditioning II: Current research and theory*. New York: Appleton-Century-Crofts, 1972.

Schneiderman, N., Fuentes, I., & Gormezano, I. Acquisition and extinction of the classically conditioned eyelid response in the albino rabbit. *Science*, 1962, **136**, 650–52.

Schoenfeld, W.N. (Ed.), *Theory of reinforcement schedules*. New York: Appleton-Century-Crofts, 1970.

Schroeder, S.R., & Holland, J.G. Reinforcement of eye movement with concurrent schedules. *Journal of the Experimental Analysis of Behavior*, 1969, **12**, 897–903.

Schusterman, R.J. Transfer effects of successive discrimination–reversal training in chimpanzees. *Science*, 1962, **137**, 422.

Scoville, W.B., & Milner, B.   Loss of recent memory after bilateral hippocampal lesions. *Journal of Neurology, Neurosurgery, and Psychiatry*, 1957, **20**, 11–19.

Scull, J.W.   The Amsel frustration effect. *Psychological Review*, 1973, **79**, 352–61.

Scull, J., Davies, K., & Amsel, A.   Behavioral contrast and frustration effect in multiple and mixed fixed-interval schedules in the rat. *Journal of Comparative and Physiological Psychology*, 1970, **71**, 478–83.

Searle, L.V.   The organization of hereditary maze-brightness and maze-dullness. *Genetic Psychology Monographs*, 1949, **39**, 279–325.

Sechenov, I.M.   *Reflexes of the brain.* Cambridge: M.I.T. Press, 1965, (originally published in 1863).

Seidal, R.I.   A review of sensory preconditioning. *Psychological Bulletin*, 1959, **56**, 58–75.

Seligman, M.E.P.   On the generality of the laws of learning. *Psychological Review*, 1970, **77**, 406–18.

Seligman, M.E.P.   Phobias and preparedness. *Behavior Therapy*, 1971, **2**, 307–20.

Seligman, M.E.P., & Beagley, G.   Learned helplessness in the rat. *Journal of Comparative and Physiological Psychology*, 1975, **88**, 534–41.

Seligman, M.E.P., & Groves, D.   Nontransient learned helplessness. *Psychonomic Science*, 1970, **19**, 191–92.

Seligman, M.E.P., & Hager, J.L.   (Eds.), *Biological boundaries of learning.* New York: Appleton-Century-Crofts, 1972.

Seligman, M.E.P., & Johnston, J.C.   A cognitive theory of avoidance learning. In F.J. McGuigan & D.B. Lumsden (Eds.), *Contemporary approaches to conditioning and learning.* Washington, D.C.: V.H. Winston & Sons, 1973.

Seligman, M.E.P., Maier, S.F., & Geer, J.   The alleviation of learned helplessness in the dog. *Journal of Abnormal and Social Psychology*, 1968, **73**, 253–62.

Seligman, M.E.P., Maier, S.F., & Solomon, R.L.   Unpredictable and uncontrollable aversive events. In F.R. Brush (Ed.), *Aversive conditioning and learning.* New York: Academic Press, 1971.

Seligman, M.E.P., Rosellini, R.A., & Kozak, M.J.   Learned helplessness in the rat: Time course, immunization, and reversibility. *Journal of Comparative and Physiological Psychology*, 1975, **88**, 542–47.

Seward, J.P.   Conditioning theory. In M.H. Marx (Ed.), *Learning: Theories.* London: Collier-Macmillan, Ltd., 1970.

Seward, J.P., & Levy, N.   Sign learning as a factor in extinction. *Journal of Comparative and Physiological Psychology*, 1949, **39**, 660–68.

Seybert, J.A., Mellgren, R.L., & Jobe, J.B.   Sequential effects on resistance to extinction at widely spaced trials. *Journal of Experimental Psychology*, 1973, **101**, 151–54.

Shaffer, W.O., & Shifrrin, R.M.   Rehearsal and storage of visual information. *Journal of Experimental Psychology*, 1972, **92**, 292–96.

Shanab, M.E., & Biller, J.D.   Positive contrast in the Lashley maze under different drive conditions. *Psychonomic Science*, 1972, **3**, 179–84.

Shanab, M.E., & Birnbaum, D.W.   Durability of the partial reinforcement and partial delay of reinforcement extinction effects after minimal acquisition training. *Animal Learning and Behavior*, 1974, **2**, 81–85.

Shanab, M.E., Melrose, S., & Young, T.   The partial reinforcement effect sustained through blocks of continuous water reinforcement. *Bulletin of the Psychonomic Society*, 1975, **6**, 261–64.

Shanab, M.E., Sanders, R., & Premack, D.   Positive contrast in the runway obtained with delay of reward. *Science*, 1969, **164**, 724–25.

Shapiro, M.M.   Temporal relationship between salivation and lever pressing with differential reinforcement of low rates. *Journal of Comparative and Physiological Psychology*, 1962, **55**, 567–71.

Shapiro, S.R., & Erdelyi, M.H.   Hypermnesia for pictures, not words. *Journal of Experimental Psychology*, 1974, **103**, 1218–19.

Sheer, D.E.   In D.E. Sheer (Ed.), *Electrical stimulation of the brain.* Austin: University of Texas Press, 1961.

Sheffield, F.D.   A drive induction theory of reinforcement. In R.N. Haber (Ed.), *Current research in motivation.* New York: Holt, Rinehart & Winston, 1966.

Sheffield, V.F.   Extinction as a function of partial reinforcement and distribution of practice. *Journal of Experimental Psychology*, 1949, **39**, 511–26.

Sherman, J.G.   *The temporal distribution of responses on fixed-interval schedules.* Unpublished doctoral dissertation, Columbia University, 1959.

Shettleworth, S.J. Conditioning of domestic chicks to visual and auditory stimuli: Control of drinking by visual stimuli and control of conditioned fear by sound. In M.E.P. Seligman & J.L. Hager (Eds.), *Biological boundaries of learning.* New York: Appleton-Century-Crofts, 1972.

Shettleworth, S.J. Reinforcement and the organization of behavior in golden hamsters: Hunger, environment and food reinforcement. *Journal of Experimental Psychology,* 1975, **104,** 56–87.

Shull, R.L., & Pliskoff, S.S. Change over delay and concurrent schedules: Some effects on relative performance measures. *Journal of the Experimental Analysis of Behavior,* 1967, **10,** 517–27.

Sidman, M. Avoidance conditioning with brief shock and no exteroceptive warning signal. *Science,* 1953, **118,** 157–58.

Siegal, S. Conditioning of insulin-induced glycemia. *Journal of Comparative and Physiological Psychology,* 1972, **78,** 223–41.

Siegal, S. Conditioning insulin effects. *Journal of Comparative and Physiological Psychology,* 1975, **89,** 189–99.

Siegel, S. Morphine analgesic tolerance: Its situation specificity supports a Pavlovian conditioning model. *Science,* 1976, **193,** 323–25.

Skinner, B.F. *The behavior of organisms. An experimental analysis.* New York: Appleton-Century-Crofts, 1938.

Skinner, B.F. Are theories of learning necessary? *Psychological Review,* 1950, **57,** 193–216.

Skinner, B.F. *Science and human behavior.* New York: Macmillan, 1953.

Skinner, B.F. *Cumulative record.* New York: Appleton-Century-Crofts, 1961.

Skinner, B.F. *Contingencies of reinforcement.* New York: Appleton-Century-Crofts, 1969.

Slotnick, B.M., & Katz, H.M. Olfactory learning-set in rats. *Science,* 1974, **185,** 796–98.

Small, W.S. An experimental study of the mental processes of the rat. *American Journal of Psychology,* 1899, **11,** 133–65.

Smith, M.C., Coleman, S.R., & Gormezano, I. Classical conditioning of the rabbits' nictitating membrane response. *Journal of Comparative and Physiological Psychology,* 1969, **69,** 226–31.

Snyder, H.L. Saccharine concentration and deprivation as determinants of instrumental and consummatory response strengths. *Journal of Experimental Psychology,* 1962, **63,** 610–15.

Solomon, R.L. Punishment. *American Psychologist,* 1964, **19,** 239–53.

Solomon, R.L., & Turner, L.H. Discriminative classical conditioning in dogs paralyzed by curare can later control discriminative avoidance responses in the normal state. *Psychological Review,* 1962, **69,** 202–19.

Solomon, R.L., & Wynn, L.C. Traumatic avoidance learning: The principles of anxiety conservation and partial irreversibility. *Psychological Review,* 1954, **61,** 353–85.

Spear, N.E. Verbal learning and retention. In M.R. D'Amato (Ed.), *Experimental psychology: Psychophysics, methodology and learning.* New York: McGraw-Hill, 1970.

Spear, N.E. Forgetting as retrieval failure. In W.K. Honig & H.P.R. James (Eds.), *Animal memory.* New York: Academic Press, 1971.

Spear, N.E. Retrieval of memory in animals. *Psychological Review,* 1973, **80,** 163–94.

Spear, N.E. Retrieval of memories. In W.K. Estes (Ed.), *Handbook of memory and cognitive processes* (Vol. IV). *Memory processes.* Hillsdale, N.J.: Lawrence Erlbaum Associates, 1976.

Spear, N.E., & Parsons, P. Analysis of a reactivation treatment: Ontogeny and alleviated forgetting. In D. Medin, R. Davis, & W. Roberts (Eds.), *Coding processes in animal memory.* Hillsdale, N.J.: Lawrence Erlbaum Associates, 1976.

Spear, N.E., & Spitzner, J.H. Effect of initial nonreward trials: Factors responsible for increased resistance to extinction. *Journal of Experimental Psychology,* 1967, **74,** 525–37.

Spear, N.E., Hill, W.F., & O'Sullivan, D.J. Acquisition and extinction after initial trials without reward. *Journal of Experimental Psychology,* 1965, **69,** 25–29.

Spence, K.W. The nature of discrimination learning in animals. *Psychological Review,* 1936, **43,** 427–49.

Spence, K.W. The differential response of animals to stimuli differing within a single dimension. *Psychological Review,* 1937, **44,** 430–44.

Spence, K.W. An experimental test of the continuity and noncontinuity theories of discrimination learning. *Journal of Experimental Psychology,* 1945, **35,** 253–66.

Spence, K.W. *Behavior theory and conditioning.* New Haven: Yale University Press, 1956.

Spence, K.W. Cognitive and drive factors in the extinction of the conditioned eye blink in human subjects. *Psychological Review,* 1966, **73**, 445–58.

Spence, K.W., & Ross, L.E. A methodological study of the form and latency of eyelid responses in conditioning. *Journal of Experimental Psychology,* 1959, **58**, 376–81.

Sperling, G. The information available in brief visual presentations. *Psychological Monographs,* 1960, **74** (Whole No. 498).

Sperling, S.E. Reversal learning and resistance to extinction: A review of the rat literature. *Psychological Bulletin,* 1965a, **63**, 281–97.

Sperling, S.E. Reversal learning and resistance to extinction: A supplementary report. *Psychological Bulletin,* 1965b, **64**, 310–12.

Spivey, J.E. Resistance to extinction as a function of number N–R transitions and percentage of reinforcement. *Journal of Experimental Psychology,* 1967, **75**, 43–48.

Springer, A.D. *Vulnerability of skeletal and autonomic manifestation of CER to the amnesic effects of ECS.* Unpublished doctoral dissertation, Brooklyn College, 1973.

Stengel, E. Psychogenic loss of memory. In C.W.M. Whitty & O.L. Zangwill (Eds.), *Amnesia.* London: Butterworth, 1966.

Stollnitz, F. Forgetting of discrimination learning set by Rhesus monkeys. Paper presented at meetings of the Psychonomic Society, San Antonio, November, 1970.

Suboski, M.P. UCS intensity and the latency of the classically conditioned eyelid response. *Journal of Experimental Psychology,* 1967, **74**, 31–35.

Sutherland, N.S., & Mackintosh, N.J. *Mechanisms of animal discrimination learning.* New York: Academic Press, 1971.

Swadlow, H., Schneiderman, E. & Schneiderman, N. Classical conditioning of a discrimination between electrically stimulated lateral geniculate bodies in the rabbit. *Proceedings of the 76th Annual Convention of the American Psychological Association,* 1968, **3**, 313–14. In N. Schneiderman (Ed.), Chapter 14. In A.H. Black & W.F. Prokasy (Eds.), *Classical conditioning: II. Current theory and research.* New York: Appleton-Century-Crofts, 1972.

Terrace, H.S. Discrimination learning with and without "errors." *Journal of the Experimental Analysis of Behavior,* 1963a, **6**, 1–27.

Terrace, H.S. Errorless discrimination learning in the pigeon: Effects of chlorpromazine and imipramine. *Science,* 1963b, **140**, 318–19.

Terrace, H.S. Stimulus control. In W.K. Honig (Ed.), *Operant behavior: Areas of research and application.* New York: Appleton-Century-Crofts, 1966a.

Terrace, H.S. Behavioral contrast and the peak shift. Effects of extended discrimination training. *Journal of the Experimental Analysis of Behavior,* 1966b, **9**, 613–17.

Terrace, H.S. Discrimination learning, the peak shift, and behavioral contrast. *Journal of the Experimental Analysis of Behavior,* 1968, **11**, 727–41.

Terrace, H.S. By-products of discrimination learning. In G. Bower & J. Spence (Eds.), *The psychology of learning and motivation,* (Vol. 5). New York: Academic Press, 1971a.

Terrace, H.S. Escape from S⁻. *Learning and Motivation,* 1971b, **2**, 148–63.

Terrace, H.S. Conditioned inhibition in successive discrimination learning. In R.A. Boakes & M.S. Halliday (Eds.), *Inhibition and learning.* New York: Academic Press, 1972.

Terrace, H.S. On the nature of nonresponding in discrimination learning with and without errors. *Journal of the Experimental Analysis of Behavior,* 1974, **22**, 151–59.

Terris, W., & Barnes, M. Learned resistance to punishment and subsequent responsiveness to the same and novel punishments. *Psychonomic Science,* 1969, **15**, 49–50.

Terris, W., & Wechkin, S. Learning to resist the effects of punishment. *Psychonomic Science,* 1967, **7**, 169–70.

Theios, J. The partial reinforcement effect sustained through blocks of continuous reinforcement. *Journal of Experimental Psychology,* 1962, **64**, 1–6.

Theios, J. Simple conditioning as two stage /and-or-none learning. *Psychological Review,* 1963, **70**, 403–17.

Theios, J., & Blosser, D. The overlearning reversal effect and magnitude of reward. *Journal of Comparative and Physiological Psychology,* 1965, **59**, 252–57.

Theios, J., Lynch, A.D., & Lowe, S.F., Jr. Differential effects of shock intensity on one-way and shuttle avoidance conditioning. *Journal of Experimental Psychology,* 1966, **72,** 294–99.

Thomas, D.R., & Switalski, R.W. Comparison of stimulus generalization following variable-ratio and variable-interval training. *Journal of Experimental Psychology,* 1966, **71,** 236–40.

Thomas, D.R., Burr, D.E., & Eck, K.O. Stimulus selection in animal discrimination learning: An alternative interpretation. *Journal of Experimental Psychology,* 1970, **86,** 53–62.

Thomas, E. Role of postural adjustments in conditioning of dogs with electrical stimulation of the motor cortex as the unconditioned stimulus. *Journal of Comparative and Physiological Psychology,* 1971, **76,** 187–98.

Thomas, G.V., & Cameron, G.N. Response rate, reinforcement frequency and behavioral contrast. *Journal of the Experimental Analysis of Behavior,* 1974, **22,** 427–32.

Thompson, T. Visual reinforcement in Siamese fighting fish. *Science,* 1963, **141,** 55–57.

Thompson, T., & Sturm, T. Classical conditioning of aggressive display in Siamese fighting fish. *Journal of the Experimental Analysis of Behavior,* 1965, **8,** 397–403.

Thompson, W.R. Influence of prenatal maternal anxiety on emotionality in young rats. *Science,* 1957, **125,** 698–99.

Thorndike, E.L. Animal intelligence: An experimental study of the associative processes in animals. *Psychological Review Monograph,* 1898, Suppl. **2,** 1–109.

Thorndike, E.L. Reward and punishment in animal learning. *Comparative Psychology Monographs,* 1932, 8 (4, Whole No. 39).

Thorpe, W.H. *Learning and instinct in animals.* London: Methuen, 1963.

Tinbergen, N. *The study of instinct.* Oxford: University Press, 1951.

Tinbergen, N. *The herring gull's world: A study of the social behavior of birds.* Garden City, N.Y.: Doubleday, 1967.

Tinklepaugh, O.L. An experimental study of representative factors in monkeys. *Journal of Comparative Psychology,* 1928, 8, 197–236.

Tolman, E.C. *Purposive behavior in animals and men.* New York: The Century Co., 1932.

Tolman, E.C. Principles of purposive behavior. In S. Koch (Ed.), *Psychology: A study of a science* (Vol. 2), *General systematic formulations, learning, and special processes.* New York: McGraw-Hill, 1959.

Tracy, W.K. Wavelength generalization and preference in monochromatically reared ducklings. *Journal of the Experimental Analysis of Behavior,* 1970, **13,** 163–78.

Trafton, C.L. Effects of lesions in the septal area and cingulate cortical areas on conditioned suppression of activity and avoidance behavior in rats. *Journal of Comparative and Physiological Psychology,* 1967, **63,** 191–97.

Trapold, M.A. Reversal of an operant discrimination by noncontingent discrimination reversal training. *Psychonomic Science,* 1966, **4,** 247–48.

Trapold, M.A., & Carlson, J.G. Proximity of manipulandum and food cup as a determinant of the generalized S^D effect. *Psychonomic Science,* 1965, **2,** 327–28.

Trapold, M.A., Carlson, J.G., & Myers, W.A. The effect of noncontingent fixed- and variable-interval reinforcement upon subsequent acquisition of the fixed-interval scallop. *Psychonomic Science,* 1965, **2,** 261–62.

Travis, R.C. Practice and rest periods in motor learning. *Journal of Psychology,* 1936, **3,** 183–87.

Trowill, J.A., Panksepp, J., & Gandelman, R. An incentive model of rewarding brain stimulation. *Psychological Review,* 1969, **76,** 246–81.

Tryon, R.C. The genetics of learning ability in rats. *University of California Publication on Psychology,* 1929, **4,** 71–89.

Tryon, R.C. Genetic differences in maze learning ability in rats. *Yearbook of the National Society for the Study of Education,* 1940, **39,** 111–19.

Tulving, E. Episodic and semantic memory. In E. Tulving & W. Donaldson (Eds.), *Organization of memory.* New York: Academic Press, 1972.

Tulving, E. Cue-dependent forgetting. *American Scientist,* 1974, **62,** 74–82.

Tulving, E., & Thomson, B.M. Encoding specificity and retrieval processes in episodic memory. *Psychological Review,* 1973, **80,** 352–73.

Tyler, D.W., Wortz, E.C., & Bitterman, M.E. The effect of random and alternating partial reinforcement on resistance to extinction in the rat. *American Journal of Psychology,* 1953, **66,** 57–65.

Underwood, B.J. The effect of successive interpolations on retroactive and proactive inhibition. *Psychological Monographs*, 1945, **59**, (3, Whole No. 273).

Underwood, B.J. Interference and forgetting. *Psychological Review*, 1957, **64**, 49–60.

Underwood, B.J. Degree of learning and the measurement of forgetting. *Journal of Verbal Learning and Verbal Behavior*, 1964, **3**, 112–29.

Underwood, B.J. *Experimental psychology* (2nd ed.). New York: Appleton-Century-Crofts, 1966.

Underwood, B.J. Are we overloading memory? In A.W. Melton & E. Martin (Eds.), *Coding processes in human memory*. Washington, D.C.: V.H. Winston & Sons, 1972.

Ungar, G. Chemical transfer of learning: Its stimulus specificity. *Federation Proceedings*, 1966, **25**, 207.

Ungar, G., Ho, I.K., & Galvan, L. Isolation of a dark avoidance inducing brain peptide. *Federation Proceedings*, 1970, **29**, 658.

Valenstein, E.S., Kakolewski, J.W., & Cox, V.C. Sex differences in taste preference for glucose and saccharine solutions. *Science*, 1967, **156**, 942–43.

Vogel, J.R., Mikulka, P.J., & Spear, N.E. Effects of shifts in sucrose and saccharine concentrations on licking behavior in the rat. *Journal of Comparative and Physiological Psychology*, 1968, **66**, 661–66.

Wagner, A.R. The role of reinforcement and nonreinforcement in an "apparent frustration effect." *Journal of Experimental Psychology*, 1959, **57**, 130-36.

Wagner, A.R. Effects of amount and percentage of reinforcement and number of acquisition trials on conditioning and extinction. *Journal of Experimental Psychology*, 1961, **62**, 234–42.

Wagner, A.R. Frustrative nonreward: A variety of punishments? In B.A. Campbell & R.M. Church (Eds.), *Punishment*. New York: Appleton-Century-Crofts, 1969.

Wagner, A.R., & Rescorla, R.A. Inhibition in Pavlovian conditioning: Application of a theory. In R.A. Boakes & M.S. Halliday (Eds.), *Inhibition and learning*. London: Academic Press, 1972.

Wagner, A.R., Logan, F.A., Haberlandt, K., & Price, T. Stimulus selection in animal discrimination learning. *Journal of Experimental Psychology*, 1968, **76**, 171–80.

Wagner, A.R., Rudy, J.W., & Whitlow, J.W. Rehearsal in animal conditioning. *Journal of Experimental Psychology Monograph*, 1973, **97**, 407-26.

Wagner, A.R., Siegel, S., Thomas, E., & Ellison, G.D. Reinforcement history and the extinction of a conditioned salivary response. *Journal of Comparative and Physiological Psychology*, 1964, **58**, 354–58.

Wagner, A.R., Thomas, S.E., & Norton, T. Conditioning with electrical stimulation of motor cortex: Evidence of a possible source of motivation. *Journal of Comparative and Physiological Psychology*, 1967, **64**, 191–200.

Walker, E.G. Eyelid conditioning as a function of intensity of conditioned and unconditioned stimuli. *Journal of Experimental Psychology*, 1960, **59**, 303–11.

Wansley, R.A., & Holloway, F.A. Multiple retention deficits following one-trial appetitive training. *Behavioral Biology*, 1975a, **14**, 135–49.

Wansley, R.A., & Holloway, F.A. Oscillation in retention performance after passive avoidance training. *Learning and Motivation*, 1975b, in press.

Warren, J.M. Perceptual dominance in discrimination learning by monkeys. *Journal of Comparative and Physiological Psychology*, 1954, **46**, 484–86.

Warren, J.M., & McGonigle, B. Attention theory and discrimination learning. In R.M. Gilbert & N.S. Sutherland (Eds.), *Animal discrimination learning*. New York: Academic Press, 1969.

Warrington, E.K., & Sanders, H.I. The fate of old memories. *Quarterly Journal of Experimental Psychology*, 1971, **23**, 432–42.

Warrington, E.K., & Weiskrantz, L. Amnesic syndrome: Consolidation or retrieval? *Nature*, 1970, **228**, 628–30.

Warrington, E.K., & Weiskrantz, L. Organizational aspects of memory in amnesic patients. *Neuropsychologia*, 1971, **9**, 67–73.

Warrington, E.K., & Weiskrantz, L. An analysis of short-term and long-term memory effects in man. In J.A. Deutsch (Ed.), *The physiological basis of memory*. New York: Academic Press, 1973.

Wasserman, E.A. Pavlovian conditioning with heat reinforcement produces stimulus-directed pecking in chicks. *Science*, 1973, **181**, 875–77.

Watkins, M.J. When is recall spectacularly higher than recognition? *Journal of Experimental Psychology*, 1974, **102**, 161–63.

Watkins, M.J., & Tulving, E. Episodic memory: When recognition fails. *Journal of Experimental Psychology: General*, 1975, **104**, 5–29.

Watson, J.B. Psychology as the behaviorist views it. *Psychological Review*, 1913, **20**, 158–77.

Watson, J.B. The effect of delayed feeding upon learning. *Psychobiology*, 1917, **1**, 51–60.

Watson, J.B., & Raynor, R. Conditioned emotional reactions. *Journal of Experimental Psychology*, 1920, **3**, 1–14.

Watson, J.D. *The double helix*. New York: Atheneum, 1968.

Waugh, N.C., & Norman, D.A. Primary memory. *Psychological Review*, 1965, **72**, 89–104.

Weinstock, S. Resistance to extinction of a running response following partial reinforcement under widely spaced trials. *Journal of Comparative and Physiological Psychology*, 1954, **47**, 318–23.

Weiskrantz, L. Experimental studies of amnesia. In C.W.M. Whitty & O.L. Sangwill (Eds.), *Amnesia*. London, Butterworth, 1966.

Weiskrantz, L. A long-term view of short-term memory in psychology. In G. Horn & R.A. Hinde (Eds.), *Short term changes in neural activity and behavior*. Cambridge: Cambridge University Press, 1970.

Weiskrantz, L. Comparison of amnestic states in monkey and man. In L.E. Jarrad (Ed.), *Cognitive processes in nonhuman primates*. New York: Academic Press, 1971.

Weisman, R.G. Factors influencing inhibitory stimulus control: Differential reinforcement of other behavior during discrimination training. *Journal of the Experimental Analysis of Behavior*, 1970, **14**, 87–91.

Weisman, R.G., Denny, M.R., Platt, S.A., & Zerbolio, D.J., Jr. Facilitation of extinction by a stimulus associated with long nonshock confinement periods. *Journal of Comparative and Physiological Psychology*, 1966, **62**, 26–30.

Weisman, R.N., Hamilton, L.W., & Carlton, P.L. Increased gustatory aversion following VMH lesions in rats. *Physiology and Behavior*, 1972, **9**, 801–4.

Weiss, J.M., Stone, E.A., & Harrel, N. Coping behavior and brain norepinephrine level in rats. *Journal of Comparative and Physiological Psychology*, 1970, **72**, 153–60.

Weiss, R.F. Deprivation and reward magnitude effects on speed throughout the goal gradient. *Journal of Experimental Psychology*, 1960, **60**, 384–90.

Weiss, S.J. Stimulus compounding in free operant and classical conditioning: A review and analysis. *Psychological Bulletin*, 1972, **78**, 189–208.

Wendt, G.R. Two and one-half year retention of a conditioned response. *Journal of General Psychology*, 1938, **17**, 178–80.

Whiting, J.W.M., & Mowrer, O.H. Habit progression and regression: A laboratory study of some factors relevant to human socialization. *Journal of Comparative Psychology*, 1943, **36**, 229–53.

Whitty, C.M.W., & Lishman, W.A. Amnesia and cerebral disease. In C.M.W. Whitty & O.L. Zangwill (Eds.), *Amnesia*. London: Butterworth, 1966.

Wickelgren, W.A. Trace resistance and the decay of long-term memory. *Journal of Mathematical Psychology*, 1972, **4**, 418–55.

Wickens, D.D. The transference of conditioned excitation and conditioned inhibition from one muscle group to the antagonistic muscle group. *Journal of Experimental Psychology*, 1938, **22**, 101–23.

Wickens, D.D. Classical conditioning as it contributes to the analyses of some basic psychological processes. In F.J. McGuigan & D.B. Lumscled (Eds.), *Contemporary approaches to conditioning and learning*. New York: Wiley, 1973.

Wike, E.L., & Kintsch, W. Delayed reinforcement and runway performance. *Psychological Review*, 1959, **9**, 179–87.

Wilcock, J., & Fulker, D.W. Avoidance learning in rats: Genetic evidence for two distinct behavioral processes in the shuttle box. *Journal of Comparative and Physiological Psychology*, 1973, **82**, 247–53.

Wilcoxin, H.C., Dragoin, W.B., & Kral, P.A. Illness induced aversions in rat and quail: Relative salience of visual and gustatory cues. *Science*, 1971, **7**, 489-93.

Williams, D.R. Classical conditioning and incentive motivation. In W.F. Prokasy (Ed.), *Classical conditioning: A symposium*. New York: Appleton-Century-Crofts, 1965.

Williams, D.R., & Williams, H. Automaintenance in the pigeon: Sustained pecking despite contingent nonreinforcement. *Journal of the Experimental Analysis of Behavior*, 1969, **12**, 511–20.

Wilson, M.P. Periodic reinforcement interval and number of periodic reinforcements as parameters of response strength. *Journal of Comparative and Physiological Psychology*, 1954, **47**, 51–56.

Wilton, R.N., & Strongman, K.T. Extinction performance as a function of reinforcement magnitude and a number of training trials. *Psychological Reports*, 1967, **20**, 235–38.

Wiseman, S., & Tulving, E. A test of confusion theory of encoding specificity. *Journal of Verbal Learning and Verbal Behavior*, 1976, in press.

Wolfe, J.B., & Kaplon, M.D. Effect of amount of reward and consummative activity on learning in chickens. *Journal of Comparative Psychology*, 1941, **31**, 353–61.

Woods, S.C., Makous, W., & Hutton, R.A. Temporal parameters of conditioned hyperglycemia. *Journal of Comparative and Physiological Psychology*, 1969, **69**, 301–7.

Woodworth, R.S., & Schlosberg, H. *Experimental psychology*. New York: Holt, 1954.

Worsham, R.W., & D'Amato, M.R. Ambient light, white noise, and monkey vocalization as sources of interference in visual short-term memory of monkeys. *Journal of Experimental Psychology*, 1973, **99**, 99–105.

Wynne, L.D., & Solomon, R.L. Traumatic avoidance learning: Acquisition and extinction in dogs deprived of normal peripheral autonomic function. *Genetic and Psychological Monographs*, 1955, **52**, 241–84.

Yarczower, M., Dickson, J.F., & Gollub, L.R. Some effects on generalization gradients of tandem schedules. *Journal of the Experimental Analysis of Behavior*, 1966, **9**, 631–39.

Yarczower, M., Gollub, L.R., & Dickson, J.F. Some effects of discriminative training with equated frequency of reinforcement. *Journal of the Experimental Analysis of Behavior*, 1968, **11**, 415–23.

Yates, F.A. *The art of memory*. Chicago: University of Chicago Press, 1966.

Zeaman, D. Response latency as a function of the amount of reinforcement. *Journal of Experimental Psychology*, 1949, **39**, 466–83.

Zeaman, D., & Wegner, N. Strength of cardiac conditioned responses with varying stimulus duration. *Psychological Review*, 1958, **65**, 238–41.

Zener, K. The significance of behavior accompanying conditioned salivary secretion for theories of the conditioned response. *American Journal of Psychology*, 1937, **50**, 384–403.

Zornetzer, S.F., & McGaugh, J.L. Retrograde amnesia and brain seizures in mice. *Physiology and Behavior*, 1971, **7**, 401–8.

Author Index

Jasper, H. H., 222
Jaynes, J., 305, 387
Jenkins, H. M., 242, 257, 301, 302
Jensen, D. D., 50
Jiulian, D., 175
Jobe, J. B., 127, 128
Johnston, J. C., 250, 252
Jones, J., 72
Jong, E., 197
Jung, J., 355, 371

Kakolewski, J. W., 278
Kalat, J. W., 210, 211
Kalish, H. I., 291, 292, 293, 294, 295, 296,
 300, 301, 304, 305, 311
Kamin, L. G., 53, 55, 64, 76, 159, 164,
 165, 166, 167, 177, 184, 190, 337, 338,
 339, 340, 342, 343, 344, 345, 346, 379,
 380, 381, 384
Kanarek, R., 141
Kaplan, S., 376
Kaplon, M. D., 97
Karas, G. G., 283
Katz, H. M., 403
Katz, J., 365
Katzev, R. D., 180
Kausler, D., 355
Keehn, J. D., 178
Keenan, B., 223
Keesey, R. E., 110, 147
Keller, D., 169
Keller, J. V., 313
Keller, K., 318
Kelly, J., 103
Keppel, G., 371, 375
Kimble, G. A., 7, 45, 67, 69, 70, 72, 91,
 180, 214, 250
Kimmel, E., 31
Kimmel, H. D., 31, 48, 51, 70, 223
Kincaid, W. D., 114
King, M. G., 160
Kintsch, W., 114, 238
Kitto, G., 459
Klein, M., 307
Kleinsmith, L., 376
Kling, J. W., 147
Klipec, W. D., 311
Knapp, R. K., 171, 178
Knarr, F. A., 94, 239
Knouse, S. B., 135

Koelling, R. A., 198, 199, 205
Koffka, K., 363
Konorski, J., 256
Konstantinas, T., 286
Koresko, M. B., 296, 300
Korn, J. H., 160, 161
Kostansek, D. J., 246
Kozak, M. J., 192
Kral, P. A., 206
Krane, R. V., 203, 259
Krecek, J., 278
Krech, D., 284, 285
Krechevsky, I., 320, 321, 322, 324, 327,
 330, 343
Kremer, E. F., 76
Krippner, R. A., 125

Lamoreaux, R. R., 169, 177
Largen, J., 98, 102, 105
Lashley, K. S., 300, 320, 321, 324, 327,
 330, 334, 335, 336, 343, 344, 348, 364,
 460, 461, 462, 463, 464, 465, 466
Lawrence, D., 325, 326, 345
Leaf, A., 452
Leaf, R., 68, 159, 233
Leao, A., 473
Lenneberg, E. H., 259
Levey, A. V., 26
Levine, M., 333
Levine, S., 102, 278, 283, 287
Levy, M., 57, 233
Lewis, D. J., 387, 388, 448
Linden, D. R., 186, 187, 188
Lishman, W. A., 429
Little, L., 318
Liu, I-M., 72
Liu, S., 38
Locke, J., 18
Logan, F. A., 86, 101, 111, 113, 114, 121,
 186, 237
Longo, N., 58
Lord, J., 110, 318
Lordahl, D. S., 49
Lorenz, K., 243, 264
Love, T., 353
Lovejoy, E., 324, 325, 345, 348
Lowe, S. F., 169
Ludvigson, H. W., 103, 125
Luria, A., 353, 392
Lynch, A. D., 169

Subject Index

Mike H
427-6542